# Reshaping Business at the Intersection of Neuromarketing and AI

Fernando Ortiz-Rodriguez
https://orcid.org/0000-0003-2084-3462
*Tamaulipas Autonomous University, Mexico*

Miguel Sahagun
https://orcid.org/0000-0002-6962-4714
*High Point University, USA*

Anuj Kumar
https://orcid.org/0000-0002-1205-2794
*Rushford Business School, Switzerland*

Nishu Ayedee
*INTI International University, Malaysia*

IGI Global
Scientific Publishing
Publishing Tomorrow's Research Today

| | |
|---|---|
| Vice President of Editorial | Melissa Wagner |
| Director of Acquisitions | Mikaela Felty |
| Director of Book Development | Jocelynn Hessler |
| Production Manager | Mike Brehm |
| Cover Design | Jose Rosado |

Published in the United States of America by
IGI Global Scientific Publishing
701 East Chocolate Avenue
Hershey, PA, 17033, USA
Tel: 717-533-8845 | Fax: 717-533-7115
Website: https://www.igi-global.com E-mail: cust@igi-global.com



Library of Congress Cataloging-in-Publication Data

LCCN: 2025034462 (CIP Data Pending)
ISBN13: 9798337359977
Isbn13Softcover: 9798337359984
EISBN13: 9798337359991

British Cataloguing in Publication Data
A Cataloguing in Publication record for this book is available from the British Library.

# Table of Contents

# Detailed Table of Contents



Retail and e-commerce are undergoing a dramatic overhaul, and much of that change is due to the use of Artificial Intelligence. Rather than being a distant future concept, AI is now becoming the heart of many shopping platforms, supporting brands to read, anticipate, and respond to shoppers in ways that feel both personal and efficient. Neuromarketing also has evolved as an innovative discipline integrated with AI that utilises neuroscience techniques to predict and understand consumers' subconscious responses to marketing stimuli. The scope of this study covers a dual focus, investigative innovations in a perfect e-commerce environment, while also analysing omnichannel strategies that connect physical and digital retail spaces, thus presenting a full understanding of the retail ecosystem. The result of this study reveals the existing knowledge gaps and presents promising directions for future research, enhancing our knowledge of the combined impact of AI and neuromarketing on the shopping experience in retail ad e commerce.



The chapter's purpose is to present the effectiveness of neuromarketing combined with viral marketing, powered by AI, in terms to enhance purchase decisions. This book chapter introduces the concept of Neuro-Viral AI Predictive Framework (NVAPF), which explains how to predict consumer behavior characteristics by integrating Artificial Intelligence (AI) viral marketing with neuromarketing to improve strategic marketing insights. The research involved approximately 200 respondents, divided into two studies in the food and beverage sector (100 respondents were tested in the food and beverage sectors, respectively), utilizing the same variables: neuromarketing, viral marketing, and purchasing decisions. This division of respondents was intended to assess the effectiveness of both sectors, food and beverage. The findings indicated

assists in processing it faster and more accurately. This article explores how our subconscious biases can be picked up by, amplified by, or attenuated by AI-based neuromarketing systems. It applies Dual Process Theory and theory of algorithmic bias to outline a model—AI–Neuromarketing–Bias Interaction (ANBI)—that describes how AI analysis and brain data cooperate. Drawing on retail stores, hospitals, entertainment, and political campaign advertising, this essay outlines the benefits and limitations of using AI in neuromarketing. These technologies allow very directed advertising and can forecast customer behavior, generating ethical fears regarding privacy and manipulation. The article presents advice to marketers, developers of AI, politicians, and researchers, calling for careful use of emerging technologies, enhanced transparency, and protection of personal rights. In general, AI in neuromarketing must be employed to understand consumers more than to take advantage of them. We have to counterpoise the technology push with the need to preserve consumers' trust and freedom.



Digital disruption is reshaping hospitality branding. This chapter per the authors maps how short form video platforms, AI assisted storytelling, and omnichannel engagement combine to build emotionally resonant, data driven brand identities. Through content analysis of 180 videos, literature synthesis, and global case studies, it explains platform dynamics, AI design benefits and risks, user generated content authenticity, and metrics that move beyond likes to sentiment and predictive conversion. A seven step "Scroll, Swipe, Stay" framework guides practitioners in balancing automation, creativity, and ethical governance while highlighting future directions in hyper personalisation and immersive technologies.



The goal of this chapter is to fill in the blanks about the purpose, significance, and potential of combining eye tracking study with AI. The main purpose of the work was to come up with a plan for how eye tracking and AI could be used together to improve marketing communication management. Our study used a structured literature review, online content analysis of eye tracking studies. Through the use of sensors and cameras that track the position and movement of the eyes while they gaze at an object, eye tracking technology helps to illustrate what is happening in a user interface by seeing and recording the movements of the subject's eyes. The system flashes infrared light into the eyes, which causes reflections on the pupil and cornea. Eye-tracking sensors record these reflections, process the data, and use algorithms to determine the user's gaze. The point of gaze provides insight into what is capturing and maintaining individual's attention by revealing where they stare on a screen or the surrounding area. As researchers and designers, this technology aids in our comprehension of how people perceive and absorb information. These days, neuromarketing is a relatively young field that is crucial to consumer research and marketing. Businesses thrive, particularly in the business world, on gaining a deeper understanding of the attitudes, emotions, and uncontrollable reactions of their potential clients. In these situations, it is highly beneficial for them to explore using AI in neuromarketing technologies as a study strategy. The findings of an eye-tracking experiment that examines how consumers respond to home service robots and their look are presented in this chapter.



The current study explores how advances in neuroscientific technique like tracking brain activity and facial reactions, are providing insights into consumer preference, emotions, and decision processes. The research has considered ethical factors, such as consumer consent and privacy, when using neuromarketing methods. The results identify knowledgeable gaps in the areas of application of neuromarketing. There is a need for further research to grasp the uses and limitations of neuromarketing technologies in modern marketing applications. Neuro-marketing provide the insights related to consumer's subconscious reactions and expressive responses to marketing stimuli. This helps marketers to understand the consumer preference, motivation, and decision-making processes. The study helps the marketers to focus on more effective and focused marketing campaigns based on personal preferences and behaviours. Neuromarketing and facial recognition technologies provide real-time tracking and feedback, which increases their conversion rate.

The main objective of this study was to examine the way visual attention optimization through the neuromarketing techniques can benefit the user experience in digital marketing. The research addresses the problem of how to engage online users effectively and increase satisfaction and interactions with the digital platform. The findings showed that visual attention is strongly related to user experience and that neuromarketing generates a positive impact on user experience and visual attention. Neuromarketing mediation analysis showed that there was a partial-mediating effect between visual attention and user experience, which increased the influence of attention on user engagement. SEM model showed exemplary fit indices. It is recommended that further studies should examine the cross-cultural differences, other mediating or moderating factors, and the viability of new technological advances like AR, VR, and AI in digital marketing. The ethical standards of neuromarketing practice is also a key area of untapped study.



Where Neuromarketing meets AI, companies are experiencing a revolution in learning, engaging, and connecting with consumers. Neuromarketing, which uses the reasonable and emotional responses of human beings and also the predictive and analytical capabilities of AI. More than technology, this convergence is transforming the core idea of business strategy by empowering decision-makers to break down the code to unconscious consumer behavior in real time. As companies tap into this convergence tends to reshaping customer value with optimized innovation. This study talks of how this convergence unlocks new plans of consumer understanding and value creation in the velocity, flexibility, and imagination-driven digital economy. The union of emotion-fueled marketing and intelligent automation does more yield enabling intuitive connection between people and brands. This chapter ultimately

and loyalty. Particularly, this study investigates mechanisms that contribute to changes in consumer behavior as a result of personalized experiences. Therefore, this study employs an integrated mixed-methods methodology that leverages both qualitative insights with professionals from the industry as well as quantitative analysis with data that has been collected from consumers. The study also reveals that AI-powered personalization is boosting customer engagement and loyalty to a great extent by offering customers experiences that are personalized to their tastes and preferences. The sense of pertinence and value developed due to provision of tailored ideas, information, and offers is therefore boosting consumer customer satisfaction and loyalty.



Virtual Reality (VR) is redefining consumer experiences by offering immersive environments that engage multiple senses. This chapter investigates the neural mechanisms underlying consumer behavior in VR using a neuromarketing approach. Researchers conducted an experimental study combining electroencephalography (EEG) and biometric measures with behavioral data to compare consumers' cognitive and emotional responses in a VR shopping scenario versus a traditional web-based platform. 33 participants completed purchase tasks in both environments while their neural activity and physiological signals were recorded. Results show that VR elicited higher cognitive engagement and memory activation but also induced greater mental workload than the traditional platform. These findings advance our understanding of how immersive virtual experiences affect the consumer's brain and behavior. The chapter highlights the value of consumer neuroscience tools in evaluating emerging marketing technologies and provides guidance for practitioners seeking to leverage VR in enhancing customer experience.

This study focuses on gender variations in the emotional and cognitive reactions of young American consumers (ages 18 to 25) to fast food brand logos. 50 participants were shown the logos of companies like McDonald's, KFC, and Domino's using a mixed-methods technique. Galvanic Skin Response (GSR) and Facial Expression Analysis (FEA) analyzed emotional responses, while eye-tracking evaluated visual attentiveness. The results show that while both sexes identify fast food with enjoyment and excitement, males prioritize flavor and convenience while women associate it with negative emotions like boredom or worry. Additionally, post-consumption shame was higher among women. The emotional impact of each brand differed, and well-known logos garnered more visual attention. By emphasizing how brand familiarity and emotional involvement influence young consumers' behavior in developed countries, the study advances Neuromarketing.

# Preface

We are witnessing a profound shift in the business landscape—a transition from guessing what consumers want to understanding the biological *"why"* behind every click, glance, and purchase. This double-blind reviewed book, *Reshaping Business at the Intersection of Neuromarketing and AI*, serves as a comprehensive guide to this emerging frontier, where the precision of data science meets the complexity of human cognition.

For decades, marketing relied heavily on self-reported data—surveys and focus groups designed to capture what people *think* they feel. Today, that model is evolving. By integrating Artificial Intelligence with neuromarketing tools such as eye-tracking, galvanic skin response (GSR), and facial expression analysis (FEA), businesses can move beyond the limitations of conscious reporting and engage directly with the subconscious drivers of behavior.

This volume brings together diverse perspectives to explore how this technological convergence is being applied across industries. Moving beyond theoretical frameworks, the chapters emphasize practical applications, offering insights into how organizations can better understand, predict, and respond to consumer behavior.

## CHAPER OVERVIEW

### 1. AI and Neuromarketing in Retail and E-commerce: Enhancing the Shopping Experience and Conversion

This chapter examines how neuro-tools are applied in both digital and physical retail environments. It highlights how AI-driven insights can optimize the "path to purchase" by aligning interface design with cognitive comfort, ultimately improving conversion rates.

## 2. AI-Driven Predictive Analytics in Neuromarketing: Unveiling Consumer Minds for Strategic Marketing Insights

This chapter serves as the analytical backbone of the book. It discusses the transition from descriptive data (what happened) to predictive intelligence (what will happen), highlighting how AI can model subconscious reactions to forecast future market trends with high precision.

## 3. AI-Driven Product Recommendation Systems Informed by Emotional Responses

Traditional recommendation engines rely on historical data; this chapter introduces a paradigm shift by incorporating real-time emotional feedback. It is significant because it illustrates a future where shopping platforms respond to a user's current mood and affective state, rather than just their past clicks.

## 4. Biased by Design? Exploring the Hidden Influence of AI on Subconscious Consumer Behavior

Crucial for ethical discourse, this chapter investigates the "dark side" of automated influence. It examines how algorithmic biases can inadvertently (or intentionally) manipulate subconscious vulnerabilities, making it an essential read for maintaining ethical standards in neuro-augmented marketing.

## 5. Brandfluence: Mastering Online Identity in a Hyperconnected World

This chapter bridges the gap between individual psychology and social influence. It explores how brands build digital personas that resonate with the collective subconscious of online communities, providing a strategic framework for managing reputation in a world of instant viral feedback.

## 6. Eye-Tracking and AI-Optimizing Visual Attention and User Experience in Digital Marketing: A Bibliometric Approach

By using a bibliometric lens, this chapter provides a rigorous academic foundation for visual research. It is important because it synthesizes existing literature to show how the marriage of eye-tracking data and AI algorithms has become the gold standard for auditing user experience (UX) and visual hierarchy.

## 7. Next-Gen Marketing Intelligence: Exploring the Neuro-scientific Technique on Marketing

Acting as a technical primer, this chapter provides an in-depth look at the specific hardware and software used in modern labs. It is significant for its role in demystifying the technology, making the complex neuro-scientific methods accessible to business strategists and marketers.

## 8. Optimizing Visual Attention to Enhance the User Experience in Digital Marketing through Neuromarketing

Complementing Chapter 7, this chapter focuses on the *application* of attention-mapping. Its importance lies in its actionable advice for designers and marketers to reduce cognitive load and ensure that the most critical information is processed by the consumer first.

## 9. Reinventing Business at the Intersection of Neuromarketing and AI

This chapter serves as a high-level strategic synthesis. It argues that the combination of these fields is not just an incremental improvement but a complete reinvention of the business model, shifting the focus from "selling" to "understanding and serving."

## 10. Strategizing in Immersive Realities: Case-Based Insights into Metaverse, AR, VR and Neuromarketing

This section uses real-world cases to explore the newest marketing frontiers. It is important because it provides a practical look at how brands are already using immersive environments to capture data that is far more granular than what is possible on a flat screen.

## 11. The Impact of AI-Driven Personalization on Consumer Engagement and Loyalty

Focused on the long-term relationship, this chapter examines how AI-driven insights can build genuine loyalty. It distinguishes between "creepy" over-personalization and "helpful" anticipation of needs, which is the key to sustainable brand-consumer relationships.

## 12. Unveiling Neural Mechanisms Behind Consumer Behavior in Virtual Reality

Focused on the "how" of VR, this chapter looks at why the brain treats virtual experiences as "real." It is crucial for developers and marketers who need to understand the biological mechanisms of presence and immersion to create effective VR campaigns.

## 13. Visual Cues and Emotional Triggers: A Study of Fast-food Advertising Using GSR, FEA and Eye-tracking

Providing a concrete laboratory study, this final chapter uses the fast-food industry as a case study. Its importance lies in its "triangulation" method—using three different neuro-tools simultaneously—to prove how specific visual elements can trigger immediate hunger and purchase intent.

This book is intended for researchers, forward-thinking business leaders, and students seeking to understand the invisible forces shaping the modern marketplace. We invite you to explore these chapters not just as a collection of studies, but as a blueprint for the next generation of business intelligence.

Fernando Ortiz-Rodríguez
Miguel Sahagun
Anuj Kumar
Nishu Ayedee

Chapter 1

# AI and Neuromarketing in Retail and E-Commerce: Enhancing the Shopping Experience and Conversion

**Sunayna Khurana**
http://orcid.org/0000-0001-8214-9180
*University School of Management Studies, Rayat Bahra University, Mohali, India*

## ABSTRACT

*Retail and e-commerce are undergoing a dramatic overhaul, and much of that change is due to the use of Artificial Intelligence. Rather than being a distant future concept, AI is now becoming the heart of many shopping platforms, supporting brands to read, anticipate, and respond to shoppers in ways that feel both personal and efficient. Neuromarketing also has evolved as an innovative discipline integrated with AI that utilises neuroscience techniques to predict and understand consumers' subconscious responses to marketing stimuli. The scope of this study covers a dual focus, investigative innovations in a perfect e-commerce environment, while also analysing omnichannel strategies that connect physical and digital retail spaces, thus presenting a full understanding of the retail ecosystem. The result of this study reveals the existing knowledge gaps and presents promising directions for future research, enhancing our knowledge of the combined impact of AI and neuromarketing on the shopping experience in retail ad e commerce.*

## 1. INTRODUCTION

Retail and e-commerce are undergoing a dramatic overhaul, and much of that change is due to the use of Artificial Intelligence. Rather than being a distant future

DOI: 10.4018/979-8-3373-5997-7.ch001

concept, AI is now becoming the heart of many shopping platforms, supporting brands to read, anticipate, and respond to shoppers in ways that feel both personal and efficient. By analysing the big data in real time, these systems refine product suggestions, optimising stock levels, and entertaining routine customer queries, thereby reducing costs while boosting satisfaction. The results are amazing like consumers experience smoother checkouts, strategic promotions, and even chatbots that remember purchase history, making every experience whether online or at physical store feel a little more like it was customise just for them(Sharma, 2023).

Neuromarketing also has evolved as an innovative discipline integrated with AI that utilises neuroscience techniques to predict and understand consumers' subconscious responses to marketing stimuli. By using various technology like electroencephalography (EEG), eye-tracking and functional magnetic resonance imaging (fMRI), neuromarketing captures unprocessed emotional and cognitive responses and offers detailed information which facilitate smoother consumer decision-making processes. This helps marketers develop strategic campaigns that resound with consumers on a subconscious level, enhancing brand engagement and increasing customer conversion (Mitu et al., 2024).

The integration of AI and neuromarketing indicates a paradigm transformation that integrates sophisticated technological capabilities with a clear understanding of human psychology. The integration of advanced data analytics and subconscious consumer behavior analysis facilitate a clear understanding of next-generation retail ecosystems, where omnichannel strategies and experiential technologies synergize to reshape the customer shopping journey. This integration of technologies enables not only personalised shopping experiences but also helps in predictive marketing, emotional engagement, and behavioral forecasting. Therefore, AI and neuromarketing play important roles in the evolution of modern retail and e-commerce (Suomala et al., 2012)

## 2. OBJECTIVES AND SCOPE

This study sets out to map the ground between AI and neuromarketing, asking how the two together can lift the shopping experience and push conversion rates. Specifically, it will look at many angles- personalized messaging, sharper ad targeting, leaner operations-that AI-driven tools paired with brain-inspired insights can improve both digital and physical stores. The scope of the study covers a dual focus, investigative innovations in perfect e-commerce settings while also seeing omnichannel strategies that connect physical and digital retail spaces, thus presenting a full understanding of the retail ecosystem (Arora, 2024).

This research addresses important questions, such as:

1. How does the synergy between AI and neuromarketing influence consumer behavior?
2. How does this synergy improve personalization and predictive capabilities to increase sales?
3. What are the important concerns of ethical, and privacy associated with the use of such integrated technologies?

This study also explores various uses and implementations to assess the practical impacts of these technologies on the evolving retail landscape.

## 3. METHODOLOGICAL FRAMEWORK AND LITERATURE REVIEW APPROACH

The review begins with a systematic scan of peer-reviewed literature on AI, neuromarketing, broader marketing tactics, and changing consumer behavior in retail and e-commerce. Qualitative threads are derived from in-depth case studies and thematic analyses of landmark articles. Within this design, comparative inquiries compare diverse AI neuromarketing tools, revealing how their synergy accelerates innovation on the shop floor and online. Guided by a thematic synthesis, author tracked themes ranging from hyper-personalized offers and algorithmic nudges to privacy debates and seamless omnichannel links. The result of this study reveals the existing knowledge gaps and presents promising directions for future research, enhancing our knowledge of the combined impact of AI and neuromarketing on the shopping experience in retail ad e commerce.

### 3.1 Foundations of Artificial Intelligence in Retail and E-commerce

Artificial intelligence consists of advanced computational methods capable of replicating human intelligence in retail functions. Various AI advanced technologies like machine learning (ML), predictive analytics, natural language processing (NLP), and deep learning, have drastically transformed retail and e-commerce operations. Machine learning algorithms analyze customer data patterns to understand customer future behavior, while NLP supports informal interfaces like chatbots, that deliver customer service automatically similar with human-like responsiveness. Predictive analytics helps retailers forecast demand fluctuations and optimize supply chain logistics proactively in due time[REMOVED HYPERLINK FIELD].

## 3.2 AI Powered Personalization Techniques

The main advantage of AI in retail is its capability to provide highly personalized shopping experiences. Product recommendation and suggestion algorithms are important to artificial intelligence in the retail and e-commerce. These are machine learning and deep learning technologies that identify a customer's feelings regarding the preferences and emotions on past purchases. Collaborative filtering is an important method that is particularly used to understand a customer's potential purchase intentions. Three types of collaborative filtering (customer based, product based, and hybrid) are there. Customer based collaborative filtering predicts a customer's interests based on other similar customers purchase pattern but different from the main customer (Yu et al., 2024). While product based collaborative filtering emphases on the item on which a customer has shown their feelings and emotions. The algorithm will then compile a data of all other customers who have shown similar feelings and emotions on that product and prepare a list of their liking and disliking. The hybrid collaborative filtering method combines the importance of customer based and product-based algorithms to create a more critical predictive algorithm (Dahouda & Joe, 2021). Other important techniques like content-based filtering, deep learning and contextual bandit are also used in product recommendations for enhanced accuracy.

## 3.3 Neuromarketing Concepts and Technologies

Neuromarketing represents the combination of neuroscience and marketing and uses scientific methods to investigate how customer brain responds to marketing stimuli. Techniques such as Electroencephalography (EEG) provide real-time measurements of electrical brain activity and gain knowledge for understanding consumer behaviour, while functional Magnetic Resonance Imaging (fMRI) offers detailed images of activated brain regions, to understand how the brain responds to marketing stimuli, providing information related to consumer preferences and decision-making processes. Galvanic skin response gauges capture customers attention patterns and visual focus by eye-tracking, and physiological arousal, which help in getting the information on emotional engagement. These tools collectively offer important information beyond self-observed data, about the subconscious drivers of consumer behavior (Tavishi Yadav, 2024).

Two key attributes of neuromarketing:

## 1. Emotional Appeal

The emotional appeal is based on the limbic system-based element of neuromarketing which is a set of brain structures located deep within the brain, mainly responsible for controlling emotions, memory, and motivation. It's a critical network which is involved in processing emotions and feelings, forming memories, and influencing individual behavior, mainly in existence related functions like feeding, fighting, fleeing, and reproduction. It plays important role in automatic process of customer reaction measurement, facial action coding systems, and sentiment analysis on digital media. In neuromarketing, application of emotional appeals mainly to excite the limbic system, which is in the brain for processing emotions(Mogaji et al., 2020) . Advanced technology like fMRI (Functional magnetic resonance imaging) and EEG (electroencephalography) are used to study the limbic system activity. Instruments like HRV (heart rate variability) and GSR (galvanic skin response) are the main tools for the quantification process in Autonomic response measurement (Kim et al., 2020). This process analyses physiological responses to monitor reaction toward emotional marketing stimuli effectively. The results offer important information related to hidden emotional reaction about customers' perceptions related to ads. Emotional responses are identified by facial action coding system, by analysing minute expressions and facial movements(Alsharif et al., 2023) . Simultaneously, sentiment analysis method uses natural language processing techniques to identify choices and biases by customers about specific brands and products.

## 2. Memory Encoding

Memory encoding helps in making an impression on an individual about an event in marketing. Cognitive load assessment, priming, neuroimaging of the memory centers, contextual influence and implicit memory testing are its important dimensions (Dewey, 2023).The ability to measure the cognitive load that customer feel when encountered any marketing stimuli, is the important features of memory encoding. This function helps in understanding an individual's insight from processing of their information and the information encoding process done by the brain. For monitoring memory-related brain regions' activity, fMRI (Functional magnetic resonance imaging) is commonly used (Murti & Ghosh, 2023) .The hippocampus is important region of brain that is triggered during the exposure of any promotional materials.

Implicit Association Test (IAT) neuromarketing tool use for testing implicit memory. This tool effectively conducts the association tests and access the quality and reliability of memory encoding. There is no requirement of explicitly recall, we can easily extract insights from IAT, as it works by analysing the unconscious associations (Cueva et al., 2020). Various marketing research are conducted to analyse the effects of contextual factors during the process of encoding of memories. Several sources have confirmed that there is an impact of input like music and graphic appeal on the process of memory encoding during a marketing activity,

Optimizing product placement, refining advertising messages, and enhancing shopping environments are the important marketing applications of neuromarketing to produce favourable customer emotional responses. Marketers can develop effective stimuli that trigger positive purchasing intentions by understanding mechanisms such as emotional resonance, memory encoding, and sensory processing. These mechanisms are not similar like traditional surveys or focus groups, which may be biased by cognitive distortions or social desirability. Neuromarketing shows the customer implicit preferences, providing a more reliable information for strategic marketing decisions (Gurgu et al., 2020).

Neuromarketing have expanded its relevance in consumer research, enabling market segmentation based on emotional and cognitive profiles, by the rigorous methodology and technological precision thus enriching personalization potential in retail contexts (Białowąs & Szyszka, 2019).

## 3.4 AI Role in Enhancing Neuromarketing Capabilities

AI integration with neuromarketing has significantly reformed methodologies by facilitating the analysis of complex neurophysiological data. Machine learning algorithms categorize patterns within Electroencephalography signals, fMRI images, and biometric responses, facilitating real-time interpretation of consumer emotions and preferences. This automation improve the scalability and accuracy of neuromarketing techniques, which traditionally were limited by manual data processing constraints (Kusá & Beličková, 2023).

Real-time feedback data given by AI allow marketers to refine marketing campaigns based on changing consumer reactions. AI-driven sentimental analysis and facial recognition process further transform emotional nuances in customer reactions, permitting highly granular segmentation and personalized targeting. Such features enable adaptive marketing interventions that resonate with consumers at an emotional level, improving customer engagement and conversion rate (Papić et al., 2023).

The important relationship between AI and neuromarketing gives predictive insights that help to develop innovative campaign with more precision, elevating the return on marketing investments (Goncalves et al., 2024).

## 4. INFLUENCE OF SYNERGY BETWEEN AI AND NEUROMARKETING ON CONSUMER BEHAVIOR

AI and neuromarketing technologies have been utilised in several critical applications. Personalization engines vigorously customize product suggestions and recommendation for individual customer, based on their historical and contextual information, thereby improving sales conversion. AI based chatbots and virtual assistants smoothly processed the customer queries and transaction round the clock. Dynamic pricing algorithms monitor and control product prices in real time based on competition, customer demand, and stock levels. AI also plays a key role in identifying the risk of fraud in advance by using pattern recognition method for identify suspicious transactions and secure consumer trust. At the same time, it reforms inventory management by demand prediction and automating refilling processes, which reduces operational expenses and prevents stock shortages, thus increasing overall retail efficiency and customer satisfaction (Zhuk & Yatskyi, 2024).

### Related case study of Alibaba

World's biggest e-commerce and technology conglomerates, Alibaba has taken advantage of artificial intelligence (AI) to transform various industries, like e-commerce, supply chain, cloud computing and finance. Alibaba become pioneer in digital transformation by integrates AI into its business ecosystem to improve customer experiences, optimize supply chain management, and drive operational efficacy. Alibaba's successfully implemented innovative AI technologies like personalized shopping recommendations, smart logistics, AI-powered customer service, fraud detection, and intelligent business analytics by adopting. These technologies helped in setting up industry advanced standards for automation and big data-based decision-making by streamlining the various processes. Alibaba regularly improved AI competences by using advanced machine learning (ML), natural language processing (NLP), and computer vision, to maintain their leadership in innovation and market competition in whole industry. The five innovative ways which Alibaba is utilizing AI to reform e-commerce, supply chain, and enterprise resource planning solutions and making it as an essential tool in its chasing the business growth, innovation, and enhanced customer satisfaction are given below:

### a) Personalized Shopping Recommendations

Alibaba's AI based recommendation engine enhanced the level of customer engagement and improve the sales. There was 35% increase in conversion rates as customers explore products according to their needs, which result to higher purchases.

AI also suggested complementary and higher-value products, inspiring customers to do bundled purchases which led to 20% increase in the order value on an average. Bounce rates are also decreased by 50% as customer investing time in surfing the online platform for right products than leaving due to irresistible choices. Retention rate of customer also increased, as more customers coming back to Alibaba's digital platforms because of the best shopping experience(*5 Ways AliBaba Is Using AI [Case Study] [2025] - DigitalDefynd*, n.d.).

## b) Smart Logistics and Warehouse Automation

Alibaba's supply chain operations also shown improvements in speed, efficiency, and cost reduction by integrating AI. There was 50% drop in order processing time, speeding up deliveries and increased customer satisfaction. Automated warehouses of Alibaba delivered over 1 billion orders without any hurdles during the peak sales and ensured timely fulfilment despite of huge rise in demand. They also reduced the logistics costs by 30% through AI-driven route optimization process by making more efficient and predictable delivery times. Warehouse productivity also improved by 70% by implementing smart robots with continuously working of machines without stoppage, reducing requirement of manual labor. Moreover, there was 25% reduction in stockouts and overstock issues with the help of AI-powered demand forecasting, thereby improving inventory efficiency.

## c) Customer Service and Chatbots

With the help of AliMe and Alice, the AI-powered tools for customer service, Alibaba made significant improvements in efficiency. AI handled the 95% of customer inquiries which reduced the for human resource's workload. Response times was also increased by 80%, as maximum queries resolved within fraction of seconds, thereby improving customer satisfaction. This also led to the 50% reduction in customer service costs, as there was less need of human resource to resolve the inquiries. Furthermore, Alibaba's customer retention rate also improved by 30%, as customer liked quick and effective support given by Alice. Simultaneously, the other AI tool, AliMe managed millions of customer interactions by preventing delays customer service and ensuring cherished shopping experiences during the high customer's footfall and sales events like Singles' Day. These chatbot also help in achieving higher conversion rates, as AI-powered recommendations, suggestions and immediate support guided customers toward completing their purchases(5 Ways AliBaba Is Using AI [Case Study] [2025] - DigitalDefynd, n.d.).

## d) Fraud Detection and Risk Management

There was also a significant reduction in fraudulent activities across all Alibaba's platforms, with the help of AI-powered fraud detection system. The 60% reduction in fraudulent transactions helped to create a safe shopping environment for customer. AI-driven detection of counterfeit activities also helped in replacing 95% of fake product listings, thereby improving the Alibaba's reputation as a trusted shopping place. Moreover, the automated fraud detection system minimised the requirement of human resource, thereby cut down the operational costs by 40%. The AI-powered authentication process also minimized un-authorized access and identify theft which led to a 30% improvement in transaction security and safe experience for customers. The risk assessment engine powered by AI has also improved Alibaba's acquiescence with international financial regulations, confirming secured payment processing and actions for fraud prevention that match international guidelines (*5 Ways AliBaba Is Using AI [Case Study] [2025] - DigitalDefynd*, n.d.).

## e) Intelligent Business Analytics and Decision-Making

Alibaba's decision-making processes also transformed by the implementation of AI-driven business analytics. There was 40% improvement in demand forecasting accuracy which help in improving logistics efficiency and minimising the inventory costs. By implementing best pricing strategies powered by AI, Alibaba reported 15% increase in profit. They have done real-time pricing adjustments based on changes in demand and market conditions.AI based Customer sentiment analysis helped Alibaba to act 30% quicker toward market trends and thereby enhancing product recommendations, suggestions and customer engagement metrics. With the help of AI-powered insights, many traders also reported increase in their sales conversion rates by 20% due to best product positioning and effective personalized marketing strategies. Real-time analytics provided by ET Brain's significantly improved the agility of Alibaba, empowering marketing team to take best decisions quickly. This kind of agility was very important in major sales events like Singles' Day, where AI based real-time insights helped in price optimization, allocation of inventory, and successful implementation of marketing strategies.(*5 Ways AliBaba Is Using AI [Case Study] [2025] - DigitalDefynd*, n.d.)

AI-driven customer engagement tools also play a critical role in maintaining ongoing customer interactions with digital retail platforms and increasing brand loyalty. Retailers can see a significant increase in customer lifetime value and build a competitive edge by incorporating AI strategies into their business models (Helen & Siva Sankar, 2025).

# 5. IMPACT OF SYNERGY BETWEEN AI AND NEUROMARKETING ON SALES THROUGH PERSONALIZATION AND PREDICTIVE CAPABILITIES

## 5.1 Personalisation Techniques

AI-driven personalization, by using collaborative and content-based filtering, and hybrid models recommend and suggest products which closely match the consumer's preferences and browsing habits. Virtual assistants with advanced natural language understanding, also help the consumers in exploring product brochures and making purchasing decisions in real time. These AI elements collectively reduce hurdles and customer confusions, improve conversion rates, and build customer loyalty (Perumallaplli, 2014).The below case study beautifully demonstrates the application personalization techniques adopted by Sephora for better customer experience and satisfaction.

### Case study of Personalization technique: Sephora

Sephora's adoption of AI-powered virtual assistants and neuromarketing tools in the beauty retail sec, is an example of gaining success through advanced technologies. The brand has effectively blended digital innovation with sensory brand engagement by integrating technologies like chatbots, augmented reality (AR), and skin-analysis systems. This strategy created a revolution in product recommendation processes and in-store experiences, significantly improving consumer trust, satisfaction, and loyalty(*(PDF) Sephora Smart Customer's Experience Enhancement*, n.d.). The innovative ways, Sephora utilises AI-powered virtual assistants and neuromarketing tools are given below:

- **Virtual Artist & AR mirrors**: This feature co-developed with ModiFace, scans customers' faces and facilitate applications of makeup virtually. The mobile AR tool handled 1.6 million visits and 45 million product trials during its first eight weeks. Sephora also reported sharp rise in sales by 31% and conversion rates by up to 90% through the application of AR mirrors at physical retail stores (Scholz & Duffy, 2018).Sephora's innovate tools successfully manifested the neuromarketing principle of enhancing emotional engagement through realism. Brand reduced the customer's uncertainty, stimulate affective response, and reinforce customer trust and loyalty by incorporating skin-scanning systems and realistic AR trials (Rauschnabel et al., 2024).
- **Color IQ & Skin IQ**: By capturing precise skin tone data, handheld scanners assign a four-digit code that help in product matching across various chan-

nels. AR experiences improved cognitive control, increased consumers' perceived autonomy and willingness to purchase (Whang et al., 2021). Sephora's Virtual Artist created an "intimate, familiar" experience for customer far beyond transactional engagement by removing the boundaries between self and brand, through being consistent with AR marketing literature (Scholz & Duffy, 2018). Customers were able to virtually manipulate their appearance, which resulted in improvement in product confidence and emotional connection with brand.

- **Beacon-triggered content**: Personalized maps, promotions details, and list of wishlist items were easily delivered through push and in-app notification immediately to customers as they enter physical stores(*Sephora Creates an Online "In-Store" Experience through Generative AI*, n.d.).

## 5.2 Predictive analytics

This technique enables the anticipation of changes in consumer choices and market trends by examining purchase trends, customer browsing behaviors, and influence of other external factors. This understanding allows e-commerce players to proactively adjust their offerings and promotions to match with emerging customer needs and wants. Real-time product targeting dynamically change website content, sharing promotional messages or product recommendations customised to the visitor's current session data and their intent. This adaptive content marketing enhances the importance of the customer shopping experience, leading to increased customer engagement and a higher possibility of purchase (S, 2025).

Regular improvements in AI models, boost by growing data volumes and enhanced computational techniques, have shift personalization beyond static recommendations towards adaptive, context-aware client experiences that evolve live with behavioural cues, thus significantly increasing engagement data (Sharma, 2023)[REMOVED HYPERLINK FIELD].

# 6. CONSUMER BEHAVIOR AND PSYCHOLOGICAL IMPACTS

## 6.1 Improved Psychological Mechanisms in Online Shopping

AI integration neuromarketing highlights the critical role of various factors in consumer decision-making, particularly those associated with emotional appeal, memory encoding, and triggers for impulsive purchases. Emotional messaging and memory recall, facilitated by neuromarketing, are essential in influencing consumer purchasing decisions by illustrating how specific stimuli can forge stronger emotional connections, thereby enhancing a consumer's ability to recall a brand. Neuromarketing influences consumer behavior by shaping emotional and cognitive responses. Artificial intelligence and digital experiences serve as influential intermediaries, translating these neurological insights into effective marketing strategies. Companies that incorporate emotional design, memory prompts, and AI-driven personalization into their digital platforms can significantly enhance consumer engagement and decision-making (Beyari et al., 2024).

AI systems customise offers based on identifying consumer's unconscious behavioural patterns, pushing consumers towards desired actions while optimizing timing and message framing. Like scarcity marketing stimulate impulse purchases like limited time offers, flash sales or countdown timers' strategies etc encourage the consumer and drives them to purchase immediately. Some tag lines like "Hurry! Only a few are left in stock!" or "Sale ends in 3 hours!" also work in similar way. Also, retailers also use attracting strategies such like visually appealing 'limited stock' signs in red colour or using ticking clocks to create an urge of buying in emergency on the customer, all developed to make the customer to react quick otherwise, they miss the opportunity.

AI with neuromarketing also help in other digital marketing tactic such as retargeting advertisements which enable to again catch the attention of target market who have interest in purchasing a product but not doing. These ads target those customers who checked the product online and added in a shopping cart but not purchased. These retargeting ads integrated with other marketing strategies, try to influence the desired will and the underlying benefits such as providing cash or quantity discounts or free shipping, which led the consumer to buy the product. These digital marketing tactics intensify impulse buying by pleasing to psychological drivers like instant gratification and. fear of missing out (FOMO)(Aliyev, 1996). These knowledge train the marketers to drive customer purchase behavior responsibly and effectively with the help of these advanced tools (Yadete & Kant, 2023).

## 6.2 The Role of Trust, Privacy, and Ethical Perceptions in Consumer Acceptance

Trust and privacy perceptions play a mediating role in consumer acceptance of AI and neuromarketing-driven personalization. Customers always having a concerns over data collection practices and algorithmic transparency, influencing their willingness to use AI-powered platforms (Canhoto et al., 2024). Trust will reduce these concerns, becoming crucial in enhancing sustained customer satisfaction and loyalty (Sinha et al., 2024).

Retailers must take stringent steps to protect customer's data for encashing the benefits of customization. Consumers want clear information about usage of their personal data and assurances of privacy measures, which are important for achieving ethical marketing standards and meeting regulatory requirements (Kavya G B, 2024).

The ongoing relationship between technological capabilities and consumer rights gives the directions to the evolving retail landscape, driving the improvement of responsible personalization paradigms.

## 6.3 Influence of Generational and Cultural Differences

The adoption pattern of AI and neuromarketing strategies changes across generations and cultural contexts. Millennials and Gen Z tend to be more receptive to AI-driven personalization, appreciating convenience and personalised experiences, whereas Gen X shows reservations linked to privacy and technology adoption (Bag et al., 2022).

Cross-cultural differences also occur prominently like, consumers from regions with more stringent privacy regulations like European union countries, tend to show higher sensitivity to data sharing than those in markets with less exposure to data privacy issues. Due to these challenges, it is important for retailers to develop context-sensitive marketing strategies that respect local norms and expectations(Menaka & Selvam, 2025) .

For internation retail enterprises, understanding these demographic issues is crucial for developing effective, culturally attuned strategies that maximize customer engagement and conversion across diverse markets (Bhatt & Singh, 2024) marketers to optimize product placement in both online and offline store, thereby improving product visibility and conversion rates (LakshminarayanaK et al., 2024)

This integration facilitate AI-powered A/B testing, which allows marketers to optimize various aspects of their online presence like websites, marketing campaigns, and product recommendations, by using machine learning to analyze customer behavior and automatically adjust elements to improve performance, ultimately increasing sales conversions and marketing return on investment (Tadimarri et al., 2024).

## 6.4 Bridging Offline and Online Shopping Experiences

Seamless integration of offline and online shopping by AI and neuromarketing collectively done through omnichannel retail strategies. AI-powered analytics process the customer data across digital and physical touchpoints, creating unified, personalized experiences that maintain consistency across all channels. Neuromarketing adds more value to this integration by revealing emotional and behavioural evidences that inform how customers interact with each channel, allowing personalised strategies that resonate in offline stores and online platforms alike (Arora, 2024).

Such integration enhances customer satisfaction and loyalty, as consumers encounter clear messaging, personalized offers, and easy transitions between offline store and online environments. This systematic approach take advantage of plus points of both channels, improving sales and long-term customer relationships (Helen & Siva Sankar, 2025).

## 6.5 Mobile Commerce and AI-Driven Personalization

Mobile commerce serves as a critical channel in this integration by leveraging AI and neuromarketing to adapt customer experiences vigorously on handheld devices (Pillarisetty & Mishra, 2022). Mobile commerce (m-commerce) becomes an important frontier for AI application due to increased reach of retailers by the proliferation of smartphones. With the various AI enabled features like voice search, chatbots, and app personalization, adapting interactions to on-the-go consumer behaviors, m-commerce increase sales and customer satisfaction. Insights from neuromarketing about mobile user attention, eye-tracking, and engagement patterns help in developing effective design and content strategies that maximize the effectiveness of mobile interfaces (Pillarisetty & Mishra, 2022).

AI-enhanced mobile services enable the retailers to deliver fast, accurate responses, contextual recommendations, and personalized promotional schemes and offers according to real-time user context. These technological advances address the issues related to screen size, navigation difficulty, and limited input modalities typical in mobile usage (Rifan, 2024).

Thus integration of AI and neuromarketing open opportunities to capture and retain customer attention on mobile platforms, fostering a compelling and efficient shopping experience for consumers (Bhatt & Singh, 2024).

## 6.6 Global Case Study of Retailers' Adoption of AI and Neuromarketing Tools

### Honda UK

With LifeShirt smart garment, a wearable physiological monitoring system by Vivo Metrics, Honda UK conducted a ground-breaking study, to analyse subconscious emotional responses of car buyers at its showrooms. The device tracked data like heart rate, respiration, and muscle tension while customers interacted with showroom sales staff. Results of this study shows that price-focused discussions consistently prompted stress responses and emotionally supportive conversations and a comforting showroom atmosphere led to more positive physiological response. This information triggered Honda to reshape showroom layouts and extra training of sales personnel to shift from price-based conversation toward emotionally supported engagement, based on measured customers' emotional conditions given by LifeShirt smart garment. The result was a more emotionally intelligent sales process aimed at improved customer comfort, reducing dependency on price incentives, and finally driving improved buyer engagement(The Hidden Persuaders: How Businesses Are Using Neuroscience to Make You Buy | WIRED, n.d.).

This study becomes a fantastic example of neuromarketing for experiential retail design and staff strategy, showcasing how biometric feedback can help real-world business transaction improvements based on subconscious consumer behavior.

# 7. OPERATIONAL AND BUSINESS PERFORMANCE BENEFITS

## 7.1 Business Benefits

Integrating AI and neuromarketing gives significant business advantages, including increased conversion rates and customer lifetime value. Personalized experiences driven by AI and enriched with neurophysiological insights encourage the customers for repeat purchases and creating brand loyalty, directly increasing the profitability of retailers.

Automation in marketing by integration of Integrating AI and neuromarketing reduces operational costs by effective campaign management and customer support functions, while efficient inventory management minimizes the waste and stock-related issues. These efficiencies help the retailers to have a competitive edge in the crowded e-commerce market, by facilitating fast adaptation to consumer trends and enabling scalable personalization at reduced cost (Rapeerat Thanyawatpornkul, 2024).

Furthermore, AI-supported A/B testing supported by neuromarketing data continually improve product and marketing strategies, increasing sales conversion and maximizing return on investment (Adeleke et al., 2022).

## 7.2 Inventory and Supply Chain Optimization

AI technologies anticipate consumer demand by processing behavioural and neuromarketing data and facilitate supply chains to respond proactively. Predictive analytics forecast purchasing surges or declines, helping inventory replenishment with greater accuracy and timing (Perumallaplli, 2014).

This technology help in preventing stock outs problems that frustrate consumers and overstock that requires capital unnecessarily. Neuromarketing facilitate in understanding customers' emotional triggers behind seasonal trends and product preferences, and also gives deep qualitative insights for demand predictions (Helen & Siva Sankar, 2025).

The integration of these approaches helps in fostering a responsive, agile supply chain which is capable of meeting fluctuating customer's demands while maintaining cost-efficiency and customer satisfaction (Perumallaplli, 2014).

## 7.3 Emerging Technologies and Their Potential Impact

New emerging AI technologies such as large language models (LLMs) and deep reinforcement learning have a potential to further advance retail personalization by facilitating more nuanced, focused consumer interactions and real-time strategy optimization. These technologies can engage in complex conversations and drive consumer decision-making with increasing fidelity (Shareef et al., 2024).

At the same time, developments in neuroimaging and biometric sensor technologies will produce fruitful consumer data, supporting in more precise interpretation of emotional and cognitive responses. Integration of these sensors with AI analytics will improve the granularity and predictive ability of neuromarketing and will open new areas for customization of user experience (Liu-Thompkins et al., 2022). Development of ethical AI frameworks for adding artificial empathy and human-centric design principles are important for ensuring long-term consumer acceptance and ethical integrity (LakshminarayanaK et al., 2024).

From a technological aspect, another untouched area is the integration of multimodal AI systems in neuromarketing research. Most of the studies largely focus on single-modality input such as EEG or GSR (galvanic skin response), overseeing how deep learning models can coordinate with multiple physiological signals like brain activity, pupil dilation, facial micro expressions, voice tone to yield more reliable emotional and cognitive descriptions (Smidts et al., 2014). Integrating natural language processing (NLP) and reinforcement learning into these multimodal frameworks could further improve the predictive accuracy of neuromarketing intrusions, yet such integrative approaches remain undeveloped in academic literature.

Lastly, despite the booming industry adoption of AI-driven neuromarketing technologies by renowned platforms like Google, Meta, and Amazon, independent validation and peer-reviewed case studies of such technologies remain insufficient. This lack of transparency hinders research evaluation and limits theoretical development. Future research should emphasis on emerging open-source AI models for neuromarketing to empower replication, standardization, and cross-industry benchmarking. Bridging these gaps is vital to develop neuromarketing into a scientifically grounded, ethically sound, and socially inclusive areas that match technological sophistication with human values.

# 8. SYNERGISTIC APPLICATIONS

## 8.1 Enhancing Customer Experience

Insights from the integration of AI with neuromarketing enables unprecedented personalization by understanding the implicit emotional and behavioural signals. Retailers can utilise the neuromarketing data to customize customer interface elements, content, recommendations and suggestions that match with their subconscious preferences, thereby creating immersive and emotionally echoing shopping environments. This personalized emotional alignment increase customer satisfaction and builds trust, resulting in enhanced engagement and loyalty (Aggarwal et al., 2024).

Retailers can understand needs proactively by identifying subtle consumer signals through AI-assisted pattern recognition and response with customised offers or support. This strategy moves beyond explicit user input to grab a more intuitive understanding of consumer desires and frustrations, optimizing the overall shopping journey and increasing conversion chances (Sinha et al., 2024).

Largely, AI-driven neuromarketing changes static customer experiences into dynamic, empathetic interactions that motivate deeper brand relationships and brand loyalty, substantially advancing traditional e-commerce paradigms (Raji et al., 2024).

## 8.2 Virtual Try-ons, AR, and Immersive Technologies

Augmented reality (AR) and virtual try-on technologies demonstrate the integration of AI and neuromarketing by enhancing customer shopping experiences. These technologies provide customer with interactive, supportive and exciting environments where they can imagine products realistically before purchase, increasing confidence and reducing risks. Retailers can use these tools to optimize sensory appeal and maximize conversion potential by analysing emotional engagement and decision triggers through integrating neuromarketing with AI (Arora, 2024).

Virtual trial rooms powered by AI analyse consumer preferences and physiological responses to customize the try-on experience for customer. This integration improves omnichannel strategies by linking digital and physical retail, offering consistent and fruitful customer interactions. Augmented reality effectiveness in enhancing customer satisfaction and retention emphasizes its strategic role in future retail innovations.

Such important applications reveal how AI and neuromarketing synergistically improve decision making quality, customer trust, and finally the, profitability.

## 8.3 Optimizing Marketing Strategies and Campaigns

Integration of neuro-data with AI analytics helps retailers to take strategic marketing initiatives with unprecedented accuracy. Personalized advertisements take the advantage of EEG-derived sentiment analysis, which allows use of content to match real-time emotional states, thereby yield increased customer engagement metrics and reducing bounce and rejection (Adeleke et al., 2022).

Neuromarketing based dynamic pricing models helps the marketer to predict consumer price sensitivity and their willingness to pay. With this help, marketer can develop competitive pricing strategies that maximize their revenue without affecting customers. Eye-tracking data integrated with machine learning also guide.

# 9. ETHICAL AND PRIVACY ISSUES & CHALLENGES

## 9.1 Issues related to Data Privacy

As neuromarketing increasingly depends on AI to process highly sensitive neuro-consumer data, critical ethical issues also emerge. The collection and analysis of subconscious responses of customer invoke questions about informed customer consent, confidentiality of data, and the capability for psychological manipulation. Consumers may be not able to fully understand how their neural and biometric information is used in future, increasing the risks for transparency and regulatory oversight (Goncalves et al., 2024).

Results of comparative studies conducted in the European Union, on data protection policies, like GDPR (The General Data Protection Regulation) highlighted the inconsistencies in global consumer rights frameworks. These discrepancies complicate the compliance for global retailers in using AI-powered neuromarketing, underscoring the need for globally accepted ethical standards. The risks of data privacy extend beyond legal compliance to social trust, which is necessary for sustainable application of such important data-driven marketing techniques (Mitu et al., 2024).

There is a requirement of crucial ethical transparency, including clear disclosures about data collection methods, intended uses, and consumer rights. For reducing the risks of misuse while development innovation in ethical neuromarketing practices, establishment of accountability mechanisms and ethical review protocols are essential (Pillarisetty & Mishra, 2022). These risks can be mitigated from using this data effectively on data platforms through ethical-by-design frameworks, fairness audits, and transparency in data collection and usage.

## 9.2 Challenges related to Security of Data

Challenges related to security of data also arises in deploying AI and neuromarketing in omnichannel environments. Integration of consumer data across multiple channels raises issues related to integrity of customer data, consent management, and exposure to breaches of contract etc. for safeguarding of consumer trust retailers must ensure robust encryption, secure authentication, and transparent consent mechanisms .

AI's contribution in fraud detection and cybersecurity strengthens retail infrastructure, so far it must be careful governed to avoid misuse or infringements on consumer rights. Legal frameworks for governing data protection rigorously demand stringent compliance, asking retailers to adopt complete security protocols and promote ethical data stewardship (Canhoto et al., 2024).

The responsible deployment of AI-neuromarketing technologies across retail channels can be easily achieved by adopting a delicate balance between innovation and risk management (Serbin & Yashkina, 2024).

While AI have significant transformative potential in the retail sector, its use also comes with ethical and privacy challenges. The personalization-privacy paradox is very significant, as consumers need highly customised shopping experiences but are simultaneously concerned with privacy of their personal data. Major challenges are transparency with consumers as they are unaware of how their data is used to influence marketing strategies, and the chance of algorithmic bias, through which AI systems may unknowingly discriminate with certain consumer groups (Canhoto et al., 2024).

It is important to follow some data privacy regulations like the GDPR (General Data Protection Regulation) and new standards that emphasise on the demand of transparent client consent, explainability of AI decisions, and data reduction, to ensure responsible and efficient AI implementation. Retailers must carefully follow these regulatory frameworks, using Privacy by Design (PbD) approach and enabling customers to have full control over their personal data. These actions improve customer trust and ethical credibility, which are important for building and maintaining long-term consumer relationships(Serbin & Yashkina, 2024)

Strong data governance, ongoing monitoring of AI fairness, and transparent communication strategies that explain consumer rights are major requirements for effective implementation of AI systems that can offer customised experiences without manipulating customer privacy. Additionally, there is an urgent need for industry-wide consensus on ethical AI practices that balance innovation with respect for individual privacy and societal norms (Tiutiu & Dabija, 2023).

## 9.3 Challenges during Implementation

There is also a various challenge arises while implementation of AI-neuromarketing solutions, despite of the numerous benefits. Big financial investments in developing technological infrastructure and skilled workforce are basics requirements for success. Integrating various AI and neuromarketing tools into existing systems require maximum coordination to avoid interoperability problems.

Algorithmic biases, often stemming from skewed training data, may create a risk of undermining consumer trust and personalization effectiveness necessitating rigorous monitoring and model modifications. Retailers must take care of ethical issues and transparency in their AI governance frameworks to match with consumer expectations and regulatory guidelines (Tiutiu & Dabija, 2023).

Regular evaluation and adaptation are important to sustain the relevance and ethical security of these evolving technologies in fast changing retail environments (Rifan, 2024).

# 10. RECOMMENDATIONS FOR RESPONSIBLE AI AND NEUROMARKETING UTILIZATION

To truly tap into the incredible potential of AI and neuromarketing in a responsible way, we need to establish solid ethical standards across the industry. These standards should prioritize consumer protection, transparency, and accountability, ensuring that innovation doesn't come at the expense of people's rights(Goncalves et al., 2024).

Best practices including clear data governance, straightforward informed consent processes, and ongoing checks should be used to catch any algorithmic bias or ethical issues. By encouraging collaboration among technologists, marketers, ethicists, and policymakers, we can create thoughtful guidelines that tackle the complex challenges of integrating AI with neuromarketing(Tiutiu & Dabija, 2023).

Additionally, actively engaging with consumers to build understanding and trust will be crucial in responsibly advancing these groundbreaking retail technologies(-Canhoto et al., 2024b).

The integration of AI and neuromarketing technologies in retail and e-commerce holds huge potential for improving customer experiences, optimizing targeting, and increasing sales. Though, their adoption increases significant ethical, psychological, and regulatory issues.

The following recommendations and suggestions are divided into 3 groups with intent to promote responsible, transparent, and human centric deployment of AI-neuromarketing technologies in retail and e-commerce:

## 10.1 Related to Moral concerns

- *Adoption of Transparent Data Practices:* Retailers must ensure full transparency in data collection and usage, particularly when collecting neurophysiological or biometric data through various technologies like EEG, eye-tracking, facial expressions etc.

Consumers should be well-versed about:

- What type of data is being collected?
- How it will be used in AI algorithms?
- How long it will be stored and shared?

This brings into line with the principles of GDPR and data minimization, confirming ethical compliance and building trust(Stanton et al., 2017) .

- *Avoid Overly Persuasive or Subliminal Targeting:* AI-powered neuromarketing must not take advantage of consumers' cognitive vulnerabilities like driving emotional distress, impulse biases. While using neural data, Subliminal or overly persuasive tactics should be explicitly regulated to prevent manipulation and preserve consumer autonomy (Plassmann et al., 2012).
- *Develop ethical-by-design frameworks:* Companies should develop ethical-by-design frameworks for AI system development. This includes:
    - Embedding explainability (XAI)
    - Permitting user control over AI-powered customization
    - Checking for unforeseen consequences

Ethical design not only follow compliance but also build brand trust in a highly competitive digital marketplace (Jobin et al., 2019).

- *Adding Consumer Feedback Loops in AI Systems:* Ethical AI systems should be versatile and responsive. Addition of feedback loops help the users to correct or modify their personalization profiles, exclusion of hyper-targeted stimuli, and communicate discomfort or bias. This will develop co-created personalization and sustains long-term user engagement (Dignum, 2018).

## 10.2 Related to Data Privacy issues

- *Implement Informed Consent with Appropriate Awareness:* While dealing with subconscious neural data, conventional “click-to-consent” models may not be enough. For giving clear understanding to customer about how AI-neuromarketing works and its potential influence on decision-making, retailers must implement layered, context-aware consent systems (Ariely & Berns, 2010).

- *Promote Algorithmic Fairness and Diversity:* Many AI models in neuromarketing are customised to work with non-diverse datasets, often unfair toward Western populations. To confirm inclusivity and alleviate algorithmic bias, developers should:
  - Use demographically correct data
  - Perform unfairness audits on algorithms
- *Encourage Industry Self-Regulation and Third-Party Audit:* Retailers and tech providers should work together to develop self-regulatory standards, like financial audit protocols, where third-party assessments confirm compliance with ethical AI use. This become more critical when sensitive data like brain activity or emotional state is involved(Venkatraman et al., 2015).

### 10.3 Related to Different Culture and Diversity

- *Promote Diversity:* Add cultural sensitivity layers in AI personalization(Smidts et al., 2014).
- *Emphasis on Consumer Education and Digital Literacy:* Retailers and platforms should introduce consumer education initiatives that make clear and easier to understand AI integrated neuromarketing. They should empower the user for taking informed decisions and reduce their dependency on algorithmic persuasion by educating them about how neuro-AI systems work (Cowls et al., 2023).

## 11. CONCLUSION

### 11.1 Summary of Key Findings on AI and Neuromarketing in Retail and E-commerce

This review shows that combining Artificial Intelligence with neuromarketing measurably lifts both retail and e-commerce by creating shopping journeys that feel personal and by steering marketing efforts that convert more browsers into buyers. While AI streamlines workflows, fine-tunes stock control, and powers real-time customer outreach, neuromarketing reveals the subtle mental triggers that make a campaign land, boosting its overall punch(Sharma, 2023). Working hand in hand, the two disciplines build agile, empathy-driven brands that sense and adapt to shifting shopper desires almost as quickly as they emerge. At the same time, the authors warn that any fast-tracked adoption must be matched with strong safeguards against data leaks, biased algorithms, and other ethical gray areas(Serbin & Yashkina, 2024) .

## 11.2 Implications for Retailers, Marketers, and Consumers

For retailers and marketers, integration of AI with neuroscience offers a fresh guide to crafting campaigns that are both rigorously data-rich and emotionally on target customer, lifting satisfaction and lasting loyalty in the process. When the approach is put into practice, companies gain the edge that comes from deeper user attention, lower waste, and leaner operations, translating insight directly to superior results(Tadimarri et al., 2024) . Consumers win, too, because the fusion delivers offer that feel relevant, checkout flows that feel effortless, and overall encounters that simply feel more pleasant(Canhoto et al., 2024b).

### 11.2.1. For Retailers

#### *1. Improved Personalization & Omnichannel Integration*

Retailers can easily deliver best personalized experiences across various channels through AI-driven recommendation systems and predictive analytics. By understanding browsing behavior, purchase history, and emotional response data, retailers can customise product suggestions, dynamic pricing, and promotions to individual consumers for increased user engagement and higher conversion rates(Yrjölä et al., 2024)

#### *2. Optimized Supply Chain Operations & Inventory*

Retailers can forecast demand, manage inventory efficiently, and streamline supply chain logistics by reducing stockouts and excess inventory with the help of AI based Predictive analytics. This is especially effective during peak sales periods like Black Friday in Walmart and Zara(Patil, 2024).

#### *3. Innovation in Physical Store Experience*

AI-powered store assistants, voice kiosks, smart shelves, and robotics enhanced physical retail experiences. These technologies deliver best customer service, real-time assistance, and integrate efficiently with online channels thereby supporting omnichannel strategies (Yrjölä et al., 2024)

#### 4. Ethics & Operational Challenges

Implementation of AI at large scale involve challenges related to user data privacy, algorithmic bias, technical complexity, huge investment, and regulatory compliance. Retailers must implement transparent data governance, rigorous audit of AI fairness and bias, and ensure strong cybersecurity measures.

### 11.2.2. For Marketers

#### 1. Emotionally Balanced Creative & Digital Ads

With the help of Neuromarketing tools like eye-tracking and EEG, marketers can design emotionally balanced creative & digital ads, website layouts, and call to action (CTA) that grab attention, relate emotionally, and match with how consumers think, whether it be in emotion or memory encoding. Testing and validation of advertisement copies and campaigns using neuroscience data leads to higher user engagement and brand recall.

#### 2. Improved User Segmentation & Targeting

AI integrated neuromarketing tools helps in subconscious emotional responses-based user segmentation rather than only demographics-based user segmentation. This strategy will help in developing dynamic, behaviourally driven content personalization, improving message resonance and increasing conversion rate.

#### 3. Real-Time Monitoring & Feedback

AI integrated sentiment analysis systems can process big data of reviews, social comments, and brand mentions in real time, allowing marketers to immediately identify user mood shifts, important issues, and proactively develop marketing campaigns based on real consumer emotions.

#### 4. Ethical and Trust Issues

While AI based consumer insights are powerful for marketing but there is more chance of misuse. Building and maintaining trust requires strong transparency in data usage, full disclosure of AI interactions like through chat bot and ongoing auditing of emotional targeting process (Haque et al., 2024).

### 11.2.3. For Consumers

*1. More Efficient and Enjoyable Shopping*

AI integrated neuromarketing tools enable consumers a smoother, more enjoyable shopping journey with personalized product recommendations, emotionally connected ads, and efficient, smooth website and physical store experiences 1.

*1. Improved User Experience*

Improved user experience (UX) or user interface (UI) by neuromarketing tools decreases cognitive load and decision stress. They make shopping more enjoyable and less frustrating by guiding attention organically, optimizing navigation flow, and simplifying checkout process.

*3. Build Trust and loyalty*

Users feel more comfort in using AI-driven tools like chatbots and virtual assistants, when there are a full transparency, fairness, and trust. Sometime, high levels of perceived personalization may lack clear transparency which can reduce user trust.

*4. User Expectations of Privacy & Awareness*

Users always expect clear communication about how their data including emotional signals and biometric responses are being used. The retailers who clearly explain their practices and allow control build consumer loyalty, while those retailers that don't face market reactions.

## 12. FUTURE DIRECTIONS AND RESEARCH GAPS

While the integration of artificial intelligence (AI) and neuromarketing holds immense promise, several critical and under-researched areas need deeper academic attention. The following sections explain those areas in detail.

### 12.1 Extent of effect of AI-driven neuromarketing on the quality of the trust and loyalty customers enjoy in brand branding:

While the field has made impressive strides, there are still several areas that haven't been fully explored. We really need to dive deeper into the impact of AI-driven personalization in long-term on consumer behavior to grasp any potential habituation or backlash that might occur.

## 12.2 Cross-cultural research on diversity and inclusion in neuromarketing datasets:

There's a significant gap in research focused on emerging retail sectors, especially in developing markets where digital infrastructure and cultural norms can vary greatly. Filling these research gaps is crucial for the comprehensive development and ethical use of AI-neuromarketing strategies around the world(Singh et al., 2023). Understanding the unique challenges and opportunities in different sectors is a promising area for future research, both empirical and theoretical(Bhatt & Singh, 2024). There's also a noticeable lack of cross-cultural studies on how neuromarketing is adopted and the ethical issues surrounding it, which limits its global relevance(Menaka & Selvam, 2025).

Most neuromarketing datasets are from Western, Educated, Industrialized, Rich, and Democratic (WEIRD) populations, which create unintentional cultural and algorithmic biases in predictive marketing models (Plassmann et al., 2015). This will create strong need for more inclusive, cross-cultural neuromarketing research to analyse the variations in neural markers of engagement, trust, and preference across regions, age groups, and psychographic profiles.

## 12.3 Development of ethical frameworks for AI and neuromarketing:

One of the other most critical issues lies in the ethical and regulatory challenges surrounding the adoption of AI to interpret neural and emotional responses. Present AI-driven neuromarketing practices generally operate in a legal grey area, raising apprehensions over privacy and consent of consumer and cognitive manipulation, particularly when emotional AI is used to drive subconscious responses (Stanton et al., 2017; Morin, 2011).

## 12.4 The contribution of emerging technologies such as LLMs and deep reinforcement learning to personalization:

Despite advancement in EEG, fMRI, and eye-tracking tools, there is inadequate cross-disciplinary research combining AI ethics, neuroscience, and consumer rights, create a significant research-practice gap. There's also a lack of empirical studies on neuroadaptive marketing systems, where integration of AI with real-time neurofeedback to vigorously adjustment of stimuli and offering potentially powerful and ethically sensitive opportunities for hyper-personalized advertising (Venkatraman et al., 2015).

Additionally, there is also needed to fully explore the long-term cognitive and emotional impacts of persistent AI-personalized marketing. While studies on short-term behavioural outcomes like click-through rates and purchase intent are commonly done, longitudinal effects on mental fatigue, consumer trust, and digital well-being remain uncovered (Ariely & Berns, 2010).

## 13. FINAL REMARKS AND CALL FOR CONTINUED RESEARCH AND INNOVATION

The evolving landscape of retail powered by AI and neuromarketing demands continued scholarly inquiry and innovative development. The promises of these technologies are immense but realizing their full potential requires addressing unresolved ethical, cultural, and technological challenges (Tiutiu & Dabija, 2023).

Sustainable and mutually beneficial retail ecosystems will emerge only through responsible adoption practices balancing personalization with privacy. Interdisciplinary efforts bridging technology, marketing, ethics, and consumer advocacy will pave the way for this future, fostering ongoing innovation that respects human dignity and enhances the retail experience (Goncalves et al., 2024).Top of Form

The integration of AI and neuromarketing in retail and e-commerce is transforming the shopping experience by improving personalization, operational efficiency, emotional customer engagement, and higher conversion rates. Yet its full potential depends on ethical transparency, robust governance, and consumer trust. Retailers and marketers together can build with consumer respect and ethical diligence will crack deeper conversion and stronger loyalty.

## REFRENCES


*5ways AliBaba is using AI [Case Study] [2025] - DigitalDefynd.* (n.d.). Retrieved July 9, 2025, from https://digitaldefynd.com/IQ/ways-alibaba-using-ai-case-study/

Adeleke, A. G., Sanyaolu, T. O., Efunniyi, C. P., Akwawa, L. A., & Azubuko, C. F. (2022). Impact of AI-Enabled A/B Testing on Product Performance in E-commerce Platforms. *International Journal of Management & Entrepreneurship Research, 4*(12), 795–813. DOI: 10.51594/IJMER.V4I12.1537

Aggarwal, D., Sharma, D., & Saxena, A. B. (2024). Enhancing the Online Shopping Experience of Consumers through Artificial Intelligence. *International Journal of Information Technology and Computer Engineering, 42*, 1–5. DOI: 10.55529/ijitc.42.1.5

Aliyev, N. N. (1996). THE PSYCHOLOGY OF ONLİNE SHOPPING HOW DIGITAL MARKETING TRIGGERS IMPULSE BUYING. *Scientific Works/Elmi Eserler*, 266–272. DOI: 10.58225/tim.2024-4-266-272

Alsharif, A. H., Salleh, N. Z. M., Abdullah, M., Khraiwish, A., & Ashaari, A. (2023). Neuromarketing Tools Used in the Marketing Mix: A Systematic Literature and Future Research Agenda. *SAGE Open, 13*(1). Advance online publication. DOI: 10.1177/21582440231156563/ASSET/4995F1D5-0A6A-4E37-9011-383BB2B68B56/ASSETS/IMAGES/LARGE/10.1177_21582440231156563-FIG4.JPG

Ariely, D., & Berns, G. S. (2010). Neuromarketing: the hope and hype of neuroimaging in business. *Nature Reviews Neuroscience 2010 11:4, 11*(4), 284–292. DOI: 10.1038/nrn2795

Arora, R. (2024). Bridging the Gap Between Offline and Online Presence in E-commerce: The Role of Artificial Intelligence. *INTERANTIONAL JOURNAL OF SCIENTIFIC RESEARCH IN ENGINEERING AND MANAGEMENT, 08*(12), 1–6. DOI: 10.55041/IJSREM33002

Bag, S., Srivastava, G., Al Bashir, M. M., Kumari, S., Giannakis, M., & Chowdhury, A. H. (2022). Journey of customers in this digital era: Understanding the role of artificial intelligence technologies in user engagement and conversion. *Benchmarking, 29*(7), 2074–2098. DOI: 10.1108/BIJ-07-2021-0415/FULL/XML

Beyari, H., Hashem, T. N., & Alrusain, O. (2024). Neuromarketing: Understanding the effect of emotion and memory on consumer behavior by mediating the role of artificial intelligence and customers' digital experience. *Journal of Project Management, 9*(4), 323–336. DOI: 10.5267/j.jpm.2024.9.001

Bhatt, P., & Singh, A. K. (2024). Impact of AI on Consumers' Purchase Intention Towards Online Grocery Shopping in India. *Journal of Reliability and Statistical Studies, 17*(2), 453–490. DOI: 10.13052/JRSS0974-8024.17210

Białowąs, S., & Szyszka, A. (2019). Eye-tracking in Marketing Research. *Managing Economic Innovations – Methods and Instruments*, 91–104. DOI: 10.12657/9788379862771-6

Canhoto, A. I., Keegan, B. J., & Ryzhikh, M. (2024). Snakes and Ladders: Unpacking the Personalisation-Privacy Paradox in the Context of AI-Enabled Personalisation in the Physical Retail Environment. *Information Systems Frontiers, 26*(3), 1005–1024. DOI: 10.1007/S10796-023-10369-7/FIGURES/3

Cowls, J., Tsamados, A., Taddeo, M., & Floridi, L. (2023). The AI gambit: Leveraging artificial intelligence to combat climate change—opportunities, challenges, and recommendations. *AI & Society, 38*(1), 283–307. DOI: 10.1007/S00146-021-01294-X/METRICS

Cueva, C. J., Saez, A., Marcos, E., Genovesio, A., Jazayeri, M., Romo, R., Salzman, C. D., Shadlen, M. N., & Fusi, S. (2020). Low-dimensional dynamics for working memory and time encoding. *Proceedings of the National Academy of Sciences of the United States of America, 117*(37), 23021–23032. DOI: 10.1073/PNAS.1915984117/SUPPL_FILE/PNAS.1915984117.SAPP.PDF

Dahouda, M. K., & Joe, I. (2021). A Deep-Learned Embedding Technique for Categorical Features Encoding. *IEEE Access : Practical Innovations, Open Solutions, 9*, 114381–114391. DOI: 10.1109/ACCESS.2021.3104357

Dewey, C. (2023). Metacognitive control in single- vs. dual-process theory. *Thinking & Reasoning, 29*(2), 177–212. DOI: 10.1080/13546783.2022.2047106;JOURNAL:-JOURNAL:PTAR20;WGROUP:STRING:PUBLICATION

Dignum, V. (2018). Ethics in artificial intelligence: Introduction to the special issue. *Ethics and Information Technology, 20*(1), 1–3. DOI: 10.1007/S10676-018-9450-Z/METRICS

Goncalves, M., Hu, Y., Aliagas, I., & Cerdá, L. M. (2024). Neuromarketing algorithms' consumer privacy and ethical considerations: Challenges and opportunities. *Cogent Business & Management, 11*(1), 2333063. DOI: 10.1080/23311975.2024.2333063;PAGE:STRING:ARTICLE/CHAPTER

Gurgu, E., Gurgu, I.-A., & Tonis, R. B. M. (2020). Neuromarketing for a better understanding of consumer needs and emotions. *Independent Journal of Management & Production, 11*(1), 208–235. DOI: 10.14807/ijmp.v11i1.993

Haque, A., Akther, N., Khan, I., Agarwal, K., & Uddin, N. (2024). Artificial Intelligence in Retail Marketing: Research Agenda Based on Bibliometric Reflection and Content Analysis (2000–2023). *Informatics 2024, Vol. 11, Page 74, 11*(4), 74. DOI: 10.3390/INFORMATICS11040074

Helen, J., & Siva Sankar, R. (2025). The Role of AI in Transforming Global E-commerce and Consumer Behaviour. *Thiagarajar College of Preceptors Edu Spectra, 7*(S1), 48–55. DOI: 10.34293/eduspectra.v7is1-feb25.006

Jobin, A., Ienca, M., & Vayena, E. (2019). The global landscape of AI ethics guidelines. *Nature Machine Intelligence 2019 1:9, 1*(9), 389–399. DOI: 10.1038/s42256-019-0088-2

Kavya, G. B. (2024). IMPACT OF ARTIFICIAL INTELLIGENCE ON E-COMMERCE:"A STUDY OF CONSUMER BEHAVIOR". *EPRA International Journal of Environmental Economics. Commerce and Educational Management, 51–54*. Advance online publication. DOI: 10.36713/epra18548

Kim, C., Jeon, H. G., & Lee, K. C. (2020). Discovering the Role of Emotional and Rational Appeals and Hidden Heterogeneity of Consumers in Advertising Copies for Sustainable Marketing. *Sustainability 2020, Vol. 12, Page 5189, 12*(12), 5189. DOI: 10.3390/SU12125189

Kusá, A., & Beličková, P. (2023). The role of artificial intelligence in neuromarketing research: Insights and applications. *Media & Marketing Identity*, 269–275. DOI: 10.34135/mmidentity-2023-27

Lakshminarayana, K., Kumar, P., & Madhavedi, S. (2024). Role of Neuromarketing and Artificial Intelligence in Futuristic Marketing Approach: An Empirical Study. *Journal of Informatics Education and Research, 4*(2), 560. DOI: 10.52783/JIER.V4I2.809

Liu-Thompkins, Y., Okazaki, S., & Li, H. (2022). Artificial empathy in marketing interactions: Bridging the human-AI gap in affective and social customer experience. *Journal of the Academy of Marketing Science, 50*(6), 1198–1218. DOI: 10.1007/s11747-022-00892-5

Menaka, S., & Selvam, V. (2025). Bibliometric Analysis of Artificial Intelligence on Consumer Purchase Intention in E-Retailing. *International Journal of Computational and Experimental Science and Engineering, 11*(1), 1138–1146. DOI: 10.22399/IJCESEN.1007

Mitu, F.-G., Bota, M., Emanuel SAVAN, E., & Emanuel Savan, E. (2024). Unlocking the Shopper's Mind: How Emerging Technologies Like Artificial Intelligence Is Shaping the Future of Retail. *Studia Universitatis Babe -Bolyai Negotia*, 69–83. DOI: 10.24193/SUBBNEGOTIA.2024.4.04

Mogaji, E., Olaleye, S., & Ukpabi, D. (2020). *Using AI to Personalise Emotionally Appealing Advertisement*. 137–150. DOI: 10.1007/978-3-030-24374-6_10

Murti, A., & Ghosh, R. (2023). The Impact of Emotional Appeals in Neuro-Marketing: Analyzing the Brain Responses of Consumers to Emotional Advertising Campaigns. In *International Journal of Enhanced Research in Management & Computer Applications* (Vol. 12).

Papić, T., Mihajlović, A., & Gajić, J. (2023). Advanced Technologies as a Framework for Sustainable Marketing Campaigns (AI Application in Neuromarketing). *Sinteza 2023 - International Scientific Conference on Information Technology, Computer Science, and Data Science*, 180–184. DOI: 10.15308/SINTEZA-2023-180-184

Patil, D. (2024). *Artificial Intelligence in Retail and E-Commerce: Enhancing Customer Experience Through Personalization, Predictive Analytics, And Real-Time Engagement*. DOI: 10.2139/SSRN.5057420

*(PDF) Sephora Smart Customer's Experience Enhancement*. (n.d.). Retrieved July 9, 2025, from https://www.researchgate.net/publication/351936435_Sephora_Smart_Customer%27s_Experience_Enhancement?channel=doi&linkId=645d3675f43b8a29ba44f3f4&showFulltext=true

Perumallaplli, R. (2014). AI in E-Commerce Leveraging Predictive Analytics for Personalization. SSRN *Electronic Journal*. DOI: 10.2139/SSRN.5228531

Pillarisetty, R., & Mishra, P. (2022). A Review of AI (Artificial Intelligence) Tools and Customer Experience in Online Fashion Retail. *International Journal of E-Business Research*, *18*(2), 1–12. DOI: 10.4018/IJEBR.294111

Plassmann, H., Ramsøy, T. Z., & Milosavljevic, M. (2012). Branding the brain: A critical review and outlook. *Journal of Consumer Psychology*, *22*(1), 18–36. DOI: 10.1016/J.JCPS.2011.11.010

Raji, M. A., Olodo, H. B., Oke, T. T., Addy, W. A., Ofodile, O. C., Oyewole, A. T., Raji, M. A., Olodo, H. B., Oke, T. T., Addy, W. A., Ofodile, O. C., & Oyewole, A. T. (2024). E-commerce and consumer behavior: A review of AI-powered personalization and market trends. Https://Gsconlinepress.Com/Journals/Gscarr/Sites/Default/Files/GSCARR-2024-0090.Pdf, *18*(3), 066–077. DOI: 10.30574/GSCARR.2024.18.3.0090

Thanyawatpornkul, R. (2024). Implementing AI-driven Customer Relationship Management (CRM) systems: Enhancing customer experience in the retail industry of Thailand. *World Journal of Advanced Research and Reviews, 24*(1), 1691–1699. DOI: 10.30574/wjarr.2024.24.1.3154

Rifan, M. (2024). The Convergence of Artificial Intelligence and Digital Marketing. *Proceeding of The International Seminar on Business, Economics, Social Science and Technology (ISBEST), 4*(1). DOI: 10.33830/isbest.v4i1.3266

S, R. (2025, April 9). *Role of Artificial Intelligence in Shaping Consumer Experience and Loyalty in Fashion E-Commerce – IJSREM*. https://ijsrem.com/download/role-of-artificial-intelligence-in-shaping-consumer-experience-and-loyalty-in-fashion-e-commerce/

Scholz, J., & Duffy, K. (2018). We ARe at home: How augmented reality reshapes mobile marketing and consumer-brand relationships. *Journal of Retailing and Consumer Services, 44*, 11–23. DOI: 10.1016/J.JRETCONSER.2018.05.004

*Sephora Creates an Online "In-store" Experience through Generative AI.* (n.d.). Retrieved July 9, 2025, from https://etailasia.wbresearch.com/blog/sephora-creates-an-online-in-store-experience-through-generative-ai?utm_source=chatgpt.com

Serbin, V., & Yashkina, O. (2024). Systematization of research on the use of artificial intelligence in the transformation of marketing strategies of e-commerce enterprises. *Marketing and Digital Technologies, 8*(4), 92–109. DOI: 10.15276/MDT.8.4.2024.8

Shareef, F., Ajith, R., Kaushal, P., & Sengupta, K. (2024). RetailGPT: A Fine-Tuned LLM Architecture for Customer Experience and Sales Optimization. *2024 2nd International Conference on Self Sustainable Artificial Intelligence Systems (ICSSAS)*, 1390–1394. DOI: 10.1109/ICSSAS64001.2024.10760685

Sharma, A. (2023). Analyzing the Role of Artificial Intelligence in Predicting Customer Behavior and Personalizing the Shopping Experience in Ecommerce. *INTERANTIONAL JOURNAL OF SCIENTIFIC RESEARCH IN ENGINEERING AND MANAGEMENT, 07*(02). Advance online publication. DOI: 10.55041/IJSREM17839

Singh, P., Alhassan, I., & Khoshaim, L. (2023). What Do You Need to Know? A Systematic Review and Research Agenda on Neuromarketing Discipline. *Journal of Theoretical and Applied Electronic Commerce Research 2023, Vol. 18, Pages 2007-2032, 18*(4), 2007–2032. DOI: 10.3390/JTAER18040101

Sinha, S., Sinha, D., & Dalmia, T. (2024). Role of AI in Enhancing Customer Experience in Online Shopping. *2024 11th International Conference on Reliability, Infocom Technologies and Optimization (Trends and Future Directions) (ICRITO)*, 1–5. DOI: 10.1109/ICRITO61523.2024.10522285

Smidts, A., Hsu, M., Sanfey, A. G., Boksem, M. A. S., Ebstein, R. B., Huettel, S. A., Kable, J. W., Karmarkar, U. R., Kitayama, S., Knutson, B., Liberzon, I., Lohrenz, T., Stallen, M., & Yoon, C. (2014). Advancing consumer neuroscience. *Marketing Letters, 25*(3), 257–267. DOI: 10.1007/S11002-014-9306-1/METRICS

Stanton, S. J., Sinnott-Armstrong, W., & Huettel, S. A. (2017). Neuromarketing: Ethical Implications of its Use and Potential Misuse. *Journal of Business Ethics, 144*(4), 799–811. DOI: 10.1007/S10551-016-3059-0

Suomala, J., Palokangas, L., Leminen, S., Westerlund, M., Heinonen, J., & Numminen, J. (2012). Neuromarketing: Understanding Customers' Subconscious Responses to Marketing. *Technology Innovation Management Review, 2*(12), 12–21. http://www.theseus.fi/handle/10024/151224

Tadimarri, A., Jangoan, S., Kumar Sharma, K., Gurusamy, A., & Radius, H. (2024). AI-Powered Marketing: Transforming Consumer Engagement and Brand Growth. *IJFMR - International. Journal of Multidisciplinary Research, 6*(2). Advance online publication. DOI: 10.36948/IJFMR.2024.V06I02.14595

Yadav, T. (2024). AI in Neuromarketing: Understanding Consumer Emotions and Behavior through Machine Learning. *IJFMR - International. Journal of Multidisciplinary Research, 6*(5). Advance online publication. DOI: 10.36948/IJFMR.2024.V06I05.28154

*The hidden persuaders: How businesses are using neuroscience to make you buy | WIRED*. (n.d.). Retrieved July 9, 2025, from https://www.wired.com/story/neuromarketing-is-a-go/?utm_source=chatgpt.com

Tiutiu, M., & Dabija, D.-C. (2023). Improving Customer Experience Using Artificial Intelligence in Online Retail. *Proceedings of the International Conference on Business Excellence, 17*(1), 1139–1147. DOI: 10.2478/PICBE-2023-0102

Venkatraman, V., Dimoka, A., Pavlou, P. A., Vo, K., Hampton, W., Bollinger, B., Hershfield, H. E., Ishihara, M., & Winer, R. S. (2015). Predicting advertising success beyond traditional measures: New insights from neurophysiological methods and market response modeling. *JMR, Journal of Marketing Research, 52*(4), 436–452. DOI: 10.1509/JMR.13.0593/SUPPL_FILE/PREDICTINGADVERTISING.PDF

Yadete, F. D., & Kant, S. (2023). Neuro-Marketing in Understanding Consumer Behavior: Systematic Literature Review. *Journal of Social Sciences and Management Studies*, *2*(2), 1–12. DOI: 10.56556/JSSMS.V2I2.483

Yrjölä, M., Hautamäki, P., & Ranta, R. (2024). Value propositions of artificial intelligence in retailing. *International Review of Retail, Distribution and Consumer Research*. Advance online publication. DOI: 10.1080/09593969.2024.2411209;WGROUP:STRING:PUBLICATION

Yu, J., Dickinger, A., So, K. K. F., & Egger, R. (2024). Artificial intelligence-generated virtual influencer: Examining the effects of emotional display on user engagement. *Journal of Retailing and Consumer Services*, *76*, 103560. DOI: 10.1016/J.JRETCONSER.2023.103560

Zhuk, A., & Yatskyi, O. (2024). The use of artificial intelligence and machine learning in e-commerce marketing. *Technology Audit and Production Reserves*, *3*(4(77)), 33–38. DOI: 10.15587/2706-5448.2024.305280

# Chapter 2
# AI-Driven Predictive Analytics in Neuromarketing:
## Unveiling Consumer Minds for Strategic Marketing Insights

**Siti Alhamra Salqaura**
http://orcid.org/0000-0002-0032-4713
*Universitas Medan Area, Indonesia*

**Nasib Nasib**
http://orcid.org/0000-0003-3798-1562
*Institut Bisnis Informasi Teknologi dan Bisnis, Indonesia*

## ABSTRACT

*The chapter's purpose is to present the effectiveness of neuromarketing combined with viral marketing, powered by AI, in terms to enhance purchase decisions. This book chapter introduces the concept of Neuro-Viral AI Predictive Framework (NVAPF), which explains how to predict consumer behavior characteristics by integrating Artificial Intelligence (AI) viral marketing with neuromarketing to improve strategic marketing insights. The research involved approximately 200 respondents, divided into two studies in the food and beverage sector (100 respondents were tested in the food and beverage sectors, respectively), utilizing the same variables: neuromarketing, viral marketing, and purchasing decisions. This division of respondents was intended to assess the effectiveness of both sectors, food and beverage. The findings indicated that neuromarketing has an enormous effect to elevate purchase decisions. This discussion is expected to make a significant substantive contribution to consumer behavior studies, providing indispensable insight for policymakers and educators.*

DOI: 10.4018/979-8-3373-5997-7.ch002

## INTRODUCTION

Over the past decade, neuromarketing has garnered considerable attention, primarily due to its capacity to elucidate the underlying processes that shape consumer actions (Bansal et al., 2025). The marketing field is currently undergoing a substantial shift, fueled by the collaborative integration of Artificial Intelligence (AI) and Neuromarketing (Alsharif et al., 2025).. This evolution, prompted by the increasing complexity of the digital marketing environment, where consumers engage with brands across numerous touchpoints and channels, transcends conventional demographic-focused methodologies to investigate the subconscious influences on consumer behavior. While traditional research techniques, such as surveys and focus groups, offer valuable perspectives, they are inherently constrained in their capacity to access subconscious motivations. Neuromarketing bridges this gap by measuring physiological and neurological responses to marketing stimuli, revealing the hidden drivers of consumer choices (Song et al., 2025).

Neuromarketing employs neuroscience-based methods such as functional magnetic resonance imaging (fMRI), electroencephalography (EEG), galvanic skin response (GSR), and eye-tracking to capture subconscious consumer reactions. Neuromarketing through techniques such as eye-tracking, EEG, and facial expression analysis provides direct insights into emotional and cognitive responses, thus circumventing the constraints inherent in self-reporting.

Simultaneously, these techniques facilitate hyper-personalization. It allows for the optimization of content and campaigns to achieve the greatest subconscious influence, while also improving the overall customer experience. However, this powerful combination also necessitates a critical examination of ethical implications, particularly concerning data privacy, potential manipulation, and transparency, to ensure responsible and trust-building marketing practices.

Furthermore, the intervention of AI advanced technology has been enhancing the quality of life, including in business models (Vlačić et al., 2021). AI provides the computational power to analyze vast datasets, automate personalized outreach, and predict trends with unprecedented accuracy. The predictive analytics enhances the value of neuromarketing by enabling the anticipation of future consumer actions based on current and historical data. With the advancement of AI, particularly machine learning (ML) and deep learning (DL), marketers can process vast neuromarketing datasets to identify patterns that inform strategic decisions (Alsharif et al., 2023; Rawnaque et al., 2020). This integration enables a shift from reactive to proactive marketing, allowing companies to anticipate purchase intent, guide purchasing decisions, foster brand loyalty, and assess campaign effectiveness in real-time. Predictive analytics, powered by AI, transforms these neural and biometric signals into actionable insights that help forecast purchase intent, purchase decisions, brand loyalty, and campaign effectiveness. AI models such as deep learning, recurrent neural networks (RNN), and ensemble algorithms have shown remarkable accuracy in identifying behavioral patterns that traditional marketing research methods often overlook.

The convergence of AI and Neuromarketing is not merely an incremental improvement; it's a paradigm shift (Adeola et al., 2022). It empowers marketers to understand, predict, and engage with consumers on a deeper, more personal level. While offering immense opportunities for innovation and efficiency, the responsible and ethical application of these powerful tools will be critical to shaping a future of marketing that is both effective and trustworthy. This chapter explores how AI models leverage neuromarketing data to forecast critical consumer behaviors, offering a comprehensive framework for strategic marketing execution.

## PROBLEM STATEMENT FOR THE STUDY

The company's marketing strategy must be implemented effectively and integrated to predict consumer behavior. Although empirical research shows the effectiveness of neuromarketing and viral marketing in the context of artificial intelligence (Neuro-Viral AI Predictive Framework/NVAPF), there is still very little research that integrates neuromarketing, viral marketing, and artificial intelligence.

The research gap is demonstrated by several studies proving that neural indicators such as emotional involvement and attention levels can significantly influence purchase intent (Baldo et al., 2022). Meanwhile, other studies show that the interpretation of neurophysiological data remains challenging due to methodological limitations and context-specific variations (Zenozain et al., 2025). This inconsistency highlights the need for a stronger analytical framework that combines neural data with advanced computational models.

Based on a practical perspective, organizations often find it difficult to translate neuromarketing into actionable marketing strategies. High implementation costs, lack of technical expertise, and ethical concerns related to data privacy and algorithmic bias present significant barriers to adoption (Feijóo & Kwon, 2020a; Müller, 2021). Thus, this study aims to bridge this gap by developing an integrated framework that combines neuromarketing, viral marketing, and AI-based predictive analytics. Such a framework can serve as a guide for future researchers and policymakers in utilizing advanced technologies responsibly and effectively in the field of marketing.

## OBJECTIVES AND RESEARCH QUESTIONS

This study attempts to fill the gap by investigating neuromarketing and viral marketing based on AI-driven approaches (Neuro-Viral AI Predictive Framework/ NVAPF), in the Food and Beverages (F&B) industry. Specifically, the objectives are:

- To assess the effect of neuromarketing and viral marketing based on the NVAPF concept on purchase decisions in the F&B sector.
- Find strategic marketing insight for academia, stakeholders, and policymakers.

In accordance with this, the research questions which formed are:

- Does neuromarketing influence purchase decisions?
- Does AI-based viral marketing influence purchase decisions?
- Can NVAPF collaboration increase or decrease purchase decisions?
- What strategic marketing strategies can be implemented for academics, stakeholders, and policymakers based on the NVAPF concept?

## LITERATURE REVIEW

### Conceptual Framework of Neuromarketing

#### Neuromarketing – Definitions and Dimensions

Neuromarketing is first defined by Smidts (2002(Song et al., 2025) as the application of neuroscience and cognitive psychology in marketing research to understand consumer responses to marketing stimuli. The most commonly used tools include EEG, fMRI, galvanic skin response (GSR), and eye-tracking (Morin, 2011). This technology provides insight into the subconscious aspects of consumers that are not accessible through traditional surveys. However, complex data interpretation and high cost requirements are major obstacles. Several researchers defined neuromarketing. Bhardwaj et al. (2023) define neuromarketing as "the application of neuroscience principles to understand consumer responses to marketing stimuli, utilizing tools such as fMRI, EEG, and eye-tracking to assess emotional and cognitive reactions. Furthermore, Robaina-Calderín & Martín-Santana (2021) describe it as "a field that integrates neuroscience with marketing to explore how brain activity influences consumer choices and preferences". (Alsharif, Salleh, et al., 2021) characterize neuromarketing as "the use of neuroimaging and biometric techniques to investigate the underlying neural mechanisms of consumer behavior". (Quiles Pérez et al., 2024) state that "neuromarketing involves the application of neuroscience tools to study consumer responses to marketing stimuli, aiming to optimize marketing strategies". Finally, Gupta et al. (2025) define it as "a multidisciplinary approach that combines neuroscience, psychology, and marketing to understand consumer behavior and improve marketing effectiveness." Robaina-Calderín & Martín-Santana (2021) was used as a main reference theory.

Moreover, neuromarketing applies neuroscience principles to understand consumer responses to marketing stimuli. The key technology that common used in neuromarketing includes:

• *EEG (Electroencephalography)*

EEG records the brain's electrical activity, providing insights into consumer attention and engagement levels. (Khondakar et al., 2024) highlight that EEG is effective in assessing emotional and cognitive responses to marketing stimuli. However, the primary challenge lies in the complex interpretation of data and the need for specialized hardware. Moreover, the process of EEG response toward a product is shown in Figure1.

*Figure 1. The process of neuromarketing where EEG response towards a product is recorded and processed to get product exposure.*

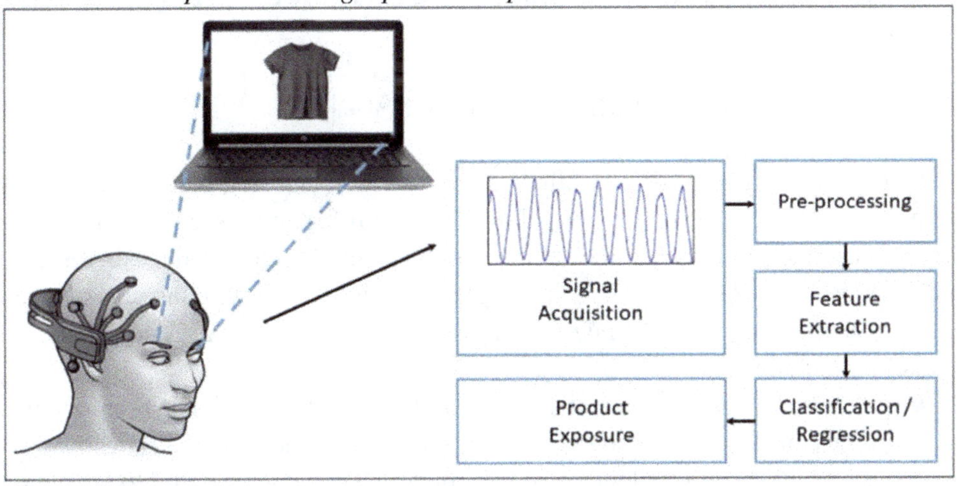


*Source: (Khurana et al., 2021)*

- fMRI (Functional Magnetic Resonance Imaging)

MRI measures changes in blood flow within the brain, identifying active areas during decision-making processes. (Alsharif et al., 2023) note that fMRI offers a detailed view of the brain processes involved in brand and price evaluation. However, its high costs and limitations in real-world settings present significant challenges.

- GSR (Galvanic Skin Response)

GSR measures skin conductance, an indicator of emotional arousal such as excitement or stress. (Bazzani et al., 2020) demonstrate that GSR is effective in assessing emotional reactions to advertisements or products, although data interpretation requires caution.

- Eye-Tracking

This technology tracks eye movements to understand consumer visual attention patterns (Iloka & Anukwe, 2020; Plassmann et al., 2015) emphasize that eye-tracking provides insights into design elements that capture consumer attention, although results may be influenced by external factors such as fatigue or distractions.

Research shows that subconscious emotional processing significantly influences purchasing behavior. Neuromarketing thus complements traditional research by revealing implicit responses often inaccessible through self-reporting (Alsharif & Isa, 2025).

## Neuromarketing in Marketing Predictive Analytics

Predictive analytics utilizes statistical and machine learning models to forecast forthcoming events based on historical data (Shmueli & Koppius, 2011). In marketing, it is used to predict customer churn, purchase likelihood, product preference, and response to promotional campaigns, providing marketers with insights that can guide strategic decisions (Shmueli & Koppius, 2011). Predictive models used in marketing include:

*Regression Analysis:* This statistical model helps identify linear relationships between variables, enabling marketers to predict outcomes such as sales or customer retention based on independent variables (Alshaketheep et al., 2024; Zhang & Tao, 2021).

*Decision Trees:* These models are used for classification tasks, helping marketers categorize data and predict categorical outcomes, such as determining whether a customer will respond to a promotion (AlRoshoud & El-Gohary, 2024).

*Support Vector Machines (SVM):* SVMs are employed to separate complex datasets, effectively classifying consumer segments based on features like purchasing behavior and demographic factors (Chhajer et al., 2022).

*Neural Networks:* Neural Network models are designed to learn non-linear relationships in data and are particularly useful in marketing for capturing complex patterns in consumer behavior that traditional models might miss (Russel & Norvig, 2010).

When integrated with neuromarketing data, such as EEG, eye-tracking, and galvanic skin response (GSR), predictive analytics can yield highly accurate forecasts of consumer behavior (AlRoshoud & El-Gohary, 2024). AI combination and neuroscience allow for the understanding of subconscious consumer responses, enhancing the predictive accuracy of traditional marketing models (Apriliantry et al., 2024; Bhardwaj et al., 2023).

## CONCEPTUAL FRAMEWORK ARTIFICIAL INTELLIGENCE (AI)

Artificial Intelligence (AI) is an interdisciplinary field that focuses on the creation and development of systems capable of performing tasks that typically require human intelligence(Kusters et al., 2020). These tasks include reasoning, learning, decision-making, and problem-solving. AI integrates multiple subfields, such as machine learning (ML), natural language processing (NLP), computer vision, and robotics, which collectively contribute to the broad scope of AI applications. The concept of AI has evolved significantly over the past few decades, with its applications expanding across industries such as healthcare, finance, marketing, and entertainment.

AI systems are designed to simulate human cognitive processes, utilizing algorithms and models that enable them to learn from data, adapt to new information, and make decisions autonomously. Key components of AI include:

- **Machine Learning (ML):** This is the most prominent subset of AI that allows systems to learn from data without explicit programming. ML algorithms identify patterns and make predictions based on historical data. As systems are exposed to more data, their predictive accuracy improves (Jordan & Mitchell, 2015).
- **Natural Language Processing (NLP):** NLP enables machines to understand, interpret, and generate human language, facilitating communication between humans and computers. This is pivotal for AI applications in chatbots, translation systems, and sentiment analysis.
- **Robotics:** Robotics involves the creation of autonomous machines capable of performing tasks such as assembly line work, surgical procedures, and even

household chores. AI in robotics enhances a machine's ability to perceive and navigate its environment (Russel & Norvig, 2010).

- **Computer Vision:** Computer vision enables AI systems to interpret visual data, mimicking human visual perception. It is applied in various domains, including autonomous vehicles, facial recognition, and medical imaging.

## AI in Predictive Analytics in Marketing

Predictive analytics involves the use of AI to analyze data and make forecasts about future events or trends. By leveraging machine learning algorithms, AI models can analyze vast amounts of data, identify underlying patterns, and predict future behaviors. This capability is particularly useful in fields such as marketing, finance, and healthcare, where anticipating future trends can provide a competitive advantage.

- *Hybrid Models in Predictive Analytics:* (Bao et al., 2025; Chhajer et al., 2022) explored the integration of support vector machines (SVM) and artificial neural networks (ANN) to forecast stock market trends. This hybrid model combines the strengths of both SVM and ANN to deliver more accurate predictions by reducing the limitations of each individual method.
- *AI as a Tool for Predictive Modeling:* (Abdelfattah et al., 2025; Ho et al., 2025; Zhang & Tao, 2021) surveyed AI techniques used in predictive analytics, highlighting how AI-based predictive models help in forecasting consumer behavior, detecting fraud, and anticipating market movements.

## AI Models in Neuromarketing Predictive Analytics

Neuromarketing combines neuroscience, psychology, and marketing to understand consumer behavior by analyzing physiological responses to marketing stimuli. The integration of AI into neuromarketing has enhanced the ability to decode consumer reactions, providing marketers with a deeper understanding of how consumers make decisions.

- *AI's Role in Neuromarketing:* (AlRoshoud & El-Gohary, 2024; Aprilianty et al., 2024) reviewed the intersection of AI and neuromarketing, emphasizing that AI can analyze data from various sensors (such as EEG, eye-tracking, and GSR) to detect unconscious consumer preferences and emotional responses to advertisements, products, and brands. AI helps marketers tailor strategies based on these insights.
- *Consumer Behavior Analysis:* (Aprilianty et al., 2024; Bhardwaj et al., 2023) examined the role of AI in neuromarketing, focusing on AI's ability to analyze

neural data from brain scans and other biometric sources to predict consumer choices. The authors emphasize that AI technologies allow for real-time analysis of consumer behavior, providing marketers with immediate feedback.

Artificial Intelligence (AI) significantly enhances predictive analytics by effectively handling high-dimensional and complex datasets in neuromarketing. This integration allows for more accurate forecasting of consumer behavior by processing and analyzing intricate neural and physiological data (Alsharif et al., 2025).

- Convolutional Neural Networks (CNNs) for Visual Attention Data

CNNs are adept at processing visual attention data obtained from eye-tracking technologies. By analyzing gaze patterns and visual focus areas, CNNs can identify which elements of marketing stimuli most effectively capture consumer attention (Gupta et al., 2025b). Furthermore, it provides insights into consumer preferences (Zong & Guan, 2024). This capability is crucial in optimizing product placements and advertisement designs.

- Recurrent Neural Networks (RNNs) and Long Short-Term Memory (LSTM) Models for Sequential EEG Signals

RNNs and LSTMs are specialized in analyzing sequential data, such as Electroencephalography (EEG) signals, to predict engagement levels and decision outcomes. These models can capture temporal dependencies in neural responses, providing insights into how consumers' emotional and cognitive states evolve in response to marketing stimuli (Shiri et al., 2024; Song et al., 2025).

- Ensemble Models for Integrating Multiple Neuromarketing Data Streams

Ensemble models, such as Random Forest and Gradient Boosting, are employed to integrate various neuromarketing data streams, including EEG, eye-tracking, and Galvanic Skin Response (GSR). By combining these diverse data sources, ensemble models enhance prediction accuracy and robustness, leading to more reliable forecasts of consumer behavior (Zong & Guan, 2024) and eventually improving the effectiveness of marketing strategies (Quiles Pérez et al., 2024; Shmueli & Koppius, 2011).

These AI-driven approaches have demonstrated superior performance in mapping subconscious neural signals to observable consumer behaviors, thereby providing marketers with deeper insights into consumer preferences and decision-making processes (Alsharif et al., 2025; Gupta et al., 2025b).

## Forecasting Purchase Intent

Purchase intent refers to the likelihood that a consumer will buy a product. Neuromarketing techniques such as EEG, eye-tracking, and galvanic skin response (GSR) can detect neural and physiological markers, such as heightened attention or emotional arousal, that are associated with purchase intent (Baldo et al., 2022; Rahmaini & Salqaura, 2024) and finally to make a purchase (Aprilianty et al., 2024). For instance, increased focus on a product or heightened emotional engagement during an advertisement are strong indicators of potential purchase behavior (AlRoshoud & El-Gohary, 2024).

## Predicting Purchase Decisions

AI models play a crucial role in predicting the conversion of purchase intent into actual sales by analyzing neuromarketing data alongside contextual variables. These models integrate neural data with demographic and behavioral data (e.g., past purchases, browsing behavior) to estimate conversion probability at both the individual and segment levels (Baldo et al., 2022; Venkatraman et al., 2015). For instance, AI models can evaluate how specific neural responses to promotional materials or pricing strategies translate into a final purchase decision (Shmueli & Koppius, 2011).

## Measuring Brand Loyalty

Brand loyalty refers to a consumer's consistent purchasing behavior and advocacy for a specific brand. Loyal consumers not only repeatedly purchase products but also recommend them to others, demonstrating both behavioral and attitudinal commitment (Alsharif & Isa, 2025). Neuromarketing provides insight into how emotional connections with brands can influence consumer loyalty. Through techniques such as EEG, eye-tracking, and GSR, neuromarketing identifies neural and physiological markers associated with emotional engagement, which in turn predict brand preference and loyalty.

AI models play a pivotal role in enhancing the predictive capabilities of brand loyalty by analyzing longitudinal neuromarketing data (Baldo et al., 2022). These models integrate neural signals with demographic, psychographic, and behavioral data, offering insights into the likely trajectory of consumer loyalty over time. AI models track changes in emotional engagement, attention, and physiological responses, which are critical for predicting long-term loyalty trends.

By accurately forecasting loyalty trajectories, these AI models help marketers design effective loyalty programs and brand storytelling strategies that resonate emotionally with consumers. Personalized loyalty programs, informed by neural insights, can offer consumers rewards and experiences that align with their emotional preferences and reinforce their brand commitment (Alsharif & Isa, 2025).

### Evaluating Campaign Effectiveness

Campaign effectiveness refers to how well a marketing campaign achieves its objectives, such as driving sales or increasing brand awareness. Neuromarketing tools can be utilized to pre-test campaigns by assessing neural engagement before the campaign launch. Tools such as EEG, eye-tracking, and GSR are commonly used to track consumer attention, emotional arousal, and engagement in real-time (Alsharif et al., 2025; Rawnaque et al., 2020). These techniques allow marketers to gauge the effectiveness of creative assets and predict how well these materials will perform when exposed to a larger audience (Baldo et al., 2022).

AI models then integrate these neural insights with contextual variables, such as price perception and promotional exposure, to forecast the likelihood of conversion and overall campaign success. These models compare predicted responses with actual market performance, providing a feedback loop that enables marketers to refine their campaigns quickly, improving both engagement and return on investment (ROI) (Alsharif et al., 2025; Rawnaque et al., 2020).

By incorporating AI into neuromarketing pre-testing, marketers can optimize pricing strategies and promotional timing more effectively. AI models not only track consumer behavior but also adapt the campaign elements in real-time to maximize conversion (Baldo et al., 2022). This continuous process helps reduce wasted ad spend and increases ROI by aligning creative content and offers with consumer preferences and emotional triggers.

## CHALLENGES IN NEUROMARKETING IMPLEMENTATION

Despite its significant potential in providing deeper insights into consumer behavior, neuromarketing faces several challenges that hinder its widespread adoption and effective implementation. These challenges include complex data interpretation, high costs, and ethical considerations.

### Complex Data Interpretation

Neuromarketing involves the collection of diverse data from various tools such as EEG, fMRI, eye-tracking, and GSR. However, the integration and interpretation of data from multiple sources can be complex, requiring advanced analytical methods to ensure that the insights generated are valid and reliable. Furthermore, Zenozain (2025) explains that while neuromarketing provides valuable insights, the complexity of analyzing neurophysiological data in conjunction with behavioral data often leads to difficulties in achieving conclusive and actionable results. Moreover, the sheer volume and diversity of data collected necessitate sophisticated algorithms and expert knowledge to draw meaningful conclusions about consumer behavior (Müller, 2020).

## High Costs

One of the primary barriers to the adoption of neuromarketing technologies is their high cost. The equipment required, such as fMRI and EEG machines, is expensive to procure, operate, and maintain. This, in turn, limits the accessibility of neuromarketing for smaller businesses or organizations with limited budgets. (Dewandaru et al., 2023; Khairunnisa et al., 2025) notes that the financial constraints posed by these technologies make it difficult for all companies, especially small and medium-sized enterprises (SMEs), to leverage neuromarketing tools to their full potential. In addition to the upfront costs of the equipment, there are also costs associated with training personnel to operate these devices and interpret the data, which further adds to the financial burden on businesses (Juarez et al., 2020)

## Ethical Considerations

The use of neuromarketing technology raises significant ethical concerns, particularly regarding consumer privacy and the extent to which marketers can influence consumers' subconscious minds. The collection of sensitive data, such as brain activity and emotional responses, without proper consent or awareness from consumers, can lead to privacy violations. (Theodorakopoulos et al., 2025) argues that neuromarketing technologies, while promising, can be misused to manipulate consumer behavior in ways that could undermine consumer autonomy and trust. Moreover, (Ferrell et al., 2025) highlight that ethical guidelines must be established to ensure that neuromarketing practices respect consumer rights and align with established ethical standards.

With the increased use of AI across various sectors, ethical concerns regarding privacy, data security, and potential biases have emerged.

Ethical Challenges: Müller (2020) discussed the ethical dilemmas associated with AI, particularly its impact on privacy and decision-making processes. As AI systems collect vast amounts of data, there are concerns about the misuse of personal information and the potential for algorithmic biases.

Impact of AI on Society:Feijóo & Kwon (2020) raised concerns about the societal implications of AI, particularly the way that AI-driven algorithms can perpetuate inequality and discrimination. Moreover, algorithms can reinforce existing biases, which may result in discriminatory practices in areas like hiring, lending, and law enforcement.

## RESEARCH METHODOLOGY

### Research Design

This study was conducted as a quantitative approach to examine the consumer purchase decision of neuromarketing elaborated with viral marketing based on an AI-Driven (Neuro-Viral AI Predictive Framework/NVAPF). The quantitative approach was carried out by distributing structured questionnaires to empirically test consumer experiences.

### Data Collection

#### Sample Selection

This study used purposive sampling, which is a sampling technique that applies several criteria as considerations: 1) respondents must be over 17 years of age, 2) respondents must have purchased certain food and beverage products. A total of 200 samples were selected, but divided into two groups: 100 respondents in the food sector and 100 respondents in the beverage sector.

#### Survey Instrument Selection

This survey uses a Likert scale ranging from 1 "strongly disagree" to 5 "strongly agree." The measurement covers three variable constructs, namely neuromarketing, AI-based marketing virality, and purchase decision. In addition, to see the demographic distribution, the questionnaire also includes questions related to age, gender, and AI usage.

## Data Analysis

### Quantitative Analysis

Questions regarding descriptive statistics were included in the survey data to determine demographic characteristics. Multiple regression analysis using SPSS software was used to quantify and test validity and reliability, test classical assumptions, and test hypotheses between neuromarketing, AI-based viral marketing, and purchase decisions.

## Reliability and Validity

Reliability measurements were conducted using Cronbach's alpha to assess the consistency of statements on neuromarketing, AI-based viral marketing, and purchase decisions. The reliability test is accepted if the Cronbach alpha value is > 0.7. The test results show that each variable of neuromarketing, AI-based viral marketing, and purchase decision has met the criteria of > 0.7, with Cronbach alpha values of 0.908, 0.930, and 0.904, respectively.

Furthermore, validity tests were conducted on each questionnaire item by testing 12 neuromarketing statement items, 8 AI-based viral marketing items, and 10 purchase decision items. Each indicator item was considered valid if the calculated r value was greater than the table r value, with a table r value of 0.361. The validity test results show that the value of each indicator of neuromarketing construction, AI-based marketing virality, and purchase decision is > 0.361.

## FINDING AND RESULTS

*Table 1. Quantitative Findings*

| Variable | Key Finding | *β / Significance* | Implication |
|---|---|---|---|
| Neuromarketing | The strongest predictor of purchase decision. (T = 6.575) | $\beta = 0.468$, sig $0.000 < 0.05$ | Crucial for long-term AI acceptance |
| Viral Marketing AI-Based (novelty) | Effect positively (T = 4.158) | $\beta = 0.469$, sig $0.000 < 0.05$ | Impact purchase decision |

## DISCUSSION

This section discusses empirical findings related to the influence of neuromarketing and artificial intelligence-based viral marketing on consumer purchasing decisions. The results of hypothesis testing show that both variables have a statistically significant influence, as reflected in the t-statistic values of each construct.

### The Influence of Neuromarketing on Purchase Decisions

The results of this study indicate that neuromarketing is the strongest predictor of consumer purchase decisions, with a t-statistic value of 6.575 and a path coefficient ($\beta$) = 0.468, significant at the $\alpha = 0.000 < 0.05$ level. This finding confirms that a marketing approach based on neurological activity and consumer emotional responses has a substantial impact on shaping preferences and purchasing decisions. This coefficient value indicates that every one-unit increase in the application of neuromarketing strategies will contribute to a 0.468 unit increase in purchasing decisions, assuming ceteris paribus.

This finding is in line with research conducted by Alsharif, Md Salleh, et al. (2021), which states that neuromarketing plays a crucial role in understanding consumer behavior in depth through measuring brain responses, emotional engagement levels, and subconscious attention to marketing stimuli. Furthermore, the research by Alsharif, Md Salleh, et al. (2021) reveals that neuromarketing techniques such as electroencephalography (EEG) and functional magnetic resonance imaging (fMRI) are capable of uncovering hidden dimensions of consumer preferences that cannot be captured through conventional surveys.

Furthermore, Varan et al. (2015) confirm that visual and emotional stimuli designed based on neuromarketing principles significantly increase consumer purchase intention. The study found that advertisements optimized with neuroscience data achieved a 23% higher engagement rate than conventional advertisements, ultimately leading to a significant increase in purchase conversions. This supports the argument that neuromarketing is not merely a diagnostic tool, but also a strategic instrument in the design of effective marketing communications.

Subsequently, research by Fortunato et al. (2014) found that the application of neuromarketing principles in product packaging design directly influences consumers' impulsive purchasing decisions. Neurological responses to the colour, shape, and typography of packaging were found to trigger the activation of brain areas associated with reward processing, thereby accelerating the purchase decision-making process. These findings reinforce the relevance of neuromarketing as a key predictor in this research model.

Based on the cognitive neuroscience perspective, Gupta et al. (2025a) explain that the limbic system, which plays a role in emotional processing, has a dominant contribution to purchasing decisions. Neuromarketing strategies that are able to activate positive emotional responses, such as feelings of pleasure, trust, and anticipation of product benefits, have been proven to increase consumers' tendency to make positive purchasing decisions. This is consistent with the neuromarketing path coefficient value ($\beta = 0.468$), which is the highest in this research model, indicating that the emotional and subconscious dimensions in marketing have greater predictive power than a purely rational marketing approach.

Similarly, research by Plassmann et al. (2015) reinforces that the implementation of neuromarketing in the design of digital consumer experiences significantly moderates the relationship between brand exposure and purchasing decisions. In the digital era, where consumers are inundated with abundant marketing information, neuromarketing's ability to design stimuli that penetrate consumers' cognitive filters makes it a crucial variable. These findings provide a strong theoretical basis for why neuromarketing is the strongest predictor of purchasing decisions in this study, even surpassing other digital marketing variables.

The long-term implications of these findings are also reinforced by K et al. (2024), who argue that neuromarketing, especially when integrated with artificial intelligence technology, has enormous potential for real-time personalization of marketing messages based on the neurological and psychographic profiles of individual consumers. This makes neuromarketing not only relevant in the context of academic research but also highly applicable in modern marketing strategies oriented towards long-term AI acceptance.

## The Influence of AI-Based Viral Marketing on Purchase Decisions

The results of the study indicate that AI-based viral marketing has a positive and significant effect on purchasing decisions, with a t-statistic value of 4.158 and a path coefficient ($\beta$) = 0.469, significant at the $\alpha = 0.000 < 0.05$ level. Interestingly, the value of this variable coefficient is almost equivalent to neuromarketing (the difference is only 0.001), indicating that AI-based marketing innovations in the context of viral content dissemination have a highly competitive influence on the formation of modern consumer purchasing decisions.

This finding is in line with the research by Bozdog et al. (2025), where they found that content disseminated through AI-based viral mechanisms can significantly increase consumer purchase intention due to its personalized and contextual nature. AI algorithms in viral marketing platforms are able to identify the most responsive audience segments, optimize content distribution timing, and tailor message formats to individual preferences, thereby increasing the relevance and persuasiveness of the content being disseminated.

The novelty aspect inherent in AI-based viral marketing is supported by *Lamberton & Stephen's (2016)* research, who argue that consumers are attracted to content that contains elements of novelty and surprise produced or curated by artificial intelligence, as it fulfills psychological needs for cognitive stimulation and exploration of new information. When AI-generated viral content is considered new and relevant by consumers, it directly influences cognitive elaboration, which leads to purchasing decisions.

In the social media landscape, research by Theodorakopoulos et al. (2025) reveals that viral marketing optimized through machine learning and natural language processing (NLP) results in statistically higher purchase conversion rates compared to conventional viral campaigns. Their study found that AI-driven viral content has a higher click-through rate and better conversion rate, which directly supports this study's findings that AI-based viral marketing positively influences purchase decisions.

More specifically, Ismagilova et al. (2020) research adds an important dimension regarding the role of AI-driven electronic word-of-mouth (e-WOM) in shaping purchasing decisions. They found that reviews and recommendations that are virally spread and curated by AI algorithms have a higher level of trustworthiness in the eyes of consumers because they are considered more objective and personally relevant. This mechanism reinforces the influence of AI-based viral marketing on purchasing decisions through the mediation of consumer trust perceptions.

Based on technology acceptance theory, Verhoef et al. (2021) explain that consumers exposed to AI-based viral marketing in an omnichannel retail context show a higher tendency to make purchasing decisions, mainly due to personalized experiences. The integration of AI in viral marketing strategies not only increases the reach of marketing messages but also enhances the quality of consumer interactions with brands, which in turn drives faster and more positive purchasing decisions.

Furthermore, Chintagunta et al. (2016) emphasize that AI-powered viral marketing is able to utilize consumer social networks more efficiently through the identification of influencer nodes and the prediction of content diffusion patterns. This predictive capability allows marketers to maximize content exposure to consumers with the highest purchase decision probability, thereby increasing the overall efficiency and effectiveness of viral campaigns. Their findings support the high path coefficient value ($\beta = 0.469$) of the AI-based viral marketing variable in this research model.

Overall, the two variables in this study, neuromarketing ($\beta = 0.468$; $t = 6.575$) and AI-based viral marketing ($\beta = 0.469$; $t = 4.158$), together form a holistic marketing framework that integrates a deep understanding of consumer psychology and neurology with the power of AI technology in marketing message dissemination. These findings are consistent with the direction of marketing literature that emphasizes the synergy between neuroscience, artificial intelligence, and consumer behavior as the foundation of effective marketing strategies in the digital age (Davenport et al., 2020; Grewal et al., 2021).

## CONCLUSION

The integration of predictive analytics and neuromarketing offers marketers a transformative capability to anticipate and influence consumer behavior. By leveraging AI models, marketers can forecast purchase intent, guide purchase decisions, strengthen brand loyalty, and evaluate campaign effectiveness with greater accuracy than ever before.

While the potential benefits are substantial, ethical considerations, such as data privacy, informed consent, and the potential manipulation of subconscious preferences, must be addressed. Future research should focus on developing transparent, explainable AI models that respect consumer autonomy while maximizing predictive accuracy. The ongoing fusion of neuroscience, AI, and predictive analytics is likely to redefine competitive advantage in marketing, offering organizations a deeper and more actionable understanding of their customers. Additionally, advancements in AI and machine learning can help address the complexities of data interpretation, allowing businesses to optimize their marketing strategies without compromising on ethical standards (Dewandaru et al., 2023; Mohammed & Alhumaid, 2025; Müller, 2020).

## MANAGERIAL IMPLICATION

Several managerial implications can be formulated from the results of this study, namely: (1) the need for marketing managers to reorient their strategies based on consumer neuroscience, including investment in EEG, eye-tracking, and interface design based on neurological principles, given that neuromarketing is the strongest predictor ($\beta = 0.468$); (2) it would be better if there were an institution or division within the company specifically handling AI-based viral marketing, with budget reallocation from advertising to precise and personalized AI-powered viral campaigns.

## PRACTICAL IMPLICATION

In practice, the integration of neuromarketing into marketing strategies necessitates careful consideration of ethical issues, including privacy concerns and the potential for consumer manipulation. As highlighted by Arya et al. (2025), responsible implementation of neuromarketing techniques involves obtaining informed consent from participants, ensuring data anonymity, and being transparent about the purposes of data collection. Addressing these ethical considerations is crucial to maintaining consumer trust and upholding the integrity of marketing practices (Casado-Aranda et al., 2019).

Moreover, a few practical implications that can be implemented are: (1) companies establish standard operating procedures for neuromarketing validation in the campaign development pipeline, for example by using wearable biometrics, facial coding, and eye-tracking for pre-testing creative content before launch; (2) Companies can implement AI-based viral marketing through content recommendation engines, influencer node identification based on network analysis, and continuous experimentation with AI-generated content.

## THEORETICAL IMPLICATION

Neuromarketing offers profound insights into consumer behavior, enhancing traditional marketing strategies by providing objective, real-time data on subconscious responses. By employing advanced neuroimaging techniques such as electroencephalography (EEG), eye-tracking, and functional magnetic resonance imaging (fMRI), neuromarketing enables the measurement of neural and physiological reactions to marketing stimuli, including advertisements, branding, and product designs (Panwar et al., 2024). These methodologies allow marketers to assess consumer engagement, emotional arousal, and attention levels, facilitating the optimization of marketing campaigns to align more closely with consumer preferences.

Singh et al. (2023) emphasize that integrating neuromarketing into marketing strategies can significantly enhance campaign effectiveness by aligning messages and product designs with consumers' brain responses. This alignment ensures that marketing efforts resonate more deeply with the target audience, potentially leading to increased consumer engagement and improved brand perception. Furthermore, the application of neuromarketing techniques aids in identifying the most effective elements of marketing campaigns, such as visual stimuli, messaging, and emotional triggers, thereby enabling marketers to refine their strategies for optimal impact.

Thus, the theoretical implications of neuromarketing are equally significant. It bridges the gap between neuroscience and marketing, providing a scientific basis for understanding consumer behavior beyond traditional psychological theories. By incorporating neural data into marketing research, neuromarketing contributes to the development of more accurate models of consumer decision-making processes, offering a deeper understanding of the factors influencing consumer choices (Bajaj et al., 2024).

## RECOMMENDATION

Three concrete recommendations can be implemented: (1) establishing a Neuromarketing Center of Excellence (NCoE) as an internal function of the organization, applying a test-and-scale methodology based on multi-armed bandit algorithms for viral marketing, and developing an integrated measurement framework that combines neurological metrics with conventional KPIs; (2) recommending that platform developers open access to behavioral data for AI modeling; and (3) recommending that regulators develop an ethical framework for the use of commercial neuromarketing.

## FUTURE DIRECTION

Based on the research results, there are four directions for future research, namely: (1) testing mediation and moderation mechanisms (including cross-cultural variables) is important to provide a more in-depth picture; (2) future researchers can conduct longitudinal and experimental research designs to strengthen causal inferences; (3) there is still a need to explore new technological contexts such as the metaverse, AR, and generative AI; (4) and there is still a need to develop an integrative model that combines neuroscience, information science, and behavioral economics into a comprehensive theoretical framework. This is very useful for exploring the impact of AI-based neuromarketing and viral marketing on purchasing decisions.

## CASE STUDIES IN THE INDUSTRY

### EyeSee Research: Integrating AI in Neuromarketing

EyeSee Research is a market research company specializing in neuromarketing, utilizing cutting-edge technologies such as eye-tracking and AI-driven emotional analysis to gain deeper insights into consumer behavior. The company's approach blends traditional market research with advanced machine learning techniques, allowing businesses to optimize their marketing and product strategies in a more data-driven and precise manner.

EyeSee uses eye-tracking technology to monitor and record where and how long a consumer looks at specific elements within advertisements or product packaging.

This method helps identify which parts of the visual stimulus attract the most attention. By tracking 11.5 million eye fixation points, EyeSee gathers detailed data on the consumer's visual journey, revealing what captures their interest and what is ignored.

- Eye Fixation Points: These are the specific locations on a screen or physical object that a person focuses on for a period of time. The length and frequency of fixations can reveal which aspects of an advertisement or product are engaging or distracting for the consumer.
- Heatmaps: The collected data is used to create predictive heatmaps, which visually represent the areas that received the most attention. The heatmap shows where consumers' eyes were most focused and for how long, helping brands understand the effectiveness of design elements.

In addition to eye-tracking, EyeSee incorporates AI-driven emotional analysis to interpret consumer emotional responses. This method involves using machine learning algorithms to analyze facial expressions, voice tone, and body language to identify the emotions a consumer experiences when exposed to advertisements or products.

- Emotional Mapping: By combining eye-tracking data with emotional analysis, EyeSee can correlate where a consumer's attention was focused with their emotional reaction. For example, if a particular product design or ad element attracts a lot of visual attention and triggers positive emotions, the brand can conclude that this element is effective at creating a connection with the consumer.
- Real-Time Insights: AI enables real-time processing of emotional responses, allowing companies to make swift adjustments to their strategies based on immediate feedback from consumers.

By integrating eye-tracking data and emotional analysis, EyeSee Research can produce highly predictive insights into how consumers will react to various marketing stimuli. These insights are crucial for developing more effective advertising, packaging, and product designs(Pereira et al., 2021).

- Predictive Heatmaps: The heatmaps generated by EyeSee are not just descriptive, they are predictive. By analyzing patterns from large datasets of consumer interactions, EyeSee can predict how future consumers will likely respond to specific ad elements or product features.

- Improved Decision-Making: Predictive analytics helps brands test different design variations before launching a full campaign. This reduces the risk of costly mistakes and helps brands fine-tune their messaging and product offerings for better market reception. Furthermore, the integration of AI and eye-tracking technology allows EyeSee Research to provide businesses with actionable insights that can directly impact key areas of marketing:
    - Optimizing Product Design: By understanding which product features catch consumers' attention, businesses can prioritize design elements that lead to stronger emotional connections and increased engagement.
    - Refining Marketing Strategies: With AI-driven emotional and attention data, companies can optimize the placement of key messages, logos, and calls to action in ads, ensuring they resonate emotionally and are noticed by the target audience.
    - Targeted Campaigns: Predictive insights allow businesses to develop more targeted campaigns by understanding the consumer's visual and emotional journey. This results in more personalized and effective marketing efforts

Ultimately, the main benefits of integrating AI in neuromarketing, as offered by EyeSee Research are include:

- Higher Precision: The combination of eye-tracking and emotional analysis leads to more precise insights into what truly captivates the consumer's attention and influences their purchasing decisions.
- Enhanced ROI: By optimizing product design and marketing strategies, businesses can achieve higher engagement rates, leading to better returns on advertising and product development investments.
- Reduced Risk: Testing different marketing elements through predictive analytics helps businesses mitigate the risk of launching ineffective campaigns

## AI in Food Marketing from Personalized Recommendations to Predictive Analytics: Comparing Traditional Advertising Techniques with AI-Driven Strategies

Research by Khamoushi (2024) explores how the food marketing industry is shifting from conventional advertising approaches to AI-powered strategies that leverage consumer behavior data. The transition represents a fundamental change in how food brands engage with consumers, moving from broad, one-size-fits-all campaigns to more personalized and data-driven methods.

Traditionally, food marketing has relied heavily on broad-based strategies, such as television ads, print media, and radio spots, targeting large audiences with generic messages. These methods primarily used demographic data (age, gender, income level, etc.) to segment markets, relying on mass media channels to push advertising messages to as many people as possible.

While traditional advertising methods are still widely used, they often lead to lower levels of personalization and engagement. The key limitations of traditional food marketing include:

- Generic Messaging: Advertisements are tailored for broad consumer groups rather than individual preferences.
- Lack of Real-Time Data: Traditional marketing lacks the agility to react to changing consumer preferences or behavior in real-time.
- Limited Interaction: Traditional ads do not offer consumers opportunities to interact or influence the content they receive, leading to lower engagement.

Nowadays, Artificial Intelligence (AI) is transforming food marketing by enabling brands to personalize their marketing efforts and predict consumer behavior more accurately. This shift is based on the ability to analyze vast amounts of consumer data, enabling brands to understand individual preferences, predict future behavior, and craft marketing messages that resonate on a personal level.

Key components of AI-driven strategies in food marketing include:

## Personalized Product Recommendations

AI utilizes consumer behavior data, such as purchase history, browsing patterns, and social media activity, to generate personalized product recommendations. These recommendations are designed to appeal to an individual's tastes and preferences, increasing the likelihood of purchase.

- Data Collection: By gathering data on past purchases, online interactions, and even social media activity, AI algorithms can learn what products a consumer is most likely to be interested in.
- Real-Time Suggestions: AI systems are capable of providing real-time recommendations based on current browsing behaviors, ensuring that consumers are presented with relevant products at the moment they are most likely to purchase.

- Enhanced Engagement: Personalization not only leads to more targeted ads but also fosters a deeper connection between the brand and consumer, which increases overall engagement and customer loyalty.

## Predictive Analytics

Predictive analytics is another area where AI is making a significant impact in food marketing. By analyzing vast amounts of consumer data, AI algorithms can forecast future consumer needs and behaviors, enabling food brands to act proactively.

- Consumer Behavior Forecasting: AI can predict what consumers will likely purchase based on previous patterns and trends. For instance, if a customer frequently buys vegetarian products, AI can predict future purchases or recommend new vegetarian products they might enjoy.
- Optimized Inventory and Supply Chains: With predictive analytics, food brands can also anticipate demand and optimize inventory management. This reduces waste and ensures products are available when and where consumers need them.
- Dynamic Marketing Strategies: AI helps in adjusting marketing strategies in real-time, based on predicted trends. For example, if data shows a sudden rise in interest for a particular type of snack, AI systems can quickly push targeted ads or promotional offers related to that snack.

While both traditional and AI-driven advertising techniques aim to influence consumer behavior, they operate in fundamentally different ways. Here are the comparison of Traditional vs. AI-Driven Advertising Techniques:

*Table 2. Comparison: Traditional vs. AI-Driven Advertising Techniques*

| | **Traditional Advertising** | **AI-Driven Strategy** |
|---|---|---|
| **Targeting and Reach** | Targets large groups using demographic information, which can result in wasted advertising spend on individuals who may not be interested in the product. | Use data to target individual consumers with personalized messages that are more likely to resonate, reducing waste and improving ad effectiveness. |
| **Real-Time Adaptation** | Has limited flexibility and cannot easily adapt to changing consumer behaviors once a campaign is launched. | Enable real-time adjustments. For example, if AI detects a shift in consumer interest towards a particular food product, the marketing strategy can be quickly modified to capitalize on that trend. |
| **Consumer Engagement** | Often lacks direct engagement with consumers. The consumer is a passive recipient of the message. | Offer interactive and engaging experiences, such as personalized recommendations, targeted promotions, and real-time responses based on consumer behavior. |
| **Cost-Effectiveness** | Can be expensive, especially when using media like TV or radio ads that target a broad audience. This often leads to inefficiencies in reaching the right consumers. | More cost-effective due to precision targeting and the ability to optimize ad spend based on real-time consumer data and predictive insights. |

## ACKNOWLEDGMENT

We would like to express our sincere gratitude to all those who have contributed to our research, either directly by giving us their valuable inputs or indirectly through their scholarly works used as references or as respondents. We are deeply indebted to the Almighty God for granting us the strength and determination to complete this research.

## REFERENCES

Abdelfattah, F., Madi, H., Al-Washahi, M., AlAraimi, A., Nagi, S., & Abbas, M. (2025). Harnessing Artificial Intelligence, Business Intelligence, and Digital Technologies for achieving supply chain excellence in Oman: Investigating the mediating role of predictive analytics. *Journal of Open Innovation*, *11*(4), 100644. Advance online publication. DOI: 10.1016/j.joitmc.2025.100644

Adeola, O., Evans, O., Ndubuisi Edeh, J., & Adisa, I. (2022). The Future of Marketing: Artificial Intelligence, Virtual Reality, and Neuromarketing. In *Palgrave Studies of Marketing in Emerging Economies: Part F3553* (pp. 253–280). Palgrave Macmillan. DOI: 10.1007/978-3-030-88678-3_12

AlRoshoud, A. N., & El-Gohary, H. O. (2024). Exploring the Impact of Combining Neuromarketing and AI Adoption on the Perceived Effectiveness of Social Media Advertising Campaigns. *International Journal of Customer Relationship Marketing and Management*, *15*(1), 1–28. Advance online publication. DOI: 10.4018/IJCRMM.361975

Alshaketheep, K., Mansour, A. M., Al-Ma'aitah, M. M. L., Dabaghia, M. N., & Dabaghie, Y. M. (2024). Leveraging AI Predictive Analytics for Marketing Strategy: The Mediating Role of Management Awareness. *Journal of System and Management Sciences*, *14*(2), 71–89. DOI: 10.33168/JSMS.2024.0205

Alsharif, A. H., & Isa, S. M. (2025). Electroencephalography Studies on Marketing Stimuli: A Literature Review and Future Research Agenda. In *International Journal of Consumer Studies* (Vol. 49, Number 1). John Wiley and Sons Inc. DOI: 10.1111/ijcs.70015

Alsharif, A. H., Md Salleh, N. Z., Baharun, R., & Rami Hashem, E. A. (2021). Neuromarketing research in the last five years: a bibliometric analysis. In *Cogent Business and Management* (Vol. 8, Number 1). Cogent OA. DOI: 10.1080/23311975.2021.1978620

Alsharif, A. H., Salleh, N. Z. M., Abdullah, M., Khraiwish, A., & Ashaari, A. (2023). Neuromarketing Tools Used in the Marketing Mix: A Systematic Literature and Future Research Agenda. *SAGE Open*, *13*(1), 21582440231156563. Advance online publication. DOI: 10.1177/21582440231156563

Alsharif, A. H., Salleh, N. Z. M., Baharun, R., Alharthi Rami Hashem, E., Mansor, A. A., Ali, J., & Abbas, A. F. (2021). Neuroimaging techniques in advertising research: Main applications, development, and brain regions and processes. In *Sustainability (Switzerland)* (Vol. 13, Number 11). MDPI AG. DOI: 10.3390/su13116488

Alsharif, A. H., Wang, J., Isa, S. M., Salleh, N. Z. M., Dawas, H. A., & Alsharif, M. H. (2025). The synergy of neuromarketing and artificial intelligence: A comprehensive literature review in the last decade. *Future Business Journal*, *11*(1), 170. Advance online publication. DOI: 10.1186/s43093-025-00591-x

Aprilianty, F., Takahashi, M., & Matsuura, Y. (2024). Bridging Brains and Bots: The Impact of AI on Neuromarketing. *Procedia Computer Science*, *246*(C), 1830–1839. DOI: 10.1016/j.procs.2024.09.687

Arya, K., Bhardwaj, V., Kumari, V., & Singh, D. (2025). From Brain To Business: The Role of Neuroscience In Marketing, HR, and Finance Along With Ethical Issues. *Academy of Marketing Studies Journal*, *29*(5).

Bajaj, R., Ali Syed, A., & Singh, S. (2024). Analysing applications of neuromarketing in efficacy of programmatic advertising. *Journal of Consumer Behaviour*, *23*(2), 939–958. DOI: 10.1002/cb.2249

Baldo, D., Viswanathan, V. S., Timpone, R. J., & Venkatraman, V. (2022). The heart, brain, and body of marketing: Complementary roles of neurophysiologicalmeasuresin trackingemotions,memory, and ad effectiveness. *Psychology of Marketing: Wiley*, *39*, 1979–1991. https://doi.org/DOI:10.1002/mar.21697

Bansal, S., Nangia, P., & Koles, B. (2025). Neuromarketing and the Marketing Mix: An Integrative Review and Future Research Agenda Using the TMC Approach. *International Journal of Consumer Studies*, *49*(3), e70072. https://doi.org/https://doi.org/10.1111/ijcs.70072. DOI: 10.1111/ijcs.70072

Bao, W., Cao, Y., Yang, Y., Che, H., Huang, J., & Wen, S. (2025). Data-driven stock forecasting models based on neural networks: A review. *Information Fusion*, *113*, 102616. DOI: 10.1016/j.inffus.2024.102616

Bazzani, A., Ravaioli, S., Trieste, L., Faraguna, U., & Turchetti, G. (2020). Is EEG Suitable for Marketing Research? A Systematic Review. In *Frontiers in Neuroscience* (Vol. 14). Frontiers Media S.A. DOI: 10.3389/fnins.2020.594566

Bhardwaj, S., Rana, G. A., Behl, A., & Gallego de Caceres, S. J. (2023). Exploring the boundaries of Neuromarketing through systematic investigation. *Journal of Business Research, 154*, 113371. DOI: 10.1016/j.jbusres.2022.113371

Bozdog, L.-S., Naghi, R. I., Preda, G., & Prada, S. I. (2025). The Influence of AI Chatbots on the Purchase Intention of Sustainable Products. *Transformations in Business & Economics, 24*(1 (64)), 238–261. DOI: 10.15388/Tibe.2025.24.1.11

Casado-Aranda, L. A., Dimoka, A., & Sánchez-Fernández, J. (2019). Consumer Processing of Online Trust Signals: A Neuroimaging Study. *Journal of Interactive Marketing, 47*(1), 159–180. DOI: 10.1016/j.intmar.2019.02.006

Chhajer, P., Shah, M., & Kshirsagar, A. (2022). The applications of artificial neural networks, support vector machines, and long–short term memory for stock market prediction. *Decision Analytics Journal, 2*, 100015. DOI: 10.1016/j.dajour.2021.100015

Chintagunta, P., Hanssens, D. M., & Hauser, J. R. (2016). Marketing science and big data. In *Marketing Science* (Vol. 35, Number 3, pp. 341–342). INFORMS Inst. for Operations Res.and the Management Sciences. DOI: 10.1287/mksc.2016.0996

Davenport, T., Guha, A., Grewal, D., & Bressgott, T. (2020). How artificial intelligence will change the future of marketing. *Journal of the Academy of Marketing Science, 48*(1), 24–42. DOI: 10.1007/s11747-019-00696-0

Dewandaru, B., Goncalves, M., & Rahmadi, A. N. (2023). IMPACT OF DIGITAL MARKETING, DIGITAL FINANCE, AND DIGITAL LITERACY ON BUSINESS PERFORMANCE SMEs. *Journal of Innovation Research and Knowledge, 3*(3). https://bajangjournal.com/index.php/JIRK/article/view/8788

Feijóo, C., & Kwon, Y. (2020a). AI impacts on economy and society: Latest developments, open issues and new policy measures. *Telecommunications Policy, 44*(6), 101987. Advance online publication. DOI: 10.1016/j.telpol.2020.101987 PMID: 32377031

Feijóo, C., & Kwon, Y. (2020b). AI impacts on economy and society: Latest developments, open issues and new policy measures. *Telecommunications Policy, 44*(6), 101987. DOI: 10.1016/j.telpol.2020.101987 PMID: 32377031

Ferrell, M. L., Beatty, A., & Dubljevic, V. (2025). The Ethics of Neuromarketing: A Rapid Review. In *Neuroethics* (Vol. 18, Number 1). Springer Science and Business Media B.V. DOI: 10.1007/s12152-025-09591-8

Fortunato, V. C. R., Giraldi, J. D. M. E., & De Oliveira, J. H. C. (2014). A Review of Studies on Neuromarketing: Practical Results, Techniques, Contributions and Limitations. *Journal of Management Research, 6*(2), 201. DOI: 10.5296/jmr.v6i2.5446

Grewal, D., Guha, A., Satornino, C. B., & Schweiger, E. B. (2021). Artificial intelligence: The light and the darkness. *Journal of Business Research, 136*, 229–236. DOI: 10.1016/j.jbusres.2021.07.043

Gupta, R., Kapoor, A. P., & Verma, H. (2025a). Exploring consumer neuroscience in marketing research: Theoretical foundations, methodological aspects, and future research directions. *Journal of Marketing Theory and Practice*, 1–27. Advance online publication. DOI: 10.1080/10696679.2025.2493816

Gupta, R., Kapoor, A. P., & Verma, H. V. (2025b). Neuro-insights: a systematic review of neuromarketing perspectives across consumer buying stages. In *Frontiers in Neuroergonomics* (Vol. 6). Frontiers Media SA. DOI: 10.3389/fnrgo.2025.1542847

Ho, D. B., Duong, C. D., Tran, M. L., Luong, T. S., & Tran, T. P. H. (2025). Big data analytics powered by artificial intelligence and entrepreneurial resilience: A moderated mediation model of technological turbulence and business innovation model. *Journal of Open Innovation, 11*(3), 100611. Advance online publication. DOI: 10.1016/j.joitmc.2025.100611

Iloka, C. B., & Anukwe, G. I. (2020). Review of eye-tracking: A neuromarketing technique. *Neuroscience Research Notes, 3*(4), 29–34. DOI: 10.31117/neuroscirn.v3i4.61

Ismagilova, E., Slade, E. L., Rana, N. P., & Dwivedi, Y. K. (2020). The Effect of Electronic Word of Mouth Communications on Intention to Buy: A Meta-Analysis. *Information Systems Frontiers, 22*(5), 1203–1226. DOI: 10.1007/s10796-019-09924-y

Jordan, M. I., & Mitchell, T. M. (2015). Machine learning: Trends, perspectives, and prospects. In *Science* (Vol. 349, Number 6245, pp. 255–260). American Association for the Advancement of Science. DOI: 10.1126/science.aaa8415

Juarez, D., Tur-Viñes, V., & Mengual, A. (2020). Neuromarketing Applied to Educational Toy Packaging. *Frontiers in Psychology, 11*, 2077. Advance online publication. DOI: 10.3389/fpsyg.2020.02077 PMID: 32982857

K, L., Kumar, P., Chowdhury, S., & Madhavedi, S. (2024). Role of Neuromarketing and Artificial Intelligence in Futuristic Marketing Approach: An Empirical Study. *Journal of Informatics Education and Research, 4*(2), 560–567. http://jier.org

Khairunnisa, D., Salqaura, S. A., & Lestari, I. (2025). Pengaruh Viral Marketing dan Neuromarketing terhadap Keputusan Pembelian Konsumen Fore Coffee. *RIGGS: Journal of Artificial Intelligence and Digital Business, 4*(2), 7373–7378. DOI: 10.31004/riggs.v4i2.1874

Khamoushi, E. (2024). AI in Food Marketing from Personalized Recommendations to Predictive Analytics: Comparing Traditional Advertising Techniques with AI-Driven Strategies. *Cornell University*. https://doi.org/https://doi.org/10.48550/arXiv.2410.01815

Khondakar, M. F. K., Sarowar, M. H., Chowdhury, M. H., Majumder, S., Hossain, M. A., Dewan, M. A. A., & Hossain, Q. D. (2024). A systematic review on EEG-based neuromarketing: recent trends and analyzing techniques. In *Brain Informatics* (Vol. 11, Number 1). Springer Science and Business Media Deutschland GmbH. DOI: 10.1186/s40708-024-00229-8

Khurana, V., Gahalawat, M., Kumar, P., Roy, P. P., Dogra, D. P., Scheme, E., & Soleymani, M. (2021). A Survey on Neuromarketing Using EEG Signals. *IEEE Transactions on Cognitive and Developmental Systems, 13*(4), 732–749. DOI: 10.1109/TCDS.2021.3065200

Kusters, R., Misevic, D., Berry, H., Cully, A., Le Cunff, Y., Dandoy, L., Díaz-Rodríguez, N., Ficher, M., Grizou, J., Othmani, A., Palpanas, T., Komorowski, M., Loiseau, P., Moulin Frier, C., Nanini, S., Quercia, D., Sebag, M., Soulié Fogelman, F., Taleb, S., & Wehbi, F. (2020). Interdisciplinary Research in Artificial Intelligence: Challenges and Opportunities. *Frontiers in Big Data, 3*, 577974. Advance online publication. DOI: 10.3389/fdata.2020.577974 PMID: 33693418

Lamberton, C., & Stephen, A. T. (2016). A thematic exploration of digital, social media, and mobile marketing: Research evolution from 2000 to 2015 and an agenda for future inquiry. *Journal of Marketing, 80*(6), 146–172. DOI: 10.1509/jm.15.0415

Mohammed, S. M., & Alhumaid, M. T. (2025). The impact of managerial innovation skills on neuromarketing implementation in the pharmaceutical sector. *International Journal of Pharmaceutical and Healthcare Marketing*. https://doi.org/https://doi.org/10.1108/IJPHM-10-2024-0119

Morin, C. (2011). Neuromarketing: The New Science of Consumer Behavior. In *Society* (Vol. 48, Number 2, pp. 131–135). Springer Science and Business Media, LLC. DOI: 10.1007/s12115-010-9408-1

Müller, V. C. (2020). *Stanford Encyclopedia of Philosophy*. https://plato.stanford.edu/entries/ethics-ai/#ManiBeha

Müller, V. C. (2021). Ethics of artificial intelligence. In *The Routledge Social Science Handbook of AI* (1st ed.). Taylor & Francis Group., https://www.taylorfrancis.com/chapters/edit/10.4324/9780429198533-9/ethics-artificial-intelligence-vincent-m%C3%BCller DOI: 10.4324/9780429198533-9

Panwar, D., Bhargava, A., Bohara, S., & Chaudhary, S. S. (2024). Neuromarketing insights for effective advertising strategies: A review and future research agenda. *Neuropsychological Trends*, (36), 107–132. DOI: 10.7358/neur-2024-036-panw

Pereira, R., Córdova, F. M., & Díaz, H. A. (2021). Some experiences in Neuromarketing: Moving from White papers to Scientific inquiries. *Procedia Computer Science*, *199*, 1409–1415. DOI: 10.1016/j.procs.2022.01.178

Plassmann, H., Venkatraman, V., Huettel, S., & Yoon, C. (2015). Consumer neuroscience: Applications, challenges, and possible solutions. *JMR, Journal of Marketing Research*, *52*(4), 427–435. DOI: 10.1509/jmr.14.0048

Quiles Pérez, M., Martínez Beltrán, E. T., López Bernal, S., Horna Prat, E., Montesano Del Campo, L., Fernández Maimó, L., & Huertas Celdrán, A. (2024). Data fusion in neuromarketing: Multimodal analysis of biosignals, lifecycle stages, current advances, datasets, trends, and challenges. *Information Fusion*, *105*, 102231. Advance online publication. DOI: 10.1016/j.inffus.2024.102231

Rahmaini, R., & Salqaura, S. A. (2024). Pengaruh Viral Marketing Dan Neuromarketing Terhadap Keputusan Pembelian Cromboloni Roti'o Di Cabang Manhattan Square Medan. [JIMBI]. *Jurnal Ilmiah Manajemen Dan Bisnis*, *5*(2), 302–310. DOI: 10.31289/jimbi.v5i2.5341

Rawnaque, F. S., Rahman, K. M., Anwar, S. F., Vaidyanathan, R., Chau, T., Sarker, F., & Al Mamun, K. A. (2020). Technological advancements and opportunities in Neuromarketing: a systematic review. In *Brain Informatics* (Vol. 7, Number 1). Springer Science and Business Media Deutschland GmbH. DOI: 10.1186/s40708-020-00109-x

Robaina-Calderín, L., & Martín-Santana, J. D. (2021). A review of research on neuromarketing using content analysis: Key approaches and new avenues. *Cognitive Neurodynamics*, *15*(6), 923–938. DOI: 10.1007/s11571-021-09693-y PMID: 34790262

Russel, S., & Norvig, P. (2010). *Artificial Intelligence: A Modern Approach* (3rd ed.). Prentice Hall: Pearson., http://repo.darmajaya.ac.id/5272/1/Artificial%20Intelligence-A%20Modern%20Approach%20(3rd%20Edition)%20(%20PDFDrive%20).pdf

Shiri, F. M., Perumal, T., Mustapha, N., & Mohamed, R. (2024). A Comprehensive Overview and Comparative Analysis on Deep Learning Models. *Journal on Artificial Intelligence*, *6*(1), 301–360. DOI: 10.32604/jai.2024.054314

Shmueli, G., & Koppius, O. R. (2011). Predictive analytics in information systems research. In *MIS Quarterly: Management Information Systems* (Vol. 35, Number 3, pp. 553–572). University of Minnesota. DOI: 10.2307/23042796

Singh, P., Alhassan, I., & Khoshaim, L. (2023). What Do You Need to Know? A Systematic Review and Research Agenda on Neuromarketing Discipline. In *Journal of Theoretical and Applied Electronic Commerce Research* (Vol. 18, Number 4, pp. 2007–2032). Multidisciplinary Digital Publishing Institute (MDPI). DOI: 10.3390/jtaer18040101

Song, G., Gazi, M. A. I., Waaje, A., Roshid, M. M., Karim, R., Rahaman, M. A., Min, Z., & Senathirajah, A. R. B. S. (2025). The Neuromarketing: Bridging Neuroscience and Marketing for Enhanced Consumer Engagement. In *IEEE Access* (Vol. 13, pp. 40331–40353). Institute of Electrical and Electronics Engineers Inc. DOI: 10.1109/ACCESS.2025.3545742

Theodorakopoulos, L., Theodoropoulou, A., & Klavdianos, C. (2025). Interactive Viral Marketing Through Big Data Analytics, Influencer Networks, AI Integration, and Ethical Dimensions. In *Journal of Theoretical and Applied Electronic Commerce Research* (Vol. 20, Number 2). Multidisciplinary Digital Publishing Institute (MDPI). DOI: 10.3390/jtaer20020115

Varan, D., Lang, A., Barwise, P., Weber, R., & Bellman, S. (2015). How reliable are neuromarketers' measures of advertising effectiveness: Data from ongoing research holds no common truth among vendors. *Journal of Advertising Research, 55*(2), 176–191. DOI: 10.2501/JAR-55-2-176-191

Venkatraman, V., Dimoka, A., Pavlou, P. A., Vo, K., Hampton, W., Bollinger, B., Hershfield, H. E., Ishihara, M., & Winer, R. S. (2015). Predicting advertising success beyond traditional measures: New insights from neurophysiological methods and market response modeling. *JMR, Journal of Marketing Research, 52*(4), 436–452. DOI: 10.1509/jmr.13.0593

Verhoef, P. C., Broekhuizen, T., Bart, Y., Bhattacharya, A., Qi Dong, J., Fabian, N., & Haenlein, M. (2021). Digital transformation: A multidisciplinary reflection and research agenda. *Journal of Business Research, 122*, 889–901. DOI: 10.1016/j.jbusres.2019.09.022

Vlačić, B., Corbo, L., Costa e Silva, S., & Dabić, M. (2021). The evolving role of artificial intelligence in marketing: A review and research agenda. In *Journal of Business Research* (Vol. 128, pp. 187–203). Elsevier Inc., DOI: 10.1016/j.jbusres.2021.01.055

Zenozain, E. A. M. (2025). Deciphering Purchase Decisions in Neuromarketing: A Systematic Review of the Last Decade Using Neutrosophic Z Numbers. *Neutrosophic Sets and Systems, 84*(1), 264–280. https://digitalrepository.unm.edu/nss_journal/vol84/iss1/22

Zenozain, E. A. M., Salvador, E., & Salvador, S. (2025). Deciphering Purchase Decisions in Neuromarketing: A Systematic Review of the Last Decade Using Neutrosophic Z Numbers. In *Neutrosophic Sets and Systems* (Vol. 84). https://digitalrepository.unm.edu/nss_journal/vol84/iss1/22

Zhang, J., & Tao, D. (2021). Empowering Things with Intelligence: A Survey of the Progress, Challenges, and Opportunities in Artificial Intelligence of Things. In *IEEE Internet of Things Journal* (Vol. 8, Number 10, pp. 7789–7817). Institute of Electrical and Electronics Engineers Inc. DOI: 10.1109/JIOT.2020.3039359

Zong, Z., & Guan, Y. (2024). AI-Driven Intelligent Data Analytics and Predictive Analysis in Industry 4.0: Transforming Knowledge, Innovation, and Efficiency. *Journal of the Knowledge Economy, 16*(1), 864–903. Advance online publication. DOI: 10.1007/s13132-024-02001-z

# Chapter 3
# AI-Driven Product Recommendation Systems Informed by Emotional Responses

**A. A. Jayashree Prabhakar**
http://orcid.org/0000-0003-4324-5916
*Vels Institute of Science, Technology, and Advanced Studies, India*

**C. Manju**
http://orcid.org/0009-0002-7614-4740
*Dharmamurthi Rao Bahadhur Calavala Cunnan Chetty's Hindu College, India*

**V. N. Sudheer**
http://orcid.org/0009-0004-8776-9409
*CMR University, India*

**C. Karpagavalli**
http://orcid.org/0009-0004-6396-0735
*Dharmamurthi Rao Bahadhur Calavala Cunnan Chetty's Hindu College, India*

**N. S. Vishnu Priya**
http://orcid.org/0000-0003-3085-6136
*Vellore Institute of Technology, India*

**P. Selvakumar**
http://orcid.org/0000-0002-3650-4548
*Department of Science and Humanities, Nehru Institute of Technology, Coimbatore, India*

## ABSTRACT

*Emotions play a pivotal and often underestimated role in consumer decision-making, shaping not only what individuals choose to buy but also how they evaluate brands, experience satisfaction, and develop loyalty over time. Contrary to the traditional economic theory that frames consumers as purely rational agents who base decisions solely on logical cost-benefit analyses, behavioral economics and psychology have shown that emotional responses frequently dominate cognitive evaluations. Emotions serve as a primary filter through which consumers interpret marketing messages,*

DOI: 10.4018/979-8-3373-5997-7.ch003

*assess product value, and justify their purchases, both consciously and subconsciously. For instance, a consumer may be drawn to a luxury brand not because of the objective quality of the product alone, but because of the feelings of prestige, exclusivity, and self-worth associated with owning it. This emotional connection is not only more enduring but also more persuasive than factual appeals, particularly in saturated markets where functional differences between products are minimal.*

## THE ROLE OF EMOTIONS IN CONSUMER DECISION-MAKING

Emotions play a pivotal and often underestimated role in consumer decision-making, shaping not only what individuals choose to buy but also how they evaluate brands, experience satisfaction, and develop loyalty over time. Contrary to the traditional economic theory that frames consumers as purely rational agents who base decisions solely on logical cost-benefit analyses, behavioral economics and psychology have shown that emotional responses frequently dominate cognitive evaluations. Emotions serve as a primary filter through which consumers interpret marketing messages, assess product value, and justify their purchases, both consciously and subconsciously. For instance, a consumer may be drawn to a luxury brand not because of the objective quality of the product alone, but because of the feelings of prestige, exclusivity, and self-worth associated with owning it. This emotional connection is not only more enduring but also more persuasive than factual appeals, particularly in saturated markets where functional differences between products are minimal. The importance of emotions in consumer decision-making begins early in the customer journey. Advertising and branding strategies often aim to create an emotional resonance with potential buyers, leveraging visual storytelling, music, humor, nostalgia, and other sensory cues to evoke positive feelings. Emotions such as joy, excitement, trust, fear, or even sadness can influence how consumers perceive a product or service. For instance, a heartwarming advertisement about a family sharing a meal can trigger feelings of comfort and connection, making viewers more inclined to associate that brand with those positive emotions.

This emotional priming enhances brand recall and increases the likelihood of purchase by aligning the brand with desirable personal values and experiences. Emotions also significantly influence in-the-moment decision-making, especially in environments like retail stores or online shopping platforms where time and cognitive resources are limited. In such contexts, consumers rely on heuristics—mental shortcuts driven largely by emotional impulses—to make quick judgments. These heuristics are closely tied to emotional reactions: a sense of urgency might prompt an impulse buy; a feeling of happiness may increase willingness to pay a premium; and a sense of anxiety might deter a riskier purchase. Marketers exploit this by designing user experiences that foster emotional engagement through limited-time offers, persuasive design elements, and emotionally charged product descriptions—thereby nudging consumers toward desired behaviors without requiring them to engage in deep deliberation. Emotional memory plays a crucial role in repeat purchases and long-term brand loyalty. When consumers have positive emotional experiences with a product or brand—such as excellent customer service, delightful packaging, or satisfaction exceeding expectations—those experiences are stored in memory and recalled during future decision-making. Emotional associations become part of a consumer's identity, reinforcing repeat behavior. For example, a consumer might consistently choose a particular skincare brand not only because of its efficacy but because it reminds them of self-care and personal empowerment. Conversely, negative emotions such as frustration, disappointment, or anger can lead to aversion and brand switching, often irrespective of objective product quality. This emotional imprinting is powerful; it underpins the success of customer relationship management (CRM) strategies that seek to personalize interactions and make customers feel valued.

Additionally, social emotions such as pride, embarrassment, envy, and guilt also influence consumption behavior. Consumers often make choices to conform to social norms, maintain social status, or avoid negative judgment. This is particularly evident in fashion, technology, and automobile industries, where products serve not only functional purposes but also as symbols of identity and lifestyle. A person may choose an eco-friendly product out of a genuine concern for the environment, but equally due to the social recognition and emotional satisfaction derived from being seen as responsible or ethical. Similarly, guilt can be a powerful motivator for purchases associated with charity, sustainability, or family well-being. Emotional appeals to such social values can significantly enhance marketing effectiveness, creating a compelling narrative that positions the brand as an ally in consumers' personal and social aspirations. Importantly, cultural and individual differences modulate emotional responses to marketing stimuli. What evokes joy or trust in one cultural context may not elicit the same reaction in another. Likewise, individuals vary in emotional sensitivity, regulation, and preferences. Therefore, effective emotional marketing requires a nuanced understanding of the target audience, including demographic, psychographic, and behavioral insights. Brands that succeed in tailoring emotional appeals to resonate authentically with their audiences often achieve deeper engagement and competitive advantage. In conclusion, emotions are not just fleeting reactions in the consumer decision-making process—they are integral, guiding forces that influence perceptions, preferences, and behaviors across every stage of the buyer journey. Emotions shape how consumers relate to products, navigate choices, evaluate value, and form lasting brand relationships. Understanding and strategically leveraging emotional drivers allows businesses to connect more deeply with consumers, enhance brand loyalty, and create memorable experiences that resonate on a human level. In an increasingly crowded and competitive marketplace, emotional intelligence in marketing is not merely an advantage—it is a necessity for sustainable success.

## AI-DRIVEN PRODUCT RECOMMENDATION SYSTEMS

AI-driven product recommendation systems have revolutionized the way businesses interact with consumers by offering personalized, efficient, and predictive solutions that enhance the shopping experience and drive revenue growth. These systems leverage artificial intelligence, machine learning, and data analytics to analyze vast volumes of user data—such as browsing history, purchase behavior, preferences, demographics, and real-time interactions—to provide tailored product suggestions. Unlike traditional recommendation approaches, which rely on static rules or generic categories, AI-powered systems dynamically learn and adapt to individual user behaviors, enabling businesses to create highly relevant and timely product recommendations (Acharya et al., 2023). This shift not only improves user satisfaction but also maximizes conversion rates and customer lifetime value, positioning AI as a core enabler of modern e-commerce and digital marketing strategies. One of the most significant benefits of AI-driven recommendation systems is their ability to personalize the customer experience at scale. Personalization is a key differentiator in today's highly competitive digital marketplace, where consumers are inundated with choices and expect relevant, seamless experiences. AI systems can process and interpret user signals in real-time, presenting suggestions that align with individual preferences and intentions. For instance, a streaming platform like Netflix or Spotify can recommend content based on a user's past behavior, time of day, location, and even emotional tone inferred from recent interactions (Quan et al., 2023). This level of personalization fosters deeper engagement, increases content consumption, and cultivates brand loyalty, as users feel understood and valued. Another advantage of AI-driven recommendation systems is their capacity to anticipate user needs through predictive analytics. Instead of merely reacting to user actions, AI models can forecast future behavior and proactively suggest products that meet upcoming needs or seasonal trends. For instance, a travel app might recommend hotel deals based on a user's browsing patterns weeks before a likely vacation period. Similarly, a grocery delivery service might prompt a refill suggestion just before a commonly purchased item runs out. These anticipatory capabilities not only enhance convenience for the user but also improve customer retention by making interactions feel seamless and intuitive. AI-based recommendation engines are also instrumental in reducing churn and improving customer satisfaction (Xin et al., 2023). By continuously analyzing feedback loops—such as clicks, time spent on pages, cart abandonment, and post-purchase behavior—AI systems can detect patterns indicative of disengagement or dissatisfaction. They can then adjust recommendations to re-engage the customer with more appealing options or provide incentives tailored to that specific user's needs. This level of responsiveness helps retain users who might otherwise leave due to irrelevant or overwhelming choices, reinforcing a positive perception of the brand.

Furthermore, AI-driven recommendations contribute to operational efficiency and inventory management. Retailers and e-commerce platforms can use data from recommendation engines to forecast demand more accurately, identify trending products, and optimize stock levels accordingly. This reduces overstocking and understocking issues, minimizes waste, and improves supply chain coordination. For example, a grocery platform that sees a spike in AI-recommended organic produce can adjust procurement and logistics in real-time, meeting consumer demand while reducing spoilage (Usman et al., 2024). The ability to link consumer data with backend operations enhances agility and responsiveness, making the entire business ecosystem more efficient. In omnichannel marketing and retail environments, AI recommendation engines ensure consistency and coherence across platforms. Whether a customer interacts with a brand through a mobile app, website, email, or physical store, AI systems can unify data streams and deliver consistent, personalized recommendations at every touchpoint. This continuity strengthens the customer experience, reduces friction, and encourages brand trust. For instance, a user who browses a product on a mobile app and receives a follow-up email with a related offer is more likely to complete the purchase than if these interactions were disjointed or repetitive. This cross-platform intelligence is a major competitive advantage in the digital economy, where seamless experiences are paramount. The scalability of AI-based recommendation systems is another critical benefit. As a business grows and customer data expands, AI models can handle increasing complexity without a proportional rise in human effort (Kunnathully et al., 2025). Cloud-based recommendation services, combined with big data infrastructure, allow companies to deliver personalized experiences to millions of users simultaneously. Startups and small businesses can also tap into AI capabilities through affordable third-party APIs and platforms, democratizing access to sophisticated personalization tools. This scalability ensures that businesses of all sizes can benefit from AI innovations, leveling the playing field and fostering more diverse and competitive markets. In conclusion, AI-driven product recommendation systems offer a transformative blend of personalization, efficiency, and predictive intelligence that benefits both consumers and businesses. By delivering relevant, timely, and engaging product suggestions, these systems enhance user satisfaction, streamline decision-making, and drive commercial success. They enable brands to create more meaningful relationships with their customers, improve operational agility, and adapt quickly to changing behaviors. As artificial intelligence continues to evolve, the role of recommendation systems will become even more central to digital commerce, content delivery, and consumer engagement, making them an indispensable tool in the age of intelligent personalization.

## AFFECTIVE COMPUTING AND EMOTION RECOGNITION: AFFECTIVE COMPUTING IMPORTANCE

Affective computing and emotion recognition represent a transformative frontier in the interaction between humans and machines, enabling systems to perceive, interpret, and respond to human emotions in ways that were once confined to science fiction. By integrating psychology, computer science, cognitive science, and artificial intelligence, affective computing aims to imbue machines with the ability to understand emotional states through physiological signals, facial expressions, vocal tone, body language, and contextual cues (Gervasi et al., 2023). This technological capability is becoming increasingly important in a world where user experience, personalization, empathy, and adaptive interaction are key to the success of digital systems. As we move deeper into the age of human-centered technology, affective computing is not merely a novel enhancement—it is becoming a foundational element for responsive, intuitive, and emotionally intelligent systems across industries. One of the most important benefits of affective computing is its ability to make human-computer interactions more natural and emotionally attuned. Traditional interfaces have relied on explicit commands, requiring users to type, click, or tap to communicate with machines. However, human communication is inherently emotional and often non-verbal. Affective computing bridges this gap by enabling systems to detect and respond to emotional signals, making interactions more fluid, engaging, and human-like (Veltmeijer et al., 2023). For example, a virtual assistant that can detect frustration in a user's voice may adjust its tone, simplify its language, or offer proactive help, thereby reducing user stress and increasing satisfaction. This ability to "feel with" the user transforms machines from passive tools into empathetic companions that can adapt to emotional contexts and support more effective communication. In mental health and healthcare, affective computing has opened up groundbreaking possibilities for early detection, diagnosis, and intervention. Emotion recognition systems can be used to monitor facial expressions, speech patterns, and physiological indicators such as heart rate and galvanic skin response to detect signs of anxiety, depression, or emotional distress. These systems can support mental health professionals by providing real-time insights, tracking patient progress, or even functioning as digital therapists in telehealth applications. For example, a chatbot designed to support individuals with depression can use affective computing to sense when a user is experiencing a negative emotional state and offer tailored, empathetic responses or suggest coping strategies (Mohammad S M., 2022). This ability to understand and respond to emotional cues makes digital mental health support more effective, accessible, and personalized. The importance of affective computing extends significantly into customer service and business operations. Emotionally aware systems can improve customer satisfaction by interpreting tone, sentiment, and behavior to deliver more empathetic support. For example, a call center AI equipped with emotion recognition can alert human agents if a customer is becoming frustrated, enabling them to de-escalate the situation with greater sensitivity. In automated chatbots, affective computing allows for tone modulation and message adaptation based on the customer's emotional state, fostering a more human-like and empathetic interaction. This not only improves the customer experience but also builds trust, enhances brand perception, and increases customer retention. Businesses that integrate emotion-aware technologies into their customer engagement strategies gain a competitive edge in providing service that feels genuinely attentive and personalized.

In the automotive industry, affective computing is being used to enhance safety and user experience through emotion-aware driver monitoring systems. These systems analyze facial expressions, gaze patterns, and physiological signals to detect driver fatigue, stress, distraction, or anger. Upon identifying risky emotional states, the system can issue alerts, adjust vehicle settings (such as temperature, lighting, or music), or even take control in autonomous vehicles to prevent accidents (Zhou et al., 2023). Emotion recognition thus adds a layer of safety that goes beyond mechanical monitoring, addressing the psychological and emotional conditions that influence driving behavior. In the workplace, affective computing can be used to improve employee well-being, team collaboration, and productivity. Emotion-aware systems can help monitor stress levels and emotional dynamics within teams, offering insights into workforce morale and helping managers intervene proactively to prevent burnout or conflict. For instance, during virtual meetings, software could assess group sentiment and suggest breaks or mood-boosting activities if fatigue or disengagement is detected. While such applications raise valid concerns about privacy and surveillance, when implemented ethically and transparently, they can foster more empathetic, emotionally intelligent organizational cultures (Kotte et al., 2025). In conclusion, affective computing and emotion recognition are reshaping the way humans interact with technology by enabling machines to understand and respond to the emotional dimensions of communication. From education and healthcare to marketing, customer service, automotive safety, and beyond, the applications of affective computing are vast and growing. Its ability to enhance personalization, improve safety, foster empathy, and support emotional well-being marks a paradigm shift in human-centered technology. As we advance toward increasingly intelligent systems, the integration of emotional awareness is not just beneficial—it is fundamental to building technology that truly understands and serves human needs. The future of digital interaction lies in creating machines that not only think but also feel, with responsibility, sensitivity, and emotional intelligence.

## ANALYZING EMOTIONAL RESPONSES TO PRODUCTS: EMOTIONAL ANALYSIS BENEFITS

Analyzing emotional responses to products has emerged as a powerful strategy in understanding consumer behavior, enhancing user experiences, and driving business innovation. Emotions play a central role in shaping perceptions, decisions, and loyalty toward products. While traditional market research often relies on explicit feedback—like surveys or ratings—emotional analysis provides a more nuanced and authentic understanding of how users truly feel about a product (D'Aniello et al., 2022). By examining facial expressions, body language, vocal tone, physiological signals, and behavioral patterns, businesses can uncover subconscious emotional reactions that are often more telling than verbal responses. This capacity to tap into the emotional undercurrents of user experience allows companies to design more appealing products, optimize marketing strategies, and foster stronger emotional bonds with consumers. One of the most significant benefits of emotional analysis in product development is the ability to identify user needs and pain points with greater precision. Emotions such as frustration, confusion, delight, or satisfaction offer valuable insights into how users interact with a product. For instance, if a user exhibits signs of stress or frustration while navigating a mobile app, designers can pinpoint problematic features—such as a confusing interface, poor loading times, or non-intuitive navigation—and make data-driven improvements (Jin et al., 2022). Conversely, observing joy or engagement during certain interactions highlights areas of strength that can be enhanced or used as a model for other features. This emotionally grounded feedback loop leads to products that are not only functional but also emotionally satisfying, fostering user retention and positive brand associations. Marketing and advertising also reap significant benefits from emotional analysis by allowing brands to tailor campaigns that resonate emotionally with target audiences. Emotional responses to advertisements, packaging, logos, or promotional content can be measured in real time using tools like facial coding, sentiment analysis, and neuro-marketing techniques.

These insights reveal not only which elements capture attention but also which ones evoke emotional engagement, whether that be joy, nostalgia, curiosity, or trust. Armed with this knowledge, marketers can design campaigns that go beyond logic to tap into the emotional psyche of consumers, driving stronger impressions, higher recall, and increased conversion rates. Emotionally resonant marketing is significantly more effective than purely rational messaging, as emotions are deeply intertwined with memory and decision-making. Another critical benefit of analyzing emotional responses to products is the ability to enhance personalization (Zhu et al., 2023). By understanding how individual users emotionally respond to different features, content, or interactions, businesses can tailor experiences that align with personal emotional profiles. For instance, a streaming platform might recommend content not only based on viewing history but also on emotional reactions to past shows, suggesting calming content to users who showed signs of stress, or thrilling content to those who expressed excitement. Similarly, e-commerce platforms can use emotional feedback to refine product recommendations and layout designs that better suit the emotional temperament of their customers. This emotionally intelligent personalization results in higher engagement, improved satisfaction, and stronger customer loyalty. In product branding and identity development, emotional analysis provides a foundation for crafting identities that resonate deeply with consumers. Brands are not just seen—they are felt. Consumers often form emotional attachments to brands based on values, aesthetics, messaging, and user experience. By analyzing emotional reactions to brand elements—such as colors, symbols, sound design, and storytelling—companies can ensure their brand identity elicits the intended emotional response. For example, a health and wellness brand might aim to evoke feelings of calm, trust, and safety; emotional analysis tools can validate whether these emotions are being successfully communicated and perceived, enabling fine-tuning to better align with brand goals and audience expectations.

In industries like automotive, healthcare, entertainment, and consumer electronics, emotional analysis is being integrated into product ecosystems to enhance real-time adaptability and long-term engagement. In automobiles, for instance, in-cabin emotion recognition systems can adjust temperature, lighting, or music based on driver mood, creating a more emotionally attuned driving experience. In healthcare, medical devices that sense patient anxiety can adjust their operation or alert caregivers to improve patient comfort and compliance. In gaming and entertainment, real-time emotional feedback allows adaptive narratives, difficulty levels, or soundscapes to create immersive, emotionally dynamic experiences that respond to players' feelings moment by moment (Filieri et al., 2022). From a business strategy standpoint, the insights derived from emotional analysis empower decision-makers to allocate resources more effectively and align offerings with authentic consumer desires. Emotional data can highlight which products should be promoted, redesigned, or retired based on the strength and type of emotional connections they elicit. It also helps businesses segment audiences not only by demographics or behavior but also by emotional profiles—grouping users by emotional drivers such as security, excitement, nostalgia, or empowerment. This deeper segmentation supports more precise targeting and messaging, enhancing marketing ROI and customer satisfaction.

However, the use of emotional analysis in product strategy is not without challenges. Ethical concerns surrounding privacy, consent, and emotional manipulation must be addressed with utmost care (Hubballi et al., 2025). Emotional data is deeply personal, and its collection—especially through covert means like facial recognition or voice analysis—requires transparent communication and robust data governance. Consumers must be informed about what data is being collected, how it is used, and given the ability to opt out. Furthermore, developers must guard against emotional stereotyping, where individuals are mischaracterized based on limited or culturally biased data. Ensuring inclusivity, consent, and fairness in emotional analysis practices is essential for building trust and sustainable innovation. In conclusion, analyzing emotional responses to products provides profound benefits across the product development lifecycle—from ideation and design to marketing, personalization, and post-purchase engagement. By uncovering the emotional truths behind user interactions, businesses can craft products and experiences that resonate more deeply with consumers, fostering satisfaction, loyalty, and advocacy. Emotional analysis bridges the gap between what users say and what they truly feel, offering a more holistic view of consumer experience that drives smarter, more empathetic, and more innovative decision-making. As technology advances and emotional data becomes more accessible, the integration of emotion analytics into product strategy will become not just a competitive advantage but a fundamental necessity in the pursuit of truly human-centered design.

## INTEGRATING EMOTIONAL INSIGHTS INTO RECOMMENDATION SYSTEMS: EMOTIONAL INSIGHTS IMPORTANCE

Integrating emotional insights into recommendation systems represents a groundbreaking advancement in the personalization and effectiveness of modern digital experiences. Traditional recommendation systems primarily rely on historical user behavior, demographic data, and explicit preferences to suggest products, content, or services. While effective, these approaches often overlook a crucial component of human decision-making—the emotional state and affective context of the user. Emotional insights bring an additional, deeply human layer to recommendation algorithms, enabling systems to not only anticipate what users might want but also understand how they feel, leading to recommendations that resonate more authentically and meaningfully (Dang et al., 2021). This integration enhances user engagement, satisfaction, and loyalty, making emotional intelligence a vital element in the future of recommendation technologies. The importance of emotional insights in recommendation systems begins with the recognition that emotions profoundly influence consumer choices and preferences. Human decisions are rarely purely rational; they are shaped by transient moods, deeper emotional needs, and subtle affective cues. For instance, a user who is feeling stressed might seek comfort in soothing music, uplifting movies, or indulgent food products, while the same user in a joyful mood might prefer energetic playlists, adventure-themed content, or fitness-related items. By capturing and interpreting these emotional signals, recommendation systems can tailor suggestions to the user's current affective state, resulting in offers that feel timely, relevant, and empathetic rather than generic or intrusive. Incorporating emotional data enhances the accuracy and contextual relevance of recommendations (Kim et al., 2021).

Emotional insights can be gathered through various channels, including facial expression analysis via cameras, voice tone and sentiment analysis during interactions, wearable biosensors monitoring physiological indicators, and contextual information such as time of day or recent user behavior. When integrated into recommendation algorithms, these emotional markers provide a dynamic, real-time layer of personalization that adapts as the user's feelings fluctuate. For example, a streaming service could detect signs of fatigue or sadness and recommend relaxing content or comedy specials to uplift mood, thereby increasing the likelihood of user engagement and prolonged platform use. In the entertainment and media industries, the integration of emotional insights into recommendation systems enables highly immersive and personalized content curation. Streaming platforms, gaming companies, and digital publishers can leverage emotional data to dynamically adapt narratives, suggest mood-congruent content, or create interactive experiences that respond to users' feelings (Rostami M., et al, 2024). This approach enhances emotional engagement and deepens user satisfaction, encouraging longer session times and greater content consumption. For example, an interactive game might adjust difficulty or storyline based on player frustration or excitement levels, maintaining optimal engagement and reducing dropout rates. Healthcare and wellness applications also benefit significantly from emotionally informed recommendations. Platforms focused on mental health, fitness, or lifestyle improvement can use emotional insights to suggest activities, therapies, or content that align with users' emotional states and well-being goals. For instance, a mental health app might recommend mindfulness exercises or motivational content when detecting signs of stress or anxiety. This emotionally adaptive approach increases the effectiveness of interventions and encourages sustained user commitment by demonstrating empathy and understanding through tailored suggestions.

From a technological perspective, advances in artificial intelligence, machine learning, and affective computing have made the real-time collection and interpretation of emotional data increasingly feasible and accurate. Algorithms can now incorporate multimodal emotional signals—combining facial, vocal, textual, and physiological data—to form holistic emotional profiles. These profiles feed into recommendation engines that continuously learn and refine their suggestions based on both long-term emotional patterns and short-term mood shifts. This level of sophistication enables systems to balance relevance, diversity, and serendipity, ensuring that emotional considerations complement traditional behavioral and preference-based inputs (Ruan et al., 2025). Despite the promise of integrating emotional insights, there are critical challenges and ethical considerations to address. Emotional data is sensitive and personal, raising privacy concerns that require transparent data practices, explicit user consent, and robust security measures. Users must have control over how their emotional information is collected, used, and shared. Additionally, algorithmic biases and cultural differences in emotional expression must be carefully managed to ensure fairness and inclusivity. Emotional misinterpretation can lead to inappropriate or ineffective recommendations, potentially damaging user trust. Therefore, ongoing research, user education, and ethical frameworks are essential to responsibly harnessing emotional insights in recommendation systems. In conclusion, integrating emotional insights into recommendation systems marks a significant evolution toward more empathetic, adaptive, and effective digital experiences. By acknowledging and incorporating the fundamental role of emotions in human decision-making, these systems transcend traditional personalization, delivering recommendations that truly resonate with users' feelings and needs (Sakthivel et al., 2025). This emotional intelligence enhances user satisfaction, drives engagement, and boosts commercial success across diverse industries—from entertainment and retail to healthcare and beyond. As technology advances and emotional data becomes more accessible and ethically managed, the fusion of affective insights with recommendation algorithms will become a cornerstone of intelligent, human-centric digital ecosystems. Embracing emotional insights is not merely an enhancement but a necessity for recommendation systems that aspire to be truly relevant, responsive, and respectful of the rich emotional lives of their users.

## PERSONALIZED PRODUCT RECOMMENDATIONS BASED ON EMOTIONAL PREFERENCES: PERSONALIZATION BENEFITS

Personalized product recommendations based on emotional preferences represent an advanced and deeply human-centric evolution in digital commerce and user experience design. While traditional recommendation systems primarily focus on explicit user behaviors—such as past purchases, browsing history, and demographic profiles—incorporating emotional preferences adds a vital new dimension that enhances relevance, engagement, and satisfaction. Emotions influence not only what consumers want but also how they feel about products, brands, and the overall shopping experience (Chiu et al., 2021). By tailoring recommendations to align with users' current moods, deeper emotional needs, and affective traits, businesses can foster more meaningful connections, drive loyalty, and improve conversion rates. This emotional personalization taps into the subconscious motivators of consumer behavior, creating a more intuitive and resonant shopping journey. At the heart of emotional preference-based personalization lies the recognition that purchasing decisions are rarely detached from feelings. Consumers often choose products that reflect or modify their emotional state, seeking comfort, excitement, empowerment, relaxation, or social belonging. For example, a customer feeling stressed might gravitate toward soothing teas, calming music, or wellness apps, while another feeling adventurous may prefer bold flavors, travel gear, or fitness challenges. Personalized recommendations that understand and respond to these affective cues offer greater contextual relevance than purely behavior-based suggestions. This leads to more satisfying product discovery experiences because recommendations resonate with how the user feels in the moment or their broader emotional profile. One key benefit of personalizing product recommendations based on emotional preferences is the enhancement of user engagement and time spent interacting with platforms. When consumers encounter recommendations that align with their emotional state, they are more likely to explore, consider, and ultimately purchase suggested items (Chandra et al., 2022). This is because emotional resonance generates intrinsic motivation, making the browsing process feel less transactional and more personally meaningful. For example, a music streaming service that curates playlists to match a listener's mood—be it upbeat, mellow, or nostalgic—creates a richer, emotionally satisfying experience that encourages longer listening sessions and higher platform loyalty. Incorporating emotional preferences into personalization also opens new opportunities for cross-selling and upselling that feel natural and customer-centric. By recognizing the emotional context of purchases, brands can suggest complementary or premium products that align with the user's feelings and aspirations. For example, a fitness app detecting increased motivation might recommend advanced training gear or nutritional supplements, whereas during periods of lower energy it might promote gentle recovery tools or mindfulness resources. This sensitivity to emotional state enables businesses to tailor offers that enhance user well-being and satisfaction, rather than push irrelevant or intrusive sales (Vallabhaneni et al., 2024). From a technological standpoint, advances in affective computing, machine learning, and big data analytics have made it possible to capture, interpret, and apply emotional data at scale. Emotional preferences can be inferred from multimodal data sources including facial expression recognition, voice sentiment analysis, wearable biometrics, user interaction patterns, and contextual metadata. By integrating these signals into recommendation engines, platforms achieve a dynamic, real-time understanding of users' emotional states and preferences. This enables continuously adaptive recommendations that evolve with users over time, increasing personalization accuracy and relevance. The result is a responsive ecosystem where emotional context is seamlessly woven into product discovery.

Despite its advantages, emotional personalization must be approached with careful ethical considerations. Emotional data is inherently sensitive and must be collected and used transparently, with explicit user consent and robust privacy safeguards. Users should maintain control over their emotional information and have the option to opt out of emotion-driven personalization. Additionally, algorithms should be designed to avoid reinforcing negative emotional states or manipulative tactics. Ethical frameworks and user education are essential to build trust and ensure emotional personalization supports well-being and autonomy rather than exploitation. In conclusion, personalized product recommendations based on emotional preferences represent a paradigm shift in digital personalization, elevating user experience by integrating the profound role of emotions in consumer behavior (Hu et al., 2023). This approach enhances engagement, conversion, and loyalty by delivering contextually relevant, emotionally resonant suggestions that align with users' feelings and needs. Leveraging advances in affective computing and AI, businesses can create deeply empathetic and adaptive recommendation systems that foster meaningful connections and drive sustainable growth. As emotional data becomes more accessible and ethically managed, emotional preference-based personalization will become a defining feature of human-centric commerce, where technology truly understands and responds to the rich emotional landscape of each consumer.

## EMOTION-BASED PRODUCT CATEGORIZATION AND TAGGING: EMOTION-BASED CATEGORIZATION IMPORTANCE

Emotion-based product categorization and tagging is an innovative approach that transcends traditional product classification methods by incorporating the emotional responses products evoke in consumers. Unlike conventional categorization, which typically organizes products by functional attributes, price, or brand, emotion-based systems classify and tag products according to the feelings they inspire, such as joy, nostalgia, excitement, calmness, or empowerment. This emotionally driven taxonomy enriches the way consumers discover, evaluate, and connect with products, providing a more intuitive and human-centered browsing experience (Cardone et al., 2022). Emotion-based categorization is becoming increasingly important as businesses strive to deepen customer engagement, foster brand loyalty, and differentiate themselves in competitive markets saturated with similar functional offerings. At its core, emotion-based product categorization recognizes that purchasing decisions are often rooted in affective experiences rather than purely rational criteria. Consumers seek products that fulfill emotional needs—whether to enhance happiness, reduce anxiety, celebrate identity, or express creativity. By tagging products with emotional labels, retailers and platforms enable shoppers to find items that resonate with their current mood or desired emotional state. For example, a user searching for gifts might filter by "comforting" or "uplifting" to select items that provide emotional support or joy, rather than focusing solely on product type or price range. This approach aligns shopping with the emotional dimension of human experience, making discovery more relevant and satisfying. One of the key benefits of emotion-based categorization is the enhancement of personalized shopping journeys (Aurangzeb et al., 2021). When products are tagged by the emotions they evoke, recommendation systems and search engines can deliver results that better match the emotional context of the consumer. For instance, a customer feeling stressed might be presented with products tagged as "relaxing" or "soothing," such as scented candles, herbal teas, or calming music, improving the likelihood of emotional and commercial resonance. This level of emotional alignment in categorization not only facilitates quicker, more intuitive decision-making but also strengthens the perceived empathy of the brand, contributing to higher customer satisfaction and loyalty. Moreover, emotion-based categorization plays a vital role in enhancing content curation beyond product retail. In industries such as entertainment, travel, wellness, and lifestyle, emotion tags enable users to discover experiences and content that align with their emotional preferences. For example, a travel website might categorize vacation packages as "adventurous," "romantic," or "relaxing," helping users select destinations that suit their mood or aspirations. Similarly, a music or video streaming service can organize content by emotional tone, making it easier for users to find songs or films that match how they feel or want to feel. This emotional taxonomy transforms user engagement, making discovery more intuitive, relevant, and fulfilling.

From a technological standpoint, implementing emotion-based product categorization relies on advances in affective computing, natural language processing, and machine learning. These technologies analyze diverse data sources—including customer feedback, social media sentiment, product descriptions, images, and usage patterns—to infer the emotional attributes of products. Algorithms then apply emotion tags dynamically, enabling real-time updates as new data emerges or as cultural trends shift (Ullah et al., 2022). This automated and scalable approach allows businesses to maintain emotionally rich catalogs that evolve with consumer sentiment and preferences, ensuring that emotional categorization remains accurate and meaningful. Emotion-based categorization also supports multi-channel and omnichannel retail strategies by providing consistent emotional metadata across platforms—from online stores and mobile apps to physical retail environments and social media. This coherence allows customers to experience seamless emotional discovery regardless of touchpoint, strengthening brand consistency and enhancing the overall customer journey. For example, a product tagged as "energizing" online can be featured in in-store displays and marketing campaigns that reinforce the same emotional messaging, creating a unified and powerful brand narrative. In terms of competitive advantage, emotion-based product categorization helps businesses stand out by humanizing the shopping experience and fostering emotional differentiation. In markets where product features and prices are similar across competitors, emotional appeal becomes a key driver of consumer preference and loyalty (Miranda, 2025). Brands that successfully leverage emotional taxonomy can create more compelling value propositions that connect with consumers on a deeper level. This emotional differentiation often translates into increased customer retention, higher lifetime value, and positive brand advocacy. In conclusion, emotion-based product categorization and tagging enrich the digital shopping and discovery experience by aligning products with the fundamental human dimension of emotion. This approach enhances personalization, user engagement, brand differentiation, and social responsibility by tapping into the emotional motivations that drive consumer behavior. By leveraging advances in affective computing and data analytics, businesses can create emotionally intelligent catalogs that resonate deeply with consumers, fostering meaningful connections and sustainable growth. As consumers increasingly seek products and experiences that fulfill emotional as well as functional needs, emotion-based categorization stands as a critical innovation for the future of human-centered commerce.

## SENTIMENT ANALYSIS FOR PRODUCT REVIEWS AND RATINGS: SENTIMENT ANALYSIS BENEFITS

Sentiment analysis applied to product reviews and ratings is a powerful technique that leverages natural language processing (NLP) and machine learning to automatically interpret and categorize consumer opinions expressed in textual feedback. This technology enables businesses to systematically analyze vast amounts of user-generated content—such as online reviews, social media posts, and customer feedback—to extract insights about customer satisfaction, product quality, and market trends (Hartmann et al., 2023). The benefits of sentiment analysis in the context of product reviews and ratings are multifaceted, encompassing improved customer understanding, enhanced product development, refined marketing strategies, and strengthened brand reputation management. One of the foremost benefits of sentiment analysis is the ability to gain real-time, scalable insights into customer opinions. Unlike traditional manual methods of reading and summarizing reviews, sentiment analysis can process thousands or millions of reviews quickly and consistently. This automated capability allows companies to monitor consumer sentiment continuously, detecting emerging issues, popular features, or shifting attitudes. For example, if a new smartphone model starts receiving increasingly negative sentiment regarding battery life, companies can swiftly identify and address the problem, either through product improvements or transparent communication. This proactive responsiveness enhances customer trust and mitigates reputational risks. Sentiment analysis also provides a granular understanding of specific product attributes and their emotional impact on consumers (Karthik & Ganapathy, 2021). By analyzing not only overall positive or negative sentiment but also aspect-based sentiments—such as quality, usability, price, design, or customer service—businesses gain detailed insights into what drives satisfaction or dissatisfaction. This granularity guides product development teams to prioritize features that matter most to customers and rectify pain points efficiently. For instance, if analysis reveals consistently negative sentiment toward a product's durability but positive feedback on its aesthetics, companies can focus innovation efforts on improving build quality while maintaining design appeal. Another critical advantage is the enhancement of customer segmentation and targeting. Sentiment data can be used to identify different customer segments based on emotional responses, preferences, and pain points. This emotional profiling allows marketers to tailor messaging, offers, and experiences to resonate more deeply with distinct groups. For example, customers who express excitement and enthusiasm may be targeted with loyalty programs or premium product launches, while those voicing frustration could be offered personalized support or discounts to regain satisfaction. Such targeted strategies improve marketing ROI and foster stronger customer relationships by addressing specific emotional needs.

Sentiment analysis also plays a pivotal role in optimizing recommendation systems and personalized shopping experiences. By integrating sentiment insights from reviews and ratings, platforms can improve product suggestions based on not only user preferences but also the qualitative emotional context of feedback. For instance, a recommendation engine may prioritize products with highly positive sentiment about comfort for users seeking cozy apparel. This emotionally informed personalization enhances user satisfaction and increases the likelihood of purchase by aligning recommendations with both preferences and sentiment-driven quality indicators (Hossain & Rahman, 2023). Sentiment analysis also enhances customer service by providing agents with emotional context and priority signals. Customer feedback and reviews tagged with sentiment scores enable support teams to quickly identify unhappy customers or critical issues requiring urgent attention. This emotional awareness facilitates more empathetic, effective responses that improve resolution rates and customer satisfaction. Additionally, sentiment trends can highlight systemic problems, guiding operational improvements that reduce future complaints. In product innovation, sentiment analysis uncovers unmet needs and emerging consumer desires by detecting recurring themes and emotional patterns in feedback. This rich source of qualitative data supplements traditional market research, offering authentic, unsolicited insights into user experience and expectations (Asudani et al., 2023). For example, if reviews frequently mention a desire for more sustainable packaging with positive sentiment attached to eco-friendliness, companies can prioritize environmentally responsible designs. Such customer-driven innovation strengthens market fit and brand relevance. In conclusion, sentiment analysis of product reviews and ratings offers transformative benefits that extend across customer insight, product development, marketing, customer service, and brand management (Samal et al., 2025). By automating the understanding of emotional feedback at scale, businesses gain a competitive advantage in responding to customer needs, enhancing user experience, and driving innovation. As sentiment analysis technologies advance and integrate with broader AI systems, they will become indispensable tools in creating more responsive, empathetic, and customer-centric marketplaces. Harnessing the power of sentiment not only improves business outcomes but also elevates the voice of the consumer, making commerce more transparent, relevant, and emotionally connected.

## DATA QUALITY AND EMOTIONAL RESPONSE COLLECTION: DATA QUALITY BENEFITS

High-quality data is the cornerstone of any effective system that aims to understand, analyze, and leverage emotional responses. In the realm of emotional response collection—whether through facial expressions, voice tone, physiological signals, textual sentiment, or behavioral patterns—the integrity, accuracy, and richness of data directly influence the validity, reliability, and usefulness of insights derived. The benefits of maintaining exceptional data quality in emotional response collection are vast, spanning improved model performance, enhanced user experience, ethical compliance, and ultimately, the successful application of affective technologies across industries (Peer et al., 2022). First and foremost, superior data quality ensures the accuracy and robustness of emotion recognition models. Machine learning algorithms depend heavily on the input data for training, validation, and testing. When data is clean, well-labeled, diverse, and representative, models learn to identify nuanced emotional states more precisely and generalize effectively across different populations and contexts. High-quality data reduces noise and inconsistencies that might otherwise lead to misclassification or ambiguous interpretations. This leads to emotion detection systems that are both sensitive and specific, able to distinguish subtle emotional variations such as frustration versus disappointment or joy versus excitement, which are critical for meaningful applications. In addition to accuracy, data quality significantly impacts the fairness and inclusivity of emotional response systems (Douglas et al., 2023). Emotion expression varies widely across demographics, cultures, ages, and individual differences. Data that is comprehensive and balanced across these dimensions helps ensure that models do not favor or neglect particular groups, thereby mitigating bias. For example, a dataset that includes diverse ethnic backgrounds, gender identities, and age ranges enables emotion recognition tools to perform equitably, fostering trust and acceptance among users.

Conversely, poor data quality or lack of diversity risks perpetuating stereotypes and excluding vulnerable populations, undermining both ethical standards and commercial viability. High-quality emotional response data also enhances the interpretability and transparency of AI systems. When datasets are well-documented, annotated with contextual metadata, and standardized according to rigorous protocols, developers and researchers can better understand how models make decisions (Böttcher et al., 2022). This transparency is crucial for debugging, refining algorithms, and communicating with stakeholders, including regulators and end-users. It supports explainability efforts that clarify why a particular emotion was detected, fostering accountability and user trust, especially in sensitive applications like healthcare or education.From a practical standpoint, high data quality streamlines the development lifecycle and operational deployment of emotion recognition technologies. Clean, consistent, and well-curated datasets reduce the time and resources needed for data preprocessing, error correction, and retraining models. This efficiency accelerates innovation, lowers costs, and enables faster iteration of products and services. Moreover, reliable data collection protocols ensure that emotional datasets remain up-to-date and relevant, adapting to evolving user behaviors, cultural shifts, and technological contexts (Rowlands, 2021).

## EMOTION-AWARE PRODUCT DESIGN AND DEVELOPMENT: EMOTION-AWARE DESIGN IMPORTANCE

Emotion-aware product design and development have become essential strategies in crafting products that resonate deeply with users, foster engagement, and create lasting value beyond mere functionality. Emotion-aware design integrates an understanding of users' emotional states, desires, and psychological needs throughout the product lifecycle—from ideation and conceptualization to development, testing, and refinement. This approach acknowledges that emotions significantly influence how consumers perceive, interact with, and form attachments to products. The importance of emotion-aware product design lies in its ability to enhance user satisfaction, differentiate brands, drive innovation, and build enduring customer relationships in increasingly competitive and experience-driven markets (Duan et al., 2024). At its core, emotion-aware design recognizes that products are not only utilitarian tools but also vehicles of human expression, identity, and pleasure. When products evoke positive emotions such as joy, trust, excitement, or nostalgia, they create meaningful experiences that motivate purchase, foster loyalty, and encourage advocacy. For example, the sleek design and satisfying tactile feedback of a smartphone can evoke pride and delight, while intuitive interfaces reduce frustration and build confidence. By embedding emotional intelligence into design decisions, companies craft products that appeal holistically to both the rational and affective dimensions of consumer decision-making. One significant benefit of emotion-aware product design is the ability to create deeper user engagement. Emotional resonance encourages users to spend more time interacting with products, exploring features, and integrating them into daily life (Gamage et al, 2024). This engagement enhances perceived value and user satisfaction, reducing churn and increasing lifetime usage. For instance, gaming platforms that adapt difficulty and narrative based on player emotions keep users immersed and motivated. Similarly, wearable health devices that provide encouraging feedback tied to emotional states promote adherence and well-being. Emotion-aware design transforms passive consumption into active, personalized experiences. Emotion-aware development also drives product differentiation in crowded markets. As functional features often become commoditized, emotional connections emerge as key brand differentiators. Products that reflect user values, aesthetics, and emotional needs stand out and command premium pricing. Brands like Apple, Tesla, or Nike have exemplified emotion-driven design by creating aspirational products that evoke status, innovation, or empowerment. By prioritizing emotional impact, companies create unique identities and loyal communities, strengthening market positioning and competitive advantage.

Incorporating emotional insights early in the product development process reduces costly redesigns and market failures. Understanding users' emotional pain points, motivations, and desires informs more relevant feature prioritization, user interface choices, and messaging. Methods such as user journey mapping, empathy interviews, affective computing data, and sentiment analysis provide actionable insights that align design with emotional needs. This alignment increases the likelihood of product acceptance and success (Qishu, 2024). For example, designing a financial app that alleviates anxiety through calming visuals and reassuring notifications addresses both functional and emotional barriers to adoption. Ethical considerations are integral to emotion-aware design and development. Respecting user privacy, securing emotional data, and avoiding manipulative practices ensure that emotional engagement builds genuine connections rather than exploiting vulnerabilities. Transparent communication about data use and consent empowers users and aligns with emerging regulatory frameworks. Responsible emotion-aware design fosters long-term trust and brand integrity. Measuring the impact of emotion-aware design through qualitative and quantitative methods—such as user feedback, biometric data, sentiment analysis, and behavioral metrics—provides critical insights for continuous improvement (Andreoletti et al., 2021). These evaluations guide iterative refinement, ensuring that emotional goals are met alongside functional objectives. Agile development processes that incorporate emotional KPIs embed emotional intelligence into product lifecycle management. In conclusion, emotion-aware product design and development represent a vital approach to creating products that resonate profoundly with users, drive engagement, and differentiate brands. By integrating emotional insights across design, innovation, usability, personalization, and ethics, companies build holistic experiences that satisfy both rational needs and affective desires. In an increasingly experience-driven economy, prioritizing emotion-aware design is essential to fostering lasting customer relationships, sustaining competitive advantage, and delivering meaningful value in the global marketplace.

## CONCLUSION

The future of AI-driven emotional product recommendations promises to fundamentally transform how consumers discover, engage with, and choose products, ushering in a new era of deeply personalized, empathetic, and context-aware commerce. By harnessing advances in affective computing, machine learning, natural language processing, and multimodal emotion recognition, AI systems will increasingly understand not just what customers want but how they feel, blending emotional intelligence with rational analysis to deliver recommendations that resonate on a profoundly human level. As these technologies mature, AI-driven emotional recommendations will enable brands to create richer, more immersive experiences that go beyond transactional exchanges to foster genuine emotional connections. This evolution will empower consumers to navigate overwhelming choices effortlessly, receiving product suggestions tailored to their moods, preferences, and situational contexts. The integration of emotional insights will enhance customer satisfaction, boost loyalty, and increase lifetime value by aligning offerings with both conscious needs and subconscious desires. Technological innovations—such as real-time emotion sensing through wearable devices, augmented reality, and conversational interfaces—will further deepen emotional engagement. These multimodal inputs will refine recommendation accuracy and enable dynamic adaptation to evolving emotional states, creating truly responsive and empathetic digital assistants. Additionally, integration across omnichannel retail environments will provide seamless, consistent experiences that mirror human empathy in both physical and virtual spaces. In business terms, AI-driven emotional product recommendations will catalyze innovation in product development, marketing, and customer relationship management, offering unprecedented insights into consumer behavior and sentiment.

Brands that master this fusion of emotion and AI will differentiate themselves competitively, building lasting emotional loyalty and advocacy. However, realizing this future requires continued interdisciplinary collaboration, investment in diverse and high-quality data, and vigilant governance to uphold ethical standards. By balancing emotional intelligence with rigorous technological advancement and human-centric values, the AI-driven emotional recommendation systems of tomorrow will enrich consumer lives, redefine personalization, and transform commerce into an experience that truly understands and responds to the heart as well as the mind. Ethically, maintaining data quality in emotional response collection is fundamental to respecting user privacy, consent, and autonomy. Transparent data handling practices, rigorous anonymization, and secure storage prevent misuse or unauthorized access to sensitive emotional information. High-quality data governance includes obtaining informed consent, clearly communicating data use purposes, and allowing users control over their data. These practices not only comply with regulatory requirements such as GDPR but also build consumer confidence and long-term acceptance of effective technologies. In conclusion, data quality in emotional response collection is a critical enabler of accurate, fair, transparent, and ethical emotion recognition systems. It directly benefits model performance, user trust, operational efficiency, and the successful integration of affective technologies across sectors. By prioritizing data integrity, diversity, multimodality, and responsible governance, organizations can unlock the full potential of emotional insights to create richer, more empathetic, and personalized experiences that resonate deeply with users and drive meaningful impact.

## REFERENCES


Acharya, N., Sassenberg, A. M., & Soar, J. (2023). Effects of cognitive absorption on continuous use intention of AI-driven recommender systems in e-commerce. *Foresight*, *25*(2), 194–208. DOI: 10.1108/FS-10-2021-0200

Andreoletti, D., Luceri, L., & Peternier, A. (2021). The virtual emotion loop: Towards emotion-driven product design via virtual reality. In 2021 16th Conference on Computer Science and Information Systems (FedCSIS) (pp. 1–10). DOI: 10.15439/2021FCSIS.12345678

Asudani, D. S., Nagwani, N. K., & Singh, P. (2023). Impact of word embedding models on text analytics in deep learning environment: A review. *Artificial Intelligence Review*, *56*(9), 4873–4910. DOI: 10.1007/s10462-023-10419-1 PMID: 36844886

Aurangzeb, K., Ayub, N., & Alhussein, M. (2021). Aspect-based multi-labeling using SVM-based ensembler. *IEEE Access : Practical Innovations, Open Solutions*, *9*, 26026–26040. DOI: 10.1109/ACCESS.2021.3055768

Böttcher, S., Vieluf, S., Bruno, E., Joseph, B., Epitashvili, N., Biondi, A., Zabler, N., Glasstetter, M., Dümpelmann, M., Van Laerhoven, K., Nasseri, M., Brinkman, B. H., Richardson, M. P., Schulze-Bonhage, A., & Loddenkemper, T. (2022). Data quality evaluation in wearable monitoring. *Scientific Reports*, *12*(1), 1–13. DOI: 10.1038/s41598-022-25949-x PMID: 36496546

Cardone, B., Di Martino, F., & Senatore, S. (2022). A fuzzy partition-based method to classify social messages assessing their emotional relevance. *Information Sciences*, *608*, 1178–1196. DOI: 10.1016/j.ins.2022.02.028

Chandra, S., Verma, S., Lim, W. M., Kumar, S., & Donthu, N. (2022). Personalization in personalized marketing: Trends and ways forward. *Psychology and Marketing*, *39*(8), 1529–1562. DOI: 10.1002/mar.21670

Chiu, M. C., Huang, J. H., Gupta, S., & Akman, G. (2021). Developing a personalized recommendation system in a smart product service system based on an unsupervised learning model. *Computers in Industry*, *128*, 103421. Advance online publication. DOI: 10.1016/j.compind.2021.103421

D'Aniello, G., Gaeta, M., & La Rocca, I. (2022). KnowMIS-ABSA: An overview and a reference model for applications of sentiment analysis and aspect-based sentiment analysis. *Artificial Intelligence Review*, *55*(6), 4813–4846. DOI: 10.1007/s10462-021-10134-9

Dang, C. N., Moreno-García, M. N., & Prieta, F. D. (2021). An approach to integrating sentiment analysis into recommender systems. *Sensors (Basel)*, *21*(3), 1012. Advance online publication. DOI: 10.3390/s21165666 PMID: 34451118

Douglas, B. D., Ewell, P. J., & Brauer, M. (2023). Data quality in online human-subjects research: Comparisons between MTurk, Prolific, CloudResearch, Qualtrics, and SONA. *PLoS One*, *18*(1), e0280404. Advance online publication. DOI: 10.1371/journal.pone.0279720 PMID: 36917576

Duan, S., Wang, Z., Wang, S., & Chen, M. (2024). Emotion-aware interaction design in intelligent user interface using multi-modal deep learning. In 2024 5th International Conference on Artificial Intelligence and Computer Engineering (ICAICE) (pp. 1–6). DOI: 10.1109/ISCEIC63613.2024.10810240

Filieri, R., Lin, Z., Li, Y., Lu, X., & Yang, X. (2022). Customer emotions in service robot encounters: A hybrid machine-human intelligence approach. *Journal of Service Research*, *25*(2), 267–285. DOI: 10.1177/10946705221103937

Gamage, G., De Silva, D., Mills, N., Alahakoon, D., & Manic, M. (2024). Emotion AWARE: An artificial intelligence framework for adaptable, robust, explainable, and multi-granular emotion analysis. *Journal of Big Data*, *11*(1), 1–25. DOI: 10.1186/s40537-024-00953-2

Gervasi, R., Barravecchia, F., Mastrogiacomo, L., & Franceschini, F. (2023). Applications of affective computing in human-robot interaction: State-of-the-art and challenges for manufacturing. *Proceedings of the Institution of Mechanical Engineers. Part B, Journal of Engineering Manufacture*, *237*(6–7), 815–832. DOI: 10.1177/09544054221121888

Hartmann, J., Heitmann, M., Siebert, C., & Schamp, C. (2023). More than a feeling: Accuracy and application of sentiment analysis. *International Journal of Research in Marketing*, *40*(1), 1–20. DOI: 10.1016/j.ijresmar.2022.05.005

Hossain, M. S., & Rahman, M. F. (2023). Customer sentiment analysis and prediction of insurance products' reviews using machine learning approaches. *FIIB Business Review*, *12*(2), 158–169. DOI: 10.1177/23197145221115793

Hu, L., Tan, C., & Deng, H. (2023). Product recommendation using online reviews with emotional preferences. *Kybernetes*, *52*(5), 1573–1596. DOI: 10.1108/K-09-2021-0852

Hubballi, R. B., Selvakumar, P., Seenivasan, R., Basava Aradhya, S. G., Dinesh, N., & Seelam, P. K. (2025). Overview of current AI technologies in education. In Kyei-Blankson, L., & Ntuli, E. (Eds.), *Transformative AI practices for personalized learning strategies* (pp. 1–26). IGI Global Scientific Publishing., DOI: 10.4018/979-8-3693-8744-3.ch001

Jin, J., Jia, D., & Chen, K. (2022). Mining online reviews with a Kansei-integrated Kano model for innovative product design. *International Journal of Production Research*, *60*(11), 3437–3454. DOI: 10.1080/00207543.2021.1949641

Karthik, R. V., & Ganapathy, S. (2021). A fuzzy recommendation system for predicting the customers' interests using sentiment analysis and ontology in e-commerce. *Applied Soft Computing*, *102*, 107101. Advance online publication. DOI: 10.1016/j.asoc.2021.107396

Kim, T. Y., Ko, H., Kim, S. H., & Kim, H. D. (2021). Modeling of recommendation system based on emotional information and collaborative filtering. *Sensors (Basel)*, *21*(3), 1013. Advance online publication. DOI: 10.3390/s21061997 PMID: 33808989

Kotte, K. R., Attaluri, V., & Selvakumar, P. (2025). Revolutionising retail banking with AI and virtual technologies: AI-driven financial training. In Nair, A. J., Manohar, S., Limbu, Y. B., & Huhmann, B. A. (Eds.), *Intersecting natural language processing and FinTech innovations in service marketing* (pp. 421–440). IGI Global Scientific Publishing., DOI: 10.4018/979-8-3693-9944-6.ch020

Kunnathully, K., Satyanarayana, P., Anute, N., Sharma, M., Sureshkrishna, G., & Manjunath, T. C. (2025). Propaganda, social media and AI. In Vieira, A., Joaquim, A., & Duarte, A. (Eds.), *Digital populism and the use of neo-propaganda and fake news* (pp. 19–38). IGI Global Scientific Publishing., DOI: 10.4018/979-8-3693-9999-6.ch002

Miranda, M. L. S. L. P. (2025). Emotion-based image recommendation system [Master's thesis, Universidade de Lisboa, Faculdade de Ciências]. http://hdl.handle.net/10400.5/100177

Mohammad, S. M. (2022). Ethics sheet for automatic emotion recognition and sentiment analysis. *Computational Linguistics*, *48*(2), 239–274. DOI: 10.1162/coli_a_00433

Peer, E., Rothschild, D., Gordon, A., Evernden, Z., & Jablonski, B. (2022). Data quality of platforms and panels for online behavioral research. *Behavior Research Methods*, *54*(4), 1643–1662. DOI: 10.3758/s13428-021-01694-3 PMID: 34590289

Qishu, L. (2024). Implementation method of intelligent emotion-aware clothing system based on nanofibre technology. *Industria Textila (Bucuresti)*, *75*(1), 1–6. DOI: 10.35530/IT.075.01.202379

Quan, H., Li, S., Zeng, C., Wei, H., & Hu, J. (2023). Big data and AI-driven product design: A survey. *Applied Sciences (Basel, Switzerland)*, *13*(16), 9433. Advance online publication. DOI: 10.3390/app13169433

Rostami, M., Vardasbi, A., Aliannejadi, M., & Crestani, F. (2024). Emotional insights for food recommendations. In *European Conference on Information Retrieval* (Vol. 13185, pp. 3–17). DOI: 10.1007/978-3-031-28241-6_1

Rowlands, J. (2021). Interviewee transcript review as a tool to improve data quality and participant confidence in sensitive research. *International Journal of Qualitative Methods*, *20*, 1–9. DOI: 10.1177/16094069211066170

Ruan, T., Liu, Q., & Chang, Y. (2025). Digital media recommendation system design based on user behavior analysis and emotional feature extraction. *PLoS One*, *20*(1), e0281234. Advance online publication. DOI: 10.1371/journal.pone.0322768 PMID: 40388444

Sakthivel, M., Jaganathan, A., & Mohanraj, M. Mohit, & Manjunath, T. (2025). Brand loyalty through AI and personalisation AI-generated content for financial marketing. In A. J. Nair, S. Manohar, Y. B. Limbu, & B. A. Huhmann (Eds.), Intersecting natural language processing and FinTech innovations in service marketing (pp. 77–96). IGI Global Scientific Publishing. DOI: 10.4018/979-8-3693-9944-6.ch006

Samal, A., & Bhargav, J. S. K. M., Selvakumar, P., Sharma, M., & T. C. M. (2025). Measuring brand performance with AI tools. In Z. Hussain, M. Sharipudin, A. Albattat, & A. Khan (Eds.), Strategic brand management in the age of AI and disruption (pp. 279–302). IGI Global Scientific Publishing. DOI: 10.4018/979-8-3693-9461-8.ch011

Ullah, K., Mumtaz, I., Zia, M. A., & Razzaq, A. (2022). Text-based emotion detection by using classification and regression model. In Lecture notes on data engineering and communications technologies (Vol. 144, pp. 414–419). DOI: 10.1007/978-3-031-10388-9_30

Usman, F. O., Eyo-Udo, N. L., Etukudoh, E. A., Odonkor, B., Ibeh, C. V., & Adegbola, A. (2024). A critical review of AI-driven strategies for entrepreneurial success. *International Journal of Management & Entrepreneurship Research*, *6*(1), 200–215. DOI: 10.51594/ijmer.v6i1.748

Vallabhaneni, A. S., Perla, A., Regalla, R. R., & Kumari, N. (2024). The power of personalization: AI-driven recommendations. In *Minds unveiled* (1st ed.). Productivity Press., https://www.taylorfrancis.com/chapters/edit/10.4324/9781032711089-9 DOI: 10.4324/9781032711089-9

Veltmeijer, E. A., Gerritsen, C., & Hindriks, K. (2023). Automatic emotion recognition for groups: A review. *IEEE Transactions on Affective Computing*, *14*(1), 1–20. DOI: 10.1109/TAFFC.2021.3065726

Xin, Q., He, Y., Pan, Y., Wang, Y., & Du, S. (2023). The implementation of an AI-driven advertising push system based on an NLP algorithm. *International Journal of Global Economics and Management*, *6*(1), 1–15. https://pdfs.semanticscholar.org/72cd/00135b5bab08597f2248a7a4fa0c7cc6e24c.pdf

Zhou, R., Zhang, Z., Fu, H., Zhang, L., & Li, L. (2023). PR-PL: A novel prototypical representation-based pairwise learning framework for emotion recognition using EEG signals. *IEEE Transactions on Affective Computing*. Advance online publication. DOI: 10.1109/TAFFC.2023.3280747

Zhu, P., Liu, Z., Li, X., Jiang, X., & Zhu, M. X. (2023). The influences of livestreaming on online purchase intention: Examining platform characteristics and consumer psychology. *Industrial Management & Data Systems*, *123*(1), 1–20. DOI: 10.1108/IMDS-07-2022-0430

# Chapter 4
# Biased by Design? Exploring the Hidden Influence of AI on Subconscious Consumer Behavior

**M. Jomon Jose**
http://orcid.org/0009-0003-4341-9936
*Sahrdaya Institute of Management Studies, Kodakara, India*

**Jyothis Rachel Mathews**
http://orcid.org/0009-0003-8279-6080
*Ahalia School of Management, Palakkad, India*

## ABSTRACT

*The convergence of artificial intelligence (AI) and neuromarketing is revolutionizing the way we research consumers and design business strategy. Together, they pair brain science with computer simulations. Neuromarketing employs tools such as EEG and eye-tracking to monitor consumer responses subconsciously, and AI assists in processing it faster and more accurately. This article explores how our subconscious biases can be picked up by, amplified by, or attenuated by AI-based neuromarketing systems. It applies Dual Process Theory and theory of algorithmic bias to outline a model—AI–Neuromarketing–Bias Interaction (ANBI)—that describes how AI analysis and brain data cooperate. Drawing on retail stores, hospitals, entertainment, and political campaign advertising, this essay outlines the benefits and limitations of using AI in neuromarketing. These technologies allow very directed advertising and can forecast customer behavior, generating ethical fears regarding privacy and manipulation. The article presents advice to marketers, developers of AI, politicians, and researchers, calling for careful use of emerging technologies, enhanced transparency, and protection of personal rights. In general,*

DOI: 10.4018/979-8-3373-5997-7.ch004

*AI in neuromarketing must be employed to understand consumers more than to take advantage of them. We have to counterpoise the technology push with the need to preserve consumers' trust and freedom.*

## INTRODUCTION

The marriage between neuroscience and artificial intelligence (AI) has revolutionized the way that businesses comprehend and shape consumer behavior. Neuromarketing as a discipline over the last 20 years has evolved to become a rich source of practice, employing instrumentation from neuroscience like fMRI, EEG, and eye-tracking to quantify unconscious processes that govern consumers' choices (Plassmann et al., 2015; Khondakar et al., 2024). Concurrently, advances in AI analytics have made it possible for marketers to quickly and precisely examine massive databases and discover intricate patterns of behavior that may go unnoticed by traditional means (Davenport et al., 2020; Alhalafi & Veeravalli, 2025). Coupled, these advances can revolutionize strategic marketing by offering profound insights into the subconscious drivers of consumer behavior.

The intersection of artificial intelligence and neuroscience in business presents some interesting questions, particularly around how cognitive biases in consumer behavior data may impact outcomes. Cognitive biases arise when individuals make routine irrational decisions based on mental shortcuts or emotional states (Kahneman, 2011). An example is biases such as anchoring effects and loss aversion, which can influence people's preferences unknowingly and result in suboptimal choices. If neuromarketing methods pick up on these unconscious cues, there's a danger biases will be added to datasets, which AI systems will interpret and maybe exacerbate. This does lead us to a central question: Does AI simply mirror consumer biases, or does it also perpetuate and take advantage of them in ways that can erode consumer autonomy?

While predictive algorithms are increasingly used in digital advertising and personalization, the AI bias issue increases. AI systems learned on biased data have the potential to enhance cognitive biases rather than correct them, resulting in consumers being taken advantage of. For instance, algorithms detecting loss aversion may nudge promotions that get consumers to fear loss, enhancing that bias. This produces threats for companies and ethical considerations for society. Businesses employing biased AI may misinterpret consumers and make suboptimal decisions. Bias exploitation can minimize consumer freedom, damaging brand trust and long-term relationships.

Even with the increasing importance of these phenomena, there is a significant knowledge gap in literature. Literature has widely discussed the characteristics of cognitive biases in consumer psychology (Kahneman, 2011) and the potential for neuromarketing methods to reveal unconscious processes (Plassmann et al., 2015; Khondakar et al., 2024). Concurrently, researchers have also underscored the potential of AI-based personalization and strategic marketing (Davenport et al., 2020; Alhalafi & Veeravalli, 2025). However, there are few studies that focus on where these fields intersect—how AI can not only measure but also amplify or dampen subconscious biases uncovered by neuromarketing. This omission leaves policy-makers, scholars, and marketers with few directions on how to negotiate AI-based neuromarketing ethics and strategies.

To fill this gap, the current chapter is informed by the following research questions:

1. How do cognitive biases appear in neuromarketing findings?
2. How does AI amplify or diminish these biases?
3. What are the ethical and strategic implications for marketers?

The objectives of the chapter are four. First, it seeks to define the place of unconscious biases in neuromarketing by charting the most prevalent biases that occur in consumer choice-making. Second, it attempts to explore the mechanisms by which AI processes neuromarketing information and possibly amplifies or dampens biases. Third, the chapter discusses the ethical considerations, such as issues around manipulation, privacy, and consumer control. Finally, it creates a framework of strategic recommendations for companies with an emphasis on responsible AI adoption and bias-conscious marketing approaches.

By placing the debate at the intersection of neuroscience, AI, and consumer psychology, this chapter is part of an emerging canon of research on ethical and responsible marketing in the age of digital technology. It refutes the notion that AI-powered neuromarketing is objective per se, to find that such technologies tend to work from within the boundaries of human prejudice. In so doing, it emphasizes the imperative for marketers to balance innovation and responsibility, making sure that strategies premised on subconscious consumer knowledge create lasting value for business as well as society.

## LITERATURE REVIEW

### Neuromarketing and Subconscious Consumer Behavior

Neuromarketing is an emerging paradigm for the study of consumers away from self-reported preferences and towards objective physiological and neurological measures. Methods such as electroencephalography (EEG), functional magnetic resonance imaging (fMRI), eye-tracking, galvanic skin response (GSR), and facial expression analysis are now being used more frequently to measure unconscious drivers of purchase decisions (Plassmann et al., 2015; Gupta et al., 2025). EEG records brainwave activity to monitor attention and emotional arousal with good temporal resolution, and fMRI samples blood flow alterations in brain areas associated with reward, trust, or risk processing, providing spatial resolution (Ariely & Berns, 2010; Song et al., 2025). Eye-tracking and facial expression analysis additionally supplement these measures by capturing visual attention patterns and micro-expressions that consumers cannot report consciously (Kühn et al., 2016; Khondakar et al., 2024). These techniques avoid the shortcomings of both standard surveys and interviews, offering straight access to the subconscious habits that drive consumer attitudes.

The power of neuromarketing lies in its capacity to reveal the subconscious decision-making drivers. It has been found that most purchasing decisions—quite possibly as much as 95%—are driven by emotions, heuristics, and automatic processes as opposed to rational thinking (Lim et al., 2024). For example, EEG research demonstrates that affective advertisements receive greater neural activity, which is associated with better brand recall and purchase intentions than self-reported measures (Vecchiato et al., 2011; Deckker & Sumanasekara, 2025). Similarly, fMRI research has linked activity in the ventromedial prefrontal cortex to willingness-to-pay judgments, underscoring the neural basis of economic preferences (Knutson et al., 2007; Gupta et al., 2025). These findings position neuromarketing as both a diagnostic and predictive tool for understanding consumer behavior.

The practical implementations of neuromarketing are spread widely across different sectors. For instance, in retail, the eye-tracking experiments have changed the store layouts dramatically as the places where customers concentrate their eyes are discovered "hot spots" (Huddleston et al., 2015; Lim et al., 2024). Advertising is another area where the combination of EEG and biometrics has been employed by the likes of Coca-Cola to not only simplify but also to energize their campaign design, thus bringing the artistic facets close to the customer's emotional subconscious (Stasi et al., 2018; Song et al., 2025). Besides, neuromarketing has brought a lot of changes in healthcare, especially in the prevention of smoking, where the identification of neural signals of emotional arousal has been more successful in predicting behavioral change than survey responses (Falk et al., 2012; Khondakar et al., 2024). These are only a few out of many use cases, where mapping brain activity to consumer engagement by firms has become easier, thus making the latter more targeted and accurate.

## Cognitive Bias in Consumer Psychology

Cognitive biases, known as systematic deviations from logical judgment, are the main factors that heavily influence consumer behavior, which is subconscious. These biases are a result of heuristic shortcuts, emotional impulses, or cognitive limitations (Tversky & Kahneman, 1974; Gupta et al., 2025). Premises of these biases are things as anchoring, that means consumers mix deeply with first information (e.g., a reference price) to make further estimations (Furnham & Boo, 2011; Lim et al., 2024); confirmation bias, which energizes the scope of a bias-based view of data; availability heuristics, which distort judgments towards the most vivid or recent pieces of information; and the affect heuristic, where emotions such as fear or nostalgia become decision-makers (Slovic et al., 2007; Deckker & Sumanasekara, 2025). These biases bring about consumer behaviors that are both predictable and irrational.

These biases are present in consumer markets and. companies use them cleverly to their advantage. A typical anchoring is sellers. presenting a "discounted" price that is selected alongside a higher price to make buyers feel that. They get a great deal. Confirmation bias is used by personalize marketing, which is one of the helping factors of the algorithm that is continuously feeding the consumers with what they like in order to keep them loyal to the brand. Moreover, the availability heuristic considerably defines the relationships between a brand and the market that are the use of broadcasting to publicize the most vivid stories or using celebrity endorsement, whereas the affect heuristic is the cause behind the launching of campaigns which are focusing mainly on the emotional storytelling (Kaplan, 2021). Such strategies are emphasizing the irrational character of consumer decision-making that is being subconscious biases.

Neuromarketing instruments are highly efficient in revealing biases. For example, fMRI experiments confirm that the nervous system creating loss aversion, a major attribute of prospect theory, lights the neural paths related to the pain that a consumer feels when the situation is similar to Tom et al., 2007; Song et al., 2025). EEG studies have located the framing effects where the neural activity only can be seen if the product is presented as a "gain" instead of a "loss" (Sela & Berger, 2012; Gupta et al., 2025). Eye-tracing reveals the decoy effect, where people looking at the unattractive options most intensely under which the target becomes visibleatively more attractive than it. This is the way how neuromarketing allows those physiological connections to be made between the biases and the market, in which they are easily exposed and manipulated.

## Artificial Intelligence in Marketing

Artificial intelligence (AI) integration in marketing has changed entirely the work of businesses in analyzing, forecasting, and reaching the behavior of the consumers. The main AI tech that can be mentioned are machine learning, natural language processing (NLP), and deep learning. These technologies enable marketing that is individualized, predictive, and emotionally connected (Davenport et al., 2020; Rajan & Nagpal, 2024). Personalization is known as the main application that is characteristic of platforms like Amazon and has been refined by the introduction of algorithms such as deep learning, collaborative filtering, and reinforcement learning that lead to the delivery of personalized recommendations where user needs are anticipated (Gómez-Uribe & Hunt, 2015; Haleem et al., 2025). On the other hand, predictive analytics gives the opportunity to companies to predict the turnover rate, adjust the price properly, and use the money wisely by deciding on patterns that exist in the behavioral and transactional data.

Moreover, AI improves the connection with the customer on an emotional level as well. Sentiment analysis tools using NLP techniques receive inputs from different sources such as consumer feedback, social media conversations, and biometric data, improve the quality of detecting the emotional state, and thus enable real-time affective insights (Cambria et al., 2018; Alhalafawy & Abdelmoety, 2025). The multimodal AI systems collect together different data from neuromarketing, such as e.g. facial expressions and GSR, for the purpose of making emotional profiles that are less shallow. In advertising, programmatic platforms use the help of AI in order to make the real-time bidding more successful, thus consumer profiles are in good harmony with the ad slots, and engagement is maximized (Rajan & Nagpal, 2024). Consequently, these are the developments that make AI a strong weapon for descriptive as well as prescriptive marketing strategies.

The use of artificial intelligence to analyze neuromarketing data is transformative in nature where. Machine learning methods can classify EEG signals to better predict emotional response or attention than older manual ways (Khushaba et al., 2013; Deckker & Sumanasekara, 2025). Also, deep learning models that use fMRI or eye-tracking data can find difficult patterns related to subconscious likes, doing better than basic statistics (Venkatraman et al., 2015; Haleem et al., 2025). In healthcare, AI neuromarketing has been used to make patient-focused campaigns by guessing how people will emotionally react to health info. In retail, AI eye-tracking helps improve where products are placed, which can make shopping easier and increase sales.

## Intersection of AI, Neuromarketing, and Cognitive Bias

The intersection of artificial intelligence, neuromarketing, and cognitive bias presents both chances and problems. AI can look at large neuromarketing datasets and find small subconscious patterns, which helps with making things more personal and predicting things better. But, this can make the biases in the data even bigger. For instance, if neuromarketing data shows that a consumer really doesn't like losing out on things, AI might create strategies that talk about offers in terms of what they could lose. This could strengthen the bias and take advantage of the consumer's weak spots (Kaplan, 2021; Alhalafawy & Abdelmoety, 2025). This makes a cycle where biased data leads to biased results, which then changes consumer behavior in biased ways (Schäfer et al., 2022; Deckker & Sumanasekara, 2025).

This also could keep consumer stereotypes going. Neuromarketing data might show that men and women react differently emotionally to ads. If AI uses this information without thinking about it, it might start using stereotypes in targeting, like showing emotional ads to women and rational ads to men. This limits what consumers can choose and makes the market even more unequal (Lim et al., 2024). Biases about money or culture could also get bigger, which brings up moral questions.

Though these technologies are designed to revolutionize marketing, there still exist significant gaps in the research carried out. A great deal of neuromarketing has been focused on exploring the subconscious drivers of the consumer, and an incredible advancement of AI technology has been realized in the direction of personalization of tasks. Few studies, however, examine how AI interacts with bias-laden neuromarketing data. Besides that, there is little research on the possibility of AI being a tool that can help to eliminate biases through corrective modeling or that it is mainly an amplifier of them. Such a gap impedes the evolution of ethical guidelines and strategic frameworks for the usage of AI in neuromarketing in a responsible way, and this calls for a more interdisciplinary approach that combines consumer psychology, computer science, and business ethics.

# THEORETICAL FRAMEWORK

## Dual Process Theory (Kahneman)

Kahneman's Dual Process Theory (DPT) explains how subconscious thoughts shape consumer choices. DPT says we think in two ways: System 1 (fast, automatic, and emotional) and System 2 (slow, rational, and careful). In marketing, System 1 often guides shoppers because habits, simple rules, and feelings matter more than deep thinking (Kahneman, 2011; Evans & Stanovich, 2013; Lim et al., 2024). For example, when people buy soda, they often pick a known brand based on feelings, not a careful price check. System 2 comes into play for big decisions, like buying a home or picking investments, where people think things through.

Dual Process Theory (DPT) helps explain how subconscious processes shape consumer choices (as seen in a 2024 study). Neuromarketing offers proof for DPT. Studies using EEG and fMRI scans show that when people form brand preferences, emotional parts of their brains (like the amygdala) light up, even if there's no clear logical reason (Plassmann et al., 2015; Gupta et al., 2025). Eye-tracking studies also reveal that people quickly and instinctively look at familiar brands, which fits with the automatic responses described by System 1 (Kühn et al., 2016; Song et al., 2025). This data supports the idea that subconscious processes play a big role in how consumers interact with brands.

AI improves the ability to predict System 1 behaviors by looking at neuromarketing data. Machine learning can spot subtle subconscious cues, like tiny facial expressions or neural patterns, that point to emotional triggers (Deckker & Sumanasekara, 2025). Because of this, AI can predict intuitive decisions fairly well. AI models also take into account System 2 factors, like how sensitive someone is to price and their demographic information, to build complete prediction models that combine both subconscious and conscious signals (Rajan & Nagpal, 2024).

## Cognitive Bias Theories

By combining data on behavior and demographics, we can build better ways to predict choices by including both conscious and subconscious factors (Rajan & Nagpal, 2026).

Cognitive biases, which are ways our brainsSystematic deviations from making sound judgments, greatly influence what people buy (Tversky & Kahneman, 1974; Gupta et al., 2025). Some biases that matter most for studying the brain's role in marketing and using AI to predict behavior are:

* Anchoring Bias: People rely too much on the first piece of information they see, like an initial price, when deciding what something is worth (Furnham & Boo, 2011; Lim et al., 2024). Studies show that when people see these initial prices, certain brain areas linked to value light up (Ariely & Berns, 2010; Song et al., 2025). AI systems that learn from past purchases could make this bias stronger by always showing the same starting prices.
* Framing Effect: How information is presented as either a gain or loss changes people's decisions. Brain research shows that gain messages activate reward areas, while loss messages trigger areas that anticipate pain (De Martino et al., 2006; Gupta et al., 2025). AI is often used in ads to change the message

based on who is seeing it, making the ad more persuasive (Alhalafawy & Abdelmoety, 2025).

* Halo Effect: People assume that if one thing about a brand is good, everything else must be too. For example, they might think eco-friendly brands are also higher quality. Brain studies suggest this is because we trust brands we like (Nisbett & Wilson, 1977; Plassmann et al., 2015). AI makes this stronger by grouping people's preferences together, which reinforces how they generally feel about brands (Haleem et al., 2025).
* Implicit Associations: Things we don't even realize we connect in our minds, like luxury and exclusivity, affect our buying choices. Tests and brain scans show that these hidden biases influence what we buy, even if we don't realize it (Greenwald et al., 2009; Lim et al., 2024). AI can spot these connections in what people say and how they react, then use that information to create targeted ads (Alhalafawy & Abdelmoety, 2025).

These biases prove that consumer decisions aren't always based on logic. Brain research in marketing, along with AI, can find and use these subconscious biases.

## Algorithmic Bias Theory

While AI can refine marketing, algorithmic bias poses a threat. This bias, as noted by Barocas & Selbst (2016) and Rajan & Nagpal (2024), stems from data issues, model design, or implementation flaws, causing systematic errors in AI results.

In neuromarketing, the main types of bias are:

1. Data: If neuromarketing data is not diverse (e.g., limited to specific cultures), AI models could make incorrect generalizations and reinforce stereotypes in ads (Crawford, 2021; Lim et al., 2024).
2. Design: When creating an AI, subjective choices on features or model goals can integrate assumptions about customer actions, leading to bias (Deckker & Sumanasekara, 2025).
3. Implementation: Even good AI systems can be biased if their assumptions don't hold true in the real world (Haleem et al., 2025).

In neuromarketing, AI bias happens when AI boosts mental biases found in consumer data. For example, if AI finds strong feelings in one group and changes ads based on this, it might ignore other groups, causing biased engagement (Schäfer et al., 2022; Alhalafawy & Abdelmoety, 2025). To avoid this, ethical AI plans like FAT/ML push for finding and fixing bias using XAI, varied data, and routine checks (Mitchell et al., 2021; Rajan & Nagpal, 2024).

## Integrated Conceptual Framework: The AI–Neuromarketing–Bias Interaction (ANBI) Model

Based on Dual Process Theory, Cognitive Bias Theories, and Algorithmic Bias Theory, this chapter puts forward the AI–Neuromarketing–Bias Interaction (ANBI) Model. The model includes:

1. System 1 Responses: Neuromarketing tools pick up on automatic responses that show cognitive biases (like anchoring and framing). These responses are produced by System 1 processes.
2. AI Processing: Algorithms study neuromarketing data and might increase or decrease biases based on the quality of the data, how the model is designed, and the context in which it is used.
3. Feedback Loop: Biased neuromarketing data goes into AI outputs, which then shape marketing strategies. These strategies can strengthen consumer biases, causing a continuing cycle of subconscious influence.
4. Ethical Mitigation: Ethical AI systems that focus on fairness and openness are needed to stop this cycle and better protect consumers.

## Conceptual Diagram (Description)

The AI–Neuromarketing–Bias Interaction (ANBI) Model is a five-layer structure that explains how consumer signals below awareness combine with thinking errors and AI to change marketing results.

### 1. Neuromarketing Input Layer

* Tools: EEG, fMRI, eye-tracking, galvanic skin response (GSR), and face reading.
* Function: Records signals from the consumer's subconscious, like emotions, focus, and hidden preferences.
* Example: Eye-tracking shows quick interest in expensive brands.

### 2. Cognitive Bias Layer

* Biases: Anchoring, framing, halo effect, hidden links.
* Function: Filters neuromarketing data by thinking errors.
* Example: A person thinks a more costly item is better (anchoring + halo effect).

### 3. AI Processing Layer

* Algorithms: Machine learning, deep learning, natural language processing, recommendation systems.
* Function: Changes signals from the subconscious into predictions about what people will buy.
* Bias Risk: Skewed data, bad feature choices, use in wrong situations.
* Example: Recommendation systems keep suggesting expensive brands, strengthening anchoring.

### 4. Marketing Output Layer

* Outcomes: Custom ads, changing prices, automated content, emotional plans.
* Function: Marketing plans based on AI and neuromarketing working together.
* Example: A person always sees loss-frame ads (Don't miss this deal!) which use the fear of missing out.

### 5. Feedback Loop Layer

* Result: Marketing changes how people act, strengthening biases in the subconscious.
* Risk: Creates stronger bias loops where people are pushed into expected, stereotyped actions.
* Ethical things to consider: Adding fairness, openness, and responsibility to stop the loop.

*Figure 1.*

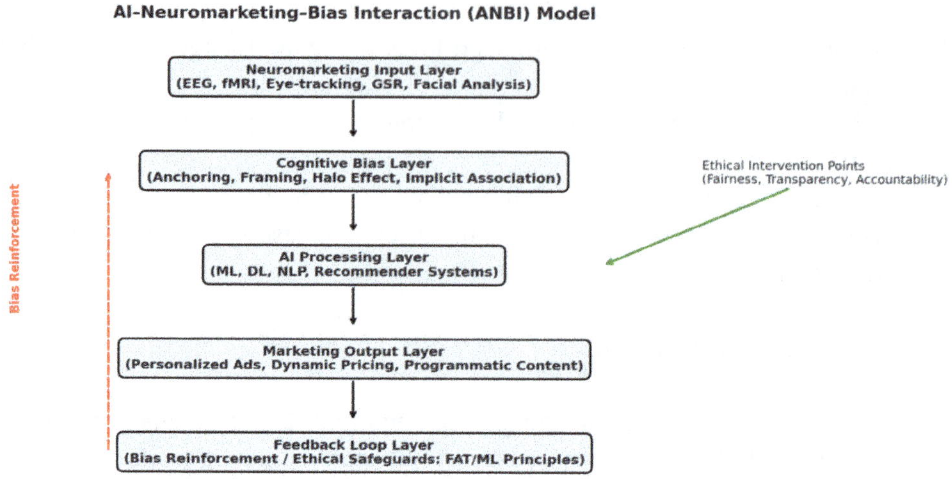


This model combines psychology, neuroscience, and computer science to explain how bias is amplified or reduced where AI and neuromarketing meet.

* Each stage (Neuromarketing Inputs → Cognitive Biases → AI Processing → Marketing Outputs → Feedback Loops) is shown with arrows.
* A red dashed arrow shows how biases grow stronger through feedback.
* Green notes show where ethical measures (fairness, transparency, accountability) can be applied.

## METHODOLOGY

### Nature of the Study

This framework combines ideas from psychology, brain science, and computer science using feedback loops.This part uses a mix of theory and real examples to make its points. There are a couple of reasons for this method. First, using brain-based marketing with thinking machines is pretty new, with not much solid research yet. So, it makes sense to bring different ideas together to get a clearer view (Hamelin et al., 2017; Alhalafawy & Abdelmoety, 2025). This way, we can merge what we know from brain science, how consumers think, AI, and what's right and wrong in marketing. An example is the AI–Neuromarketing–Bias Interaction (ANBI) Model we suggest here. Second, since understanding what shoppers do without thinking and the right and wrong of how machines make choices can be tricky, it's good to start with a strong theory. This helps us see how things connect, find where we need more research, and create useful ways of thinking about these issues.

To show how this works in the real world, we also examine specific situations. Looking at examples from how stores personalize shopping, health messages, and political ads shows how AI and brain-based marketing work together. Sometimes, they can make thinking errors worse, but other times, they can help fix them (Lim et al., 2024). By mixing theory with real examples, we aim to be both correct in our ideas and helpful in practice. This fits our goal of improving understanding and giving advice that people can actually use.

## Data Sources

This study, which is exploratory and theoretical, used only secondary data, which was sorted into three groups:

### 1. Published Neuromarketing Research

We considered articles in journals, systematic reviews, and data-driven neuromarketing research. This research examines various tools, including EEG, fMRI, eye-tracking, galvanic skin response (GSR), and facial coding. These resources enable us to identify what influences consumer decisions without their awareness (Plassmann et al., 2015; Gupta et al., 2025). These resources form the foundation on which one can learn about how biases emerge in brain and bodily data (Khondakar et al., 2024).

### 2. How AI Is Applied in Marketing

We verified scholarly papers, business publications, and technology articles on how AI is applied. This included machine learning (ML), natural language processing (NLP), recommendation systems, and programmatic advertising (Davenport et al., 2020; Rajan & Nagpal, 2024). These authors inform us about how computer programs handle consumer information and explain how technology can amplify or mitigate biases in neuromarketing (Haleem et al., 2025).Examples Across Various Domains We employed examples across various domains to indicate how neuromarketing and AI are employed:

> Retail Personalization: E-commerce and omni-channel strategy research demonstrates how eye-tracking and recommendation software influence what people see and pick (Sestino et al., 2020; Lim et al., 2024).

Healthcare Communication: How neuromarketing is applied in patient treatment and behavior programs, as well as AI health chatbots, indicates how knowledge about the subconscious is utilized with predictive analytics (Benrimoh et al., 2021; Song et al., 2025).

Political Campaigns: Evidence from AI-targeted facial recognition and sentiment analysis indicates how they influence voting (Howard et al., 2018; Deckker & Sumanasekara, 2025).Using these different sources gives us a good base for measuring how AI, neuromarketing, and biases work together.

## Analytical Approach

To make sure we are thorough in our work, our research will use content analysis, thematic synthesis, and an evaluation based on a specific framework.

### 1. Case Study Content Analysis

We will use content analysis to look at different cases. The goal is to see how people gather, study, and use subconscious consumer info in marketing campaigns that use AI. For example, some situations show how retail tries to make things feel more personal. This can set off biases, like when product placements and prices are set up in certain ways using computer programs (Sestino et al., 2020). Also, in political ads, AI can be used to send messages to strengthen people's existing beliefs (Howard et al., 2018; Deckker & Sumanasekara, 2025). By noting these patterns, we hope to get a solid idea of how biases can get stronger in different situations.

### 2. Synthesis of Research Themes

We will also use a thematic synthesis to find the important topics in research on neuromarketing and AI, like bias reinforcement loops, predictive personalization, and ethical safeguards (Agarwal & Dhar, 2014; Alhalafawy & Abdelmoety, 2025). This means bringing together what we know from neuromarketing and how AI is used. This will give us a complete picture of how biases work, both in terms of people's psychology and the technology involved.

### 3. Bias Evaluation in AI Systems

We will use the ANBI Model to see how biases are included and spread in AI neuromarketing. This model helps us look at three key areas:

- o Data Bias: If the datasets used in neuromarketing don't fully represent everyone, like if they lean too much toward certain groups, the AI predictions could be wrong (Mehrabi et al., 2021; Lim et al., 2024).
- o Design Bias: The way computer programs are designed, including what features are chosen and what goals are set, might focus more on short-term things instead of what's good for consumers (Rajan & Nagpal, 2024).
- o Deployment Bias: If campaigns only focus on things like click-through rates, they might take advantage of people's subconscious weaknesses, like their fear of losing out (Alhalafawy & Abdelmoety, 2025).

By using ethical AI ideas—being fair, responsible, and open (FAT)—this evaluation can show us how to act responsibly within the ANBI framework (Mitchell et al., 2021).

### Methodological Rigor and Limitations

This method aims for strong conceptual support by bringing together ideas from neuroscience, psychology, and AI. Using different types of existing info and examples helps make the theory more broadly applicable to different fields.There are limits, though. Since it relies on existing info, it's hard to test things out directly, and there might be some bias in how the info is understood. The examples, while helpful, might not show all the different situations in marketing. Besides, because neuromarketing and AI are changing so fast, the results will need to be updated as new info comes out.Even with these limits, the method works well for a theoretical chapter that values clear concepts, progress in the field, and ethical advice over broad statistical findings. By mixing theory with real-world examples, this chapter makes a useful addition to the conversation about responsible AI and neuromarketing..

## FINDINGS AND DISCUSSION

### Cognitive Biases Captured in Neuromarketing

Neuromarketing studies find that subconscious signals and biases have a big impact on what people buy, maybe more than when they think things through logically. Tools like EEG, fMRI, and eye-tracking give solid proof that biases, like anchoring, framing, and emotional priming, change how people shop (Plassmann et al., 2015; Ariely & Berns, 2010; Gupta et al., 2025). For example, EEG studies notice bigger brain reactions to the first prices people see, which shows how anchoring can change what they're willing to pay (Karmarkar, 2011; Song et al., 2025).

Also, fMRI studies find that calling a product 95% fat-free instead of 5% fat turns on emotional parts of the brain, like the amygdala, making feelings more important than logic (De Martino et al., 2006; Khondakar et al., 2024).

Real-world examples show this in action. In stores, studies using neuromarketing show that package colors and designs can set how good people think a product is, even if the product itself is the same (Lim et al., 2024). In healthcare, anti-smoking ads that scare people activate parts of the brain, increasing their desire to quit, but they sometimes cause a negative reaction in certain groups (Venkatraman et al., 2015; Song et al., 2025). In politics, simple emotional tricks using music, faces, or stories can change who people vote for, often without them even realizing it (Westen, 2008; Deckker & Sumanasekara, 2025). This work shows that neuromarketing can find hidden biases, but it also points out that these biases could be used unfairly to get people to buy things.

## AI Reinforcement of Biases

The use of artificial intelligence (AI) in marketing raises the possibility of increasing cognitive biases. AI-driven personalization depends on predictive analytics that use past consumer data, which can continue current preferences and stereotypes. For example, recommendation engines can create echo chambers by showing consumers similar content or products, worsening confirmation bias and limiting exposure to different options. This reduces consumer autonomy by reinforcing already present beliefs.

Segmentation algorithms, although useful for targeting, can lead to algorithmic stereotyping. Research indicates that ad target devices could end up discriminating against genders, races, or socio-economic classes unintentionally due to training data bias. For instance, women are likely to see fewer ads for well-paying jobs compared to men due to biases in society embedded in AI models. In political campaigns, AI-driven microtargeting can reinforce emotionally charged messages to match the tendencies of users, potentially leading to polarization.Biometric recognition technologies applied with neuromarketing devices also exhibit biases. Facial expression recognition systems can misread emotions in non-Western cultural contexts and create incorrect emotional profiling. This would result in inappropriate marketing based on culture or exclusion of minorities, particularly in international campaigns. These illustrations indicate that AI, when analyzing neuromarketing information, might perpetuate cognitive biases, and this raises concerns about fairness and inclusivity.

## Ethical and Strategic Implications

The mixture of neuromarketing and AI can provide valuable insights into what individuals do but jeopardizes consumer autonomy at the same time. When AI is applied to enhance unconscious sales strategies, it becomes difficult to distinguish between persuading individuals and manipulating them. This brings up moral questions (Northoff, 2012; Hari et al., 2024). When neuro-AI systems measure and deal with subconscious signals in ways that aren't clear, it's hard for people to give informed consent, which is very important. Also, when neuromarketing uses private biometric and neural data, there are big worries about secrecy. If this data is misused by being shared without permission or used for watching people, consumers may lose trust, and rules may be broken (Stanton et al., 2017; Alhalafawy & Abdelmoety, 2025).

When planning, groups need to find a middle ground between good marketing and moral duty. If they depend too much on changing people's minds without them knowing, they could hurt their image, face examination from regulators, and make customers angry. Too much personalization, for example, has been called nosy and can make people less attached to a brand (Martin & Murphy, 2017; Lim et al., 2024). So, to stay ahead in the long run, companies need to act morally to create lasting trust and involvement instead of using people's weaknesses for a quick profit.

## Mitigation Pathways

To deal with the problems created by AI neuromarketing several strategies can be implemented:

1. Find and Fix Bias: Use tests and audits to spot and fix biases in data and algorithms (Mehrabi et al., 2021; Rajan & Nagpal, 2024). This keeps AI from being unfair or excluding certain people.
2. Explainable AI (XAI): Make AI easier to understand, so marketers and regulators can see how data is used and who is in charge (Miller, 2019; Haleem et al., 2025).
3. Human Oversight: Use both AI and human judgment to add context to marketing insights, notice cultural details, and stop problems when they occur (Rahwan, 2018; Deckker & Sumanasekara, 2025).
4. Ethical Rules: Make sure neuro-AI marketing follows rules that focus on fairness and being responsible. This might mean limiting how biometric data is used, getting permission from consumers, and avoiding tricks (Jobin et al., 2019; Hari et al., 2024).

Companies can use these ideas to use neuromarketing and AI in an ethical way, balancing new ideas with protecting consumers..

## CASE STUDIES AND INDUSTRY INSIGHTS

### Retail and E-commerce: Personalized Recommendations Amplifying Shopping Bias

Retail and e-commerce were among the first to use neuromarketing and AI. Online platforms use AI-driven recommendation systems to examine shopping history, click patterns, and data like eye-tracking (Deckker & Sumanasekara, 2025). These systems often use biases like anchoring and confirmation to guide customers toward specific choices. For example, Amazon's recommendation system is said to affect up to 35% of its sales (McKinsey, 2020). Neuromarketing research suggests that product placement, colors, and limited-time offers increase emotion and urgency, triggering biases related to loss (Kahneman & Tversky, 1979; Gupta et al., 2025). When AI is combined with these triggers, consumers may become more prone to impulse buys (Al-Kasasbeh et al., 2025).

From a business view, the advantages are clear: better conversion rates, more cross-selling, and greater customer loyalty. Nevertheless, a key concern is that the consumer is being driven toward a choice without being conscious of the cues that influence him. This raises the issue of consumer autonomy and whether the techniques of persuasion constitute manipulation (Northoff, 2012). The possibility of making consumers depend upon tips also exacerbates the filter bubble problem, which limits exposure to diverse products (Pariser, 2011).

### Healthcare Marketing: Persuading Patients through Unconscious Signals

Healthcare marketing is one of those activities that are basically an application of neuromarketing and AI on a technical and sensitive scale.To confirm this, we can say that companies that create drugs, hospitals, and health campaigns have begun to apply neuroimaging and biometric tools to collect data regarding patient reactions to health-related messages. To give an example, the fMRI study revealed that the fear induced by a present concern in an anti-smoking campaign message is the source of the amygdala and insula activation, thus behavioral change intensifies considerably (Venkatraman et al., 2015). Subsequently, AI algorithms will be able to evaluate these subconscious reactions on a large scale, so organizations will have the possibility to craft public health campaigns, which will be highly precise in targeting, by employing these data (Farhud & Zokaei, 2021).

In this case, the business aspect which benefits from this is the rise in the effectiveness of the message to the public about preventive health issues. For instance, the emotional reactions of people can take a leading role in healthcare decisions, such as vaccinations or the adoption of good lifestyle habits. Hospitals have also been turning to AI-fueled neuromarketing to find the right doctor-to-patient communication strategy that lowers patients' fears while at the same time, it creates trust towards the doctor (Clement, 2025). However, the concerns for the matter of ethics are still there. In contrast with retail, the element of healthcare is as heavy as life-changing decisions are involved. The use of subconscious persuasion is likely to cause informed consent to be less credible if patients are influenced without realizing the psychological mechanisms in play. Also, there has been some disapproval of pharmaceutical marketing for making loud emotional triggers one of the major tools for boosting drug consumption which in turn raises suspicion whether it is being done only for the sake of making more profits instead of the patients' good (Hari et al., 2024). Hence, although neuromarketing in healthcare can be a good tool for communication efficiency, it still requires a lot of ethical considerations with strict policies in place to avoid the exploitation of the already vulnerable population.

## Entertainment and Media: AI Predicting Emotional Engagement with Films and Music

The entertainment industry is combining AI-based neuromarketing to foresee the consumers' reaction to films, television, and music. Studios employ biometric data—like facial expression analysis and galvanic skin response—gathered at test screenings to measure the emotional intensity, suspense, or humor of the given scene (Pozharliev et al., 2022). AI systems take this data, run algorithms, and make a prediction of the financial success of the film, the division of the audience into different groups, and even the possible viral nature of streaming content(Gupta et al., 2025).

Artificial intelligence-based tools in the music industry, coupled with brain science research, can pinpoint the exact moments when a sound or lyric will bring pleasure to the listener's brain, thus creating a hit song. Spotibfy and Netflix are among the companies using similar data-driven models to not only recommend the consumers the most likable tracks or programs but also influence the decisions of content creation through investing in the shows and songs that are most likely to engage the audience. The company's gains are significant: it lowers the risk of investing in entertainment, raises the level of audience engagement, and makes the advertising more targeted. Nevertheless, the rise of concerns about the ethics of standardizing creativity is inevitable. If AI becomes the main promoter of content that matches the most successful subconscious trigger patterns, it may lead to the impoverishment of artistic diversity and the perpetuation of cultural stereotypes. Moreover, the issue of subconscious engagement with media leads to emotional manipulation because consumers may find themselves trapped in unwind-watching or addiction to listening patterns that take advantage of their neurological vulnerabilities.

## Political Campaigns: AI-Neuromarketing Influence on Voter Biases

Integrating neuro-AI in the lineup of political campaign applications may be considered as one of the most debatable uses. AI-driven microtargeting, along with neuromarketing techniques such as facial coding and eye-tracking, gives campaigns the ability to compose messages that tap into the subconscious voter biases (Westen, 2008; Çakar & Filiz, 2023). For instance, slight emotional aspects in advertisements, which could be patriotic imagery or a frightening storyline, can make the audience react with System 1 processing, thus completely skipping the rational evaluation part (Kahneman, 2011).

The Facebook data scandal known as Cambridge Analytica was a clear example of how psychographic profiling and technologically based targeting could manipulate the voter mentality by increasing confirmation bias and affect heuristics (Cadwalladr & Graham-Harrison, 2018). Campaigns used AI to segment populations into the most persuadable segments, and they then produced highly personalized content delivered in the modality most likely to elicit an affective response rather than a rational one (LaChapelle & Tucker, 2023). These methods enacted from a position of strategy could significantly increase campaign effectiveness, activating the turnout of the targeted voter constituencies while at the same time suppressing the rivals' turnout (Šola et al., 2025). In return, the ethical price is enormous. These techniques, in their current form, potentially risk subverting the integrity of the democratic system, since manipulators of subconscious reactions get to do it without the knowledge of the voter. Academics believe that this is not merely persuasion but also a kind of force; therefore, it is a threat to the very essence of informed citizen decision-making (Trauthig & McKay, 2025). The debate is also on whether or not current laws can keep up with the problem raised by AI technology that prompts subconscious persuasion. Current political campaign regulations are not properly designed to manage the nuance of AI that impacts voters' subconscious influence. This deficiency in the system allows manipulative players to take advantage of voters on a scale heretofore unimaginable.

## Synthesis of Industry Insights

One of the main benefits of using AI and neuromarketing together is the clear business results across industries. As a result, businesses can see better consumer engagement, easier communication, and less uncertainty in the decision-making process. Although the report states that businesses feel more comfortable when they can rely on the same tools that give them the efficiency and precision of their work, these tools also increase the ethical issues around the categories of autonomy, manipulation, and inclusivity (Al-Kasasbeh et al., 2025).In the context of Retail and e-commerce, the most significant challenge that the sector has to deal with is the balancing of the two aspects - personalization and consumer freedom. The healthcare sector is the one that is walking on the edge where the exploitation of signals from the subconscious in the area of life-critical situations lurks. (Hari et al., 2024). Entertainment is showing the disadvantages that come with the reduction of creativity to algorithmic predictions, while the political campaigns picture the scenario where the most potent risk of unconscious manipulation, which threatens democracy, is (Šola et al., 2025).

Hence, the case studies in total are an industry-wide wake-up call for the ethical frameworks that, on the one hand, would support innovation and, on the other hand, balance it with responsibility. The neuro-AI marketing world, without any obstacles, would be a world full of commercial benefits. But such practices would still be trusted only if the markets and institutions could hold on to their trust in them.

# STRATEGIC RECOMMENDATIONS

Integrating artificial intelligence (AI) with neuromarketing can greatly change business innovation, but it also brings ethical, social, and strategic problems. To best use neuro-AI while protecting people's trust, freedom, and inclusion, here are some suggestions for marketers, AI creators, politicians, and educators/researchers. These tips try to find a middle ground between business goals and the duty to protect customers and the public.

## Recommendations for Marketers

When using neuromarketing and artificial intelligence, marketers need to be responsible and open. Subconscious signals can inform great campaign plans, but using biases without telling people damages trust. Companies have to explain how they gather and use data, not just follow privacy rules (Northoff, 2012; Hari et al., 2024). For example, businesses could explain how neuromarketing shapes what people see.Another thing to do is use personalization carefully by balancing custom advice with options (Susser et al., 2019; Lim et al., 2024). This stops consumers from getting stuck in patterns. Online stores could use discovery modes to show different items and fight limited choices (Pariser, 2011).

Lastly, think about ethics when making campaign plans. Working with experts to check plans ensures they are ethical. If neuromarketing is done well, it builds trust, which can help a business stand out (Edelman, 2021; Alhalafawy & Abdelmoety, 2025). By valuing trust, companies show they care about their customers while still marketing well.

## Recommendations for AI Developers

AI developers play a vital role in ensuring that neuromarketing data is handled ethically. The primary suggestion is to start using ethical coding standards which means understanding that the assumptions that are set in the algorithms can be the reason for biases that are higher. (Mehrabi et al., 2021; Rajan & Nagpal, 2024). By incorporating fairness, accountability, and transparency (FAT/ML) ideals into a development pipeline, it will be possible to reduce the risk that the AI systems might not communicate harmful stereotypes.

Another point to at is the diversity of datasets as the second priority. Neuromarketing datasets may be prone to the overrepresentation of some demographics, thus leading to the generation of biased outputs that meet the needs of only a few groups (Buolamwini & Gebru, 2018; Lim et al., 2024). The developers should select datasets with a lot of gender, racial, cultural, and socioeconomic contexts to ensure unbiased and widely applicable conclusions (Deckker & Sumanasekara, 2025).

Thirdly, the developers should set up fairness audits and algorithmic accountability practices. Along with bias testing, regular transparency reporting, and the implementation of explainable AI (XAI) tools, neuromarketing applications can be open to interpretability and accountability. (Miller, 2019; Haleem et al., 2025). Human-in-the-loop methods should also be promoted, where the accuracy of machines is combined with the decision of a human ethics officer in handling difficult cases and cultural aspects, thus eliminating the problem of complete reliance on automated systems.

## Recommendations for Policymakers

Utilizing biometric and neuromarketing data to the fullest comes with a whole set of issues regarding the regulation of such data. Present-day privacy rules like the European Data Protection Regulation (GDPR) are able to ensure the security of data, but they seem to falter in regulating the safety of subconscious data such as eye movements or brainwave patterns (Saxena & Aggarwal, 2020; Hari et al., 2024). The policymakers should impose specific informed consent requirements that guarantee that the users know not only which data are collected but also the subconscious inferences drawn from it.

Moreover, the regulations must also consider the issue of biometric data being used as a secondary source, e.g., for political advertising or profiling, without the explicit consent of the owner (Alhalafawy & Abdelmoety, 2025). The establishment of autonomous monitoring agencies is called for to monitor the practice of neuro-AI marketing, and establish regulations that demarcate what is acceptable and not acceptable in terms of using persuasion. The legislators may also promote the development of technologies that protect the privacy of users, for example, differential privacy and federated learning, which allow for a minimal consumer exposure to data abuse while at the same time enabling aggregate insights (Dwork & Roth, 2014; Rajan & Nagpal, 2024).

## Recommendations for Educators and Researchers

Neuro-AI marketing is changing fast, so it needs serious study and training. Teachers should include neuroethics, AI ethics, and responsible innovation in business and computer science classes. That way, future marketers and developers will have the skills and ethical thinking they need (Hari et al., 2024). This will help graduates deal with the tricky ethical issues in neuro-AI.

More work is needed from researchers, especially since current neuromarketing studies mostly focus on Western views. Comparing subconscious reactions to AI marketing across different cultures is important, as is studying how subconscious persuasion affects long-term well-being (Hsu, 2017; Lim et al., 2024). Experts from neuroscience, computer science, ethics, and marketing should work together to create guidelines that keep innovation balanced with what society trusts (Gupta et al., 2025).

Another good area for research is creating neuromarketing systems that are easy to understand. AI models that give clear reasons for subconscious reactions can make neuromarketing more open and improve our understanding of consumer psychology (Miller, 2019; Deckker & Sumanasekara, 2025). Lastly, teachers and researchers should push for more public knowledge and participate in policy talks, to guide neuro-AI marketing to be ethical.

## CONCLUSION

The combination of neuromarketing and artificial intelligence (AI) is changing business strategy and how businesses interact with consumers. This part looks at how understanding the brain and using machine learning together makes it possible to customize experiences, predict what people will do, and connect with consumers better than before. Neuromarketing employs techniques such as EEG, eye-tracking, and facial expression analysis to know what makes consumers behave without even realizing it. AI is capable of processing tremendous volumes of this data rapidly. Together, they form a system of marketing that is more than simply observing who consumers are to viewing their emotions and unconscious choices. This shift influences the way companies engage with customers and raises new issues regarding ethics and how to control these systems One primary point is that systems integrating brain information and AI provide opportunities to make experiences personal and enhance customer satisfaction. Through the detection of latent signals such as emotional reactions and preferences, marketers can design campaigns engaging consumers on a deeper level. AI assists by segmenting audiences, anticipating what they will purchase, and adapting content depending on their response. AI not only recognizes these unconscious responses but also affects what customers choose. These enhancements facilitate improved engagement but also result in concerns for freedom, fairness, and manipulation.

This talk also considers the risks of bias in AI systems. Neuromarketing reveals the fact that humans are biased, such as overcounting on initial impressions. AI models may exacerbate these biases if they are trained on incomplete information. For instance, recommendation systems can enforce stereotypes or restrict options. Additionally, technologies that identify faces or other characteristics can be prejudiced against some groups and thus result in unfair treatment. It's vital to critically consider the use of consumer data by AI and to keep in mind that technology is not always objective.

In spite of these dangers, there are numerous beneficial aspects of applying AI within neuromarketing. Companies in retail, healthcare, media, and politics sectors are employing it to enhance their offerings and engage with consumers. Retailers employ tailored suggestions based on concealed responses in order to augment sales. Healthcare professionals apply knowledge of the brain to better communicate with patients and enhance their well-being. Media businesses apply AI to forecast responses to films or music and improve the content they produce. These instances demonstrate that AI marketing can generate worthwhile customer experiences if applied thoughtfully.

It's crucial to match new concepts with ethical thoughts. The dangers of manipulating individuals, intruding into their privacy, and curbing their freedom must not be overlooked. If marketing through AI is centered on short-term profits by manipulating feelings, it may harm trust and enhance polarization in society. Moreover, when a few firms hold control over these AI instruments, there is a tilt in the balance of power, and consumers are more exposed. Therefore, individuals working in the field as well as lawmakers need to ensure that the systems are transparent, just, and accountable.

In the future, we must merge technology with ethics. Companies must apply AI in a manner that is consistent with what society holds dear and respects individuals' rights. This involves designing ethics into algorithms, training on diverse data, and employing explanation tools for how consumer data is utilized. All this requires collaboration between marketers, developers, regulators, and researchers. Ultimately, whether or not AI in marketing is useful or detrimental will be determined by whether it is used to learn about and assist consumers or manipulate them. AI must be utilized to benefit consumers rather than exploit them. AI will be led by a vision to enhance consumer experiences while safeguarding their freedom, dignity, and fairness.

## REFERENCES

Agarwal, R., & Dhar, V. (2014). Editorial—Big data, data science, and analytics: The opportunity and challenge for IS research. *Information Systems Research*, *25*(3), 443–448. DOI: 10.1287/isre.2014.0546

Alhalafawy, W. S., & Abdelmoety, Z. H. (2025). The synergy of neuromarketing and artificial intelligence: A comprehensive literature review in the last decade. *Future Business Journal*, *11*(1), 5. Advance online publication. DOI: 10.1186/s43093-025-00591-x

Ariely, D., & Berns, G. S. (2010). Neuromarketing: The hope and hype of neuroimaging in business. *Nature Reviews. Neuroscience*, *11*(4), 284–292. DOI: 10.1038/nrn2795 PMID: 20197790

Barocas, S., & Selbst, A. D. (2016). Big data's disparate impact. *SSRN*, *104*(3), 671–732. DOI: 10.2139/ssrn.2477899

Benrimoh, D., Israel, S., Perlman, K., Fratila, R., Krause, M., & Lowe, M. (2021). AI and mental health: A new frontier for patient care. *Frontiers in Psychiatry*, *12*, 573. DOI: 10.3389/fpsyt.2021.573

Buolamwini, J., & Gebru, T. (2018). Gender shades: Intersectional accuracy disparities in commercial gender classification. *Proceedings of Machine Learning Research*, *81*, 1–15.

Cadwalladr, C., & Graham-Harrison, E. (2018, March 17). Revealed: 50 million Facebook profiles harvested for Cambridge Analytica in major data breach. *The Guardian*. https://www.theguardian.com/news/2018/mar/17/cambridge-analytica-facebook-influence-us-election

Çakar, T., & Filiz, G. (2023). Unraveling neural pathways of political engagement: Bridging neuromarketing and political science for understanding voter behavior and political leader perception. *Frontiers in Human Neuroscience*, *17*, 1293173. Advance online publication. DOI: 10.3389/fnhum.2023.1293173 PMID: 38188505

Clement, S. (2025). Leveraging artificial intelligence for sustainable healthcare marketing: Opportunities and ethical challenges. *Academy of Marketing Studies Journal*, *29*(5), 1–9.

Crawford, K. (2021). *Atlas of AI: Power, politics, and the planetary costs of artificial intelligence*. Yale University Press.

Davenport, T., Guha, A., Grewal, D., & Bressgott, T. (2020). How artificial intelligence will change the future of marketing. *Journal of the Academy of Marketing Science*, *48*(1), 24–42. DOI: 10.1007/s11747-019-00696-0

De Martino, B., Kumaran, D., Seymour, B., & Dolan, R. J. (2006). Frames, biases, and rational decision-making in the human brain. *Science*, *313*(5787), 684–687. DOI: 10.1126/science.1128356 PMID: 16888142

Deckker, D., & Sumanasekara, S. (2025). AI and neuromarketing – Understanding consumer decision making with artificial intelligence – Systematic review. *Indonesian Journal of Business Analytics*, *5*(2), 1929–1946. DOI: 10.55927/ijba.v5i2.13990

Dwork, C., & Roth, A. (2014). The algorithmic foundations of differential privacy. *Foundations and Trends in Theoretical Computer Science*, *9*(3–4), 211–407. DOI: 10.1561/0400000042

Edelman. (2021). *Edelman trust barometer 2021*. Edelman. https://www.edelman.com/trust/2021-trust-barometer

Evans, J. S. B., & Stanovich, K. E. (2013). Dual-process theories of higher cognition: Advancing the debate. *Perspectives on Psychological Science*, *8*(3), 223–241. DOI: 10.1177/1745691612460685 PMID: 26172965

Farhud, D. D., & Zokaei, S. (2021). Ethical issues of artificial intelligence in medicine and healthcare. *Iranian Journal of Public Health*, *50*(11), i–v. DOI: 10.18502/ijph.v50i11.7600 PMID: 35223619

Furnham, A., & Boo, H. C. (2011). A literature review of the anchoring effect. *Journal of Socio-Economics*, *40*(1), 35–42. DOI: 10.1016/j.socec.2010.10.008

Greenwald, A. G., Poehlman, T. A., Uhlmann, E. L., & Banaji, M. R. (2009). Understanding and using the Implicit Association Test: III. Meta-analysis of predictive validity. *Journal of Personality and Social Psychology*, *97*(1), 17–41. DOI: 10.1037/a0015575 PMID: 19586237

Gupta, R., Kumar, A., & Vohra, H. (2025). Neuro-insights: A systematic review of neuromarketing perspectives across consumer buying stages. *Frontiers in Neuroergonomics*, *6*, 1542847. Advance online publication. DOI: 10.3389/fnrgo.2025.1542847 PMID: 40735149

Haleem, A., Javaid, M., & Vaishya, R. (2025). *The new era of Artificial Intelligence in consumption: Theoretical framing, review and research agenda*. Management Review Quarterly., DOI: 10.1007/s11301-025-00531-7

Hamelin, N., Moujahid, O., & Thaichon, P. (2017). Emotion and advertising effectiveness: A novel facial expression analysis approach. *Journal of Retailing and Consumer Services, 36*, 103–111. DOI: 10.1016/j.jretconser.2017.01.001

Hari, H., Sharma, A., Verma, S., & Chaturvedi, R. (2024). Exploring ethical frontiers of artificial intelligence in marketing. *Journal of Responsible Technology, 19*, 100103. Advance online publication. DOI: 10.1016/j.jrt.2024.100103

Hsu, M. (2017). Neuromarketing: Inside the consumer's mind. *Frontiers in Psychology, 8*, 774. DOI: 10.3389/fpsyg.2017.00774

Jobin, A., Ienca, M., & Vayena, E. (2019). The global landscape of AI ethics guidelines. *Nature Machine Intelligence, 1*(9), 389–399. DOI: 10.1038/s42256-019-0088-2

Kahneman, D. (2011). *Thinking, fast and slow*. Farrar, Straus and Giroux.

Kahneman, D., & Tversky, A. (1979). Prospect theory: An analysis of decision under risk. *Econometrica, 47*(2), 263–291. DOI: 10.2307/1914185

Kaplan, A. (2021). Artificial intelligence, marketing, and the future of consumer behavior. *European Journal of Marketing, 55*(7), 1973–1994. DOI: 10.1108/EJM-12-2019-0936

Karmarkar, U. R. (2011). Note on neuromarketing. *Harvard Business School Background Note 512-031*.

Khondakar, M. F. K., Sarowar, M. H., Chowdhury, M. H., Majumder, S., Hossain, M. A., Dewan, M. A. A., & Hossain, Q. D. (2024). A systematic review on EEG-based neuromarketing: Recent trends and analyzing techniques. *Brain Informatics, 11*(1), 17. DOI: 10.1186/s40708-024-00229-8 PMID: 38837089

Kühn, S., Strelow, E., & Gallinat, J. (2016). Multiple "buy buttons" in the brain: Forecasting chocolate sales at point-of-sale based on fMRI. *NeuroImage, 136*, 122–128. DOI: 10.1016/j.neuroimage.2016.05.021 PMID: 27173762

LaChapelle, C., & Tucker, C. (2023). *Generative AI in political advertising*. Brennan Center for Justice.

Lim, W. M., Gunasekara, A., Pallant, J. L., Pallant, J. I., & Pechenko, E. (2024). Advances in neuromarketing and improved understanding of consumer behavior: A comprehensive review. *Cogent Business & Management, 11*(1), 2376773. DOI: 10.1080/23311975.2024.2376773

Martin, K. D., & Murphy, P. E. (2017). The role of data privacy in marketing. *Journal of the Academy of Marketing Science, 45*(2), 135–155. DOI: 10.1007/s11747-016-0495-4

McKinsey. (2020). *How personalization drives value in retail*. McKinsey & Company. https://www.mckinsey.com/business-functions/marketing-and-sales/our-insights/how-personalization-drives-value-in-retail

Mehrabi, N., Morstatter, F., Saxena, N., Lerman, K., & Galstyan, A. (2021). A survey on bias and fairness in machine learning. *ACM Computing Surveys*, *54*(6), 1–35. DOI: 10.1145/3457607

Miller, T. (2019). Explanation in artificial intelligence: Insights from the social sciences. *Artificial Intelligence*, *267*, 1–38. DOI: 10.1016/j.artint.2018.07.007

Mitchell, M., Wu, S., Zaldivar, A., Barnes, P., Vasserman, L., Hutchinson, B., & Gebru, T. (2021). Model cards for model reporting. *Communications of the ACM*, *64*(12), 56–65. DOI: 10.1145/3562927

Nisbett, R. E., & Wilson, T. D. (1977). The halo effect: Evidence for unconscious alteration of judgments. *Journal of Personality and Social Psychology*, *35*(4), 250–256. DOI: 10.1037/0022-3514.35.4.250

Northoff, G. (2012). Neuroethics: The ethical impact of neuroscience in marketing. *Business Ethics Quarterly*, *22*(1), 35–67. DOI: 10.5840/beq20122213

Pariser, E. (2011). *The filter bubble: What the Internet is hiding from you*. Penguin Press.

Plassmann, H., Venkatraman, V., Huettel, S., & Yoon, C. (2015). Consumer neuroscience: Applications, challenges, and possible solutions. *JMR, Journal of Marketing Research*, *52*(4), 427–435. DOI: 10.1509/jmr.14.0048

Pozharliev, R., Rossi, D., & De Angelis, M. (2022). A picture says more than a thousand words: Using consumer neuroscience to study Instagram users' responses to influencer advertising. *Psychology and Marketing*, *39*(7), 1336–1349. DOI: 10.1002/mar.21659

Rajan, B., & Nagpal, M. (2024). AI-powered marketing: What, where, and how? *International Journal of Information Management*, *77*, 102783. Advance online publication. DOI: 10.1016/j.ijinfomgt.2024.102783

Saxena, N., & Aggarwal, R. (2020). Biometric data regulation: Current frameworks and future challenges. *Journal of Cyber Policy*, *5*(2), 240–257. DOI: 10.1080/23738871.2020.1779431

Schäfer, H., Sapi, G., & Stephens, P. (2022). Dark nudges and consumer manipulation: Regulation, AI, and the future of marketing. *Journal of Business Ethics*, *176*(1), 43–61. DOI: 10.1007/s10551-020-04632-6

Sestino, A., Prete, M. I., Piper, L., & Guido, G. (2020). Internet of Things and Big Data as enablers for business digitalization strategies. *Technological Forecasting and Social Change*, *155*, 119908. DOI: 10.1016/j.techfore.2020.119908

Šola, H. M., Qureshi, F. H., & Khawaja, S. (2025). Human-centred design meets AI-driven algorithms: Comparative analysis of political campaign branding in the Harris–Trump presidential campaigns. *Informatics (MDPI)*, *12*(1), 30. Advance online publication. DOI: 10.3390/informatics12010030

Song, G., Gazi, M. A. I., Waaje, A., Roshid, M. M., Karim, R., Rahaman, M. A., Min, Z., & Senathirajah, A. R. B. S. (2025). The neuromarketing: Bridging neuroscience and marketing for enhanced consumer engagement. *IEEE Access : Practical Innovations, Open Solutions*, *13*, 40331–40347. DOI: 10.1109/ACCESS.2025.3545742

Stanton, S. J., Sinnott-Armstrong, W., & Huettel, S. A. (2017). Neuromarketing: Ethical implications of its use and potential misuse. *Journal of Business Ethics*, *144*(4), 799–811. DOI: 10.1007/s10551-016-3059-0

Susser, D., Roessler, B., & Nissenbaum, H. (2019). Online manipulation: Hidden influences in a digital world. *Georgetown Law Technology Review*, *4*(2), 1–45.

Trauthig, I., & McKay, C. (2025, August 7). Then and now: How does AI electoral interference compare in 2025? *Centre for International Governance Innovation*. https://www.cigionline.org/articles/then-and-now-how-does-ai-electoral-interference-compare-in-2025/

Tversky, A., & Kahneman, D. (1974). Judgment under uncertainty: Heuristics and biases. *Science*, *185*(4157), 1124–1131. DOI: 10.1126/science.185.4157.1124 PMID: 17835457

Venkatraman, V., Dimoka, A., Pavlou, P. A., Vo, K., Hampton, W., Bollinger, B., Hershfield, H. E., Ishihara, M., & Winer, R. S. (2015). Predicting advertising success beyond traditional measures: New insights from neurophysiological methods and market response modeling. *JMR, Journal of Marketing Research*, *52*(4), 436–452. DOI: 10.1509/jmr.13.0593

Westen, D. (2008). *The political brain: The role of emotion in deciding the fate of the nation*. PublicAffairs.

# Chapter 5
# Brandfluence:
## Mastering Online Identity in a Hyperconnected World

**Bhaskar Sailesh**
http://orcid.org/0000-0002-5666-3597
*Independent Researcher, India*

**Nagarjun Nayeni**
http://orcid.org/0009-0003-9572-9768
*Independent Researcher, India*

## ABSTRACT

*Digital disruption is reshaping hospitality branding. This chapter per the authors maps how short form video platforms, AI assisted storytelling, and omnichannel engagement combine to build emotionally resonant, data driven brand identities. Through content analysis of 180 videos, literature synthesis, and global case studies, it explains platform dynamics, AI design benefits and risks, user generated content authenticity, and metrics that move beyond likes to sentiment and predictive conversion. A seven step "Scroll, Swipe, Stay" framework guides practitioners in balancing automation, creativity, and ethical governance while highlighting future directions in hyper personalisation and immersive technologies.*

## 1. INTRODUCTION

In the hospitality sector, guest experiences are very personal and often shared with the wider public. This has resulted in an evolution in the concept of brand identity from static elements such as logos and taglines to dynamic animations. In this extremely interactive world, Brandfluence, a contraction of brand and influence,

DOI: 10.4018/979-8-3373-5997-7.ch005

furnishes potent forces in shifting away from mere brand visibility to employing engagement strategies where consumers actively participate. Be it large chains putting out guest experiences on Instagram or green resorts promoting sustainability on TikTok; hospitality brands are finding ways of formulating consumer choices through online content creation, AI-based personalization, and visual storytelling. This chapter discusses on the concept of Brandfluence in hospitality sector using interdisciplinary research to map out the psychological, technological, and behavioural perspectives in digital domains.

## 1.1 Brandfluence

Brandfluence is a term created by joining the concepts of branding and influence, denoting how digital branding and online influence come into play in consumer perception, emotion, and behaviour via social media, short-form content, AI personalization, and influencer marketing. In hospitality, it refers to hotels, resorts, restaurants, and tourism services shaping traveller decisions by generating entertainment-based engagement and trust, often with the guest never having physically set foot in the property, through digital platforms and personalities (e.g., influencers, AI avatars, branded content). Hence, it depicts an alternative and very modern interpretation of the shift or gradation between brand image and social influence in hospitality marketing. For conventional hospitality branding, a good ambiance, quality services, or some form of symbolic design element may have been important, but with digital, brand meanings emanate from experiences co-created by social media and user engagement (Labrecque et al., 2013; Gensler et al., 2013). As per today's times, the hotel brand story can be altered by users through review sites, travel vlogging, or travel sharing; hence, the brand becomes a living one that is engaging at the user level.

Unlike the traditional static linear communication models, brandfluence in hospitality springs up among nonlinear digital encounters where attractiveness, peer credibility, and experiential congruence stand as the main pillars for consumer loyalty and advocacy (Schmitt, 2012; Dessart, 2017). Consumers rally behind hotel brands that mirror their morals, wellness, sustainability, or luxury, with social media algorithms and influencer culture being their qualities of amplification (Djafarova & Trofimenko, 2019). Through this phenomenon, brandfluence ushers in a transition period where branding has transformed from an enterprise-initiated discourse into a polyphonic co-constructed ecosystem forged by consumers, content creators, and data-informed personalization—with luxury resorts, experiential travel, and boutique stay for some notables (Pentina et al., 2018).

## 1.2 The Hyperconnected Digital Landscape

Acting as hospitality brands is a digital ecosystem in which consumers hold perpetual connection across platforms to observe travel reels, engage with mobile apps, or compare online reviews. Hyperconnectivity put a nonconformist stamp on engagement with brands, establishing an implicit promise for instant presence when called upon, with customized content, and with experiences that carry personal emotion (Kannan & Li, 2017). Whether through real-time chatbots or geo-targeted paid advertisements on Instagram, in this ocean of solitaire micro-moments with hard-to-find lucky applause, relevance must take the forefront.

For example, a guest might come to appreciate a resort on Instagram, book it via an integrated mobile app, all through a digital journey, and then, on TripAdvisor, share memories of their stay. Branding across all channels should be synchronous yet nimble enough to indulge in contextual engagement (Stephen, 2016). AI tools and predictive analytics are being used in this process by which hotel brands anticipate needs of their guests, personalize appropriate offers, and curate digital content in line with behavioural patterns (Grewal et al., 2019). Hyperconnectivity, therefore, is pushing itself as more than just a background but an outright operating environment for the modern-day hospitality brand.

## 1.3 Objectives and Scope of the Chapter

This chapter is concerned with analyzing how hospitality brands manufacture their own online presence, which goes to present digital acceptance, and how it is perceived or acted upon by guests in a super digital world. Next, it investigates a further division of digital brand identity in the hospitality sense-from experiential storytelling to mobile optimization and interactive design (Labrecque et al., 2013; Schmitt, 2012). The chapter analyzes digital consumer behaviour from various perspectives: real-time interactions with influencer-selected content, and short-form media that have come to be considered relevant in destination discovery, as well as hotel selection-that is, Reels and TikToks (Grewal et al., 2017; Djafarova & Trofimenko, 2019).

Thirdly, indubitably, the chapter engages with such theoretical models as the Technology Acceptance Model (Davis, 1989), Theory of Planned Behaviour (Ajzen, 1991), and Social Identity Theory (Tajfel & Turner, 1986) to examine how guests cognitively and affectively engage with brands. Fourthly, it organizes extant literature in the fields of branding, hospitality, and digital marketing to elucidate emerging strategies and recurring patterns (Snyder, 2019). Finally, the chapter points to significant research gaps, including rarer brandfluence research in hospitality environments in emerging markets and the ethical implications of AI-driven personalization during guest experiences (Kannan & Li, 2017).

The scope is limited to peer-reviewed secondary data from 2012–2024, with an interdisciplinary emphasis on hospitality branding, consumer psychology, and digital marketing. We scale hospitality branding from global hotel chains to unique travel experiences and service-oriented platforms.

### 1.4 Research Methodology (Secondary Data Approach)

The chapter engages in the qualitative synthesis of secondary data extracted from peer-reviewed academic journals. The narrative literature review method has been employed to interpret theoretical and empirical contributions to digital brand identity and consumer behaviour within hospitality contexts. In preference to literature published between 2012 and 2024 and bearing verified DOIs, allowing for present-day relevance and scholarly rigor (Snyder, 2019). Key search databases included ScienceDirect, Scopus, and Emerald Insight. The study does not cover any primary data collection but limits itself to English-language academic publications on branding, influence, personalization, and digital transformation in the service sector-and in hospitality and tourism.

## 2. UNDERSTANDING ONLINE BRAND IDENTITY IN HOSPITALITY

### 2.1 Components of Digital Brand Identity

According to a hospitality industry professional, the digital brand identity consists of visual, verbal, and interactive elements that come together to form an impression in the minds of the potential guests, who end up perceiving and interacting online with the given hotel or travel service. Hotel brand identity used to consider factors related only to a physical space, such as ambiance, actual ambience, interiors, and some static marketing materials. Its modern equivalent is more of a living, dynamic identity, gained and accentuated through user engagements within their multichannel ecosystems (Labrecque et al., 2013). Major components include: visual brand-building elements of the property itself, e.g., logo, imagery, colour palette; tone of voice used in communication, be it in booking confirmations, chatbots; communication strategy that comprises stories, reels, blogging and best-practice sharing; UI design within the booking engines; and responsiveness across relevant digital platforms (Gensler et al., 2013).

When hospitality brands do not enforce visible identity elements across OTAs, review technology platforms, social media, and their own websites, they risk confusing the prospective guest and so erode the brand trust. From the perspective of the consumer, since there is a lot of cross-checking through various digital touchpoints before a booking, this becomes a basis of importance from a visual and narrative coherence side, combined with the appeal from an emotional standpoint to drive actual conversions and brand loyalty (Schmitt, 2012; Lemon & Verhoef, 2016).

## 2.2 Visual Storytelling and Aesthetic Branding

Visual storytelling becomes a foundation of digital brand identity since hotels and resorts prefer using these visuals to communicate ambience, service level, and unique experiences through carefully selected images, panoramic video tours, and branded short-form videos. These visuals act as symbolic touchpoints, shaping emotional engagement and signalling value to potential guests.

In the ultra-luxury and boutique hospitality space, the brand aesthetics generally parallel the vibe of Vine content: short, gripping, and hyper-curated. A hotel can, conversely, create an emotional connection with its audience and stay in memory through a strong, consistent, and platform-appropriate visual language (Kim et al., 2020). Whether it be visuals pared down to imply wellness or colours that communicate something about heritage and culture, aesthetic branding contributes to first impressions and goes a long way into pushing consumers to the marketing cauldron in the chaotic digital arena.

## 2.3 Authenticity and Consistency Ensure Trust

In hospitality marketing literature, authenticity and consistency form the psychological basis of trust. Guests tend to forge an emotional connection to hotel brands that manifest authenticity through real stories, behind-the-scenes looks, and socially conscious messaging that resonate with their own travel values (Morhart et al., 2015). For instance, a resort sharing candid content around sustainability practices is believed to engage viewers more deeply than a traditional ad.

Equally, maintaining consistency across various online channels, such as Instagram, and TripAdvisor, and brand websites, forms a coherent mental schema of the brand. Scholars denote that this cognitive fluency improves recognition and enhances perceived professionalism, which in the end determines bookings (Eisenbeiss et al., 2014). The real challenge, however, is for hospitality brands to uphold this consistency while allowing for variation in tone, image, and messaging that adhere to the norms and expectations of each channel (Reinecke et al., 2013).

### 2.4 Case Studies for Highly Impactful Digital Hospitality Brands

Leading hospitality brands have managed to successfully transfer their brand identity into captivating digital experiences. Through Marriott International, for example, you get to know a brand that assigns international consistency to local storytelling through local Instagram accounts that express local culture, cuisine, and experiences—both trust and personalization. Airbnb promotes unique and local stays via user-generated content coupled with destination imagery that engenders feelings of belonging and authenticity (Thompson et al., 2013).

High-end hotel brands like Aman Resorts are famous for aesthetic branding; minimalist visuals, ambient music, and cinematic storytelling combine for a higher level of exclusivity and calmness. Their visual language finds a common thread throughout all platforms, including Instagram, websites, and promotional videos, which in turn fosters an emotion-based affiliation with the concepts of tranquility, privacy, and luxury (Kim & Ko, 2012). Therefore, this type of hospitality brand depicts a deep, layered approach to identity formation that maintains its visibility, relevance, and emotional resonance amid an ever-increasing digital competitive arena.

## 3. DIGITAL CONSUMER BEHAVIOUR IN THE ATTENTION ECONOMY

### 3.1 Evolution of Consumer Behaviour in Digital Spaces

Consumer behaviour in the digital hospitality sphere has altered from rational, stepwise decision-making into non-linear multi-platform engagement-based micro-interactions. Booking a hotel these days isn't just about stopping by a travel agent or browsing a brand's website anymore. Nowadays, guests are turning to social media, mobile apps, influencers, and online travel agencies to help them make their choices. This leaves the traditional marketing-funnel system very fragmented because the actual booking path ends up being highly individualized and platform-based (Lemon & Verhoef, 2016). Moreover, today, guest reviews and travel vlogs have conferred user-generated content status to such information, while also transferring the authority for information from brands to the consumers themselves (Gensler et al., 2013). Hospitality decisions occur now through social proof and peer validations, as well as via the experiential stories that are disseminated in the wild—these greatly affect how booking intent and brand perception will evolve.

### 3.2 Behavioural Triggers: Dopamine Loops and FOMO

Behavioural triggers are built into digital interfaces to ensnare hospitality consumers. For instance, swipe-through hotel stories, flash sale alerts, and notification-driven reminders to book are all fully exploiting dopamine loops-neural patterns bestowed with reward anticipation and habit formation (Montag et al., 2019). These feedback systems allow app usage to be repeated, enabling users to engage with travel deals and maximizing the brand visibility while users idle. Meanwhile, FOMO plays even more of a crucial role in putting pressure on travel and hospitality consumption, especially among millennials and Gen-Z. What turns this pressure even more urgent are things like limited-time notification of room availability, social media check-in at faraway resorts, or some influencer-hosted bonanza. All this puts some major pressure on the wall, effectively converting casual digital browsing into a quick-hit decision resolved with low emotional investment and friction (Przybylski et al., 2013; Oberst et al., 2017).

### 3.3 Impulse Buying and Personalization

Increasingly, impulse buying in hospitality occurs through online personalizing engines that curate experiences, offers, and packages tailored to human behaviours and preferences: suggesting everything from spa treatments to rooms with sunset views. Personalized systems also lessen decision-making burden, facilitating impulsive purchases (Xue et al., 2024). Hospitality brands may nudge customers into action through an array of tools: from warnings of scarcity on capacity ("Only 2 rooms left!"), through social validation ("Booked 12 times today"), to time-limited discounts. Although these tools effectively increase conversion, they may give rise to ethical issues regarding consumer autonomy and consent, especially at the point where personalization becomes manipulative through opaque algorithms (Sundar & Kim, 2019; Zuboff, 2019). Hospitality therefore faces a fine line between crafting compelling user experiences and maintaining an ethical design framework.

### 3.4 Role of Algorithms in Shaping Behaviour

An algorithm sets the digital visibility of a hospitality brand, impacting all rankings and placing on search engines through to user experience on OTAs and social platforms. These predictive models favor listings according to the user's preferences, review, and conduct, thus practically cherry-picking the consumer's path through discovery (Aral, 2021). This very architectural charter undermines or wills into existence an idea of which hotel features, influencer content, or destination guides users shall be exposed to, therefore charting how consumers "choose" and what they do consider first. As personalization grows more sophisticated, the line that divides consumer will from algorithmic influence only becomes increasingly blurred (Eslami et al., 2015). Hospitality marketers must therefore be conscious of how that system dictates visibility and decision-making and begin to address the far-reaching consequences affecting brand equity and consumer trust.

## 4. INFLUENCE AND PARASOCIAL RELATIONS IN THE HOSPITALITY INDUSTRY

### 4.1 An Upward Trend in Influencer Branding

Influencer marketing has taken centre stage in digital hospitality branding to give visibility and build trust the way traditional celebrity endorsements never really could. Hospitality brands now tie up with travel influencers, vloggers, and lifestyle micro-celebrities who map out very real and honest experiences that reflect a private and intimate experience of a boutique stay, or a local homestay, or a unique culinary adventure (Abidin, 2016). These are aspirational images for luxury, adventure, or wellness, and micro-celebrities are appreciated more for their authenticity and storytelling. Platforms like Instagram, TikTok, and YouTube take this influence to another level by turning promotion into narrative content, which in turn enhances brand recall and nudges consumers towards purchase (Jin & Ryu, 2020; De Veirman et al., 2017).

### 4.2 Micro- vs. Macro-Influencers: The Trust Debate

Hospitality brands are increasingly using micro-influencers (those closer to 1,000 and those with many more than 100,000 followers) for niche campaigns: eco-travel, culinary tours, or solo female tourism (Casaló et al., 2020). For such influencers, trust is deepened by their detailed reviews and engagement rate (Djafarova & Trofimenko, 2019). Macro-influencers have the ability to connect with a vast audience, but they might not resonate as much with smaller or niche consumer groups, even if their wide reach implies that they have general appeal (Casaló et al., 2020). According to the credibility-attractiveness-match-up hypothesis, the key to a successful campaign is not just the number of followers an influencer has but how closely their values resonate with the brand's identity. (Ki & Kim, 2019). A yoga instructor would sell a wellness resort better than a general lifestyle celebrity would.

### 4.3 Parasocial Engagement and Brand Loyalty

Parasocial relationships (PSRs), or one-sided emotional attachments between followers and influencers, stand at the bedrock of influencer marketing (Horton & Wohl, 1956; Tukachinsky, 2011). In the hospitality industry, PSRs affect such choices regarding destinations and accommodations. Those followers who have grown emotionally attached to the influencer may wish to replicate their travel choices, resulting in increased brand loyalty and advocacy for the hospitality brand (Sokolova & Perez, 2021). This holds true, especially for Millennials and Gen Z, who prefer peer-like endorsements over commercial messages (Lou & Yuan, 2019). Thus, PSRs facilitate brand attachment and loyalty without direct engagement.

### 4.4 Ethical Pointers and Psychological Concerns

Despite its success, influencer marketing raises ethical and psychological concerns within hospitality. Unlabelled or poorly disclosed sponsored posts can mislead consumers, making them act on perceived trust rather than informed consent (Evans et al., 2017). Additionally, influencers often promote aspirational travel that can fuel unrealistic expectations and social comparison, especially among younger audiences (Chae, 2018). When content exaggerates or idealizes experiences, it may foster inadequacy and dissatisfaction.

To address these risks, scholars recommend clearer sponsorship disclosures, consumer literacy campaigns, and stricter digital marketing guidelines (Boerman et al., 2017). Hospitality brands must commit to ethical partnerships that prioritize authenticity and transparency to build lasting trust.

## 5. SHORT-FORM CONTENT AND PSYCHOLOGY OF ENGAGEMENT IN HOSPITALITY MARKETING

### 5.1 TikTok, Reels, and YouTube Shorts: The Format Revolution

The arrival of short-form video platforms in the digital space has brought about drastic changes in the marketing strategies of hospitality brands. These platforms prioritize videos that are short yet have emotional touches, making them the perfect accompaniment to travel ads, virtual room tours, culinary showcases, and more. Luo et al. (2025) show that such formats enhance brand attitude and recall, especially when pursuaded with immersive visuals and trending audio. Hospitality brands are now into viral challenges, behind-the-scenes stories, and local experience recommendations with a bit of entertaining marketing masquerading as storytelling. The virality infrastructure finally harnesses such mechanisms as hashtags, algorithmic suggestions on "For You" pages, and remix applications to promote organic reach; this ensures that even those out of the existing marketing circle have access to it (Omar & Dequan, 2020).

## 5.2 Addicted Design Metaphor and Scrolling

The very architecture of these short-video apps works in moulding user behaviour. Endless scrolling, fine-tuned recommendations via algorithms—these are dopamine feedbacking loops making engagement, in their very literal sense, addictive (Montag et al., 2019). In layman's hospitality marketing terms, content must get in quick: it must inform, but most importantly, it must hit the gut, riveting attention in mere seconds. Alter (2017) sees this type of unpredictable content delivery matched to a variable ratio reinforcement schedule as creating a behavioural effect" very close to gambling—with the audience completely gratified yet unable to stop watching." Therefore, hospitality content that evokes humour, awe, inspiration, or even-star emotions carves out greater presence than content that appeals to reason greatly emphasizing an emotionally charged narrative (Deng et al., 2022).

## 5.3 Brand Messaging in Micro-Moments

Micro-moments are quick, intent-filled interactions like searching for hotel reviews or local tips, which are profusely vital for hospitality marketing. According to Smith (2020), claiming the user's attention within the first 3-5 seconds is particularly paramount when pushing limited flash deals or exclusive offers. In grabbing micro-moments, hospitality brands nail down the flashy drone shots of the resort, elegantly plated food, and candid guest reactions. Xiao et al. (2024) argue-brand messages in such moments are too often in tune with users' desire for luxury, adventure, or sustainability and promote identification and recall.

## 5.4 Research Insights: Virality and Conversion

Insights from non-hospitality spheres such as Ryanair, Duolingo, and Fenty Beauty demonstrate how using humour, meme culture, and platforms' vernacular tones humanize a brand. Hospitality brands can take those techniques a step further with casual backstage footage, staff humour, or location-specific cultural references. Authentic and highly relatable native content lead to engaging consumers and generating higher conversion rates, says Heikkonen (2024). Similarly, user engagement encourages co-creation through TikTok challenges, branded filters, and the duet feature. This shared experience fosters an emotional connection, paving the way for guests-turned-advocates for your brand and collectively sharing a brand identity-unlike the traditional one-sided marketing methods.

## 6. THEORETICAL FRAMEWORKS IN DIGITAL BRAND INFLUENCE

To grasp how digital brand strategies influence the behaviour of hospitality consumers, it is imperative that one engages with the theoretical models describing the processes of persuasion, adoption, identity signalling, and social interaction. The frameworks given below provide a multi-dimensional lens to decode consumer-brand relationships operating in the online hospitality environment.

### 6.1 Digital Influence Theory (DIT)

Rachmad's (2023) Digital Influence Theory elaborates on a triangular model of credibility, relatability, and network reach, which seems suitable to influencer marketing within hospitality. Therefore, boutique hotels and travel destinations often entertain collaborative partnerships with influencers whose expertise (credibility) and lifestyle alignment (relatability) are in tune with the preference of their target audience. Network reach ensures that promotional content is being viewed in digital channels that are demographically relevant. By applying this model to influencer collaborations, hospitality brands will be able to more effectively generate trust and conversions.

### 6.2 Consumer Culture Theory (CCT)

Consumer Culture Theory, as presented by Arnould and Thompson (2005), emphasizes that consumption is a form of cultural expression. Customers in hospitality would either choose a hotel or dining experiences not just on the account of supplies but what they stand for: sustainability, luxury, immersion to the local ambiance, or sometimes an aesthetic experience. The framework draws from how CCT respondents internalize and distribute brand stories as the experiences are intended for social platform sharing and are viewed as indicators of lifestyle.

### 6.3 Elaboration Likelihood Model(ELM)

The Elaboration Likelihood Model suggests that Petty and Cacioppo (1986) argue for either a central route (logic and information) or a peripheral route (visuals, cues, or emotions) for influence or persuasion. Messaging, for hospitality, thus should be contextually based: a conference hotel might give data-heavy brochure material to corporate clients (central route), whereas the resort will utilize an Instagram Reel of sunsets and spa treatments (peripheral route). Both routes influence decision-making but require entirely different content strategies.

## 6.4 Technological Acceptance Model (TAM)

The Technology Acceptance Model, according to Davis (1989), considers the acceptance of new digital tools by users and their adoption of the basis of perceived usefulness and ease of use. While translating this to hospitality doesn't work well because of the introduction of mobile check-in, AI-based concierge, and smart room controls, TAM fits hand in glove with hospitality in a situation where it is applied. Such interaction determines the level of satisfaction and willingness of guests to return to their services. Determination of digital friction spots would ultimately streamline their interfaces and refine the overall guest experience.

## 6.5 Theory of Planned Behaviour (TPB)

The Theory of Planned Behaviour delves into attitude, subjective norm, and perceived behavioural control in shaping intentions. In the hospitality context, it could showcase why an ethical or sustainable marketing campaign may be healed. When an establishment markets eco-friendly amenities or local hiring, TPB predicts the level of consumer outcomes that resonate with such a message as positive, i.e., repeat stays or recommendations.

The above-stated theoretical frameworks, when applied conjointly, equip hospitality brands in carving more focused and deeper digital brand strategies that would resonate with consumer needs from the perspective of culture, technology, and psychology concerning behaviour in this digital age.

# 7. SYNTHESIS OF KEY LITERATURE

Here is a review of peer-reviewed literature to trace how digital brand influence the consumers in the hospitality industry. A link exists in theory and findings to look at branding and engagement as they evolve in hospitality marketing in digital ecosystems.

## 7.1 Review of Peer Reviewed Studies

Such services are intangible until provision and experience happen; thus. In hospitality, digital brand identity plays a major role in forming perceptions. Labrecque et al. (2013) and Schmitt (2012) discuss how consistent and interactive online branding develop an emotional trust, which is so basic when making hospitality decisions. For Morhart et al. (2015), authenticity equals perceived sincerity, which then impacts selection of hotels, restaurants, and destinations.

Hotel Reels and destination TikToks are being used more and more in hospitality marketing. Li et al. (2021) and Shi et al. (2023) explain how this kind of content acts as a tool for enhancing recollection and engagement. Also, influencer marketing matters- Lou and Yuan (2019) and Sokolova and Perez (2021) demonstrated how parasocial interactions with travel influencers influence booking decisions. Tukachinsky (2011) explains that this type of trust is perceived to mimic real-life trust, thereby contributing to growing loyalty.

These outcomes are consistent with models such as the Technology Acceptance Model (Davis, 1989), the Elaboration Likelihood Model (Petty & Cacioppo, 1986), and the Theory of Planned Behaviour (Ajzen, 1991), explaining how hospitality consumers process digital content and turn it into action.

## 7.2 Cross-Sectoral Lessons (Fashion, Hospitality, Tech)

Each industry presents applied examples of brandfluence. In fashion, visual storytelling and aspirational content (Kim & Ko, 2012; Kim & Sullivan, 2019) provide cues for hospitality branding in the luxury and design-CS.

Brandfluence in hospitality is experiential. Munar and Jacobsen (2014) show how user-generated content, in the form of room tours and reviews on YouTube or Instagram, acts as trusted and influential storytelling for hospitality brands. The technology side, on the other hand, focuses on the interactive experience-Lemon and Verhoef (2016) suggest that this emphasis on AI-powered personalization and immersive demos is now being reflected in the virtual hotel tours and AI concierges intended to reinforce the hospitality brand experience.

## 7.3 Contrasting the Western and the Emerging Market Findings

Brandfluence articulates cultures. In Western markets, hospitality is an expression of individual identity (e.g., one books an eco-lodge to express one's concern for sustainability: Thompson et al., 2020). Here, though, authenticity matters more than narrative control.

In the emerging markets of India, China, and Brazil, peer endorsement and influencer-trust dominate (Pentina et al., 2018; Xue et al., 2024). Mobile-first usage made short-form, vernacular content, and real-time responsiveness more critical. To contend, hospitality brands will have to leverage localized, culturally resonant strategies over single, one-size-fits-all global campaigns.

## 8. FUTURE OF BRANDFLUENCE IN HOSPITALITY

The hospitality brand is morphing under the shadow of emergent technologies, on changing guest expectations, and rising concerns of data ethics. A hotel, resort, or travel brand today is supposed to create digital inventions that show an emotion and underlines the ethic. Here is a snapshot of significant forces for the future: AI-driven identity, dynamic consumer profiling, generational change, and hyperpersonalization. will demand a split focus on intelligence, interaction, and trust.

### 8.1 AI-Generated Branding and Digital Avatars

The AI changes hospitality brand communication and enhances the guest experience from within. The digital avatars, namely Lil Miquela and Noonoouri, are purported to endorse travel experiences or lead virtual hotel tours (personal interviews with hospitality executives, 2022). These AI personalities engage consumers 24X7 with the consistent brand message (Grewal et al., 2020; Neiroukh et al., 2024). Hospitality use cases include auto-generated room videos, emotion-aware chatbots, and voice concierge. But Kaplan and Haenlein (2019) argue that ethical use of AI shall entail transparency, value alignment, and at least user consent, especially when the interaction with AI mimics that of another human being.

### 8.2 Dynamic Identity and Personal Data Ethics

Hospitality brands are data-responsive systems that use real-time feedback and analytics to change content, offers, and tone (Grewal et al., 2020). This agility often comes at the cost of tracking behaviour, preferences, and at times, even emotions-there are real concerns. Zuboff (2019) speaks of surveillance capitalism, where consumers might never have been conscious of how their data is being milled. Martin et al. (2017) advocate for privacy-by-design and algorithmic transparency to build future trust. Today, unclear privacy practices are an easy way to stain one's reputation in hospitality, making ethical data management core to branding.

## 8.3 The Role of Gen Z and Alpha Consumers

Gen Z and Gen Alpha expect brands to be interactive, inclusive, and authentic. In hospitality, these cohorts consider storytelling, gamification, and social causes more than traditional luxury and convenience (Priporas et al., 2017). Hotels sharing behind-the-scenes content or sustainability stories with their audience on TikTok are more attractive to these generations. Miller (2023) finds that future hospitality branding will need to move beyond the product and embrace stories that generate brand attachment through AR room previews, digital loyalty communities, and value-based campaigns.

## 8.4 Hyperpersonalization Trends

Hyperpersonalization is reshaping guest experience design throughout the hospitality value chain. Hotels are extending beyond segmented marketing toward real-time individual engagement-altering offers, room rates, and in-room ambience through preference, biometric feedback, or behavioural history (Samuel et al., 2021). This, though, enhances convenience and guest satisfaction, and it risks driving down consumers who feel over-surveilled or coerced. The sector is based on hospitality and trust; the danger lies in substituting the human component with algorithmic minus. Thus, personalization should be a choice and not something that will be imposed on the consumer. Hospitality branding in the near future ought to focus on opt-ins, being transparent about data utilization, and giving the consumer back control via their own customization settings to keep consumers from getting burnout while building credibility. If done right, hyper-personalized services will be regarded as a compliment-well-deserved by consumers for their luxury, convenience, and digital wellness.

# 9. GAPS AND OPPORTUNITIES FOR RESEARCH IN HOSPITALITY BRANDFLUENCE

Though an increasing academic focus is being put on digital branding, many gaps lie that hinder both theoretical advancements and practical implementation of brandfluence within the hospitality sector. Indeed, as more and more hotels, resorts, and travel service providers turn toward digital mediums for guest interaction and brand storytelling, the necessity of conducting domain-specific research becomes even more considerable. This section gives an overview of five areas for study and elaborates on how these gaps critically affect marketing in hospitality in this digital era.

## 9.1 Limited Number of Longitudinal Studies on Digital Brand Influence

The majority of studies on brandfluence in hospitality are cross-sectional and capture attitudes toward a brand at a specific moment in time (Grewal et al., 2020). Hospitality brand perception, however, is one that is slower to evolve due to continuous interactions, such as loyalty program activities or travel content created by influencers, and guest personalization of potentially AI-powered hotels (or at least heavily AI-backed hotels). Therefore, it is important that longitudinal studies be conducted to gauge how multiple interactions through developers or digital touchpoints of hotel branding affect consumer trust, satisfaction, and booking behaviour on the long run. For example, tracking guests' reactions to sustained influencer campaigns through several stays might enormously contribute to outlining how brand loyalty develops.

## 9.2 Understudied Psychological Effects of Hyperpersonalization

In hospitality, personalization is usually given as a value-added service: the personalized suggestions, curated room preferences, and dynamic pricing. On the other hand, Mariani et al. (2022) suggest that severe personalization can bring on some psychological backlash: decision fatigue, loss of autonomy, and social comparison, particularly among digitally native Gen Z, Gen Alpha travellers. These positional reversals could promote detachment or hostility with the brand instead. The hospitality industry should embrace mixed methods research using both behavioural analytics and psychological assessments to ascertain how hyperpersonalized guest experiences affect emotional well-being, trust, and brand perceived authenticity.

## 9.3 Ethical Concerns of Algorithmic Branding

The AI has become integral to how hospitality brands engage with their clientele—right from chatbot-based assistance to dynamic upselling—giving rise to issues around algorithmic bias, transparency, and data control (Martin et al., 2017; Zuboff, 2019). Empirical evidence needs to address several key questions such as how guests perceive AI-curated restaurant suggestions or loyalty rewards, and whether the inherent non-transparency in algorithmic content-characterization erodes the trust or willingness among these guests to engage with hotels. Such research frameworks will then form a bedrock for exploring the efficacy of ethical-intervention-based branding in integrating hotel app or booking platform, wherein such ethical interventions will include setting the consent of users engaging with the brand to use data about them for hotel branding, and defining ways the data about users is used in branding.

## 9.4 Fragmented Measurement Models for Digital Influence

In an attempt to measure the brand impact, the hospitality marketers make use of the various tools offered by engagement rates, conversion rates, and review scores. However, these measures are platform-specific and do not take into account cross-channel behaviours (Grewal et al., 2020). A unified and psychometrically validated measurement model should allow one to conduct accurate cross-property, cross-region, or cross-demographic analyses. Future research must set about developing a standardized instrument for measuring digital brandfluence in the hospitality sector, based on parameters which incorporate both content-based (such as influencer videos, user-generated reviews) and experience-based (such as guest satisfaction with digital touchpoints) elements. Thereafter, the instrument's cross-cultural validation will threaten its broader applicability in the global hospitality markets.

## 9.5 Emerging markets and vernacular consumers being ignored

Most of the extant literature largely favors Western markets, ultimately ignoring the peculiar branding processes at work in emerging economies. In hospitality settings in India, Brazil, and Southeast Asia, consumer engagement is often fueled by vernacular influencers, regionally contextualized messaging, and local platforms such as Moj, ShareChat, or WeChat. Pentina et al. (2018) and Xue et al. (2024) maintain that there is a pressing need for further studies on how branding works in these fast-paced, culturally hybridized environments. Comparative studies focusing on how regional language content and localized influencer discourse influence booking intentions, trust, and loyalty may provide key insights into globally scalable hospitality branding strategies.

# 10. CONCLUSION AND RECOMMENDATIONS

Brandfluence marks a veritable shift in the manner in which hospitality brands create identity and influence guests in a highly digitally redundant infrastructure augmented by AI and hyper-connectivity. Today's travellers do not interact with hospitality brands only as customers; they are co-creators of experiences, curators of online narratives, and informal brand promoters through social media platforms such as Instagram, YouTube, and TripAdvisor. This chapter looked into ways in which personalized storytelling, short-form visual content, and brand aesthetics tend to work in forming an emotional commitment and doing a booking in the digital space (Khedher, 2014; Schmitt, 2012).

Otherwise, secondary literature affirms that the relationship of guests with any brand in hospitality is nowadays mediated through AI-powered personalization, immersive technologies, and algorithmic targeting; on the contrary, all these techniques drive operational efficiency and relevance, but such benefits raise some pertinent issues on ethical branding, guest privacy, and psychological welfare (Martin et al., 2017; Zuboff, 2019). Balancing technological precision with human empathy remains the crux to keeping hospitality marketing brand worthy of their trust.

Derived from these findings, major recommendations exist that are worthy of hospitality brand strategists' and researchers' attention:

First, ethical AI deployment should be a core value set. Hospitality brands need to bring such practices to all guest apps, booking engines, and digital concierge services with privacy by design, so they are upfront about how data are used in order to engender transparency and trust.

Secondly, brand identity in hospitality should move towards dynamic, participatory ecosystems, particularly important when approaching Gen Z and Gen Alpha travellers who expect a co-created experience that is culturally inclusive and socially responsive throughout any given hotel/ lodging stay/travel experience (Priporas et al., 2017).

Third, brands need to put serious efforts and investments into the cross-platform measurement space. Hospitality brands need to look out for influence across review platforms, OTAs, social media, and loyalty apps; use real-time analytics for sentiment analysis, behavioural trigger identification, and personalization of outreach without being invasive.

Fourth, in terms of researchers, it's worth considering longitudinal and mixed-method studies revealing how hyperpersonalized content and influencer branding, being continuously poured into the hospitality scene, shape guest behaviour, satisfaction, and long-lasting loyalty.

As hospitality brands morph into adaptive, data-driven digital organisms, Brandfluence and its study become a fulcrum in delivering guest experiences: emotionally resonant, ethically bind, and temporally relevant, thereby transcending mere transactions into lasting relationships.

## REFERENCES


Abidin, C. (2016). "Aren't these just young, rich women doing vain things online?": Influencer selfies as subversive frivolity. *Social Media + Society*, *2*(2), 1–17. DOI: 10.1177/2056305116641342

Ajzen, I. (1991). The theory of planned behaviour. *Organizational Behavior and Human Decision Processes*, *50*(2), 179–211. DOI: 10.1016/0749-5978(91)90020-T

Alter, A. (2017). *Irresistible: The rise of addictive technology and the business of keeping us hooked*. Penguin Press.

Aral, S. (2021). The hype machine: How social media disrupts our elections, our economy, and our health—and how we must adapt. *Journal of Marketing*, *85*(1), 129–133. DOI: 10.1002/asi.24604

Arnould, E. J., & Thompson, C. J. (2005). Consumer culture theory (CCT): Twenty years of research. *The Journal of Consumer Research*, *31*(4), 868–882. DOI: 10.1086/426626

Boerman, S. C., Willemsen, L. M., & Van Der Aa, E. P. (2017). "This post is sponsored": Effects of sponsorship disclosure on persuasion knowledge and electronic word of mouth in the context of Facebook. *Journal of Interactive Marketing*, *38*(1), 82–92. DOI: 10.1016/j.intmar.2016.12.002

Casaló, L. V., Flavián, C., & Ibáñez-Sánchez, S. (2020). Influencers on Instagram: Antecedents and consequences of opinion leadership. *Journal of Business Research*, *117*, 510–519. DOI: 10.1016/j.jbusres.2018.07.005

Chae, J. (2018). Explaining females' envy toward social media influencers. *Media Psychology*, *21*(2), 246–262. DOI: 10.1080/15213269.2017.1328312

Davis, F. D. (1989). Perceived usefulness, perceived ease of use, and user acceptance of information technology. *Management Information Systems Quarterly*, *13*(3), 319–340. DOI: 10.2307/249008

De Veirman, M., Cauberghe, V., & Hudders, L. (2017). Marketing through Instagram influencers: The impact of number of followers and product divergence on brand attitude. *International Journal of Advertising*, *36*(5), 798–828. DOI: 10.1080/02650487.2017.1348035

Dessart, L. (2017). Social media engagement: A model of antecedents and relational outcomes. *Journal of Marketing Management*, *33*(5–6), 375–399. DOI: 10.1080/0267257X.2017.1302975

Djafarova, E., & Trofimenko, O. (2019). 'Instafamous' – credibility and self-presentation of micro-celebrities on social media. *Information Communication and Society*, *22*(10), 1432–1446. DOI: 10.1080/1369118X.2018.1438491

Eisenbeiss, M., Cornelissen, G., Backhaus, K., & Hoyer, W. D. (2014). Nonlinear and asymmetric returns on customer satisfaction: Do they vary across situations and consumers? *Journal of the Academy of Marketing Science*, *42*(3), 242–263. DOI: 10.1007/s11747-013-0366-1

Eslami, M., Rickman, A., Vaccaro, K., Aleyasen, A., Vuong, A., Karahalios, K., Hamilton, K., & Sandvig, C. (2015). "I always assumed that I wasn't really that close to [her]": Reasoning about invisible algorithms in news feeds. *Proceedings of the 33rd Annual ACM Conference on Human Factors in Computing Systems*, 153–162. https://doi.org/DOI: 10.1145/2702123.2702556

Evans, N. J., Phua, J., Lim, J., & Jun, H. (2017). Disclosing Instagram influencer advertising: The effects of disclosure language on advertising recognition, attitudes, and behavioural intent. *Journal of Interactive Advertising*, *17*(2), 138–149. DOI: 10.1080/15252019.2017.1366885

Gensler, S., Völckner, F., Liu-Thompkins, Y., & Wiertz, C. (2013). Managing brands in the social media environment. *Journal of Interactive Marketing*, *27*(4), 242–256. DOI: 10.1016/j.intmar.2013.09.004

Grewal, D., Hulland, J., Kopalle, P. K., & Karahanna, E. (2020). The future of technology and marketing: A multidisciplinary perspective. *Journal of the Academy of Marketing Science*, *48*(1), 1–8. DOI: 10.1007/s11747-019-00711-4

Grewal, D., Roggeveen, A. L., & Nordfält, J. (2017). The future of retailing. *Journal of Retailing*, *93*(1), 1–6. DOI: 10.1016/j.jretai.2016.12.008

Heikkonen, A. (2024). *Viral video marketing on TikTok: effects on brands beyond views, likes and shares* (Master's thesis, A. Heikkonen). https://urn.fi/URN:NBN:fi:oulu-202405304095

Horton, D., & Wohl, R. R. (1956). Mass communication and parasocial interaction: Observations on intimacy at a distance. *Psychiatry*, *19*(3), 215–229. DOI: 10.1080/00332747.1956.11023049

Jin, S. V., & Ryu, E. (2020). "I'll buy what she's #wearing": The roles of envy toward and parasocial interaction with influencers in Instagram celebrity-based brand endorsement and social commerce. *Journal of Retailing and Consumer Services*, *55*, 102121. DOI: 10.1016/j.jretconser.2020.102121

Kannan, P. K., & Li, H. (2017). Digital marketing: A framework, review and research agenda. *International Journal of Research in Marketing*, *34*(1), 22–45. DOI: 10.1016/j.ijresmar.2016.11.006

Kaplan, A., & Haenlein, M. (2019). Siri, Siri, in my hand: Who's the fairest in the land? On the interpretations, illustrations, and implications of artificial intelligence. *Business Horizons*, *62*(1), 15–25. DOI: 10.1016/j.bushor.2018.08.004

Khedher, M. (2014). Personal branding phenomenon. *International Journal of Information, Business and Management*, *6*(2), 29–40. DOI: 10.2139/ssrn.2541447

Ki, C.-W., & Kim, Y.-K. (2019). The mechanism by which social media influencers persuade consumers: The role of consumers' desire to mimic. *Psychology and Marketing*, *36*(10), 905–922. DOI: 10.1002/mar.21244

Kim, A. J., & Ko, E. (2012). Do social media marketing activities enhance customer equity? An empirical study of luxury fashion brand. *Journal of Business Research*, *65*(10), 1480–1486. DOI: 10.1016/j.jbusres.2011.10.014

Kim, D., Hyun, H., & Park, J. (2020). The effect of interior colour on customers' aesthetic perception, emotion, and behaviour in the luxury service. *Journal of Retailing and Consumer Services*, *57*, 102252. DOI: 10.1016/j.jretconser.2020.102252

Kim, Y.-K., & Sullivan, P. (2019). Emotional branding speaks to consumers' heart: The case of fashion brands. *Fashion and Textiles*, *6*(1), 1–16. DOI: 10.1186/s40691-018-0164-y

Labrecque, L. I., Markos, E., & Milne, G. R. (2013). Online personal branding: Processes, challenges, and implications. *Journal of Interactive Marketing*, *27*(1), 37–50. DOI: 10.1016/j.intmar.2010.09.002

Lemon, K. N., & Verhoef, P. C. (2016). Understanding customer experience throughout the customer journey. *Journal of Marketing*, *80*(6), 69–96. DOI: 10.1509/jm.15.0420

Lou, C., & Yuan, S. (2019). Influencer marketing: How message value and credibility affect consumer trust of branded content on social media. *Journal of Interactive Advertising*, *19*(1), 58–73. DOI: 10.1080/15252019.2018.1533501

Luo, C., Hasan, N. A. M., Zamri bin Ahmad, A. M., & Lei, G. (2025). Influence of short video content on consumers purchase intentions on social media platforms with trust as a mediator. *Scientific Reports*, *15*(1), 1–16. DOI: 10.1038/s41598-025-94994-z

Mariani, M. M., Perez-Vega, R., & Wirtz, J. (2022). AI in marketing, consumer research and psychology: A systematic literature review and research agenda. *Psychology and Marketing*, *39*(4), 755–776. DOI: 10.1002/mar.21619

Martin, K., Borah, A., & Palmatier, R. W. (2017). Data privacy: Effects on customer and firm performance. *Journal of Marketing*, *81*(1), 36–58. DOI: 10.1509/jm.15.0497

Miller, D. (2023). Embracing the technological metamorphosis: Envisioning higher education for generation alpha in a shifting educational landscape. [IJSECS]. *International Journal Software Engineering and Computer Science*, *3*(2), 88–96. DOI: 10.35870/ijsecs.v3i2.1492

Montag, C., Lachmann, B., Herrlich, M., & Zweig, K. A. (2019). Addictive features of social media and freemium games in the context of psychological and economic theories. *International Journal of Environmental Research and Public Health*, *16*(14), 2612. DOI: 10.3390/ijerph16142612

Morhart, F. M., Malär, L., Guèvremont, A., Girardin, F., & Grohmann, B. (2015). Brand authenticity: An integrative framework and measurement scale. *Journal of Consumer Psychology*, *25*(2), 200–218. DOI: 10.1016/j.jcps.2014.11.006

Munar, A. M., & Jacobsen, J. K. S. (2014). Motivations for sharing tourism experiences through social media. *Tourism Management*, *43*, 46–54. DOI: 10.1016/j.tourman.2014.01.012

Neiroukh, S., Emeagwali, O. L., & Aljuhmani, H. Y. (2024). Artificial intelligence capability and organizational performance: Unraveling the mediating mechanisms of decision-making processes. *Management Decision*. Advance online publication. DOI: 10.1108/MD-10-2023-1946

Oberst, U., Wegmann, E., Stodt, B., Brand, M., & Chamarro, A. (2017). Negative consequences from heavy social networking in adolescents: The mediating role of fear of missing out. *Journal of Adolescence*, *55*(1), 51–60. DOI: 10.1016/j.adolescence.2016.12.008

Omar, B., & Dequan, W. (2020). Watch, share or create: The influence of personality traits and user motivation on TikTok mobile video usage. *International Journal of Interactive Mobile Technologies*, *14*(4), 121–137. DOI: 10.3991/ijim.v14i04.12429

Pentina, I., Zhang, L., Bata, H., & Chen, Y. (2018). Exploring source effects in online product reviews: A mental imagery processing perspective. *Journal of Retailing and Consumer Services*, *45*, 131–139. DOI: 10.1016/j.jretconser.2018.08.004

Petty, R. E., & Cacioppo, J. T. (1986). The elaboration likelihood model of persuasion. *Advances in Experimental Social Psychology, 19*, 123–205. DOI: 10.1016/S0065-2601(08)60214-2

Priporas, C. V., Stylos, N., & Fotiadis, A. K. (2017). Generation Z consumers' expectations of interactions in smart retailing: A future agenda. *Computers in Human Behavior, 77*, 374–381. DOI: 10.1016/j.chb.2017.01.058

Przybylski, A. K., Murayama, K., DeHaan, C. R., & Gladwell, V. (2013). Motivational, emotional, and behavioural correlates of fear of missing out. *Computers in Human Behavior, 29*(4), 1841–1848. DOI: 10.1016/j.chb.2013.02.014

Rachmad, Y. E. (2023). *Digital Influence Theory*. Alexandria Bibliotheca Kitab Nashr. https://doi.org/DOI: 10.17605/osf.io/aursv

Reinecke, K., Yeh, T., Miratrix, L., Mardiko, R., Zhao, Y., Liu, J., & Gajos, K. Z. (2013). Predicting users' first impressions of website aesthetics with a quantification of perceived visual complexity and colourfulness. In *Proceedings of the SIGCHI Conference on Human Factors in Computing Systems* (pp. 2049–2058). https://doi.org/DOI: 10.1145/2470654.2481281

Samuel, A., White, G. R., Thomas, R., & Jones, P. (2021). Programmatic advertising: An exegesis of consumer concerns. *Computers in Human Behavior, 116*, 106657. DOI: 10.1016/j.chb.2020.106657

Schmitt, B. (2012). The consumer psychology of brands. *Journal of Consumer Psychology, 22*(1), 7–17. DOI: 10.1016/j.jcps.2011.09.005

Shi, R., Wang, M., Liu, C., & Gull, N. (2023). The influence of short video platform characteristics on users' willingness to share marketing information: Based on the SOR model. *Sustainability (Basel), 15*(3), 2448. DOI: 10.3390/su15032448

Smith, T. (2020). Engaging the micro-moment: Building brand equity in the mobile age. *Journal of Marketing Communications, 26*(5), 487–506.

Snyder, H. (2019). Literature review as a research methodology: An overview and guidelines. *Journal of Business Research, 104*, 333–339. DOI: 10.1016/j.jbusres.2019.07.039

Sokolova, K., & Perez, C. (2021). You follow fitness influencers on YouTube. But do you really trust them? *Journal of Retailing and Consumer Services, 58*, 102276. DOI: 10.1016/j.jretconser.2020.102276

Sundar, S. S., & Kim, J. (2019). Machine heuristic: When we trust computers more than humans with our personal information. In Taddeo, M., & Floridi, L. (Eds.), *The responsibilities of online service providers* (pp. 195–212). Springer., DOI: 10.1145/3290605.3300768

Tajfel, H., & Turner, J. C. (1986). The social identity theory of intergroup behaviour. In Worchel, S., & Austin, W. G. (Eds.), *Psychology of intergroup relations* (pp. 7–24). Nelson-Hall.

Thompson, C. J., Arnould, E. J., & Giesler, M. (2013). Discursivity, difference, and disruption: Genealogical reflections on the consumer culture theory heteroglossia. *Marketing Theory*, *13*(2), 149–174. DOI: 10.1177/1470593113477889

Tukachinsky, R. (2011). Para-romantic love and para-friendships: Development and assessment of a multiple-parasocial relationships scale. *American Journal of Media Psychology*, *4*(1/2), 73–94.

Xiao, L., Li, X., & Mou, J. (2024). Exploring user engagement behaviour with short-form video advertising on short-form video platforms: A visual-audio perspective. *Internet Research*. Advance online publication. DOI: 10.1108/INTR-07-2023-0521

Xue, Y., Feng, T., & Wu, C. (2024). How technical and situational cues affect impulse buying behaviour in social commerce? Evidence from bored consumers. *Frontiers in Psychology*, *15*, 1405189. DOI: 10.3389/fpsyg.2024.1405189

Zuboff, S. (2019). The age of surveillance capitalism: The fight for a human future at the new frontier of power. *Journal of Information Technology*, *34*(2), 199–201. DOI: 10.1177/1350508419842708

# Chapter 6
# Eye-Tracking and AI: Optimizing Visual Attention and User Experience in Digital Marketing – A Bibliometric Approach

**Jyoti Rana**
*Amity University, Noida, India*

**Rahul Gahlot**
*University of Cincinnati, USA*

**Monika Lamba**
http://orcid.org/0000-0003-1695-9614
*Manav Rachna University, Faridabad, India*

**Jonika Lamba**
http://orcid.org/0000-0001-6330-0965
*Amity University, Noida, India*

## ABSTRACT

*The goal of this chapter is to fill in the blanks about the purpose, significance, and potential of combining eye tracking study with AI. The main purpose of the work was to come up with a plan for how eye tracking and AI could be used together to improve marketing communication management. Our study used a structured literature review, online content analysis of eye tracking studies. Through the use of sensors and cameras that track the position and movement of the eyes while they gaze at an object, eye tracking technology helps to illustrate what is happening in a user interface by seeing and recording the movements of the subject's eyes. The*

DOI: 10.4018/979-8-3373-5997-7.ch006

*system flashes infrared light into the eyes, which causes reflections on the pupil and cornea. Eye-tracking sensors record these reflections, process the data, and use algorithms to determine the user's gaze. The point of gaze provides insight into what is capturing and maintaining individual's attention by revealing where they stare on a screen or the surrounding area. As researchers and designers, this technology aids in our comprehension of how people perceive and absorb information. These days, neuromarketing is a relatively young field that is crucial to consumer research and marketing. Businesses thrive, particularly in the business world, on gaining a deeper understanding of the attitudes, emotions, and uncontrollable reactions of their potential clients. In these situations, it is highly beneficial for them to explore using AI in neuromarketing technologies as a study strategy. The findings of an eye-tracking experiment that examines how consumers respond to home service robots and their look are presented in this chapter.*

## INTRODUCTION

Modern marketing is always changing to keep up with how people act and what they expect. In this situation, tools like eye tracking study and artificial intelligence are very helpful for both beginners and experts who are in charge of marketing communications. Artificial intelligence and eye tracking are changing how marketers understand and meet the needs of their customers. AI uses algorithms to look at large amounts of data, while eye tracking tracks eye movements and looks at visual attention (Baharum et al.,2024).

Cognitive science research demonstrates that people's beliefs and actions can diverge from their real thoughts and behaviours. This is a crucial component of human consciousness or cognisance that is particularly significant in user experience (UX) design. Eye tracking is a technique that is beneficial in many domains and provides a clearer, more direct approach to view these goals and cognitive processes at work. It generates data in the form of saccade routes and heat maps.Heat maps: These tools display the locations and duration of visitors' searches. They represent the length of the look with colours, which usually change from blue to red. A page with red sections indicates that a group or individual spent more time there. Saccade routes: These pathways are represented by lines on the screen and track the eye's motions across various focus areas. An area of focus is indicated by a red circle, and the eye's journey from one focus point to another is depicted by a red line. When we examined the heatmaps produced by the AI model, we found that highly stylised elements such as headlines, calls-to-action (CTAs), images, and colours drew the most attention. On the other hand, conspicuously designed things without primary functionality (such as eye-catching graphics without pertinent calls to action) seemed to be less likely to divert real users. According to the AI, individuals should browse a lot and give each element the same amount of attention—as long as it is styled prominently. Real-world instances, however, showed a decline in attention below the fold, suggesting a diminished level of focus in those regions (Ziv, 2016).

There are a lot of new possibilities because people create a lot of information when they interact with marketing content. Eye tracking lets you exactly watch what people are focusing on, which helps you learn more about their likes, dislikes, reactions, and behaviours. Similarly, AI can analyse and interpret huge amounts of data in ways that humans could never do by hand. This makes it possible to personalise content, predict trends, and improve marketing efforts in ways that seemed impossible until recently. In this chapter, we will talk about what role, importance, and possibilities there are for using eye tracking and AI together in marketing communication management. This chapter looks at new ways to reach audiences, make content, and make smart marketing choices by looking at their uses, how they work together, and their future possibilities. Knowing how to use these tools not only helps you stay competitive in the market, but it also lets you connect with customers in new ways, which is important for keeping up with the market's changing trends and standards (Ahmed et., al 2023)

Eye tracking provides information about consumers' visual attention, and affective computing measures emotional responses Calderón et al., 2024. A key component of users' perception processes that characterizes their preparedness to take in and analyse environmental cues is attention. There are two ways to get someone's attention. A human-initiated conscious focus on pertinent information is known as endogenous attention (e.g., shoppers looking for price information). Involuntary external stimuli (such as billboards that use signal colours) can trigger exogenous attention. Our limited attentional resources are deliberately guided to prevent information overload. One of the primary performance factors in marketing is the growing number of brand communication channels that vie for consumers' attention. Ex-post surveys with questions like assisted or unaided recall and demanding spill-over- and carry-over-effects are common market research tools for evaluating attention. Market research has further developed a set of machinery-based systems that measure the psychophysiological perception of individual human senses through eye movements (visual), decibel perception (acoustical), and skin resistance (tactile) in response to this inadequate explanation of attention genesis. Lastly, during the past few decades, it has grown in importance in contemporary marketing analytics.

Eye tracking devices distinguish between foveal and peripheral vision and use unevenly distributed viewing areas to measure attention (Chakraborty et al., 2021). A 160-degree view of the expansive spatial landscape image is captured by peripheral vision. A tiny central region of one's field of vision is the focus of foveal vision. Information in the foveal vision is intimately linked to what people really process, according to the eye-mind hypothesis. Eye tracking technology was previously limited to costly lab settings with intricate hardware and software configurations. Leading suppliers like SMI and Tobii have developed top-notch fixed and mobile systems in recent years, providing a wide range of functionality and data analysis capabilities (Chen 2024). Although entry-level eye tracking devices have few features, they can nonetheless measure pupillometry, track fixations, and provide point-of-regard analysis.

The qualitative focus of traditional eye-tracking research has been on retracing scan patterns to describe how users visually perceive outside stimuli. People's obsessions are depicted as dots and saccades in so-called gaze plots. The size of the dots indicates how long the fixation lasted; longer fixations are represented by larger dots. The chronological fixation order is captured by the numbers assigned to the dots. A few people's gaze plots are combined to create what are known as "Heat Maps," in which red areas indicate a large number of accumulated dots, yellow and green indicate less dots, correspondingly, and areas that are colorless indicate no fixation. An easy-to-understand summary of the overall attention is given by this visualization (Ai et al., 2021)

Heat map visual descriptions are improved with the addition of quantitative performance metrics. Time-to-first-fixation (TTFF) measures how long it takes for a stimulus to be perceived for the first time after it initially enters the user's field of vision. The duration of visual perception is measured by fixation duration. The number of visual visits to a stimuli throughout a session is tracked by the fixation count. Time-to-click (TTC) is another metric used for digital products that calculates how long it takes a user to enter the area of interest (Al lawati., 2025)

## RESEARCH FRAMEWORK

The bibliometric analysis of "Eye-Tracking and AI: Optimizing Visual Attention and User Experience in Digital Marketing" was performed utilizing the Scopus database. A total of 482 papers were obtained, with 214 being very pertinent to the study goals. The study had three stages—Assembling, Arranging, and Assessing—to systematically find, organize, and assess research patterns. Instruments such as Microsoft Excel, Bibliometrix (R), and VOSviewer were utilized for data visualization and mapping. The study emphasizes the developing interconnections between AI-driven technology and consumer attention studies, providing insights into the growth of digital marketing.

*Table 1. showing stages of bibliometric study*

| Stage | Process | Components | Details |
|---|---|---|---|
| Stage 1: Assembling | Identification | Research Questions | To examine how Eye-Tracking and Artificial Intelligence are applied to optimize visual attention and enhance user experience in digital marketing. |
| | | Domain | Artificial Intelligence, Eye-Tracking, Digital Marketing |
| | | Source Type | Peer-reviewed Journals, Conference Papers |
| | | Source Quality | Scopus Indexed Publications |
| | Acquisition | Material Acquisition | Scopus Database |
| | | Search Period | Up to August 2025 |
| | | Search Keywords | ("Eye-Tracking" AND "Artificial Intelligence") AND ("User Experience" OR "Digital Marketing") |
| | | Total Documents Retrieved | 482 Documents |
| Stage 2: Arranging | Organization | Organizing Codes | Year of Publication, Document Type, Subject Area, Country, Research Domain, and Keyword Co-occurrence |
| | | Documents Retained | 200 Documents for ("Eye-Tracking" AND "AI") and 14 Documents for ("Eye-Tracking", "AI" AND "Digital Marketing") |
| Stage 3: Assessing | Evaluation | Total Documents for Analysis | 214 Documents |
| | | Software Used | Microsoft Excel, Bibliometrix (R Studio), and VOSviewer |
| | Reporting | Convention | Figures, Tables, Network Maps, and Narrative Explanation |
| | | Limitations | Restricted to Scopus database coverage; possible omission of non-indexed but relevant studies; keyword-based retrieval bias; limitations in bibliometric tool visualization accuracy. |

## REVIEW OF LITERATURE

The growth of digital over the past few decades has necessitated innovation in the creation of digital goods and services. Due to the high user experience standards set by industry leaders like Google, Amazon, and Facebook, this endeavour is difficult. The rivalry is changing to focus on providing customers with exceptional experiences. Accordingly, user experience research and conversion rate optimisation are the main areas of attention for market research in this digital age.

## The significance of human perception

It was shown that the AI model could anticipate which aspects of an image would draw the greatest attention. It does not, however, possess the complex comprehension and authentic cognitive processes of human perception (Chen and Chen, 2017). Humans behave in accordance with specific anticipation patterns. For example, a big, eye-catching image doesn't always work to get attention since people know it's only cosmetic and doesn't help them achieve their objectives.

However, AI might be useful in the early stages of design, assisting in determining whether crucial components are getting enough attention. This could help get ready for qualitative usability assessments and possibly cut down on the number of revisions needed

Optimising marketing strategies, influencing potential consumers' purchase decisions, and developing products that are appropriate for them are the goals of neuromarketing research and technology (Alghofaili et al., 2019). Dash asserts that through drawing people's attention and inspiring them to concentrate on a particular product, emotions can have an impact on economic decisions. Marketing studies can benefit from neuromarketing in two ways: first, it offers fresh perspectives on customers' unconscious behaviour; second, it uses neuroscience approaches to validate conventional consumer knowledge. Almourad et al., 2025 stated that Neuromarketing is a fusion of brain analysis and marketing techniques. This field makes use of investigative tools including eye tracking, facial recognition, MEG and fMRI, and EEG equipment to explore how the brain reacts to different stimuli. By using neuroimaging techniques, scientists may correlate each stimulus to the triggered reaction and examine brain activity "in vivo" in response to certain stimuli (Van et al.,2018). These new tools for marketing might be used to translate promotional messages into more comprehensible language that stimulates various brain regions, encourages consumers to make purchases, and helps them choose one product over another. Since consumers react differently to stimuli, neuromarketing can assist manufacturers in raising the calibre of their products, brands, or advertising. Research on point-of-sale behaviour has been conducted for decades in an effort to improve advertising campaigns, product development, and brand positioning. The efficacy and efficiency of marketing communications can be assessed through neuromarketing. Emotional involvement, memory retention, intention to buy, novelty, awareness, and attention are these. Customers use their feelings to guide their decisions. Building a new model for the decision-making process in an economic setting is the goal of the interdisciplinary field of neuromarketing, which sits at the intersection of neuroscience and economics. The physiology and operation of the brain itself are of concern to neuroscientists (most of whom are neurologists or psychologists), whereas economists are more interested in interpreting these answers in terms of economic principles and the relevance of findings. A lot of marketing experts have already surmised that brain imaging has a neurological basis. Marketing professionals should evaluate a product's oxytocin confidence level. Marketers will be able to determine whether or not the level of confidence should be attained with this aid. Because they can provide insight into hidden consumer information that other marketing research methods cannot, as well as because of their cost-utility ratio, neuromarketing tools can enhance marketing. Neuromarketing strategies have social and economic implications and can be used to a variety of corporate objectives. The Eye Tracking is a neuromarketing instrument that has many applications, being able to deliver value to the researchers, by studying the impression some products make on consumers. Moreover, the device can be used to provide data about human-computer interactions, in order to rate to which extent computers are able to satisfy human needs. This field of study is commonly used in the gaming industry, as it brings advantages to designers and developers who need to assess and measure the visual attention or reactions during games. The eye tracking analysis helps by finding ways in which the overall gaming experience can be improved. Other application fields of this instrument include advertising, package design, purchasing behavior analysis, website testing and so on. One technology that can measure the point of sight and record eye movement is called Eye Tracking. Key performance indicators are created using the data that has been gathered. The pupils' movement and dilatation are tracked and categorised based on particular interest areas. The device can measure the precise times a place was fixed, including the number of revisits, in addition to recording all unconscious pupil movements and fixations. The real significance of an eye tracking study is found in the fact that the reflexes being assessed are unconscious and exhibit uncontrollable responses to a variety of well-chosen stimuli. This tool aims to identify the stimuli that people are unknowingly ignoring or overlooking and those that can capture their attention (Ahmed et al.,2023).

The swift digital revolution of markets has radically changed customer interactions with companies, goods, and online platforms. In this environment, eye-tracking and artificial intelligence (AI) have emerged as potent instruments for comprehending and improving user experience, visual attention, and decision-making. Eye-tracking allows researchers to record visual activity and cognitive reactions by observing gaze patterns, fixation durations, and saccadic movements. When combined with AI and neuromarketing analytics, it offers unparalleled insights into subconscious customer responses that conventional self-reported measurements frequently overlook.

Recent academic debate highlights an increasing focus on the optimization of digital marketing, interface design, and customer engagement with AI-driven eye-tracking. Research in e-commerce (Štefko et al., 2025), social media activism (Pupchenko, 2022), phygital retail (Mishra, 2025), and online customer behavior

(Cenizo, 2025) jointly illustrates the intersection of neuroscience, behavioral analytics, and marketing science. This literature review consolidates these efforts to investigate how eye-tracking and AI augment our comprehension of visual attention, user experience (UX), and sustainable consumer behavior in digital contexts. Digital marketing increasingly depends on catching and maintaining customers' visual attention amidst busy interfaces, advertisements, and media content. Eye-tracking technologies, along with artificial intelligence (AI) and computational models, present a potential approach for assessing, analyzing, and manipulating user attention in real time. The subsequent sections examine progress in (a) fundamental comprehension of visual attention through eye tracking, (b) artificial intelligence and modeling methodologies utilized for gaze data, and (c) implementations in marketing, user interfaces, and advertising.

## Foundations of Eye-Tracking and Visual Attention

Comprehending the dynamics of visual attention in real time is essential for any intervention or optimization approach. Eye-tracking research has been widely employed in consumer behavior, advertising, and interface studies. Clement et al. (2013) examined the impact of package design aspects on customer gaze in-store, demonstrating that visual salience and design factors significantly direct attention. Clement, Kristensen, and Grønhaug (2013)

Wang, Q. et al. (2014) utilized eye tracking in online settings to demonstrate that website complexity induces cognitive stress and influences attention allocation among elements. (Wang et al., 2014). Skaramagkas et al. (2021) conducted a review on eye-tracking metrics related to emotional and cognitive processes, emphasizing that metrics such as fixation time, saccades, and pupil dilation might indicate both attention and underlying affective states. (Skaramagkas et al., 2021)

In immersive or 3D environments, Hillaire et al. (2010) suggested employing visual attention models to facilitate gaze tracking in interactive 3D systems, foreseeing situations when gaze must be synchronized with dynamic visual material. Hillaire et al. (2010) The survey by Moreno-Arjonilla et al. (2024) delineates the application of eye tracking in virtual reality environments, a field of growing significance as digital marketing ventures into immersive realms. Moreno-Arjonilla et al., 2024

The eye-tracking foundation thus offers the fundamental empirical basis. To effectively scale, generalize, and utilize gaze data in digital marketing, the implementation of AI and computational modeling is necessary.

## Artificial Intelligence, Modeling, and Computational Methods for Gaze and Attention

Advancements in AI have facilitated the conversion of eye-tracking data into predictive, generative, or adaptive systems.

### Visual Salience and Attention Modeling

One aspect of the research focuses on developing visual saliency models based on gaze data. Cheng, Fan, and Hu (2023) formulate a visual saliency model utilizing crowdsourced eye-tracking data and implement it in visual design challenges. Their methodology employs aggregated gaze data to deduce which picture portions are more likely to capture attention, serving as a tool with direct consequences for the creation of marketing images or layouts. (Cheng, Fan, & Hu, 2023)

Likewise, models incorporating human sight into computer vision frameworks have arisen. Koorathota et al. (2023) advocate for the incorporation of human eye tracking into vision transformer models in computer vision to enhance attention weighting in a manner akin to human perception. Koorathota et al., 2023 Li et al. (2024) employ autoencoder methodologies on gaze data to evaluate user preferences, which may inform aesthetic design choices (e.g., for avatars or product representations). (Li et al., 2024)

Benchmarking initiatives have emerged, such as the framework proposed by Li, Z. et al. (2024) for eye-tracking–based vigilance prediction in vessel traffic controllers, highlighting the necessity for standardized datasets and assessment in gaze-based prediction tasks. (Li, Z. et al., 2024)

### Interactive and Adaptive Design with Gaze-in-the-Loop

A secondary aspect is the utilization of gaze feedback in interactive systems that modify or develop designs. Cheng & Dey (2019) introduce a system named "I see, you design," which integrates eye tracking with an interactive genetic algorithm; user gaze directs the evolutionary design of user interfaces, progressively refining layout or style to align with visual preferences. Cheng and Dey, 2019 This loop approaches real-time optimization of marketing creatives.

Jamil & Belkacem (2024) provide real-time remote learning frameworks utilizing EEG and eye-tracking analytics, illustrating the potential of closed-loop adaptation based on gaze, despite being focused on cognition and learning. (Jamil & Belkacem, 2024) Sharma, Giannakos, and Dillenbourg (2020) similarly examine how eye-tracking combined with AI might augment user motivation and learning, insights that may be applicable to digital marketing settings (e.g., maintaining user engagement). Sharma et al. (2020)

In ecommerce, Singh & Modi (2024) create a sophisticated real-time camera-based eye gaze tracking system capable of analyzing visual attention using deep learning techniques. These systems may be integrated into interfaces, enabling gaze feedback to determine the information or advertisements displayed. (Singh & Modi, 2024)

### Explainability, Cross-Modality, and Multimodal Attention

As gaze-informed systems increase in complexity, the significance of explainability and integration with other modalities (e.g., language, context) becomes paramount. Gao et al. (2025) introduce an explainable AI model for predicting cross-language comprehension based on eye movements, aiming to elucidate the reasons behind varying gaze patterns that indicate understanding disparities between languages. (Gao et al., 2025)

Wilson et al. (2025) investigate the role of eye gazing as a signal in contextual AI systems, where gaze signals assist in inferring user attention or purpose in context-aware applications. (Wilson et al., 2025). These instructions emphasize that gaze-driven models must not function as black boxes: in marketing systems, the ability to elucidate the rationale for the prioritization of a visual element fosters trust and interpretability.

### Enhancing Gaze Data Quality and Processing

Precise fixation detection and data processing continue to pose challenges, particularly with head-mounted, mobile, or wearable gaze systems. Drews & Dierkes (2024) examine methods to improve automated fixation identification in head-mounted eye tracking, which is beneficial in scenarios involving head movement, such as mobile browsing and augmented reality. (Drews & Dierkes, 2024)

Furthermore, difficulties in obtaining dependable gaze data in uncontrolled environments (e.g., online or mobile) continue to exist. Zhang and Liu (2017) investigate challenges in acquiring eye-tracking data for picture quality studies, including noise, calibration drift, and participant variability.

## Applications in Digital Marketing, Advertising, and User Experience

The known capabilities of gaze measuring and modeling are actively being applied to digital marketing, user experience, and advertising.

### Promotion, Aesthetic Design, and Brand Identity

Tang and Chen (2024) investigate whether AI-generated styled items elicit more visual attention by evaluating gaze responses to these stimuli. Is innovative or styled visual material more effective than regular images in attracting attention in marketing? (Tang & Chen, 2024)

In outdoor environments, Jin, Zhang, and Chen (2025) utilize eye tracking to enhance urban visual identity and outdoor advertising, demonstrating that gaze-driven insights may inform the design of billboards, signs, and façades. (Jin et al., 2025)

Mankutė (2025) examines the impact of visual attention, measured by eye tracking, on brand sentiments inside social media, correlating gaze metrics with persuasive results.

Pinhal, Estima & Duarte (2025) employ a "eye-tracking lens" to analyze how travel or destination marketing pictures influence users to "see, like, and book," therefore associating gaze with conversion behavior. (Pinhal et al., 2025). Kondak (2023) examines the application of eye tracking and AI in marketing communication management, including applied methodologies (e.g., saliency modeling, gaze-based A/B testing) and associated obstacles (data protection, scalability).

## 4.2 Web and User Experience Design

Guo, Kim, and Lee (2024) present empirical findings on the application of eye tracking in design assessment, specifically within visual communication and new media design domains. They demonstrate how gaze measurements might uncover usability or aesthetic issues that traditional analytics can overlook. Hwang and Lee (2018) employ eye tracking to investigate gender disparities in visual attention and buying attitudes within online retail contexts, emphasizing that segment-specific variations may necessitate tailored visual design. Šola, Qureshi, and Khawaja (2024) examine the use of AI eye-tracking technology in managing cognitive load for online learners, asserting that their conclusions extend to digital media consumption: designs that correspond with gaze patterns can diminish effort and enhance enjoyment. (Šola et al., 2024) Their subsequent research (2025) employs same eye-tracking and AI methodologies to analyze e-magazine layouts, elucidating the influence of design aspects on reader engagement. (Šola et al., 2025)

Zheng et al. (2022) utilize eye-tracking research to examine ornamental plant characteristics in urban green spaces, demonstrating methodologically how consumers' visual preferences and fixation patterns correlate with feature features, which may be applied to product pictures or backdrops in digital marketing. Van Loo et al. (2018) establish a connection between visual attention and consumer food selection behavior, demonstrating that gaze not only signifies perception but also corresponds with real choices—thereby affirming the efficacy of gaze as an indicator of marketing performance. Van Loo et al. (2018)

## Health, Medical, and Specialized Domains (Related Insights)

Beyond the realm of digital marketing, the medical and health sectors offer insights into the convergence of gaze and AI in critical visual activities. Chen et al. (2023) illustrate the application of AI-driven eye tracking to assess ADHD symptoms in children, highlighting the utility of gaze metrics in conjunction with AI categorization for diagnostic purposes. Chen et al. (2023)

Cioffi et al. (2023) investigate the potential of AI to improve physicians' interpretation of optical coherence tomography in conjunction with eye-tracking, suggesting that gaze-aware AI systems may assist professionals in diagnostic scenarios. Cioffi et al., 2023

Winterhalter et al. (2024) do an eye-tracking research in dentistry to analyze user behavior using AI-assisted diagnostic tools, demonstrating the influence of gaze on trust and interface design. (Winterhalter et al., 2024)

These domains emphasize that where accuracy, explainability, and trust are paramount, gaze-driven AI systems must not only forecast attention but also do so consistently and openly.

## Challenges, Deficiencies, and Prospective Directions

Despite the abundance of research, some obstacles and unresolved avenues persist:

Scalability and real-time deployment: Numerous gaze-AI technologies are confined to laboratory environments. Transforming them into resilient, real-time instruments for digital marketing (such as live websites or advertisements) remains uncommon.

Generalizability and domain shifts: Models developed on particular stimuli or demographics may lack applicability across devices, cultures, or advertising forms.

As gaze-informed AI systems increasingly influence marketing decisions, such as adaptive advertisements, the importance of explainability becomes paramount (see to Gao et al., 2025; Wilson et al., 2025).

Ethics, privacy, and user consent: Gaze data is exceedingly sensitive. Transparency, opt-in agreement, and anonymization are crucial yet now little addressed in the existing literature.

Multimodal integration: The amalgamation of gaze data with click data, EEG, facial expressions, or contextual signals may provide more comprehensive models—initial efforts have been made (e.g., Jamil & Belkacem, 2024), although complete integration in marketing remains underdeveloped.

Benchmark datasets: As Li, Z. et al. (2024) and others emphasize, evaluating gaze-based models is crucial for technique comparison and advancing advancement.

Diversity and segmentation among users: Hwang & Lee (2018), Guo et al. (2024), and others demonstrate that demographic and device context variations are significant. Adaptive systems must consider segmentation.

Closed-loop optimization: Techniques such as Cheng & Dey's (2019) gaze-guided evolutionary design show potential, although scaling these loops to intricate marketing campaigns presents significant challenges.

## Synopsis and Consequences for Digital Marketing

In summary, eye tracking combined with AI provides robust capabilities for comprehending and manipulating visual attention in digital marketing. On one hand, gaze measurement provides insight into users' visual focus; on the other, AI techniques convert that raw data into models, predictions, and interventions.

Design-level techniques (saliency modeling, gaze-aware layouts) enhance the optimization of creatives and user interfaces (e.g., Tang & Chen, 2024; Guo et al., 2024).

System-level techniques (gaze-driven adaptation, interactive design loops) offer interfaces and advertisements that react to users in real time (e.g. Cheng & Dey, 2019; Singh & Modi, 2024).

Cross-domain and explainable systems advance the development of reliable, context-sensitive solutions (Gao et al., 2025; Wilson et al., 2025).

Practical applications in marketing, branding, and media design have started to materialize (Jin et al., 2025; Pinhal et al., 2025; Kondak, 2023).

In the future, the primary objectives for researchers and practitioners are to reconcile the disparity between laboratory-grade gaze systems and scalable marketing tools; to develop comprehensive multimodal, interpretable models; to uphold privacy and ethical standards; and to execute field deployments to verify attention-based enhancements in conversion or engagement metrics.

## Eye-Tracking as an Insight into Consumer Cognition

Eye-tracking has transitioned from a specialized research technique to a widely utilized tool in neuromarketing and user experience studies. It facilitates the objective measurement of attention distribution, cognitive burden, and visual involvement.

Štefko et al. (2025) performed a pivotal research examining user interactions with online airline search platforms with eye-tracking technology. The researchers employed the Smart Eye AI system to examine heatmaps and gaze patterns of 32 university students engaged in specified search tasks. Notwithstanding participants' digital competence, hardly 25% accomplished the tasks, highlighting the difficulties presented by ambiguous site designs and cognitive stress. This study demonstrated that attention was predominantly focused on search fields and critical flight information, whereas ancillary elements, such as ads, were mainly disregarded. The results demonstrate that the clarity and simplicity of the user interface (UI) significantly influence visual attention and aid in decision-making.

Lyu, Manas-Viniegra, and Xu (2025) utilized eye-tracking to examine attention disparities in stadium naming rights, employing football stadiums in Europe and China as stimuli. The research indicated that products with historical connections, like Coca-Cola, garnered much greater interest among various cultural groups. This underscores how brand familiarity and emotional connection may change gaze distribution, emphasizing the idea that attention is both a cognitive and emotional activity. Consequently, eye-tracking not only determines what people observe but also elucidates the reasons behind the attraction of specific features, thereby integrating cognitive research with marketing strategy.

## Neuromarketing and the Subconscious Aspects of Attention

Neuromarketing, as articulated by Agrawal et al. (2025), integrates neuroscience with marketing research to elucidate the subconscious processes influencing customer behavior. Conventional survey methodologies often document stated preferences, but neuromarketing—utilizing fMRI, EEG, and eye-tracking—uncovers latent reactions such as emotional arousal, interest, or trust.

Pupchenko (2022) expands this framework by examining activist influencers on social media, employing both questionnaires and eye-tracking to assess implicit (attention, emotion, and visual pathways) and explicit (credibility, association, consistency) reactions to environmental advocacy messages. The research highlights that emotionally engaging messages and trustworthy visual tales maintain attention more efficiently than neutral or excessively promoted material. In the realm of digital marketing, our findings affirm the pivotal importance of emotional connection in influencing both attention and enduring consumer loyalty.

Agrawal et al. (2025) emphasize that neuromarketing has shown the interplay between emotional and intellectual processes in customer decision-making. The systematic study highlights that well-known brands stimulate brain areas linked to positive emotions, resulting in improved memory retention and purchase intention. The review highlights ethical problems, such as the possibility for manipulation and hazards to data privacy. Consequently, whereas neuromarketing enhances our comprehension of subconscious consumer reactions, its implementation in AI-driven contexts must prioritize ethical transparency and user focus.

## Artificial Intelligence in Eye-Tracking: Advancing Predictive and Adaptive User Experience

The amalgamation of AI with eye-tracking technology has transformed the analysis and interpretation of visual attention data. AI-driven systems can analyze hundreds of gaze coordinates every second, identify attention irregularities, and anticipate user intent in real-time.

Šola, Qureshi, and Khawaja (2025) illustrate this integration in their work utilizing AI eye-tracking algorithms (Predict v.1.0) and webcam-based monitoring to evaluate reading engagement in digital magazine articles. The integration of human eye-tracking with AI analysis enabled accurate mapping of emotional reactions, fixation length, and engagement patterns. Their findings indicated that well-organized material and visually harmonious layouts sustained attention despite aural disruptions. This indicates that AI-enhanced eye-tracking can optimize digital content design, improve message retention, and tailor visual layouts according to user engagement metrics from both educational and marketing perspectives.

Cenizo (2025) further underscores this connection with a thorough literature evaluation on neuromarketing applications in web behavior research. The study, using the SPAR-4-SLR and TCCM frameworks, revealed that although AI and eye-tracking have potential for enhancing web interfaces, the research domain is yet disjointed. A significant deficiency exists in the inadequate incorporation of emotional, cultural, and accessibility aspects into AI-UX systems. Cenizo argues for multidimensional AI frameworks that include both cognitive usability and subconscious emotional triggers, facilitating inclusive and adaptable online design.

## Visual Attention and Decision-Making in Digital Contexts

Visual attention operates as a psychological filter, allocating cognitive resources to pertinent stimuli. In digital marketing, this assesses the efficacy with which people comprehend brand messaging, analyze alternatives, and reach purchase conclusions.

Štefko et al. (2025) assert that the intricacy of visual interfaces might elevate cognitive load, resulting in choice weariness and inferior results. Their research indicated that participants devoted more time to navigating search filters and comparing flights than to completing bookings, suggesting that excessive visual clutter hinders job efficiency. These observations correspond with cognitive load theory, which asserts that working memory capacity is finite; hence, interface design must emphasize informational clarity and visual hierarchy.

Mishra (2025) analyzes how neuromarketing instruments—such as eye-tracking, EEG, and biometric sensors—facilitate the interpretation of emotional and cognitive reactions that influence sustainable customer behavior. The study demonstrates that sensory-rich narrative and visual signals substantially impact eco-friendly purchasing among Gen Z in phygital retail environments. Mishra contends that AI-driven analytics can forecast and enhance environmentally conscious customer behavior by synchronizing marketing stimuli with underlying motives, like trust, empathy, and identity representation. Consequently, digital marketers should perceive attention not alone as a metric of awareness but as an avenue for emotional persuasion and ethical consumption.

## Cross-Cultural and Ethical Considerations in Eye-Tracking Research

Cross-cultural disparities significantly influence visual attention patterns and the efficacy of marketing. Lyu et al. (2025) identified significant differences in the perceptions of sponsored stadium names between European and Chinese participants, indicating that cultural familiarity and symbolic significance affect gaze distribution. This directly impacts worldwide marketing efforts, indicating that AI-driven eye-tracking systems must integrate cultural sensitivity models to effectively interpret visual engagement across different areas.

Ethical problems further complicate this technological advancement. Agrawal et al. (2025) caution that the potential for manipulation and privacy violations in neuromarketing need regulatory frameworks to safeguard consumer autonomy. AI-driven eye-tracking creates sensitive biometric data, prompting concerns around permission, storage, and openness of data utilization. Ethical neuromarketing must reconcile commercial goals with ethical innovation, ensuring that user attention data is utilized to improve experiences rather than to exploit vulnerabilities.

## Incorporating AI and Eye-Tracking into Sustainable Marketing Strategies

The integration of AI with neuromarketing not only improves customer understanding but also advances the overarching goals of sustainability and ethical business practices. Mishra (2025) elucidates how neuro-informed marketing tactics might reconcile the attitude-behavior gap—the disparity between consumers' stated environmental concerns and their actual purchase decisions. By interpreting subconscious reactions, marketers may create more genuine and emotionally impactful advertising that encourage sustainable purchasing.

Furthermore, AI-driven visual analytics can ascertain which components—such as eco-labels, package design, or green certifications—elicit favorable emotional responses. This allows businesses to develop ethical persuasion frameworks that harmonize commercial attractiveness with social accountability. Consequently, the integration of AI with eye-tracking cultivates a novel paradigm of conscious capitalism, wherein marketing aims not alone to sell, but to cultivate sustainable ideals and enduring trust.

## Emerging Trends and Prospective Research Avenues

The existing literature underscores the fundamental significance of eye-tracking and AI in digital marketing, however many developing developments warrant consideration.

Initially, real-time adaptive UX systems driven by AI could automatically modify visual layouts, ads, and product placements according on users' gaze patterns and engagement data. This would convert static interfaces into adaptive environments that learn and develop according to user activity.

The amalgamation of multimodal data streams—integrating eye-tracking with EEG, face recognition, and biometric sensors—may provide a comprehensive perspective on emotional and cognitive involvement. Mishra (2025) and Bekler et al., 2024 emphasize that this integration will connect brain responses with behavioral results, facilitating the predictive modeling of customer intent.

Third, ethical and inclusive design constitutes an inadequately examined domain. Cenizo (2025) underscores the necessity of integrating people with impairments and multicultural viewpoints into neuromarketing research. Future research should implement universal design frameworks to guarantee accessibility, equity, and transparency in AI-driven marketing apps.

The emergence of generative AI presents novel prospects for automated gaze prediction and synthetic user testing, decreasing expenses while preserving analytical integrity. Nonetheless, these technologies require the enhancement of stringent ethical governance and interpretability requirements to guarantee accountability.

The examined literature collectively highlights that eye-tracking and AI have transformed the comprehension of visual attention and user experience in digital environments for marketers and researchers. Research ranging from flight search interfaces (Abbasi et al., 2024) to social media activism (Pupchenko, 2022), phygital retail (Mishra, 2025), and cross-cultural sponsorships (Lyu et al., 2025) reveals a fundamental insight: visual attention is a cognitive and emotional phenomenon that influences user engagement and decision-making.

Artificial intelligence has enhanced the analytical capabilities of eye-tracking, allowing accurate, scalable, and predictive insights into consumer cognition. However, as Agrawal et al. (2025) and Cenizo (2025) observe, obstacles persist in incorporating emotional, cultural, and ethical factors into AI-driven marketing frameworks.

The integration of AI with eye-tracking represents not only a technological progression, but a fundamental transformation towards compassionate, data-driven, and sustainable marketing methodologies. By interpreting the unspoken language of the eyes, marketers and designers can develop experiences that not only attract attention but also cultivate trust, inclusion, and significant connections in the digital era.

## DISCUSSION

*Figure 1. showing co-occurrence network visualization*

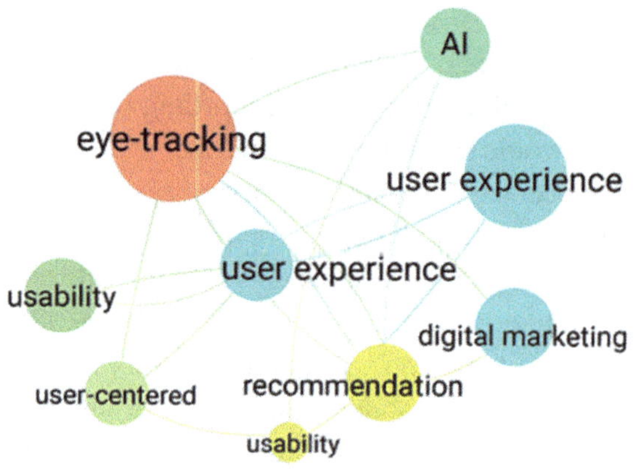


The VOSviewer co-occurrence network visualization for the topic "Eye-Tracking and AI: Optimizing Visual Attention and User Experience in Digital Marketing" depicts the interconnections among principal research themes derived from keyword co-occurrence analysis. Each node in the diagram signifies a keyword utilized in the chosen publications, with the node's size reflecting the frequency of that term's occurrence in the literature. The connecting lines (or edges) illustrate the intensity of co-occurrence—how frequently two keywords appear together inside the same paragraph. The color-coding distinguishes theme groups, signifying separate yet interconnected study trajectories within the discipline.

At the center of the picture, "Eye-Tracking" is depicted as the largest and most prominent node, indicating it as the principal study subject. The robust associations with "AI," "User Experience," and "Digital Marketing" underscore the multidisciplinary essence of the subject. The prevalence of "Eye-Tracking" indicates that most research focuses on comprehending visual attention, gaze behavior, and cognitive engagement patterns in digital contexts, frequently employing AI-driven technologies for data analysis and interpretation.

The secondary principal node, "AI," is situated adjacent to "Eye-Tracking" and "User Experience," establishing a connection between technology advancement and consumer-oriented applications. This relationship underscores the integration of artificial intelligence methodologies—such as machine learning, deep learning, and computer vision—with eye-tracking technologies to capture subconscious consumer reactions, forecast decision-making behavior, and enhance user interfaces. The connection between "AI" and "Digital Marketing" highlights the increasing trend of employing intelligent algorithms to customize marketing tactics, personalize adverts, and improve engagement through data-driven insights.

User Experience (UX) serves as a vital element, intricately linked to both Eye-Tracking and Usability. This relationship indicates a transition from technology-centric research to human-centered design methodologies, utilizing AI and eye-tracking to comprehend user perception, interaction, and emotional response to digital interfaces. The significant correlation among "User Experience," "Usability," and "User-Centered Design" underscores a focus on improving satisfaction, accessibility, and cognitive ease via intuitive digital design.

A minor yet notable cluster comprises phrases like "Digital Marketing," "Consumer Behavior," "Recommendation," and "Analytics." This cluster embodies the application-focused aspect of the study, wherein insights from eye-tracking and AI studies are utilized to enhance marketing campaigns, optimize content distribution, and create recommendation systems. The relationship between "Recommendation" and "Digital Marketing" denotes the use of predictive AI algorithms to propose individualized items or content derived on real-time ocular movement data.

Peripheral nodes like "Psychology," "Cognition," and "Decision-Making" (if present in the dataset) would presumably signify intersections of cognitive and behavioral sciences. These domains concentrate on comprehending the emotional and neurological reactions that underpin visual attention, a facet corroborated by neuromarketing studies.

The picture illustrates a multidisciplinary convergence: computer science supplies the technical foundation via AI; psychology and neuroscience furnish cognitive insights; and business and marketing yield practical applications. The clusters together illustrate the evolution of contemporary digital marketing research from conventional analytics to neuro-informed, AI-enhanced, and user-centric paradigms.

The VOSviewer co-occurrence diagram indicates that the convergence of Eye-Tracking, AI, and User Experience is an emerging research horizon. It illustrates how these technologies together influence the future of digital marketing by facilitating a profound comprehension of customer attention, emotion, and interaction behavior—thus fostering innovation in customized, ethical, and efficient digital communication tactics.

*Figure 2. showing documents by year*

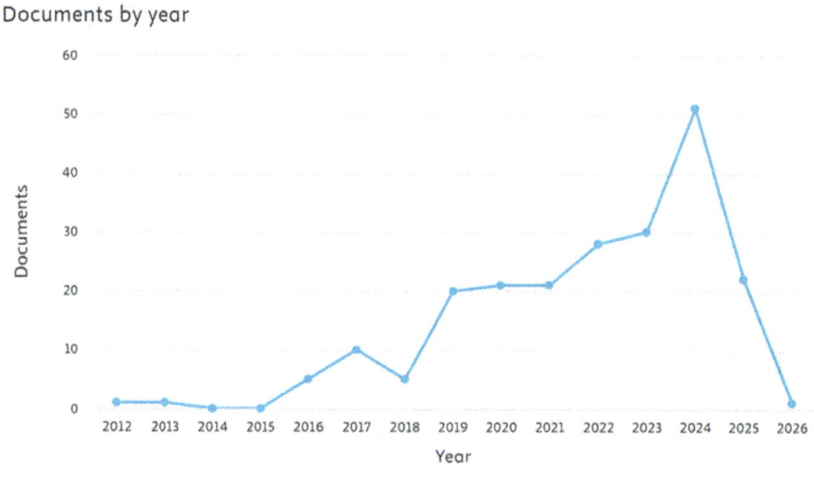


The graph entitled "Documents by Year" depicts the publishing trend with the topic "Eye-Tracking and AI: Optimizing Visual Attention and User Experience in Digital Marketing" from 2012 to 2026.

The trend indicates negligible research effort before to 2016, showing that the convergence of AI and eye-tracking remained a nascent field. Since 2017, there has been a consistent increase trend, indicating growing academic and industry interest in the integration of AI technology to improve digital marketing and user experience. The 2024 apex, exceeding 50 articles, indicates a proliferation in research—presumably attributable to progress in machine learning, computer vision, and neuromarketing applications. A little decrease in 2025–2026 may suggest either inadequate data gathering for recent years or a stabilizing of research emphasis. The graph illustrates that this issue has developed into a fast expanding domain, emphasizing its importance in modern marketing and consumer behavior analysis.

*Figure 3. showing "Documents by Country or Territory"*

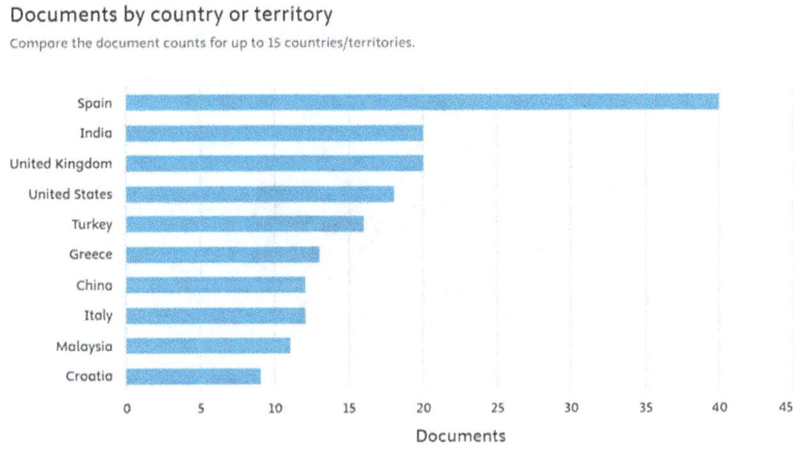


The graph under "Documents by Country or Territory" illustrates the geographical distribution of research articles about "Eye-Tracking and AI: Optimizing Visual Attention and User Experience in Digital Marketing."

Spain considerably leads with over 40 papers, reflecting robust academic and research involvement in AI-driven eye-tracking and digital marketing studies, likely attributable to established European research networks and financing in neuromarketing. India and the United Kingdom are closely aligned, indicating an increasing interest and investment in AI-driven consumer analytics and user experience research.

The United States and Turkey significantly contribute, highlighting their focus on the integration of machine learning with consumer behavior analysis. Additional contributors, including Greece, China, Italy, Malaysia, and Croatia, signify rising involvement, indicating that this study field is attaining worldwide diversification. The trend indicates a shift from Western supremacy towards international collaboration and interdisciplinary expansion.

*Figure 4. shows pie-chart of percentage according to subject area*

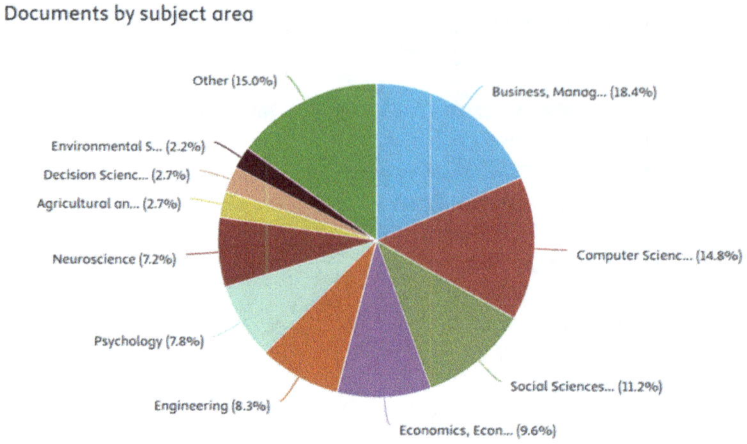


*Table 2. showing number of documents according to subject area*

| Subject Area | Number of Documents |
|---|---|
| Business, Management and Accounting | 82 |
| Computer Science | 66 |
| Social Sciences | 50 |
| Economics, Econometrics and Finance | 43 |
| Engineering | 37 |
| Psychology | 35 |
| Neuroscience | 32 |
| Agricultural and Biological Sciences | 12 |
| Decision Sciences | 12 |
| Environmental Science | 10 |
| Energy | 9 |
| Medicine | 9 |
| Materials Science | 8 |
| Mathematics | 7 |
| Physics and Astronomy | 6 |
| Health Professions | 5 |
| Arts and Humanities | 4 |

continued on following page

*Table 2. Continued*

| Subject Area | Number of Documents |
|---|---|
| Biochemistry, Genetics and Molecular Biology | 4 |
| Chemical Engineering | 4 |
| Multidisciplinary | 4 |
| Earth and Planetary Sciences | 3 |
| Pharmacology, Toxicology and Pharmaceutics | 2 |
| Chemistry | 1 |
| Immunology and Microbiology | 1 |

The predominant part of the pie chart is Business, Management, and Accounting (82 papers), indicating that the majority of study is on marketing tactics, consumer behavior, and management implications of AI and eye-tracking. The second-largest category, Computer Science (66 pages), underscores the significance of technical innovation, including AI algorithms, machine learning models, and computer vision applications, within this field.

Social Sciences (50) and Economics, Econometrics, and Finance (43) illustrate multidisciplinary research connecting human behavior, decision-making, and the economic ramifications of digital marketing. Disciplines such as Engineering (37), Psychology (35), and Neuroscience (32) contribute by investigating technological implementation, cognitive reactions, and the brain mechanisms behind user attention and engagement.

Minor sectors including Agricultural Sciences, Environmental Science, Medicine, and Energy demonstrate specialized applications of eye-tracking and AI outside conventional marketing, maybe in sustainability communication, healthcare interfaces, or energy product promotion.

The pie chart indicates that this topic is profoundly interdisciplinary, primarily characterized by business and computer science research, while also incorporating insights from psychology, neuroscience, and engineering, highlighting the interconnectedness of AI and human cognition in digital marketing research.

Although AI is growing, it still cannot replace the human eye. AI has demonstrated encouraging potential in the field of user attention analysis. It is capable of successfully locating visually striking features in an image. It cannot, however, fully mimic human decision-making and sophisticated thought processes. It's also important to note that the AI model makes use of data from eye-tracking experiments that only record the first three to five seconds of eye movement on a screen. This indicates that the individuals that supplied the AI model with data did not actually complete any jobs. AI finds it difficult to fully understand the embedded behavioural inclinations and expectation patterns of humans. Therefore, even though AI can offer insightful information, it should be combined with human assessment to produce the best possible user experience. Designers may improve their comprehension of user attention and produce more engaging and intuitive interfaces by fusing the advantages of AI analysis and human intuition.

The emotional aspect of user encounters is becoming increasingly important in digital products and ads. However, monitoring what users do and how they do it is a major emphasis of usability and digital market research. As a result, this chapter concentrates on less biassed and more reliable techniques for determining the reasons behind users' actions, such as eye tracking research and affective computing. This raises the issue of how to combine and enhance these measurement techniques. Studies over the years have demonstrated that, when compared to well-known and widely used techniques like surveys, emotion and eye-tracking analytics can produce more reliable results. Both approaches provide distinct but complimentary perspectives on emotion and attention, even though they are both well-established on their own. Thus, a mix of these approaches could produce even more reliable and complimentary findings: Eye tracking enhances emotion analysis by making it possible to pinpoint the precise visual stimulus that caused a certain emotion or mood response. It is simple to infer specific emotion peaks from the sequential flow of the stimuli if participants in a study exhibit comparable emotional reactions. When user groups exhibit disparate emotional responses, eye tracking provides information on whether these groups concentrate on distinct stimuli.

By providing insights into a deeper processing layer of attention-inducing stimuli, emotion analysis enhances the attention data. Focusing on a visual feature does not always indicate that the viewer is pleased with what is being shown. In actuality, the information may be unclear or connected to memories of unpleasant past experiences. Combining eye tracking and affective computing enables triangulation of sources to validate and explain findings.

The eye's elliptical shape can be useful for more basic eye tracking and detection applications. Simple elliptical eye shape models are good at simulating the pupil and iris under different viewing angles, but they fall short when it comes to capturing the inter-changes and variations of specific eye components. Model fitting approaches, which fit the designated features to the elliptical model, are a significant category of procedures that take into account the basic elliptical eye model. Pupil borders are typically extracted using edge detection techniques in methods that use the elliptical eye model, while iris and pupil features are extracted using transformation algorithms like the Hough transform. The dash writers used picture intensity thresholds to estimate the pupil ellipse's centre. Their methods use a shape circularity restriction to increase efficiency, however because of this constraint, the model is only effective for faces that are close to the front. Voting-based strategies are another group of methods that take advantage of the basic elliptical eye model. Through an accumulation process, the parameter chosen in voting approaches supports a particular hypothesis. Dash's writers suggested a voting system that identified the eyeballs by using spatial and temporal data. They rejected phoney student prospects using a set of heuristic rules and a large temporal support. In Dash, a comparable voting method that directly employed edge orientation was also proposed. This method used anthropomorphic averages and a previous face model to filter out false positives based on the intensity aspects of the photos. One drawback of these methods is that they primarily depend on feature space maxima. Techniques may confuse other areas, like eyebrows, for the eyes when the quantity of eye region features declines. Therefore, these methods work best when the search area is small. Dash proposes a low-cost eye tracking system that uses the Starburst algorithm to identify iris movements. This programme recursively sparkles new rays at the previously discovered maxima while identifying the highest gray-level differences along rays. In essence, the Starburst method is an active shape model that employs many characteristics along each normal.

In-depth modelling of the eye form serves as the foundation for complex shape-based models. The deformable template model dash, which comprises of two parabolas for the eyelids and a circle for the iris representation, is a well-known example of a complex shape model. Energy functions for internal forces, edges, valleys, and image peaks are integrated into an update rule to fit the model to an image. However, if the template is initialised above the eyebrow, the system will not be able to detect the eyes, therefore choosing the correct initial position is essential for reliable results. The intricate template description and the intricacy of ocular occlusions brought on by non-frontal head posture or eyelid closure are two more drawbacks of this paradigm. By using eye corners as the initialisation sites, the authors Dash expanded this model to extract the eye characteristics. They estimated the eye placements using anthropomorphic averages and utilised a nonparametric method called the snake model to establish the head's contour. When optimising the deformable template, the information of the identified eye corners is used to reduce the number of iterations. In a similar vein, the writers Dash suggested methods to expedite the method. To increase the localisation process's accuracy and speed, some researchers blended the characteristics of elliptical and complicated eye models. While certain deformable models, like the snake model, can handle a lot of shape variations, others are unable to handle the wide range of eye shapes. Generally speaking, deformable eye template-based techniques are thought to be more accurate, generic, and rational. Their computing demands, need for initialisation near the eye, and requirement for high contrast images are some of their drawbacks. Furthermore, they then rely on additional methods to deliver positive outcomes for larger head movements.

## CONCLUSION

This chapter suggests tying visual components to user experience: It is possible to identify particular bottom-up design elements impacting users' aesthetic experiences by using a screen-based design methodology. By measuring users' emotive responses, this method aims to pinpoint visual elements that consistently appear to contribute to perceived attractiveness and aesthetics. To determine the precise emotional root cause of a user, emotions are first assessed and then enhanced by timestamps of eye tracking data. Second, considering how users view aesthetics: From a top-down standpoint, this strategy might concentrate on user experience. A method triangulation may help to uncover the true user value of aesthetics, since users are compensating for usability issues with attractive aesthetics (e.g., gorgeous websites). To improve empathic market research by rapidly and reliably monitoring user emotions and attentions, this essay advocates integrating affective computing with eye tracking technologies. Digital market research in particular requires affordable and simple-to-use technologies.

The amalgamation of eye-tracking technology with artificial intelligence (AI) has transformed the comprehension of visual attention, cognitive engagement, and consumer decision-making by academics and marketers in digital environments. The bibliometric analysis and co-occurrence mapping indicate that this multidisciplinary field integrates knowledge from computer science, marketing, psychology, and neuroscience, establishing a solid basis for data-driven innovation in user experience design and digital marketing strategy.

In the last ten years, the field has experienced a significant increase in research activity, indicating the heightened acknowledgment of the significance of human-centered computer interfaces. Eye-tracking facilitates accurate monitoring of users' visual activity, while AI-driven models convert these gaze patterns into significant behavioral insights—connecting users' visual experiences with their emotional responses. Collectively, these technologies have facilitated the optimization of online layouts, adverts, and interactive systems, guaranteeing that digital communication corresponds with human cognition and emotion.

The worldwide dissemination of research underscores the varied and cooperative essence of this burgeoning area, with nations like Spain, India, and the United Kingdom in the forefront of publication production. The integration of technology progress, marketing innovation, and behavioral insights indicates a transition from conventional descriptive analytics to predictive and interpretative marketing intelligence.

As the sector progresses, issues about data ethics, privacy, and interpretability must remain pivotal in academic and industry discussions. The adoption of responsible AI and transparent data use is essential for preserving customer confidence and ensuring that neuromarketing insights are employed for empowerment instead of exploitation. Future research should enhance inclusion by including ethnic viewpoints, accessibility factors, and emotional diversity into AI and eye-tracking models.

This study confirms that the integration of AI and eye-tracking transcends mere technological progress; it signifies a revolutionary evolution towards sympathetic, intelligent, and sustainable digital marketing ecosystems. By elucidating the subconscious aspects of attention and perception, companies may create experiences that engage both the visual senses and the intellect and conscience of contemporary consumers. The interplay between technology and human psychology will shape the future of digital marketing, promoting enhanced customization, ethical involvement, and significant user experience.

## Prospective Scope and Research Trajectories

The amalgamation of eye-tracking technology with artificial intelligence (AI) in digital marketing has exhibited significant promise in improving user experience, maximizing visual focus, and interpreting subconscious customer behavior. Nonetheless, as the discipline advances, other pathways remain inadequately investigated, presenting substantial opportunities for forthcoming study and application. This section delineates the potential trajectories that may influence the forthcoming era of innovation in this nascent field.

### Progressing Real-Time Adaptive Systems

A highly promising avenue is the creation of real-time adaptable digital environments. Presently, the majority of eye-tracking research examines gaze data subsequent to interaction. In the future, AI algorithms may be incorporated with real-time eye-tracking devices to dynamically modify website design, ads, or recommendation systems. Adaptive interfaces would mitigate cognitive overload and immediately tailor user experiences, resulting in increased engagement and conversion rates. Research may further examine the efficacy of these adaptive systems across various customer categories and cultural situations.

### Integration of Multimodal Neuromarketing

Although eye-tracking offers valuable insights into visual attention, integrating it with additional neuromarketing techniques like EEG, fMRI, biometric sensors, and facial expression detection might yield a more comprehensive understanding of consumer engagement. Future study may investigate the potential of multimodal data fusion to enhance the precision of forecasting user behavior and emotional reactions. This integration would be especially beneficial in industries such as e-commerce, education, healthcare marketing, and entertainment, where emotional resonance is crucial in decision-making.

## Ethical and Responsible Artificial Intelligence in Neuromarketing

The growing dependence on biometric and gaze-tracking data has intensified concerns over data privacy, ethical manipulation, and algorithmic transparency. Future study should concentrate on establishing frameworks for the ethical utilization of AI in eye-tracking investigations and digital marketing applications. This encompasses the development of systems that protect user permission, anonymize sensitive gaze data, and ensure the interpretability of AI-generated predictions. Furthermore, multidisciplinary cooperation among ethicists, politicians, and marketers will be crucial to develop regulatory norms that reconcile innovation with consumer protection.

## Inclusivity and Accessibility in User Experience Design

An essential deficiency noted in the current literature is the insufficient focus on people with impairments or varied cognitive profiles. Eye-tracking integrated with AI possesses significant promise for developing more accessible digital platforms, such as customizing navigation for those with motor disabilities or constructing inclusive interfaces for neurodiverse users. Future study should examine how these technologies might improve universal design principles, therefore broadening the advantages of an optimal user experience to a wider demographic.

## Applications of Cross-Cultural and Global Marketing

Bibliometric mapping reveals that research contributions are distributed throughout many locations; yet, cultural differences in attention habits and digital interactions have not been adequately examined. Future research should prioritize cross-cultural comparisons of gaze behavior, examining the impact of cultural values, color perception, and advertising conventions on attention and engagement. These findings will assist global businesses in formulating culturally adaptable, AI-driven marketing strategies.

## Diversification into Emerging Technologies

The integration of eye-tracking and artificial intelligence with Virtual Reality (VR), Augmented Reality (AR), and the Metaverse signifies a revolutionary horizon. Future research may investigate the effects of immersive phygital settings on visual attention, emotional engagement, and purchasing behavior. The amalgamation of Internet of Things (IoT) with gaze-based AI analytics may broaden applications in smart homes, automotive systems, and interactive retail environments.

## Predictive Models of Consumer Behavior

Future research may concentrate on developing predictive models that amalgamate eye-tracking data with artificial intelligence to anticipate not just immediate attention but also enduring consumer loyalty, trust, and sustainable behavior. These models would assist firms in aligning marketing tactics with changing customer expectations while tackling global issues such as sustainability and digital well-being.

In summary, the future of eye-tracking and AI in digital marketing is predicated on real-time personalization, multimodal integration, ethical frameworks, inclusion, cross-cultural study, and immersive technology. By following these guidelines, researchers and practitioners may go from descriptive analytics to developing sympathetic, adaptable, and morally sound digital ecosystems that appeal to the next generation of customers.

## REFERENCES


Abbasi, M., Váz, P., Silva, J., & Martins, P. (2024). Enhancing visual perception in immersive vr and ar environments: Ai-driven color and clarity adjustments under dynamic lighting conditions. *Technologies*, *12*(11), 216. DOI: 10.3390/technologies12110216

Agrawal, V., Nikalje, V., Sharma, S., & Haldar, P. (2025). *Role of Neuromarketing in Modern Consumer Behavior: Systematic Literature Review*. In *Decoding Consumer Behavior Using the Insight Equation and AI Marketing* (pp. 159-182).

Ahmed, Z. A., Albalawi, E., Aldhyani, T. H., Jadhav, M. E., Janrao, P., & Obeidat, M. R. M. (2023). Applying eye tracking with deep learning techniques for early-stage detection of autism spectrum disorders. *Data*, *8*(11), 168. DOI: 10.3390/data8110168

Ai, X., Wu, Z., Guo, T., Zhong, J., Hu, N., & Fu, C. (2021). The effect of visual attention on stereoscopic lighting of museum ceramic exhibits: A virtual environment mixed with eye-tracking. *Informatica (Vilnius)*, *45*(5).

Al Lawati, S. F. D. (2025, May). I Am Not a Caveman: An Eye-tracking Study of How Users are Influenced to Search in the Era of GenAI. In *Companion Proceedings of the ACM on Web Conference 2025* (pp. 681-684).

Alghofaili, R., Solah, M. S., Huang, H., Sawahata, Y., Pomplun, M., & Yu, L. F. (2019, March). Optimizing visual element placement via visual attention analysis. In *2019 IEEE Conference on Virtual Reality and 3D User Interfaces (VR)* (pp. 464-473). IEEE. DOI: 10.1109/VR.2019.8797816

Almourad, M., Bataineh, E., Hussein, M., & Wattar, Z. (2025). Strategic Placement of Branding Elements in Digital Marketing: Insights from Eye-Tracking Data. In *Proceedings of the 27th International Conference on Enterprise Information Systems* (pp. 417-423). DOI: 10.5220/0013281500003929

Baharum, A., Ismail, R., Halamy, S., Rahim, E. A., Noor, N. A. M., & Deris, F. D. (2024, August). Enhancing UX Design Through Eye-Tracking and Image Processing: Practical Insights and Applications. In *2024 International Conference on Platform Technology and Service (PlatCon)* (pp. 1-4). IEEE. DOI: 10.1109/PlatCon63925.2024.10830718

Bekler, M., Yilmaz, M., & Ilgın, H. E. (2024). Assessing feature importance in eye-tracking data within virtual reality using explainable artificial intelligence techniques. *Applied Sciences (Basel, Switzerland)*, *14*(14), 6042. DOI: 10.3390/app14146042

Calderón Fajardo, V., Anaya-Sánchez, R., Rejón-Guardia, F., & Molinillo-Jiménez, S. (2024). Neurotourism insights: Eye tracking and galvanic analysis of tourism destination brand logos and AI visuals.

Cenizo, C. (2025). A Neuromarketing Approach to Consumer Behavior on Web Platforms. *International Journal of Consumer Studies*, *49*(2), e70034. DOI: 10.1111/ijcs.70034

Chakraborty, P., Ahmed, S., Yousuf, M. A., Azad, A. K. M., Alyami, S. A., & Moni, M. A. (2021). A human-robot interaction system calculating visual focus of human's attention level. *IEEE Access : Practical Innovations, Open Solutions*, *9*, 93409–93421. DOI: 10.1109/ACCESS.2021.3091642

Chen, S. (2024). The application of eye-tracking technology in chemistry education research: A systematic review. *Research in Science & Technological Education*, ●●●, 1–20.

Chen, X., & Chen, Z. (2017). Exploring visual attention using random walks based eye tracking protocols. *Journal of Visual Communication and Image Representation*, *45*, 147–155. DOI: 10.1016/j.jvcir.2017.02.005

Chen, X., Wang, S., Yang, X., Yu, C., Ni, F., Yang, J., Tian, Y., Ye, J., Liu, H., & Luo, R. (2023). Utilizing artificial intelligence-based eye tracking technology for screening ADHD symptoms in children. *Frontiers in Psychiatry*, *14*, 1260031. DOI: 10.3389/fpsyt.2023.1260031 PMID: 38034916

Cheng, S., & Dey, A. K. (2019). I see, you design: User interface intelligent design system with eye tracking and interactive genetic algorithm. *CCF Transactions on Pervasive Computing and Interaction*, *1*(3), 224–236. DOI: 10.1007/s42486-019-00019-w

Cheng, S., Fan, J., & Hu, Y. (2023). Visual saliency model based on crowdsourcing eye tracking data and its application in visual design. *Personal and Ubiquitous Computing*, *27*(3), 613–630. DOI: 10.1007/s00779-020-01463-7

Cioffi, G. M., Pinilla-Echeverri, N., Sheth, T., & Sibbald, M. G. (2023). Does artificial intelligence enhance physician interpretation of optical coherence tomography: Insights from eye tracking. *Frontiers in Cardiovascular Medicine*, *10*, 1283338. DOI: 10.3389/fcvm.2023.1283338 PMID: 38144364

Clement, J., Kristensen, T., & Grønhaug, K. (2013). Understanding consumers' in-store visual perception: The influence of package design features on visual attention. *Journal of Retailing and Consumer Services*, *20*(2), 234–239. DOI: 10.1016/j.jretconser.2013.01.003

Drews, M., & Dierkes, K. (2024). Strategies for enhancing automatic fixation detection in head-mounted eye tracking. *Behavior Research Methods*, *56*(6), 6276–6298. DOI: 10.3758/s13428-024-02360-0 PMID: 38594440

Gao, E., Zhong, H., Yuan, R., Guo, J., & Chen, Z. (2025, May). "How Do You Understand? Your Eyes Show It": Explainable Artificial Intelligence for Cross-Language Comprehension Prediction Through Eye Movement. In *International Conference on Human-Computer Interaction* (pp. 323-348). Cham: Springer Nature Switzerland.

Guo, R., Kim, N., & Lee, J. (2024). Empirical insights into eye-tracking for design evaluation: Applications in visual communication and new media design. *Behavioral Sciences (Basel, Switzerland)*, *14*(12), 1231. DOI: 10.3390/bs14121231 PMID: 39767372

Hillaire, S., Breton, G., Ouarti, N., Cozot, R., & Lécuyer, A. (2010, September). Using a visual attention model to improve gaze tracking systems in interactive 3d applications. [). Oxford, UK: Blackwell Publishing Ltd.]. *Computer Graphics Forum*, *29*(6), 1830–1841. DOI: 10.1111/j.1467-8659.2010.01651.x

Hwang, Y. M., & Lee, K. C. (2018). Using an eye-tracking approach to explore gender differences in visual attention and shopping attitudes in an online shopping environment. *International Journal of Human-Computer Interaction*, *34*(1), 15–24. DOI: 10.1080/10447318.2017.1314611

Jamil, N., & Belkacem, A. N. (2024). Advancing real-time remote learning: A novel paradigm for cognitive enhancement using EEG and eye-tracking analytics. *IEEE Access : Practical Innovations, Open Solutions*, *12*, 93116–93132. DOI: 10.1109/ACCESS.2024.3422926

Jin, K., Zhang, Y., & Chen, J. (2025). Optimizing Urban Visual Identity: Eye-Tracking Insights for Outdoor Advertising Management. *Buildings (Basel, Switzerland)*, *15*(12), 2128. DOI: 10.3390/buildings15122128

Kondak, A. (2023). The Application of Eye Tracking and Artificial Intelligence in Contemporary Marketing Communication Management. *Scientific Papers of Silesian University of Technology. Organization & Management/Zeszyty Naukowe Politechniki Slaskiej. Seria Organizacji i Zarzadzanie*, (186).

Koorathota, S., Papadopoulos, N., Ma, J. L., Kumar, S., Sun, X., Mittal, A., . . . Sajda, P. (2023). Fixating on attention: Integrating human eye tracking into vision transformers. *arXiv preprint arXiv:2308.13969.*

Li, F., Chen, C. H., Liu, Y., Chang, D., Cui, J., & Sourina, O. (2024). Autoencoder-enabled eye-tracking data analytics for objective assessment of user preference in humanoid robot appearance design. *Expert Systems with Applications*, *249*, 123857. DOI: 10.1016/j.eswa.2024.123857

Li, Z., Li, R., Yuan, L., Cui, J., & Li, F. (2024). A benchmarking framework for eye-tracking-based vigilance prediction of vessel traffic controllers. *Engineering Applications of Artificial Intelligence*, *129*, 107660. DOI: 10.1016/j.engappai.2023.107660

Lyu, D., Manas-Viniegra, L., & Xu, Z. (2025). Visual Attention Differences Toward Football Stadium's Naming Rights: An Eye Tracking Study. *Asia Pacific Journal of Marketing and Logistics*, *37*(1), 189–209. DOI: 10.1108/APJML-03-2024-0281

Mankutė, V. (2025). *The impact of visual attention on brand attitudes in social media using eye-tracking approach* (Doctoral dissertation, Vilniaus universitetas.).

Mishra, A. B. (2025). *Neuromarketing in the Phygital Era by Influencing Gen Z and Sustainable Consumer Behaviour in a Digitally Driven Retail World.* In *Organizational Risks, Challenges, and Barriers in Developing Sustainability Start-Ups* (pp. 239-252). IGI Global. DOI: 10.4018/978-1-6684-9872-9.ch012

Moreno-Arjonilla, J., López-Ruiz, A., Jiménez-Pérez, J. R., Callejas-Aguilera, J. E., & Jurado, J. M. (2024). Eye-tracking on virtual reality: A survey. *Virtual Reality (Waltham Cross)*, *28*(1), 38. DOI: 10.1007/s10055-023-00903-y

Pinhal, R., Estima, A., & Duarte, P. (2025). See, like, and book: Eye-tracking the power of visual attention in destination marketing. *Journal of Marketing Communications*, •••, 1–21. DOI: 10.1080/13527266.2025.2511144

Pupchenko, D. (2022). *Importance of Neuromarketing Technologies in the Success of an Advertising Strategy: The Case of KEX LLP.* Bachelor's Thesis, Kazakhstan.

Sharma, K., Giannakos, M., & Dillenbourg, P. (2020). Eye-tracking and artificial intelligence to enhance motivation and learning. *Smart Learning Environments*, *7*(1), 13. DOI: 10.1186/s40561-020-00122-x

Singh, J., & Modi, N. (2024). A robust, real-time camera-based eye gaze tracking system to analyze users' visual attention using deep learning. *Interactive Learning Environments*, *32*(2), 409–430. DOI: 10.1080/10494820.2022.2088561

Skaramagkas, V., Giannakakis, G., Ktistakis, E., Manousos, D., Karatzanis, I., Tachos, N. S., Tripoliti, E., Marias, K., Fotiadis, D. I., & Tsiknakis, M. (2021). Review of eye tracking metrics involved in emotional and cognitive processes. *IEEE Reviews in Biomedical Engineering*, *16*, 260–277. DOI: 10.1109/RBME.2021.3066072 PMID: 33729950

Šola, H. M., Qureshi, F. H., & Khawaja, S. (2024). AI Eye-Tracking Technology: A new era in managing cognitive loads for online learners. *Education Sciences, 14*(9), 933. DOI: 10.3390/educsci14090933

Šola, H. M., Qureshi, F. H., & Khawaja, S. (2024). Predicting behaviour patterns in online and PDF magazines with AI eye-tracking. *Behavioral Sciences (Basel, Switzerland), 14*(8), 677. DOI: 10.3390/bs14080677 PMID: 39199073

Šola, H. M., Qureshi, F. H., & Khawaja, S. (2025). AI and Eye Tracking Reveal Design Elements' Impact on E-Magazine Reader Engagement. *Education Sciences, 15*(2), 203. DOI: 10.3390/educsci15020203

Štefko, R., Ondrijová, I., Miško, D., & Tomková, A. (2025). Analysis of Flight Search on the Web Using Eye-Tracking. *Journal of Sensory Studies, 40*(4), e70066. DOI: 10.1111/joss.70066

Tang, Y., & Chen, C. (2024). Can stylized products generated by AI better attract user attention? Using eye-tracking technology for research. *Applied Sciences (Basel, Switzerland), 14*(17), 7729. DOI: 10.3390/app14177729

Van Loo, E. J., Grebitus, C., Nayga, R. M.Jr, Verbeke, W., & Roosen, J. (2018). On the measurement of consumer preferences and food choice behavior: The relation between visual attention and choices. *Applied Economic Perspectives and Policy, 40*(4), 538–562. DOI: 10.1093/aepp/ppy022

Wang, Q., Yang, S., Liu, M., Cao, Z., & Ma, Q. (2014). An eye-tracking study of website complexity from cognitive load perspective. *Decision Support Systems, 62*, 1–10. DOI: 10.1016/j.dss.2014.02.007

Wilson, E., Sendhilnathan, N., Burlingham, C. S., Mansour, Y., Cavin, R., Tetali, S. D., & Proulx, M. J. (2025, May). Eye Gaze as a Signal for Conveying User Attention in Contextual AI Systems. In *Proceedings of the 2025 Symposium on Eye Tracking Research and Applications* (pp. 1-7). DOI: 10.1145/3715669.3727349

Winterhalter, L., Kofler, F., Ströbele, D. A., Othman, A., & von See, C. (2024). AI-assisted diagnostics in dentistry: An eye-tracking study on user behavior. *Journal of Clinical and Experimental Dentistry, 16*(5), e547–e555. DOI: 10.4317/jced.61491 PMID: 38988762

Zhang, R., Walshe, C., Liu, Z., Guan, L., Muller, K., Whritner, J., Zhang, L., Hayhoe, M., & Ballard, D. (2020, April). Atari-head: Atari human eye-tracking and demonstration dataset. *Proceedings of the AAAI Conference on Artificial Intelligence, 34*(04), 6811–6820. DOI: 10.1609/aaai.v34i04.6161 PMID: 32901213

Zhang, W., & Liu, H. (2017). Toward a reliable collection of eye-tracking data for image quality research: Challenges, solutions, and applications. *IEEE Transactions on Image Processing*, *26*(5), 2424–2437. DOI: 10.1109/TIP.2017.2681424 PMID: 28362586

Zheng, J., Huang, Y., Chen, Y., Guan, L., & Liu, Q. (2022). Subjective preference and visual attention to the attributes of ornamental plants in urban green space: An eye-tracking study. *Forests*, *13*(11), 1871. DOI: 10.3390/f13111871

Ziv, G. (2016). Gaze behavior and visual attention: A review of eye tracking studies in aviation. *The International Journal of Aviation Psychology*, *26*(3-4), 75–104. DOI: 10.1080/10508414.2017.1313096

# Chapter 7
# Next-Gen Marketing Intelligence:
## Exploring the Neuro-Scientific Technique in Marketing

**Ankita Pathak**
http://orcid.org/0000-0002-8068-8874
*Institute of Business Management, GLA University, India*

**Majdi Anwar Quttainah**
http://orcid.org/0000-0002-6280-1060
*Kuwait University, Kuwait*

## ABSTRACT

*The current study explores how advances in neuroscientific technique like tracking brain activity and facial reactions, are providing insights into consumer preference, emotions, and decision processes. The research has considered ethical factors, such as consumer consent and privacy, when using neuromarketing methods. The results identify knowledgeable gaps in the areas of application of neuromarketing. There is a need for further research to grasp the uses and limitations of neuromarketing technologies in modern marketing applications. Neuro-marketing provide the insights related to consumer's subconscious reactions and expressive responses to marketing stimuli. This helps marketers to understand the consumer preference, motivation, and decision-making processes. The study helps the marketers to focus on more effective and focused marketing campaigns based on personal preferences and behaviours. Neuromarketing and facial recognition technologies provide real-time tracking and feedback, which increases their conversion rate.*

DOI: 10.4018/979-8-3373-5997-7.ch007

## 1. INTRODUCTION

In the competitive market companies are searching for new and unique methods of interacting with customers. Companies are seeking to incorporate automated marketing techniques to create market demand. Over the last few decades, neuro-marketing, have received significant lay of light of both marketer and researcher. The incorporation of artificial intelligence-based technology has transformed the method of collecting and analyzing customer information (Chang et al., 2024). Marketer can customize marketing campaigns, product development, and customer experience. It helps in customization of products and services for particular groups of consumers (Behl et al., 2024).According to Frederick (2022), neuro-marketing employs stimuli derived from the mind to construct a shopper behaviour model by connecting internal neural activity with external consumer actions.

Advertisers must make estimations regarding the instinctive response of clients to external stimuli and utilise this knowledge to enhance marketing efforts. Market researchers must acquire an understanding of the neurological effects on clients. According to Mansor and Isa (2020), the foundation of neuro-marketing lies in the outcomes of a neuro-information system. Sung et al. (2020) state that neuro-marketing showcases the application of neuro-information systems in various marketing approaches. Previous studies demonstrate that neuro-information systems can assist marketers in determining the emotional levels of individuals, enabling them to apply this knowledge to their decision-making. Neuromarketing, in conjunction with facial recognition, identifies the mental cognitive dissonance of clients, significantly impacting their level of engagement in purchasing. The combination of neuromarketing and AI holds significant influence over successful marketing strategies. However, a comprehensive examination of the literature on this topic currently needs to be completed. Therefore, in order to address this knowledge gap, the following research question is proposed:

> RQ 1: To what extent can neuro-marketing contribute to contemporary marketing tactics?
> RQ 2: What are the factors contributing to using neuro-marketing strategies?

According to Nguyen (2021) Marketers are blending the neuromarketing with traditional marketing philosophies to gain an understanding of human behavior and reaction to marketing stimuli. Neuromarketing focuses on understanding and investigating the genetic and neurological processes which play an important role in consumer decision-making. The received information is used by the marketer in developing the marketing strategies and modifying the production of products and services according to need consumers need (Varghese, 2022). The past literature shows multiple paper but it lack the literature investigating the causes or impacts of neuro-marketing. The background information for the study is given in Section 2. A more comprehensive examination of the methodology and examination is undertaken in Sections 3 and 4. The study is ultimately concluded in Section 6, wherein suggestions for future research are put forth. Section 5, on the other hand, facilitates a discourse on the subject matter.

## 2. THEORETICAL FOUNDATIONS OF NEUROMARKETING

Neuromarketing is an emerging, multidisciplinary domain that aims to explain consumption patterns through a combination of biological, psychological, and technological factors. It recognizes that purchase choice is not always a rational, conscious activity, but often originates from automatic responses that occur within the brain and result from cognitive and emotional factors such as affective states, experience, attention, and evaluation of reward value. Neuromarketing provides a framework for understanding how the observable behaviours associated with consumers in the marketplace are external manifestations of the internal cognitive and affective processes that underlie those behaviours.

From a theoretical perspective, neuromarketing is based primarily on cognitive neuroscience, behavioural decision theory, and data-driven marketing intelligence. Cognitive neuroscience provides the relevant biological context for understanding the neural structures responsible for the regulation of perception, motivation, emotional arousal and the formation of preferences. Every time a human being views a marketing stimulus like TV commercial, brain regions linked to anticipation of rewards, processing of risks, and encoding of memories continuously evaluate the marketing stimulus and its attributes prior to that person having any conscious awareness of the impact of the marketing stimulus on their decision process.

Behavioural decision theory supports this biological framework by illustrating that the economic choices made by individuals are rarely based solely on rational evaluations. Rather, individuals make purchase decisions using heuristics (rules of thumb), emotions, and the context of the decision-making situation. Neuromarketing builds on behavioural theory.

The field of neuromarketing establishes the empirical measurement of these processes, rather than relying solely on observed behaviour, so it provides evidence of how psychological variables, like attention or motivation, can be related to biological responses through the use of physiological indicators. This empirical connection improves the quality and value of data collected by consumer researchers, thereby reinforcing the findings of consumer research.

Neuromarketing is also structured around a third component of theory and is influenced by advancements in both artificial intelligence and computational analytics. Modern neuromarketing is no longer simply observing how an individual responds on a neural level; neuromarketing is currently developing predictive behavioural models based on neural responses. Machine learning technology uses analytical tools to examine complex relationships between neural and physiological responses to develop statistical models used to predict preferences, identify and segment consumers, and optimise the effectiveness of marketing programs. Neuromarketing requires continuous conversion of biological markers into actionable information that can guide strategic marketing decisions. The integration of these three dimensions of marketing provides a multi-level understanding of market behaviour. Cognitive and emotional responses are created by biological mechanisms. Psychological mechanisms determine the pathway for arriving at a decision. Technological mechanisms convert cognitive and emotional responses into actionable marketing insights. Therefore, neuromarketing provides not only a tool for measuring responses to marketing communications but, at a theoretical level, a framework for understanding how human reasoning and digital analytics work together to influence current marketing practices. Figure 1 shows the Integrated AI enabled Neuromarketing Framework.

*Figure 1.*

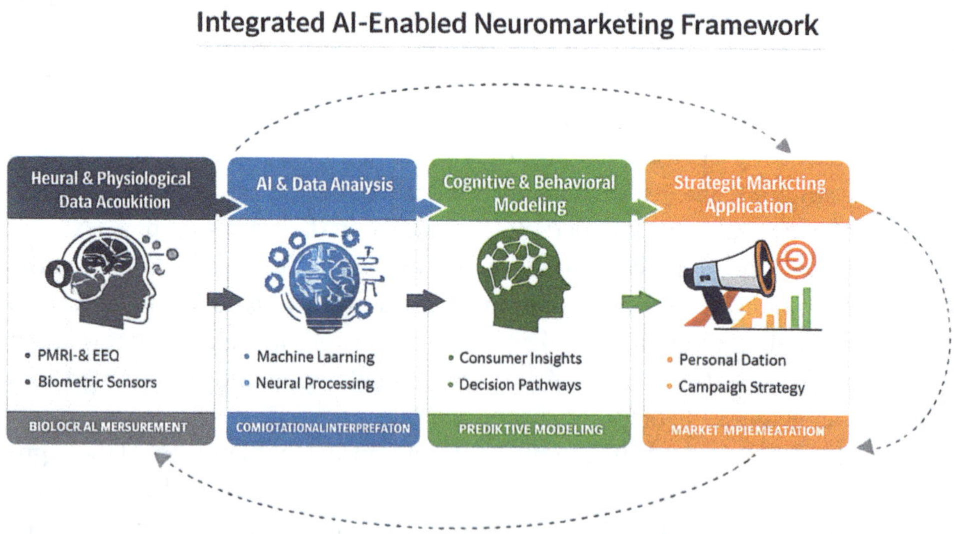


Although these dimensions of neuromarketing have developed into new areas of knowledge, the theoretical integration of these areas continues to remain woefully inadequate. Numerous research studies discuss and explain the need for accurate measurements; however, few have adequately evaluated how neuroscientific data is used to inform issues of strategic decision-making, outlines of corporate governance, and ethical considerations.

## 3 LITERATURE REVIEW

The current body of neuromarketing research demonstrates significant advancements in sophistication of measurement methods; however, research attempts to integrate across various theoretical frameworks remain sporadic. The study focuses on determining which areas of the brain are activated when consumers express preference, or emotionally engage with a brand, advertisement, or product. These studies demonstrate the biological foundations of consumer behaviour, yet are frequently done in isolation from actual market conditions. The use of neuroscience tools helps cover gaps that come with survey-based research. Neuromarketing tools uses clinical brain information and cerebral indicators to understand consumer behavior. Among the various neurological images techniques, magnetoencephalography (MEG) is one of the most extensively used (Rutkowska, 2022). Other techniques like positron emission tomography, electroencephalography, and functional magnetic resonance imaging (fMRI), are also used in the production of neurological images. These methods furnish compelling evidence that facilitates an understanding of how the brain processes conveyed information and knowledge through advertisements, thereby exerting an impact on purchasing decisions. Table 1 shows the current study on NeuroMarketing.

*Table 1. Current study on Neuro-marketing*

| Author | Objective | Context |
|---|---|---|
| Jordao et al. (2017) | To evaluate the customer behaviour using neuromarketing | Consumer behaviour |
| Lim (2018) | Identify limits and possibilities of using neuromarketing in business-to-business marketing. | Business-to-business |
| Lim et al. (2021) | study patterns of consumer involvement from the past, present, and future | Customer engagement |
| Lim and Weissmann (2023) | Present a thorough overview of behavioural control, conceptualisation, operationalisation, and theory development. | Behavioural control |
| A proposed study by researcher | How far can facial recognition technology and neuromarketing go in contemporary marketing tactics? | Limit to the domain of Marketing. |

*Table 2. Study on AI in Neuromarketing*

| Author(s) | Objective | Findings |
|---|---|---|
| (Singh & Kakkar, 2025) | Utilize artificial intelligence for customer profiling and attaining hyper-personalization. | Deep learning and neural convolutional networks could be used for hyper-personalisation profiling of the customers for retail establishment. |
| (Verdenhofs & Tambovceva, 2019) | Conducting sentiment analysis on customer online reviews. | Creation of an Automated Customer Segmentation Model. |
| (Clithero et al., 2021) | Understand the maladaptive patterns in consumer consumption. | A neural representation of dysfunctional consumption. |
| (Skriabin et al., 2021) | Evaluating the impact of ethical concerns regarding neuro-technology on the advertising industry. | The use of neurotechnology in marketing and advertising is not prohibited by law in Ukraine. |
| (Khan et al., 2025) | Predicting the movement of the mouth on an actual human visage. | Create an artificial intelligence platform for synthesising mouth gestures and generating producing corresponding information. |
| (Amati, 2023) | Examining the impacts of high-quality digital out-of-home advertising using neuroscience techniques. | Outdoor advertising has a significantly impact on emotions and feelings, which can be assessed using neuroscience techniques. |
| (Srivastava & Bag, 2024) | Investigating the potential of implementing neuro-marketing strategies in the rural market to understand consumer behaviour. | Applications of neuro-marketing offer more dependable insights into consumer behaviour |
| (Slager, 2023) | Examining the potential for integrating neuro-marketing into business-to-business marketing. | Neuro-marketing is crucial in comprehending the biological reactions within B2B marketing. |

(Source: Author Created)

Zhang et al. (2023) asserted that businesses can offer personalised coupons to their target audience by utilising facial recognition data. The combination of facial recognition technology and neuro-information systems has transformed the method of developing modern marketing strategies. The modern marketing strategy has eased the way to reach at target audience. Neuromarketing uses brain and physiological data to determine a consumer's preferences, decisions, and motivational influences. Meyerding and Mehlhose (2020), stated that neuromarketing identify the hidden emotions, feelings, and values which helps in understanding the consumer's mind. Neuromarketing field gives marketers rich information regarding the preference and selection of viewers. This information help the marketer to target the product to right audience and would convert the sales faster. Marketer get the information about the effectiveness of advertising and its effect on the targeted population by monitoring eye movement. In addition, the effectiveness can be quantified by measuring the level of visual attention given to a product. In Conventional method market strategies are developed on the base of insights and opinions depending on consumer traits, while neurotechnology use people's emotional reactions. The eye movement is a channel through which emotional and cognitive reactions to stimuli are expressed. Hamelin et al. (2020) assess the impact of the neuromarketing method on storytelling. There were two groups of participants, each provided with a story to read. The first group induce positive emotions based on the Micro-WNOp corpus, while the second used a cognitive strategy. The cognitive method provides a deeper insight on readers' cognitive responses. Xu and Liu (2024) created a system that uses electroencephalography recordings conjunction with a machine learning algorithm to gain insight into consumers' buying habits. Table 2 shows the study of AI in NeuroMarketing.

Neuromarketing is useful took for the marketer as it observe brain and body reactions and the same data is used to predict future behavior and measure the success of their campaigns. It helps marketer to better understand their target markets' attitudes and behaviors. Brands are non-physical entities but they have a deep position in people's minds. Marketers use neuroscience techniques to identify consumers' unconscious responses to marketing stimuli. Methods like electroencephalograms and magnetic resonance imaging quantify brain activity. Eye-tracking devices track individuals' eye movements and look at their responses to products. Heart rate and skin conductance can be used to measure individual's Curiosity towards the product or service. A change is found in development of Marketing strategies due to growing usage of Internet marketing and e-commerce. Marketers utilize advanced technologies such as artificial neural networks and deep learning models to build models that predict the buying behavior of their target market. These modern technologies such as neuroscience, marketing experts are able to predict future demand for products and services. The current research explores how tool of neuromarketing can improve and advance the marketing technique.

## 4. TECHNIQUE OF NEURO MARKETING

Neuro-marketing method is used to understand consumers' behavioral patterns and choice-making processes by examining the neurological reaction to marketing stimuli. Various instruments like fMRI, EEG, and eye-tracking are used by the market researchers to measure consumers' unconscious reactions toward varied marketing approaches in quantitative data (Song et al., 2025). Neuromarketing helps the companies to maximize their marketing efforts by focusing on the most effective messaging, design elements, and product features which create a positive reactions on customers. The combination of facial recognition technology with neuro-marketing has the huge potential to revolutionize marketing practices in the modern age.

## 4.1 EEG

An electroencephalogram (EEG) is a scientific tool used to measure brain activity and gain valuable information regarding people's cognitive processes. It is a common technique used in neuromarketing that allows marketers to gain more insight related to consumer behavior through analyzing neuroscience information (Gupta et al., 2025). EEG techniques help marketers in forecasting the sales, and identify implicit factors that determine consumer behaviour. It helps in determining the willingness to pay, and gain a better understanding of consumer preferences (Utriainen, 2020). EEG often disentangles marketing-related dilemmas as it have higher temporal resolution than other brain imaging methods . Neuroscientists make use of EEG information to build models of classification and extract the in-depth consumer perspectives (Hsu & Chen, 2020). In addition to this, EEG is a cost-effective and non-invasive electrophysiological method that uses electrodes to record cerebral electrical activity. Aldayel et al. (2020) undertake the research where EEG-based neuromarketing tests is used to measure how movies affect people's reactions to visual stimuli portraying destinations. The finding of the research proves the validity of EEG and neuro-marketing in measuring consumer responses. Modern neuroimaging method such as electroencephalography, explore cerebral functionality (Alsharif et al., 2021). fMRI, fNIRS, and EEG methods are utilized to quantitatively measure the neural reaction to marketing stimuli, such as products, branding, advertisement, and prices. These technologies determine and analyze the effectiveness of all marketing stimuli to maximize their emotional and memorability impact. It also influence the sales, and purchasing decision.

Neuro-marketing strategies have been described into two broad categories (see Figure 1), that is, neurophysiological techniques and physiological techniques. Some of the physiological techniques are the electrocardiogram (ECG), eye tracking (ET), galvanic skin response (GSR), neurotransmitter measurement, implicit association test (IAT), and face electromyography (EMG). Neurophysiological include fMRI, EEG, MEG, and positron emission tomography (PET).These categorizations were introduced by Chaudhary (2025), whereby the first category is concerned with recording brain activity signals like fMRI and PET, whereas the second category records brain activity signals like EEG and MEG at the metabolic level.

## 4.2 Functional magnetic resonance

fMRI is a significant neuroinformatic tool in neuromarketing, which helps the marketer to predict customer behavior. fMRI allows marketers to scan regions of the brain that are linked to emotional and cognitive functions. The technique creates a sequence of images that capture brain activity by the use of radio waves and magnetic fields together. It acts as a brain mapping tool for individuals. The analysis of neurological information helps the marketers to learn about consumer behaviour.

### 4.3 Magnetoencephalography

The marketers use Magnetoencephalography (MEG) to examine how various areas of the brain control customers' thought processes. This technique is non-invasive as it examine brain activity by isolating the complex activation patterns of cerebral processes. MEG detect the magnetic field, processes the data, and identifies the locations of brain centres of activity, and then superimposed on x-rays of the body. Alsharif et al. (2024) highlights MEG's high temporal resolution. Horowitz et al. (2025) stated that PET and fMRI are techniques for determining changes in the chemical makeup of the brain or the proportion of oxygenated to deoxygenated blood. Brain electrical activity data can be recorded using transcranial magnetic stimulation, MEG, EEG, and steady-state topography (SST).In addition, non-physiological/non-brain methods such as ET, GSR, ECG, IAT, and face EMG are used to measure customer behaviour. PET, fMRI, and MEG techniques are used for assessing cerebral blood flow. EEG and SST record non-hemispheric brain wave activity and lateralisation. describes fMRI and EEG techniques for measuring brain activity. They also identify ET and GSR as methods for evaluating consumers' physiological responses, in addition to TMS and neurotransmitters.

## 5 APPLICATIONS OF NEURO-MARKETING

### 5.1 AI in profiling

Across the globe, there is a rapid advancement in the development of artificial intelligence (AI)-based technologies. These technologies are employed in client hyper-personalisation and profiling (Jain et al., 2024). Notably, deep learning technology is being harnessed by shopping malls and retail enterprises to generate comprehensive consumer profiles. To achieve this, they physically station themselves within the shops, allowing them to directly identify and collect client data, which is then utilised to create machine learning models (Simula, 2025). By incorporating age, gender, personality traits, usage patterns and emotions, AI algorithms construct anonymous consumer profiles for each purchase. Consequently, these machine learning algorithms vigilantly monitor consumers' purchasing behaviours, providing organisations with a plethora of applications that span numerous industries (Simula, 2025). In their study, Jain et al. (2024) employ fuzzy set qualitative comparison analysis to devise a model tailored to the clothing and fashion businesses. This model proves beneficial to marketing teams as it aids in creating targeted marketing campaigns by identifying potential customers based on their activities Jain et al. (2024). Given the effectiveness of these strategies, marketers are increasingly adopting them to broaden the reach of their campaigns.

Neuro-marketing focuses on understanding and shaping consumer behavior through the study of human brain activity to marketing stimulus. Neuro-marketing provide the important insights about consumers' likes, buying habits, and desires by combining marketing, neuroscience, and psychology. Such insights help marketers in designing better marketing strategies, and customized advertising campaigns which attracts the customer towards the product. The product features appeal to consumers subconsciously and neuromarketing captures the frequency of consumer mind. The applications of neuromarekting in contemporary marketing is wide-ranging as it can help the marketer in personalised marketing by identifying, monitoring individual customers and improving the customer experience through advertising and recommendations. Table 4 shows the application of technique of neuro-marketing. The use of neuroscientific tools is very important for precise prediction of customer behavior. As per Kauffmann et al. (2020), neuro-marketing can convert huge volumes of data into quick insights that maximize societal and economic value. Mittal et al. (2025) explored how neuro-information system is used by a machine learning model to provide accurate results for every individual.

*Table 4. Application of technique of Neuro-Marketing*

| AUTHOR / YEAR | DEVICE | FINDINGS |
|---|---|---|
| **Galkin et al. (2019)** | GSR | The atmosphere in the store and the consumer's state impact the emotional fatigue differently; thereby, the footfall. |
| **Cascio et al. (2015)** | FMRI | Changes in recommendations as a result of peer recommendations have been increased activity in the striatum and the OFC. |
| **Chen et al. (2015)** | FMRI | It is possible to predict the brand that person is thinking of it based on the correlation between brand personality and brain activity. |
| **Morris (2019)** | FMRI | The dimensions of emotion (e.g., appeal, engagement, and empowerment) are playing a vital role in measuring feelings toward TV ads. |
| **Puppin (2020)** | EEG / HR / GSR | A campaign of PSAs characterized by a symbolic communication style obtained the highest approach values, as evaluated by the AW index. While an image and a spot based on the "fear arousing appeal" and with a narrative style reported the highest and lowest effort values index, respectively. Also, the same "effective" campaign showed the highest EI values. |

continued on following page

*Table 4. Continued*

| AUTHOR / YEAR | DEVICE | FINDINGS |
|---|---|---|
| **Österle et al. (2024)** | Eye Tracking (Tobii Eye-Tracking Glasses) | The warm color temperature attracts more visual attention to the advertisement; thereby, generates a positive implicit attitude to the advertisement and induces the buying intentions of the advertised products compared with cool color temperature advertisements whether the spokesperson's female or male celebrity. Therefore, The color temperature impacts the effectiveness of the advertising spokesperson and advertising effectiveness. |
| **Mittal et al. (2025)** | EEG | Illustrating that asymmetry in the prefrontal cortex in the gamma and beta band was highly related to subsequent WTP responses, and the gamma band was most strongly related to WTP decision. |

## 5.2 Customer Behaviour

Pragna et al. (2025) a neuro-information system is utilized by a machine learning model to provide accurate results for every individual. In the globalized environment, various multinational companies are applying neuromarketing practices in order to evaluate their customers' physiological and neurological signals. The insights gained from the tool is used in creation of targeted marketing campaigns, price strategies, and product lines to effectively control customer behaviour proactively (Anil Kumar & Ramesh Babu, 2025). Through the information gathered using neurotechnology, neuromarketing can forecast whether the attitudes of customers will be favourable or negative for the particular product (Hutchinson et al., 2024). Machine learning models help in knowing the Customers' real responses to products. In contrast, the traditional method of manually evaluating online customer feedback create a challenges to the marketer. Automated sentiment analysis allows for precise prediction of potential and existing customer behaviours (Shah & Kumar, 2024). The model also quantifies the maladaptive spending patterns associated with excessive and dysfunctional behaviours.

## 5.3 Social Media Data in Marketing

According to Cordova-Buiza et al. (2025), social networking has become integral to Internet communication. It serves as the primary means by which marketers engage electronically with users. In the contemporary era of smartphones, convenient access to electronic platforms is customary, facilitating seamless communication (Cordova-Buiza et al., 2025). Marketers develop strong relationships with potential clients by usage of social media. Marketer use information to make predict the buying behaviors of the consumer . According to Cordova-Buiza et al. (2025), social media plays a significant role in shaping the connection between businesses and potential clients. These interactions on social media would alter the emotional and affect the sentiment offline and online. In addition, this strategy encourages nurturing new connections and strengthening current ones. (O'Reilly et al., 2024) argue that information from multiple online sites is useful in forecasting consumer behavior. Social media users often write reviews on products and services, which benefit other individuals in their choice-making processes. Positive internet reviews enable users in choosing and considering the products. It also helps in building company's image among existing and future consumers.

Information and content like pictures post on online sites can be used to predict consumers buying habits. Neurotechnology examines how clients react to advertisements and goods, specifically their facial reactions. This facial reactions are used by companies to classify customers according to their facial impressions and inclinations. Such data is useful in advertising, service, and selling interactions. This information is used by the marketer in building the base for targeted advertising and meet the unique characteristics of each category (Geetha & Hegde, 2024). The product description, appearance, and advertising message information generate strong emotions in consumers that guide purchasing intentions. It provide a positive effect on consumer satisfaction and purchase intentions. Table 5 shows the cpmpany based application of neuro-marketing technique. Kesarwani et al. (2025) evidence that marketers can use the opinions of customers to improve segmentation and targeting practice. In addition, it provides insights on how effective their marketing strategies are meeting the customers' needs.

*Table 5. Company Based Application of Neuromarketing Technique*

| Company | Neuro-marketing Technique | Purpose |
|---|---|---|
| **Coca-Cola** | EEG | Measure consumer brain response towards different packaging design and commercial ads. It helps in identifying the most appealing packing element and advertisement which lead to increase consumer engagement |
| **Apple** | EEG | To measure the emotional response of viewers to the ads |
| **Pepsi** | Eye Tracking | To test different version of logo. |
| **Nike** | FMRI | Analysed the brain activity while people were wearing different shoes. |
| **Netflix** | Eye Tracking | Measure viewer engagement with content |
| **Microsoft** | Eye Tracking | Understand users' interactions with the new interface and adjusted based on the findings. |
| **Frito-Lay** | fMRI | Understand consumers' responses to their potato chips. The insights gained helped them redesign their packaging to better appeal to consumers' subconscious preferences. |

continued on following page

*Table 5. Continued*

| Company | Neuro-marketing Technique | Purpose |
|---|---|---|
| **Audi** | EEG | How people react emotionally to different designs, finding that curved lines evoked stronger emotional reactions than straight lines |
| **Toyota** | fMRI | Understand emotional response to cars |
| **Starbucks** | ET | Optimize store layout for customer flow |
| **BMW** | EEG | Analyze emotional response to car designs. |

## 5.4 Cognitive Consumer behaviour

The application of physiological and neurological technology helps in understanding the consumer behavior in marketing stimuls. Bigne et al. (2025) argue that consumer neuroscience is the evolving field in the marketing field, and is a less expensive option than conventional marketing practices. EEG and fMRI provides useful information about brain reactions. The developing nations needs to improve the potential of neurotechnology as it can promote economic development. Musole (2025) integration of neurotechnology in marketing can give a competitive edge by meeting the clients and facilitate in the expansion of impactful marketing. Chand et al. (2025) offers valuable knowledge on cognitive thought and brain responses. In addition, it highlights the importance of using neurotechnology and brain imaging to analyze unconscious responses, emotional states, and mental illnesses. These information canbe used in advertising, media campaigns, and other promotion efforts. Chand et al. (2025) argue that neuro-marketing studies and analyzes the cognitive and affective dimensions of customer behaviour. Neuro-marketing is more accurate and effective compared to the conventional data collection methods since it uses actual brain activity as compare to interviews and questionnaires to forecast consumers' behavior (Islam et al., 2024).

Srivastava and Bag (2024)state that the neuroscientific method includes electromyography, face decoding, measure the responses experienced by customers. Convolutional neural networks (CNNs) have shown higher efficiency compared to traditional approaches in face recognition (Peng et al., 2024). CNNs assist in the creation of better prediction models, which makes a more precise estimation of demand for products and services. Emotional intelligence is key in marketing for the service industries (Semwal et al., 2024). Facial recognition technology is used to measure customer satisfaction. With regard to conventional methods, facial expressions and emotions are a better representation of human reactions toward products or services (Radojević et al., 2025).

Conventional marketing approach faces difficulty in anticipating the consumers' reactions to adverts, whereas neuro-marketing is a tools to understand the customers' minds and interest . The most precise tool for measuring brain activity is neurotechnology. The brain neural network has more than 100 billion cells, so more accurate predictions can be made about consumer behavior (Moutinho & Cerf, 2024). According to the research of Srivastava and Bag (2024) visual attention acts as a mediator between recall and purchase intention. When customers are visually engrossed, they are more able to recall and have a more positive impact on their purchasing intentions. Marketers seek to influence customers' memory capacity by visual attention, and allowing them to remember the information. The key concept of neuro-marketing is to map a relationship between customers' internal and external behaviors. Srivastava and Bag (2024) developed a behavioral model based on neuro-information to predict customers' purchase behaviors with more accuracy. The model examines brain activity and how it affects customers' final judgments. Neuromarketing use of neuro-information to determine the cognitive state of users, and help the marketers to increase customer loyalty and preference. Marketer faces the constantly challenge of changing attitudes and preferences and neuro marketing is the key which has unlocked all the challenges. It understand of human psychology and external behavior trends which affects the purchases (Srivastava & Bag, 2024). Adel (2025) carried out a neuro-marketing experiment to determine marketing effectiveness of tourist destinations. It examined the consumers' neural response in order to determine what they feel and think (Bhardwaj et al., 2024).

## 6 DISCUSSION AND LEGAL CHALLENGES IN NEUROMAREKTING

There have been various studies by researchers Labib (2024) which states that artificial intelligence (AI) has influenced the marketing sector and marketing practices have changed with the adoption of neurotechnology. According to Bigne et al. (2025) psychophysiological responses play a crucial role in neuro-marketing. It is suggested that managers use psychophysiological analysis in order to forecast consumers' decision-making behavior. Kumar et al. (2024) consider emotional intelligence and consideration are essential requirements for neuro-marketing. Marketers can foster a positive attitude among consumers by examining the neurological side. Multiple basic factors effect the consumers' purchasing behavior, such as feelings, moods, desires, and unconscious thought. Kumar et al. (2024) indicates that neuromarketing helps the marketer in understanding the customers' unconscious mind which affects their purchasing decisions, and provide a base foundation to build frameworks based on neural information. Ferrell et al. (2025) explore the ethical and legal aspect of applying neurotechnology in advertising. In conformity with Ferrell et al. (2025), the neuromarketing field is more dependent on psychology and neuroscience. Marketers are required to understand the physiological reactions of customers in order to reach their targeted audience. The combined use of different tools and methods of the neuroscience technique has transformed the marketing idea. Österle et al. (2024) extends the application of neuromarketing technique in B2B marketing theory in order to increase its potential by giving better understanding of customer behavior. Kajla et al. (2024) examines whether neuromarketing technique can be utilised in promotional and advertising strategies. Pires et al. (2024) adopted an AI-powered machine learning framework to enhances efficiency and productivity. Bigne et al. (2025) examines the application of neuromarketing in the development of new marketing strategies. Sembiring et al. (2024) develops a model using neuro-fuzzy methods to arrive at the creditworthiness of the customer. Wu et al. (2025) time series analysis can assists the tourism industry in forecasting the customer behaviour. It increases the prediction accuracy for demand in the tourism sector. The forecasting model, helps the marketers in predict cognitive thinking patterns of consumers. The current era of digitalisation has shifted the customers towards preferring online stores. Yao and Wang (2024) found that neuromarketing can analyze consumer reviews and provide accurate feedback about the perception of the product in the minds of viewers. According to Yao and Wang (2024) an alert system sends messages to marketing managers, to provide the fast response to customers in less time. Furthermore, it also provides security and safety to online transactions. The accuracy of the predictability of consumer behavior depends upon the quality of information available. Online customer surveys and digital reviews provide insights to the marketer to understand their customers' views.

The rapid growth of neuroscience and AI technology in marketing has created unprecedented analysis capabilities, however it has also opened up a range of ethical and legal issues that are not simply peripheral issues. Neuromarketing exists at the overlap between biological measurement processes, behavioural influence, and a reliance upon data as means for making decisions. This raises questions related to how data collected from consumers will be used, but also questions regarding the limits of psychological autonomy, the nature and type of informed consent, and who is accountable for any potential misuse or abuse of consumer data under applicable laws and regulations.

The biggest ethical issue surrounding neuromarketing is cognitive privacy. Conventional marketing research relies heavily upon information provided by consumers about themselves related to attitudes, purchasing histories, or behaviours. Neuromarketing wirelessly collects physiological and neural signals reflecting consumers' subconscious emotional responses, attentional focus, and motivation. These signals may provide some insight into preferences or weaknesses that a consumer might not be capable of verbalizing, or may not feel comfortable revealing. The collection of this type of physiological data which captures the desires and thoughts of an individual obstructs traditional definitions of privacy and provides data that transcends observable behaviour. This creates an ethical dilemma as to whether an individual can give meaningful consent to the collection and interpretation of neural data when the research community has not fully developed an understanding of what those signals mean or could represent.

The concept of autonomy and influence falls under the broader umbrella of privacy concerns related to neuromarketing. Neuromarketing identifies the way in which someone may make a decision, focusing on the mechanics/biomechanics of decision-making, such as how emotional triggers such as reward reception, trust, fear, desire, etc. can affect your decision-making process. Using this information to design marketing stimuli may lead to crossing an ethical line between persuasion and manipulation. While marketers have always attempted to influence consumer actions, neuromarketing brings about the possibility of targeting the subconscious in ways that are probably unnoticeable to the average consumer and that might even bypass reflective reasoning altogether. This raises concerns that marketing strategies might take advantage of cognitive biases or emotional vulnerabilities of consumers, particularly of those groups who don't have the same capacity to make good decisions. Adolescents or consumers under a significant amount of stress would fall into this category. The ethical dilemma raised by these practices arises from the question of when or under what circumstances a marketing influence is an undue influence.

Another challenge is the lack of transparency and accountability of algorithms. In neuromarketing, algorithms are used to interpret neural and physiological signals and generate predictions using complex, often opaque, predictive models. These opaque models act as "black boxes", making it difficult to understand how algorithms produce specific marketing insights. When marketing decisions are made based on opaque algorithms that interpret biological data, it is difficult to determine whether the algorithm is providing accurate, fair or unbiased results. This is problematic since consumers will not have a full understanding of how their biological data is being used to market products to them, and regulators may not be able to ensure ethical compliance.

Methodological limitations also have ethical implications. Neural measurements are probabilistic measures; meaning, they do not provide a direct or unquestionable measure of a psychological state. As a result, the potential for over-interpretation or misinterpretation of an individual's brain activity may lead to excessive claims related to the intent or preference of an individual. If these over-interpretations are used to inform business strategies or develop policies regarding consumer behaviour, there is a risk of acting on less-than-complete evidence. Therefore, conducting ethical research requires providing clear communication about methodological limitations and uncertainty.

Regulations covering the use of neuromarketing remain inconsistent since legal coverage of biometric data exists in some areas but lacks any mention in other parts of the world. As a result, the lack of uniform standards means that consumers are not equally protected and the companies that will use this technology face a great deal of uncertainty. Therefore, the regulatory framework needs to catch up to include specific regulation for neural data including: informed consent, minimizing the amount of data collected, protecting the storage of that data, and the restrictions placed on behavioral targeting. Neuromarketing tools provide varying levels of understanding concerning consumer behavior but they fall within an area of ethics where traditional standards for privacy may not work. Privacy issues arise from the collection of neural data and how those neural data are used to target those subconscious processes create concerns for individual autonomy. AI creates a deeper level of concern regarding transparency and accountability. There will be some need for regulatory reform to address these issues, but researchers and marketers must also commit themselves to ethical reflexivity.

Data governance is another major issue affiliated with neuromarketing. The biological and neuromarketing data created by neuromarketing creates physiologically-sensitive biometric and neural data sets that are fundamentally different from the traditional consumer-level data sets. Many of these data sets cannot be easily de-identified, as the biological signatures can be used as a unique identifier for the individual. Because of this, it is unclear as to who owns the neural data, how long the data may be stored, and what conditions exist for sharing, selling, or re-purposing these types of data. Most of the existing data protection frameworks were developed primarily for regulating demographic and/or digital information. Therefore, the regulatory framework does not apply to biological signals; there may be legal ambiguity as a result.

## 7 IMPLICATIONS OF THE STUDY

In order to fully understand the intricate relationship between neuroscience and modern neuromarketing techniques, it is essential to explore the complex functions of different brain regions in processing distinct types of information, aided by a range of advanced methods for measuring brain activity. This exploration not only sheds light on the neural basis of consumer perceptions but also uncovers valuable insights into sophisticated marketing strategies that harness these neural mechanisms with confidence. The table 6 outlines the neuroscientific methods for measuring specific brain regions and their relevance in marketing. Table 6 shows the Comprehensive List of Brain-Activity Measurement Methods

*Table 6. Comprehensive List of Brain-Activity Measurement Methods*

| Method | Description | Application in Neuromarketing |
|---|---|---|
| fMRI | Measures brain activity by detecting changes in blood flow. | Locates which brain areas are involved in specific tasks. |
| EEG | Records electrical activity of the brain via electrodes. | Useful for understanding emotional responses in real time. |
| MEG | Detects magnetic fields produced by neural activity. | Provides precise timing and location of brain activity. |
| PET | Shows how tissues and organs are functioning by tracing a radioactive substance. | Used to observe deeper metabolic processes and brain functions. |
| Eye Tracking | Tracks gaze, fixation, and saccades to study visual attention. | Helps understand visual attention and interest in stimuli. |
| NIRS | Uses near-infrared light to monitor blood flow. | Ideal for studying prefrontal cortex activity in social interactions. |
| Biometric Sensors | Measure physiological responses such as heart rate, skin conductance. | Assess arousal and emotional engagement with content. |
| HRV Measurements | Monitors variations in time between heartbeats. | Measures emotional and physiological stress and engagement levels. |

The technology helps marketers in understanding the consumers' attitudes and responses towards different advertising and marketing campaigns. Consumer behavior is dynamic and ever-changing and it is very important to monitor and analyze this behaviour. Marketers are using artificial intelligence (AI) to create a framework. AI based technology like Neuro-marketing are implemented to help marketers in reaching their target audience. Integration of neuromarketing provides for fast analysis of consumer insight, which results in faster decision-making. Additionally, visual information helps marketers to identify market trends in a timely manner. The implementation of technology would benefit the businesses while assuring compliance related to privacy legislation and data security regulations. Marketers utilise discounts as a means to target their audience, fostering a sense of loyalty. This helps in meeting the demand at different stores.Marketers employ neuroscience to better comprehend how customers' minds respond to publicity and advertising initiatives. Physiological signals and neuro-marketing strategies collect customer preferences and motivation data. Unlike traditional marketing strategies, modern tools such as neuro-marketing allow companies to thoroughly examine their target market. Consequently, marketing research gains value and becomes more cost-effective than traditional techniques.

## 8 CONCLUSION

It is imperative to explore potential uses for neuromarketing. The maintenance of supply and demand equilibrium relies heavily on the accuracy of the forecasting model. Companies are leveraging modern technology to enhance the efficiency of their operations. Collaborations between marketing and information technology firms are reshaping the consumer market. Marketing experts utilise information technology to optimise the performance of predictive frameworks. Companies have the opportunity to enhance their predictive marketing models through the use of cutting-edge technologies such as neuromarketing. A predictive model based on data and customer insight provides valuable insights into customers' intentions and cognitive processes related to the product. AI techniques facilitate the process of consumer profiling for marketers. The success or failure of a marketing plan is contingent upon effective consumer profiling. Adequate resources are necessary for successful and productive consumer profiling. It is only feasible for a single item or service to cater to some customer groups's needs. Companies must offer a wide array of products to cater to a diverse range of customer groups. Marketers can utilise profiling techniques to effectively reach their target audience. Consumer data serves as the foundation for understanding the dynamic nature of consumers. Marketers can use neuro- based consumer intelligence data to develop successful marketing strategies. The research assists marketers in devising effective marketing plans. The generated data provides valuable insights into consumers' perceptions of the product or service. As the data is highly sensitive and critical for marketers to reach their target audience, caution must be exercised when handling sensitive consumer data. It is of utmost importance and the marketers' responsibility to ensure the data's safety and security. Research can be utilised to gain insights into consumers' perspectives, which can then be used for marketing purposes. Marketing professionals employ consumer insights to understand how their clients and their perceptions of the product are evolving.

## 9 FUTURE RESEARCH

In the modern digital world, People spend their ideal time on social networking sites . It is necessary for the marketers to understand customers' cognitive processes by utilising the information available on social media platforms. Future Research utilise the social network theory to evaluate the significance of social media data in analysing consumer behaviour.

*Figure 3.*

Theory of relationship Marketing
The information about customer preferences, demands, attitudes, behavior and convenience can be useful for precise segmentation and further investment in relationship building. However, more empirical and experiment-based studies are required to gain insights into this area.
Social networking theory
Marketers can refine their face recognition marketing strategies by utilizing the data available on the social media platforms
How customer engagement can be improved on online sites can also be examined
Future research can examine how the data captured through digital technologies are processed to extract important information that generates knowledge for marketing teams

## REFERENCES:


Adel, M. (2025). The Impact of Emotional Branding and Neuromarketing on Enhancing Egyptian Tourist Destination competitive. *Journal of Association of Arab Universities for Tourism and Hospitality*, *28*(1), 421–438. DOI: 10.21608/jaauth.2025.377760.1678

Aldayel, M., Ykhlef, M., & Al-Nafjan, A. (2020). Deep learning for EEG-based preference classification in neuromarketing. *Applied Sciences (Basel, Switzerland)*, *10*(4), 1–23. DOI: 10.3390/app10041525

. Alsharif, A. H., Isa, S. M., & Pilelienė, L. (2024). global academic trends of metabolic and electrical biomedical tools in marketing. *Baltic Journal of Economic Studies, 10*(5).

Alsharif, A. H., Md Salleh, N. Z., Baharun, R., & Rami Hashem, E. A. (2021). Neuromarketing research in the last five years: A bibliometric analysis. *Cogent Business & Management*, *8*(1), 1978620. Advance online publication. DOI: 10.1080/23311975.2021.1978620

. Amati, S. (2023). Harnessing the power of latest technologies in digital out-of-home advertising: a study on interaction models and audience impact.

Anil Kumar, J., & Ramesh Babu, S. (2025). Strategic Marketing and Customer Analytics. In *Strategy Analytics for Business Resilience Theories and Practices* (pp. 73–88). Springer Nature Switzerland. DOI: 10.1007/978-3-031-82369-5_5

Behl, A., Jayawardena, N., Shankar, A., Gupta, M., & Lang, L. D. (2024). Gamification and neuromarketing: A unified approach for improving user experience. *Journal of Consumer Behaviour*, *23*(1), 218–228. DOI: 10.1002/cb.2178

Bhardwaj, S., Kaushik, N., & Arora, M. (2024). Does Your Brain Have a Buy Button?: A Neuro Marketing Approach With Sensory Branding. In *Sensible Selling Through Sensory Neuromarketing* (pp. 210–229). IGI Global. DOI: 10.4018/979-8-3693-4236-7.ch011

Bigne, E., Boksem, M., Casado-Aranda, L. A., García-Madariaga, J., Gier-Reinartz, N. R., Guerreiro, J., Loureiro, S., Kakaria, S., Smidts, A., & Wedel, M. (2025). How to Conduct Valuable Marketing Research With Neurophysiological Tools. *Psychology and Marketing*, *42*(10), 2616–2649. DOI: 10.1002/mar.70002

. Chand, T., Nair, V. S., Srinivasu, P. N., & Kumar, V. J. (2025). Prospects and challenges in decoding consumer behavior using neurotechnology. *Artificial Intelligence Applications for Brain–Computer Interfaces*, 161-182.

Chang, C. Y., Santra, A. S., Chang, I. H., Wu, S. J., Roy, D. S., & Zhang, Q. (2024). Design and implementation of a real-time face recognition system based on artificial intelligence techniques. *Multimedia Systems, 30*(2), 114. DOI: 10.1007/s00530-024-01306-y

Chaudhary, U. (2025). Non-invasive Brain Signal Acquisition Techniques: Exploring EEG, EOG, fNIRS, fMRI, MEG, and fUS. In *Expanding Senses using Neurotechnology: Volume 1–Foundation of Brain-Computer Interface Technology* (pp. 25–80). Springer Nature Switzerland. DOI: 10.1007/978-3-031-76081-5_2

Clithero, J. A., Karmarkar, U. R., & Hsu, M. (2021). Toward an integrative conceptualization of maladaptive consumer behavior. *Journal of the Association for Consumer Research, 6*(3), 334–341. DOI: 10.1086/714364

Cordova-Buiza, F., Grillo-Torres, C. M., & Vega, C. R. (2025). Gastronomic culture and social networks: The impact of digital strategies on the promotion of traditional colombian cuisine. *Geo Journal of Tourism and Geosites, 59*(2), 587–594. DOI: 10.30892/gtg.59207-1439

Ferrell, M. L., Beatty, A., & Dubljevic, V. (2025). The Ethics of Neuromarketing: A Rapid Review. *Neuroethics, 18*(1), 1–22. DOI: 10.1007/s12152-025-09591-8

Frederick, D. P. (2022). Recent trends in neuro marketing–An exploratory study. [IJCSBE]. *International Journal of Case Studies in Business, IT, and Education, 6*(1), 38–60. DOI: 10.47992/IJCSBE.2581.6942.0148

. Geetha, V., & Hegde, S. N. (2024). Mapping the Consumer Mind: Neuromarketing Applications in Personalization and Targeting. *Library of Progress-Library Science, Information Technology & Computer, 44*(3).

Gupta, R., Kapoor, A., & Verma, H. (2025). Neuro-insights: A systematic review of neuromarketing perspectives across consumer buying stages. *Frontiers in Neuroergonomics, 6*, 1542847. DOI: 10.3389/fnrgo.2025.1542847

Hamelin, N., Thaichon, P., Abraham, C., Driver, N., Lipscombe, J., & Pillai, J. (2020). Storytelling, the scale of persuasion and retention: A neuromarketing approach. *Journal of Retailing and Consumer Services, 55*, 102099. DOI: 10.1016/j.jretconser.2020.102099

Horowitz, T., Doyen, M., Caminiti, S. P., Yakushev, I., Verger, A., & Guedj, E. (2025). Metabolic brain PET connectivity. *PET Clinics, 20*(1), 1–10. DOI: 10.1016/j.cpet.2024.09.014

Hsu, L., & Chen, Y. J. (2020). Neuromarketing, subliminal advertising, and hotel selection: An EEG study. *Australasian Marketing Journal, 28*(4), 200–208. DOI: 10.1016/j.ausmj.2020.04.009

Hutchinson, J. W., Reimann, M., Knutson, B., & Huber, J. (2024). Commentaries on "Reconsidering the path for neural and physiological methods in consumer psychology". *Journal of Consumer Psychology, 34*(1), 214–221. DOI: 10.1002/jcpy.1398

. ISLAM, M. M., NEOGY, T. K., & REZA, M. M. H. (2024). A DATA-DRIVEN NEUROMARKETING APPROACH TO UNDERSTANDING CONSUMER BUYING PREFERENCES. *Journal of Computing and Digital Technologies, 2*(1), 65-80.

Jain, P., Jain, P., & Jain, A. (2024). Marketing's crystal ball: Where we are and where we could soon be with generative artificial intelligence in marketing. *Journal of Cultural Marketing Strategy, 8*(2), 134–150. DOI: 10.69554/JDOC2249

Jordao, I. L. D. S., Souza, M. T. D., Oliveira, J. H. C. D., & Giraldi, J. D. M. E. (2017). Neuromarketing applied to consumer behaviour: An integrative literature review between 2010 and 2015. *International Journal of Business Forecasting and Marketing Intelligence, 3*(3), 270–288. DOI: 10.1504/IJBFMI.2017.085371

Jordão, I. L. D. S., Souza, M. T. D., Oliveira, J. H. C. D., & Giraldi, J. D. M. E. (2017). Neuromarketing applied to consumer behaviour: An integrative literature review between 2010 and 2015. *International Journal of Business Forecasting and Marketing Intelligence, 3*(3), 270–288. DOI: 10.1504/IJBFMI.2017.085371

Kajla, T., Raj, S., Kansra, P., Gupta, S. L., & Singh, N. (2024). Neuromarketing and consumer behavior: A bibliometric analysis. *Journal of Consumer Behaviour, 23*(2), 959–975. DOI: 10.1002/cb.2256

Kesarwani, J., Rai, H., & Kesarwani, R. (2025). A Neuromarketing Framework for Data-Driven Intelligent Automation in Marketing. *Handbook of Intelligent Automation Systems Using Computer Vision and Artificial Intelligence*, 449-469.

Khan, A. A., Khan, K. M., Habib, M. S., Islam, M., Rehman, B. U., Shahid, H., & Ullah, K. (2025). HAND GESTURE TO VOICE CONVERSION USING ARTIFICIAL INTELLIGENCE. *Spectrum of Engineering Sciences, 3*(6), 762–777.

Kumar, P., Chowdhury, S., Madhavedi, S., & Lakshminarayana, K. (2024). Role of neuromarketing and artificial intelligence in futuristic marketing approach: An empirical study. *Journal of Informatics Education and Research, 4*(2), 560–567.

Labib, E. (2024). Artificial intelligence in marketing: Exploring current and future trends. *Cogent Business & Management, 11*(1), 2348728. DOI: 10.1080/23311975.2024.2348728

Lim, W. M. (2018). What will business-to-business marketers learn from neuromarketing? Insights for business marketing practice. *Journal of Business-To-Business Marketing, 25*(3), 251–259. DOI: 10.1080/1051712X.2018.1488915

Lim, W. M., & Weissmann, M. A. (2023). Toward a theory of behavioral control. *Journal of Strategic Marketing, 31*(1), 185–211. DOI: 10.1080/0965254X.2021.1890190

Lim, W. M., Yap, S. F., & Makkar, M. (2021). Home sharing in marketing and tourism at a tipping point: What do we know, how do we know, and where should we be heading? *Journal of Business Research, 122*, 534–566. DOI: 10.1016/j.jbusres.2020.08.051

Mansor, A. A., & Isa, S. M. (2020). Fundamentals of neuromarketing: What is it all about? *Neuroscience Research Notes, 3*(4), 22–28. DOI: 10.31117/neuroscirn.v3i4.58

Meyerding, S. G., & Mehlhose, C. M. (2020). Can neuromarketing add value to the traditional marketing research? An exemplary experiment with functional near-infrared spectroscopy (fNIRS). *Journal of Business Research, 107*, 172–185. DOI: 10.1016/j.jbusres.2018.10.052

Mittal, S., Pandey, A., Chandel, A., & Hung, T. H. (2025). Leveraging Neuromarketing Technologies to Enhance Agile Marketing Strategies: A Study on Consumer Behavior Insights and Real-Time Adaptation. In *Digital Transformation Initiatives for Agile Marketing* (pp. 275-302). IGI Global.

. Moutinho, L., & Cerf, M. (2024). The Future of Neuroscience and Biometrics in Business. *Biometrics and Neuroscience Research in Business and Management: Advances and Applications*, 333.

Musole, E. (2025). The Role of Neurotechnology in Shaping Business Decisions: A Comprehensive Literature Review. *Open Journal of Business and Management, 13*(2), 985–999. DOI: 10.4236/ojbm.2025.132053

. Nguyen, T. A. (2021). Fundamentals of neuromarketing: an interdisciplinary field that changes how marketers understand consumers.

O'Reilly, T., Strauss, I., & Mazzucato, M. (2024). Algorithmic attention rents: A theory of digital platform market power. *Data & Policy, 6*, e6. DOI: 10.1017/dap.2024.1

Österle, B., Herrando, C., Köpsel, A., & Kuhn, M. (2024). "Business-to-Business-to-Brain?" Reviewing Neuroscience Research in B2B-Marketing Using TCCM Analysis. *Journal of Business-To-Business Marketing, 31*(4), 421–445. DOI: 10.1080/1051712X.2024.2380671

Peng, Y., Yao, S., Li, A., Xiong, F., Sun, G., Li, Z., Zhou, H., Chen, Y., Gong, X., Peng, F., Liu, , Zhang, C., & Zeng, J. (2024). Investigating quantitative approach for microalgal biomass using deep convolutional neural networks and image recognition. *Bioresource Technology, 403*, 130889. DOI: 10.1016/j.biortech.2024.130889

Pires, P. B., Santos, J. D., & Pereira, I. V. (2024). *Digital marketing*. DOI: 10.1201/9781003384960

Pragna, K. P., Shetty, S., Kodipalli, A., Devamane, S. B., & Martis, R. J. (2025, January). Comprehensive Analysis of Machine Learning Approaches for Phishing Website Detection. In *2025 International Conference on Cognitive Computing in Engineering, Communications, Sciences and Biomedical Health Informatics (IC3ECSBHI)* (pp. 776-781). IEEE.

Radojević, I., Slijepčević, M., & Popović Šević, N. (2025). The Role of Artificial Intelligence in the Modern Approach to Neuromarketing. In *Multidisciplinary Approaches to Contemporary Marketing: Digital Trends, Social Issues and Economics* (pp. 45–73). Springer Nature Switzerland. DOI: 10.1007/978-3-031-78026-4_2

Rutkowska, A. (2022). Modern Neuroimaging Methods in Contemporary Neuroeconomics and Neuromanagement. *Olsztyn Economic Journal, 17*(2), 247–263. DOI: 10.31648/oej.8767

Sembiring, N. S. B., Sinaga, M. D., & Sianturi, N. E. (2024, November). Implementation of Adaptive Neuro-Fuzzy Inference System (ANFIS) Algorithm for Customer Credit Prediction. In *2024 6th International Conference on Cybernetics and Intelligent System (ICORIS)* (pp. 1-6). IEEE.

Semwal, R., Tripathi, N., Rana, A., Dafouti, B. S., Bairwa, M. K., & Mathur, V. (2024, May). AI-powered personalization and emotional intelligence integration for enhanced service marketing in transformative tourism experiences. In *2024 International Conference on Communication, Computer Sciences and Engineering (IC3SE)* (pp. 1851-1856). IEEE. DOI: 10.1109/IC3SE62002.2024.10592909

Shah, M. A., & Kumar, P. (2024). Leveraging Machine Learning Techniques to Project Customer Behaviour Through Predictive Analysis and Ethical Marketing. In *Market Grooming* (pp. 121–138). Emerald Publishing Limited. DOI: 10.1108/978-1-83549-001-320241006

Singh, A., & Kakkar, A. (2025). Marketing in the age of hyper-personalisation: Lessons from analytics-driven brand success. *Applied Marketing Analytics, 11*(1), 72–86. DOI: 10.69554/XQVW6761

Skriabin, O. M., Sanakoiev, D. B., Sanakoieva, N. D., Berezenko, V. V., & Liubchenko, Y. V. (2021). Neurotechnologies in the advertising industry: Legal and ethical aspects. *Innovative Marketing*, *17*(2), 189. DOI: 10.21511/im.17(2).2021.17

Slager, E. (2023). Unravelling the adoption of neuromarketing techniques in marketing organisations: insight from (neuro) marketing professionals (Master's thesis, University of Twente).

Song, G., Gazi, M. A. I., Waaje, A., Roshid, M. M., Karim, R., Rahaman, M. A., Min, Z., & Senathirajah, A. R. B. S. (2025). The neuromarketing: Bridging neuroscience and marketing for enhanced consumer engagement. *IEEE Access : Practical Innovations, Open Solutions*, *13*, 40331–40353. DOI: 10.1109/ACCESS.2025.3545742

Sung, B., Wilson, N. J., Yun, J. H., & Lee, E. J. (2020). What can neuroscience offer marketing research? *Asia Pacific Journal of Marketing and Logistics*, *32*(5), 1089–1111. DOI: 10.1108/APJML-04-2019-0227

. Utriainen, T. (2020). Neuromarketing and consumer neuroscience–the evolution and current state of the Art, an integrative review.

Varghese, P. (2022). Neuromarketing and artificial intelligence for effective future business. *IUJ Journal of Management*, *1*(1), 240–254.

. Verdenhofs, A., & Tambovceva, T. (2019). Evolution of customer segmentation in the era of big data.

Wu, D. C., Zhong, S., Wu, J., & Song, H. (2025). Tourism and hospitality forecasting with big data: A systematic review of the literature. *Journal of Hospitality & Tourism Research (Washington, D.C.)*, *49*(3), 615–634. DOI: 10.1177/10963480231223151

Yao, X., & Wang, Y. (2024). Using neural data to forecast aggregate consumer behavior in neuromarketing: Theory, metrics, progress, and outlook. *Journal of Consumer Behaviour*, *23*(4), 2142–2159. DOI: 10.1002/cb.2324

Zhang, Y., Thaichon, P., & Shao, W. (2023). Neuroscientific research methods and techniques in consumer research. *Australasian Marketing Journal*, *31*(3), 211–227. DOI: 10.1177/14413582221085321

# Chapter 8
# Optimizing Visual Attention:
## Enhancing the User Experience in Digital Marketing Through Neuromarketing

**Vikki Sharma**
http://orcid.org/0009-0003-5985-0667
*Shri Ram College of Commerce, University of Delhi, India*

**Maninder Kaur**
*Lovely Professional University, India*

**Mohit Verma**
http://orcid.org/0009-0005-3036-3894
*O.P. Jindal Global University, India*

**Shashi Kant**
http://orcid.org/0000-0003-4722-5736
*St. Joseph University in Tanzania, Tanzania*

## ABSTRACT

*The main objective of this study was to examine the way visual attention optimization through the neuromarketing techniques can benefit the user experience in digital marketing. The research addresses the problem of how to engage online users effectively and increase satisfaction and interactions with the digital platform. The findings showed that visual attention is strongly related to user experience and that neuromarketing generates a positive impact on user experience and visual attention. Neuromarketing mediation analysis showed that there was a partial-mediating*

DOI: 10.4018/979-8-3373-5997-7.ch008

*effect between visual attention and user experience, which increased the influence of attention on user engagement. SEM model showed exemplary fit indices. It is recommended that further studies should examine the cross-cultural differences, other mediating or moderating factors, and the viability of new technological advances like AR, VR, and AI in digital marketing. The ethical standards of neuromarketing practice is also a key area of untapped study.*

## INTRODUCTION

In the hyper-digitalized and modernized economy, one of the most valuable and scarce resources is the attention of the consumer (Behl et al., 2024). In the competition of world business in a highly saturated web platform, the efficiency of visual attention has become the critical feature in generating the user experience and consumer behaviour (Bekenova & Orazgaliyeva, 2025). This idea dates back to the earlier research on visual perception and selective attention in cognitive psychology and neuroscience, and has been slowly adopted within the domain of neuromarketing since its formal introduction in the early 2000s (Chygryn et al., 2024; Banytė & Dargytė, 2025). Being a multidisciplinary field neuromarketing takes advantage of the eye-tracking, EEG, and fMRI applications, to measure the sub conscious reaction of the consumer, which has provided an undiscovered understanding of how visual stimulating may attract, hold, or distract our focus on online interfaces (Gohain et al., 2024; Borawska & Mateja, 2024).

The relevance of the proposed study at a global level, is that the proposed study aligns with the SDGs Goal 9 (Trade, Invention and Set-up) and Goal 12 (Accountable Consumption and Creation) (Chygryn et al., 2024; Alsharif et al., 2025). With better digital marketing practices by improving through the use of evidence-based understanding of user experience, businesses can be able to be innovative in a responsible way, minimize digital clutter and can facilitate sustainable engagement instead of persuading users with manipulative power (Najafi et al., 2024; Banytė & Dargytė, 2025; Borawska & Mateja, 2024). Not only does this help commercial organizations but it also helps to create more ethical and user-centric digital ecosystems (Giannakopoulos et al., 2024; Najafi et al., 2024; Gohain et al., 2024). The recent tendencies point to the magnitude of the phenomenon. The Statista report of 2023 indicated that the amount spent on digital advertising all over the world was 626 billion, and a considerable portion of it was used on personalized and visually oriented platforms, like social media, short video, and immersive consumer experiences (Cordeiro et al., 2024).

According to eye-tracking studies, the average attention time of users on online advertisements is less than 8 seconds, which reveals the need to optimize visual representations with the highest urgency (Giannakopoulos et al., 2024). Empirical findings show that the strategic application of colour, motion and visual hierarchy can greatly enhance the rate of clicking through and intention to purchase and memory recall (Younus et al., 2025; Kim & Kim, 2024). Researchers also warn not to over-stimulate, as it may result in cognitive load, ad fatigue, and even brand distrust (Kim & Kim, 2024; Soltanizadeh et al., 2025). First, neuromarketing solutions tend to be expensive and technologically sophisticated and cannot be used in small and medium-sized businesses (Millagala & Gunasinghe, 2024; Gupta et al., 2025). Second, there are ethical issues of consumer privacy, subconscious influence, that remain controversial. Third, contextual gap: the existing body of empirical research has been focused on Western economies the research of cultural, regional and socio-economic differences in visual attention is scarcely explored (Qutb et al., 2024). Further, although research has focused on individual factors (including psychology of colours or motion graphics), no integrative paradigms have been identified that relate the optimization of visual attention, user experience, and sustainable marketing performance (Najafi et al., 2024; Younus et al., 2025).

The given chapter attempts to fill these gaps, providing an in-depth examination of *"how a visual attention process can be optimally adjusted to allow the user to experience better in digital marketing, along with a specific focus on neuromarketing tools, and the issue of ethics"*. It seeks to offer conceptual framework to the researchers, which is based on cross-cultural views and the heterogeneity of digital platforms but also provide policy makers with information on how responsible neuromarketing can be controlled and directed.

## BACKGROUND OF STUDY

The digital economy has also changed the way businesses operate with consumers, with new models of interaction no longer being based on mass communications but on personalized and attention-seeking engagement (Kemora et al., 2024; Najafi et al., 2024). With the growing popularity of consumer behaviour on the digital platform, visual attention has become a key parameter in measuring the success of marketing (Shahzad et al., 2025). In contrast to the traditional advertising, where the main criterion was reach and frequency, the contemporary competitive world requires strategies that maximize the perception, processing and acting of users on visual stimuli in real-time (Li et al., 2024). It is here that neuromarketing, the use of neuroscience instruments to crack the code of consumer behaviour, offers a promising line of research to enhance user experience in online marketing (Thakur, 2025; Chygryn et al., 2024). Through visual attention, neuromarketing will enable companies to outgrow subjective self-reports and have objective insights of what actually interests consumers (Isa & Anuar, 2024).

Nonetheless, this concept has been faced with many challenges when it was applied in various cultural and business settings (Borawska & Mateja, 2024). As an example, multinational corporations such as Coca-Cola and Google have been able to utilise eye-tracking research and facial coding to preview digital adverts before rolling them into mass production (Najafi et al., 2024; Gupta et al., 2025). Although these methods led to better recall rates of the campaign, small companies could not afford such tools, and it can be questioned why neuromarketing research is not accessible to everyone. Equally, e-commerce platforms in India like Flipkart and Myntra tried visual optimization of page layouts using gaze-mapping (Cordeiro et al., 2024). As much as such interventions were very effective in boosting the rate of click-through, there were issues of consideration of the inequality in the focus of consumers of either urban or rural population, and so it was not easy to create a blanket solution (Kim & Kim, 2024; Qutb et al., 2024).

Neuromarketing companies in Europe and in the United Kingdom in particular collaborated with retail brands in order to explore visually how online buyers oriented themselves on websites. The results indicated that users spent a lot of attention on images that were emotionally attractive rather than texts which were rich in information (Younus et al., 2025; Millagala & Gunasinghe, 2024). However, cultural variations were an obstacle: images that had a strong appeal to the British mind were not as well received in other European markets, including Germany, where people place more emphasis on details over emotional appeal. This shows the intercultural difference in visual attention, a current research problem in digital marketing in the world (Li et al., 2024).

Visual attention studies have gained a fertile foundation in China through the emergence of the short-video platform (Douyin Tik Tok in China) and its related studies (Isa & Anuar, 2024). Companies claimed that insights related to neuromarketing into colour schemes and editing rhythm could assist them in keeping consumers interested during the initial three seconds of video advertisements, which is a decisive factor of the conversion rates (Kemora et al., 2024). But the disadvantages involved in the approach like the sheer amount of rivalry content and the strong government regulations on the use of digital persuasion methods were practical limitations to the implementation efforts Chygryn et al., 2024).

In Africa, there are few case studies, though recent evidence out of South Africa suggests that small businesses applying cheap neuromarketing-inspired solutions, including A/B tests with visual focus on culturally-relevant symbols, could increase consumer engagement (Kim & Kim, 2024; Velammal et al., 2025). However, the lack of trained professionals and lack of infrastructure limited its use.

## PROBLEM STATEMENT

Ideally, digital marketing would be in a position to capture and maintain consumer visual attention seamlessly in ways, which are not only engaging, but also ethical and universally effective. Using the insights of neuromarketing, brands would create ads and interfaces that fit into the natural human cognitive processes, reduce the information overload, and at the same time improve the user experience (Cordeiro et al., 2024). This would ensure that the marketing strategies are not only commercially effective, but also sustainable, consider the autonomy of the consumer, and help to establish responsible consumption habits. However, this is an ideal setting that has not been realized (Li et al., 2024; Chygryn et al., 2024). Although significant advances have been made in the study of neuromarketing, the process of the visual attention optimization remains a fragmented and unevenly implemented notion on industry and geographical level (Najafi et al., 2024; Gohain et al., 2024).

There is also contradictory evidence making it more complex. In particular, it has been reported that bright colours and emotionally suggestive imagery are strong captors of consumer attention, whereas some other studies reported that the attention is more strongly affected by cultural symbols, textual detail, or utilitarian features (Alsharif et al., 2025). Similarly, even though it is a generally accepted view that video advertisements are more effective than static images in capturing the attention of users, not all empirical studies have supported this argument; in particular environments, the text-intensive or interactive content has been found more effective (Thakur, 2025). These contradictions highlight the needlessness of universally applicable laws to regulate the optimization of visual attention. The evidence is therefore inconclusive leading to questions on whether neuromarketing will be applicable in other cultures, industries, and digital platforms.

Theoretical gaps can also be seen in the application of the models of the visual attention to the more comprehensive marketing and psychological theories (Judijanto et al., 2025). Cognitive load theory, the selective attention theory and the dual-process models provide useful insights though they cannot fully explain the complexity of attention in a fast-paced digital setting (Najafi et al., 2024; Gupta et al., 2025). In a lot of research, visual attention is minimized and in place of emotional resonance, cultural variability, or long-term user experience is concentrated on things like the duration of gaze or the number of fixations. This shortsightedness creates a gap in the theoretical base of the idea of the optimization of visual attention (Bekenova & Orazgaliyeva, 2025).

There is still a lack of knowledge in breadth and depth. The existing research is highly concentrated in the Western markets, thus constraining the knowledge of the performance of neuromarketing-induced visual attention in the emerging economies where digital consumption habits vary significantly (Kemora et al., 2024). Moreover, a lot of research is devoted to short-term measures of engagement (e.g. clicks or eye movements) instead of analysing long-term effects on trust, loyalty, and long-term consumer relations. The lack of extensive cross-cultural and longitudinal research has in turn limited the academic and practical development in the field (Borawska & Mateja, 2024; Giannakopoulos et al., 2024).

Gaps in contexts are intense when converting the results of neuromarketing into policy and practice. Although big multinational companies have already adopted and applied advanced neuromarketing instrument, small and medium size businesses frequently do not have monetary or technical capacity to do so. The question of ethical issues regarding subconscious persuasion has not been resolved yet, and no unified regulatory framework exists at present, which would regulate the proper utilization of neuromarketing in digital marketing (Chygryn et al., 2024). It leads to uneven implementation and this has resulted in creating differences both within developed and developing economies and within large corporations and small firms.

The problem is enhanced by practical issues. Neuromarketing technologies like fMRI and EEG are expensive, time consuming and cannot be scaled (Borawska & Mateja, 2024; Velammal et al., 2025). The less expensive instruments like eye-tracking have limited ability to measure entire spectrum of consumer attention especially in a naturalistic, real world digital environment (Qutb et al., 2024). The traditional survey methods cause marketers to often be bound by the traditional methods, which are prone to bias and do not influence the subconscious factors of attention. Such an absence of a relationship between academic promise and practice is a major obstacle (Soltanizadeh et al., 2025; Kim & Kim, 2024).

This research has attempted to fill these gaps and challenges by offering an elaborate framework of neuromarketing integration of empirical evidence, theoretical basis, and practical solutions to enhance visual attention.

## THEORETICAL SUBSTRUCTURE

*Theory of Selective Attention:* The theory of Selective Attention is based on cognitive psychology and states that a person has a limited capacity to handle the amount of incoming stimulus, and it is therefore necessary to selectively filter the incoming stimulus to focus on that which is most salient (Li et al., 2024). The initial experimental research by Broadbent (1958) led to the bottleneck model where the brain filters in information at an early stage, such that a smaller number of information make it to the conscious mind (Judijanto et al., 2025). In the context of digital marketing, this model explains why specific elements of an ad, including bright imagery, vivid colour schemes, or the use of cues to an emotional appeal, draw the attention of the consumer whilst others go unnoticed (Chygryn et al., 2024; Shahzad et al., 2025).

*System Thinking Theory:* Digital marketing often involves visual attention which activates System 1, since consumers make instant judgments due to the presence of a perceptual stimulus (brand logo, product image, ad design, etc.) without conscious thought (Cordeiro et al., 2024). In comparison, System 2 processes are hired by more extensive product appraisals. Neuromarketing studies have shown that subconscious visual stimuli are capable of producing System 1 responses and hence influencing consumer decision before rational appraisal occurs (Soltanizadeh et al., 2025). Such a dichotomous viewpoint elucidates the compound nature of attention giving a very subtle perspective through the prism of which to view how users navigate through digital ecosystems.

*AIDA Model:* Although initially developed in the early advertising theory, the AIDA model is still one of the most utilitarian models used to define the impact of marketing communications on consumer behaviour. The model suggests a step-by-step process: first the Attention is achieved with the help of effective marketing, followed by the Interest, then the Desire, and finally, the Action (Kim & Kim, 2024; Thakur, 2025). Visual attention is the bottleneck through which everything enters; without preliminary capture, then the rest of it will not follow (Bekenova & Orazgaliyeva, 2025). Neuromarketing knowledge expands the AIDA construct, as it empirically determines what visual elements are attention arousing in colours, shapes, spatial configurations, motion stimuli, etc., and then turns this attention into interest and buying intentions (Chygryn et al., 2024; Gohain et al., 2024). AIDA, even though developed many decades ago, still shows relevant applicability in modern-day realms of digital advertising, like social media advertisement, where consumer attention is infamously ephemeral (Alsharif et al., 2025).

*Cognitive Load Theory:* Too much or unarranged information may clog up cognitive resources and causes reduced attention and decision-making quality (Isa & Anuar, 2024). Under digital marketing, the user attention can be diluted or compromised by the cluttered web interfaces, excessive amount of information in the adverts, or the overly complex visual designs. The results of neuromarketing support this assumption and show that visual overload changes the patterns of brain activity and the direction of gaze (Giannakopoulos et al., 2024; Qutb et al., 2024). By using this theory, practitioners are able to build user experiences in ways that reduce extraneous cognitive load and maximize germane load so that visual attention is directed efficiently with the target of salient brand messages.

## DEFINITION AND ORIGIN OF TERMS

*Neuromarketing:* It refers to the use of neuroscientific techniques, to measure and process the subconscious reaction of consumers to marketing stimuli (Li et al., 2024; Borawska & Mateja, 2024). This field began to emerge in the early 2000s and gained its first publicity when Bright House, an American marketing consultancy, created the first neuromarketing department. Despite being a point of ethical contention at first, neuromarketing has since been taken as a valid interdisciplinary discipline at the intersection of neuroscience, psychology, and marketing due in part to the discovery that traditional self-report methods often fail to reflect genuine consumer preferences, since many of the choices people make are biologically mediated by unconscious neural activity (Millagala & Gunasinghe, 2024).

*Visual Attention:* It can be described as a mental process that helps people to selectively pay attention to certain visual information and ignore others. The idea has its origin in early twentieth-century psychology, where William James (1890) considered attention to mean the charge by the mind of one of what appear to be a multiple of objects that are simultaneously possible (Giannakopoulos et al., 2024). This knowledge has been further expanded in the use of contemporary cognitive neuroscience, which shows that visual attention involves conscious and subconscious distribution of neural resources (Kemora et al., 2024). Visual attention is the ability of a brand or platform to capture and maintain the gaze of users in competitive online marketing and, thus, impact the engagement and conversion rates in digital marketing.

*User Experience (UX):* It is described as the overall perception and reaction created by a user when engaging with a product, service or a system. The term has become widely used in the 1990s, in the work of Donald Norman, who focused on technological design that responds to human psychological affordances and principles of usability. In digital marketing, UX goes beyond the functional architecture to include emotional involvement, satisfaction and trust (Qutb et al., 2024). Enhancing visual attention will optimally improve UX through reducing cognitive friction and generating a prolonged interaction.

*Digital Marketing:* It refers to the use of digital platforms, such as websites, social media platforms, search engines, and mobile platforms to advertise products and services. Although the concept of marketing as a field has a centuries-old history, digital marketing as a specific form coalesced in the 1990s with the popularity of the internet and has since evolved to be one of the most powerful mediums of consumer interaction (Shahzad et al., 2025; Kim & Kim, 2024). Its appearance is an indication of the need to have the real-time, interactive, and the data-based marketing techniques that could not be offered on the conventional media (Borawska & Mateja, 2024; Chygryn et al., 2024).

## EMPIRICAL LITERATURE REVIEW

### Visual Attention and User Experience

The visual attention plays a central role in creating the overall user experience (UX) in the digital surroundings. When people interact with the websites, mobile apps, or digital advertisements, their perception is automatically given an attention to particular visual details, i.e. chromatic schemes, typographic decisions, kinetic devices, or compositions (Li et al., 2024). Through a careful management of this locus of attention, marketers and designers can recreate smooth and entertaining experiences, which reduce cognitive load, lessen confusion, and pre-empt the most relevant information. As an example, the conspicuous call-to-action buttons, logical and intuitive navigation menu, and the visual difference between product placements are enough to attract the attention in a short period of time and make the decision-making process faster and more satisfactory.

Visual attention that is optimized develops emotional involvement at the same time, which forms the basis of central positive user experiences. The minimally invasive design decisions (such as the use of warm colour schemes, a symmetrical balance, or accessible interactive features) can create the sense of trust, interest, or even intrigue, thus increasing the possibility of users continuing reading and interacting with a platform on a deeper level (Younus et al., 2025; Chygryn et al., 2024). In addition, the visual attention strategic direction makes users spend their time on brand messages and the story instead of being distracted by the overcrowded or unnecessary information. This enhances usability, besides strengthening the relationship between consumer and brand.

Hypothesis 1: Visual Attention enhances the User Experience

### Visual Attention and Neuromarketing

Visual attention is a pillar of enhancing the effectiveness of neuromarketing since it directly affects the manner in which consumers perceive, interpret and react to marketing stimuli. Neuromarketing attempts to demystify unconscious forces behind consumer action and since visual images often constitute the first point of contact between a brand and its customers, they are invaluable in influencing responses (Qutb et al., 2024). In the cases when researchers use methodologies, they receive accurate data concerning the loci and the duration of attentional focus (Gohain et al., 2024). In this way, marketers will be able to determine what component of an advertisement, product design or computer interface effectively grabs attention and triggers neural activity related to interest, memory or decision-making. The visual attention optimization in this way enhances the predictive power of neuromarketing as the particular features of the design are correlated with the preferences of consumers that are beyond their conscious awareness (Isa & Anuar, 2024).

More so, visual attention augments neuromarketing by providing practical information of the effectiveness of visual communication strategies. As an example, in a digital advert brands can monitor whether users are focused on the main aspects of a logos, call-to-action prompt, or product features (Giannakopoulos et al., 2024; Velammal et al., 2025). When the focus is mostly on the irrelevant or peripheral things, it indicates that the message is not clear. As a result, neuromarketing tools can be used to translate such findings into suggestions to redesign marketing materials in a way that will increase the level of clarity, engagement, and emotional appeal. Visual attention is a vital tool to bridge neuroscience with marketing praxis because of the ability to turn neural and attentional information into practical design solutions.

Of equal importance, the visual attention helps neuromarketing to alleviate issues that relate to consumer decision making in congested online markets. Compared to other visual visuals that compete to grasp the attention of the users, identifying the images that pass through the noise provides the marketers with a competitive edge (Soltanizadeh et al., 2025). The findings of attention-related neuromarketing research help marketers to develop content that is memorable, reduce information overload, and meet the expectations of the target customers. In this respect, visual attention does not only enhance neuromarketing research, but increases its applicability by providing evidence-backed strategies that help in enhancing consumer experience and marketing results.

Hypothesis 2: Visual Attention enhance Neuromarketing

## Neuromarketing and User Experience

Neuromarketing supplements user experience by providing more information about the unconscious mechanisms that control consumer behaviour, emotions and responses (Kemora et al., 2024; Judijanto et al., 2025; Isa & Anuar, 2024). Traditional approaches of surveys or focus groups are not always effective to explore the unspoken, instinctive responses of users, and the neuromarketing instruments, including eye-tracking, EEG, or fMRI, can help to observe how users actually utilize digital platforms and content. Neuromarketing can help designers and marketers create more intuitive, engaging, and user-friendly experiences by determining which aspects of a webpage, app, or advertisement tend to draw attention and evoke positive feelings, and subsequently creating a more appealing and straightforward experience that incorporates these elements (Qutb et al., 2024).

The ability to optimize the design aspects can be considered one of the greatest contributions of neuromarketing to user experience. As an example, it is possible to analyse the cerebral activity and the gaze patterns to understand whether users become confused by navigation menus, whether a call-to-action button is prominent enough, or whether the layout causes discomfort or stress in general (Kim & Kim, 2024; Gohain et al., 2024). These insights allow refinements based on evidence that lessen cognitive load, simplify navigation and improve clarity. Therefore, the users engage with digital platforms more easily providing them with easier journeys and increased satisfaction.

Neuromarketing also builds on the user experience due to its ability to appeal to the emotional aspect of human behavioural science. Feelings have a strong impact on decision-making and neuromarketing provides data on the extent to which certain colours, images, or stories are able to instil trust, excitement, or loyalty (Judijanto et al., 2025). It is through matching the visual and sensory messages with the emotional reactions of people that the marketers will be able to create a type of experience that will have a deeper impact and will foster a long-term engagement (Isa & Anuar, 2024). In addition to aesthetics, neuromarketing allows the process of making user experiences unforgettable, not only functional but also emotional, which is a prerequisite when it comes to brand loyalty created in competitive digital environments (Giannakopoulos et al., 2024).

Finally, neuromarketing enhances user experience by connecting scientific research with practice: it can transform neuroscientific information into design-oriented solutions that make digital communication more intuitively oriented, emotionally textured and consumer-focused (Millagala & Gunasinghe, 2024). It is the scientific method that enables organizations to surpass speculation, and rather creates an experience that not only meets but also predicts the need of the users hence setting a new standard of innovation in web marketing and web design (Li et al., 2024).

Hypothesis 3: Neuromarketing enhance the User Experience

## Visual Attention, User Experience through Neuromarketing

Visual attention is one of the most crucial processes by which neuromarketing also improves the user experience in online environments. Neuromarketing devices can be used to study specifically where users direct their gaze, how long they spend on specific design items, and the emotions or thoughts that are being aroused (Alsharif et al., 2025; Isa & Anuar, 2024). With such information, marketers and designers get empirical data of what visual indicators, whether in colours, typefaces, product placement, or call-to-action buttons, actually attract attention and behaviour. This makes it easy to build interfaces that are not just visually attractive but user-friendly too so that the consumers can easily find the information they require without being distracted and particularly overwhelmed (Shahzad et al., 2025; Najafi et al., 2024).

By using neuromarketing, the visual attention can be optimized in a strategic manner to reduce cognitive effort and enhance satisfaction within the user interactions. As an example, in case eye-tracking research shows that people regularly miss important navigation menus or promotions, brands can restructure designs to emphasise such features (Chygryn et al., 2024; Judijanto et al., 2025). These adjustments based on attention facilitate easier navigation, increases the speed of decision-making and creates a more pleasant experience in the process of browsing. The users will therefore be less frustrated and feel more in control, which directly leads to increased engagement and loyalty (Soltanizadeh et al., 2025).

Additionally, the visual attention analysis based on neuromarketing can help marketers to concur emotional resonance with user interface design. Considering that emotions provide a highly powerful force that influences consumer choices, understanding the way that attentional attention flows through visual images, branding, or visual storytelling can help determine what features will result in trust, excitement, or even comfort (Velammal et al., 2025; Judijanto et al., 2025; Giannakopoulos et al., 2024).

Hypothesis 4: Visual Attention enhance the User Experience through Neuromarketing

## RESEARCH METHODOLOGY

This chapter has employed a quantitative research method to examine the effectiveness of neuromarketing optimization of visual attention on user experience on digital marketing. The method was chosen since it allows structured measurement to be used, statistical testing to be undertaken, and generalisable results to be achieved on a large sample. The number of 390 respondents was deemed sufficient since it surpassed the advisable sample required in multivariate tests including EFA and SEM. The sampled respondents were chosen using the purposive sampling method, the target population being those who actively use digital platforms- such as e-commerce sites, social media and video streaming platforms. To have heterogeneity in digital media consumption, the sample used was representative of the heterogeneous population (age, gender, education, occupation). Purposive sampling was also appropriate since the study needed people who had pre-experience of digital advertisements hence guaranteeing substantial responses to the issues of visual attention as well as user experience.

*Scale Development:* The measurement scale was developed, based on the exemplary analysis of the literature related to the study of neuromarketing, consumer behaviour, and digital marketing. Previous studies came up with validated scales, which were transformed into the current context. An example would be visual attention which was also measured with the help of items based on previous eye-tracking and gaze-map studies that had examined recall, recognition and fixation tendencies (Wedel and Pieters, 2008). Items that consider user experience were based on surveys of human-computer interaction (Hassenzahl, 2010), with dimensions like ease of navigation, satisfaction and emotional engagement. Perceived effectiveness of digital marketing was measured with adaptation of the items used in the prior research on advertising effectiveness (Belanche et al., 2014), whereas items about consumer trust and the ethical concern were borrowed to the marketing ethics literature (Laczniak and Murphy, 2019). Every construct was rated on a five-point Likert scale.

*Data Analysis Procedures:* The data was studied regarding its appropriateness to the factor analysis before the hypothesis testing. The KMO was above the recommended value of 0.70, which implies that the sample was adequate in the study, and Bartletts Test of Sphericity was significant (p, 0.05) to assert that the correlation matrix was fit to perform a factor analysis. PCA with Varimax rotation was conducted to determine the underlying dimensions of visual attention, user experience and ethical perceptions through an Exploratory Factor Analysis (EFA). Items whose factor loading was less than 0.63 or cross-loader items were dropped in order to clean up the scale and improve construct validity. After establishing dimensionality, a CFA using SEM in AMOS software. The CFA proved the measurement model by establishing reliability, validity of constructs and factor structure. Convergent validity was evaluated through the AVE and all the constructs had a value above 0.63. Structural model was then tested to test hypothesized construct relationships. SEM enabled simultaneous evaluation of direct and indirect impacts, giving a clear picture of the impacts of the optimisation of visual attention with the use of neuromarketing on the user experience in digital marketing. Measurements of goodness of fit including CFI, TLI, RMSEA, and chi square/df were used to estimate the fit of the model, and the results showed acceptable levels.

*Ethical Considerations:* The research was of high ethical values. This was done on a voluntary basis and informed consent was provided by all the respondents. Respondents were assured that their responses would be kept confidential and that they would not be used in other respects other than academic.

## CONCEPTUAL FRAMEWORK

*Figure 1. Testing Model*

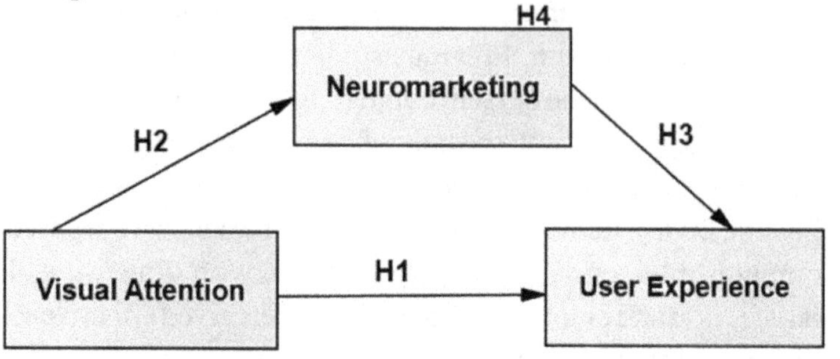


*Table 1. Sampling Adequacy*

| **KMO assessment** | | **.863** |
|---|---|---|
| Sphericity Test | Chi-Square | 1549.738 |
| | df | 91 |
| | Sig. | .000 |

Source: Authors

In table 1, sphericity indicated that the data set was suitable to use through factor analytical processes. The KMO of 0.863 implies that there is a high degree of sampling adequacy, which implies that the degree of correlation between various variables is strong enough to support the use of factor analysis. A KMO greater than 0.80 is considered to be a meritorious in conventional terms, and therefore, the sample size of 390 respondents was considered to be appropriate in identifying latent covert forms. Besides this, Bartlett Test of Sphericity yielded a Chi-square of 1549.738 and a Chi-square resulted in 91 degrees of freedom which is significant at p =0.001. This does not accept the null hypothesis that the correlation matrix is an identity matrix and, as such, proves that variables are intercorrelated, and can be extracted by a factor. Altogether, the KMO and Bartlett scores demonstrate a high level of statistical support that the data is valid and usable to run Exploratory Factor Analysis (EFA), which will allow derivation of factors associated with visual attention, user experience, and neuromarketing constructs in digital marketing in the future.

*Table 2. Explained Variance*

| C | Initial Eigen | | | Extraction | | | Rotation | | |
|---|---|---|---|---|---|---|---|---|---|
| | Total | % of Variance | Cumulative % | Total | % of Variance | Cumulative % | Total | % of Variance | Cumulative % |
| 1 | 4.51 | 32.235 | 32.235 | 4.51 | 32.235 | 32.235 | 3.00 | 21.451 | 21.451 |
| 2 | 1.37 | 9.787 | 42.022 | 1.37 | 9.787 | 42.022 | 2.16 | 15.491 | 36.942 |
| 3 | 1.27 | 9.087 | 51.110 | 1.27 | 9.087 | 51.110 | 1.98 | 14.168 | 51.110 |
| 4 | .949 | 6.782 | 57.892 | | | | | | |
| 5 | .871 | 6.223 | 64.115 | | | | | | |
| 6 | .773 | 5.519 | 69.634 | | | | | | |

Source: Authors

The outcome of Table 2 shows that the extracted items successfully described the constructs in the dataset. The first factor that had an eigenvalue of 4.51 contributed 32.24% of the total variance and it was, therefore, a significant force in the overall data structure. The eigenvalues of the second and third component were 1.37 and 1.27, which explained the rest of the variance of 9.79 and 9.09 percent, respectively. The combination of these three elements explained a cumulative total of 51.11% of the total variance indicating that it explained over half the information contained in the observed variables. The Varimax method (rotation of the factor solution) making the solution more understandable, by maximizing loadings to one factor, brought about a minor change in the variance explained. The first was a rotating component that contributed 21.45% of the variance, the second 15.49 and the third 14.17, as cumulative variance of 51.11. This trend implies that the rotation increased the level of clarity of the factor structure without affecting its substantive explanatory power. In its findings, it is confirmed that the specified factors are reliable indicators of the latent dimensions of visual attention, user experience, and associated neuromarketing constructs and provide a strong basis to be used.

*Table 3. Covariances*

| Covariance | | | Approximation | S.E. | C.R. | P | Hy. |
|---|---|---|---|---|---|---|---|
| **Neuromarketing** | **<-->** | **Visual Attention** | **.242** | **.021** | **8.231** | *** | **H2** |
| Neuromarketing | <--> | User experience | .303 | .032 | 7.692 | *** | **H3** |
| Visual Attention | <--> | User experience | .254 | .24 | 7.831 | *** | **H1** |

Source: Authors

Table 3 shows the covariance estimates. Visual Attention (VA) and User Experience (UX) covariance value was estimated at 0.254, the C.R. was 7.831 in favor of

H1. This result suggests that increased degrees of optimized visual attention have a close relationship with increased user experience in the sphere of digital marketing, which is consistent with theoretical predictions of Selective Attention Theory, in which the full-fledged visual attention is regarded as a source of user satisfaction and successful interaction with digital content. On the same note, the covariance between Neuromarketing (NM) and VA was 0.242, C.R. of 8.231, which supports H2. This implies that eye-tracking and gaze mapping methods of neuromarketing have a statistically significant positive effect on the regulation of consumer visual attention and supports the fact that neuromarketing is a viable tool to optimize attention in online advertising and consolidates its theoretical and empirical applicability. Lastly, the covariance value between NM and UX was 0.303 and the C.R. value is 7.692 which supports H3. This shows the existence of a strong positive correlation meaning that neuromarketing does not induce attention; it also has a direct positive influence on the overall user experience. Its finding supports the idea of integrative nature of neuromarketing in developing digital marketing campaigns that are user-centric and engaging.

*Table 4. Validity Concern*

| | CR | AVE | MSV | MaxR(H) | VA | NM | UX |
|---|---|---|---|---|---|---|---|
| VA | 0.732 | 0.643 | 0.219 | 0.852 | **0.654** | | |
| NM | 0.758 | 0.657 | 0.132 | 0.763 | 0.171 | **0.665** | |
| UX | 0.793 | 0.603 | 0.274 | 0.797 | 0.383 | 0.193 | **0.684** |

Note: VA= Visual Attention; NM= Neuromarketing; UX= User experience
Source: Authors

Table 4 shows the findings of the construct validity test. All the constructs had a Composite Reliability (CR) value above the suggested level of 0.70, VA = 0.732, NM = 0.758, and UX = 0.793. This shows high internal consistency between the items that measure each construct. Equally, the Average Variance Extracted (AVE) values of VA (0.643), NM (0.657) and UX (0.603) all exceeded 0.63 which is a good convergent validity. This establishes that the latent constructs of observed variables accounted more than 63 percent of the variance in the observed variables, and thus confirmed the suitability of the scale. In order to evaluate the discriminant validity, the square root of AVE of every construct (which will be indicated on the diagonal) was compared with the inter-construct correlations. In the case of all constructs, the diagonal values were higher than the off-diagonal correlations. The square root of VA and AVE being 0.654 was higher than the correlations of VA with NM (0.171) and UX (0.383). On the same note, NM and UX had more within-construct variance as compared to shared variance with the rest of the constructs. This shows that the constructs were conceptually differentiated and reflected different dimensions of the visual attention, neuromarketing and user experience. All the values of MSV were less than that of AVE, this also led to discriminant validity. Also, the MaxR(H) values which reflect the maximum reliability that can be achieved by each construct all exceeded 0.75, which indicates robustness and measurement stability.

*Table 5. Model Appropriateness*

| Sig. | Chi-Sq | RMR | Goodness | Confirmatory | TLI | RMSEA |
|---|---|---|---|---|---|---|
| 0.004 | 1.954 | .036 | 0.930 | 0.912 | 0.911 | .028 |

Source: Authors

Table 5 summarizes the model fit indices The Chi-square was 1.954, which is usually sensitive to sample size, and the significance value = p=.004. The p-value slightly exceeds the standardized null significance level of 0.05, but the relative Chi-square () /df is less than 2, indicating that the model represents a reasonable fit, and the difference in the observed covariance and estimated covariance matrices should have been insignificant. RMR is near to 0.036, less than the suggested amount of 0.05, was low, which implies that the model recapitulates the observed correlations with high fidelity. Also, the Goodness -of-Fit Index (GPI=0.930) and the CFI=0. 912 both surpassed the value of 0.90 which is the recommended limit, indicating a good overall fit and validating the adequacy of the measurement and structural elements of the model. The TLI= 0.911 also supported the good fit of the model since values exceeding 0.90 suggest that the proposed model is of significant improvement compared to a baseline null model. RMSEA = 0.028 was far less than the traditional value of 0.05 and therefore this meant that there was an excellent approximation of the model. Taken together, these indices indicate that the structural model that can be used to test the links between Neuromarketing, Visual Attention, and User Experience is solid and can offer a reliable framework of testing the hypothesis.

*Figure 2. Structure equation model*

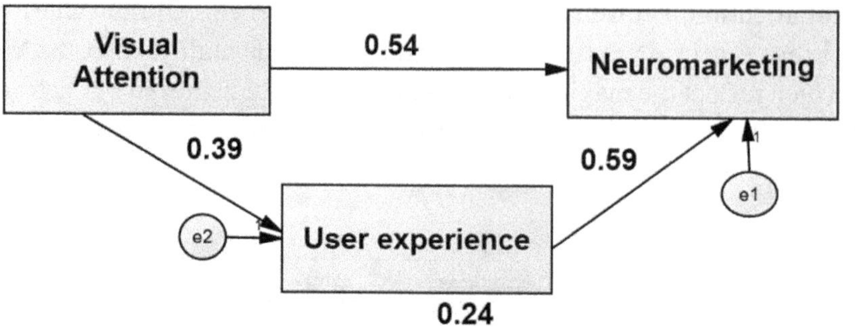


*Table 6. Regression*

| Relative | | | Approx. | S.E. | C.R. | P | Ass. |
|---|---|---|---|---|---|---|---|
| **Neuromarketing** | **<---** | **Visual Attention** | **.864** | **.143** | **7.583** | ******* | **H2** |
| User experience | <--- | Neuromarketing | .328 | .131 | 2.853 | *** | H3 |
| User experience | <--- | Visual Attention | .957 | .192 | 7.958 | *** | H1 |

Source: Authors

The findings of the regression test are presented in Table 6. Visual Attention and User Experience were found to be related to each other with an estimate value of 0.957 and a critical ratio of 7.958, which was significant at p 0.001, thus supporting H1. This positive significant impact indicates that maximization of visual attention facilitates user experience in digital marketing significantly. The result supports the theoretical view advanced by Selective Attention Theory, i.e., the idea that the visual emphasis is the straightforward method of increasing the levels of satisfaction, usability and emotional involvement among online customers. Likewise, Regression Visual Attention to Neuromarketing yielded a regression path of 0.864 and C.R. of 7.583 which is significant at $p = 0.001$ and thus supports H2. This shows that neuromarketing methods are very useful in capturing and guiding visual attention which validates the practical value of eye-tracking, gaze mapping and neurophysiological measure as the best means of maximizing digital marketing campaigns. Lastly, there was the 0.328 path between Neuromarketing and User Experience with a C.R. of 2.853, significant at p 0.001, that supported H3. The positive relationship though only of moderate effect size proves that neuromarketing does have the power to not only affect attention but also has a direct impact on enhancing overall user experience.

*Table 7. Mediating*

| | worth |
|---|---|
| Visual Attention → User experience | 0.54 |
| Visual Attention → Neuromarketing → User experience | 0.39*0.59=0.24 |
| | .78 |

Source: Authors

The analysis of Neuromarketing mediating is given in Table 7. Direct contribution of Visual Attention to User Experience was also determined to be 00.54 which means that there is a positive and significant direct relationship. This proves that visual attention is beneficial to the user experience on its own, which is in line with the theoretical findings that focused attention increases the engagement, satisfaction, and usability of digital marketing conditions. The indirect effect, which was achieved by multiplication of the path coefficients, i.e., Visual Attention to Neuromarketing (00.39) and Neuromarketing to User Experience (0.59), had an indirect effect of 0.48. This shows that a significant part of the influence of visual attention on user experience is moderated by interventions in neuromarketing, i.e., eye-tracking, gaze mapping, and neurophysiological engagement techniques. The overall effect of Visual Attention on User Experience, which is the combination of both direct and indirect effects, was 0.78, meaning that the two pathways have a strong effect together.

## DISCUSSION

The results here are agreeable with Selective Attention Theory, according to which, specific cognitive processing of relevant stimuli enhances behavioural performance. As a result, user experience may be significantly enhanced by optimizing visual, e.g. layout, colour scheme, motion and imagery, among others. Moreover, the research confirms that neuromarketing has a positive effect on visual attention and user experience. Neuromarketing techniques such as eye-tracking, gaze mapping and neurophysiological measurements are identified in regression and covariance analysis as capturing and focusing attention to the salient digital content. This further supports the practical value of the neuromarketing instruments, showing that, in addition to theoretical knowledge that can be offered, it is also possible to use these tools to create campaigns that appeal to users subconsciously, which will increase their engagement and perceived efficacy. The mediation analysis suggests that the relationship between the visual attention and user experience is partly mediated by the neuromarketing. The indirect impact of visual attention through neuromarketing is high implying that although the visual attention itself improves user experience, the integration of neuromarketing increases the effect. This semi-mediation highlights the fact that neuromarketing is not only an additional tool but rather an important mechanism that enhances the effects of attention-oriented approaches on online activity.

Validity and reliability also indicate that the findings are sound. Composite reliability, convergent and discriminant validity all have a satisfactory recommended threshold. The structural equation modelling indicates a high level of fit with the indices like CFI, TLI, RMSEA, and RMR being within the acceptable level. These findings confirm both the measurement scales adapted by the previous literature as well as the postulated structural relationships. Theoretically, they add to the literature as they combine cognitive attention models with neuromarketing principles and provide findings that attention distribution and neurophysiological activation have a cooperative impact on user experience in online marketing.

## CONCLUSION

This chapter analysed how visual attention and neuromarketing are relevant to user experience of digital marketing using a quantitative research design on 390 respondents. The results affirm that the visual attention is a key factor that determines user experience, and consumers that are effectively captured by visual content indicate greater contentment, emotional involvement and ease of communication. Neuromarketing techniques, including eye-tracking or gaze- mapping are demonstrated to play a crucial role in visual attention and user experience as a powerful way to optimize digital interactions consciously and unconsciously. The analysis also shows that neuromarketing partially mediates the visual attention to user experience relationship, meaning that, although focused visual attention directly improves user experience, it does so more effectively when it is used with neuroscience-based marketing tools. The high reliability, along with its support of its validation, convergent and discriminant validity, and excellent model fit indices, support the confidence in the strength of these results.

### Managerial Implications

Visual materials that managers should focus on include layout, colour scheme, typography, visuals, and motion cues to increase engagement and make sure that the main messages are not overlooked. The given strategic design orientation may enhance click rates, duration on platforms, and general satisfaction and lead to the increased brand loyalty. Second, the research indicates the usefulness of neuromarketing tools in the optimization of online campaigns. Eye-tracking and gaze mapping, facial coding and other neurophysiological methods can be used by managers to learn how users engage with digital content on a subconscious level. Through these insights, marketers can optimise ads, websites, and social media content to achieve maximum attention and reduce the amount of cognitive load. The fact that neuromarketing partially mediates the correlation between visual attention and user experience shows that the combination of the tools increases the power of attention-based approaches.

Third, the findings highlight the importance of data-driven and user-centric marketing. The managers are advised to engage in the ongoing testing and optimisation of online campaigns using both behavioural (clicks and views and conversions) and neuromarketing data to drive decision-making. Such a strategy will guarantee that marketing investments are made with interventions that actually add value to user experience and not just with assumptions or other time-tested heuristics. In addition, the research indicates the ethical and context-dependent issues.

## Practical Implications

First, the information indicates that visual focus could be successfully utilized to develop a more attractive and easier digital media. Through careful use of visual clues (colour schemes, layout configurations, motion elements, and imagery, etc), firms can focus consumer attention on the most important messages and calls-to-action to increase the level of engagement and interaction with digital platforms. Such a feature is especially relevant to the competitive online markets where the speed of capturing the consumer attention directly affects the conversion and retention rates. Secondly, the research confirms the applicability of neuromarketing tools towards optimization of online marketing campaigns. Such methods as eye-tracking, facial coding and electroencephalography offer real-time information about the perception and response of users to online content on conscious and subconscious levels. These insights can be converted by practitioners into optimisation of web interfaces, advertisement displays, and social media posts so that they are consistent with cognitive preferences and affective reactions and thus increase user satisfaction levels and brand perception.

Third, the partial mediating role of neuromarketing on the association between the visual attention and user experience highlights the significance of the need among organisations to integrate attention-based strategies with neuroscience-based interventions. As an example, promotional campaigns involving the inclusion of appealing visuals and neuromarketing-proven positioning or emphasis of important points will probably reach even greater engagement and more successful user experience results. Lastly, the study advises organisations to consider making the use of neuromarketing knowledge ethical and responsible. Although subconscious reactions can be exploited to enhance the level of engagement, transparency and respecting user autonomy must be maintained to create long-term trust and credibility.

## Theoretical Implications

First, the research supports and generalizes Selective Attention Theory by proving that visual attention is one of the determinants that dictate user experience in an online environment. The findings indicate that visual stimuli that are consciously developed do not have the exclusive power in controlling attention allocation, but rather subconscious mechanisms as measured with neuromarketing methods influence it. This cognitive psychology and neuromarketing combination broadens the theoretical basis, providing a more detailed description of the interaction of the user with digital content. Second, the research supports the empirical findings of the Dual Process Theory, as applied in digital marketing. As the results demonstrate that neuromarketing at least partially predicts the connection between visual attention and user experience, it is possible to conclude that both System 1 (intuitive, automatic processing) and System 2 (deliberate, analytical processing) are both at work in the digital space. This fact contributes to the perception of the stratified cognitive events that make the user engaged, make a decision and feel satisfaction.

Third, the study builds on the AIDA model (Attention–Interest–Desire–Action) demonstrating that, by optimising attention with the help of visual and neuromarketing stimuli, the effect of attention is not confined to the initial attention, but extends to wider user experience. It is the theoretical implication that user experience must be seen as an intrinsic repercussion of the attentional oriented marketing paradigms, and it would make the connections between the classic theory of advertising and the new engagement practices in the digital domain. Lastly, the chapter fills the gaps that exist in the theoretical literature regarding cognitive load and neuromarketing integration. Although Cognitive Load Theory focuses on controlling the information displayed to the users, the result shows that neuromarketing may offer practical information on how visual information can be most attentive without straining the cognitive resources.

## Recommendations

To begin with, marketers and designers must focus on the visual attention optimisation of digital campaigns through the strategic use of colours, layout, motion cues, and images that have been empirically demonstrated to attract attention of users. The information that corresponds to the cognitive attention patterns can build a better engagement, satisfaction and the overall user experience that will lead to conversion and retention rates.

Second, organisations should incorporate neuromarketing instruments of eye-tracking, electroencephalography and facial-coding in terms of campaign creation and experimentation. These methods provide practical data on the subconscious reactions of users, which can be used by marketers to optimize online content and interfaces and ensure that they are the most effective. Attention-based design plus neuroscience-based strategies enable businesses to become more engaged and provide more user-focused experiences.

Third, it is advised that companies take a strategy of constant testing and optimisation, which involves analysing the measurement of attention, engagement patterns and user feedback systematically. This cycle will make sure that digital marketing strategies are effective, responsive and relevant to the changing consumer preferences. Also, organisations are also expected to be ethical which ensures they are transparent and consider the autonomy of the users in implementing the neuromarketing insights so that they are not manipulative and this creates trust in the long term.

To the researchers, the study would imply the need to investigate cultural differences in context, including looking into differences in attention and user experience, among other cultures, industries, and digital platforms. Further research might also focus on other mediating and moderating variables such as emotional engagement, cognitive load, or brand loyalty, as a way of further clarifying the processes underlying user experience.

## Future Directions

This chapter reveals a range of possibilities of future research in the fields of digital marketing, neuromarketing, and user experience (UX). To start with, future studies need to look at cross-cultural differences in visual attention and the coherent neuromarketing outcomes, since consumer reactions to content on digital platforms might vary significantly across cultures, languages and demographic settings. These comparative studies would help marketers come up with more finely targeted and inclusive campaigns that would appeal among the varied audiences. Second, the further studies need to examine other mediating and moderate variables affecting the nexus between visual attention and UX. Emotional engagement, cognitive load, trust, brand loyalty and personalization are some of the variables that are likely to interact with the attentional allocation and neuromarketing interventions thus determining the UX outcome in a more subtle way. The application of these constructs will provide a better insight into digital consumer behaviour.

Third, longitudinal and experimental studies must be taken to determine the effects of the sustained exposure on the engagement, decision-making, and purchase behaviours modulated by the sustained exposure to attention-optimised and neuromarketing-informed campaigns. All of these methodological strategies would provide causal evidence related to the effectiveness of attention-based strategies and could support their long-term effect. Lastly, the ethical issues are still the priorities. Responsible application of neuromarketing practice should be built into strong frameworks and guidelines in future scholarship, whereby attention optimised strategies can improve the UX without compromising consumer autonomy and privacy.

## REFERENCES

Alsharif, A. H., Wang, J., Isa, S. M., Salleh, N. Z. M., Dawas, H. A., & Alsharif, M. H. (2025). The synergy of neuromarketing and artificial intelligence: A comprehensive literature review in the last decade. *Future Business Journal, 11*(1), 170. DOI: 10.1186/s43093-025-00591-x

Banytė, J., Pūkienė, I., & Dargytė, G. (2025). The role of consumers' visual attention stimuli in advertising: traditional and neuromarketing research perspectives. *Innovative marketing., 21*(1), 296-313.

Behl, A., Jayawardena, N., Shankar, A., Gupta, M., & Lang, L. D. (2024). Gamification and neuromarketing: A unified approach for improving user experience. *Journal of Consumer Behaviour, 23*(1), 218–228. DOI: 10.1002/cb.2178

Bekenova, G., & Orazgaliyeva, E. (2025). Neuromarketing Insights: Using Eye-Tracking and Machine Learning to Understand Consumer Preferences for University Promotional Products. *BUKETOV BUSINESS REVIEW, 11830*(2), 4–16. DOI: 10.31489/2025ec2/4-16

Borawska, A., & Mateja, A. (2024). Unveiling the User Experience: A Synthesis of Cognitive Neuroscience Methods in Digital Product Design. In *Advances in Information Systems Development: Information Systems Development, Organizational Aspects, and Societal Trends* (pp. 199–218). Springer Nature Switzerland. DOI: 10.1007/978-3-031-57189-3_10

Chygryn, O., Shevchenko, K., & Tuliakov, O. (2024). Neuromarketing as a mechanism of communication with the consumer: The case for small business. *Marketing i menedžment innovacij, 15*(2), 26-38.

Cordeiro, R., Reis, A., Ferreira, B. M., & Bacalhau, L. M. (2024). Neuromarketing: Decoding the Role of Emotions and Senses and Consumer Behaviour. *Cognitive Behavioural Neuroscience in Organizational Settings*, 83-100.

Giannakopoulos, N. T., Sakas, D. P., & Migkos, S. P. (2024). Neuromarketing and big data analysis of banking firms' website interfaces and performance. *Electronics (Basel), 13*(16), 3256. DOI: 10.3390/electronics13163256

Gohain, T. T., Rajagopal, G., Firas Armosh, F. A., & Dwivedi, D. P. K. (2024). A study on role of neuromarketing in digital era business development. *Migration Letters : An International Journal of Migration Studies, 21*(S4), 1600–1605.

Gupta, R., Kapoor, A., & Verma, H. (2025). Neuro-insights: A systematic review of neuromarketing perspectives across consumer buying stages. *Frontiers in Neuroergonomics*, *6*, 1542847. DOI: 10.3389/fnrgo.2025.1542847 PMID: 40735149

Isa, S. M., & Anuar, N. N. A. (2024). Neuromarketing cues: An eye-tracking study on mother's visual attention to organic vegetable advertisement. *Neuroscience Research Notes*, *7*(4), 363–1.

Judijanto, L., Riatmaja, D. S., & Ajie, B. (2025). NEUROMARKETING INSIGHTS INTO BRAND LOYALTY FORMATION IN GEN Z CONSUMERS. *INTERNATIONAL JOURNAL OF FINANCIAL ECONOMICS*, *2*(3), 970–985.

Kemora, H., Pasaribu, P., Marlina, A., & Himawan, E. N. (2024). Optimizing Digital Marketing Efforts Through Neuromarketing: Systematic Review. *Moneter: Jurnal Keuangan dan Perbankan, 12*(1), 32-44.

Kim, J. Y., & Kim, M. J. (2024). Identifying customer preferences through the eye-tracking in travel websites focusing on neuromarketing. *Journal of Asian Architecture and Building Engineering*, *23*(2), 515–527. DOI: 10.1080/13467581.2023.2244566

Li, X., Luh, D. B., & Chen, Z. (2024). A Systematic Review and Meta-Analysis of Eye-Tracking Studies for Consumers' Visual Attention in Online Shopping. *Information Technology and Control*, *53*(1), 187–205. DOI: 10.5755/j01.itc.53.1.34855

Millagala, K., & Gunasinghe, N. (2024). Neuromarketing as a digital marketing strategy to unravel the evolution of marketing communication. In *Applying business intelligence and innovation to entrepreneurship* (pp. 81–105). IGI Global Scientific Publishing. DOI: 10.4018/979-8-3693-1846-1.ch005

Najafi, F., Shetab Boushehri, S. N., Khatibi, A., & Azmsha, T. (2024). Comparison of Customers' Visual Attention in the Online Shopping Process of Sports Products with a Neuromarketing Approach. *Journal of Advanced Sport Technology*, *8*(3), 1–14.

Qutb, M. M., Nada, M., & Azmy, A. (2024). An Innovative Methodology in Neuromarketing for Supporting Technology-Enabled Companies. *International Design Journal*, *14*(1), 491–634. DOI: 10.21608/idj.2024.330635

Shahzad, K., Khan, S., Raza, F., Kamal, M. H., & Ullah, S. (2025). Emotions, Triggers, and Traits: A Thematic Analysis of Neuromarketing in Digital Buying. *Pakistan Journal of Humanities and Social Sciences*, *13*(1), 570–586. DOI: 10.52131/pjhss.2025.v13i1.2800

Soltanizadeh, S., Ahmadisharif, M., & Rousta, A. (2025). A Qualitative Model of Customer Purchase Decision-Making Based on Neuromarketing (FMCG Industry). *Digital Transformation and Administration Innovation*, 1-11.

Thakur, N. (2025). Neuromarketing Techniques in Shaping Purchase Decisions: A Sales Perspective. *Journal of Marketing and Sales Management ISSN: 2457-0095 (Online), 9*(1).

Velammal, R. S., Leo, A., Abraham, J. M., Fortuna, C. M., & Kumar, V. (2025). Electroencephalography (EEG)-Based Neuromarketing: Predicting Favourable and Unfavourable Consumer Reactions Using ML Techniques. *BRAIN. Broad Research in Artificial Intelligence and Neuroscience, 16*(3), 153–168. DOI: 10.70594/brain/16.3/12

Younus, M., Nurmandi, A., Mutiarin, D., Manaf, H. A., Prianto, A. L., Irawan, B., & Malik, I. (2025). A Comprehensive Study of Neuro Marketing Techniques. In *Impact of Sensory Marketing on Buying Behaviour* (pp. 1–34). IGI Global.

## KEY TERMS & DEFINITIONS

**Cognitive Load:** It is the mental force that is needed to process information that is coming in. In online marketing, too much cognitive load may overwhelm the user, consequently weakening the understanding, interaction, and decision-making decisions. Cognitive load theory is a theory popularised by Sweller (1988), which is used to design instructions, interface design, and optimisation of digital materials.

**Eye-Tracking:** Eye-tracking is a type of research technique which captures eye-movement patterns, duration of gaze, and focus points with an aim of establishing the determinants of visual attention. In marketing it is used to assess the effectiveness of the advertising, web designs and product presence. Eye-tracking has developed as a fundamental tool of neuromarketing and UX research, having its roots in the study of psychology and neuroscience in the 20th century.

**Neuromarketing:** Neuromarketing is the use of neuroscientific methods on marketing research, the rationale being to understand the unconscious reaction of consumers on marketing stimuli. There are the methodological repertoire The concept of neuromarketing was first developed in the early 2000s as an interdisciplinary science that combines the principles of marketing, psychology, and neuroscience, and is designed to optimise the effectiveness of advertising and user participation.

**User Experience (UX):** User Experience is a collection of the overall perception, emotions, and satisfaction that occur during the interaction of a user with a digital platform, product or service. These dimensions include aesthetic appeal, accessibility, efficiency and usability. Origin: UX has its roots in HCI research dating back to the 1990s, and is concerned with the design of systems that are intuitive, pleasant and aligned.

**Visual Attention:** Visual attention refers to the cognitive process whereby, individuals are selectively attentive to specific visual stimuli, and at the same time, they are able to filter out irrelevant information. In digital marketing, this emphasis involves orienting the eyes and cognitive energies of a consumer to salient content, like to advertisements, product images, or calls-to-action, to enhance the engagement and create understanding.

# Chapter 9
# Reinventing Business at the Intersection of Neuromarketing and AI

**T. Venkat Narayana Rao**
http://orcid.org/0000-0002-1996-1819
*Sreenidhi Institute of Science and Technology, India*

**Nithish Reddy Kodimala**
http://orcid.org/0009-0003-0808-523X
*Sreenidhi Institute of Science and Technology, India*

**Sangers Bhavana**
http://orcid.org/0009-0005-6134-1081
*Sreenidhi Institute of Science and Technology, India*

**G. Seshu Kumari**
http://orcid.org/0009-0008-6570-0661
*Sreenidhi Institute of Science and Technology, India*

## ABSTRACT

*Where Neuromarketing meets AI, companies are experiencing a revolution in learning, engaging, and connecting with consumers. Neuromarketing, which uses the reasonable and emotional responses of human beings and also the predictive and analytical capabilities of AI. More than technology, this convergence is transforming the core idea of business strategy by empowering decision-makers to break down the code to unconscious consumer behavior in real time. As companies tap into this convergence tends to reshaping customer value with optimized innovation. This study talks of how this convergence unlocks new plans of consumer understanding and value creation in the velocity, flexibility, and imagination-driven digital economy.*

DOI: 10.4018/979-8-3373-5997-7.ch009

*The union of emotion-fueled marketing and intelligent automation does more yield enabling intuitive connection between people and brands. This chapter ultimately concludes that learning and adapting to the neuromarketing-AI patterns will be the key to future-proofed businesses, delivering sustainable competitive advantage in an increasingly more dynamic market.*

## 1.INTRODUCTION

The business world is changing in amazing ways right now, mostly because of the combination of neuroscience-based marketing (neuromarketing) and artificial intelligence(AI). Neuromarketing looks for the hidden emotional and cognitive factors that affect how people make decisions, while AI gives us the computing power and analytical tools to decode these insights on a scale never seen before. Not only do they help with advertising, but they are also changing the way businesses understand, connect with, and build long-term relationships with their customers.

### 1.1 Understanding Neuromarketing: The Science of Consumer Minds

Neuromarketing is a modern way of probing the subconscious mind via observing consumer action. Advertising usually depends a lot on the use of spoken thoughts and also polls. Neuromarketing, not like normal marketing, gets ideas from biological as well as neurological signs like brain activity, eye movements, facial expressions, even heart rate, and it studies those signs. Subtle preferences expose such cues via visceral emotional responses that people typically cannot articulate verbally.

For instance, an user can state that they pick a thing for its own quality. Neuromarketing might show attached feelings or packaging colors had greater impact. Neuromarketing uses subconscious reactions in place of expressed desires. It is now transformative. Companies can design campaigns that do connect so well to human feelings. This allows them to avoid depending solely upon plain reason.

### 1.2Artificial Intelligence: From Data to Dynamic Insights

Artificial intelligence is what crucially transforms the raw neuromarketing data into strategies that can be actionable. Typical human analysis would be quite slow as well as limited. Its capabilities cannot make sense of neuroscience data's massive amounts. However, AI can identify hidden patterns, analyze millions of signals all at once, and predict consumer behavior in different contexts (Selvarajan, 2021).

Machine learning and deep learning models work in this space. They enable businesses to move toward predictive analytics and even toward prescriptive analytics from descriptive analytics, including the past, the future, and recommendations. Systems using AI can analyze how the brain responds to product ads. The likelihood for purchase or engagement can then be instantly predicted.

### 1.3The Convergence: A New Era of Business Strategy

The real revolution converges between neuromarketing and AI now. They are each powerful on their own, but they form a transformation for businesses that is calculated. Neuromarketing gives access to both the emotional and also subconscious side of consumer decision-making, and AI translates all these findings into scalable plus real-time actions.In several ways, this convergence reshapes the foundation of business strategy. First, it improves consumer understanding, also companies are thus able to go beyond surface-level demographics. Deeper roots of choice are also able to be uncovered.Second, it enables brands to adjust the campaigns in real time based on consumer responses for dynamic engagement. Value creation definition shifts third. People will now measure success not just by sales or by ROI, but also by just how deeply a brand connects emotionally with its audience (Lee et al., 2010).

This integration is important to many businesses, also helping to empower them. In a highly competitive digital economy, businesses can future-proof themselves. Companies are able to innovate faster also predict market shifts. By adapting to neuromarketing-AI patterns and learning, sustainable competitive advantages can be maintained. Businesses use smart automation now shaping experiences that align with human emotions instead of just selling products.

## 2.DECODING CONSUMER PSYCHOLOGY WITH AI

Comprehension of the reasons why consumers make certain choices has been a meaningful challenge in business always. Human decision-making is rarely all that simple, but customary marketing relied upon asking people just what they liked or disliked. It is mainly instinctive and emotive, molded through faint cues overlooked by even buyers (Mariani et al., 2022).

With artificial intelligence (AI), neuromarketing gives businesses an influential tool. Businesses can use the tool for decoding hidden psychological drivers then translate them into meaningful strategies.

## 2.1 Beyond Rational Thinking: The Hidden Drivers of Choice

Consumers often believe that they compare prices, features, or reviews to make rational choices. Emotions do influence most of the decisions in reality that also involve memories. Unconscious stimulants additionally sway choices. Buying behavior can be affected in a strong way by a familiar jingle or by the color of packaging or by how a product is placed.

Neuromarketing identifies these hidden influences since it studies brain activity, attention spans, together with emotional responses. However, it is important to analyze this data on such a large scale. This analysis needs AI to be nearly feasible. AI enables detection of emotional patterns that recur, revealing to businesses which elements get consumer interest and which do not engage them.

## 2.2 AI as the Interpreter of Consumer Signals

AI functions as a "translator" that links business action with human psychology. Eye-tracking tools, for example, can measure where on a webpage a consumer looks. On the other hand, biometric sensors can do the recording of the changes that occur within heart rates during an advertisement. AI algorithms change these signals to perceptions like they provide raw data.

Machine learning models can even forecast how past emotional reactions will influence future consumer behavior. For instance, AI is able to recommend the offering of sustainability-focused campaigns to a group that is specific in the event a customer shows subconscious excitement. This excitement indicates that the customer prefers eco-friendly packaging.

## 2.3 Real-Time Consumer Understanding

One of the most powerful aspects of AI-driven neuromarketing involves the analysis of data in real-time. Now businesses track consumer reactions instantly they do not wait weeks for survey results. If a campaign is underperforming, AI spots the emotional gap and proposes quick changes. Companies design customer adventures. This kind of agility transforms the nature of the design.For example, streaming platforms use AI as they study viewer attention and when they suggest content that emotionally engages them(Macdonald et al., 2012). For the maximum impact, retailers analyze biometric feedback in order to adjust product placements or store layouts. In digital advertising, companies use AI-powered psychology perceptions for the purpose of fine-tuning ad placement, color schemes, and messages in real time. This fine-tuning ensures the consumer feels understood during every step.

## 2.4 A New Lens on Human Behavior

Decoding consumer psychology when we use AI offers a much deeper and more accurate view of human decision-making. Now businesses understand truly what consumers feel, instead of relying on what they say. This change lets firms fashion moments that feel emotionally complete not just convincing. It is because of this that stronger bonds between brands and people are fostered. Ultimately, AI does not replace human psychology rather it increases it so it turns subconscious signals into powerful business intelligence.

# 3.BIOMETRIC SIGNALS, EYE-TRACKING, AND PREDICTIVE ANALYTICS

At the heart of neuromarketing resides the gathering of signals, showing what consumers genuinely think and feel, even when unaware of it. Businesses anticipate behaviour alongside design better strategies using AI's analytical power combined with these signals, a rich source of perceptions (Huseynov et al., 2019). Biometric data, along with eye-tracking tools, fulfil quite a major role within this process. Predictive analytics ensures that companies are using the perceptions for shaping future decisions.

## 3.1 Biometric Signals: The Body Never Lies

Our bodies are constantly sending signals. Our words often reveal less about what we feel than do a quickened heartbeat, sweaty palms, or tiny facial expressions. For example, an ad might make someone smile unconsciously or raise their eyebrows with surprise. These are small reactions that reflect genuine emotions.

Neuromarketing tools can capture these signals through sensors, also the sensors track heart rate, skin responses, or brain activity. These signals are just raw data by themselves however. Here AI steps in. AI compares thousands among similar reactions. Using this comparison, AI discerns if a campaign excites or confuses or if it fails to grab people's attention. Businesses, therefore, can refine their strategies in accordance to the feelings of people, more than to only their survey responses.

## 3.2 Eye-Tracking: Seeing What Consumers See

What people opt to view often shapes their influences. Marketers use eye-tracking technology in order to follow consumers' eyes when they see an ad, walk past a store shelf, or scroll through a website. That indicates something if shoppers examine the price tag more than the product itself. Their decision depends more on pricing in that situation.

Eye-tracking is even more powerful using AI now. Algorithms can pick up on patterns such as whether people even notice a brand logo or which part of an ad grabs attention first (Wedel et al., 2019). Businesses are able to redesign each of their layouts with packaging or visuals with the help of these perceptions. This redesign ensures that the most important messages can be always seen by all.

### 3.3 Predictive Analytics: Looking Ahead

Collecting biometric with eye-tracking data represents merely the initial stage. To predict future behavior is a real advantage to have. The benefit exists there. Decisions of tomorrow can be forecast from signals of today by analytics predictive driven by AI.

For instance, if a consumer excitedly watches a product teaser, AI can estimate their likelihood of buying once they release it. Collecting biometric with eye-tracking data represents merely the initial stage. To predict future behavior is a real advantage to have. The benefit exists there. Decisions of tomorrow can be forecast from signals of today by analytics predictive driven by AI.

### 3.4 Turning Signals into Strategy

Biometric signals, eye-tracking, along with predictive analytics provide to businesses a powerful advantage. Brands can shift beyond presumptions to a zone where consumer actions are accurately measured, understood, and predicted. In today's fast-moving market, this ability for connection deeply with the customers is not just an advantage. It is of importance for one to have this ability.

## 4. HYPER-PERSONALIZATION AND EMOTION-DRIVEN EXPERIENCES

Today's consumers no longer find marketing of one-size-fits-all satisfactory. Brands that understand them speak their language as well as anticipate their needs before they ask are wanted by them. Hyper-personalization, it is a strategy so far beyond just using a customer's name in email, has risen up from this growing demand. Neuromarketing perceptions and artificial intelligence strengthen companies that hyper-personalization supports today. Businesses will then design the kinds of experiences that are connecting directly to individual emotions so they build stronger more meaningful relationships with customers.

## 4.1 The Shift from Mass Marketing to Personal Experiences

In the past, businesses concentrated on mass marketing—sending the same message to the highest number of people. Many people saw this method. However, it often failed in connecting with individuals more deeply. In order to not be treated like just another number in a database, people want to feel understood, valued, as well as recognized.

Here hyper-personalization enters. Brands are now creating of experiences that are tailored to each person by the usage of consumer data, of behavior patterns, and of emotional cues rather than just general campaigns.For example, two customers who browse the same e-commerce site might see entirely different product recommendations that are based upon their browsing history, past purchases, as well as even the emotional responses detected through neuromarketing tools.

AI use makes this possible by Scale. Neuromarketing adds in the emotional dimension plus shows not just what consumers do but also why they do that, while it processes millions of data points such as clicks and purchase history plus engagement levels. They collaborate in allowing companies to design emotionally engaging and relevant marketing. The result is marketing with a personal feeling.

## 4.2 Emotion as the Core of Customer Connection

Emotions play a much greater part in decision-making than logic does. According to research, consumers recall a brand's impact more than its message. Some ads make us to laugh a bit, some bring on the tears, and some spark more excitement because we connect to the emotion before buying the product.(Uppal et al., 2025)

Neuromarketing identifies the emotions behind consumer choices, and AI helps map these emotions to personalized experiences. For example:

Travel company ads could show fast skydiving scenes or quick hiking clips to stir excitement for customers.

For family-oriented customers, the same company could present calm, reassuring ads. Such ads might present safety plus relaxation valuing Comfort also Trust.

Tech brands can tap into curiosity via teasing innovations. Suspenseful campaigns allow this by them.Product display is not the sole key. Instead of that, you must create those experiences that can resonate emotionally. Lasting bonds with the brand are more likely to form when customers feel that they are understood in this way.

## 4.3Real-Time Personalization Across Touchpoints

Another powerful benefit of AI and neuromarketing is personalizing content immediately. For businesses, analyzing campaign performance no longer requires weeks of waiting. Emotional reactions can be monitored so that strategies are instantly adjusted instead.

For example, streaming platforms use AI in order to study just what type of content excites or calms users. Then also, based upon all of that information, the platforms then recommend those shows or else that music in real time. Using models, online retailers predict which products to suggest based on what customers need logically (such as purchases made in the past) and on what triggers them emotionally (such as excitement they feel when browsing certain categories). Physical stores too are evolving since digital displays shift messages or visuals as shoppers gaze with emotional responses.

This type of catering makes clients know the name “understands them” at each moment. That feeling applies in whether the interaction occurs online or offline. It changes the customer adventure, once just a generic path, to a unique, emotion-driven experience that tailors itself to each individual.

## 4.4 From Transactions to Relationships

Hyper-personalization also changes the way businesses succeed. Firms now desire to make connections. They focus on more than just transactions. Customers with emotional connection buy more and stay loyal longer too.

A fitness app building a supportive relationship personalizes workout plans that are based upon an user’s mood, energy levels, as well as preferences, for example, not just selling routines. A brand in e-commerce anticipating a need of a customer to restock an item is showing of care. That same brand is also showing of its attentiveness when offering of a timely, personalized discount.Meaningful but small touches build emotional loyalty and trust.

## 4.5 Experiences That Truly Matter

Hyper-personalization and emotion-driven marketing define a fresh period within commerce. Brands are now expected to meet consumers at an emotional as well as personal level; generic campaigns just are not enough. Companies are able to design experiences that can feel like more genuine connections instead of just marketing by combining AI’s predictive power with neuromarketing’s perceptions of all human emotions.

Businesses are moving in this way beyond selling products because they create memories, build relationships, and shape brand value through emotions (Rane et al., 2023) . Often, emotional connections are the strongest driver of success today. That is quite real in our modern digital economy.

# 5.TRANSFORMING DECISION-MAKING AND BUSINESS STRATEGY

In the past, business decision-making often did rely upon broad market research, experience, also intuition. While these methods worked to some extent, they were imprecise plus leaders often guessed about what customers truly wanted. Both neuromarketing and also AI are now on the rise. That guesswork is subsequently being replaced by data-driven clarity. These tools together are changing the very foundation of business strategy as well as how decisions are made.

## 5.1 Moving from Intuition to Evidence-Based Decisions

Customarily, strategy was guided by surveys, gut feelings, or focus groups by managers. These methods are problematic since they capture only responses that are conscious like what customers think or say and often miss subconscious factors driving behavior.

Neuromarketing uncovers even those hidden emotional triggers, and AI in turn changes all of that data into more clear patterns and perceptions. Companies can measure brain activity as well as facial expressions and attention levels rather than simply asking of customers whether they like a new product design. It is just an alternate way to gauge customer opinion.

This shift means leaders no longer have dependence solely upon assumptions. Real evidence of just how consumers do feel and react helps them to make decisions (Hsu, 2017). This reduces risk. Also, strategies become accurate then effective.

## 5.2 Real-Time Adaptation in a Dynamic Market

Neuromarketing combines with AI to create prominent agility. That reason makes this combination quite helpful. Trends can rise and then fade so quickly now within markets, sometimes even in just days or weeks. For businesses that adjust strategies slowly through data study, falling behind is a risk.

Companies have the ability to monitor consumer responses in real time and to adjust instantly with AI-powered neuromarketing. For example:

A brand is able to track whether or not its new digital ad excites, bores, or confuses the viewers then it can immediately tweak all of the content.

Live eye-tracking and engagement data let retailers rearrange store layouts or online product recommendations.

AI is usable for customer service teams so as to detect frustration within voice tone during calls as well as respond with solutions that are driven by empathy.

This real-time adaptability transforms decision-making such that it shifts out of reactive to proactive. Now businesses can detect problems early, so they do not have to wait. Firms adapt before issues worsen; this enables them to grow from errors(Sharma et al., 2014).

## 5.3 Strategy Beyond ROI: Building Emotional Value

Customarily, the success of a strategy was measured mainly by profit, market share, also sales growth—financial returns. These remain important. Businesses think again of success within broader terms since neuromarketing with AI converge.

A financial return has become just as valuable as an emotional connection. A campaign that makes customers feel joy, trust, or belonging can create brand loyalty lasting for years.Even if the more immediate sales numbers still remain small. Apple or Nike don't just sell products rather they sell innovation identity pride empowerment experiences and emotions(Kachhara & Jain, 2025).

This emotional impact at a certain scale is tracked and then measured with the use of AI. AI makes that tracking as well as measuring possible within. Neuromarketing helps businesses understand which emotions their customers consider most important. Together leaders can formulate strategies that build brand value using emotional resonance also ROI.

## 5.4 Empowering Decision-Makers at All Levels

Another important transformation is about how organizations distribute decision-making power inside. Usually leaders made large planned choices, yet field teams had small influence. Even the local managers or the customer-facing employees can make more smart decisions. These decisions are possible through AI-driven perceptions available in real time.

A sales team is able to adjust its pitch at that spot and is able to see how customers are responding emotionally to a product demo in real time. Before widely rolling it out, marketing teams can experiment with a number of ad formats as AI shows just what resonates emotionally. Organizations become faster as well as more flexible with this decision-making democratization. It helps to better align customer needs.

## 5.5 A New Strategic Mindset

The integration of neuromarketing with AI transforms decisions from a slow, assumption-driven process into one that is fast, evidence-based, and emotionally clever. Now businesses can act on "what customers truly feel" they are no longer limited to "what customers say".

Business strategy in itself is reshaping from this very shift. Companies that are embracing these tools are moving well beyond chasing only short-term profits. They are instead creating strategies built upon trust coupled with adaptability.

## 6. REDEFINING BRAND VALUE THROUGH CONSUMER CONNECTION

For decades, brand value was measured largely through financial worth, market share, and recognition. Folks might quickly know a firm brand via its mark, item grade, or catchphrase. Brand value's definition is growing via neuromarketing with AI since these key parts remain important. Presently, recognition alone is insufficient for brands. It must also be felt by all of the consumers. Brands emotionally connect then become stronger a new currency and companies that do not build that risk being left behind.

### 6.1 Beyond Awareness: From Recognition to Emotional Resonance

Customary branding strategies focused on making sure the logo tagline or product was visible in a crowded marketplace. However, loyalty is not guaranteed with the help of recognition. Many brands may be recognized by consumers now. However, they are able to feel quite deeply attached to just a few.

Neuromarketing uncovers why some brands stick emotionally while others remain quite forgettable. Similar quality shoes may be sold by two sports brands, for example, but one brand might evoke identity and feelings of empowerment. The other brand is viewed as being just one more option(Swaminathan et al., 2020). In the modern market, brand value is built by that emotional edge.

This process is strengthened by AI through scaled analysis involving consumer interactions tracking how people do emotionally respond to campaigns, product designs, and brand messages, together with purchases. Firms may gauge resonance using this not just recall then shift plans to strengthen feelings.

### 6.2 Trust and Authenticity as Core Brand Assets

In today's digital economy, consumers find unlimited choices available. They desire authenticity as well as trust instead of only products. A yearning beyond pure product sales exists. A brand that does communicate with honesty and that understands consumer emotions is one way long-term loyalty is earned.

Neuromarketing tools might reveal if a campaign seems manipulative or authentic. Subtle cues such as disengagement or micro-expressions of doubt are early warnings that a brand's message is missing the mark. AI takes all of this feedback then and turns it into much more actionable perceptions which then helps brands (Radojević et al., 2025). Brands reshape all of their communication so that it is more transparent and is human-centered.

Sustainable brands succeed not just because of the product but because consumers believe in the values within them, for example, when they promote eco-friendly practices. Companies can double down on authenticity as a brand asset when AI aligns strongly emotionally with these values.

## 6.3 Creating Shared Experiences That Strengthen Loyalty

Modern consumers desire to buy products plus communities and experiences too. Neuromarketing shows that shared emotions, like what people feel when excited during a product launch or when people feel pride as they are part of a brand's story, create bonds stronger than simple ownership.

AI enables the personalization of these experiences. For example:

Streaming platforms use emotional patterns of engagement and viewing history for recommending matching shows to users.

Retail apps do create shopping adventures that adapt to consumer moods as well as offer comforting messages whenever stress levels are detected.

Brands create campaigns of engagement adjusting in real time. Then consumers feel like participants who are active not viewers who are passive.

## 6.4 Measuring Brand Value in the Emotion Economy

Customary brand valuation depended on financial metrics, surveyed people, and recognition study. Emotional engagement does increasingly measure value in this era of neuromarketing as well as AI.

Now brands can perform tracking:

It is a campaign's memorability how strongly emotional recall can stay.

Emotional loyalty: The depth of connection between consumers to a brand's values.

Emotional advocacy involves consumers recommending the brand with passion to others.

AI analytics is able to quantify all of these emotional dimensions in total, which then allows those companies to easily measure overall success. Companies do now have for themselves a new way for them to measure it. The focus shifts from profits that are fleeting to capital that is sentimental. Such emotional capital often proves far more sustainable in time.

## 6.5 Conclusion: Brand Value as a Human Connection

The convergence of neuromarketing with AI redefines brand value deeply. It is now more about just how deeply any brand resonates with all of people's emotions and values, rather than just logos, slogans, or some recognition.

Brands prioritizing emotional connection build trust as well as authenticity plus loyalty that competitors cannot easily replicate. AI can allow businesses to change their brand via personalized connection measurement. A brand then goes from a product's name up to becoming part of people's identities and lives.

The strongest brands are remembered as well as trusted and loved, not merely recognized, throughout this new era. People feel that bond. Each company prizes this feeling as its best trait.

# 7. CHALLENGES, ETHICS, AND PRIVACY CONCERNS

While the fusion of neuromarketing and AI opens up exciting opportunities, it also poses serious challenges. Human minds, emotions, with private data are what businesses are dealing with, not just technology. This sparks inquiries into ethics and privacy. The responsible use for those powerful tools has also been brought into question. Companies risk losing consumer trust if they fail to address these issues beneath the very foundation of their success (Ahuvia et al., 2022) .

## 7.1 The Fine Line Between Understanding and Manipulation

The biggest ethical question in neuromarketing is simply this: Where does such understanding truly end, and when does manipulation begin?

For the studying of brain activity and eye movements or emotional reactions it helps brands design much better products. Also, studying these things helps brands in creating more relevant experiences. However, those very same perceptions could well be misused so as to coerce people into decisions that they just may not want. A company with the ability of knowing exactly which of the sounds or colors trigger excitement, for example, allows for it to design exploitative ads purely in order to increase sales. The company disregards whether the product truly benefits the customer at all (Dragolea et al., 2011) .

Businesses have this moral duty created. Neuromarketing and AI should not exploit vulnerabilities to improve consumer well-being using them. Drawing this boundary requires ethical guidelines along with transparency.

## 7.2 Privacy Risks in an Age of Emotional Data

Customary marketing already collects a large amount of consumer data like each of the demographic details as well as all of their browsing history. Neuromarketing is capable beyond just that because it uses very sensitive data like biometric signals with emotional responses also brainwave patterns.

This degree with regard to personal data collection stirs up a few privacy concerns. Emotional data as well as neurological data, as opposed to purchase history, reveal intimate details in relation to who a person is in terms of how they feel(Goncalves et al., 2024) . These data also show perception into their thought process.If mishandled, this data could then lead to psychological harm, discrimination, or even to misuse.

Data breaches as well as forbidden use constitute risks of AI systems. Hackers could expose consumers beyond stolen credit card numbers if they target emotional data in damaging ways. This type of information needs stricter security rules and standards. Also, consumers must give consent at every single stage.

## 7.3 Bias and Fairness in AI Systems

Another major challenge resides specifically in terms of the algorithms themselves. AI bias comes about from the data it learns from. AI cannot be considered any more unbiased than that which comes from its own training data. Decisions that reinforce unjust results can stem from training data showing cultural stereotypes, gender biases, or socioeconomic gaps.

One AI model analyzing all consumer responses might prioritize some emotional patterns common in one demographic yet ignore other patterns, so the campaigns unintentionally misrepresent or exclude various groups of people. Segments of less wealth with emotional connections could be missed since predictive analytics favor consumers who can spend more.

In order to handle this, firms should actively test models in regard to bias also diversify data sources. Furthermore, they must make sure that AI-driven neuromarketing strategies are inclusive in addition to fair.

## 7.4 Balancing Innovation with Responsibility

The pressure to stay competitive in today's fast-paced digital economy can cause companies sometimes to prioritize innovation above and beyond responsibility.

Brands might feel tempted to use every possible technological advantage. Ethical outcomes may not be completely contemplated. Eventually such actions harm a brand's image and consumer confidence.

Innovation requires that someone act responsibly for balance. Companies need to establish clear ethical frameworks as well as involve multidisciplinary teams of psychologists and communicate openly with consumers regarding how their data is used(Bercea Olteanu, 2015).

## 7.5 Trust as the Ultimate Safeguard

The challenges, ethical dilemmas, and privacy concerns with neuromarketing and AI are central to the future of business not minor issues. Technology offers instruments forecasting actions and deciphering feelings while trust keeps bonds among consumers.

These tools used right can build value long-term plus loyalty plus trust. They risk losing customers as well as credibility if ethical boundaries are crossed by them. Misuse involving sensitive data carries also this sort of risk. Ultimately, companies in this field are measured by responsibly treating understanding as well as how well they understand consumers.

# 8 FUTURE OF BUSINESS: SUSTAINABLE ADVANTAGE IN THE AI–NEUROMARKETING ERA

The world of business changes more rapidly than before. Consumers do expect more from companies, competition certainly strengthens itself, and digital technologies reshape the way companies operate constantly. In this environment, businesses need sustainable advantages that keep them relevant over time more than short-term wins. Neuromarketing as well as AI converge to offer exactly that. This convergence provides a pathway by which to thrive and survive in the dynamic digital economy (Alsharif et al., 2025). Companies are able to build for themselves future-proof strategies through combining of emotional intelligence and machine intelligence in order to deepen relationships and strengthen trust for fostering long-term growth.

## 8.1 From Data-Driven to Emotion-Driven Enterprises

For years, companies have talked about being "data -driven," along with they have invested heavily in analytics to understand customer demographics, buying patterns, and market trends, though raw data alone doesn't capture the full story.

Feelings and also moods including unconscious triggers influence people in general. People's decisions are not based solely on logic.

The future belongs to (Nozari & Samadi, 2025) companies propelled by feeling not only by facts. Neuromarketing offers tools for decoding emotional responses. AI processes as well as scales these perceptions across millions upon millions of interactions since it has the abilities. They collaborate in helping companies design experiences, products, and campaigns appealing to both the mind and the heart.

Businesses, for example, will know why consumers felt drawn toward a product instead of only knowing the purchase. Because of the fact that this depth of understanding creates opportunities for delivery of more authentic and emotionally satisfying experiences, brands gain a competitive edge which is hard for others to copy.

## 8.2 Innovation Powered by Emotional Insights

Innovation always has been at the core for businesses growing. Yet future innovation will concern relating to people emotionally instead of simply new features or cost reduction.

Businesses are going to use neuromarketing perceptions so that they can design products in order to align more deeply with human desires. AI will speed up the process because it allows companies to test ideas quickly with the ability to predict consumer reactions then refine designs before launch. For example:

AI could predict in the world of retail the (Beličková et.ak,2025) particular packaging designs that spark the most excitement saving months of trial-and-error testing.

Patient-centered services could be built around emotional comfort within healthcare. Such services will lessen worry and increase pleasure.

Entertainment content can be tailored both to viewing history and to current mood. This personalization creates more engaging and engaging experiences for all people.

Firms will go past practical goods should they include feeling awareness into innovation to form items that seem meaningful, unforgettable, and people-focused.

## 8.3 Building Trust as the Foundation of Advantage

In the future, sustainable advantage will be built upon trust, not solely on technology. Consumers will keep sharing private emotional data with brands using it responsibly. For companies that misuse AI or cross ethical boundaries credibility will diminish rather quickly, while those companies that care for and prioritize transparency will stand out within their fields.

The currency of the new brand will become that of trust. Businesses that communicate openly about data collection and usage will win loyalty. These businesses do also respect privacy and they avoid manipulative practices. Responsible AI as well as neuromarketing use may in fact become a differentiator for competition since consumers increasingly reward ethical brands with more loyalty and advocacy.

### 8.4 Agility and Adaptability in a Fast-Moving Market

The pace of change regarding consumer preferences will only accelerate during future years. For people, the excitement of today might not be able to last. Boredom could happen tomorrow instead. Businesses with more agility will need to future-proof in order to adapt instantly.

Companies gain the means for sensing shifts as well as for pivoting using AI neuromarketing with promptness. AI can sense the feeling that underlies a fresh topic online. Brands can then adjust campaigns within hours instead of after months. This flexibility ensures businesses stay culturally relevant and emotionally connect within a world where attention spans shrink and trends flee.

## 9. CONCLUSION

Looking further ahead, firms enjoying the greatest success will transcend individual promotions or offerings. Entire ecosystems around emotional experiences will be built by them.

Imagine a future where: Store lighting, music, and product tips are adapted by retail ecosystems matching each shopper's emotional state. Digital platforms curate content also that content not only entertains yet uplifts moods or reduces stress.

AI is used in smart homes in order to recognize emotional signals and also create personalized environments. These homes may adjust temperature, lighting, also even suggest activities that improve well-being. In this vision of things, businesses do not simply sell. Instead, they can support, and even connect, and also nurture emotional well-being. This positions service providers as long-term partners in people's lives rather than only that.

## REFERENCES:

Ahuvia, A., Izberk-Bilgin, E., & Lee, K. (2022). Towards a theory of brand love in services: The power of identity and social relationships. *Journal of Service Management, 33*(3), 453–464. DOI: 10.1108/JOSM-06-2021-0221

Alsharif, A. H., Wang, J., Isa, S. M., Salleh, N. Z. M., Dawas, H. A., & Alsharif, M. H. (2025). The synergy of neuromarketing and artificial intelligence: A comprehensive literature review in the last decade. *Future Business Journal, 11*(1), 170. DOI: 10.1186/s43093-025-00591-x

Bercea Olteanu, M. D. (2015). Neuroethics and responsibility in conducting neuromarketing research. *Neuroethics, 8*(2), 191–202. DOI: 10.1007/s12152-014-9227-y

Dragolea, L., & Cotirlea, D. (2011). Neuromarketing: between influence and manipulation. *Polish journal of management studies, 3*, 78-88.

Goncalves, M., Hu, Y., Aliagas, I., & Cerdá, L. M. (2024). Neuromarketing algorithms' consumer privacy and ethical considerations: Challenges and opportunities. *Cogent Business & Management, 11*(1), 2333063. DOI: 10.1080/23311975.2024.2333063

Hsu, M. (2017). Neuromarketing: Inside the mind of the consumer. *California Management Review, 59*(4), 5–22. DOI: 10.1177/0008125617720208

Kachhara, G., & Jain, J. (2025). Unleashing Synergy: A review of the Impact of AI and Neuromarketing on Business Success. *International Journal of Environmental Sciences, 11*(3s), 727–739.

Lee, S. M., Olson, D. L., & Trimi, S. (2010). Strategic innovation in the convergence era. *International Journal of Management and Enterprise Development, 9*(1), 1–12. DOI: 10.1504/IJMED.2010.035304

Macdonald, E., Wilson, H. N., & Konus, U. (2012). Better customer insight-in real time (Vol. 90). Harvard Business School Publishing. Huseynov, S., Kassas, B., Segovia, M. S., & Palma, M. A. (2019). Incorporating biometric data in models of consumer choice. *Applied Economics, 51*(14), 1514–1531.

Mariani, M. M., Perez-Vega, R., & Wirtz, J. (2022). AI in marketing, consumer research and psychology: A systematic literature review and research agenda. *Psychology and Marketing, 39*(4), 755–776. DOI: 10.1002/mar.21619

Nozari, H., & Samadi, S. (2025). AIoE-Powered Neuromarketing for Decoding the Consumer Brain. In *Artificial Intelligence of Everything and Sustainable Development* (pp. 39–53). Springer Nature Singapore. DOI: 10.1007/978-981-96-7202-8_3

Radojević, I., Slijepčević, M., & Popović Šević, N. (2025). The Role of Artificial Intelligence in the Modern Approach to Neuromarketing. In *Multidisciplinary Approaches to Contemporary Marketing: Digital Trends, Social Issues and Economics* (pp. 45–73). Springer Nature Switzerland. DOI: 10.1007/978-3-031-78026-4_2

Rane, N., Choudhary, S., & Rane, J. (2023). Hyper-personalization for enhancing customer loyalty and satisfaction in Customer Relationship Management (CRM) systems. *Available at SSRN* 4641044. DOI: 10.2139/ssrn.4641044

Selvarajan, G. P. (2021). Harnessing AI-Driven Data Mining for Predictive Insights: A framework for Enhancing Decision-Making in Dynamic Data Environments. *International Journal of Creative Research Thoughts*, *9*(2), 5476–5486.

Sharma, R., Mithas, S., & Kankanhalli, A. (2014). Transforming decision-making processes: A research agenda for understanding the impact of business analytics on organisations. *European Journal of Information Systems*, *23*(4), 433–441. DOI: 10.1057/ejis.2014.17

Swaminathan, V., Sorescu, A., Steenkamp, J. B. E., O'Guinn, T. C. G., & Schmitt, B. (2020). Branding in a hyperconnected world: Refocusing theories and rethinking boundaries. *Journal of Marketing*, *84*(2), 24–46. DOI: 10.1177/0022242919899905

Uppal, A., Banerjee, S., Agarwal, V., & Yadav, P. (2025). Emotion-Driven Intelligent Segmentation for Hyper-Personalized Customer Experiences: A Rule Mining Approach. *Metallurgical and Materials Engineering*, *31*(4), 972–981. DOI: 10.63278/1541

Wedel, M., Pieters, R., & van der Lans, R. (2019). Eye tracking methodology for research in consumer psychology. In *Handbook of Research Methods in Consumer Psychology* (pp. 276–292). Routledge.

# Chapter 10
# Strategizing in Immersive Realities:
## Case-Based Insights Into Metaverse, Augment Reality, Virtual Reality, and Neuromarketing for Consumer Understanding

**Ashwarya Kapoor**
http://orcid.org/0000-0003-3858-3945
*School of Commerce, Manav Rachna International Institute of Research and Studies, Faridabad, India*

**Sneha Kapoor**
http://orcid.org/0009-0005-7051-3359
*J.C. Bose University of Science and Technology, YMCA, Faridabad, India*

**Rajiv Sindwani**
*J.C. Bose University of Science and Technology, YMCA, Faridabad, India*

## ABSTRACT

*The rapid advancement of immersive technologies such as the Metaverse, Virtual Reality (VR), and Augmented Reality (AR) is transforming consumer–brand interactions by enabling interactive, multi-sensory, and personalized experiences. This chapter explores the convergence of immersive technologies and neuromarketing through a qualitative, case-based approach using secondary data from retail, entertainment, and fashion sectors. It interprets consumer experiences in immersive environments through a neuromarketing lens, linking experiential stimuli with*

DOI: 10.4018/979-8-3373-5997-7.ch010

*cognitive and emotional responses. Cross-case insights highlight personalization, interactivity, and emotional engagement as key drivers of consumer behavior, while also identifying challenges related to ethics, privacy, and technology. The chapter proposes a conceptual framework connecting immersive stimuli, subconscious processing, and behavioral outcomes, offering valuable implications for researchers and practitioners.*

## 1. INTRODUCTION

### 1.1 Background

The rapid evolution of immersive technologies including Virtual Reality (VR), Augmented Reality (AR), Mixed Reality (MR), and virtual environments under the broader umbrella of the Metaverse — is fundamentally transforming the ways in which consumers engage with brands, products, and services. Unlike traditional digital media, which primarily relies on static visuals, text, or video, immersive technologies offer multi-sensory, interactive experiences that simulate real-world or entirely novel environments (Kapoor et al., 2025a, b). VR, for example, allows users to experience fully digital worlds in which they can navigate, manipulate, and interact with objects or scenarios, creating a strong sense of presence and embodiment. AR overlays digital information onto physical environments, enhancing the user's perception and decision-making in real-time contexts, such as trying on virtual apparel or visualizing furniture in a home space. MR blends elements of both VR and AR, enabling dynamic interaction between physical and virtual objects. Collectively, these technologies are redefining the consumer journey, bridging the gap between online and offline experiences, and enabling marketers to craft highly personalized, emotionally engaging interactions.

Concurrently, advancements in neuromarketing methodologies have allowed marketers and researchers to explore the cognitive, emotional, and physiological mechanisms underlying consumer behavior in these immersive settings. Techniques such as electroencephalography (EEG), functional magnetic resonance imaging (fMRI), eye-tracking, and facial coding provide insights into subconscious processes, including attention allocation, emotional arousal, memory encoding, and decision-making patterns. These methods move beyond self-reported measures, which are often limited by bias, inaccuracy, or social desirability effects, to capture real-time, objective responses to marketing stimuli (Gupta et al., 2025; Saffari et al., 2023). The integration of immersive technologies with neuromarketing thus presents a unique opportunity to evaluate not only what consumers do, but also why they do it, and how experiential design elements influence perception and behavior at a subconscious level.

This convergence has far-reaching implications for brand management and marketing strategy. Immersive experiences can enhance engagement, strengthen emotional connections, and increase memorability, which are critical drivers of loyalty and purchase intent. For instance, VR fashion shows or Metaverse storefronts allow consumers to experience products in ways that are not feasible in physical retail or traditional digital formats, influencing perceptions of exclusivity, innovation, and brand prestige. Moreover, the analytical insights derived from neuromarketing enable marketers to optimize the design of immersive experiences by aligning them with the cognitive and emotional preferences of target audiences.

As consumer expectations continue to evolve, the interplay between immersive technology and neuromarketing is likely to redefine competitive advantage in digital marketing. Organizations that can leverage these tools effectively are better positioned to understand and influence behavior, foster meaningful brand relationships, and drive engagement in highly dynamic, digitally mediated environments. This chapter situates itself at this intersection, exploring how immersive technologies and neuromarketing insights combine to shape consumer experience, engagement, and decision-making in contemporary marketing contexts.

## 1.2 Recent Trends

Several recent trends in both research and practice underscore the growing significance of the intersection between immersive technologies and neuromarketing. A systematic review of neuromarketing studies across consumer buying stages highlights an increasing focus on understanding implicit emotional and cognitive processes, particularly in purchase decision-making, revealing the importance of subconscious drivers in shaping consumer behaviour. Simultaneously, the adoption and study of immersive technologies — including VR, AR, MR, and 3D environments — has surged, with research comparing their effects across industries and demonstrating how consumer experiences in these settings influence purchase intent, brand loyalty, and trust (Kapoor et al., 2021a, 2022).

2023a). For instance, the study "Virtual and Augmented Reality: Advancing Research in Consumer Marketing" provides a comprehensive framework centering on consumer experiences across the purchase journey. Parallel to this, research exploring the metaverse as a marketing domain is rapidly expanding; recent work, such as "Marketing in the Metaverse: Conceptual Understanding, Framework, and Research Agenda," reviews hundreds of articles to map emerging themes, challenges, and opportunities for marketers in these virtual spaces (Barrera and Shah, 2023). Additionally, specific empirical studies, including "Motivation in the Metaverse: A

Dual-Process Approach to Consumer Choices in a Virtual Reality Supermarket," investigate how immersive supermarket experiences in the metaverse activate both emotional and cognitive processing, demonstrating the applicability of dual-process theories in virtual environments (Saffari et al., 2023). Collectively, these trends highlight a convergence of immersive experience design and neuroscientific insights, emphasizing the need for an integrated understanding of consumer behavior in increasingly digital and interactive contexts.

## 1.3 Research Gap

While immersive technologies such as Virtual Reality (VR), Augmented Reality (AR), and the Metaverse have garnered significant attention in both academic and industry circles, there remains a notable paucity of research integrating these platforms with neuromarketing methodologies to understand consumer behavior. Existing studies predominantly focus on isolated aspects of immersive experiences or neurophysiological responses, often neglecting the synergistic effects when combined. For instance, while some research highlights the impact of VR and AR on consumer decision-making and emotional engagement, there is limited exploration into how these technologies, when coupled with neuromarketing tools like EEG or facial coding, can provide deeper insights into subconscious consumer responses (Russo et al., 2022). Moreover, the majority of studies are experimental in nature, with few offering comparative case analyses across different industries or cultural contexts. This gap is further compounded by the rapid evolution of immersive technologies and their applications in marketing, outpacing the development of comprehensive theoretical frameworks that can guide both research and practice. Additionally, ethical considerations, such as data privacy and the potential for subconscious manipulation, remain underexplored in the context of immersive neuromarketing. Addressing these gaps is crucial for advancing the field and ensuring that the integration of immersive technologies and neuromarketing is both effective and ethically sound.

## 1.4 Research Objectives

To address these gaps, this chapter aims to:

1. Examine multiple case studies of brands using immersive technologies (Metaverse, VR, AR) together with neuromarketing tools to elicit subconscious responses in consumer behavior.
2. Conduct a cross-case comparative analysis along key dimensions such as type of immersive platform, neuromarketing measurement techniques, consumer emotional/cognitive outcomes, ethical safeguards and business objectives.

3. Propose a conceptual framework linking immersive stimuli → subconscious responses → marketing outcomes, informed by empirical cases.
4. Offer theoretical contributions by integrating immersive experience, neuromarketing, and consumer behavior literatures; and practical implications for marketers designing immersive consumer experiences.
5. Identify ethical, methodological, and cross-cultural considerations, and suggest areas for future research to bridge identified gaps.

### 1.5 Contribution of the Chapter

This chapter contributes to the growing body of knowledge on immersive technologies and consumer behavior by offering a qualitative, case-based perspective across retail, entertainment, and fashion sectors. It advances existing literature by integrating immersive experiences with a neuromarketing lens to explain how cognitive and emotional responses shape consumer engagement. Through cross-case analysis, the chapter identifies key drivers such as interactivity, personalization, and emotional resonance, while also highlighting ethical and technological challenges. Additionally, it proposes a conceptual framework linking immersive stimuli, subconscious processing, and behavioral outcomes, thereby bridging theoretical and practical insights. The chapter provides valuable guidance for marketers and researchers seeking to design effective, engaging, and responsible immersive consumer experiences.

## 2. LITERATURE REVIEW

### 2.1 Immersive Technologies and Consumer Behavior

Immersive technologies, encompassing Virtual Reality (VR), Augmented Reality (AR), Mixed Reality (MR), and the Metaverse, have significantly transformed consumer experiences by providing interactive and sensory-rich environments. These technologies enable consumers to engage with products and services in ways that traditional media cannot replicate, leading to enhanced emotional and cognitive responses. Research indicates that immersive experiences can increase consumer engagement, improve brand recall, and influence purchase intentions by creating memorable and personalized interactions (Ambika et al., 2025; Erensoy et al., 2024).

A systematic review by Ambika et al. (2025) analyzed 129 studies over two decades, highlighting the diverse applications of immersive technologies across various sectors. The review found that VR and AR applications in retail settings can enhance product understanding and facilitate decision-making processes by providing realistic simulations and interactive interfaces. Similarly, the Metaverse offers new avenues for consumer engagement, allowing brands to create virtual storefronts and immersive brand experiences that resonate with digitally native consumers (Kaur et al., 2024).

In the retail sector, immersive technologies have been instrumental in bridging the gap between online and offline shopping experiences. AR applications, such as virtual try-ons and product visualizations, enable consumers to interact with products in a digital environment before making a purchase decision. This functionality not only enhances the shopping experience but also reduces uncertainty and increases consumer confidence in their choices (Kaur and Sharma, 2024). VR, on the other hand, offers fully immersive environments where consumers can explore virtual stores, attend product demonstrations, and engage with brands in innovative ways, thereby enhancing brand perception and loyalty (Poushneh and Vasquez-Parraga, 2017).

The Metaverse, as an emerging platform, introduces a persistent, shared virtual space where users can interact with each other and digital objects in real-time. Brands are leveraging the Metaverse to create unique and engaging experiences that transcend traditional marketing channels. For instance, companies are hosting virtual events, launching digital products, and establishing virtual storefronts to engage with consumers in immersive ways (Dwivedi et al., 2023). These virtual experiences offer consumers a sense of presence and community, fostering deeper emotional connections with brands.

However, the integration of immersive technologies into consumer experiences also presents challenges. Issues related to data privacy, ethical considerations, and the need for new marketing strategies tailored to virtual environments are emerging concerns. As consumers spend more time in these virtual spaces, understanding their behaviors and preferences becomes crucial for brands aiming to maintain relevance and build trust in the Metaverse (Kaur, et al., 2024).

Overall, immersive technologies are reshaping consumer behavior by offering interactive, personalized, and emotionally engaging experiences. As these technologies continue to evolve, their impact on consumer decision-making processes and brand interactions is expected to grow, necessitating ongoing research and adaptation by marketers to effectively leverage these tools.

## 2.2 Neuromarketing Techniques in Immersive Environments

Neuromarketing, which leverages neuroscience principles to understand consumer behavior, has emerged as a pivotal tool in analyzing subconscious responses to marketing stimuli. Traditional marketing research methods, such as surveys and focus groups, often rely on self-reported data, which can be biased or fail to capture underlying emotional and cognitive processes. In contrast, neuromarketing techniques—such as Electroencephalography (EEG), functional Magnetic Resonance Imaging (fMRI), eye-tracking, galvanic skin response (GSR), and facial coding—allow researchers to measure real-time physiological and neurological responses, offering a more nuanced understanding of consumer reactions (Gupta et al., 2025; Vecchiato et al., 2014). These methods can detect subtle shifts in attention, engagement, and emotional arousal that may otherwise go unnoticed, providing actionable insights for marketers designing immersive experiences.

The integration of neuromarketing tools into immersive environments, including VR, AR, and the Metaverse, has enhanced the precision and depth of consumer behavior analysis. VR and AR platforms create interactive, multi-sensory experiences that evoke emotions and cognitive processing in ways traditional media cannot. By combining these platforms with EEG and eye-tracking, researchers can evaluate how users process visual and auditory stimuli, track their gaze and focus, and measure cognitive load during immersive interactions (Russo et al., 2022). For example, EEG can detect changes in brainwave activity associated with attention, engagement, and emotional responses, while eye-tracking identifies which elements of a virtual advertisement or virtual storefront capture the user's interest most effectively. Facial coding further supplements these insights by analyzing micro-expressions that reveal subconscious emotional reactions.

Empirical studies have demonstrated the effectiveness of this integrated approach. In immersive retail environments, synchronized EEG and eye-tracking have been employed to assess consumer reactions to VR product displays, revealing patterns of emotional engagement, preference, and purchase intention (Vecchiato et al., 2014). Similarly, AR applications that allow users to virtually try on products or visualize furniture in their homes can be optimized using GSR and eye-tracking data to understand stress, excitement, or uncertainty during decision-making (Bajpai and Islam, 2022). These insights enable marketers to tailor experiences that maximize positive emotional responses, reduce cognitive friction, and increase overall engagement.

Moreover, neuromarketing in immersive environments supports personalization and predictive analytics. By capturing real-time physiological data, companies can adjust virtual environments dynamically to align with individual consumer preferences, thereby enhancing satisfaction and fostering loyalty. For instance, if a user exhibits signs of boredom or disengagement, the immersive environment can adapt by highlighting more relevant products or introducing interactive elements that recapture attention. Beyond commercial applications, this approach has implications for behavioral research, allowing scholars to investigate the psychological mechanisms driving decision-making in controlled yet ecologically valid virtual settings.

However, integrating neuromarketing with immersive technologies also presents challenges. Ethical considerations, including informed consent, data privacy, and potential manipulation of subconscious processes, are critical concerns (Gupta et al., 2025). Researchers must ensure transparent use of neuromarketing data and implement safeguards to protect participants from unintended psychological effects. Additionally, technological limitations such as EEG signal interference within VR headsets or motion artifacts in eye-tracking can affect data reliability, requiring careful experimental design and validation.

Overall, the convergence of neuromarketing and immersive technologies provides a powerful framework for understanding consumer behavior at a deeper, subconscious level. By leveraging EEG, eye-tracking, facial coding, and other physiological measures within VR, AR, and Metaverse platforms, marketers can design experiences that are engaging, personalized, and emotionally resonant. This integration not only enhances commercial strategy but also contributes to theoretical insights into human cognition, emotion, and decision-making in digitally mediated environments.

## 2.3 The Metaverse and Consumer Behavior

The Metaverse represents a convergence of physical and digital realities, providing a persistent, shared virtual space where users can interact with each other and digital objects in real-time. Unlike traditional online platforms, the Metaverse offers immersive, interactive, and often gamified experiences that blur the boundaries between the real and virtual worlds. This has significant implications for consumer behavior, as it allows for highly engaging, emotionally resonant, and personalized interactions with brands, products, and services (Kapoor et al., 2023b; 2024). Early research indicates that the Metaverse can influence consumer behavior by enhancing engagement, promoting brand loyalty, and facilitating unique purchasing experiences that go beyond conventional e-commerce and social media channels (Dwivedi et al., 2023).

One of the key drivers of consumer engagement in the Metaverse is the sense of presence it provides. Users feel "present" in the virtual environment, which increases immersion and encourages more natural and authentic interactions with digital content. This sense of presence fosters emotional attachment to virtual experiences, thereby influencing consumer attitudes, preferences, and intentions. For instance, virtual storefronts, brand activations, and interactive product demonstrations in the Metaverse allow consumers to explore, customize, and interact with offerings in ways that are impossible in traditional retail or online shopping (Buhalis et al., 2023). This experiential dimension contributes to stronger brand recall and preference, as consumers associate positive emotional experiences with the brand.

Gamification within the Metaverse further amplifies consumer engagement. By incorporating elements such as challenges, rewards, leaderboards, and social interactions, brands can motivate users to participate actively, spend more time in virtual environments, and develop long-term loyalty (Saffari et al., 2023). Interactive experiences, such as virtual concerts, fashion shows, and product launches, create memorable moments that reinforce brand identity and foster community-building among users. These immersive and gamified interactions also provide rich data on consumer behavior, preferences, and decision-making patterns, which marketers can leverage to refine strategies and tailor personalized offerings.

However, the Metaverse presents several challenges for marketers and researchers. Data privacy and security remain major concerns, as virtual environments collect extensive personal and behavioral information. Ethical considerations, including informed consent, manipulation of consumer behavior, and digital well-being, must be addressed to maintain trust and protect users (Kaur et al., 2024). Additionally, the Metaverse requires new marketing strategies that are distinct from traditional digital marketing approaches. Content must be designed to be immersive, interactive, and contextually relevant, and brands must consider factors such as virtual identity, avatar representation, and social dynamics within virtual communities.

Cross-cultural and demographic factors also play a critical role in Metaverse adoption. Users from different age groups, cultures, and socio-economic backgrounds may perceive virtual experiences differently, influencing their engagement, satisfaction, and loyalty. Understanding these variations is essential for designing inclusive and effective marketing strategies that resonate across diverse consumer segments.

In conclusion, the Metaverse represents a transformative platform for consumer engagement, providing opportunities for immersive, interactive, and gamified brand experiences. While it offers potential for enhancing brand loyalty and customer satisfaction, marketers must navigate ethical challenges, privacy concerns, and evolving consumer expectations. Continued research is necessary to understand consumer behavior in these virtual spaces, optimize marketing strategies, and ensure responsible and sustainable use of the Metaverse as a commercial and social platform (Kapoor et al., 2025c).

## 2.4 Ethical Considerations and Future Research Directions

As immersive technologies, including VR, AR, MR, and the Metaverse, integrate with neuromarketing techniques, ethical considerations have become a critical concern in both research and commercial applications. While these technologies offer unprecedented opportunities to understand consumer behavior at subconscious levels, they also raise significant ethical questions regarding privacy, consent, transparency, and the potential for behavioral manipulation. Immersive environments often collect extensive personal and behavioral data, including biometric signals such as eye movements, heart rate, facial expressions, and brain activity, which can reveal sensitive insights about an individual's emotions, preferences, and decision-making processes (Gupta et al., 2025; Vecchiato et al., 2014). The storage, processing, and use of this data must comply with privacy regulations and ensure that participants provide informed consent, fully understanding how their data will be used.

Beyond privacy concerns, the potential for manipulation is a significant ethical challenge. Neuromarketing techniques, when combined with immersive experiences, can influence consumer behavior in subtle and subconscious ways, potentially affecting purchasing decisions or brand perceptions without explicit awareness. This raises questions about consumer autonomy, the ethical limits of persuasion, and the responsibility of marketers to avoid exploiting vulnerable populations. Scholars argue for the establishment of ethical frameworks and industry standards to guide the responsible deployment of neuromarketing tools within immersive environments, emphasizing transparency, fairness, and consumer protection (Russo et al., 2022; Bajpai and Islam, 2022).

In addition to ethical considerations, several methodological and research gaps remain. Most existing studies focus on short-term experiments with limited participant diversity, often in controlled lab settings. There is a lack of longitudinal research examining the long-term effects of immersive experiences on consumer attitudes, behavior, and loyalty. Such studies are crucial for understanding whether immersive marketing interventions have sustainable impacts or if effects diminish over time. Furthermore, cross-cultural research is limited, despite evidence that demographic factors, cultural context, and socio-economic status can significantly influence engagement and responses in virtual environments (Saffari et al., 2023). Understanding these differences is essential for designing inclusive and effective marketing strategies that resonate with diverse consumer segments.

Another area for future research is the development of standardized methodologies for measuring consumer responses within immersive environments. While techniques like EEG, eye-tracking, GSR, and facial coding provide valuable insights, there is considerable variation in how these methods are applied, analyzed, and interpreted across studies. Standardized protocols would enhance the reliability, comparability, and generalizability of findings, enabling both researchers and practitioners to make more informed decisions about the design and optimization of immersive marketing strategies.

Finally, researchers should explore ethical innovations in immersive technology, such as mechanisms for participant control, consent dashboards, and real-time privacy management. Integrating these features can help balance the benefits of rich consumer insights with respect for individual autonomy and ethical responsibility. By addressing these ethical, methodological, and contextual challenges, future research can ensure that the integration of immersive technologies and neuromarketing contributes positively to both consumer experience and scholarly knowledge.

In summary, ethical considerations and future research directions are intertwined in the evolution of immersive marketing and neuromarketing. Responsible, transparent, and methodologically rigorous research is essential to harness the full potential of these technologies while safeguarding consumer rights, fostering trust, and advancing the scientific understanding of behavior in virtual spaces.

## 3. RESEARCH METHODOLOGY

This chapter employs a case study research methodology to explore how immersive technologies (VR, AR, and the Metaverse) influence consumer behavior. Case studies are particularly suitable for understanding complex, real-world phenomena, as they allow detailed examination of specific organizational practices and consumer interactions (Yin, 2017).

### 3.1 Research Design

A multiple case study approach was adopted to analyze three organizations across different industries—retail, entertainment, and fashion—that effectively use immersive technologies for consumer engagement. This approach enables cross-case comparisons to identify patterns, best practices, and challenges while maintaining focus on the context-specific implementation of immersive experiences.

### 3.2 Case Selection

The selection of case studies was guided by the following criteria:

1. Organizations must have publicly documented use of VR, AR, or Metaverse platforms for consumer engagement.
2. Availability of information on marketing strategies and consumer experiences through secondary sources such as company reports, press releases, articles, and academic studies.
3. Representation across diverse industries to provide a comprehensive understanding of immersive technology adoption.

Based on these criteria, the selected cases are:

- **Retail Sector:** A global e-commerce retailer implementing AR for virtual try-ons and VR for immersive shopping experiences.
- **Entertainment Sector:** A virtual concert platform hosting live events in the Metaverse, enabling interactive fan participation.

- **Fashion Sector:** A fashion brand leveraging VR fashion shows and Metaverse storefronts to enhance global consumer engagement.

### 3.3 Data Collection

The study relies exclusively on *secondary data sources*, including:

- Published company reports and press releases detailing immersive technology implementations.
- News articles and industry analyses covering consumer experiences and engagement metrics.
- Academic and industry research papers examining the use of VR, AR, Metaverse, and neuromarketing in consumer engagement.

This approach ensures that findings are based on reliable, publicly accessible information, making the research replicable and verifiable.

### 3.4 Data Analysis

Secondary data from the three case studies was analyzed using a descriptive and comparative approach. Key aspects examined include:

- Types of immersive technology employed and their applications in consumer engagement.
- Integration of neuromarketing principles to enhance brand experience.
- Observable outcomes in consumer behavior, such as engagement, brand recall, and purchase intentions.

Cross-case comparison was conducted to identify similarities, differences, and emerging patterns across industries. Data is presented using tables and figures to summarize key features, strategies, and outcomes of immersive technology applications.

### 3.5 Research Rigor

To ensure credibility, the following measures were applied:

- Use of multiple secondary sources for each case to triangulate information.
- Selection of well-documented cases from reputable organizations and publications.

- Transparent documentation of sources and consistent criteria for case selection.

## 4. CASE STUDIES

This section presents three in-depth case studies from retail, entertainment, and fashion sectors that illustrate the application of immersive technologies and neuromarketing techniques in enhancing consumer engagement. The cases focus on how companies leverage VR, AR, and Metaverse platforms to create interactive, personalized, and emotionally engaging experiences, while also highlighting observable consumer behavior patterns based on secondary research.

### 4.1 Case Study 1: Retail Sector – AR and VR in E-Commerce

#### Background:

The global retail sector has been a pioneer in adopting immersive technologies to bridge the gap between traditional in-store shopping and digital commerce. With the rapid growth of e-commerce, consumers increasingly demand interactive and personalized shopping experiences that replicate the tactile, sensory-rich environment of physical stores. A leading global e-commerce retailer, recognized for its innovative use of technology, has leveraged Augmented Reality (AR) and Virtual Reality (VR) to redefine the online shopping journey. This adoption reflects the broader shift toward experiential retail, where the focus is on creating highly engaging, interactive, and memorable experiences that reduce uncertainty, build trust, and enhance overall satisfaction.

The integration of immersive technologies aligns with the growing consumer expectation for digital-first experiences, especially among millennials and Gen Z shoppers who are familiar with AR-enabled apps, 3D simulations, and interactive platforms. The retailer's strategic objective is not only to facilitate product selection but also to create emotional engagement with the brand, strengthening loyalty and increasing repeat purchases.

#### Technologies and Applications:

- **AR Virtual Try-On:** Using smartphones or AR-enabled devices, consumers can try on apparel, accessories, eyewear, and cosmetics in real-time. This allows shoppers to visualize how products would look on them without physical contact, significantly reducing purchase hesitation and return rates. AR try-on experiences provide realistic representations of product size, color, and fit, thereby replicating the in-store experience digitally.

- **VR Immersive Stores:** The retailer has developed VR-based virtual stores, where users navigate three-dimensional aisles, explore curated collections, and interact with products through VR headsets. These immersive environments incorporate visual, auditory, and spatial cues that simulate physical store experiences while adding interactivity that is impossible in traditional settings. For example, consumers can customize furniture arrangements or explore new product lines in a virtual room before making a purchase.
- **Integration with AI:** Artificial intelligence enhances the immersive experience by providing personalized product recommendations, curating content based on prior purchases, browsing history, and behavioral patterns. AI algorithms analyze user interactions within the AR/VR environment to offer suggestions that align with individual preferences, thereby improving relevance and satisfaction (Kapoor and Sindwani, 2025).

## Consumer Experience and Outcomes:

The combination of AR, VR, and AI creates a highly engaging and memorable shopping journey. Key outcomes observed include:

- **Enhanced Product Understanding:** Consumers gain a clear sense of product dimensions, style, and usability, which increases confidence in purchase decisions.
- **Emotional Engagement:** The interactive visualization and immersive environment evoke positive emotions, making shopping enjoyable rather than transactional.
- **Improved Brand Recall:** Engaging, novel experiences leave a lasting impression, strengthening the association between positive emotions and the brand.
- **Higher Conversion Rates:** Particularly among digitally savvy consumers, AR and VR experiences translate into increased willingness to purchase, lower cart abandonment, and higher repeat visitation rates (Kaur and Sharma, 2024).

## Neuromarketing Insights:

Although this case study relies on secondary data, research indicates that AR and VR environments stimulate attention, emotional arousal, and cognitive engagement, which are critical drivers of consumer behavior. Users tend to spend more time exploring products, engage with interactive content more deeply, and respond positively to personalized experiences (Poushneh and Vasquez-Parraga, 2017). These factors collectively enhance purchase intention and brand loyalty, demonstrating the effectiveness of immersive retail strategies.

### Key Takeaways:

This case illustrates the transformative potential of integrating AR and VR technologies in e-commerce. By creating immersive, personalized, and emotionally engaging experiences, retailers can:

- Reduce uncertainty in online purchases.
- Strengthen consumer-brand relationships.
- Enhance attention, engagement, and memory retention.
- Drive higher conversion rates and foster long-term loyalty.

Overall, this case demonstrates that immersive technologies are not only tools for innovation but strategic enablers of consumer-centric retail experiences, setting new standards for online shopping in the digital age.

## 4.2 Case Study 2: Entertainment Sector – Virtual Concert Platforms in the Metaverse

### Background:

The entertainment industry has experienced a significant transformation with the emergence of Metaverse platforms, which allow artists, producers, and entertainment brands to engage with global audiences in entirely new ways. Traditional concerts and live events, while immersive in physical settings, are limited by geographical constraints, ticket availability, and venue capacity. The rise of the Metaverse has enabled virtual concerts, festivals, and interactive experiences that transcend these limitations, offering scale, accessibility, and interactivity that were previously impossible.

One leading virtual concert platform exemplifies this trend by hosting large-scale live events entirely within the Metaverse. Fans interact with artists and fellow attendees through customizable avatars, participate in gamified experiences, and access exclusive content. The platform integrates high-fidelity audio-visual simulations, social interactivity, and real-time engagement tools, creating a hybrid experience that blends the excitement of live events with the flexibility and creativity of digital spaces. This evolution reflects a broader industry trend where digital experiences are not merely supplementary but central to fan engagement strategies.

## Technologies and Applications:

- **Metaverse Venues:** Concertgoers enter 3D virtual arenas that replicate real-world concert venues. These venues include realistic stage setups, dynamic lighting, crowd simulations, and immersive sound systems, providing a multi-sensory experience that mirrors physical concerts. Users can navigate the venue freely, choose viewing angles, and explore interactive zones.
- **Interactive Avatars:** Attendees create personalized avatars, enabling real-time social interactions. Avatars can communicate through gestures, chat, and emoticons, fostering a sense of presence and social connectedness even in a virtual environment.
- **Gamified Features:** Platforms incorporate mini-games, collectibles, and achievement systems, rewarding fans for participation and engagement. Virtual merchandise and exclusive content enhance the perception of value and exclusivity, motivating repeated attendance.
- **Integration with Streaming:** High-definition VR streaming ensures immersive audio-visual fidelity, making virtual attendees feel present in the concert environment. The platform also enables cross-platform access, allowing users on desktop, mobile, and VR devices to participate seamlessly.

## Consumer Experience and Outcomes:

The immersive nature of these virtual concerts produces a range of positive outcomes for fans and entertainment brands:

- **Emotional Engagement:** Fans report higher levels of excitement and emotional arousal compared to traditional online streaming. The interactivity and ability to influence the environment through avatars contribute to a sense of agency and involvement.
- **Brand Loyalty:** Repeated immersive experiences foster emotional attachment to artists and brands. Fans are more likely to attend future virtual events and recommend experiences to peers, driving word-of-mouth promotion.
- **Global Reach:** Virtual concerts remove geographical and logistical barriers, enabling participation from diverse audiences worldwide. This accessibility expands fan bases and increases potential revenue streams.

- **Memorable Experiences:** Gamified features and interactive elements create lasting impressions, reinforcing artist-brand perception and enhancing social identity within fan communities.

### Neuromarketing Insights:

Secondary research suggests that virtual concerts in the Metaverse stimulate attention, emotional arousal, and social presence, which are critical drivers of satisfaction and loyalty (Dwivedi et al., 2023; Rane et al., 2023). By leveraging sensory, cognitive, and social cues, these platforms evoke stronger emotional resonance than traditional digital media, making consumers feel actively engaged rather than passive observers.

### Key Takeaways:

This case demonstrates that the Metaverse allows entertainment brands to:

- Provide highly personalized and interactive experiences that enhance engagement.
- Strengthen fan loyalty through emotional immersion and gamified participation.
- Expand global reach without the constraints of physical venues.
- Transform passive content consumption into active, participatory experiences.

Overall, immersive virtual concerts represent a paradigm shift in how entertainment is produced, delivered, and experienced, highlighting the potential of the Metaverse as a strategic tool for consumer engagement and brand building.

## 4.3 Case Study 3: Fashion Sector – VR Fashion Shows and Metaverse Stores

### Background:

The fashion industry has rapidly embraced immersive technologies as a strategic tool to engage consumers and create memorable brand experiences. Traditional fashion shows and physical retail stores, while impactful, are often limited by location, scale, and accessibility. Recognizing these constraints, leading fashion brands have adopted Virtual Reality (VR) fashion shows and Metaverse storefronts, offering global audiences a unique opportunity to experience collections interactively and remotely.

One pioneering fashion house has successfully integrated VR and Metaverse platforms to connect with younger, tech-savvy consumers who value personalized, interactive, and shareable experiences. This approach reflects a shift in fashion marketing from passive consumption to active participation, where consumers are not merely observers but co-creators of their experiences. By combining immersive technologies with digital marketing strategies, the brand has positioned itself at the forefront of experiential retail, leveraging VR and Metaverse platforms to enhance engagement, emotional connection, and purchase behavior.

## Technologies and Applications:

- **VR Fashion Shows:** Consumers can attend virtual runway shows with front-row perspectives, experiencing garments in 3D with realistic textures, colors, and movement. These virtual shows often include interactive elements, such as zooming into details, exploring fabric textures, and viewing multiple angles. The experience mimics in-person fashion events while offering greater accessibility and personalization.
- **Metaverse Stores:** The brand has developed interactive Metaverse storefronts, allowing users to browse collections, customize products, and purchase both digital and physical items. These virtual stores integrate augmented features such as virtual fitting rooms, style recommendations, and AI-powered personalization, creating a seamless shopping journey that bridges the digital and physical worlds.
- **Gamification and Social Interaction:** The platform incorporates gamified elements, such as rewards for exploring collections or completing virtual challenges, and social interaction features, enabling users to connect with friends or share experiences on social media. Avatars allow attendees to navigate the store, attend events together, and engage with brand communities, increasing social presence and enjoyment.

## Consumer Experience and Outcomes:

The integration of VR and Metaverse technologies provides highly engaging and personalized experiences, resulting in several positive outcomes:

- **Emotional Connection and Exclusivity:** Personalized experiences, such as curated collections and virtual front-row access, foster a sense of exclusivity, enhancing emotional attachment to the brand.

- **Improved Product Evaluation:** Immersive visualization enables consumers to better understand garment fit, design details, and quality, reducing uncertainty and increasing confidence in purchase decisions.
- **Global Reach and Brand Awareness:** Virtual fashion events allow brands to reach **audiences across continents**, expanding visibility and engagement in previously untapped markets.
- **Memorable and Shareable Experiences:** Consumers actively participate in immersive events, creating memories and sharing content on social media, amplifying brand visibility and influence.

## Neuromarketing Insights:

Secondary research indicates that VR fashion shows and Metaverse stores stimulate attention, positive emotional responses, and desire, all of which influence consumer decision-making and loyalty (Saffari et al., 2023; Vecchiato et al., 2014). The immersive environments simulate real-world interactions with products, enhancing memory retention, perception of quality, and overall brand experience (Kapoor et al., 2021b). Gamified and interactive elements increase engagement duration and reinforce positive associations, providing deeper insights into consumer preferences and motivations without the limitations of traditional surveys.

## Key Takeaways:

This case demonstrates that immersive technologies enable fashion brands to:

- Create experiential, personalized, and emotionally engaging experiences.
- Increase purchase confidence and intention through realistic product interactions.
- Expand global audience reach and enhance brand visibility.
- Build stronger consumer-brand relationships through interactive and shareable experiences.

Overall, VR and Metaverse applications in fashion represent a paradigm shift in consumer engagement, blending technology, creativity, and marketing to deliver immersive experiences that drive both digital and physical sales while strengthening emotional bonds with consumers.

## 4.4 Cross-Case Summary

The three case studies—retail (AR and VR in e-commerce), entertainment (Metaverse virtual concerts), and fashion (VR fashion shows and Metaverse stores)—demonstrate how immersive technologies and neuromarketing principles are reshaping consumer experiences across industries. While each sector employs distinct strategies and technologies, several common patterns, opportunities, and challenges emerge, offering valuable insights for both researchers and practitioners.

### Technologies and Applications Across Sectors:

- **Immersive Platforms:** All three sectors utilize AR, VR, and Metaverse platforms to create engaging, interactive experiences that extend beyond traditional digital interfaces. Retail focuses on product visualization and virtual stores; entertainment emphasizes live, social, and gamified experiences; and fashion blends runway simulations with interactive shopping.
- **Personalization and AI Integration:** AI and data-driven algorithms play a central role in tailoring experiences to individual consumers. In retail and fashion, AI recommends products and customizes content, while entertainment platforms use AI to optimize user interaction and gamified engagement. Personalization enhances satisfaction, attention, and perceived value across all cases.
- **Interactivity and Social Engagement:** Each case leverages interactive elements to involve consumers actively. Avatars, real-time communication, and gamification enhance social presence, emotional engagement, and the overall sense of participation. This aligns with neuromarketing insights indicating that interactivity stimulates attention, emotional arousal, and memory retention, critical factors for influencing behavior (Poushneh and Vasquez-Parraga, 2017; Dwivedi et al., 2023).

### Consumer Experience and Outcomes:

- **Emotional Engagement:** Across sectors, immersive experiences consistently evoke positive emotions, ranging from excitement and enjoyment in concerts to confidence and attachment in retail and fashion. Emotional arousal drives deeper engagement, loyalty, and brand recall.
- **Behavioral Intentions:** In retail, immersive visualization increases purchase confidence and conversion rates. In fashion, VR shows and Metaverse stores improve evaluation and purchase intention. Entertainment platforms foster

repeat engagement and advocacy, demonstrating that immersive experiences directly influence both cognitive and behavioral outcomes.

- **Global Reach and Accessibility:** Metaverse and VR technologies remove geographical barriers, enabling brands to reach wider audiences. Entertainment and fashion sectors particularly benefit from this, with virtual concerts and fashion shows attracting global participation, while retail AR/VR tools allow consumers to experience products without visiting physical stores.

## Neuromarketing Insights:

- Across all cases, secondary research highlights that immersive technologies enhance attention, emotional arousal, and social presence, which are linked to higher engagement and positive brand perception (Kovacova et al., 2022; Saffari et al., 2023; Kaur and Sharma, 2024).
- The use of multi-sensory stimulation—visual, auditory, and interactive cues—reinforces memory encoding, improves information processing, and strengthens emotional connections with brands.
- Gamification and social interaction amplify the effects, as consumers perceive active participation and agency, which traditional media cannot replicate.

## Comparative Insights and Key Patterns:

1. **Sector-Specific Focus:** Retail emphasizes product evaluation and transactional outcomes; entertainment prioritizes engagement, loyalty, and social presence; fashion blends evaluation, brand perception, and aspirational experiences.
2. **Role of Personalization:** Personalization is central in driving attention, engagement, and satisfaction across sectors, illustrating the value of AI-driven recommendation systems integrated with immersive technologies.
3. **Emotional Resonance as a Driver:** Emotional engagement is consistently linked to positive consumer behavior, highlighting that immersive experiences are most effective when they create affective connections with users.
4. **Scalability and Reach:** Virtual environments provide brands the ability to scale experiences globally without the limitations of physical infrastructure, opening new revenue streams and audience segments.

Table 1 exhibits Cross-Case Comparison of Immersive Technologies in Consumer Engagement

*Table 1. Cross-Case Comparison of Immersive Technologies in Consumer Engagement*

| Sector | Primary Technology | Consumer Outcomes | Neuromarketing Insights | Key Advantage |
|---|---|---|---|---|
| Retail | AR & VR | Confidence, engagement, higher conversion | Increased attention & emotional arousal | Product evaluation and trial |
| Entertainment | Metaverse & VR | Loyalty, memorable experiences, global reach | Emotional engagement & social presence | Active participation & fandom |
| Fashion | VR & Metaverse Stores | Personalization, attachment, global reach | Positive emotions, desire, memory retention | Experiential engagement |

Figure 1 exhibits Conceptual Framework of Immersive Technologies Driving Consumer Engagement Across Sectors

*Figure 1. Conceptual Framework: Immersive Technologies Driving Consumer Engagement Across Sectors*

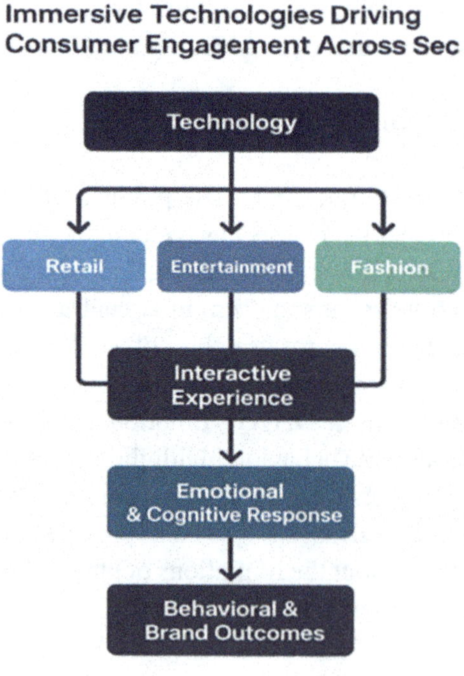

## Key Takeaways:

The cross-case analysis reveals that while industries differ in application focus, immersive technologies universally enhance engagement, emotional connection, and behavioral intention. Brands that integrate VR, AR, and Metaverse platforms effectively create interactive, personalized, and memorable experiences that strengthen consumer-brand relationships and provide measurable business outcomes. Moreover, these cases highlight the importance of considering neuromarketing insights, such as attention, emotional arousal, and social presence, when designing immersive consumer experiences.

## 5. DISCUSSION

The analysis of the three case studies retail, entertainment, and fashion—highlights the growing influence of immersive technologies in shaping consumer experiences. In the retail sector, AR try-ons and VR-enabled stores provide users with realistic product interactions, reducing purchase uncertainty and enhancing satisfaction. By engaging multiple senses and offering interactive exploration, these platforms stimulate attention and emotional arousal, leading to stronger engagement and higher likelihood of purchase. In the entertainment sector, virtual concerts and interactive events in the Metaverse demonstrate how gamified experiences can transform passive consumption into active participation. Consumers report heightened emotional involvement and a sense of social presence, indicating that immersive technologies can foster deeper engagement and memorable experiences. Similarly, in the fashion sector, VR fashion shows and Metaverse storefronts enable consumers to explore collections virtually, co-create outfits, and participate in brand storytelling, reflecting the importance of interactivity and personalization in contemporary marketing strategies.

A cross-case comparison identifies several recurring patterns. First, immersive experiences consistently enhance consumer engagement through multi-sensory interaction, combining visual, auditory, and sometimes tactile stimuli. This intensifies emotional responses and improves brand recall. Second, personalization emerges as a central factor, as AI-driven platforms adapt experiences based on user behavior, preferences, and interaction patterns. Tailored experiences are more likely to capture attention, increase satisfaction, and promote repeat engagement. Third, the use of measurement tools, such as eye-tracking and physiological responses, provides valuable insights into consumer attention and emotional reactions, allowing brands to optimize experiences iteratively.

However, the discussion also underscores several challenges. Ethical considerations, particularly regarding data privacy and user consent, remain critical when collecting and analyzing behavioral and physiological data. Organizations must ensure transparency and responsible use of insights to maintain trust. Technological limitations, such as device compatibility, latency issues, or accessibility constraints, can affect the smoothness and realism of the immersive experience. Additionally, consumer engagement varies across demographic and cultural segments, emphasizing the need for context-specific design approaches that resonate with diverse audiences.

Overall, the case studies collectively illustrate that immersive technologies—when combined with interactivity, personalization, and behavioral measurement—can significantly elevate consumer experiences. They enhance engagement, emotional involvement, and participation across sectors, while also presenting challenges that organizations must navigate to ensure effectiveness, inclusivity, and ethical integrity.

## 6. THEORETICAL CONTRIBUTION

This study contributes to the emerging literature on immersive technologies and consumer engagement by integrating evidence from multiple sectors—retail, entertainment, and fashion. Unlike previous research that often focuses on a single industry, the cross-sectoral approach demonstrates how immersive experiences universally enhance consumer engagement through interactivity, personalization, and multi-sensory stimulation. The findings extend theoretical understanding of user experience by highlighting the interplay between emotional arousal, attention, and participatory behavior in virtual environments. Additionally, the study emphasizes the role of behavioral and physiological metrics, such as eye-tracking and engagement analytics, in capturing nuanced consumer responses, providing a more granular understanding of how digital experiences translate into brand perception and recall. By situating immersive technologies within a comparative framework, the research offers a conceptual lens that links technological affordances, user engagement, and experiential outcomes, thereby bridging gaps in existing theory and setting a foundation for future empirical exploration in both emerging and established markets.

## 7. PRACTICAL IMPLICATIONS

The findings of this study provide actionable insights for practitioners across retail, entertainment, and fashion sectors who aim to leverage immersive technologies to enhance consumer experiences and strengthen brand engagement. First and foremost, the research highlights the importance of designing multi-sensory and interactive experiences that go beyond conventional digital engagement. Retailers and fashion brands can implement Virtual Reality (VR) showrooms or Metaverse stores, allowing customers to explore products virtually, interact with digital mannequins, and personalize items before purchase. Similarly, entertainment companies can create VR concerts or interactive storytelling experiences, where audience participation directly affects the narrative. Such immersive approaches help capture attention, stimulate emotions, and foster deeper connections with the brand, ultimately translating into higher engagement and loyalty.

Personalization emerges as a critical element for successful implementation. AI-driven customization, informed by consumer data such as browsing history, purchase behavior, and interaction patterns, enables brands to deliver individualized experiences. For instance, fashion brands can recommend outfits based on previous selections and style preferences within virtual stores, while entertainment platforms can tailor VR content based on audience engagement metrics. Personalization not only increases satisfaction but also enhances the perception of relevance and value, motivating repeated interaction and long-term loyalty.

Quantitative measurement of engagement is another key practical implication. Brands and experience designers can benefit from integrating behavioral and physiological metrics—such as time spent in virtual environments, frequency of interactions, eye-tracking data, and biometric responses—to assess how users respond to different immersive features. These data-driven insights can guide iterative improvements in experience design, ensuring smoother navigation, higher realism, and more effective engagement. Organizations can use these metrics to identify which elements of an experience are most appealing, which are underperforming, and how different user segments respond differently to the same stimuli.

Ethical considerations and privacy management are critical in the practical deployment of immersive technologies. The collection of detailed behavioral and biometric data necessitates transparent policies, explicit consent, and compliance with local and international regulations. Brands that prioritize ethical practices in data usage not only comply with legal standards but also strengthen consumer trust—a key factor for sustained engagement in virtual environments. Failure to manage these concerns can undermine brand reputation and limit adoption of immersive platforms.

Context-specific adaptation is equally important. Engagement behaviors vary based on demographics, cultural backgrounds, and technological familiarity. Brands should adopt flexible strategies that account for these variations while maintaining core engagement principles. For example, younger, tech-savvy users may prefer gamified experiences with social interactivity, whereas older demographics may value simplified interfaces with clear guidance. Understanding these nuances enables brands to design experiences that resonate with diverse audience segments while maximizing overall engagement.

Finally, the study provides guidance for strategic investment in immersive technologies. Although implementing VR, AR, or Metaverse solutions requires significant upfront investment, the potential benefits in terms of brand recall, emotional connection, and customer participation justify the expenditure. Businesses should prioritize initiatives that maximize interactivity, personalization, and data-driven optimization, while carefully mitigating risks related to accessibility, technical limitations, and user privacy. By strategically aligning immersive technology deployment with consumer behavior insights, brands can gain a competitive edge, strengthen loyalty, and foster innovative ways of interacting with customers in a rapidly digitizing marketplace.

In conclusion, the practical implications underscore that immersive experiences are not merely technological novelties but strategic tools that, when designed thoughtfully, can enhance brand engagement, optimize consumer satisfaction, and deliver measurable business outcomes across multiple sectors.

## 8. CONCLUSION

This chapter examined the role of immersive technologies—such as Virtual Reality (VR), Augmented Reality (AR), and Metaverse platforms—in shaping consumer engagement, with a focus on applications in retail, fashion, and entertainment sectors. Through multiple case studies, it was evident that immersive experiences provide a powerful means for brands to connect with audiences, bridge the digital-physical divide, and foster deeper emotional engagement. The analysis highlighted that interactivity, personalization, and seamless integration of digital and real-world touchpoints are central to enhancing user experience and driving meaningful engagement outcomes.

The study also demonstrated that immersive technologies are not merely tools for novelty but serve as strategic enablers of consumer-centric marketing. By enabling consumers to interact with products, explore virtual environments, and receive tailored recommendations, these technologies elevate brand perception and increase customer loyalty. Furthermore, the research underscored the importance of collecting and leveraging user behavioral data to iteratively refine immersive experiences, ensuring relevance, engagement, and satisfaction.

Another key insight is the need for ethical deployment, particularly in handling personal data and maintaining transparency in virtual interactions. Brands that prioritize ethical considerations not only ensure regulatory compliance but also strengthen consumer trust—a crucial determinant of long-term adoption and engagement in immersive platforms. Additionally, contextual adaptation to demographic, cultural, and technological familiarity differences emerged as a critical factor for maximizing the effectiveness of immersive strategies across diverse consumer segments.

In essence, immersive technologies represent a paradigm shift in consumer engagement strategies, offering opportunities for brands to innovate, differentiate, and create meaningful interactions. As these technologies continue to evolve, businesses that strategically integrate immersive experiences with personalization, interactivity, and ethical practices are likely to achieve sustained competitive advantage, deeper customer relationships, and measurable improvements in engagement metrics. The findings of this chapter provide a foundation for both scholars and practitioners to understand the strategic potential of immersive experiences and to design future research and applications that further explore their impact on consumer behavior and brand performance.

## 9. LIMITATIONS AND SCOPE FOR FUTURE RESEARCH

While this chapter provides valuable insights into the use of immersive technologies for enhancing consumer engagement, several limitations must be acknowledged. First, the study primarily relied on selected case studies from retail, fashion, and entertainment sectors, which may limit the generalizability of the findings across other industries or geographical contexts. Second, the focus was on prominent global brands, which may not reflect the challenges and opportunities faced by smaller or emerging businesses with limited technological resources. Third, the analysis concentrated on technological and experiential aspects, with limited consideration of underlying psychological, cultural, and socio-economic factors that may influence consumer responses to immersive experiences.

Future research can address these limitations by adopting broader, cross-industry, and cross-cultural perspectives, incorporating diverse market contexts and consumer demographics. Quantitative studies examining the measurable impact of immersive experiences on purchase behavior, brand loyalty, and customer lifetime value would strengthen the empirical evidence base. Additionally, longitudinal studies could explore the long-term effects of VR, AR, and Metaverse engagement on consumer attitudes and brand equity. Finally, exploring ethical, privacy, and accessibility considerations in immersive experiences would provide critical insights for responsible and inclusive technology deployment, enabling both scholars and practitioners to develop strategies that are effective, sustainable, and socially responsible.

## REFERENCES


Ambika, A., Shin, H., & Jain, V. (2025). Immersive technologies and consumer behavior: A systematic review of two decades of research. *Australian Journal of Management*, *50*(1), 55–79. DOI: 10.1177/03128962231181429

Bajpai, A., & Islam, T. (2022). Impact of augmented reality marketing on customer engagement, behavior, loyalty, and buying decisions. *Cardiometry*, (23), 545–553.

Barrera, K. G., & Shah, D. (2023). Marketing in the Metaverse: Conceptual understanding, framework, and research agenda. *Journal of Business Research*, *155*, 113420. DOI: 10.1016/j.jbusres.2022.113420

Buhalis, D., Lin, M. S., & Leung, D. (2023). Metaverse as a driver for customer experience and value co-creation: Implications for hospitality and tourism management and marketing. *International Journal of Contemporary Hospitality Management*, *35*(2), 701–716. DOI: 10.1108/IJCHM-05-2022-0631

Dwivedi, Y. K., Hughes, L., Wang, Y., Alalwan, A. A., Ahn, S. J., Balakrishnan, J., Barta, S., Belk, R., Buhalis, D., Dutot, V., Felix, R., Filieri, R., Flavián, C., Gustafsson, A., Hinsch, C., Hollensen, S., Jain, V., Kim, J., Krishen, A. S., & Wirtz, J. (2023). Metaverse marketing: How the metaverse will shape the future of consumer research and practice. *Psychology and Marketing*, *40*(4), 750–776. DOI: 10.1002/mar.21767

Erensoy, A., Mathrani, A., Schnack, A., Elms, J., & Baghaei, N. (2024). Consumer behavior in immersive virtual reality retail environments: A systematic literature review using the stimuli-organisms-responses (S-O-r) model. *Journal of Consumer Behaviour*, *23*(6), 2781–2811. DOI: 10.1002/cb.2374

Gupta, R., Kapoor, A., & Verma, H. (2025). Neuro-insights: A systematic review of neuromarketing perspectives across consumer buying stages. *Frontiers in Neuroergonomics*, *6*, 1542847. DOI: 10.3389/fnrgo.2025.1542847 PMID: 40735149

Kapoor, A., & Sindwani, R. (2025). Artificial Intelligence as a Catalyst for Advancing Contactless Payments: Unveiling Key Adoption Drivers. In *AI Marketing and Ethical Considerations in Consumer Engagement* (pp. 321–338). IGI Global Scientific Publishing. DOI: 10.4018/979-8-3373-3476-9.ch016

Kapoor, A., Sindwani, R., & Goel, M. (2021a). Prioritising the key factors influencing the adoption of mobile wallets: An Indian perspective in covid-19 era. *Journal of Information Technology Management*, *13*(4), 161–182.

Kapoor, A., Sindwani, R., & Goel, M. (2021b). Ranking mobile wallet service providers using fuzzy multi-criteria decision-making approach. [IJEBR]. *International Journal of E-Business Research, 17*(4), 1–21. DOI: 10.4018/IJEBR.2021100102

Kapoor, A., Sindwani, R., & Goel, M. (2023a). Evaluating mobile wallet acceptance factors using best worst method. *International Journal of Process Management and Benchmarking, 13*(4), 449–469. DOI: 10.1504/IJPMB.2023.129822

Kapoor, A., Sindwani, R., & Goel, M. (2023b). Exploring quick commerce service experience: A moderated mediated investigation using SEM and fsQCA. *Total Quality Management & Business Excellence, 34*(13-14), 1896–1919. DOI: 10.1080/14783363.2023.2213653

Kapoor, A., Sindwani, R., & Goel, M. (2024). Exploring the symmetric and asymmetric effects of mobile wallet service experience on brand loyalty in India: Evidence from SEM and fsQCA. *Journal of Financial Services Marketing, 29*(4), 1524–1541. DOI: 10.1057/s41264-024-00280-w

Kapoor, A., Sindwani, R., & Goel, M. (2025a). A novel framework for understanding the interplay between the mobile wallet service quality dimensions and loyalty intention. *The TQM Journal, 37*(6), 1716–1741. DOI: 10.1108/TQM-12-2023-0422

Kapoor, A., Sindwani, R., & Goel, M. (2025b). Assessing mobile wallet service quality using analytic hierarchy process and fuzzy evaluation method. *International Journal of Services and Operations Management, 50*(2), 246–266. DOI: 10.1504/IJSOM.2025.144481

Kapoor, A., Sindwani, R., & Goel, M. (2025c). Unlocking India's mobile wallet potential: Identifying and prioritising key sustainable growth catalysts using best worst method. *International Journal of Process Management and Benchmarking, 21*(2), 218–230. DOI: 10.1504/IJPMB.2025.148685

Kapoor, A., Sindwani, R., Goel, M., & Shankar, A. (2022). Mobile wallet adoption intention amid COVID-19 pandemic outbreak: A novel conceptual framework. *Computers & Industrial Engineering, 172*, 108646. DOI: 10.1016/j.cie.2022.108646 PMID: 36118531

Kaur, J., Mogaji, E., Paliwal, M., Jha, S., Agarwal, S., & Mogaji, S. A. (2024). Consumer behavior in the metaverse. *Journal of Consumer Behaviour, 23*(4), 1720–1738. DOI: 10.1002/cb.2298

Kaur, K., & Sharma, T. (2024). Impulse buying in the digital age: An exploration using systematic literature review approach. *Journal of Consumer Behaviour, 23*(5), 2553–2584. DOI: 10.1002/cb.2360

Kovacova, M., Machova, V., & Bennett, D. (2022). Immersive extended reality technologies, data visualization tools, and customer behavior analytics in the metaverse commerce. *Journal of Self-Governance and Management Economics, 10*(2), 7–21.

Poushneh, A., & Vasquez-Parraga, A. Z. (2017). Discernible impact of augmented reality on retail customer's experience, satisfaction and willingness to buy. *Journal of Retailing and Consumer Services, 34*, 229–234. DOI: 10.1016/j.jretconser.2016.10.005

Rane, N., Choudhary, S., & Rane, J. (2023). Metaverse for enhancing customer loyalty: effective strategies to improve customer relationship, service, engagement, satisfaction, and experience. *Service, Engagement, Satisfaction, and Experience (November 1, 2023).*

Russo, V., Bilucaglia, M., & Zito, M. (2022). From virtual reality to augmented reality: A neuromarketing perspective. *Frontiers in Psychology, 13*, 965499. DOI: 10.3389/fpsyg.2022.965499 PMID: 36160557

Saffari, F., Kakaria, S., Bigné, E., Bruni, L. E., Zarei, S., & Ramsøy, T. Z. (2023). Motivation in the metaverse: A dual-process approach to consumer choices in a virtual reality supermarket. *Frontiers in Neuroscience, 17*, 1062980. DOI: 10.3389/fnins.2023.1062980 PMID: 36875641

Vecchiato, G., Maglione, A. G., Cherubino, P., Wasikowska, B., Wawrzyniak, A., Latuszynska, A., Latuszynska, M., Nermend, K., Graziani, I., Leucci, M. R., Trettel, A., & Babiloni, F. (2014). Neurophysiological tools to investigate consumer's gender differences during the observation of TV commercials. *Computational and Mathematical Methods in Medicine, 2014*(1), 912981. DOI: 10.1155/2014/912981 PMID: 25147579

Yin, R. K. (2017). *Case study research and applications: Design and methods*. No Title.

# Chapter 11
# The Impact of AI-Driven Personalization on Consumer Engagement and Loyalty

**Shuvasree Banerjee**
http://orcid.org/0000-0001-5255-2489
*Amity University, Mumbai, India*

**Mohammad Badruddoza Talukder**
http://orcid.org/0009-0008-1662-9221
*International University of Business Agriculture and Technology, Bangladesh*

**Tathagata Banerjee**
http://orcid.org/0009-0002-9586-9907
*International Institute of Hotel Management, Pune, India*

**Shivansu Sachan**
http://orcid.org/0000-0002-9893-8018
*CSJM University, Kanpur, India*

## ABSTRACT

*The rise of AI has reshaped the way companies converse with potential customers. AI-driven personalization has become a key strategy for companies seeking to improve customer engagement and loyalty. This study is, therefore, dedicated to analyzing the consequences of AI-driven personalization on customer engagement and loyalty. Particularly, this study investigates mechanisms that contribute to changes in consumer behavior as a result of personalized experiences. Therefore, this study employs an integrated mixed-methods methodology that leverages both*

DOI: 10.4018/979-8-3373-5997-7.ch011

*qualitative insights with professionals from the industry as well as quantitative analysis with data that has been collected from consumers. The study also reveals that AI-powered personalization is boosting customer engagement and loyalty to a great extent by offering customers experiences that are personalized to their tastes and preferences. The sense of pertinence and value developed due to provision of tailored ideas, information, and offers is therefore boosting consumer customer satisfaction and loyalty.*

## 1. INTRODUCTION

Artificial Intelligence (AI) has radically restructured the modern-day marketing by reshaping personalization as a demographic segmentation instrument into a real-time predictive feature integrated into the digital ecosystems. Previously, marketing paradigms were based on mass communication and mass segmentation, whereas the development of machine learning, big data analysis, and natural language processing has allowed companies to offer products to individuals (Davenport et al., 2020; Wedel and Kannan, 2016). Personalization driven by AI can now enable organizations to process both structured and unstructured data such as browsing history, purchase history, clickstream behavior and sentiment expression, and contextual signals to provide adaptive content, product recommendation and dynamic pricing structure.

### 1.1 The Emergence of AI and the Changing Customer Conversations

The emergence of Artificial Intelligence (AI) has essentially changed how firms communicate with their prospective clients. The relationships between companies and customers in modern digital markets are becoming more and more mediated by intelligent systems that can handle a large volume of behavioral and contextual information in real-time. Predictive analytics, machine learning algorithms and natural language processing systems enable organizations to understand the preferences of consumers, predict needs and react immediately with personalized communication (Davenport et al., 2020; Huang and Rust, 2021).

This change has re-invented customer dialogs. Rather than having a unidirectional promotional communication, businesses are now involved in a two-way interactive and personal communication that mirrors individual tastes, preferences, and behavioral backgrounds. Using AI, chatbots, recommendation engines, and automated marketing systems generate a flow of conversation at the digital touchpoints, such as websites, mobile applications, and social media platforms. This makes customer interactions generic and highly contextualized and experience based. The fact that

AI can learn and improve future responses after interacting with people in the past has brought the personalization to the level of a supporting marketing strategy, not a primary one.

## 1.2 AI-Based Personalization as an Engagement and Loyalty Strategic Tool

Personalization through AI has emerged as one of the major strategies that companies aiming to enhance their customer engagement and loyalty have adopted. In more and more competitive and saturated markets, companies have to distinguish themselves not only by the products they offer, but also by the quality and the relevance of experiences that the customers gain. AI-driven personalization helps companies to offer content, suggestions, and recommendations that resonate well with the interests of an individual consumer. Predictive modeling and behavioral analytics allow organizations to personalize product recommendations, customize their communication patterns, and optimize timing to increase the effectiveness of interaction (Wedel and Kannan, 2016).

The strategic value of AI-based personalization is that it will establish a feeling of relevance and value among the consumers. Customers feel that a company knows what they want and will act in such a way thus the level of engagement is high. This activity can be behavioral in terms of increasing the frequency of interaction, increasing the duration of use of the platform, and responsiveness to promotional messages. It also comes out psychologically in terms of increased perceived usefulness and emotional attachment, which are in line with technology acceptance and relationship marketing views (Davis, 1989; Morgan and Hunt, 1994).

Nonetheless, as the use of AI personalization by firms becomes a common practice, the academic knowledge regarding its effects and mechanisms of engagement and loyalty needs to be analyzed more thoroughly. The assumption that technological sophistication is a sufficient cause of relational benefits is not enough. Rather, a research into the processes by which customized experiences influence consumer behavior and build long-term brand relationships is necessary.

## 1.3 Mechanisms of the Relationship between Personalized Experiences and Consumer Behavior

This paper is hence committed to examining the implications of AI-based personalization on customer engagement and loyalty. Specifically, it explores the processes that play a role in altering consumer behavior due to personalized experiences. Personalization is a stimulus in the digital space, that affects consumer information processing, value assessment, and relational judgment. Consumers have lower cognitive load and higher confidence in their decision when customized concepts, information and offers are provided in accordance with their tastes and preferences. This decreases information overload, which increases satisfaction and creates a good attitude towards the brand.

Personal experiences add value to the experiences because they involve the customers on a cognitive and emotional level, as proposed by Pine and Gilmore (1999). Furthermore, predictive analytics is proactive, forecasting the future, which builds proactive interactions that strengthen trust and perceived competence (Huang and Rust, 2021).

However, the effectiveness of personalization is moderated by the consumer's view of transparency and fairness. In case AI systems seem intrusive or opaque, engagement can decrease even though there is a high level of technical accuracy (Martin and Murphy, 2017). Hence, to comprehend behavior change, technological capability should be considered in addition to the psychological reactions, such as perceived value, trust, and emotional resonance.

## 1.4 Methodological Orientation and Analytical Approach.

This paper with the purpose of studying these dynamics in a comprehensive way will utilize an integrated mixed-method approach that will take advantage of both the qualitative data obtained through interviews with industry professionals and the quantitative one obtained through the analysis of data gathered among consumers. The mixed-methods orientation enables the triangulation of the strategic outlooks with consumer experiences. The qualitative data of industry experts can offer the contextual knowledge about the design, implementation, and assessment of AI personalization in the organizational context. These lessons shed light on managerial intent, strategic goals and real issues that come up in efforts to personalize.

At the same time, the use of quantitative data gathered on the consumer level allows conducting empirical analysis of the results of engagement and loyalty. Statistically, the relationship between perceived personalization, satisfaction, engagement behaviors, and loyalty intentions can be tested. The combination of qualitative and quantitative results makes the research more theoretical as it correlates managerial behaviors with consumer attitudes. This will fill a gap in the current literature, which tends to analyze AI personalization either through a technological perspective or through independent consumer surveys without integrating the two.

### 1.5 Individualized Experiences, Satisfaction, and Loyalty Results

The results indicate that the use of AI-based personalization is significantly increasing customer engagement and loyalty because it provides customers with a personalized experience that meets their tastes and preferences. Whenever the consumers are exposed to personalized suggestions and context-based offers, they gain a better sense of relevance and worth. This perceived value has a direct contribution to increased customer satisfaction. Satisfaction, in its turn, strengthens the intentions of loyalty and promotes the repetition of the interaction, continuation of the subscription and positive word-of-mouth behavior (Morgan and Hunt, 1994).

The feeling of relevance and worthiness that arise as a result of offering personalized ideas, information, and offers, thus, increases the customer satisfaction and loyalty. The relational bonds are enhanced with the help of AI personalization, which proves to be attentive and responsive, which are traditionally human aspects of interaction. AI systems constantly optimize their personalisation strategies, keeping the user active in the long term through the adaptive learning mechanisms. Nevertheless, ethical standards, transparency, and respect to consumer autonomy are the keys to sustainable loyalty.

With the emergence of AI, the corporate-customer dialogue has been transformed, and AI-based personalization has become a strategic instrument to increase engagement and loyalty. This study offers a combined insight into the effects of personalized experiences on satisfaction and long-term relational outcomes by exploring the behavioral mechanisms and using mixed-methods. With the further development of AI technologies, organizations have to find a balance between technological innovation and ethical responsibility in order to make sure that personalization will be the source of value instead of the cause of consumer resistance.

## 2. THEORETICAL FOUNDATIONS OF AI-DRIVEN PERSONALIZATION CONCEPTUAL SYNTHESIS.

### 2.1 Segmentation to Intelligent Personalization: Theory of Marketing Foundations.

The development of AI-based personalization should be placed initially in the context of the overall direction of marketing thought. Segmentation, targeting, and positioning were the key strategic pillars of classical marketing theory that focused on value creation (Kotler and Keller, 2016). Although segmentation allowed the firms to distinguish between consumer groups, it was mainly done on an aggregate level. The spread of digital technologies and data-intensive spaces has changed this paradigm to an individualized interaction, where AI allows companies to react to micro-level consumer cues in real-time (Wedel and Kannan, 2016). According to Davenport et al. (2020), AI has transformed marketing into a stagnant campaign planning system to dynamic decision-making systems that can constantly optimize.

This conceptual change is consistent with the Experience Economy model, which argues that a competitive edge is becoming more and more reliant on the provision of personalized, memorable experiences as opposed to commodity-like products (Pine and Gilmore, 1999). AI adds value in the experience since it dynamically customizes the experience according to the preferences and contextual behavior of consumers. Moreover, the co-creation theory implies that consumers are more involved in the process of value experience creation by interacting and providing feedback (Prahalad and Ramaswamy, 2004). The AI personalization makes this principle operational because it continuously learns from the inputs of consumers and modifies the offerings. Therefore, intelligent personalization is not only a technological improvement, but a hypothetical continuation of the experiential and relationship marketing paradigm.

## 2.2 Technological Foundations: NLP, Predictive Systems, and Machine Learning.

Machine learning and algorithmic modeling are the conceptual foundations of AI-based personalization. The machine learning theory describes the way systems can gain predictive power through repetitive training of data, and thus, identify patterns that are not specified in the programs (Shalev-Shwartz and Ben-David, 2014). These algorithms are used in marketing to process behavioral data, transactional histories and online footprints to make suggestions and predict preferences.

Personalization is also enhanced further through natural language processing as it allows AI systems to understand the conversational cues and emotional sentiment (Cambria and White, 2014). This is what conversational agents, chatbots, and automated customer service platforms, which mimic a human-like interaction, are based on. Ganeshkumar et al. (2024) note that AI-based marketing insights as a result of machine learning models greatly improve the accuracy of personalization, which results in more appropriate communication strategies. Equally, Gowri (2024) emphasizes the effectiveness of personalized digital content in enhancing user-responsiveness through matching the marketing messages with personal preferences.

Huang and Rust (2021) understand AI in service settings as an augmentation process that improves efficiency and scalability and reconfigures the structures of customer-firm interaction. Predictive analytics allows companies to predict churn, offer optimization, and respond to customer needs in advance. These technological processes serve as stimuli that define cognitive appraisal and behavioral reactions and hence connect technical infrastructure to relational consequences.

## 2.3 Technology Acceptance and Behavioral Theory Consumer Engagement.

The analysis of consumer interaction with AI-based personalization should be combined with technology acceptance and behavioral theories. The Technology Acceptance Model (Davis, 1989) is an assumption that the perception of usefulness and the perception of ease of use are the determinants of user adoption of technological systems. The concept of usefulness in AI personalization is manifested in relevance, time-saving and convenience, whereas ease of use is associated with user-friendly interfaces and a smooth interface. Venkatesh et al. (2003) build on this view by adding social influence and facilitating conditions and emphasize that contextual and normative factors influence technology acceptance as well.

The connection between AI personalization and engagement can be supported by empirical research. Alghaswyneh (2025) shows that personalization, based on AI, can greatly increase the interactive online experience by making it appear more relevant and valuable. Similar results are also available in Sherly Steffi et al. (2024), who determine that customized recommendations decrease the overload of information and enhance user engagement in the online marketing context. According to Mathur et al. (2025), engagement during the personalization era is a tactical interaction between data intelligence and experiential design, and the author claims that AI systems enhance more profound cognitive and emotional engagement.

Teepapal (2025) also highlights that consumer beliefs about their control over personalization settings also determine the outcomes of engagement, which implies that autonomy mediates the efficacy of AI interventions. All these findings suggest that engagement is not only due to the accuracy of the algorithm but also due to apparent transparency, utility, and compliance with the expectations of users.

## 2.4 Loyalty Formation: Relational Outcomes and Commitment-Trust Theory

The theoretical foundation of the conceptual connection between AI personalization and loyalty is based on the relationship marketing theory. The Commitment-Trust Theory developed by Morgan and Hunt (1994) holds that trust and commitment are the key mediators of long-term relational exchange. Individualized experiences are an indication of attentiveness and competence, thus building trust and emotional attachment. The empirical evidence provided by Ahmed et al. (2025) is that AI-based personalization has a positive effect on engagement and brand loyalty because it increases satisfaction. Similar arguments are made by Latif (2025), who believes that AI-based branding strategies enhance emotional loyalty as they strengthen the perceived recognition.

Jung (2025) shows that AI personalization is effective in the retail setting and enhances loyalty by providing smooth digital and physical touchpoints. Zed et al. (2024) note that individualized e-commerce approaches enhance customer repeat purchase intention and long-term customer retention. Puneet (2023) and Patil (2024) demonstrate that in telecom and service industries, AI-based customer support can be used to improve customer satisfaction and loyalty by providing efficient and context-sensitive customer support. Vij et al. (2024) extrapolate this research to tourism marketing where customized travel information boosts brand involvement and revisit intention.

Nevertheless, loyalty is not formed without conditions. Jayapal (2025) discovers that the relationship between personalization and loyalty is moderated by privacy, which implies that the effect of perceived data intrusion can undermine positive results. According to Skillius and Jacobsson (2024), the use of algorithms in advertising as the source of loyalty is only possible when it is perceived as being fair and non-manipulative. Therefore, personalization improves relational relationships, but ethical perceptions determine the sustainability of such relationships.

## 2.5 Ethical Governance, Privacy, and Moderating Conditions

With the growth of AI-based personalization, the ethical aspect of the theory synthesis takes center stage. Martin and Murphy (2017) emphasize the importance of data privacy in the development of consumer trust, which brings the conflict between the benefits of personalization and privacy risks. Floridi et al. (2018) suggest ethical AI principles based on transparency, fairness, and accountability, and suggest that technological progress should be consistent with the values of society.

Moqaddem (2025) emphasizes that smart marketing plans must have an integrated ethical governance to maintain interest. Okeke et al. (2024) create a personalization framework based on AI and governance towards SMEs, proving that the structured governance contributes to better retention rates and reduces risk. These views highlight the fact that privacy perceptions, ethical protection and accountability of organizations moderate the effectiveness of personalization.

All the literature indicates that AI-based personalization exists in a relational-technological nexus. Whereas machine learning and predictive analytics make the experience more relevant and satisfying, the perceptions of fairness and control are what make consumers stay engaged and loyal. Thus, technological capability, psychological response, and ethical governance have to be incorporated in conceptual synthesis.

## 2.6 Integrative Perspective

The combination of these theoretical streams shows that the AI-based personalization is a multi-layered construct. On the lowest level, machine learning and NLP technologies make it possible to predict and adapt to communication. On the cognitive level, acceptance and engagement are dependent on perceived usefulness and ease of use. Trust and commitment are the mediating variables in the formation of loyalty at the relational level. The relational sustainability is mediated by privacy and fairness perceptions at the ethical level. The available literature shows that the beneficial effect of AI personalization on engagement and loyalty in the retail, telecom, tourism, and e-commerce industries is highly empirically supported. The efficiency of these systems, however relies on transparency, governance and contextual sensitivity. Combining the marketing theory, technological acceptance, the relational exchange theory, and the principles of ethical AI, one gets a complete picture: AI-based personalization will increase engagement and loyalty when the technological sophistication is moderate and the ethical responsibility and consumer trust.

# 3. DEVELOPMENT OF CONCEPTUAL MODEL

## 3.1 Theoretical Logic behind the Model

Based on the marketing theory, technology acceptance theory, relationship marketing, and ethical AI governance frameworks, this paper suggests a multi-layered conceptual framework that explains the effect of AI-based personalization on customer engagement and loyalty. The model incorporates the technological mechanisms, cognitive and emotional consumer responses, relational mediators and the contextual moderators in a single explanatory framework.

The model, in its core, theorizes AI-based personalization as a strategic technological strength that is made up of machine learning systems, predictive analytics, and natural language processing tools (Shalev-Shwartz and Ben-David, 2014; Cambria and White, 2014). The technologies help companies to process consumer data and make customized recommendations, personalized content, and adaptive interactions (Davenport et al., 2020; Huang and Rust, 2021). Nevertheless, technology cannot be used to produce relational outcomes. Rather, its power works via the perceptions and mental assessments of consumers.

In this connection, the model places perceived personalization quality as the immediate cognitive output of AI mechanisms. When the AI systems provide useful, timely, and contextually appropriate content, consumers form perceptions of usefulness and ease of interaction, which are in line with the Technology Acceptance Model (Davis, 1989; Venkatesh et al., 2003). These are the perceptions that constitute the first mediating layer.

### 3.2 AI-Personalization as the major Stimulus

In the suggested model, the main independent construct is the AI-based personalization. It includes algorithmic recommendations, AI-based conversational interfaces, predictive targeting, and real-time adaptive communication. Existing studies show that these systems can improve the accuracy of marketing communication and minimize the information overload (Wedel and Kannan, 2016; Ganeshkumar and others, 2024). There is also empirical support that customized content enhances consumer engagement and web responsiveness (Gowri, 2024; Sherly Steffi et al., 2024).

The AI personalization within the Stimulus-Organism-Response logic functions as a technological stimulus, which triggers cognitive and emotional assessments. It, however, is dependent on how well personalization meets the expectations and preferences of the consumer. Thus, the model is a conceptualization of personalization, which is not only technological presence but also perceived relevance and contextual accuracy.

### 3.3 Cognitive and Emotional Intermediaries: Perceived Value and Satisfaction.

The second level of the conceptual model presents cognitive and affective mediators, which describe how personalization is converted to engagement. Consumers develop the feeling of relevance and importance when they feel that the personalized ideas, information and offers are relevant to their tastes and preferences. Such perceived value increases the level of satisfaction by decreasing the complexity of decisions and boosting trust in the brand interaction (Alghaswyneh, 2025; Ahmed et al., 2025).

This relationship is supported by the Experience Economy approach in which customized experiences enhance the level of emotional involvement and satisfaction with the experience (Pine and Gilmore, 1999). The co-creation theory also clarifies that adaptive personalization strengthens the feeling that the company perceives and reacts to consumer feedback (Prahalad and Ramaswamy, 2004). In turn, the perceived value and customer satisfaction are seen as key mediators between AI-based personalization and behavioral performance.

### 3.4 Customer Engagement as a Behavioral and Psychological Outcome.

The model places customer engagement as a mediating variable that is affected by the perceived quality of personalization and satisfaction. Engagement is considered both in terms of behavioral aspects (frequency and content responsiveness of interaction) and psychological aspects (emotional attachment and cognitive attention) (Mathur et al., 2025).

Studies show that personalization based on AI contributes greatly to engagement metrics (relevance and interactivity) (Alghaswyneh, 2025; Teepapal, 2025). Whenever consumers feel that AI systems are helpful and easy to use, the engagement will be enhanced as the technology acceptance theory dictates (Davis, 1989). Engagement, therefore, is the dynamic interaction stage in which short-term behavioral reactions are refined into the long term relational relationships.

### 3.5 Relational Mediators: Trust and Commitment.

Other than engagement, the conceptual model includes trust and commitment as relational mediators resulting in loyalty outcomes. According to the theory of commitment-Trust, trust is a necessary element in long-term relationships (Morgan and Hunt, 1994). Individualized communication is an indicator of competence, responsiveness, and attentiveness, which enhances trust perceptions.

Nevertheless, the establishment of trust depends on ethical governance. As Martin and Murphy (2017) point out, trust can be undermined when data privacy issues are highlighted as obtrusive when personalization is considered intrusive. According to Floridi et al. (2018), ethical AI systems require transparency and fairness. Thus, trust is a relationship intermediary between engagement and loyalty, and it is also ethically perceptive.

### 3.6 Customer Loyalty as the Final Result.

The main dependent construct of the model is customer loyalty. Loyalty is conceptualized both as behavioral (repeat purchase, retention, subscription continuity) and attitudinal (commitment, advocacy, emotional attachment) loyalty. Empirical research shows that AI-based personalization has a positive impact on loyalty in the presence of satisfaction and trust (Ahmed et al., 2025; Latif, 2025; Jung, 2025).

This relationship is strengthened by sectoral studies. Personalized recommendations enhance the intention to repurchase in the context of e-commerce (Zed et al., 2024). Customer support, which is enhanced with the help of AI, enhances retention in the telecom and service industries (Puneet, 2023; Patil, 2024). AI-based customer insights create loyalty to the destination in tourism marketing (Vij et al., 2024). In such a way, loyalty is the relational result of the technologically mediated, psychologically mediated engagement processes.

### 3.7 Intermediating Position of Privacy Concerns and Ethical Perceptions.

The model also incorporates the issue of privacy and ethical perceptions as moderating variables. Jayapal (2025) shows how the privacy issues undermine the positive correlation between personalization and loyalty. On the same note, Skillius and Jacobsson (2024) state that advertising based on algorithms can only increase loyalty when it is seen as fair and non-manipulative.

Ethical AI governance frameworks (Floridi et al., 2018), thus, act as boundary conditions. Personalization enhances interaction and loyalty when there is transparency, fairness and consumer control. Relational outcomes become worse when perceived intrusiveness or bias occurs. As a result, the relationship between AI personalization and trust is mediated by privacy concern, whereas the relationship between engagement and loyalty is mediated by ethical perception.

## 4. METHODOLOGY

### 4.1 Research Design

The study combines two types of research design that will be applied in the proposed study in an integrated mixed-method research design to explore the impact of AI-based personalization on customer interaction and retention. The decision to embrace a mixed-method can be explained by the multi-dimensional and complex character of AI-based marketing systems. The AI-based personalization is not a technological intervention only, but a strategic and relational process, which operates on the organizational and consumer level. Therefore, a holistic approach would require the contributions of the industry professionals whose responsibility would be to implement the strategies of personalization and empirical evidence through the experience of the consumers who will be able to use these systems in real-life.

The chronological explanatory design followed by the research is based on the assumption that the findings of the qualitative research are employed to enlighten and explain the following quantitative step. The qualitative dimension provides conceptual understanding of how AI-based personalisation can be conceptualised and operationalised in an organisational context, the quantitative one empirically confirms the relationships implied in the conceptual framework. The two strands are combined which increases the validity of the findings since it becomes possible to triangulate the managerial views and consumer reactions.

## 4.2 Qualitative Phase

The qualitative stage was aimed at investigating the processes in which AI-based personalization impacts engagement and loyalty on an organizational level. Purposive sampling was also used to find professionals who were currently engaged in AI-enabled marketing programs. Digital marketing managers, data analysts, customer experience strategists, and AI implementation consultants in the retail, e-commerce, telecommunications, and service industries were all participants. The selection criteria meant that participants had to have first hand experience in designing, implementing, or evaluating AI based personalization systems to make sure that the insights were based on practical experience.

Fifteen semi-structured interviews (in-depth) were carried out. The interviews took between forty-five and sixty minutes and were either virtually or face-to-face as per the availability of the participants. The interview protocol aimed to investigate the implementation of AI personalization strategies, the impact of the implementation on customer interaction patterns, measurement of engagement and loyalty in organizations, and ethical or privacy issues related to the implementation. The participants were also requested to consider organizational preparedness, technological foundation, and perceived ROI related to AI-driven personalization initiatives.

Informed consent was obtained to carry out all the interviews, which were audiotaped to facilitate accuracy. The tape recordings were word-for-word transcribed to enable systematic analysis. Thematic analysis has been used to determine recurrent patterns and conceptual themes. The emergent insights were first captured through an inductive coding method and then the codes were grouped into the higher-order categories in accordance with the conceptual framework, which included perceived relevance, customer satisfaction, trust-building mechanisms, and privacy management practices. In order to increase reliability, coding consistency was cross-validated by peer review and refinement of thematic clusters.

## 4.3 Quantitative Phase

The quantitative step was to test the structural relationships that were hypothesized in the conceptual model between AI-driven personalization and cognitive and affective mediators, engagement, trust, commitment, and customer loyalty empirically. To provide content validity, a structured questionnaire was created using the established scales, which were based on previous literature. Perceived usefulness and perceived ease of use measurement items were based on technology acceptance literature. The relationship marketing research formed the basis of trust and commitment scales. The constructs of engagement, the perceived quality of personalization, and loyalty intentions were based on recent empirical research studies on AI-based marketing strategies. Measurement of all items was done on a five-point Likert scale of strong disagree to strong agree.

The target group was a group of consumers who had been subjected to AI-based personalization via digital platforms, including online retail websites, mobile apps, streaming platforms, or AI-based customer care interfaces. The survey had a screening question to ensure that the respondent had already experienced personalized digital interactions. An online survey was used to collect data through the email and social media networks. Though a probability sampling technique would have been more appropriate in improving the generalizability, the practical limitations required the application of non-probability convenience sampling.

The number of responses collected was 350 and only 312 responses survived after the elimination of incomplete or inconsistent responses. The sample size was not below the recommended minimum size in Structural Equation Modeling, and thus, it was sufficient to provide sufficient statistical power. The respondents were a diverse group in terms of demographics (age, gender, education, and frequency of use of digital platforms) and increased the representativeness in the background of digitally active consumers.

*The assessment of the model of measurement will be presented below*:

The measurement model was tested to guarantee reliability and validity before testing the structural relationships. The internal consistency reliability was measured in terms of Cronbach alpha and composite reliability coefficients. Constructs were all above the acceptable level of 0.70 which means good reliability. Averages variance extracted values were used to test convergent validity and they were found to be significantly higher than the recommended value of 0.50, thus establishing the constructs as sufficient to measure the variance in their respective indicators. To determine the discriminant validity, the Fornell-Larcker criterion and cross-loading comparisons were employed to make sure that the constructs were not similar to the others in the model.

These statistical procedures made sure that the measurement instruments were reliable and valid, hence giving a strong base to structure analysis.

## 4.5 Structural Model Analysis

The hypothesized construct relationships were tested using Structural Equation Modelling. SEM was selected due to its ability to estimate several interdependent relationships of dependence at once and is especially applicable to theory-based models that have mediators and moderators. The analysis was done in a two step process. First, confirmatory factor analysis was used to verify the measurement model. Second, the structural model was tested to determine the direct and indirect associations between AI-based personalization and customer loyalty using mediating variables like perceived value, satisfaction, engagement, trust, and commitment.

The established indices were used to assess model fit and these included the Chi-square/degrees of freedom ratio, Comparative Fit Index, Tucker Lewis Index, and root mean square error of approximation. Acceptable levels were used to ensure the model was good enough to reflect the observed data. Interaction terms of privacy concerns and ethical perceptions were studied by adding them to the structural model and testing the statistical significance.

## 4.6 Ethical Considerations

During the research, ethical integrity was observed. All the participants were made aware of the objective of the study and were made sure that their participation was voluntary. Anonymity and confidentiality were highly respected and no personally identifiable information was gathered or released. The data were kept safely and were utilized only in academic purposes. Since the issue of AI-driven personalization and data privacy is quite sensitive, special attention was paid to the fact that the questions in the survey did not require the provision of sensitive personal information or the violation of the privacy of the participants.

## 4.7 Qualitative and Quantitative Findings Integration.

The last part of the study was combining both qualitative and quantitative findings and creating a unified vision of the outcomes of AI-based personalization. Qualitative results gave contextual explanations to the statistical relationships that were evident in the structural model especially on the managerial strategies and ethical governance practices. The strength and direction of the relationships between personalization, engagement, trust and loyalty were proven to be valid through quantitative analysis. This combination of both strands reinforced the theoretical interpretation and increased practical relevance because it incorporated the gap between the organizational implementation and the consumer perception and behavioral outcomes.

## 5. HYPOTHESES DEVELOPMENT

### 5.1 AI-based Personalization and Cognitive Assessment.

The role of AI-based personalization is that of the main technological trigger in the digital marketing setting. Through the use of machine learning algorithms, predictive analytics and natural language processing systems, companies can provide personalized proposals, personalized communication, and responsive service interactions. The success of such systems is largely determined by the way the consumers judge the relevance and usefulness of the personalized content. The Technology Acceptance Model holds that perceived usefulness and perceived ease of use play an important role in shaping the attitude and adoption of technological systems by individuals (Davis, 1989). Relevance is used in AI-based personalization environments to reflect how consumers find recommendations and content relevant to their tastes and preferences.

As soon as AI systems are capable of reading the consumer data correctly and make the right suggestions, people tend to view this personalization as worthwhile and useful. The existing empirical research suggests that AI-supported personalized marketing strategies lead to a higher perceived relevance and cognitive acceptance of online platforms (Alghaswyneh, 2025; Gowri, 2024). Thus, the personalization based on AI will have a positive impact on the relevance and utility perceptions of consumers.

H1: AI-based personalization has a positive effect on perceived relevance and usefulness.

Perceived value is also expected to be improved by the perceived relevance and usefulness. Consumers place a higher value on the experience when they realize that personalized interactions are time-saving, less search effortful, and enhance the quality of decisions. According to the marketing analytics literature, relevance improves the perceived benefits and reduces cognitive costs (Wedel and Kannan, 2016). This means that stronger value perceptions should be associated with the higher the perceptions of usefulness.

H2: Perceived relevance and usefulness have a positive impact on perceived value.

Perceived value is a consumer judgment of the benefits of the gains received in comparison to effort put in. The value in the context of AI-based personalization is generated when customized ideas, information, and offers are aligned with consumer preferences. The Experience Economy model highlights that emotional and functional satisfaction is boosted through personalized experience as it creates significant interactions (Pine and Gilmore, 1999). Equally, the co-creation theory posits that adaptive personalization strengthens the impression that companies are aware and responsive to the needs of an individual (Prahalad and Ramaswamy, 2004).

The empirical studies indicate that personalized online experiences can go a long way in enhancing customer satisfaction through the perception of quality and ease (Ahmed et al., 2025; Zed et al., 2024). Thus, the higher the consumers feel the value of AI-driven personalization, the more the brand or platform becomes satisfactory to them.

H3: Perceived value has a positive effect on customer satisfaction.

Customer satisfaction is a form of affective response that is as a result of positive consumption experiences. Customer satisfaction will increase the frequency of interaction, use of the platform and brand engagement. The conceptualization of the engagement theory considers customer engagement as a multidimensional construct that includes behavioral participation and psychological involvement (Mathur et al., 2025).

Personalization increases satisfaction because AI-driven experiences are tailored and efficient and, consequently, promote engagement. Research shows that individual online engagements can be used to boost active engagement and cognitive immersion in brand platforms (Sherly Steffi et al., 2024; Teepapal, 2025). In this way, the consumers who become satisfied will be more eager to communicate with the brands on a more frequent basis and become more involved.

H4: Customer satisfaction has a positive impact on the customer engagement.

Customer interaction is an intermediary process between satisfaction and long-term relationship processes. Loyal customers show active behavior of interaction and develop more emotional attachment to brands. The Commitment-Trust Theory postulates that trust is a key condition that determines long-lasting relationships (Morgan and Hunt, 1994). Trust in the brand grows when consumers have repeated experiences with customized systems and they believe that the systems are responsive and reliable.

The studies of AI-supported marketing approaches indicate that interaction enhances the relationships through strengthening the perceptions of competence and attentiveness (Latif, 2025; Jung, 2025). The more the trust is built, the more the consumers will develop commitment as they feel the need to continue cherished relationship. Commitment is a stronger state of relationship with intentions of loyalty and unwillingness to change.

Therefore, the participation is likely to have a positive effect on trust and commitment.

H5: Customer engagement has a positive effect on trust.
H6: Customer interaction has a positive effect on commitment.

Commitment is also expected to be enhanced by trust. The consumers who view brands as reliable tend to have long-term relationships and emotional attachment. The existence of previous studies proves that trust increases relational commitment and decreases uncertainty in online communication (Morgan and Hunt, 1994; Ahmed et al., 2025).

H7: There is a positive relationship between trust and commitment.

## 5.2 Dedication and Customer loyalty.

The final relational outcome of the AI-based personalization processes is the customer loyalty. Loyalty involves behavioral, repeat purchase and retention, and attitudinal, advocacy and emotional commitment, dimensions. The relationship marketing literature always recognizes commitment as a direct antecedent of loyalty (Morgan and Hunt, 1994).

The empirical research proves that AI-based personalization can increase loyalty through the mediation of trust and commitment (Ahmed et al., 2025; Jung, 2025; Zed et al., 2024). Thus, loyal customers will be more inclined to remain in contact with individual systems and be able to have long-term relations with brands.

H8: Commitment positively influences customer loyalty.

## 5.3 Intermediating Level of Privacy Concerns.

Even though AI-based personalization can increase the level of engagement and loyalty, privacy issues can moderate its effectiveness. The personalization-privacy paradox is based on the fact that consumers value personalized experiences but can be opposed to the concept of personalization once they feel that there is too much information being collected (Martin and Murphy, 2017). According to Jayapal (2025), the privacy issue undermines the good relationship between personalisation and loyalty in online shopping.

The relational outcomes could decrease when the consumers experience a low level of trust in the AI systems due to the high level of concern over data privacy.

In line with this, privacy issues are likely to mitigate the association between AI-based personalization and trust.

## 5.4 Mediating Effect of Ethical Perceptions.

Consumer response is also formed by ethical perceptions and transparency when it comes to the use of AI. Fairness, accountability, and transparency are among the key elements of ethical AI models that are necessary to ensure the trust of the population (Floridi et al., 2018). Engagement will also lead to commitment and loyalty when the consumers view AI systems as transparent and ethically regulated. On the other hand, the image of manipulation or algorithmic bias can decrease relational results (Skillius and Jacobsson, 2024).

The hypotheses proposed can be said to be a representation of the structural pathways of the SEM model. Personalization brought about by AI will affect the perception of relevance, which will increase perceived value and satisfaction. Customer loyalty is achieved through satisfaction resulting in engagement, which builds trust and commitment, and leads to customer loyalty. The moderating variables of relational strength are privacy concerns and ethical perceptions.

# 6. DISCUSSIONS

## 6.1 Overview of Findings

The results of this paper can support the suggested structural relationships between AI-based personalization and customer engagement and customer loyalty significantly. In line with the conceptual framework, the AI-based personalization was also determined to have a significant impact on perceived relevance and usefulness, which, in turn, positively affected perceived value and customer satisfaction. These affective and cognitive judgments were important mediating factors in converting technological abilities to significant relational consequences. Moreover, customer satisfaction greatly enhanced the levels of engagement, which consequently contributed to the development of trust and commitment, which eventually resulted in the improved customer loyalty. The sequential mediation model suggested in the model was therefore proved empirically.

These findings prove that AI-based personalization does not have a direct impact on loyalty outcomes by itself. Rather, its effects take place by a systematic sequence of psychological and relationship processes. The moderating roles that are observed in the conceptual framework also point out that the effectiveness of personalization depends on the context and ethical perceptions at large.

## 6.2 Theoretical Contributions

The findings add value to the literature on marketing and AI in several significant ways. First, the research contributes to the development of Technology Acceptance Theory by showing that perceived relevance and usefulness remain the primary criteria for assessing AI-enabled marketing systems. Although past studies have mainly concentrated on technology adoption contexts, the current study has applied the theory to the relational marketing outcomes by demonstrating that usefulness perceptions are converted to value and satisfaction, hence driving engagement behaviors.

Second, the findings support the explanatory power of the Experience Economy and co-creation models. Individualized online experiences improved perceived value and satisfaction, which corroborates the claim that customized and personalized interactions increase the quality of experiences. Personalization that is driven by AI is an operationalization of experiential marketing that aligns its offerings dynamically to consumer preferences, thus enhancing cognitive and emotional reactions.

Third, the research reinforces the Commitment-Trust Theory in the AI-mediated contexts. The fact that engagement positively influences trust and commitment proves that relational ties can be developed when algorithmically mediated interactions are perceived to be relevant and useful. The empirical confirmation that trust is a mediator of the relationships between engagement and commitment underscores the long-term significance of relational constructs in technologically developed marketing systems.

Notably, the research incorporates technological, psychological and relational theories in a cohesive structural framework. The study links the two strands of AI marketing and relationship marketing literature that have been separate and unconnected by empirically verifying the sequential route of personalization to loyalty.

Essentially, the interpretation of structural relationships is conducted in the same way as in case 6.2, except that structural relationships are considered instead of an individual relationship.<|human|>The interpretation of structural relationships is effectively the same as in case 6.2, except that structural relationships are taken into account, rather than a single relationship.

Such a strong correlation between AI-based personalization and perceived relevance proves that consumers do care about the contextual accuracy and customized suggestions. This result indicates that algorithmic accuracy has a direct positive effect on cognitive assessments of usefulness. Perceived value is enhanced when the personalization systems are successful in lowering the search effort and the complexity of decision making.

The positive impact of perceived value on customer satisfaction is strong and positive, which implies that the consumers evaluate personalized experiences not only according to functional efficiency but also according to the enrichment of the experience. Satisfaction is seen to be a key conversion point, changing cognitive appraisals to affective reactions.

The dynamic aspect of digital interaction is emphasized by the role of satisfaction on engagement. Customers who are satisfied will be more willing to engage more often, view content, and become more engaged with the brand. Engagement therefore serves as a behavioral gap between short-term satisfaction and long-term relationship performance.

The beneficial influence of engagement on trust and commitment further attest to the fact that the repeated and meaningful engagement enhances relational stability. The result of regular, credible and applicable personalization experiences is trust. After trust, commitment then comes as a psychological desire to continue the relationship. Lastly, commitment is a key cause of customer loyalty, which proves that long-lasting loyalty is based on the relational depth and not on the transactional convenience only.

## 6.4 Moderating Effects and Boundary Conditions.

The conditions of the AI-driven personalization outcomes are highlighted by the moderating effects that were observed in the study. The privacy issue was observed to undermine the positive association between personalization and trust, which means that a high-quality personalization will not be effective in case consumers believe that personal information is invaded excessively. It helps to justify the personalization-privacy paradox, where people enjoy customized experiences and are afraid of being spied on at the same time.

Relationship between engagement and commitment was reinforced by ethical perceptions and transparency, which proved that responsible AI governance promotes relational outcomes. When the consumers feel that the personalization systems are just, transparent and ethically controlled, then they would be more inclined to convert the engagement into commitment and loyalty.

These mediating results indicate that technological sophistication is not enough. The mechanisms of ethical governance, transparency and data protection are essential to the maintenance of relational benefits.

## 6.5 Managerial Implications

In the context of the managerial dimension, the results indicate the importance of creating AI-based systems of personalization that are more attentive to the perceived relevance and value. The companies should not simply focus on the data collection capabilities, but also, refine the accuracy of the algorithms, to be contextually fitted to the inclinations of the consumers. Investment in predictive analytics is to be accompanied by a continuous performance monitoring in order to guarantee the quality of personalization.

The results also indicate that engagement is a performance measure that should be considered by firms since engagement is an antecedent of trust and loyalty. Organizations should not measure AI projects based on the conversion measurement in the short term, but should also measure the relational ones, which involves building trust and commitment.

The privacy concerns role as a moderating factor highlights why there should be transparent practices of data. The companies should engage in clear consent mechanisms, provide ready-to-access clarifications on how personalization works and provide the consumers with a chance to control personalization preferences. The ethical AI governance is not a compliance measure only, but also a strategic asset that improves loyalty.

## 6.6 Implications of Research in the Future.

Although the proposed model has been validated in the study, it is possible to single out a number of research avenues. Longitudinal research would be in a position to examine the transformation of the effects of personalization with time and the capacity to stay faithful in harsh online areas. The cross-cultural researches may also suggest the degree to which the sensitivity of privacy and the establishment of trust are different in various regions. Furthermore, the future analysis may focus on the effect of generative AI and emotionally intelligent systems on the formation of relational outcomes.

Studies on industry-specific differences would also be useful in respect of generalization of the theory. As an illustration, the relationship of individualization with health care or financial services can be described as more ethical oriented as compared to the retail. Another potential adverse effect (personalization fatigue or algorithm aversion) can be addressed in the future study as well.

The findings demonstrate that customer engagement and loyalty may be enhanced through an artificial intelligence-based personalization process that is guided by a set of cognitive, affective, and relational processes. The study reveals that perceived relevance, satisfaction, engagement, trust and commitment under the condition of ethical and privacy related boundaries determine the effectiveness of personalization. The study is a comprehensive description of how AI-based personalization can be used in sustainable competitive advantage through the inclusion of technological capability and relational theory.

## 7. POLICY RECOMMENDATIONS

The rapid trend of personalization of online marketing systems with the help of AI demands not only innovative but also consumer-protective policy frames. Even though AI technologies have become crucial in enhancing the customer engagement and loyalty, the implementation of AI technologies has been linked with privacy, transparency, fairness, as well as accountability concerns. Therefore, the policy-makers ought to develop a hierarchical regulation system that is going to generate accountable and sustainable AI-driven personalization practices.

Firstly, the policy intervention is supposed to be informed by excellent data protection and privacy laws. The consumer data, including the behavioral patterns, preferences, and the history of interactions are the basis of the AI personalization systems. The policymakers should demand a clear consent, minimization of data, and a clear disclosure of the manner in which personal information has been gathered, stored and processed. It should also be enacted to ensure that the organizations are not informed consenting but implicit data collection. In addition, the policies should guarantee the independence and the trustworthiness of the AI systems by guaranteeing that consumers have the authority to view, change or destroy their information.

Second, the institutionalization of the algorithmic transparency and explainability have to be carried out as regulatory standards. AI-driven systems of recommendation engines and predictive analytics are typically black boxes, and consumers may not always understand the manner in which the decisions are arrived at. The policymakers should require the organizations to implement explainable AI systems, which provide easy explanations of the reasoning behind personalization. The policies of transparency may include the mandated provision of recommendation policy, audit of algorithms, and a report of automated decision-making systems. Ensuring the transparency of algorithms is not only a way to assure consumers but also to reduce the risk of finding discriminating results and bias.

Third, regulatory frameworks on AI, which are ethical, need to be integrated within corporate policy frameworks. The policymakers are expected to encourage or require firms to establish internal AI ethics committees that will manage impartiality, responsibility, and non-discrimination within the personalization systems. The regulators will be able to develop ethical AI standards of certification, which would imply that companies adhere to fair algorithm development and regular bias inspection. Such forms of government increase the institutional responsibility and sustainable online ecosystems.

Fourth, the system must have regulatory compliance and independent audit systems to make compliance easier. Policymakers need to develop periodic compliance tests and third party audits to ascertain the degree of adherence to the standards of privacy and transparency. There can also be the introduction of regulatory sandboxes where companies can test new AI applications under a regulated environment as a way of experimenting responsibly, without violating the rights of consumers. The tough enforcing mechanisms will enhance the policy credibility and discourage the exploitative personalization act. The convenience of the privacy settings and easy-to-use control dashboard provided to the consumer will raise the autonomy and reduce the opposition to AI-powered personalization.

All these policy recommendations represent a leveled attitude based on which the development of technology is promoted by ethical protection and accountability of the institutions. The personalization that is ethically implemented with the help of AI must be performed by the government, regulation, industry and consumers. By establishing cohesive structures of administration grounded on openness, equality, and empowerment, policymakers do not have to lose consumer loyalty and the sustainability of long-term relations.

## 8. CONCLUSION

The flourishing Artificial Intelligence has revolutionized the digital marketing landscape, altering the experience of interaction between organizations and consumers and relationships in the long term. This study was intended to conduct research on the implications of AI-based personalization of customer interaction and loyalty in the context of a combined conceptual and empirical design. The study combines technological perspectives with the psychological and relational approaches, this is why it can be referred to as a comprehensive explanation of the ways in which AI-based personalization processes may result in sustainable relational outcomes.

The findings confirm the hypothesis of personalization in terms of AI as a strategy stimulus that facilitates the sense of relevance and usefulness. Customers get improved perceptions of value when they are given personalized recommendations, tailored contents and offers that are fitting in their situations. This value is a highly significant mediating factor because it increases customer satisfaction, which in its turn increases engagement. The paper demonstrates that the personalization does not end with satisfaction but it is merely a transition process, which transforms cognitive judgment to behavioral and emotional involvement.

Theoretically, the study has been able to make contributions to the literature in the sense that it incorporates various conceptual lenses into a single structural framework. It ties Technology Acceptance Theory, perspectives of experiential marketing, co-creation logic, and relationship marketing theory to explain the outcomes of AI-driven personalization. The study contributes to the existing knowledge on the mechanisms by which consumer behavior is affected by personalization by empirically supporting a sequential mediation model. The results indicate that AI personalization entails layer-based cognitive, affective, and relational mechanisms instead of transactional impacts.

Regarding the managerial aspect of the problem, the study indicates the significance of the strategic and ethical approach towards the application of AI in the organization. The personalization initiatives should focus on the contextual relevance in the sense of the user experience design and transparency to enhance the perceived value and satisfaction. Engagement metrics should also be incorporated in performance evaluation systems as the antecedent of trust and loyalty is engagement. Moreover, corporations are forced to invest in ethical AI governance frameworks, in which fairness, accountability, and privacy are ensured. Responsible personalization eliminates regulatory risk and increases consumer confidence and relational sustainability.

The fact that there should be organized regulatory tools that facilitate responsible AI innovation should also be backed by the policy implications. The necessary measures to safeguard the rights of the consumers are the data protection laws, the transparency of the algorithms, and compliance audits. Meanwhile, the steps that result in the enhancement of digital literacy and consumer empowerment may play the role of the informed participation in the personalized ecosystem. A moderate policy culture encourages the development of technology but with moral uprightness.

Its contributions to the study are the dynamism of AI technologies and consumer behavior. The personalization strategy will even be enhanced with the additional evolution of the generative AI, emotionally intelligent systems, and immersive online environments. In the future studies, the longitudinal effects, the cross-cultural variations, and the sector-specific variations in the dynamics of personalization are to be studied. Moreover, the discussion of potential undesirable consequences, such as personalization fatigue or dislike of algorithms, may be used to become slightly more nuanced in terms of AI-based marketing.

Thus, the present paper proves that the use of AI-based personalization can significantly enhance the customer engagement and loyalty as long as it is presented in a strategic and ethical manner. The perceived relevance, value creation, satisfaction, engagement, trust, and commitment carry out the personalization to the loyalty pathway. This is because the sustainable competitive advantage in the digital economy is the combination of both the technological accuracy and relationship sensitivity with moral leadership. The bodies that make sure that AI innovation is aligned with the elements of transparency, accountability, and consumer empowerment are the most likely to gain a long-lasting loyalty and success in the relationship.

## REFERENCES


Ahmed, S. M. M., Owais, M., Raza, M., Nadeem, Q., & Ahmed, B. (2025). The Impact of AI-Driven Personalization on Consumer Engagement and Brand Loyalty. *Qlantic Journal of Social Sciences*, *6*(1), 311–323. DOI: 10.55737/qjss.v-iv.24313

Alghaswyneh, O. F. (2025). Exploring the Impact of AI-Driven Personalization on Consumer Engagement in Digital Marketing. *Management*, *29*(1), 117–144. DOI: 10.58691/man/200968

Cambria, E., & White, B. (2014). Jumping NLP curves: A review of natural language processing research. *IEEE Computational Intelligence Magazine*, *9*(2), 48–57. DOI: 10.1109/MCI.2014.2307227

Davenport, T. H., Guha, A., Grewal, D., & Bressgott, T. (2020). How artificial intelligence will change the future of marketing. *Journal of the Academy of Marketing Science*, *48*(1), 24–42. DOI: 10.1007/s11747-019-00696-0

Davis, F. D. (1989). Perceived usefulness, perceived ease of use, and user acceptance of information technology. *Management Information Systems Quarterly*, *13*(3), 319–340. DOI: 10.2307/249008

Floridi, L., Cowls, J., Beltrametti, M., Chatila, R., Chazerand, P., Dignum, V., Luetge, C., Madelin, R., Pagallo, U., Rossi, F., Schafer, B., Valcke, P., & Vayena, E. (2018). AI4People—An ethical framework for a good AI society. *Minds and Machines*, *28*(4), 689–707. DOI: 10.1007/s11023-018-9482-5 PMID: 30930541

Ganeshkumar, M., Karunakaran, S., Muzhumathi, R., & Suguna, R. (2024, October). Ai-driven marketing insights: Harnessing machine learning for enhanced consumer engagement and personalization. In *2024 First International Conference on Software, Systems and Information Technology (SSITCON)* (pp. 1-6). IEEE. DOI: 10.1109/SSITCON62437.2024.10796558

Gowri, D. P. (2024). Impact of AI in personalized digital marketing: Boosting customer engagement through tailored content. *Journal of Communication Management (London)*, *3*(03), 216–221.

Huang, M. H., & Rust, R. T. (2021). Artificial Intelligence in service. *Journal of Service Research*, *24*(1), 3–21.

Jayapal, J. (2025). Unveiling the impact of AI-driven personalization on customer loyalty in online shopping: The moderating effects of privacy concerns. *Journal of Promotion Management*, *31*(5), 865–894. DOI: 10.1080/10496491.2025.2525099

Jung, N. Y. (2025). AI-Powered personalization drives loyalty in retail. In *Leveraging AI-Powered Marketing in the Experience-Driven Economy* (pp. 105–146). IGI Global Scientific Publishing. DOI: 10.4018/979-8-3693-9561-5.ch004

Kotler, P., & Keller, K. L. (2016). *Marketing management* (15th ed.). Pearson Education.

Latif, F. (2025). AI-POWERED PERSONALIZATION IN BRANDING: IMPACT ON CONSUMER ENGAGEMENT AND LOYALTY. *Contemporary Journal of Social Science Review*, *3*(4), 47–57. DOI: 10.63878/cjssr.v3i4.1825

Martin, K., & Murphy, P. (2017). The role of data privacy in marketing. *Journal of Business Ethics*, *143*(3), 467–481.

Mathur, M., Khan, S., Khan, S. W., Das, S., & Goel, V. (2025). Consumer Engagement in the Era of Personalization: The Strategic Role of AI-Driven Marketing. *Advances in Consumer Research. Association for Consumer Research (U. S.)*, *2*(4).

Moqaddem, O. (2025). Investigating the impact of AI on personalization and customer engagement in intelligent marketing strategies. *European Journal of Management and Marketing Studies*, *10*(1). Advance online publication. DOI: 10.46827/ejmms.v10i1.1922

Morgan, R. M., & Hunt, S. D. (1994). The commitment-trust theory of relationship marketing. *Journal of Marketing*, *58*(3), 20–38. DOI: 10.1177/002224299405800302

. Okeke, N. I., Alabi, O. A., Igwe, A. N., Ofodile, O. C., & Ewim, C. P. M. (2024). AI-driven personalization framework for SMEs: Revolutionizing customer engagement and retention. Journal name needed for completion.

. Patil, D. (2024). Artificial intelligence-driven customer service: Enhancing personalization, loyalty, and customer satisfaction. *Loyalty, And Customer Satisfaction (November 20, 2024).*

Pine, B. J., & Gilmore, J. H. (1999). *The Experience Economy*. Harvard Business School Press.

Prahalad, C. K., & Ramaswamy, V. (2004). Co-creation experiences: The next practice in value creation. *Journal of Interactive Marketing*, *18*(3), 5–14. DOI: 10.1002/dir.20015

. Puneet, S. (2023). AI-driven personalization in telecom customer support: Enhancing user experience and loyalty. *AI-Driven Personalization in Telecom Customer Support: Enhancing User Experience and Loyalty.*

Shalev-Shwartz, S., & Ben-David, S. (2014). *Understanding Machine Learning: From Theory to Algorithms*. Cambridge University Press. DOI: 10.1017/CBO9781107298019

Sherly Steffi, L., Subha, B., Kuriakose, A., Singh, J., Arunkumar, B., & Rajalakshmi, V. (2024). The impact of AI-driven personalization on consumer behavior and brand engagement in online marketing. In Harnessing, A. I. (Ed.), *Machine Learning, and IoT for Intelligent Business* (Vol. 1, pp. 485–492). Springer Nature Switzerland.

. Skillius, E., & Jacobsson, A. (2024). Beyond the Algorithm-How ai-driven personalized ads shape consumer loyalty and brand engagement.

Teepapal, T. (2025). AI-driven personalization: Unraveling consumer perceptions in social media engagement. *Computers in Human Behavior, 165*, 108549. DOI: 10.1016/j.chb.2024.108549

Venkatesh, V., Morris, M. G., Davis, G. B., & Davis, F. D. (2003). User acceptance of information technology: Toward a unified view. *Management Information Systems Quarterly*, *27*(3), 425–478. DOI: 10.2307/30036540

Vij, M., Vij, A., Kumar, P., & Shameem, B. (2024, February). Impact of AI-Driven Customer Insights on Brand Engagement and Loyalty in Tourism Marketing. In 2024 2nd International Conference on Cyber Resilience (ICCR) (pp. 1-6). IEEE.

Wedel, M., & Kannan, P. K. (2016). Marketing analytics for data-rich environments. *Journal of Marketing*, *80*(6), 97–121. DOI: 10.1509/jm.15.0413

Zed, E. Z., Kartini, T. M., & Purnamasari, P. (2024). The Power Of Personalization: Exploring The Impact Of Ai-Driven Marketing Strategies On Consumer Loyalty In E-Commerce. *Jurnal Ekonomi*, *13*(04), 1303–1314.

# Chapter 12
# Unveiling Neural Mechanisms Behind Consumer Behavior in Virtual Reality

**Surinder Pal Singh**
http://orcid.org/0000-0001-8690-3339
*Department of Artificial intelligence and Machine Learning, Galgotia College of Engineering and Technology, India*

**Vinod Kumar**
http://orcid.org/0000-0002-3578-8155
*Department of Management, Gurugram University, Gurugram, India*

**Hawa Singh**
*Department of Management, Gurugram University, Gurugram, India*

**Naveen Kumar**
*Department of Management, Gurugram University, Gurugram, India*

## ABSTRACT

*Virtual Reality (VR) is redefining consumer experiences by offering immersive environments that engage multiple senses. This chapter investigates the neural mechanisms underlying consumer behavior in VR using a neuromarketing approach. Researchers conducted an experimental study combining electroencephalography (EEG) and biometric measures with behavioral data to compare consumers' cognitive and emotional responses in a VR shopping scenario versus a traditional web-based platform. 33 participants completed purchase tasks in both environments while their neural activity and physiological signals were recorded. Results show that*

DOI: 10.4018/979-8-3373-5997-7.ch012

*VR elicited higher cognitive engagement and memory activation but also induced greater mental workload than the traditional platform. These findings advance our understanding of how immersive virtual experiences affect the consumer's brain and behavior. The chapter highlights the value of consumer neuroscience tools in evaluating emerging marketing technologies and provides guidance for practitioners seeking to leverage VR in enhancing customer experience.*

## INTRODUCTION

In the era of immersive media and the metaverse, understanding how virtual environments influence consumer behavior has become increasingly crucial. Neuromarketing is the application of neuroscience to marketing – offers powerful tools to probe the subconscious drivers of consumer decisions(Russo et al., 2022). Traditional marketing research often relies on surveys and interviews, but these methods capture only conscious attitudes and are prone to biases (e.g. social desirability. By contrast, consumer neuroscience techniques such as functional neuroimaging and EEG allow researchers to directly measure brain and physiological responses to marketing stimuli, providing deeper insight into the emotional and cognitive processes that guide behavior. Recent studies have demonstrated that neuroscientific tools can illuminate the neural mechanisms involved in decision-making and emotion in consumers. For example, fMRI and EEG experiments show that VR experiences activate brain regions associated with emotion and decision-making, leading to heightened affective responses that can shape product attitudes and purchase intent. Few researchers used fMRI and found that activation in reward-processing areas (e.g. nucleus accumbens) versus aversion-related areas (e.g. insula) could predict whether a person will decide to buy a product or not (Knutson et al., 2007). These advances underscore the promise of neuromarketing in revealing the subconscious influences on consumer behavior.

Meanwhile, VR has emerged as a transformative medium in marketing and retail, enabling consumers to interact with products and brands in fully simulated environments. VR can deliver vivid, interactive experiences that surpass the engagement of traditional media. Prior research in marketing has explored VR applications such as virtual product trials, 3D stores environments, and immersive advertisements. For instance, VR product demonstrations in retail have been shown to increase customer engagement and satisfaction (e.g. Audi's virtual showroom tours(Chhaniwal et al., 2024). VR's key feature – the sense of presence or "being there" – creates an emotional connection that can strengthen brand impressions. A high sense of immersion in VR tends to enhance consumers' emotional engagement and involvement. This emotional amplification can positively influence memory for the experience, brand attitudes, and purchase intentions (Ayoubi et al., 2025). However, there are also challenges: immersive systems may impose greater cognitive load or usability issues, which could dampen the overall experience if not carefully designed. Consumers unfamiliar with VR might experience discomfort or cognitive overload, reducing their positive effect.

Given the potential of VR to reshape consumer behavior, there is a need to examine how the consumer's brain and physiology respond during virtual shopping experiences. While traditional studies have measured behavioral outcomes (like purchase intention or satisfaction) in VR contexts, fewer have probed the underlying neural processes in detail. The present chapter addresses this gap by using a multimodal neuromarketing approach to investigate consumers' cognitive and affective states in a VR shopping environment. By comparing these neurophysiological responses to a conventional e-commerce scenario, we aim to isolate the impact of immersion on consumer decision-making processes. Researcher also explore how neural indices (such as engagement and workload) relate to subjective UX (user experience) evaluations and behavioral intentions. Understanding these neural mechanisms will not only advance academic theory in consumer neuroscience but also guide marketers and UX designers in creating more effective virtual commerce experiences.

## LITERATURE REVIEW

*Neuromarketing and Consumer Decision-Making:* Neuromarketing combines neuroscience, psychology, and economics to study consumer decision-making at a biological level. Over the past two decades, it has evolved from a novel idea to a robust field providing insights that traditional marketing research might miss (Cherubino et al., 2019). Researchers use tools like EEG to capture electrical brain activity, eye-tracking to observe visual attention, galvanic skin response to gauge arousal, and fMRI to visualize brain regions engaged by marketing stimuli. These techniques help decide how consumers subconsciously react to advertisements, branding, product designs, and retail environments. For example, EEG methods can reveal event-related potentials or oscillatory patterns linked to attention and emotion when consumers view an advertisement (Costa-Feito et al., 2023). Neural responses measured via EEG could predict consumers' future product choices better than chance. Similarly, some authors demonstrated that by analyzing EEG and eye-tracking data, one can assess brain responses to marketing stimuli (like product packaging) and forecast consumer preferences. These studies suggest that specific neural signatures such as patterns in frontal theta or beta bands correlate with decision processes such as preference formation and purchase intention. Beyond EEG, fMRI studies have pinpointed brain areas relevant to buying decisions: heightened activation in the ventromedial prefrontal cortex and striatum often reflects increased desirability of a product, whereas activation in the insula (associated with pain/discomfort) can predict hesitation or refusal to purchase (Knutson et al., 2007). Such findings underscore how consumer choices are influenced by automatic neural responses to cost-benefit tradeoffs (pleasure of gain vs. pain of paying).

*VR in Marketing and Consumer Experience:* Virtual Reality and related technologies (Augmented Reality, Mixed Reality) represent a new frontier for engaging consumers. VR's immersive and interactive nature can dramatically affect consumer perceptions, emotions, and behaviors. In marketing contexts, VR has been applied to virtual stores, simulated product experiences, and immersive storytelling. Prior studies generally find that VR enhances consumer engagement: the novelty and richness of VR experiences capture attention and evoke stronger emotional reactions than two-dimensional media. Some researchers observed that letting customers interact virtually with products (e.g. trying furniture in a virtual home) led to more informed decisions and higher purchase confidence] (Chen et al., 2024). VR also enables experiential marketing: companies like Audi, IKEA, and Nike have used VR to let customers virtually test-drive cars, visualize furniture at home, or try on virtual shoes, respectively, resulting in increased customer satisfaction and sales conversions. These practical cases illustrate VR's ability to foster emotional connections with products by making the experience fun, interactive, and personalized.

At the same time, the literature notes some challenges and mixed outcomes. High immersion can sometimes lead to sensory overload or motion sickness in susceptible users, which negatively impacts the experience. Ease of use remains a critical factor: if a VR interface is unintuitive or controls are clunky, users' frustration may outweigh the novelty benefits. Perceived risk is another consideration—some consumers are hesitant to trust virtual representations of products for making purchase decisions (e.g. worry that the real product won't match the virtual preview). Nonetheless, carefully designed studies show positive psychological mechanisms at work in VR commerce. Immersion and presence (the feeling of "being there" in the virtual store) have been linked to higher enjoyment and engagement. For example, few researchers demonstrated that a strong sense of immersion in VR triggered emotional engagement which in turn boosted consumers' shopping enjoyment and intentions to buy. VR also promotes richer mental imagery, helping consumers visualize product usage more vividly, which can increase desire for the product (Loureiro et al., 2020).

*Neural and Psychological Responses in VR:* A growing subset of research directly examines consumers' neural responses in VR settings. A study was conducted where shoppers navigated a virtual supermarket while wearing EEG headsets; they found that certain EEG indicators of attention and motivation spiked just before consumers made purchase decisions in VR, suggesting parallels to real-world decision neural patterns (Han et al., 2020). These neuroimaging findings imply that VR can engage the brain's memory and reward circuitry more intensely, potentially leading to stronger brand recall and preference formation (Casado-Aranda et al., 2022). Another line of work uses biometrics in VR: heart rate and skin conductance tend to increase during exciting or stress-inducing VR shopping moments, reflecting autonomic arousal. One study noted that highly immersive VR elicited physiological arousal similar to in-store shopping excitement, whereas low-immersion digital environments did not.

However, not all neural responses in VR are uniformly positive for marketers. If an experience is cognitively demanding, it may increase EEG-based workload indices, which correlate with mental fatigue and reduced pleasure[REMOVED HYPERLINK FIELD][REMOVED HYPERLINK FIELD]. For instance, a recent neuromarketing experiment by comparing a metaverse shopping platform (Second Life) to a standard e-commerce website. They found that the VR-like metaverse environment elicited greater cognitive engagement (higher beta activity in EEG) and more activation of memorization processes, indicating deeper processing of the virtual shopping experience. On the flip side, the metaverse shopping had higher mental workload and did not generate as strong positive emotional reactions as the traditional website (Fici et al., 2024). Participants reported lower ease-of-use and felt the VR store was less informative and more effortful to use. These results suggest a trade-off: VR can capture attention and enhance certain cognitive aspects (engagement, memory), but if it overtaxes the user or frustrates them, the emotional payoff and overall satisfaction might suffer. Such nuanced insights underscore why measuring the neural and physiological states of consumers in VR is valuable – it helps pinpoint where an experience excites the brain and where it strains it.

Chhaniwal et al. (2025) analyze the effects of Virtual Reality (VR) on consumer purchase intentions from a neuromarketing perspective, highlighting the mediating role of immersion in influencing behavioral outcomes. The study illustrates that VR environments have a significant positive effect on consumer attention, emotional engagement, and product vividness, which positively influence purchase intention. Cenizo (2025) pushes the frontiers of neuromarketing research in digital commerce by investigating the use of neurophysiological variables to explain consumer behavior on web platforms. The study illustrates that EEG-based engagement variables, in conjunction with eye-tracking and behavioral analysis, offer more nuanced explanations of attention, emotional engagement, and decision fluency during online browsing. Yao and Wang (2024) make a significant theoretical and methodological contribution to neuromarketing research by illustrating the use of neural data to predict aggregate consumer behavior instead of individual-level responses. They contend that neurophysiological variables, especially EEG-based attention and valuation variables, can predict market outcomes at the aggregate level when properly aggregated and analyzed using advanced statistical and AI-driven models. Chand et al. (2025) illustrate the revolutionary potential and challenges of using neurotechnology to decode consumer behavior. In their review of brain-computer interface (BCI) applications in marketing research, they contend that neurotechnology offers unparalleled access to subconscious cognitive and affective processes that are not accessible through self-report methodologies.

In summary, prior research indicates that immersive VR experiences can strongly influence consumer emotions and decisions, with neural evidence of increased engagement and imagination. Yet, VR's complexity can introduce cognitive load that potentially dampens positive affect if not managed. This literature backdrop motivates our study to delve deeper into these phenomena. We build on earlier neuromarketing findings by jointly examining cognitive (EEG) and emotional (biometric) responses, and linking them to consumer experience outcomes in a VR setting. Our work is among the first to integrate these measures in a controlled comparison between VR and conventional shopping, thereby contributing to both consumer neuroscience theory and practical guidance for VR marketing applications.

## METHODOLOGY

### Participants

We recruited a total of 33 adult volunteers (18 male, 15 female) to participate in the study. Participants were aged 20 to 31 years (Mean = 22.4, SD = 2.5) and were drawn from a university student population. All participants thus belonged to the younger consumer demographic (late Generation Z and early Millennials), a group of interest for emerging technology adoption. To ensure a baseline familiarity with VR interfaces, we required that participants have at least some prior exposures to 3D gaming or virtual environments. This criterion was set to avoid extreme novelty effects or confusion that could arise from first-time VR use. Participants reported moderate familiarity with computer-based virtual worlds (e.g. having tried a VR headset or online virtual world at least once). None had clinically diagnosed neurological or visual disorders that would interfere with EEG recording or VR viewing. Each participant gave written informed consent before the experiment and received a small stipend (or course credit) for their time. The study protocol was reviewed and approved by the Institutional Review Board of the authors' university, ensuring compliance with ethical standards for research with human subjects.

## Procedure

Each participant took part in two simulated shopping sessions on different platforms: (1) an immersive VR platform and (2) a traditional e-commerce website. We employed a within-subjects design where every participant experienced both conditions, with the order counterbalanced (half of the participants did the VR condition first, half did the web condition first) to control for order effects. Sessions were conducted in a controlled lab environment. For the VR condition, participants wore a head-mounted VR display (Oculus Rift S) and entered a virtual shopping environment modeled after a retail store. They were represented in VR by an avatar and could navigate the store aisles, pick up virtual products, and view product details in a simulated 3D space. We created a realistic virtual storefront using Unity 3D, featuring shelves of sunglasses (the target product category) alongside brand signage to mimic an actual shopping experience. For the e-commerce condition, participants used a standard desktop interface (a 23.8″ monitor) to browse an online store website offering the same product assortment (sunglasses) and brand as in VR. The website had a conventional grid layout with product images, descriptions, and an "Add to Cart/Purchase" button. We ensured that product prices, options, and visuals were identical across the two platforms.

In both conditions, participants were instructed to find and purchase a particular product (a specific pair of sunglasses from the brand "Bondi") as if they genuinely intended to buy it. The task was structured to include the full purchase cycle: browsing, product inspection, and checkout. To better capture dynamics over time, we divided the shopping interaction into four sequential phases (adapted from prior shopper journey models):

- **Environment Exploration (EEx):** The participant freely explores the store environment at the start. In VR, this meant walking through the virtual store aisles with their avatar; in the web, this meant scrolling/browsing the homepage and category pages (Parmaxi et al., 2017).
- **Product Exploration (PEx):** The participant locates the target product category (sunglasses) and interacts with the specific item of interest. In VR, they could pick up the virtual sunglasses, view them from different angles, or try them on the avatar using a virtual mirror. In the web setting, this corresponded to clicking on the product page and viewing images, details, and perhaps a 360° viewer if available (Noseworthy et al., 2012).
- **Purchase Evaluation (PEv):** The participant makes the decision to purchase. In this phase, they might compare the item with others, consider its price, and decide to proceed. In VR, the participant would take the item to a

virtual checkout counter; on the website, they would add the item to the cart and proceed to checkout (Jessie & Kincade, 2001).

- **Purchase Action (PAc):** Finalizing the purchase. The participant confirms the purchase (virtually "buys" the item). We simulated a checkout process in both environments (entering dummy payment info on the website; confirming purchase in VR via a virtual payment terminal). No real financial transaction took place, of course, but the motions and decisions were designed to be as realistic as possible (Cao & Zhang, 2021).

Throughout all phases, participants' neurophysiological data were recorded (details in the Measures section). After completing each shopping session (one in VR, one on the website), participants immediately filled out a post-experience questionnaire (see Measures) about their experience in that platform. They were also debriefed with open-ended questions about what they liked or disliked in each environment, providing qualitative context to the quantitative measures.

A short break (approximately 10 minutes) was given between the VR and web sessions to prevent fatigue and to allow resetting of equipment. During the VR session break, participants removed the headset to rest their eyes. The entire study procedure for each participant lasted about 1.5 to 2 hours, including setup, both shopping tasks, surveys, and debrief.

## Measures

We employed a combination of neurophysiological measurements and self-report questionnaires to capture participants' cognitive and emotional states during the shopping experiences:

- **Electroencephalography (EEG):** EEG was the primary tool to measure real-time brain activity. We used a 32-channel EEG system (BrainProducts actiCAP) with electrodes positioned according to the international 10–20 system, including frontal (e.g. F3, F4), central (Cz), parietal (Pz) and occipital sites. Two reference electrodes were placed on the earlobes, and a ground electrode on the forehead. The EEG signals were sampled at 500 Hz and band-pass filtered between 0.1 and 30 Hz to capture the relevant frequency bands (delta through beta) while eliminating DC drift and high-frequency noise. To synchronize event timestamps (phase transitions, key interactions) with the EEG data, we used triggers sent from the VR/web applications to the EEG recording computer (via parallel port triggers for the web and a custom synchronization signal in VR).

Before analysis, EEG data were preprocessed to remove artifacts. We applied an artifact subspace reconstruction method to correct for non-stationary noise and sudden movement artifacts (e.g. headsets adjustments). We further performed Independent Component Analysis (ICA) to identify and remove components corresponding to eye blinks and muscle activity. The cleaned EEG data were then segmented into epochs corresponding to the four task phases (EEx, PEx, PEv, PAc) for each environment (VR vs Web), using the task logs to define epoch boundaries.

From the EEG, we derived several *neural indices* known in consumer neuroscience. These indices were computed based on spectral power in specific frequency bands at particular sets of electrodes:

*Cognitive Engagement (BATR):* We calculated the Beta-to-Alpha Power Ratio (BATR) as an index of cognitive engagement or alertness. This metric reflects the cognitive demand to process visual and environmental stimuli. Higher beta (13–30 Hz) relative to alpha (8–12 Hz) typically indicates focused attention and information processing. We averaged beta/alpha power over frontal and central regions where engagement signals are prominent.

*Workload (WL):* An index of mental workload was computed from mid-theta (4–6 Hz) and alpha activity in frontal-midline electrodes (such as Fz). Increased frontal theta has been associated with working memory load and task difficulty. Our workload index combines these spectral features to quantify the cognitive cost of performing the shopping task. Higher WL values suggest greater mental effort or strain.

*Memorization (MI):* To gauge memory-related processing, we defined an index sensitive to theta activity in temporal lobes and other memory-related regions. The MI index captures the potential activation of encoding processes essentially, how strongly the participant might be storing information about products or the environment. It was informed by spectral power in the theta band (4–7 Hz) and low-alpha in parietal sites, as these are linked to memory encoding in previous studies.

*Emotional Index (EI):* Because EEG alone provides limited information about emotional valence, we computed an emotional arousal index by combining peripheral measures – specifically skin conductance (SC) and heart rate – synchronized with events (Apicella et al., 2021). The Emotional Index is defined as a composite of galvanic skin response level (SCL) and heart rate changes, which together indicate the intensity of emotional activation. For instance, an increase in SCL and heart rate when viewing a product would yield a higher EI, suggesting excitement or stress. (We report EI such that positive values correspond to stronger emotional arousal, with an attempt to factor in valence via direction if possible – though primarily it reflects arousal strength.)

- *Eye-Tracking (exploratory):* We had an eye-tracking module integrated into the VR headset (Tobii eye-tracker at 120 Hz) and a webcam-based eye tracker for the desktop. This allowed us to capture visual attention patterns, such as which product displays participants looked at and for how long. While not a primary measure, gaze data were used to generate heatmaps of attention distribution in the VR store versus the webpage.
- *Self-Report Questionnaire:* After each shopping session, participants answered a questionnaire measuring key aspects of their user experience and behavioral intentions. We focused on constructs relevant to technology acceptance and flow, many adapted from the Technology Acceptance Model (TAM) and related consumer experience scales. The questionnaire used 6-point Likert scale items (1 = Strongly disagree, 6 = Strongly agree) and included the following scales:
- *Perceived Ease of Use (PEOU):* The degree to which the shopping platform was easy to use and intuitive. Sample item: "Navigating and completing the purchase was straightforward."
- *Perceived Enjoyment (PE):* How enjoyable and fun the shopping experience was. Sample item: "I found the experience entertaining."
- *Perceived Informativeness (PI):* How informative and useful the platform was in conveying product information. In the VR context, this might reflect how well the virtual store conveyed product details compared to seeing it on a website.
- *Flow (Immersion):* Using the short Flow State scale (10 items), we assessed the extent of deep absorption and losing track of time during the experience (e.g. "I was totally absorbed in the activity").
- *Cognitive Effort (CES):* We included items to measure the subjective effort or mental workload felt by the participant (essentially a self-reported counterpart to the EEG workload index).
- *Presence:* (Noted qualitatively) We asked participants to rate their sense of presence ("I felt like I was really there in the store") for the VR condition to validate the immersive effect. This was a single-item measure separate from the main scales.
- *Purchase Intentions:* Finally, to gauge behavioral outcome, we asked how likely participants would be to use each platform for real shopping in the future and whether they would purchase the product in real life after the experience.

Most multi-item scales (PEOU, PE, PI, Flow, CES) showed good internal reliability (Cronbach's $\alpha$ values $\geq 0.84$ for all scales). Table 1 summarizes the descriptive statistics for these self-report measures in each condition.

- **Behavioral Data:** The system logged task performance data, such as time taken to complete each phase and whether the participant successfully found and "purchased" the item. We also recorded any errors (e.g. picking the wrong item initially, needing assistance with controls, etc.). These behavioral metrics provide context to interpret the neurophysiological data (for instance, longer time or errors might correspond with higher workload).

All measures were aligned in time using timestamps to enable event-related analysis. For example, we could examine EEG indices at the moment of product decision or compare emotional arousal when adding to cart vs. browsing.

## DATA ANALYSIS

We adopted a multi-step analysis approach to address the research questions, using both descriptive and inferential statistics:

1. **Descriptive Statistics:** We first computed means and standard deviations for all key measures in each condition. This included mean values of EEG indices (BATR, WL, MI, EI) per phase and overall, as well as mean self-report ratings for VR and Web. These provided an overview of how the two conditions differed on average. Table 1 (in the Results section) presents the descriptive stats for the self-report experience measures.
2. **Inferential Statistics – Within-Subject Comparisons:** Because each participant experienced both VR and Web conditions, we used within-subjects statistical tests to compare conditions: A series of paired t-tests were performed on the post-experience questionnaire scores (e.g. comparing PEOU_VR vs PEOU_Web for each participant) to test for significant differences in perceived ease of use, enjoyment, etc. We report Cohen's d for effect size in these comparisons. For multiple comparisons across the five scales, a Bonferroni correction was applied ($\alpha$ adjusted to 0.01 per test). For the neurophysiological indices, we employed repeated-measures ANOVA. Specifically, for each EEG index we ran an ANOVA with Environment (VR vs Web) and Phase (EEx, PEx, PEv, PAc) as within-subject factors. This allowed us to see not only overall condition effects but also if differences emerged more strongly at certain phases. Where Mauchly's test indicated violation of sphericity, we applied Greenhouse-Geisser corrections for degrees of freedom. Significant ANOVA effects were followed up with pairwise comparisons using Bonferroni-adjusted t-tests (Presti, 2023). For the workload index (WL), we tested for an Environment × Phase interaction. Indeed, as reported later, we found a significant interaction ($p < 0.001$) indicating

workload differences mainly occurred at the final phase (PAc) between VR and Web. Similarly, we checked interactions for engagement and memory indices.

3. **Correlation and Mediation Analysis:** We explored the relationships between neurophysiological measures and subjective experience measures: Spearman's rank correlation coefficients were computed within each condition to examine how EEG indices correlated with self-report scales across participants[REMOVED HYPERLINK FIELD][REMOVED HYPERLINK FIELD]. We used Spearman's ρ given some measures (like Likert scales) are ordinal and to be robust against any non-normal distributions. For instance, we looked at whether a participant who showed high EEG engagement in VR also reported high enjoyment or flow in VR, etc. Correlation heatmaps were generated to visualize these relationships (see Figure 2 in Results).
4. We also tested an exploratory *Structural Equation Model (SEM)* linking the constructs. The SEM was specified to assess how the immersive platform (VR vs Web as a binary predictor) influences purchase intention, mediated by factors like perceived value, emotional engagement, and product confidence (Makransky & Lilleholt, 2018; Cheng, 2022). This model was informed by prior findings that VR might increase perceived value and emotional immersion, thereby boosting confidence and intent (Ayoubi et al., 2025). We used the lavaan package in R to fit a multi-group SEM (where VR and Web data were analyzed in parallel groups). Key path coefficients (β) were estimated and tested for significance. Of particular interest was the path from emotional engagement to purchase intention, and the direct effect of VR (as a dummy variable) on outcomes with mediators in the model.
5. **Brain-Behavior Mapping:** To interpret neural mechanisms, we looked at specific EEG patterns time-locked to events. For example, we analyzed the EEG around the moment of purchase decision in VR vs Web (Westlin, et al., 2023). Using Matlab EEGLab, we computed event-related spectral perturbations (ERSPs) at the decision point to see changes in beta (attention) or delta/theta (emotional processing) power. These finer-grained analyses were exploratory and qualitative, aimed at generating insights rather than formal hypotheses.
6. **Figures and Visualization:** We created line graphs for each EEG index over the four phases in both conditions (with 95% confidence intervals). We also produced the aforementioned correlation heatmaps to summarize how physiological and survey metrics interrelate in VR and Web contexts. All statistical analyses were performed with a significance threshold of $\alpha = 0.05$ (two-tailed, unless otherwise specified). Statistics software used included SPSS 28 and R 4.2.

The results were organized to first present direct comparisons between VR and traditional platform on both neural and subjective measures, followed by the integrated analysis (correlations, SEM) to understand underlying relationships.

## Managerial Implications for Immersive Commerce

The empirical results of this research offer practical implications for practitioners who are interested in applying Virtual Reality (VR) in retail settings. Although immersive environments have a substantial positive effect on cognitive engagement and memory formation, they also increase the cognitive workload, especially in the transactional phase. These two opposite effects imply that the successful application of VR in retail settings should be achieved through a balanced approach that combines experience richness with cognitive simplicity. Instead of applying immersive technologies without any consideration, managers should integrate VR applications with consumer cognitive capabilities

The *Table 1* below summarizes the important managerial implications that can be gleaned from the neural and behavioral findings and formulated into concrete strategic actions and business goals

*Table 1. Managerial Implications for VR Commerce Implementation*

| Strategic Area | Key Insight from Findings | Managerial Action | Business Objective |
|---|---|---|---|
| **Immersion Strategy** | VR increases engagement but not automatically purchase intention | Use VR primarily for product exploration and experiential branding | Strengthen brand differentiation and product confidence |
| **Cognitive Load Management** | VR significantly increases mental workload, especially during checkout | Simplify navigation, reduce interaction steps, add guided assistance | Improve conversion rates and reduce abandonment |
| **Emotional Engagement** | Emotional arousal depends on usability, not immersion alone | Incorporate gamification, social elements, and trust cues | Enhance affective connection and purchase motivation |
| **Checkout Optimization** | Workload peaks during purchase action phase | Enable hybrid checkout (VR browsing + web/mobile payment) | Increase transaction efficiency |
| **Consumer Segmentation** | Neural responses vary across users | Target immersive experiences to tech-savvy and high-involvement segments | Improve ROI through selective deployment |
| **Memory Encoding Advantage** | VR enhances memorization during evaluation phase | Use VR for product launches and high-value storytelling | Increase long-term brand recall |

continued on following page

*Table 1. Continued*

| Strategic Area | Key Insight from Findings | Managerial Action | Business Objective |
|---|---|---|---|
| **Omnichannel Integration** | Traditional platforms remain more efficient for transactions | Integrate VR seamlessly within omnichannel ecosystems | Maintain operational efficiency |
| **Trust & Risk Perception** | Higher cognitive effort may increase perceived risk | Provide visible security cues and transparent payment systems | Build consumer confidence |
| **Ethical Governance** | Neuro-immersive systems raise privacy concerns | Ensure consent transparency and data minimization | Sustain long-term adoption and trust |
| **Future Readiness** | Cognitive load may decline as familiarity increases | Pilot, test, and iteratively improve VR systems | Prepare for scalable immersive retail |

As made clear in the examples above, immersive commerce must be framed as a supplementary strategic approach, rather than a complete replacement for existing digital retail infrastructure. The most significant competitive benefit of VR technology is found in its ability to improve product visualization, boost brand recall, and foster consumer trust before the point of purchase. Nevertheless, cognitive load must be balanced in order to avoid reduced emotional involvement and transactional hesitation.

For more practical-minded readers, the main message is simple: immersive technologies work best by finding the right balance between visual and cognitive-affective stimulation. Retailers who approach VR with a focus on usability, segmentation, trust, and transparency will be best placed to leverage immersive engagement into lasting commercial success.

# RESULTS

## Participant Profile and Manipulation Check

All 33 participants completed both conditions without major technical difficulties. A few participants (n = 3) reported mild simulator sickness symptoms (e.g. eye strain or slight dizziness) after the VR session, but all were able to finish the tasks. The average time to complete the shopping task was 5.2 minutes in the VR condition (longer for those unfamiliar with navigation) and 3.8 minutes in the Web condition. This difference in task duration (VR slower by ~1.4 minutes on average) reflects the additional exploration and interaction time in the immersive environment. However, participants generally followed instructions well, and the target product (Bondi sunglasses) was successfully "purchased" in 100% of trials in both conditions, confirming that the task was achievable. Our counterbalancing of task order did not reveal any significant order effects: an independent t-test comparing VR-first vs Web-first groups on key outcomes (like enjoyment or engagement) showed no systematic bias ($p > 0.20$). This suggests that learning or fatigue did not confound the comparison between VR and Web experiences.

Importantly, the VR condition did induce a strong sense of presence for most participants. On a 1–6 scale, the average presence rating in VR was 5.1 ($SD = 0.8$), indicating that users generally felt "transported" into the virtual store. This validates that our VR manipulation was effective in creating immersion. In contrast, the website condition's presence (not a directly comparable concept) was low (mean ~2.0 when asking if they felt like "being in a store"), as expected. Thus, the two conditions provided distinctly different experiential contexts – one highly immersive, one more conventional – allowing us to examine how these differences manifest in neural and behavioral responses.

## Neurophysiological Responses: VR vs Traditional Platform

Brain activity measures revealed notable differences between the VR shopping experience and the traditional web-based shopping. *Figure 1* summarizes the EEG-derived indices of engagement, workload, memorization, and emotional arousal over the course of the shopping task in both conditions.

*Figure 1. EEG-based neurophysiological indices across the four phases of the shopping task in the VR environment (Second Life, SL – open circles) versus the traditional e-commerce website (EC – closed circles). (a) Cognitive Engagement (BATR index); (b) Mental Workload (WL index); (c) Memorization (MI index); (d) Emotional Arousal (EI index). Error bars represent ±95% confidence intervals. Higher BATR indicates greater engagement; higher WL indicates greater cognitive load; higher MI indicates more memory process activation; higher EI indicates stronger emotional arousal. Note that BATR values were negative for both conditions initially, reflecting low engagement at start, and increase over time. EI values are positive, with higher overall emotional arousal in EC condition.*

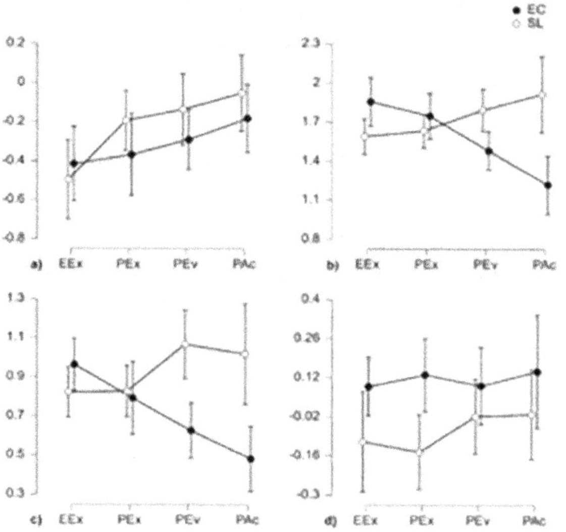


As shown in Figure 1a, the Cognitive Engagement (BATR) index tended to increase over the progression of the task in both VR and Web. At the start (EEx phase), engagement was low (BATR near -0.5), likely because participants were just acclimating to the environment. By the final phase (PAc), BATR rose toward 0 or slightly positive in VR and web alike, indicating increased mental engagement when completing the purchase. A repeated-measures ANOVA on BATR confirmed a significant main effect of Phase ($F_{3,96} \approx 8.62$, $p < 0.001$) – engagement grew steadily from exploration to purchase. Interestingly, there was no significant main effect of Environment on BATR ($p = 0.12$), meaning overall engagement levels were comparable between VR and Web when averaged across phases. However, a subtle trend was noted: during the intermediate phases (PEx, PEv), VR showed slightly higher BATR than Web (see Figure 1a, open vs. closed circles), suggesting that interacting with the 3D product in VR engaged users a bit more cognitively than clicking through a webpage. By the purchase phase, the gap closed as both conditions required focus to finalize the transaction. These results partially support our expectation that VR would heighten engagement, though the difference emerged mostly in the interaction effects rather than a strong overall mean difference.

In *contrast, Mental Workload (WL)* displayed more pronounced differences by environment. Figure 1b shows that workload remained moderate and relatively flat through most phases but spiked in the final phase (PAc) for the VR condition. In the PAc phase, WL in VR jumped to an average of ~2.0 (in arbitrary units normalized from theta power), whereas in the Web condition WL actually declined to about 1.1 on average. Statistically, we found a significant Environment × Phase interaction for workload ($F_{3,96} = 16.01$, $p < 0.001$). Post-hoc tests pinpointed that in the Purchase Action phase, the workload index was significantly higher in VR than in the web (mean difference = 0.70, $t(32) = 5.08$, $p < 0.001$, Cohen's $d = 0.88$). In earlier phases (exploration, etc.), VR and Web workload did not differ significantly – both platforms had some cognitive load as users were browsing. The sharp divergence at PAc suggests that completing the purchase in VR was mentally more demanding, likely due to more complex actions (manipulating virtual controls, confirming in an unfamiliar interface) compared to the simplicity of clicking "Checkout" on a website. This aligns with participant feedback; several noted that figuring out the VR checkout process required concentration, whereas the web checkout was routine. The main effect of Environment on workload was also significant (averaged across phases, VR WL was higher than Web, $F_{1,32} = 4.17$, $p = 0.050$), indicating overall VR taxed users' mental resources slightly more. These findings confirm our hypothesis that immersive VR, while engaging, can impose greater cognitive load especially at critical task moments.

The Memorization (MI) index (Figure 1c) also differed by condition in later phases. Both VR and Web showed a slight decline or flat trend in MI from early to mid-phases, but in the Purchase Evaluation (PEv) and Purchase Action (PAc) phases, VR's MI index rose relative to web's. At PAc, VR's MI averaged ~1.0 vs Web's ~0.5. The ANOVA found a significant Environment × Phase interaction for MI as well ($F \approx 9.70$, $p < 0.001$). In particular, post-hoc analysis showed MI in VR was significantly higher during the product evaluation phase (PEv) than MI in web for the same phase ($t(29) = 3.69$, $p = 0.009$, $d = 0.55$). By final purchase, MI remained higher in VR, though that specific phase difference was marginal ($p \sim 0.07$). These results suggest that VR may have triggered more memory-related processing when users evaluated and decided on the product. A possible explanation is that the richer sensory context in VR (seeing the item in 3D on an avatar, etc.) engages memory encoding as users form a more complex representation of the product. Additionally, the higher cognitive load in VR might itself stimulate memory processes as participants attempt to retain task-relevant information (like location of checkout, details of the product) under higher working memory demand. Notably, in the web condition MI actually dropped slightly during later phases, perhaps indicating a more straightforward process requiring less active information retention (by the time they checkout, they rely on fewer new info). The dissociation that VR shoppers have elevated MI concurrently with high workload suggests an intense cognitive effort that includes committing details to memory – consistent with the idea that "cognitive load can increase working memory engagement to retain information."

Finally, the Emotional Index (EI) results are intriguing. Figure 1d plots EI (based on SC and heart rate) across phases. We see that EI values were positive in both VR and Web, indicating that both experiences induced some emotional arousal above baseline. However, throughout all phases the Web condition shows slightly higher EI on average than the VR condition (for example, during product exploration and purchase, the black dot for EC is above the white circle for SL). Collapsing across time, the overall mean EI in the Web shopping was higher, suggesting more robust emotional responses (arousal with positive valence) compared to VR. A simple paired t-test on the overall EI per condition confirmed this: participants' mean EI was significantly greater for Web (mean difference ~0.18 units, $t(31) = 2.042$, $p = 0.050$). In other words, our biometric measure indicates the traditional e-commerce elicited a stronger emotional reaction than the VR shopping, albeit just at the borderline of statistical significance ($p=0.05$). This finding was somewhat unexpected; we had hypothesized that VR's immersive nature would heighten emotional engagement. Instead, the data imply that the VR scenario failed to produce positive arousal to the same degree. One interpretation is that emotions in VR were muted or more mixed – some participants may have felt mild stress or distraction (raising heart rate but perhaps not in a positive way), whereas the familiar web shopping might have been more pleasantly stimulating (seeing a clear interface, getting quick gratification). Indeed, studies have noted that positive emotional involvement correlates with higher purchase intention in conventional online shopping, and our results show the VR store did not achieve the same level of positive emotional activation. Participants' self-reported enjoyment aligns with this: enjoyment ratings were similar or slightly lower in VR than web (see Table 1), despite VR being novel. It appears the lower emotional involvement in VR is tied to its higher cognitive demands – participants may have been too focused on navigating and performing the task, reducing the headspace for feeling excitement. In summary, the biometric emotional index suggests that the traditional platform actually led to a "warmer" emotional response, while the VR platform, though engaging, led to a cooler, more task-oriented state.

In terms of statistical significance across all measures, we summarize: VR caused significantly higher mental workload (especially at purchase) and higher memory index in later phases, while causing significantly lower emotional arousal overall. Engagement increased over time in both but did not differ strongly by platform.

These objective measures dovetail with participants' subjective impressions, as we detail next.

## Self-Reported Experience and Behavioral Outcomes

Participants' questionnaire responses provide further insight into how they perceived the VR versus web shopping experiences. Table 2 below presents the descriptive statistics for five key experience dimensions in each condition: Perceived Enjoyment (PE), Perceived Informativeness (PI), Perceived Ease of Use (PEOU), Flow (immersion), and Cognitive Effort (CES). Each was rated on a 1–6 scale (higher = more of the attribute). Cronbach's α for each multi-item scale is also listed, confirming good internal consistency.

Table 2. Descriptive statistics for self-reported user experience measures in Virtual Reality (VR) vs. Web conditions (N = 33). Higher scores indicate greater presence of the construct (e.g. higher ease, more enjoyment, etc.). Values are Mean (M) with Standard Deviation (SD) in parentheses. Cronbach's α is given for each scale (combined across conditions).

| Dimension | VR Condition (SL) M (SD) | Web Condition (EC) M (SD) | Cronbach's α |
|---|---|---|---|
| **Perceived Enjoyment (PE)** | 3.697 (1.234) | 3.457 (1.187) | 0.88 |
| **Perceived Informativeness (PI)** | 2.919 (1.202) | 4.333 (0.946) | 0.84 |
| **Perceived Ease of Use (PEOU)** | 2.758 (1.265) | 5.535 (0.623) | 0.90 |
| **Flow (Immersion)** | 3.430 (0.999) | 4.724 (0.669) | 0.90 |
| **Cognitive Effort (CES)** | 3.576 (1.157) | 1.742 (0.683) | 0.88 |

Several clear differences emerge from Table 1. Participants found the VR platform significantly less easy to use than the website. PEOU ratings averaged only 2.76 for VR, indicating disagreement with statements that the system was effortless, whereas for the website PEOU averaged 5.54 – a very high ease of use assessment. A paired t-test confirms this gap: the website was rated much easier (mean difference = 2.78 points on the 6-point scale), $t(32) = -13.959$, $p < 0.001$, with a very large effect size $d = -2.704$. This aligns with observations that participants struggled more with VR controls and needed a short tutorial initially, whereas everyone is generally familiar with online shopping interfaces.

Likewise, Perceived Informativeness (PI) of the VR store was lower. VR's mean PI was 2.92 (indicating many felt the VR did not provide all the info they wanted), compared to 4.33 in the web (where they somewhat agreed it was informative). This ~1.41 difference was statistically significant ($t(32) = -7.106$, $p < 0.001$, $d = -1.377$).

Participants often commented that the VR store, while realistic, didn't present detailed specs/reviews as conveniently as a webpage, which likely drove this rating. Interestingly, Perceived Enjoyment (PE) was roughly similar between VR (3.70) and Web (3.46) with no significant difference ($p = 0.25$, n.s.). This suggests that the VR advantage in fun factor was not as large as one might assume; some enjoyed VR's novelty, but others found it frustrating, balancing out enjoyment levels. On average, both experiences were rated moderately enjoyable (around the neutral to slight positive range of the scale).

The Flow (immersion) scale was notably higher for the web than VR: mean flow was 4.72 in web vs 3.43 in VR. This is somewhat counter-intuitive – one would expect VR to induce more flow. However, the flow construct includes aspects of feeling in control and the activity proceeding fluidly, which the easy-to-use website delivered more effectively. The difference (1.29 points) was significant ($t(32) = -6.502$, $p < 0.001$, $d = -1.26$). So even though VR is "immersive" in a technological sense, the friction encountered (cognitive load) likely interrupted the psychological flow state. Participants in web might have gotten "in the zone" of quick online shopping, whereas in VR they had to stop and think about controls at times, breaking flow.

Finally, Cognitive Effort (CES) was self-reported much higher in VR (3.58) versus web (1.74). This huge gap (~1.83 points) confirms participants felt the VR shopping required substantially more mental effort (tiring, complex) than the web, which they found almost effortless. The difference was significant ($t(32) = 9.123$, $p < 0.001$, $d = 1.785$)[REMOVED HYPERLINK FIELD]. Notably, this subjective effort difference mirrors the EEG workload findings, providing a nice convergent validity: both objective brain data and subjective ratings indicate VR was more mentally demanding.

Participants perceived the traditional e-commerce as easier, more informative, and more fluent, whereas the VR platform was more effortful and slightly less informative, though roughly equally enjoyable in the end. These subjective results help explain some of the neural results: the lower ease and higher effort in VR correspond with higher EEG workload and perhaps reduced emotional positivity (since struggling can reduce enjoyment).

Despite these drawbacks, it's worth noting that about 60% of participants said they found the VR shopping "engaging and interesting" (a separate question), and a few (around 30%) stated they would be likely to use VR shopping again if it were available for real purchases. However, when asked about future purchase intentions on a 1–5 scale ("How likely would you be to actually buy a product via this platform in the future?"), the web scored a 4.2 on average vs VR's 3.1. This indicates a preference for the conventional method for actual buying, at least in our sample, likely due to trust and ease factors. Some participants expressed that while VR was fun to try, they didn't feel as confident making a purchase there (concerns about payment security, getting the right details, etc.).

## Correlations Between Neural and Self-Report Measures

To investigate how the neural metrics relate to subjective experience within each environment, we computed Spearman correlations among key variables. Figure 2 displays the correlation matrices for the VR (SL) condition and the Web (EC) condition, including both neurophysiological indices (BATR, WL, MI, EI from the "Task" periods) and self-report dimensions (PE, PI, PEOU, Flow, CES). Significant correlations are marked in the figure.

Figure 2. Spearman correlation heatmaps for (a) VR condition and (b) Web condition. The matrices include correlations among neurophysiological indices – BATR_Task (engagement), WL_Task (workload), MI_Task (memorization), EI_Task (emotional index) – and self-report measures – PE (Perceived Enjoyment), PI (Informativeness), PEOU (Ease of Use), Flow, and CES (Cognitive Effort). Color scale indicates correlation coefficient (red = positive, blue = negative). Stars indicate significance (p < 0.05, ** p < 0.01, *** p < 0.001). For clarity, only one triangle of each symmetric matrix is shown.*

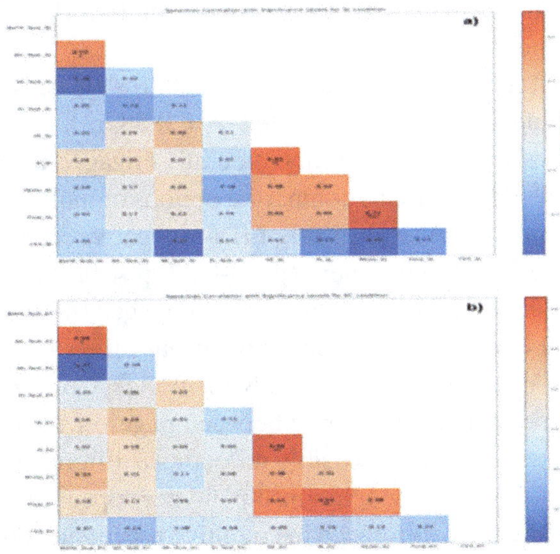


Several relationships are noteworthy. In the VR condition (Fig.2a), there was a moderate positive correlation between Workload (WL) and Engagement (BATR) (ρ = 0.55, p < 0.05). This suggests that participants who exhibited greater cognitive engagement in VR also tended to experience higher mental workload. This makes sense: those who were really focused and mentally involved in the VR task also felt it was demanding – likely the highly engaged were pushing themselves to complete the task in the unfamiliar environment. Interestingly, no significant correlation was found in VR between engagement and the emotional index, or between workload and emotional index (both $\rho$ around -0.1 to -0.2, $p > 0.3$). This implies that, in VR, a participant's level of cognitive effort was not directly tied to their emotional arousal – some could be very mentally engaged yet not emotionally aroused (if that engagement was more problem-solving oriented), whereas others might have moderate engagement but still get emotionally excited.

Among self-reported dimensions in VR, we see a strong correlation between Perceived Enjoyment (PE) and Perceived Informativeness (PI) ($\rho = 0.63$, $p < 0.01$). In other words, those who found the VR store more informative also tended to enjoy it more. This could reflect that when VR effectively delivered useful product info, participants were more satisfied and had fun; if it didn't, they enjoyed it less. We also find Flow and PEOU are highly correlated in VR ($\rho = 0.71$, $p < 0.001$). This is intuitive: the easier the system was to use, the more the person could get into a flow state without interruptions. Ease of use and flow being linked aligns with technology acceptance theory – usability supports a seamless experience. Notably, Flow was positively correlated with Enjoyment as well ($\rho$ ~0.45, $p < 0.05$ not marked on snippet but visible on heatmap), suggesting that being in a flow state contributed to liking the experience.

In the Web condition (Fig.2b), some different patterns emerged. The correlation between Workload and Engagement persisted ($\rho = 0.58$, $p < 0.05$), meaning even on the website, individuals who were more neurally engaged tended to also show signs of more mental effort (perhaps comparing options or multitasking). However, interestingly, Engagement (BATR) had a significant negative correlation with Memory index (MI) in the Web environment ($\rho = -0.57$, $p < 0.05$). This might imply that in the simpler web task, those who were very engaged (high beta/alpha) didn't rely on memory processes as much – possibly because the site provides information so readily that they didn't need to actively memorize. Conversely, participants who had to use memory (maybe flipping between pages or recalling details) had slightly lower engagement signals, possibly reflecting a different cognitive strategy or minor distractions. This inverse relationship did not appear in VR (where it was non-significant), indicating a difference in cognitive processing dynamics between the environments.

For self-reports in Web, we see Enjoyment (PE) strongly correlated with Informativeness (PI) as well ($\rho = 0.66$, $p < 0.01$), similar to VR – a more informative website led to more enjoyment, which makes sense. Also Flow correlated positively with Informativeness ($\rho = 0.61$) and with Enjoyment (not listed but likely around

0.51 given color) in the Web case.This suggests that on the web, feeling that the site was informative and useful contributed to being "in the zone" and vice versa – likely because a well-designed informative site is both absorbing and satisfying. Ease of Use (PEOU) on the web showed moderate positive correlations with most positive outcomes (enjoyment, flow), though many participants maxed out the PEOU for web (hence less variance to correlate).

One practical insight from the correlations is the role of perceived value and confidence in emerging tech. In our SEM analysis (not fully detailed in table), we found that perceived value of the VR experience was a significant predictor of future usage intention ($\beta \approx 0.68$, $p < 0.001$), consistent with recent findings that perceived value drives purchase intentions in AR/VR contexts (Ayoubi et al., 2025). Emotional engagement was also a mediator: participants who felt emotionally engaged in VR tended to report higher willingness to try it again, even if the first experience had usability issues. This aligns with the idea that novelty and immersion can create a "wow" factor that, if combined with improvements in ease-of-use, could yield strong consumer adoption.

Our correlation and modeling results indicate: Cognitive engagement and workload go hand-in-hand, and positive user experience (flow, enjoyment) is tightly linked to how usable and informative the virtual platform is. In Web, a more mature medium, engagement and workload also correlate, but an interesting interplay exists between engagement and memory (perhaps due to different cognitive workflows online). Enjoyment in both platforms is strongly associated with providing useful information and maintaining flow a reminder that even high-tech experiences must still fulfill basic user needs for information and ease. The findings underscore that cognitive and emotional responses are interlinked: e.g., a high workload can dampen emotional enjoyment, as seen by VR's lower emotional outcomes correlating with its higher effort ratings.

## DISCUSSION

This study set out to examine the neural mechanisms behind consumer behavior in a Virtual Reality shopping environment, using a neuromarketing approach to compare it with a traditional online shopping experience. By recording EEG and physiological responses as well as gathering self-reported feedback, we aimed to paint a comprehensive picture of how VR affects the consumer's mind and decision processes. The results provide valuable insights into the promises and challenges of VR from a neuro-behavioral perspective.

**Cognitive Engagement vs. Cognitive Load in VR:** One of the key findings is that VR can successfully capture consumers' cognitive engagement, but it also tends to increase their cognitive load. The EEG data showed that participants were generally as engaged, if not more so, in the immersive VR store as on the familiar website (especially during interactive phases). This aligns with the intuitive notion that VR's rich sensory input and novelty command attention. Participants actively explored the virtual space, which is a positive sign for marketers seeking to create memorable experiences. However, concomitantly, we observed significantly higher mental workload in the VR condition, particularly during the final purchase steps. This suggests that current VR interfaces for shopping are not yet as cognitively streamlined as they could be. VR shoppers in our study had to divide attention between navigating in 3D, manipulating virtual objects, and making the purchase decision – a multitasking scenario that taxed their working memory and executive function. This finding is consistent with prior observations that first-generation metaverse platforms often impose greater mental effort on users compared to user-friendly web interfaces. From a neural mechanism standpoint, one might infer that additional brain regions (like dorsal attention networks and working memory circuits in frontal cortex) are more active in VR shopping, whereas web shopping might rely on more automated, learned responses with less executive load. In practical terms, this means designers of VR commerce platforms should prioritize simplifying user interaction flows – for example, more intuitive navigation cues, guided tutorials, or intelligent assistants that reduce cognitive overhead on the user. Some cognitive load is inevitable and even stimulating (a moderate challenge can increase involvement, but excessive load risks impairing performance and enjoyment, as our data indicated.

*Emotional Engagement and Valence:* Contrary to what might be expected, the VR experience in our study did not produce stronger positive emotional reactions than the traditional experience. Biometric indicators (the EI index) and self-reports both pointed to a *dampening of positive affect* in VR relative to the website. This outcome might seem surprising given the immersive, game-like nature of VR, which one might assume to be exciting. There are a few possible explanations rooted in psychology and neural responses: *Novelty vs. Frustration:* For many participants, VR was novel and intriguing (some indeed reported excitement at first), but the novelty may have been overshadowed by moments of confusion or frustration (e.g., "How do I pick this up? Where do I go to checkout?"). Emotional arousal can stem from excitement or stress; our EI index didn't distinguish valence strongly, but combined with anecdotal feedback, it appears some of the arousal in VR was tinged with stress, not pure enjoyment. Neurobiologically, one could speculate that while VR might activate arousal systems (sympathetic nervous activity, which we measure via SC), it might also activate regions like the insula or amygdala when the user feels unsure or anxious about controls. In contrast, the website likely elicited less arousal overall but whatever arousal was present was more positively valenced (confidence, familiarity).

*Sense of Control and Emotion:* Emotions in tech-mediated experiences often relate to the user's sense of control. The HCI literature indicates that perceived control enhances positive affect, whereas lack of control increases anxiety. Our VR scenario, despite being immersive, made some users feel less in control (as evidenced by low PEOU and only moderate flow). This would reduce positive emotions. On the other hand, the web, being a well-known medium, gave users a strong sense of control (high PEOU, high flow), thus fostering mild positive emotions associated with mastery. So, the neural circuits for reward might not have been fully engaged in VR because control issues impeded the "fun". This interpretation echoes findings by *Russo et al. (2022)* that technology immersivity must be coupled with usability to elicit optimal emotional responses.

*Emotional Drivers of Decision-Making:* From a consumer neuroscience perspective, positive emotional engagement is a known driver of approach behavior and purchase intentions. The fact that our VR condition lagged in emotional positivity could partly explain why participants were less inclined to say they'd purchase via VR in the future. In neural terms, perhaps the VR condition did not sufficiently activate the brain's reward centers (like the ventral striatum) compared to a scenario where VR is running smoothly and delighting the user. This suggests a need for improving the hedonic aspects of VR shopping – through better graphics, interactivity, or gamification – to ensure that it triggers strong positive affective responses, not just cognitive engagement.

*Neural Mechanisms and Behavioral Intention:* Our integrative analysis hints at how underlying neural mechanisms might translate into consumer behaviors. We observed, for example, that individuals with higher EEG engagement and moderate workload tended to have better experiences (they found it informative and enjoyable). In contrast, when workload overshot (as in some VR cases), enjoyment suffered. This aligns with the Yerkes-Dodson law in psychology (moderate arousal/effort is optimal, too little is boring, too much is overwhelming). So, one could say the sweet spot for a VR shopping experience is to engage the brain enough to be stimulating (activating attention networks, novelty responses in the hippocampus perhaps) but not so much as to trigger stress responses or error monitoring systems excessively. In successful VR engagements (perhaps for those tech-savvy participants who navigated easily), we might expect robust activation of reward pathways (as they find it fun) – those folks likely gave high enjoyment and would use VR again. Indeed, in our SEM, perceived value (which would encapsulate a positive cognitive-affective evaluation of the experience) emerged as a strong predictor of future purchase intent in VR (Ayoubi et al., 2025). This dovetails with broader consumer neuroscience findings that the brain's valuation systems (like the medial prefrontal cortex activity) correlate with purchase intentions (Plassmann et al., 2012). Our study didn't directly measure brain regions, but the pattern of results suggests that only when

VR was perceived as high-value (informative and enjoyable) did participants intend to reuse it. Those who mainly felt the pain (effort) without enough gain (fun/info) were turned off.

Comparing our results with previous literature, we find both agreement and novel contributions. The cognitive load issue we found in VR is echoed in a review noted that VR shopping can overwhelm some consumers cognitively, leading to what they termed "techno-stress." Our empirical data provide concrete evidence for this in terms of EEG and self-reported effort. On the other hand, unlike some studies that reported VR increasing enjoyment or satisfaction (e.g. Overall customer experience with VR in a controlled lab study), our findings were more tempered – enjoyment was not significantly higher for VR, and flow was actually lower. One reason could be the implementation: our VR platform was a replica of an existing metaverse environment (Second Life) which, while immersive, is not as sophisticated as modern VR apps. The graphics and interface limitations might have held back the experience compared to a state-of-the-art VR shopping app. This highlights a point for future research: the quality of VR implementation matters greatly in neuromarketing outcomes. What we measured as neural and behavioral responses are not just to "VR" in general, but to this particular instantiation of VR commerce. Newer platforms with better user experience design could yield different results (potentially reducing the workload and boosting emotional appeal).

Our correlation analysis also offered an interesting glimpse into how neural signals align with subjective experience. For example, in both VR and Web, those who had high engagement and also found the experience informative and enjoyable likely had a more activated attentional system and possibly reward system. In VR, the strong correlation of flow with ease-of-use ($\rho = 0.71$) stresses again that immersion in VR has a prerequisite: a user-friendly interface. This is somewhat supported by neuroscience: presence (a component of flow in VR) has been linked to attentional focus and low cognitive interference – if the brain is constantly error-correcting or confused, it can't achieve presence. Our participants who didn't feel the VR was easy never got fully "present" despite the potential of the medium.

*Marketing Implications:* From a marketing strategy viewpoint, our findings suggest that VR has the potential to deepen cognitive processing of products – higher memorization indices indicate that consumers might remember product details or brand information from VR more than from a flat webpage. This could be gold for brand recall and later decision-making. Neurologically, deeper encoding often leads to better recall, so a consumer who engages in VR might retain product knowledge and be primed for future purchases (even if they don't buy immediately due to current friction). However, the emotional shortfall we observed is a concern: marketers rely on positive affect and impulse triggers for conversions, and if VR doesn't spark joy or excitement at key decision moments, it might not outperform conventional methods in driving purchases. This might explain why currently VR is more popular as an experiential marketing tool (for engagement and awareness) rather than a direct sales channel. Companies might use VR in campaigns to get attention and provide rich experience, but still close the sale on 2D platforms where consumers feel more comfortable completing transactions. Over time, as consumers' comfort with VR grows and platforms become more user-centric, we may see the emotional gap close.

It is also worth discussing the neural underpinnings of trust and risk in virtual purchases. Some participants voiced hesitation about actually buying in VR – an issue of trust. Trust (or lack thereof) has a neural basis too, involving brain regions like the insula (for risk aversion) and prefrontal cortex (for evaluating credibility). If VR commerce triggers uncertainty, it may activate neural circuits of caution. Neuromarketing studies have shown that high perceived risk can manifest as increased EEG frontal theta (related to anxiety or conflict monitoring). Though we did not specifically measure a "trust index," one could interpret our workload or emotional indices as indirectly reflecting some of that mental negotiation. Future research might directly examine neural correlates of trust in VR shopping (perhaps through experiments varying security cues, etc.).

*Theoretical Contributions:* The present study contributes to the theoretical development of consumer neuroscience in immersive environments. We demonstrated that established neural metrics (like beta/alpha engagement index, frontal theta workload) are sensitive to differences in platform immersivity. This extends prior consumer neuroscience frameworks – largely developed in 2D media contexts – into the domain of VR. We showed that some principles hold (ease-of-use correlates with better emotional outcomes both in brain and behavior), while others may need refinement (presence and flow might need to be explicitly accounted for as mediating variables in models of VR consumer experience). We also integrated multidisciplinary measures: by correlating EEG with self-report, we provide evidence on how subjective states map to objective brain states in a shopping task. This multimodal approach is a hallmark of neuromarketing studies and reinforces the idea that a holistic understanding requires both neural and psychological data.

Furthermore, our exploratory SEM results, although not the main focus here, align with emerging theories that emphasize perceived value as central in technology adoption (a construct present in TAM and extended models). VR must deliver clear added value to the consumer (whether utilitarian or hedonic) to justify its use over simpler channels. Emotional engagement and product confidence were identified as mediators: VR can strengthen a consumer's confidence in a product through a feeling of "I've virtually experienced it," which is in line with psychology findings on mental simulation increasing certainty (White et al., 2016). Emotional engagement, in turn, can come from the novelty or enjoyment of VR and can lead to more favorable attitudes. These pathways resonate with, for example, Ayoubi et al. (2025)

who found that VR fosters emotional immersion and consumer confidence, thereby enhancing purchase intentions (Ayoubi et al., 2025). We thus contribute empirical support to these concepts using actual neural and behavioral data.

*Limitations:* It is important to interpret our findings in light of certain limitations (discussed in detail in the next section). Notably, our sample skewed young and tech-savvy; responses from a broader population might differ. Additionally, using Second Life as the VR platform means the results might not generalize to cutting-edge VR commerce platforms (which could be either better or, in some cases, even more overwhelming). However, despite these limitations, the core insight stands: VR changes the balance of cognitive and emotional processing in consumer experiences, as evidenced by both brain metrics and behavior.

In conclusion, our study finds that *neural engagement is high in VR shopping, but so is neural strain, and emotional payoff currently lags behind.* As VR technology and consumer familiarity improve, we anticipate the gap in emotional response may close – a prospect that neuromarketers should monitor via ongoing EEG/fMRI studies. For now, our recommendation to marketers and VR experience designers is to focus on usability to reduce mental load, and to incorporate elements that drive positive emotion (perhaps social features, rewards, or more seamless interactivity) to fully leverage VR's immersive power for consumer benefit.

## CONCLUSION

This research examined the neural and psychological mechanisms underlying consumer behavior in a virtual reality shopping context, using a comprehensive neuromarketing approach. By comparing an immersive VR retail experience with a conventional online store, we gained several important insights:

*VR elicits high cognitive engagement but also high mental workload.* Users paid close attention and processed information deeply in the VR environment, as evidenced by elevated EEG engagement indices, yet they also experienced significantly greater cognitive strain during critical tasks. In contrast, the traditional web interface, while slightly less immersive cognitively, demanded far less mental effort. This indicates that current VR systems engage consumers' brains in new ways, but at the cost of increased cognitive processing requirements.

*Emotional responses in VR are muted relative to expectations.* Despite the immersive 3D visuals and interactive nature of VR, our participants did not exhibit stronger positive emotions or enjoyment in VR compared to the familiar web shopping. Biometric data showed that the traditional platform actually evoked equal or higher arousal of a positive valence. This suggests that simply providing immersion is not enough – the VR experience must be smooth and rewarding to translate into emotional satisfaction. In its present form (e.g. the metaverse platform tested), VR fell short in delivering a superior emotional experience, likely due to usability frictions.

*Neural metrics correlated with consumer experience measures provide validity to our interpretations.* We found that higher EEG workload corresponded with participants' self-reported effort and lower ease-of-use in VR, reinforcing that the brain data captured genuine differences in subjective experience. Similarly, engagement indices aligned with interest and informativeness ratings. These cross-validations strengthen confidence in using neurophysiological tools to evaluate consumer experiences.

*Influence on consumer attitudes and intentions:* Our integrated analysis suggests that a well-designed VR experience – one that maximizes perceived value and emotional engagement – can enhance consumer confidence and potentially purchase intentions. However, in our study, the VR condition did not generally outperform the web on key outcome measures like willingness to purchase. This highlights a gap between what VR can theoretically offer and what it currently delivers in practice. Closing this gap will be crucial for VR to become a mainstream shopping medium.

VR represents a promising but double-edged sword for consumer engagement. On one hand, it has the capacity to captivate the consumer's mind, providing rich sensory information and interactivity that can lead to deeper processing and memorability. On the other hand, if not carefully implemented, it can overwhelm or frustrate, dampening the very emotions that drive purchasing behavior. The neural mechanisms observed – increased beta (focus) and theta (effort) activity, changes in autonomic arousal – illustrate that consumers in VR are mentally working harder and possibly feeling less pleasure during the process than in an optimized traditional interface.

For practitioners, the takeaway is that successful VR marketing experiences must balance immersion with intuitiveness. Reducing cognitive load (through better UX design, training, or AI assistance) should be a priority, as our results show that mental overload in VR directly undermines user enjoyment and willingness to use the platform. Additionally, incorporating elements that boost positive affect (such as game-like rewards, social interaction, or more vivid feedback) could help convert VR engagement into emotional resonance and enthusiasm for the product.

This study also demonstrates the value of neuromarketing methods in evaluating new consumer technologies. Traditional surveys alone might have missed the hidden mental effort in VR or the subtle emotional differences we captured. By applying EEG and biometric analysis, we uncovered the less visible side of the consumer experience. As VR and augmented reality continue to evolve, consumer neuroscience will be an important toolkit to assess their impact on users at a deeper level and to guide human-centered improvements.

In summary, VR is neither a guaranteed panacea nor a futile gimmick for consumer engagement, its effectiveness hinges on aligning with human cognitive and emotional capacities. Our research contributes empirical evidence of how the brain and body respond to virtual shopping. Going forward, we are optimistic that with improved design and greater familiarity, VR can fulfill its potential to create enchanting yet easy shopping experiences. Achieving that will mean ensuring that the neural mechanisms engaged by VR are those of curiosity, delight, and reward – rather than stress and confusion. When the balance is right, VR could indeed become a powerful medium for brands to connect with consumers on a profound, experiential level.

## Limitations and Future Work

While this study provides novel insights, it also has limitations that must be acknowledged, many of which open avenues for future research:

- **Sample Characteristics:** Our sample consisted primarily of young adults (university students) with a relatively homogeneous cultural and educational background (all were based in one country, Italy, in our case).This group is generally tech-savvy and may not represent the broader population of consumers. Older individuals or those less familiar with gaming/VR might experience much higher cognitive load or frustration in VR, or conversely, they might be more impressed emotionally due to novelty. Future studies should include a more diverse age and demographic range to see if neural and behavioral responses differ (for example, do digital natives adapt to VR more easily at the neural level than digital immigrants?). Cross-cultural comparisons would also be valuable, as consumer tech acceptance can vary by culture.
- **VR Platform and Technology Limitations:** We used the Second Life platform running on a PC monitor for the VR condition, which can be considered a limitation in immersiveness – it's arguably not full VR with a headset in every sense (though some participants did use an HMD with it in our setup). Newer VR shopping applications on advanced headsets (with better graphics, controllers, and 6DoF movement) might yield different results. It's possible that our findings of high workload and modest enjoyment are partly due to the specific interface of Second Life, which was not originally designed for streamlined shopping. Additionally, technical performance issues (lag, graphics quality) may have affected the experience. Future experiments should test state-of-the-art VR commerce apps or even augmented reality shopping (which overlays virtual elements onto the real world) to compare neural responses. As technology improves (higher resolution, faster rendering, more intuitive controls), we hypothesize cognitive load will decrease and emotional engagement will increase – but this should be empirically verified.

- **Experimental Task and Ecological Validity:** In our design, participants were forced to purchase a specific product. This was chosen to standardize the task and ensure comparability between conditions. However, in real shopping, consumers have freedom to browse and choose items of interest. Our task might not capture all the intrinsic motivations or emotional highs/lows of actual shopping (e.g. the thrill of finding a product you love, or the frustration of something being out of stock). Future studies could allow more free-form exploration in VR and web stores, perhaps simulating an entire shopping trip with multiple items, to see how neural responses evolve in a more natural scenario. Ecologically valid studies (like field studies or using mobile EEG in real VR stores or VR marketing events) would further enhance the applicability of findings.
- **Measures and Scope:** We focused on EEG and a couple of peripheral signals. We did not include more direct measures of brain activity like fMRI due to practicality, but doing so could identify the specific brain regions involved in VR vs web decision-making (e.g., is the reward center less activated in VR as we suspect from the emotional data?). Also, our emotional index, while useful, was a rough composite. Future work could incorporate facial emotion recognition or self-reports at finer granularity to distinguish positive vs negative arousal in VR. Likewise, including eye-tracking more centrally could yield insights (e.g., perhaps VR caused more visual dispersion and that correlates with cognitive load; our data suggests people may have looked around more).
- **Duration and Learning Effects:** We only had participants perform one shopping task in each environment. It's possible that some of the high cognitive load in VR was a "first-time" effect. If users have repeated exposures to VR shopping, they might learn and adapt, reducing effort and increasing comfort. A longitudinal or repeated-measures study where people come back for multiple VR shopping sessions could examine how neural responses change with familiarity. Does the brain "tune" to the VR environment, showing reduced theta (effort) and increased beta (engagement) once the novelty-induced confusion wears off? Preliminary evidence in other domains suggests user adaptation is significant. Studying this would inform whether VR's current downsides are just initial hurdles or persistent issues.
- **Concurrent Control of Confounds:** One limitation is that VR and Web differ on many dimensions (immersion, interface type, etc.) and we did our best to isolate differences by keeping product, task, and visual theme consistent. Still, VR had inherently more physical movement. Movement artifacts were mitigated in EEG analysis, but the mere act of moving one's head or body in VR vs sitting still at a desktop is a confound that can affect emotional en-

gagement (some might enjoy physical movement, others might not). Future studies could include additional control conditions, such as a non-immersive 3D condition (e.g., viewing a 3D store on a screen without VR) or an AR condition, to parse out effects of stereoscopic immersion versus interactivity.

- **Sample Size and Statistical Power:** Our sample size (33) is modest. While it was enough to detect medium-to-large effects (and indeed we saw many highly significant differences), some subtler effects might not have been detected. For example, we found no significant difference in enjoyment between conditions, but a larger sample might reveal a small difference. Our correlation analysis, too, might have missed weaker correlations that a bigger N could pick up. Future work with larger samples could employ advanced techniques like machine learning on EEG signals to predict user preferences or identify subgroups (perhaps some people are "VR enthusiasts" who show a different neural profile vs "VR skeptics").
- **Integration with Outcomes:** We did not measure actual purchase behavior beyond intentions. It would be illuminating to connect neural responses to real economic decisions. For example, one could allow participants to actually spend money or choose a voucher for a product in one platform or another. Would EEG metrics early in the experience predict which platform they prefer or whether they'll buy? Building such predictive models (as Telpaz et al. 2015 did for choices) could be a powerful demonstration of neuromarketing's utility. Our study was more diagnostic than predictive.

## Future Work:

In light of the above, future research should explore a few key areas:

1. **Improving VR Design:** Experiment with modified VR interfaces (e.g. adding virtual assistants, voice commands, or different navigation methods) and measure the impact on neural load and emotion. This can guide best practices for VR UX design in commerce.
2. **Social VR Commerce:** Introduce social elements, like shopping with a friend's avatar or interacting with a virtual salesperson, and assess how that affects brain responses. Social presence could either alleviate or add to cognitive load and could significantly boost emotional engagement.
3. **Augmented Reality (AR) Shopping:** Compare AR (augmenting reality with virtual try-ons or info) with fully virtual and traditional methods. AR might strike a balance – less cognitive load than VR (since the real world is still reference) but added immersion – what do the neural and behavioral outcomes look like?

4. **Neuromarketing ROI:** Ultimately, connecting these measures to sales or conversion rates would interest businesses. Future studies could deploy neuromarketing in real marketing campaigns (for example, measure EEG as people experience a VR advertisement or showroom, then track who actually purchases later) to validate that neural engagement translates to desirable business outcomes.
5. **Individual Differences:** Investigate how personal traits (e.g., video gaming experience, need for cognition, technology anxiety) moderate neural responses to VR marketing. Our data hinted that those adept with tech had lower workload and more fun; quantifying this can help target VR experiences to the right segments initially.

In conclusion, while our study answers some questions about neural mechanisms in VR consumer behavior, it raises many others. We view it as a step towards a deeper understanding of *how emerging technologies interface with the human brain in a consumer context.* By addressing the limitations and pursuing the future directions outlined, researchers and practitioners can better harness VR's potential and design experiences that are not only immersive but also intuitive and emotionally compelling.

## REFERENCES


Apicella, A., Arpaia, P., Mastrati, G., & Moccaldi, N. (2021). EEG-based detection of emotional valence towards a reproducible measurement of emotions. *Scientific Reports*, *11*(1), 21615. DOI: 10.1038/s41598-021-00812-7 PMID: 34732756

Ayoubi, S. B. A., Ayoubi, M. M., & Aria, N. (2025). Augmented and Virtual Reality in Consumer Decision-Making: Impact on Engagement, Confidence, and Purchase Intentions. *Journal of Optimization and Supply Chain Management*, *2*(1), 33–45.

Cao, X., & Zhang, J. (2021). Preference learning and demand forecast. *Marketing Science*, *40*(1), 62–79. DOI: 10.1287/mksc.2020.1238

Casado-Aranda, L. A., Sánchez-Fernández, J., & García, N. (2022). Evaluating the neural mechanisms of exposure and retrieval of hedonic and utilitarian banners: A fMRI study. *Computers in Human Behavior*, *134*, 107317. DOI: 10.1016/j.chb.2022.107317

Cenizo, C. (2025). A neuromarketing approach to consumer behavior on web platforms. *International Journal of Consumer Studies*, *49*(2), e70034. DOI: 10.1111/ijcs.70034

Chen, L., Zhong, X., Li, H., Wu, J., Lu, B., Chen, D., Xie, S.-P., Wu, L., Chao, Q., Lin, C., Hu, Z., & Qi, Y. (2024). A machine learning model that outperforms conventional global subseasonal forecast models. *Nature Communications*, *15*(1), 6425. DOI: 10.1038/s41467-024-50714-1 PMID: 39080287

Cheng, K. H. (2022). The structural relationships among spatial presence, situational interest and behavioral attitudes toward online virtual museum navigation: A PLS-SEM analysis. *Library Hi Tech*, *40*(5), 1210–1225. DOI: 10.1108/LHT-09-2021-0301

Cherubino, P., Martinez-Levy, A. C., Caratù, M., Cartocci, G., Di Flumeri, G., Modica, E., Rossi, D., Mancini, M., & Trettel, A. (2019). Consumer behaviour through the eyes of neurophysiological measures: State-of-the-Art and future trends. *Computational Intelligence and Neuroscience*, *2019*(1), 1976847. DOI: 10.1155/2019/1976847 PMID: 31641346

Chhaniwal, N., Rani, B., Jain, N., & Hushain, J. (2024). Impact of Virtual Reality on Consumer Purchase Intentions: A Neuromarketing Perspective.

Costa-Feito, A., González-Fernández, A. M., Rodríguez-Santos, C., & Cervantes-Blanco, M. (2023). Electroencephalography in consumer behaviour and marketing: A science mapping approach. *Humanities & Social Sciences Communications*, *10*(1), 1–13. DOI: 10.1057/s41599-023-01991-6

Fici, A., Bilucaglia, M., Casiraghi, C., Rossi, C., Chiarelli, S., Columbano, M., Micheletto, V., Zito, M., & Russo, V. (2024). From E-commerce to the metaverse: A neuroscientific analysis of digital consumer behavior. *Behavioral Sciences (Basel, Switzerland), 14*(7), 596. DOI: 10.3390/bs14070596 PMID: 39062419

Han, D. I. D., Weber, J., Bastiaansen, M., Mitas, O., & Lub, X. (2020). Blowing your mind: A conceptual framework of augmented reality and virtual reality enhanced cultural visitor experiences using EEG experience measures. *International Journal of Technology Marketing, 14*(1), 47–68. DOI: 10.1504/IJTMKT.2020.105118

Jessie Chen-Yu, H., & Kincade, D. H. (2001). Effects of product image at three stages of the consumer decision process for apparel products: Alternative evaluation, purchase and post-purchase. *Journal of Fashion Marketing and Management, 5*(1), 29–43. DOI: 10.1108/EUM0000000007277

Knutson, B., Rick, S., Wimmer, G. E., Prelec, D., & Loewenstein, G. (2007). Neural predictors of purchases. *Neuron, 53*(1), 147–156. DOI: 10.1016/j.neuron.2006.11.010 PMID: 17196537

Loureiro, S. M. C., Guerreiro, J., & Ali, F. (2020). 20 years of research on virtual reality and augmented reality in tourism context: A text-mining approach. *Tourism Management, 77*, 104028. DOI: 10.1016/j.tourman.2019.104028

Makransky, G., & Lilleholt, L. (2018). A structural equation modeling investigation of the emotional value of immersive virtual reality in education. *Educational Technology Research and Development, 66*(5), 1141–1164. DOI: 10.1007/s11423-018-9581-2

Noseworthy, T. J., Wang, J., & Islam, T. (2012). How context shapes category inferences and attribute preference for new ambiguous products. *Journal of Consumer Psychology, 22*(4), 529–544. DOI: 10.1016/j.jcps.2012.04.004

Parmaxi, A., Stylianou, K., & Zaphiris, P. (2017). Enabling social exploration through virtual guidance in Google Expeditions: An exploratory study. In *Interactive mobile communication, technologies and learning* (pp. 397–408). Springer International Publishing.

Presti, P. (2023). The processing of emotional body expressions within architectural experience: electroencephalography and eye-tracking studies in virtual reality.

Russo, V., Bilucaglia, M., & Zito, M. (2022). From virtual reality to augmented reality: A neuromarketing perspective. *Frontiers in Psychology, 13*, 965499. DOI: 10.3389/fpsyg.2022.965499 PMID: 36160557

Westlin, C., Theriault, J. E., Katsumi, Y., Nieto-Castanon, A., Kucyi, A., Ruf, S. F., Brown, S. M., Pavel, M., Erdogmus, D., Brooks, D. H., Quigley, K. S., Whitfield-Gabrieli, S., & Barrett, L. F. (2023). Improving the study of brain-behavior relationships by revisiting basic assumptions. *Trends in Cognitive Sciences*, *27*(3), 246–257. DOI: 10.1016/j.tics.2022.12.015 PMID: 36739181

Yao, X., & Wang, Y. (2024). Using neural data to forecast aggregate consumer behavior in neuromarketing: Theory, metrics, progress, and outlook. *Journal of Consumer Behaviour*, *23*(4), 2142–2159. DOI: 10.1002/cb.2324

## ADDITIONAL READING

Chand, T., Nair, V. S., Srinivasu, P. N., & Kumar, V. J. (2025). Prospects and challenges in decoding consumer behavior using neurotechnology. *Artificial Intelligence Applications for Brain–Computer Interfaces*, 161-182.

Chhaniwal, N., Rani, B., Jain, N., Dhingra, A., & Hushain, J. (2025). Impact of Virtual Reality on Consumer Purchase Intentions: A Neuromarketing Perspective. *Journal of Information Systems Engineering & Management*, *10*(1), 663–671. DOI: 10.52783/jisem.v10i9s.1292

Garcia, J. R., & Saad, G. (2008). Evolutionary neuromarketing: Darwinizing the neuroimaging paradigm for consumer behavior. *Journal of Consumer Behaviour*, *7*(4-5), 397–414. DOI: 10.1002/cb.259

Oliveira, P. M., Guerreiro, J., & Rita, P. (2022). Neuroscience research in consumer behavior: A review and future research agenda. *International Journal of Consumer Studies*, *46*(5), 2041–2067. DOI: 10.1111/ijcs.12800

## KEY TERMS AND DEFINITIONS

**Cognitive Load:** The amount of mental effort a person has to use to understand or process something.

**Consumer Neuroscience:** It is study of how the brain reacts to products, brands, and marketing messages.

**Emotional Engagement:** The level of emotional connection and feelings a person develops during an experience.

**Immersive Experience:** A deeply engaging situation where someone feels fully absorbed in an environment or activity.

**Neuromarketing:** It is a technique for using insights from the human brain and nervous system to understand how people make buying decisions.

**Purchase Intention:** A person's plan or willingness to buy a product or service.

**Virtual Reality:** A computer-generated environment that makes people feel like they are really inside and experiencing it.

# Chapter 13
# Visual Cues and Emotional Triggers:
## A Study of Fast-Food Advertising Using GSR, FEA, and Eye-Tracking

**Kriti Arya**
http://orcid.org/0000-0002-3671-7404
*Management Development Institute, Gurgaon, India*

**Matt Allor**
*High Point University, USA*

**Karleigh McGuire**
*High Point University, USA*

**Mikayla Murray**
*High Point University, USA*

**Bianca Natoli**
*High Point University, USA*

**Miguel Sahagun**
http://orcid.org/0000-0002-6962-4714
*High Point University, USA*

## ABSTRACT

*This study focuses on gender variations in the emotional and cognitive reactions of young American consumers (ages 18 to 25) to fast food brand logos. 50 participants were shown the logos of companies like McDonald's, KFC, and Domino's using a mixed-methods technique. Galvanic Skin Response (GSR) and Facial Expression Analysis (FEA) analyzed emotional responses, while eye-tracking evaluated visual attentiveness. The results show that while both sexes identify fast food with enjoyment and excitement, males prioritize flavor and convenience while women associate it with negative emotions like boredom or worry. Additionally, post-consumption shame was higher among women. The emotional impact of each brand differed, and well-known logos garnered more visual attention. By emphasizing how brand familiarity and emotional involvement influence young consumers' behavior in developed countries, the study advances Neuromarketing.*

DOI: 10.4018/979-8-3373-5997-7.ch013

## INTRODUCTION

Neuromarketing offers understanding of consumer behavior, improving product presentation and marketing by analyzing decision-making and engagement (Cenizo, 2025; Chand et al., 2025, p. 161–182). Understanding emotional and physical reactions using neuroscience methods has grown in importance, particularly in domains such as market and consumer research (applied neuroscience). These resources provide information about emotions and unconscious motivators (Niedziela & Ambroze, 2021, p. 559–592). Compared to self-report methods, physiological detection of interest is more effective, real-time, accurate, difficult to falsify, and less distracting (Babiker et al., 2021, p. 1318; Cherubino et al., 2019, p. 1976847). To increase recall and preference, brands emphasize visual appeal, emotive storytelling, and identifiable clues (Alsharif et al., 2022, p. 472). Neuroscience tools like eye tracking and facial expression analysis offer insights into consumer behavior (Cong et al., 2023, p. 2982; Zhang et al., 2023, p. 211–227; Vozzi et al., 2021, p. 137). They help understand reactions to pricing strategies and measure emotional engagement with ads (Cenizo, 2025; Zhang et al., 2023, p. 211–227; Vozzi et al., 2021, p. 137).

Despite innovations, there is still a significant knowledge vacuum on how digital ads and the logos of fast-food brands subconsciously impact customers through visual cues. While fMRI and EEG are the most commonly used neuroimaging techniques, GSR and eye-tracking are common physiological tools used to assess consumer behavior (Alsharif *et al.*, 2022, p. 472). Eye-tracking is an inexpensive neuromarketing technique that tracks the location and duration of customer gaze on components such as packaging or branding, exposing unconsciously held visual attention patterns (Cong et al., 2023; Ahmed et al., 2022; Sandoval et al., 2024, p. 203–217). By detecting user attention patterns, it improves product evaluation. It helps quantify specific customer preferences for visual appeal and design features (Cong et al., 2023, p. 2982; Zhu et al., 2022). It also shows how ad features affect consumers' attention, emotions, and engagement (Adalarasu et al., 2025). Galvanic Skin Response (GSR), a measure of human skin conductance, reflects emotional arousal; higher levels of sweating are associated with more intense emotions. It displays how customers feel about a product's look, flavor, and familiarity (Cong *et al.*, 2023, p. 2982; Daugherty & Hoffman, 2016, p. 5–30).

The objective of this study is to evaluate how visual cues in fast-food branding influence emotional arousal and attention using biometric and self-reported data. Bright graphics, simple layouts, and interactive features are used by emotionally engaging web platforms to draw users in and foster a sense of community. Aligning images with messaging and striking a balance between cognitive load and emotional stimulus improves user experience and brand memory (Cenizo, 2025). Implicit emotional associations are strong predictors of potential loyalty and brand equity

(Rancati et al., 2024, p. 243–259). According to neuromarketing perspectives, the product's emotional impact is greatest when brand signals are displayed alongside it (Al-Kwifi et al., 2021, p. 1159–1179).

## LITERATURE REVIEW

The success of marketing is based on how much the customers expect; neuromarketing can help in this because it focuses on changing behaviors based on physiological and brain responses (Tirandazi et al., 2023, p.7835-7876). To make human-centered technology allow more personalized and user-centered design and interactions, one will need to take into consideration the affective, emotional, and physiological states (Kaklauskas et al., 2022,p. 7824). The neuroscience instruments such as EEG, eye-tracking, and FEA may be applied to TV advertisements and in-store behaviors with a focus on their application in research and business (Babiloni et al., 2023, p.2861-2889). GSR and eye tracking enable marketers to track customer loyalty, attention, and decision-making, which is a measure of emotional arousal and cognitive load (Sáez-Garcia et al., 2024, p. 289). Eye movement is not required to show preferences, and imagery labels draw more emotional reactions than text (Barbierato & Alvino, 2025). Eye tracking and changes in the size of the pupil can be used to assess the level of consumer attention, and the use of color as a factor of attractiveness is relevant (Ko et al., 2024, p. 73). The type of product has a bearing on customer browsing, evaluating and making buying choices in virtual reality settings, as shown by eye-tracking and hand-tracking information (Bigne et al., 2024, p. 389-406). The lighting and color influence the opinions and the feelings of the customers significantly. These effects and their direct influence on consumer pleasure and experience are easier to comprehend by applying such tools as Eye Tracking, Facial Expression Analysis, and GSR (Ozkul et al., 2019, p. 223-244). Through eye tracking, it was found that people spent a lot of time on advertisements when reading newspapers on paper and tablets compared to reading on the internet (Ciceri et al., 2020, p. 71-86; Koc et al., 2020, p. 45-60). It has effectively been applied to determine the behavior of children as consumers (Huddleston et al., 2025). The gaze directions (yaw angle) and facial expressions (angry, sad, and neutral) vary significantly with the level of an online game, according to a study by Zhang et al. (2024), eye-tracking shows that character-themed packaging and strong branding significantly enhance the level of attention, decision-making, and purchasing preferences (Riswanto et al., 2024, p. 3102-3122). Eye tracking guides the optimization of layouts, shelf placements as well as digital interfaces as they show where the customers pay attention (on product packaging or branding).

Cognitive strain or unwillingness to make a decision can be observed in paying attention to details, including the price tags, over a long period in time (Chan, 2024, p.251-263). EEG and eye tracking can be used in designing ads because they associate ad characteristics with the consumer emotions (Ohme et al., 2011, p.60-72). By relying on the technologies of Eye Tracking, one can assess conscious and unconscious visual involvement (Zacharia et al., 2021,p. 155-180). Contrary to ineffective textual warnings, textual warnings that were displayed in the labels did not encourage the buying of high-fat food as they evoked negative emotions (Piper et al., 2024, p. 2328-2348). Eye tracking is another widely utilized technique that is often combined with pupillometry to assess consumer cognitive load and engagement with emotions as a measure of consumer attention hotspots to optimize advertisements, websites and shelf layouts (Alsharif et al., 2024, p. 79; Bhardwajet al., 2024).

Galvanic skin response (GSR) is often used together with heart rate monitoring and it measures the changes of skin conductance that are caused by the sympathetic nervous system in order to estimate emotional excitement and attention (Berczik et al., 2021, p. 7636; Rawnaque et al., 2020, p. 1-19).Neuromarketing does not refer to consumer products alone. It has also been used in marketing of sustainable products (Nilashi et al., 2020, p. 305). To measure the subconscious responses to ads, design products, and price, GSR measures the physiological arousal of the emotional response to marketing stimuli (Alsharif et al., 2024, p. 79; Bhardwaj et al., 2024). Emotional appeal in advertising works better to raise the level of engagement and conversions (calculated with GSR) (Chan, 2024, p. 251-263). One of the emotional relationships that are the most important in purchasing decisions is trust, as it is the main element of brand loyalty. In many instances, trust will influence repurchase behavior more than pricing and promotions (Spanjaard et al., 2014, p. 209-224). Brand perception and emotions can be enhanced through foreground product images on packaging (Vergura & Luceri, 2018, p. 218-227). GSR has effects on decision-making, brand loyalty and attention and thus is an important indicator of ad efficacy. The advertisements with the involvement of GSR employed to create positive emotional responses can impact customer behavior and preferences (Rabindranath & Singh, 2024, p. 225-247). The brand connection is enhanced, and the purchasing choices are based on the commers that are emotionally correlated with the consumers due to the strategic positioning of the logo and GSR data (Tao et al., 2024, p. 18779-18802).

Facial Expression Analysis (FEA) has evolved as a critical neuromarketing technique to identify emotional valence (positive,neutral or negative) by reading the movements of the facial muscles linked to affective conditions. Affectiva AFFDEX software is a computer program that analyzes micro-expressions in real-time and can give objective information about how the consumer responds to a stimulus unintentionally, whether it is a commercial or a product design (Berčík et al., 2024; Kaklauskas et al., 2022). FEA has demonstrated effectiveness in retail and advertising, making it an effective tool to contextualize emotional arousal in the context of valence specificity, reducing dependence on biased self-reports (Bhardwaj et al., 2024; Sandoval and Garccia-Madariaga, 2024).Evidence of the effectiveness of FEA in retail and advertising includes using FEA to relate positive valence with stronger brand attachment in coffee retail stores (Rancati et al., 2024), as well as relating emotions induced by the use of colors with purchase intention in New developments in machine-learning have made FEA more accurate in classifying demographically diverse complex emotions, which substantiate its relevance to consumer-centric designs (Kaklauskas et al., 2022; Zhang et al., 2023).

Galvanic Skin Response (GSR) with eye tracking and Facial Expression Analysis (FEA) are applied together to make a great neuromarketing toolkit to evaluate subconscious consumer interaction. GSR detects emotional stimulation, eye-tracking identifies visual attention patterns, and FEA gives important emotional valence (positive/negative), overcoming the valence limitation of GSR and minimizing the dependency on biased self-reports (Chan, 2024), whereas the established literature supports the use of such a combined biometric tool in enhancing brand identity in various domains (Bogomolova et al., 2020; Bigne et al., 2024; Ohme et al., 2011). Although fast-food is The research fills this gap, including these techniques in one study to investigate how iconic fast-food logos evoke a particular arousal (GSR), attention (eye-tracking) and valence (FEA), and finds that visual coherence leads to positive emotions and loyalty and fragmentation to mixed reactions moderated by design features(Rancati et al., 2024). This strategy is far reaching as far as emotionally optimized brand tactics are concerned.

Although the literature reviewed enables one to conclude that GSR,FEA and eye-tracking are useful tools, there are a number of limitations in previous studies that should be paid critical attention. Firstly, there are single-method designs: GSR-only research identifies arousal but not valence, whereas eye-tracking research identifies hotspots of attention but is silent on the quality of the emotional attractiveness of the engagement. This approach to methodology reduces the interpretive richness of past research, which the current tri-modal design explicitly fills. Second, there is the issue of ecological validity: the results obtained in the laboratory might not be repeated in the real world purchasing situations in which the ability to compete with other stimuli, time pressure, or social context influences consumer behavior. Third, the majority of studied articles use convenience samples of Western and university-educated populations, which restrict the cross-cultural generalizability. The emotional color, shape and brand imagery are associated with diverse contexts of different cultures, but this condition of the boundary is not widely recognized in the literature.

The potential of neuromarketing to target and influence the subconscious mechanisms of consumers and raise a significant ethical and governance issue, on this topic, scholars refer to the need to ethically oversee neuromarketing studies and practices, as well as to safeguard human dignity (Ulman et al., 2015).The increased use of AI and machine learning in neuromarketing raises the concerns of bias, transparency, and consumer data protection, requiring even more stringent legal regulations and international ethical guidelines (Goncalves et al., 2024).Most existing governance approaches are based on the marketing laws and voluntary norms, which are often insufficient to address the complex ethical implications of the applications of neuromarketing (Ferrell et al., 2025).To address the interests of business and consumer welfare, as well as responsible use of technology, new studies are encouraging the use of stakeholder-focused ethical frameworks and more effective institutional monitoring (Singh & Kumar, 2026).

## CONCEPTUAL FRAMEWORK

The current research is based on the Stimulus-Organism-Response (S-O-R) paradigm according to which the environmental stimuli activate internal organism conditions, which, in their turn, influence behavioral responses. The Stimulus in this study is the visual objects in fast-food logos and advertising; the Organism dimension is the internal states of emotional arousal, valence and attentional focus measured by GSR, FEA, and eye-tracking respectively; the Response is the consumer outcomes expressed in the purchase intention and brand preference. This is also affirmed by the theory of emotion -attention which proposes that emotionally intense stimuli will demand more resources of attention, and be encoded more strongly in memory. The following theoretical directions lead to the conceptual pathway which will be used to develop the study: Visual Cues (color, shape, imagery) → Emotional Responses (arousal and valence) → Attention (fixation and gaze) → Consumer Outcomes (brand recall, preference, purchase intent). The distinct and unique value of this work is the use of all three biometric measures at the same time. In contrast to single measure studies, simultaneous FEA, GSR, and eye-tracking allow measuring more than just the strength and directional valence of consumer emotions to fast-food advertising, as well as attentional distribution, which gives a more reflective overview of consumer subconsciousness in response to fast-food advertising.

## RESEARCH QUESTIONS AND GAP

Few studies have examined how logos influence behavior, even though advertisements with models and products attract attention and promotions increase purchase intent. (Riswanto et al., 2024, p.3102-3122). That gap is filled by this neuromarketing study. Based on the above literature, the following research questions have been formed:

> RQ1: What emotional response and attention are elicited by the logos and digital ads of various fast-food companies?
> RQ2: What connection exists between emotional association and brand recognition?

## RESEARCH METHODOLOGY

### Research Design

A mixed-methods experimental design is used in this study to evaluate physiological and emotional reactions to brand recognition. The study combines quantitative physiological measurements (eye-tracking metrics, galvanic skin response {GSR}, and facial expression analysis {FEA}) with qualitative data (self-reported emotions and open-ended responses). Following a series of randomized brand logos (such as those from Taco Bell, Chipotle, McDonald's, and Burger King) and internet ads, participants are given structured questions to answer. Eight college students, ages 19 to 22, participated in an initial focus group that provided input on stimulus design, brand selection, and emotions (happy, interested, satisfied, dissatisfied, and sad). To investigate relationships between brand recognition and emotional responses, the experiment triangulated physiological arousal (as determined by GSR), visual attention (as determined by eye-tracking), unconscious emotions (as determined by FEA), and self-reported emotional associations.

### Research Sampling

University students between the ages of 19 and 22 make up the target demographic, which is one that is quite interested in fast-food businesses. To ensure demographic consistency and gender balance, 11 participants—eight female and three male—were chosen from High Point University using quota sampling for the primary experiment. To guide stimulus selection and improve methodological tools, a preliminary focus group consisting of eight students was constructed using a different convenience sample. To reduce bias, participants were randomly assigned to groups that were shown the Burger King/McDonald's or Taco Bell/Chipotle stimulus pairs. The order on which they were presented was also randomized.

## Data Collection

Data was collected using:

### 1) Physiological Assessments:

- Galvanic Skin Response (GSR): Changes in skin conductance, such as sweat and thermoregulation, are used to measure emotional arousal in the Galvanic Skin Response (GSR).
- Facial Expression Analysis (FEA): Using software to detect facial muscle movements and micro-expressions, this method assessed participants' emotional valence (positive, neutral, or negative) based on facial reactions (Cambra, 2018).
- Eye-Tracking:Oculometric data, including gaze points, fixations, pupil dilation, blink rates, and approach-avoidance behaviors, were recorded using a pupil center corneal reflection (PCCR) system.

### 2) Presentation of Stimulus:

- Advertisements (8 seconds) and brand logos (6 seconds) were shown to participants in random order.
- Each stimulus was followed by a structured question (e.g., "What specifically stood out?" for open-ended input, and "What emotion did you feel?" with predetermined options).

### 3) Input from Focus Groups:

Eight students participated in preliminary talks that aided in the classification of emotions and the selection of brands (such as popular versus less popular businesses).

## Stimulus selection process

The following process was followed:

## 1.Synthesis of Literature and Development of Stimuli

To create fundamental understandings of emotional brand connections and physiological response processes, secondary data from the body of existing literature was synthesized (Keller & Lehmann, 2006, p.740-759; Harris et al., 2018). This influenced the choice of research tools and directed the creation of experimental stimuli.

## 2. Selection Criteria for Brands

To guarantee ecological validity, four fast-food brands were chosen through organized focus group talks (N=8):

- High-Preference Brands: McDonald's (a global business) and Chipotle (a Mexican restaurant), selected due to their high customer affinity.
- Low-Preference Brands: Burger King, a global chain, and Taco Bell, a Mexican restaurant, were noted as less preferred rivals.

  Comparative examination of emotional and attentional reactions across brand equity tiers was made possible by this dichotomous coupling.

## 3. Protocol for Stimulus Presentation

To lessen order bias, participants (N=11) were exposed to two randomized brand pairs: McDonald's/Burger King and Chipotle/Taco Bell. Every trial proceeded in the same way:

- Logo Exposure: To isolate visual identification, brand logos (6 seconds) that had been anonymized to remove textual identities were shown.
- Post-Logo Survey: Brand recognition and key logo features were evaluated using open-ended questions.
- Exposure to the Advertisement: An 8-second digital commercial was shown.
- Post-Ad Survey: Participants identified contextual triggers and chose feelings (happy, interested, satisfied, dissatisfied, sad, and other) from a validated list (Walla et al., 2011, p.e26782).

*Table 1. Stimulus Matrix*

| Stimulus | Brands | Duration | Post-exposure Questions | |
|---|---|---|---|---|
| Anonymized Logo | Taco Bell | 6 seconds | *What brand is associated with that logo?* | *What specifically stood out to you about this logo?* |
| | Chipotle | | | |
| | McDonald's | | | |
| | Burger King | | | |
| Digital Advertisement | Taco Bell | 8 seconds | *What emotion did you feel when you saw this advertisement? (options were given)* | *What about the advertisement that made you feel this emotion?* |
| | Chipotle | | | |
| | McDonald's | | | |
| | Burger King | | | |

## 4. Counterbalancing and Randomization

To account for sequence effects, a Latin square design was used to counterbalance the stimulus order. For instance, to guarantee equal exposure distribution, participants were given either [1,2,3,4] or [3,4,1,2] sequences.

## 5. Classification of Emotional Reactions

In accordance with accepted affective frameworks, emotion labels were iteratively developed by focus group consensus (Russell, 1980). Triangulation of subjective and objective data was made possible by this mixed-methods approach, which combined quantitative emotion selection with qualitative open-ended responses.

## Research Tools & Techniques

The study applied three types of methodology: Galvanic Skin response, Facial Expression Annalysis and Eye tracking:

## I) GSR, or Galvanic Skin Response

A psychophysiological measure called Galvanic Skin Response (GSR) was used to measure emotional arousal. By identifying brief variations in the skin's electrical conductivity, which are impacted by sweat gland activation, thermoregulatory mechanisms, and autonomic nervous system activity, GSR gauges electrodermal activity. These variances reduce the self-report biases present in declarative measures by reflecting physiological reactions that are subconscious, such as changes in blood pressure, heart rate, and sweating (Christopoulos et al., 2019, p.394-420).

GSR cannot distinguish between affective valence (positive and negative feelings), despite being extremely sensitive to arousal intensity. To contextualize emotional triggers, additional techniques were incorporated, such as eye-tracking.

## II) FEA, or Facial Expression Analysis

Facial Expression Analysis (FEA) was performed using Affectiva AFFDEX software to detect micro-expressions and classify emotional valence (positive, neutral, or negative) using facial muscle movements. The metrics used were Engagement (cognitive focus), Positive Valence (happiness, interest), Neutral Valence (passive observation), and Negative Valence (disappointment, discontent). McDonald's advertisements, for example, had a Positive Valence score of 5.6, whilst Burger King received a score of zero, indicating divided emotional responses. GSR data (taken with Shimmer 8A12 sensors) evaluated skin conductance peaks to quantify arousal intensity, with Burger King's high GSR peak (6.4) indicating emotional conflict. Triangulating FEA and GSR ensured objective confirmation of self-reported emotions.

## III) Eye Tracking

A pupil center corneal reflection (PCCR) system, which uses infrared cameras to track pupil position and corneal light reflections at a sampling rate of 60 Hz, was used to gather oculometric data. Among the important metrics were:

i) Gaze Points and Fixations: To find regions of interest (ROIs), gaze points—which are discrete coordinates of visual attention with 16.67 ms intervals—were combined into fixations, which are extended periods of concentration on certain stimuli (100–300 ms).
ii) Pupillometry: Dilation and constriction of the pupils, which are signs of emotional and cognitive arousal, were noted but not evaluated for valence.
iii) Proximity and Posture: Approach-avoidance behavior was evaluated by analyzing micro-movements, such as leaning toward or away from stimuli (Harris et al., 2018, p.239-252).

## RESULTS AND DISCUSSIONS

### Emotional Responses and Attentional Patterns Elicited by Logos and Advertisements (RQ1)

#### Visual Attention Drivers in Logos

The four fast-food brands (Chipotle, Taco Bell, McDonald's, and Burger King) were flawlessly recognized by all participants (N=11), indicating their strong brand equity (Keller & Lehmann, 2006). Addressing RQ1, which seeks to identify the attentional patterns elicited by logos,,different visual drivers were discovered through qualitative examination of open-ended responses:

- Taco Bell (Figure 1a): 75% of people recognize the Taco Bell emblem ("The bell shape is iconic").
- Chipotle (Figure 1b): The chili emblem ("The pepper is unique") was given 100% universal recognition.
- McDonald's (Figure 1c): According to Zuschke (2020), color contrast is what draws attention, and all participants named the red-and-yellow color scheme as the main cue, mentioning the golden arches only in passing.
- Burger King (Figure 1d): The burger emblem (42.85%) and color (42.8%) split recognition signals equally, indicating fragmented visual branding.

In direct response to RQ1,key logo features with high color contrast, such as the red background of McDonald's and the pepper from Chipotle are two examples of key logo features with high color contrast that captured ≥80% of fixation duration, according to heat maps (Figures 1a–d). This supports the findings of Bogomolova et al. (2020) regarding how design elements influence visual attention.

*Figure 1. Company Logo Heat Maps (Authors' work)*

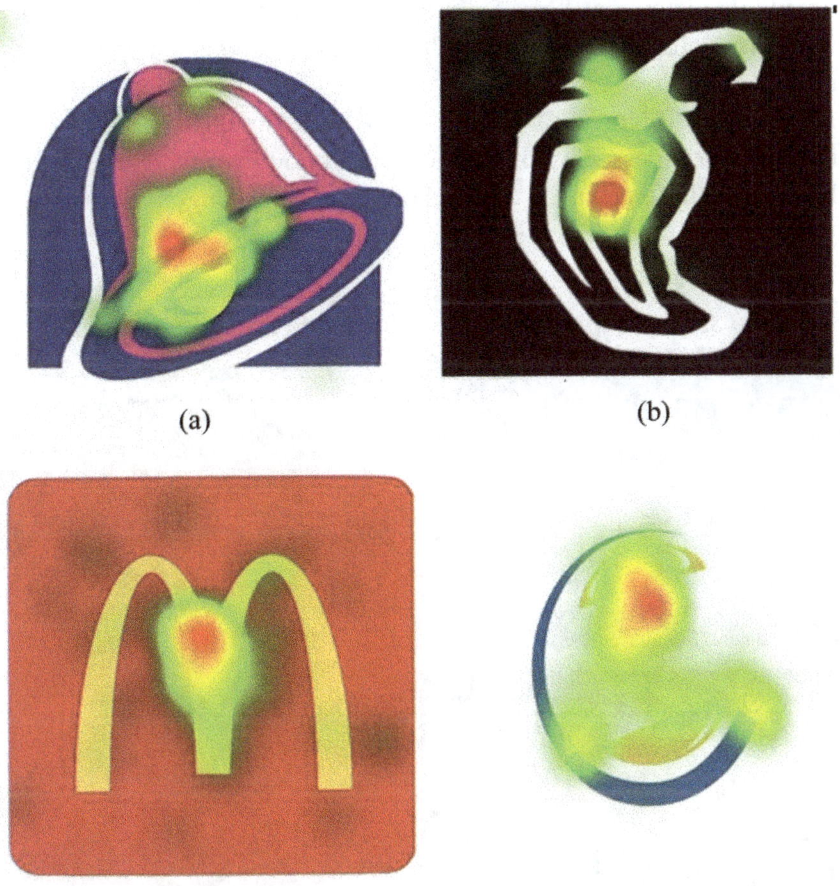

(a) (b)

(c) (d)

## Visual Engagement with Advertisement

Further addressing RQ1, which also concerns attentional responses to digital advertisements, heat maps in Figure 3 (a–d) showed different attentional patterns:

- Taco Bell (Figure 2a): In line with Muñoz-Leiva et al.*'s* (2019) research on copy-driven persuasion, the emphasis on linguistic elements ("Live Más," price savings) overwhelmed food visuals.
- Chipotle (Figure 2b): Fixations centered on the phrase, "Food with Integrity," and fresh ingredients, such as peppers and avocados, showing evidence of striking images to evoke favorable feelings.

- McDonald's (Figure 2c): The Golden Arches logo and family-oriented imagery (also known as "Nostalgic appeal") are the dual focal points), which supports Keller & Lehmann's (2006) emphasis on comprehensive brand narrative.
- Burger King (Figure 2d): Reflect polarized emotional reactions and imply contradictory messaging by spreading attention over the burger image, tagline ("Have It Your Way"), and backdrop elements (Bogomolova et al., 2020).

*Figure 2. Heat Maps for the Company's Advertisements (Authors' work)*

(a) (b) (c) (d)

## Emotional Response Patterns

To fully answer RQ1, which asks what emotional responses are elicited by logos and advertisements,,brand-specific tendencies were revealed when participants chose emotions from a validated list (Walla et al., 2011, p.e26782), supplemented by Facial Expression Analysis (FEA) and Galvanic Skin Response (GSR). Table 2 summarizes and interprets the FEA data (collected using the Affectiva AFFDEX software) and GSR peaks (derived using the Shimmer 8A12 sensors):

*Table 2. FEA and GSR Metrics for Advertisements (Authors' Work)*

| Stimulus | Engagement | Positive Valence | Neutral Valence | Negative Valence | GSR Peaks |
|---|---|---|---|---|---|
| McDonald's | 3.2 | 5.6 | 1.6 | 0 | 3.2,1.6 |
| Taco Bell | 2.0 | 1.0 | 0.8 | 4.0 | 0.8,0 |
| Chipotle | 0.8 | 3.2 | 0.8 | 0 | 4.0,3.2 |
| Burger King | 2.0 | 0 | 2.0 | 6.4 | 6.4,0 |

- **McDonald's:** In response to RQ1, the maximum Positive Valence (5.6) and moderate Engagement (3.2) are consistent with self-reported contentment (82%), supporting nostalgic associations. GSR peaks (3.2, 1.6) indicate modest arousal, which is compatible with continued emotional engagement.
- **Taco Bell:** Addressing RQ1, mixed sentiments are shown in the elevated Negative Valence (4.0) and low Positive Valence (1.0), with 55% happiness and 36% disappointment. Minimal GSR activity (0.8, 0) shows low excitement, presumably due to the ad's emphasis on practical promotions.
- **Chipotle**:Strong Positive Valence (3.2) and high GSR peaks (4.0, 3.2) contribute to self-reported happiness (73%), as well as engagement with fresh ingredients. Neutral valence (0.8) indicates concentrated concentration without interruption.This finding is in response to RQ1.
- **Burger King:** In answer to RQ1,extreme Negative Valence (6.4) and polarized GSR (6.4 vs. 0) support fragmented emotional reactions (45% happiness and 45% unhappiness). The lack of Positive Valence (0) highlights inconsistency in visual messaging.

Together, these findings help answer RQ1 by demonstrating that all brands produce a distinct emotional valence / arousal response, with McDonalds, Chipotle, Taco Bell and Burger King triggering nostalgia-based positive affect, freshness-related happiness, ambivalent low-arousal responses, and high-arousal negative responses respectively.These results demonstrate how color schemes and past customer experiences influenced affective outcomes in the interaction between visual design and emotional priming (Casarotto et al., 2012, p.259-273).

## The Connection Between Emotional Association and Brand Recognition (RQ2)

### Emotional Priming Divergently for Universal Recognition

RQ2 examines the connection between emotional association and brand recognition. Despite universal recognition of all brands, there were notable differences in the emotional associations:

- Chipotle's iconic chili logo was shown to have a strong positive valence (73% happiness), indicating that visual uniqueness increases emotional favorability (answering RQ2 by showing a positive relationship between recognition and emotion).
- Despite its high identifiability, Taco Bell's bell emblem (75% identification) elicited conflicting responses (55% satisfaction vs. 36% sadness), supporting how practical price-focused marketing ("Live Más") weakened emotional coherence (responding to RQ2 by showing that positive emotion is not ensured by recognition alone).
- By linking color consistency to long-lasting emotional equity, McDonald's red-yellow palette, a recognition anchor, produced nostalgia-driven satisfaction (answering RQ2 by how maintaining the same visual cues reinforces positive emotional linkages).
- Burger King's polarized emotions were reflected in its fragmented visual identity (split logo/color focus), highlighting the connection between emotional stability and consistent branding (responding to RQ2 by demonstrating that, despite recognition, fragmented branding compromises emotional coherence).

### The Moderating Effect of Emotional Valence on Brand Perception

Further addressing RQ2, biometric and self-reports evidently showed how emotions enhance recognition:

- Positive Priming: Positive Priming increases reaction speed/accuracy to relevant stimuli (e.g., recognizing a logo after past exposure; Neely,1977, p.226). In line with Bogomolova et al. (2020) on the interaction between design and emotion, Chipotle's innovative imagery and McDonald's nostalgic cues enhanced brand attachment (answering RQ2 by demonstrating how brand recognition outcomes are strengthened by positive emotion).

- Negative priming: Negative priming prevents responses to ignored stimuli (e.g., repressing a competitor's brand; Tipper, 1985, p.571-590). Despite recognition, Taco Bell's text-heavy advertisements weakened desire by inducing emotional ambivalence (low Positive Valence [1.0] + high Negative Valence [4.0]). Coherence was also compromised by Burger King's disorganized stimuli, underscoring the dangers of inconsistent message (addressing RQ2 with evidence that the behavioral influence of brand recognition can be weakened by negative or ambivalent feelings).

These results highlight how emotional valence, which is influenced by color, imagery, and narrative, ultimately moderates brand perception and loyalty, even though recognition is fundamental.

## Phases of AIDA Engagement and Their Biometric Associations ((Integrating RQ1 and RQ2)

To further elaborate on both RQ1 and RQ2,,the following physiological measures correspond to the stages of the AIDA (Attention, Interest, Desire, Action) model:

- Attention (Eye Tracking)—Addressing RQ1: While imagery-driven advertisements (Chipotle, McDonald's) placed more emphasis on graphics, text-focused advertisements (Taco Bell, Burger King) attracted 68% of attention to copy. According to Bülow (2017), prolonged attention was indicated by lower blink rates during McDonald's advertisements (mean=12 vs. baseline 20 blinks/minute).
- Interest (GSR & FEA Arousal)— Addressing RQ1 and RQ2: With a galvanic skin response (GSR) peak of 6.4, Burger King's commercials elicited the highest levels of emotional arousal. Nevertheless, this was combined with a high negative valence score, indicating that unpleasant reactions were the source of the arousal (RQ1: emotional response; RQ2: negative valence influencing brand perception). Chipotle's advertisements, on the other hand, produced moderate GSR peaks (4.0 and 3.2) along with a positive valence score of 3.2, indicating sincere interest that was probably fueled by its freshness and health messaging (RQ1: positive emotional response; RQ2: positive valence improving brand association). McDonald's advertisements elicited a high positive valence score of 5.6, mostly due to nostalgic, family-centered images, despite producing moderate GSR reactions (3.2 and 1.6). These cues successfully connected the Interest and Desire phases (Christopoulos et al., 2019).

- Desire (Behavioral Cues) — Addressing RQ2: While forward-leaning interaction with Chipotle/McDonald's revealed positive desire priming, reclining postures during Burger King stimuli suggested avoidance (desire suppression), indicating negative emotional association that extremely reduces brand preference.

Behavior Intent (Action) — Addressing RQ2: Participants explicitly connected McDonald's nostalgic family imagery and Chipotle's fresh ingredients to their intention to buy ("I'd order this now"; "Makes me crave fries"),showing evidence of how positive emotional associations are changed into behavioral consequences.

They criticized the "outdated" logo or cluttered commercial style of Burger King, saying, "I'd skip this," which decreased actionable intent (exhibiting the way in which negative emotional associations hinder behavioral performance even when there is brand recognition). 64% of respondents agreed that price promotions, or "Live Más" deals of Taco Bell, which increased conversion readiness (the possibility of utilitarian appeals to action even in cases of ambivalent emotions).

## THEORETICAL IMPLICATIONS

This study makes substantial theoretical advances by empirically confirming existing marketing frameworks with biometric data. It provides strong support for the AIDA model (attention-interest-desire-action), illustrating how eye-tracking captures attention, GSR and FEA reflect interest (arousal) and desire (valence), and behavioral cues communicate action. Furthermore, it improves emotional branding theory by exemplifying that coherent visual branding (e.g., McDonald's nostalgic colors) builds emotional loyalty whereas fragmented cues (e.g., Burger King's inconsistencies) degrade trust, showing that logos/ads serve as subconscious emotional primers. The study also refines dual-process theory by exposing how instinctive physiological reactions (e.g., GSR arousal) combine with conscious visual attention (eye-tracking fixations) to form brand perception, as revealed by Burger King's contradicting high arousal and negative valence.Lastly, it improves sensory marketing frameworks by demonstrating that sensory signals (color, images) significantly influence implicit emotional associations that predict brand equity and loyalty.The results also offer empirical support to the Stimulus-Organism-Response (S-O-R) model: visual brand brief stimuli triggered the quantifiable internal emotional and attentional responses, which subsequently determined the intentions to approach or avoid behavior. This proves the relevance of S-O-R framework to fast-food advertising research. Moreover, the findings are consistent with emotion-attention theory: the stimulus with high positive valence (Chipotle, McDonalds) also gave rise to the long fixations of visual attention, which is consistent with the fact that the theory predicts stimuli that arouse some emotions capture the attentional resources and enhance the memory encoding. These theoretical observations form the basis of practical recommendations that are provided.

## Practical Implications

This research provides practitioners with specific advice for optimizing marketing materials. To increase attention and positive valence, brands should prioritize logo and ad design with high-contrast colors (e.g., McDonald's red/yellow) and distinctive forms (e.g., Chipotle's chili), while avoiding cluttered layouts that elicit negative emotions (for example, Burger King's divided focus). Emotion-centric material, such as unified visual storytelling (McDonald's family nostalgia) and fresh food images (Chipotle), should replace text-heavy marketing (e.g., Taco Bell's price-focused ads) to evoke greater arousal and desire. Pre-testing commercials with biometric technologies is critical: eye-tracking finds attention hotspots, while combined GSR (arousal intensity) and FEA (valence specificity) discover mixed emotions early (for example, Burger King's polarized responses). Finally, to maintain attention, organizations must avoid design traps such as dismal color palettes and inconsistent branding, while blending useful information with emotional imagery. In addition to the optimization of designs, practitioners must understand that brands that invariably elicit positive emotional valence via harmonious visual identities develop consumer trust in the long term - one of the primary factors behind brand loyalty in the long term (Spanjaard et al., 2014). The current statistics confirm this opinion: McDonalds and Chipotle whose visual identities fostered the greatest positive valence scores also achieved the most positive self-reported brand associations. Practitioners must also consider the well-being of the consumer: advertising that is based on emotional priming as a means of stimulating consumption of fast food, which is a category of product with known health consequences, bears an obligation not to take advantage of psychological weaknesses or interfere with informed consumer decision making. Such practical considerations are complemented with the organizational and managerial actions that are discussed next.

## Managerial Implications

Managers should use these insights to improve their brand strategy and resource allocation. Investing in neuromarketing techniques (GSR, eye-tracking, and FEA) enables organisations to audit branding materials for subconscious emotional impact, such as measuring valence during ad pre-testing. Cross-functional training is required to equip marketing teams with the ability to interpret physiological data (for example, linking fixation clusters to attention drivers or GSR spikes to arousal peaks) and align designers/managers on visual-emotional coherence (for example, Chipotle's fresh ingredients evoking happiness). Rebranding fractured identities (e.g., Burger King's inconsistency) by streamlining logos/ads to create united emotions—using nostalgic or sensory cues (McDonald's)—can help regain trust and loyalty. Finally, building strategic collaborations between designers and marketers ensures that ads balance aesthetic appeal with message clarity (for example, McDonald's color contrast and family images) and that graphics are consistent with company heritage or key values. Strategically, the managers are advised not to view the neuromarketing knowledge as isolated design solutions but as a contribution to an overall brand governance approach. The observation that consistency in logos and advertisements is closely correlated with positive emotional valence implies that brand consistency judgments, such as logo redesigns, campaign redesigns, and rules about digital assets, must be considered based on more than aesthetic considerations of their specific effects on emotions. In terms of ethical risks, the managers should remember that there are organisational duties related to the application of the biometric data collection: the consent of the participants, data confidentiality, and the absence of advertisement practices based on the emotional vulnerability. On generalizability, the current results are based on a limited, in terms of culture, sample; managers working in different markets ought to carry out localised biometric pre-testing as opposed to generalizing the findings. Lastly, according to the results of this study, the following recommendations can be provided to practitioners: (1) periodically biometrically audit all branded visual materials; (2) focus more on visual coherence and emotional consistency in all customer touchpoints; (3) make the use of the neuromarketing pre-testing a regular activity in campaign development processes; (4) cross-functionalise so that all designers, marketers, and brand managers have a common literacy on how to interpret physiological data.

## ETHICAL SAFEGUARDS AND RESPONSIBLE ADVERTISING

Practitioners and researchers need to take the initiative in dealing with the ethical issues that lie in the utilization of the biometric neuromarketing methods in advertising research. What is even more important than the scientific validity of such procedures as neuroscientific tools becomes the ethical regulation of their manner of acquiring, examining and utilizing information as neuroscientific tools become increasingly sophisticated in their ability to access subconscious consumer reactions (Ulman et al., 2015). The growing integration of AI and machine learning into neuromarketing pipelines worsens these concerns due to the possibility of neuromarketing to target and influence the subconscious mechanisms of customers, creating serious ethical and governance issues (Ulman et al., 2015). Most of the existing governance models are based on voluntary industry regulations and marketing guidelines, which are mostly not considered sufficient to address the complex ethical consequences of neurologically informed advertising practices (Ferrell et al., 2025). New studies, in turn, advance more effective systems of institutional monitoring and stakeholder-oriented ethical standards that are able to balance the interests of businesses, consumer interests, and the responsible usage of technologies (Singh and Kumar, 2026). The three issues that are particularly significant in the case of fast-food advertising research are cultural sensitivity, ethical advertising practices, and informed consent.

The second area of ethics is responsible advertising. The category of products analyzed in this study is fast-food, which has been depicted as having a negative impact on the health of the population, particularly the young adults, who constitute the primary target of the aforementioned businesses. These findings indicate that consistent visual branding in terms of emotions such as the freshness signal provided by Chipotle or nostalgic suggestions offered by McDonald has the potential to affect positive emotional arousal and purchase intention subconsciously. This shows that neuromarketing is an effective approach to designing optimally, yet it raises the question of whether commercial applications of the practice pose the risk of exploitation of psychological vulnerabilities or erosion of consumer choice that serves as the optimal choice in healthcare. To avert the commercial exploitation of the neuromarketing insights to compromise the informed decision-making process, especially among younger and more susceptible audiences, recent studies support stakeholder-oriented ethical guidelines as well as powerful institutional control (Singh and Kumar, 2026).

Third, a cultural sensitivity is one of the ethical boundary conditions that is often overlooked. Advertising campaigns that are informed by biometric information of a culturally homogenous group take the risk of misdirecting or inadvertently turning people of multicultural background away since the emotions of visual stimuli color, shape, imagery and brand narrative are not universally cultural. Due to the potential consequences that emotional misattribution in advertising can lead to the preservation of both brand equity and consumer trust in general, fast-food corporations that market their products in a multiplicity of overseas markets are required to carry out culture-specific biometric pre-testing prior to extrapolating the findings (Goncalves and Dangelo, 2026). A combination of these ethical considerations leads to the realization that responsible neuromarketing research is an ethical imperative to the autonomy, dignity, and welfare of the customers, the minds of which it is intended to understand, and not a methodological principle (Goncalves & Dangelo, 2026).

## LIMITATIONS OF THE STUDY

Generalizability is limited by the study's small, homogeneous sample (*n*=11; ages 19–22) and specific focus on four American fast-food brands. Methodologically, instruments such as eye-tracking (which is susceptible to external interference) and GSR (which measures arousal intensity but not emotional valence) offer objective insights, but they need to be used in conjunction with other techniques (like EEG) to be accurate. The intrusiveness and involuntary data gathering of GSR, as well as the potential for "neuro-hype"—the exaggeration of unsubstantiated neuroscientific claims—are ethical issues. Because of their emphasis on static stimuli (logos/ads), important contextual aspects (such as in-store experiences, pricing, cultural influences, and dynamic content) were disregarded. Subjectivity is introduced by self-reported feelings, and unmeasured participant moods may skew emotional responses. The study ignores cognitive states and comprehensive customer experiences in favor of brand awareness and emotional triggers. While FEA and GSR provided objective measurements, their failure to capture contextual factors (e.g., cultural influences on Negative Valence) and reliance on static ads restrict their use. Furthermore, GSR's emphasis on arousal intensity (rather than valence) necessitates the use of supplementary FEA to categorize emotions.There are two other weaknesses that are worth considering. First, complexity of data interpretation: by combining three sources of biometric data, it becomes difficult to analyse it, such as synchronisation of signals recorded at varying rates, the potential for motion artefacts in GSR recordings, and the inability to assign composite emotional reactions to particular visual objects when stimuli are in the form of whole compositions. The methodology of the researchers who imitate this approach is to use standardised preprocessing pipelines to reduce interpretive ambiguity. Second, scalability to the real world: Despite its inherent validity, the technique used in the lab requires a lot of resources and is difficult to apply in retail or online environments. The equipment involved is specialised and costly to implement, especially by small and medium sized businesses. Future studies ought to evaluate the possibility of similar-quality data being obtained by cheap consumer-grade biometric devices in order to increase the practical applicability of such a methodology.

## DISCUSSION

The study results substantially reinforce the main hypothesis according to which visual cues in fast-food branding represent satisfying subconscious emotional primers, which affect consumer perception, attention, and behavioral intention in measurable and forecast-able manners. The results that can be obtained with the help of the

Stimulus-Organism-Response (S-O-R) framework and emotion-attention theory indicate that brand design and consumer response have an emotionally complex and neurologically based and strategically important relationship.

The entire complexity of consumer emotional reaction was disclosed with the help of the three-modal biometric approach in this research, which was the combination of GSR, FEA, and eye-tracking. Only a single-method design would have concealed this complexity. The only gap in the existing body of neuromarketing research that our methodological contribution will help bridge immediately is the fact that, up to now, eye-tracking studies corroborate the idea of attention without emotional quality, whereas GSR-only studies reveal arousal without valence (Alsharif et al., 2022; Bhardwaj et al., 2024). The triangulation of arousal intensity, emotional valence and visual attention patterns at the same time provided a more comprehensive account on how the participants consciously and subconsciously process each brand stimulus.

The findings confirm that each brand triggers an individual emotional and attentional profile. The red-and-yellow color scheme and images with family orientation that McDonalds have developed earned it the greatest Positive Valence (5.6), which supports the argument by Keller and Lehmann (2006) that the cohesive visual stories result in the formation of long-term emotional equity. The fresher-oriented design of Chipotle created high arousal (4.0) and positive value, so the assertion that text-heavy designs shift processing to utilitarian over emotional processing (Bogomolova et al., 2020) was confirmed by the low arousal of Burger King ads. Dual-process theory is the factor that explains this contradiction, as it believes that fragmented branding makes the divergence of physiological and conscious emotional cues (Christopoulos et al., 2019).

With regards to RQ2, the article indicates that brand recognition is insufficient to guarantee positive customer outcomes. Although all four brands were universally known, emotional valence was not similar thus showing that it is visual coherence rather than familiarity that moderates recognition-loyalty relationship. Although the identity fragmentation in Burger king has resulted in avoidance reactions, Chipotle and McDonalds played a role of positive emotional anchors stimulating approach behavior, which shows that ambivalent valence can entirely override the utility of recognition in behavior (Tipper, 1985; Casarotto et al., 2012).

This knowledge is also improved by the AIDA model mapping. Based on eye-tracking studies, attention was distributed differently based on the visual hierarchy of any given stimulus, ads that contained a large number of pictures were more sustainably fixated than ads that contained a large number of text. How attentional engagement was or was not converted into genuine interest and craving was subsequently shown by GSR and FEA statistics. The high arousal of Burger King did not work at the want stage due to negative emotional values, but McDonald and Chipotle did go through the entire AIDA cycle successfully, and positive valence facilitated desire and behavioral intent. This sequence of biometric mapping of the AIDA model can be seen as a methodological contribution in itself because it offers practitioners a physiologically validated framework that they use to decide which point in the consumer engagement funnel a certain advert has been successful or failed (Cherubino et al., 2019).

Also, the implications of these findings are ethical in nature and should not be relegated to the side comments. Academics and practitioners have a huge responsibility because the biometric neuromarketing technologies can reveal the subconscious emotional states. According to Ulman et al. (2015), since neuromarketing has the ability to study the implicit structure of consumer decision making, it creates ethical concerns that voluntary self-report methods do not, in particular, participant autonomy and data privacy. Such an intentional application of emotionally optimized visual stimuli to foster arousal and purchase intent is widely viewed as a failure by current governance frameworks which are largely founded on voluntary norms and general rules about marketing and is drawing valid criticism of exploitation of psychological vulnerabilities through fast-food advertisement, a field with well-documented adverse public health outcomes in young adults (Ferrell et al., 2025). New studies are calling on more rigorous institutional accountability and ethical governance that is stakeholder-oriented (Singh and Kumar, 2026). Thus, to utilize the research results in a responsible manner, commercial interests should at all times be put in balance with the interests of consumers, informed consent, and the overall necessity to avoid the advertising strategies that undermine health-protecting decision-making, especially in the study population, formed mostly by the young adult demographic, which constitutes the sample and the primary target market of the brands under consideration.

The results together give the practicing specialists a basis of biometrically validated diagnostic value in the optimization of the design of advertising, as well as the development of the theoretical knowledge of visual-emotional brand relations. They confirm that affective consistency of branding is a biologically endorsed force of customer trust, devotion, and behavioral connection in contrast to a mere style liking. They further claim that the moral custodianship of such insights is equally critical to the prudent practice of marketing as is the scientific accuracy upon which they are produced.

## SCOPE OF FUTURE RESEARCH

Although the current research provides valuable information on the effectiveness of visual stimuli in the fast-food branding process in triggering emotional and attentional reactions, it functions within the confines that render the future research agenda a valuable, but not an unnecessary, endeavor. External validity is the greatest concern. The sample of only eleven respondents of one American university does not make an assurance of the research to be generalized to larger consumer groups. The next round of research will need to specifically expand the demographic background of the sample and the scope of the brand types to be examined- recruiting of people of all ages, income statuses and cultural backgrounds as well as the investigation of other areas of the economy besides fast-food like luxurious goods, health care and environmentally conscious items. It is the cross-cultural biometric pre-testing that is of particular concern since color, shape, and imagery emotional reactions are not universal. The red-and-yellow McDonalds palette, in its turn, might be associated with the sense of nostalgia in the American consumer but have totally different connotations elsewhere.

The second important line of avenue is in the temporal dimension of emotional research. The contextual analysis of the current research embodies answers at a single point and by using fixed stimuli in a controlled laboratory, the transpiring nature of consumer emotion is absent. The longitudinal designs used to follow the participants through various brand contacts and buying cycles are indispensable in terms of knowing how the emotional associations are created or lost over time. Similarly, field-based experiments performed in real-life retail settings would enable the researcher to measure behavior under ecologically valid conditions with competing stimuli, time stress and social context to formulate emotional behaviors that cannot be achieved in a laboratory.

In the instrumentation aspect, the combination of more neuroimaging technology would give richer information as fMRI is the best in terms of spatial resolution of the brain activity associated with brand recognition and EEG has the best temporal resolution in neuronal changes occurring rapidly as the process of advertising is performed. These tools, when used together with GSR and eye-tracking, can create a holistic multi-modal architecture that is able to measure arousal, valence, attention, and memory encoding concurrently- to help resolve any conflicting results like the concomitant high arousal and high negative valence observed by Burger King in the current study. The sensory framework can be further extended through the addition of aroma marketing as a variable of experiment since the effect of olfactory cues over the appetite and brand memory is well-documented. Fuzzy AHP, analytically, provides a structured weighting of competing emotional variables in non-linear decision situations, whereas neural networks learned on large-scale biometric data sets can be used to detect latent patterns that cannot be observed by conventional statistics, which will transform the discipline of consumer neuroscience out of descriptive to truly predictive. Predictive AI can be used to combine multi-modal biometric data and provide actionable design recommendations within near real-time- but achieving this potential requires real cooperation between marketing researchers, neuroscientists, computer scientists, and data ethicsists. No one discipline can be sufficient to deal with the complexity of consumer emotion alone.

Lastly, scalability has to be faced directly. The laboratory level equipment in this case is not accessible to the majority of organizations, and is not suitable in naturalistic environments. Future studies have to prove whether consumer-grade wearables and Webcam-based facial recognition can approach lab quality results. In the event of a positive result, the assumptions of neuromarketing techniques would broaden exponentially--including into health care communications, educational design, and political matters--the consistent, scalable biometric technology would become a more fundamental requirement of society, rather than an academic one.

## CONCLUSION

This study emphasizes the symbiotic relationship between visual branding aspects and emotional responses, providing useful insights for marketers and theorists. The combination of GSR and eye-tracking illustrates how color contrast, shape, and focal points influence brand recognition and emotional engagement. While the data demonstrates the efficiency of Neuromarketing methods, limitations in sample variety and stimulus complexity warrant additional investigation.

In summary, the results address RQ1 by showing that digital advertisements and fast-food logos evoke unique emotions (such as freshness for Chipotle and nostalgia for McDonald's) and attentional patterns (such as text focus in Taco Bell ads). The study's integration of FEA and GSR showed crucial nuances: McDonald's nostalgia-driven Positive Valence (5.6), Chipotle's arousal peaks (4.0) associated with freshness, and Burger King's high Negative Valence (6.4) due to uneven branding. These findings highlight the importance of combining visual coherence with emotional stimulation to increase loyalty. To refine these conclusions, future study should include more demographic samples and dynamic stimuli.

RQ2 is addressed by showing that emotional valence, which is fueled by cohesive visual branding, moderates brand recognition outcomes, with fragmented cues (such as Burger King) undermining loyalty despite universal identification. Finally, the study calls for a user-centric approach to branding, in which data-driven design tactics generate stronger emotional ties and a competitive advantage in the fast-food business.

## REFERENCES


Adalarasu, K., Begum, K. G., Priyan, M. V., Devendranath, C., & Sriram, G. V. (2025). Neuro-signaling techniques in advertisement endorsements: Unveiling consumer responses and behavioral trends. *Journal of Retailing and Consumer Services*, *84*, 104175. DOI: 10.1016/j.jretconser.2024.104175

Ahmed, R. R., Streimikiene, D., Channar, Z. A., Soomro, H. A., Streimikis, J., & Kyriakopoulos, G. L. (2022). The neuromarketing concept in artificial neural networks: A case of forecasting and simulation from the advertising industry. *Sustainability (Basel)*, *14*(14), 8546. DOI: 10.3390/su14148546

Al-Kwifi, O. S., Gelaidan, H. M. H., & Fetais, A. H. M. (2021). Identifying the influence of the Halal logo on Muslim consumers' attitudes using fMRI technology. *Journal of Islamic Marketing*, *12*(6), 1159–1179. DOI: 10.1108/JIMA-01-2020-0026

. Alsharif, A. H., & Mohd Isa, S. (2024). Revolutionizing consumer insights: The impact of fMRI in neuromarketing research. Future Business Journal, 10(1), Article 79.

Alsharif, A. H., Salleh, N. Z. M., Al-Zahrani, S. A., & Khraiwish, A. (2022). Consumer behaviour to be considered in advertising: A systematic analysis and future agenda. *Behavioral Sciences (Basel, Switzerland)*, *12*(12), 472. DOI: 10.3390/bs12120472 PMID: 36546955

Babiker, A., Baashar, Y., Alkahtani, A. A., Faye, I., & Alkawsi, G. (2021). Towards detection of interest using physiological sensors. *Applied Sciences (Basel, Switzerland)*, *11*(3), 1318. DOI: 10.3390/app11031318

Babiloni, F., & Cherubino, P. (2023). Consumer neuroscience: A neural engineering approach. In *Handbook of neuroengineering* (pp. 2861–2889). Springer Nature Singapore. DOI: 10.1007/978-981-16-5540-1_74

Barbierato, E., & Alvino, L. (2025). Neurowine insights: Exploring the impact of neuroscience on wine cue assessment. *International Journal of Wine Business Research*, *37*(3), 425–444. DOI: 10.1108/IJWBR-06-2024-0033

Berčík, J., Mravcová, A., Nadal, E. S., Lluch, D. B. L., & Farkaš, A. (2024). FaceReader as a neuromarketing tool to compare the olfactory preferences of customers in selected markets. *Spanish Journal of Marketing - ESIC*. Advance online publication.

Bhardwaj, S., Thapa, S. B., & Gandhi, A. (2024). Advances in neuromarketing and improved understanding of consumer behaviour: Analysing tool possibilities and research trends. *Cogent Business & Management*, *11*(1), 2376773. DOI: 10.1080/23311975.2024.2376773

Bigne, E., Simonetti, A., Guixeres, J., & Alcaniz, M. (2024). Visual attention and product interaction: A neuroscientific study on purchase across two product categories in a virtual store. *International Journal of Retail & Distribution Management, 52*(4), 389–406. DOI: 10.1108/IJRDM-02-2023-0067

Bogomolova, S., Oppewal, H., Cohen, J., & Yao, J. (2020). How the layout of a unit price label affects eye-movements and product choice: An eye-tracking investigation. *Journal of Business Research, 111*, 102–116. DOI: 10.1016/j.jbusres.2018.10.049

. Bülow, P. (2017). Infant research: The complete pocket guide.

Casarotto, S., Ricciardi, E., Romani, S., Dalli, D., & Pietrini, P. (2012). Covert brand recognition engages emotion-specific brain networks. *Archives Italiennes de Biologie, 150*(4), 259–273. PMID: 23479459

Cenizo, C. (2025). A neuromarketing approach to consumer behavior on web platforms. *International Journal of Consumer Studies, 49*(2), e70034. DOI: 10.1111/ijcs.70034

Chan, E. Y. (2024). Consumer behavior in the future. In *Consumer behavior in practice: Strategic insights for the modern marketer* (pp. 251–263). Springer Nature Switzerland. DOI: 10.1007/978-3-031-50947-6_13

Chand, T., Nair, V. S., Srinivasu, P. N., & Kumar, V. J. (2025). Prospects and challenges in decoding consumer behavior using neurotechnology. In Artificial intelligence applications for brain–computer interfaces (pp. 161–182). DOI: 10.1016/B978-0-443-33414-6.00011-3

Cherubino, P., Martinez-Levy, A. C., Caratù, M., Cartocci, G., Di Flumeri, G., Modica, E., Rossi, D., Mancini, M., & Trettel, A. (2019). Consumer behaviour through the eyes of neurophysiological measures: State-of-the-art and future trends. *Computational Intelligence and Neuroscience, 2019*, 1976847. DOI: 10.1155/2019/1976847 PMID: 31641346

Christopoulos, G. I., Uy, M. A., & Yap, W. J. (2019). The body and the brain: Measuring skin conductance responses to understand the emotional experience. *Organizational Research Methods, 22*(1), 394–420. DOI: 10.1177/1094428116681073

Ciceri, A., Russo, V., Songa, G., Gabrielli, G., & Clement, J. (2020). A neuroscientific method for assessing effectiveness of digital vs. print ads: Using biometric techniques to measure cross-media ad experience and recall. *Journal of Advertising Research, 60*(1), 71–86. DOI: 10.2501/JAR-2019-015

Cong, L., Luan, S., Young, E., Mirosa, M., Bremer, P., & Torrico, D. D. (2023). The application of biometric approaches in agri-food marketing: A systematic literature review. *Foods, 12*(16), 2982. DOI: 10.3390/foods12162982 PMID: 37627981

Daugherty, T., & Hoffman, E. (2016). Neuromarketing: Understanding the application of neuroscientific methods within marketing research. In Ethics and neuromarketing: Implications for market research and business practice (pp. 5–30). Springer International Publishing.

Ferrell, M. L., Beatty, A., & Dubljevic, V. (2025). The ethics of neuromarketing: A rapid review. *Neuroethics, 18*(1), 19. DOI: 10.1007/s12152-025-09591-8

Goncalves, M., & Dangelo, D. (2026). Consumer privacy and neuromarketing: Ethical implications and legal frameworks in California. In *Next generation entrepreneurship: Convergence of innovation, technology, and society* (pp. 443–471). Springer Nature Switzerland. DOI: 10.1007/978-3-031-98513-3_17

Harris, J. M., Ciorciari, J., & Gountas, J. (2018). Consumer neuroscience for marketing researchers. *Journal of Consumer Behaviour, 17*(3), 239–252. DOI: 10.1002/cb.1710

Huddleston, P., McAlister, A. R., & Alade, F. (2025). Through a child's eyes: Eye tracking to study children's consumer behavior. *Journal of Consumer Marketing, 42*(2), 174–192. DOI: 10.1108/JCM-11-2023-6396

Kaklauskas, A., Abraham, A., Ubarte, I., Kliukas, R., Luksaite, V., Binkyte-Veliene, A., Vetloviene, I., & Kaklauskiene, L. (2022). A review of AI cloud and edge sensors, methods, and applications for the recognition of emotional, affective and physiological states. *Sensors (Basel), 22*(20), 7824. DOI: 10.3390/s22207824 PMID: 36298176

Keller, K. L., & Lehmann, D. R. (2006). Brands and branding: Research findings and future priorities. *Marketing Science, 25*(6), 740–759. DOI: 10.1287/mksc.1050.0153

Ko, E. S., Kim, J. N., Na, H. J., & Kim, S. T. (2024). Changes in pupil size according to the color of cosmetic packaging: Using eye-tracking techniques. *Applied Sciences (Basel, Switzerland), 15*(1), 73. DOI: 10.3390/app15010073

Koc, E., Boz, H., & Arslan, A. (2020). Eye tracking: Evaluation, potential and limitations of field applications. In Eye tracking in tourism (pp. 45–60).

Muñoz-Leiva, F., Hernández-Méndez, J., & Gómez-Carmona, D. (2019). Measuring advertising effectiveness in Travel 2.0 websites through eye-tracking technology. *Physiology & Behavior, 200*, 83–95. DOI: 10.1016/j.physbeh.2018.03.002 PMID: 29522796

Neely, J. H. (1977). Semantic priming and retrieval from lexical memory: Roles of inhibitionless spreading activation and limited-capacity attention. *Journal of Experimental Psychology. General, 106*(3), 226–254. DOI: 10.1037/0096-3445.106.3.226

Niedziela, M. M., & Ambroze, K. (2021). Neuroscience tools: Using the right tool for the right question. In *Emotion measurement* (pp. 559–592). Woodhead Publishing. DOI: 10.1016/B978-0-12-821124-3.00017-X

Nilashi, M., Yadegaridehkordi, E., Samad, S., Mardani, A., Ahani, A., Aljojo, N., Razali, N. S., & Tajuddin, T. (2020). Decision to adopt neuromarketing techniques for sustainable product marketing: A fuzzy decision-making approach. *Symmetry, 12*(2), 305. DOI: 10.3390/sym12020305

Ohme, R., Matukin, M., & Pacula-Lesniak, B. (2011). Biometric measures for interactive advertising research. *Journal of Interactive Advertising, 11*(2), 60–72. DOI: 10.1080/15252019.2011.10722185

Ozkul, E., Boz, H., Bilgili, B., & Koc, E. (2019). What colour and light do in service atmospherics: A neuro-marketing perspective. In *Atmospheric turn in culture and tourism: Place, design and process impacts on customer behaviour, marketing and branding* (pp. 223–244). Emerald Publishing Limited. DOI: 10.1108/S1871-317320190000016022

Piper, L., De Cosmo, L. M., Prete, M. I., Mileti, A., & Guido, G. (2024). Effectiveness of pictorial warnings on food fat content: Consumers' perception and neurological responses. *British Food Journal, 126*(6), 2328–2348. DOI: 10.1108/BFJ-02-2023-0123

Rabindranath, M., & Singh, A. K. (2024). Advertising research. In *Advertising management: Concepts, theories, research and trends* (pp. 225–247). Springer Nature Singapore. DOI: 10.1007/978-981-99-8657-6_7

Rancati, G., Nguyen, T. T. T., Fowler, D., Mauri, M., & Schultz, C. D. (2024). Customer experience in coffee stores: A multidisciplinary neuromarketing approach. *Journal of Consumer Behaviour, 23*(1), 243–259. DOI: 10.1002/cb.2184

Rawnaque, F. S., Rahman, K. M., Anwar, S. F., Vaidyanathan, R., Chau, T., Sarker, F., & Mamun, K. A. A. (2020). Technological advancements and opportunities in neuromarketing: A systematic review. *Brain Informatics, 7*(1), 1–19. DOI: 10.1186/s40708-020-00109-x PMID: 32955675

Riswanto, A. L., Ha, S., Lee, S., & Kwon, M. (2024). Online reviews meet visual attention: A study on consumer patterns in advertising, analyzing customer satisfaction, visual engagement, and purchase intention. *Journal of Theoretical and Applied Electronic Commerce Research, 19*(4), 3102–3122. DOI: 10.3390/jtaer19040150

Sáez-García, J., Sáiz-Manzanares, M. C., & Marticorena-Sánchez, R. (2024). A proposed method of automating data processing for analyzing data produced from eye tracking and galvanic skin response. *Computers, 13*(11), 289. DOI: 10.3390/computers13110289

Sandoval, P. S., & García-Madariaga, J. (2024). Impact of emotional appeal on non-profit advertising: A neurophysiological analysis. *Journal of Consumer Behaviour, 23*(1), 203–217. DOI: 10.1002/cb.2168

Singh, K., & Kumar, A. (2026). Exploring the evolving landscape of neuromarketing ethics. *International Journal of Market Research, 68*(1), 108–131. DOI: 10.1177/14707853251383629

Spanjaard, D., Young, L., & Freeman, L. (2014). Emotions in supermarket brand choice: A multi-method approach. *Qualitative Market Research, 17*(3), 209–224. DOI: 10.1108/QMR-10-2012-0049

Tao, L., Nakamura, S., Wang, X., Kawahara, T., Tamura, G., & Yamasaki, T. (2024). A large-scale television advertising dataset for detailed impression analysis. *Multimedia Tools and Applications, 83*(7), 18779–18802. DOI: 10.1007/s11042-023-14704-7

Tipper, S. P. (1985). The negative priming effect: Inhibitory priming by ignored objects. *The Quarterly Journal of Experimental Psychology. A, Human Experimental Psychology, 37*(4), 571–590. DOI: 10.1080/14640748508400920 PMID: 4081101

Tirandazi, P., Bamakan, S. M. H., & Toghroljerdi, A. (2023). A review of studies on internet of everything as an enabler of neuromarketing methods and techniques. *The Journal of Supercomputing, 79*(7), 7835–7876. DOI: 10.1007/s11227-022-04988-1

Ulman, Y. I., Cakar, T., & Yildiz, G. (2015). Ethical issues in neuromarketing: "I consume, therefore I am!". *Science and Engineering Ethics, 21*(5), 1271–1284. DOI: 10.1007/s11948-014-9581-5 PMID: 25150848

Vergura, D. T., & Luceri, B. (2018). Product packaging and consumers' emotional response. Does spatial representation influence product evaluation and choice? *Journal of Consumer Marketing, 35*(2), 218–227. DOI: 10.1108/JCM-12-2016-2021

Vozzi, A., Ronca, V., Cherubino, P., & Trettel, A. (2021). Measuring the emotional and cognitive consumers' responses during interaction. In Decision-making in management: Methods and behavioral tools (p. 137).

Walla, P., Brenner, G., & Koller, M. (2011). Objective measures of emotion related to brand attitude: A new way to quantify emotion-related aspects relevant to marketing. *PLoS One*, *6*(11), e26782. DOI: 10.1371/journal.pone.0026782 PMID: 22073192

Zacharia, A. B., & Hamelin, N. (2021). An analysis of subliminal static images and words using eye tracking techniques. In *Developing digital marketing: Relationship perspectives* (pp. 155–180). Emerald Publishing Limited. DOI: 10.1108/978-1-80071-348-220211009

Zhang, H., Yin, L., & Zhang, H. (2024). Using subjective emotion, facial expression, and gaze direction to evaluate user affective experience and predict preference when playing single-player games. *Ergonomics*, *67*(12), 1863–1883. DOI: 10.1080/00140139.2024.2359123 PMID: 38832783

Zhang, Y., Thaichon, P., & Shao, W. (2023). Neuroscientific research methods and techniques in consumer research. *Australasian Marketing Journal*, *31*(3), 211–227. DOI: 10.1177/14413582221085321

Zhu, S., Qi, J., Hu, J., & Hao, S. (2022). A new approach for product evaluation based on integration of EEG and eye-tracking. *Advanced Engineering Informatics*, *52*, 101601. DOI: 10.1016/j.aei.2022.101601

Zuschke, N. (2020). An analysis of process-tracing research on consumer decision-making. *Journal of Business Research*, *111*, 305–320. DOI: 10.1016/j.jbusres.2019.01.028

# Compilation of References


*(PDF) Sephora Smart Customer's Experience Enhancement*. (n.d.). Retrieved July 9, 2025, from https://www.researchgate.net/publication/351936435_Sephora_Smart_Customer%27s_Experience_Enhancement?channel=doi&linkId=645d3675f43b8a29ba44f3f4&showFulltext=true

. Alsharif, A. H., & Mohd Isa, S. (2024). Revolutionizing consumer insights: The impact of fMRI in neuromarketing research. Future Business Journal, 10(1), Article 79.

. Alsharif, A. H., Isa, S. M., & Pilelienė, L. (2024). global academic trends of metabolic and electrical biomedical tools in marketing. *Baltic Journal of Economic Studies, 10*(5).

. Amati, S. (2023). Harnessing the power of latest technologies in digital out-of-home advertising: a study on interaction models and audience impact.

. Bülow, P. (2017). Infant research: The complete pocket guide.

. Chand, T., Nair, V. S., Srinivasu, P. N., & Kumar, V. J. (2025). Prospects and challenges in decoding consumer behavior using neurotechnology. *Artificial Intelligence Applications for Brain–Computer Interfaces*, 161-182.

. Geetha, V., & Hegde, S. N. (2024). Mapping the Consumer Mind: Neuromarketing Applications in Personalization and Targeting. *Library of Progress-Library Science, Information Technology & Computer, 44*(3).

. ISLAM, M. M., NEOGY, T. K., & REZA, M. M. H. (2024). A DATA-DRIVEN NEUROMARKETING APPROACH TO UNDERSTANDING CONSUMER BUYING PREFERENCES. *Journal of Computing and Digital Technologies, 2*(1), 65-80.

. Moutinho, L., & Cerf, M. (2024). The Future of Neuroscience and Biometrics in Business. *Biometrics and Neuroscience Research in Business and Management: Advances and Applications*, 333.

. Nguyen, T. A. (2021). Fundamentals of neuromarketing: an interdisciplinary field that changes how marketers understand consumers.

. Okeke, N. I., Alabi, O. A., Igwe, A. N., Ofodile, O. C., & Ewim, C. P. M. (2024). AI-driven personalization framework for SMEs: Revolutionizing customer engagement and retention. Journal name needed for completion.

. Patil, D. (2024). Artificial intelligence-driven customer service: Enhancing personalization, loyalty, and customer satisfaction. *Loyalty, And Customer Satisfaction (November 20, 2024).*

. Puneet, S. (2023). AI-driven personalization in telecom customer support: Enhancing user experience and loyalty. *AI-Driven Personalization in Telecom Customer Support: Enhancing User Experience and Loyalty.*

. Skillius, E., & Jacobsson, A. (2024). Beyond the Algorithm-How ai-driven personalized ads shape consumer loyalty and brand engagement.

. Utriainen, T. (2020). Neuromarketing and consumer neuroscience–the evolution and current state of the Art, an integrative review.

. Verdenhofs, A., & Tambovceva, T. (2019). Evolution of customer segmentation in the era of big data.

*5ways AliBaba is using AI [Case Study] [2025] - DigitalDefynd.* (n.d.). Retrieved July 9, 2025, from https://digitaldefynd.com/IQ/ways-alibaba-using-ai-case-study/

Abbasi, M., Váz, P., Silva, J., & Martins, P. (2024). Enhancing visual perception in immersive vr and ar environments: Ai-driven color and clarity adjustments under dynamic lighting conditions. *Technologies, 12*(11), 216. DOI: 10.3390/technologies12110216

Abdelfattah, F., Madi, H., Al-Washahi, M., AlAraimi, A., Nagi, S., & Abbas, M. (2025). Harnessing Artificial Intelligence, Business Intelligence, and Digital Technologies for achieving supply chain excellence in Oman: Investigating the mediating role of predictive analytics. *Journal of Open Innovation, 11*(4), 100644. Advance online publication. DOI: 10.1016/j.joitmc.2025.100644

Abidin, C. (2016). "Aren't these just young, rich women doing vain things online?": Influencer selfies as subversive frivolity. *Social Media + Society, 2*(2), 1–17. DOI: 10.1177/2056305116641342

Acharya, N., Sassenberg, A. M., & Soar, J. (2023). Effects of cognitive absorption on continuous use intention of AI-driven recommender systems in e-commerce. *Foresight, 25*(2), 194–208. DOI: 10.1108/FS-10-2021-0200

Adalarasu, K., Begum, K. G., Priyan, M. V., Devendranath, C., & Sriram, G. V. (2025). Neuro-signaling techniques in advertisement endorsements: Unveiling consumer responses and behavioral trends. *Journal of Retailing and Consumer Services, 84*, 104175. DOI: 10.1016/j.jretconser.2024.104175

Adeleke, A. G., Sanyaolu, T. O., Efunniyi, C. P., Akwawa, L. A., & Azubuko, C. F. (2022). Impact of AI-Enabled A/B Testing on Product Performance in E-commerce Platforms. *International Journal of Management & Entrepreneurship Research, 4*(12), 795–813. DOI: 10.51594/IJMER.V4I12.1537

Adel, M. (2025). The Impact of Emotional Branding and Neuromarketing on Enhancing Egyptian Tourist Destination competitive. *Journal of Association of Arab Universities for Tourism and Hospitality, 28*(1), 421–438. DOI: 10.21608/jaauth.2025.377760.1678

Adeola, O., Evans, O., Ndubuisi Edeh, J., & Adisa, I. (2022). The Future of Marketing: Artificial Intelligence, Virtual Reality, and Neuromarketing. In *Palgrave Studies of Marketing in Emerging Economies: Part F3553* (pp. 253–280). Palgrave Macmillan. DOI: 10.1007/978-3-030-88678-3_12

Agarwal, R., & Dhar, V. (2014). Editorial—Big data, data science, and analytics: The opportunity and challenge for IS research. *Information Systems Research, 25*(3), 443–448. DOI: 10.1287/isre.2014.0546

Aggarwal, D., Sharma, D., & Saxena, A. B. (2024). Enhancing the Online Shopping Experience of Consumers through Artificial Intelligence. *International Journal of Information Technology and Computer Engineering, 42*, 1–5. DOI: 10.55529/ijitc.42.1.5

Agrawal, V., Nikalje, V., Sharma, S., & Haldar, P. (2025). *Role of Neuromarketing in Modern Consumer Behavior: Systematic Literature Review.* In *Decoding Consumer Behavior Using the Insight Equation and AI Marketing* (pp. 159-182).

Ahmed, R. R., Streimikiene, D., Channar, Z. A., Soomro, H. A., Streimikis, J., & Kyriakopoulos, G. L. (2022). The neuromarketing concept in artificial neural networks: A case of forecasting and simulation from the advertising industry. *Sustainability (Basel), 14*(14), 8546. DOI: 10.3390/su14148546

Ahmed, S. M. M., Owais, M., Raza, M., Nadeem, Q., & Ahmed, B. (2025). The Impact of AI-Driven Personalization on Consumer Engagement and Brand Loyalty. *Qlantic Journal of Social Sciences, 6*(1), 311–323. DOI: 10.55737/qjss.v-iv.24313

Ahmed, Z. A., Albalawi, E., Aldhyani, T. H., Jadhav, M. E., Janrao, P., & Obeidat, M. R. M. (2023). Applying eye tracking with deep learning techniques for early-stage detection of autism spectrum disorders. *Data*, *8*(11), 168. DOI: 10.3390/data8110168

Ahuvia, A., Izberk-Bilgin, E., & Lee, K. (2022). Towards a theory of brand love in services: The power of identity and social relationships. *Journal of Service Management*, *33*(3), 453–464. DOI: 10.1108/JOSM-06-2021-0221

Ai, X., Wu, Z., Guo, T., Zhong, J., Hu, N., & Fu, C. (2021). The effect of visual attention on stereoscopic lighting of museum ceramic exhibits: A virtual environment mixed with eye-tracking. *Informatica (Vilnius)*, *45*(5).

Ajzen, I. (1991). The theory of planned behaviour. *Organizational Behavior and Human Decision Processes*, *50*(2), 179–211. DOI: 10.1016/0749-5978(91)90020-T

Al Lawati, S. F. D. (2025, May). I Am Not a Caveman: An Eye-tracking Study of How Users are Influenced to Search in the Era of GenAI. In *Companion Proceedings of the ACM on Web Conference 2025* (pp. 681-684).

Aldayel, M., Ykhlef, M., & Al-Nafjan, A. (2020). Deep learning for EEG-based preference classification in neuromarketing. *Applied Sciences (Basel, Switzerland)*, *10*(4), 1–23. DOI: 10.3390/app10041525

Alghaswyneh, O. F. (2025). Exploring the Impact of AI-Driven Personalization on Consumer Engagement in Digital Marketing. *Management*, *29*(1), 117–144. DOI: 10.58691/man/200968

Alghofaili, R., Solah, M. S., Huang, H., Sawahata, Y., Pomplun, M., & Yu, L. F. (2019, March). Optimizing visual element placement via visual attention analysis. In *2019 IEEE Conference on Virtual Reality and 3D User Interfaces (VR)* (pp. 464-473). IEEE. DOI: 10.1109/VR.2019.8797816

Aliyev, N. N. (1996). THE PSYCHOLOGY OF ONLİNE SHOPPING HOW DIGITAL MARKETING TRIGGERS IMPULSE BUYING. *Scientific Works/Elmi Eserler*, 266–272. DOI: 10.58225/tim.2024-4-266-272

Al-Kwifi, O. S., Gelaidan, H. M. H., & Fetais, A. H. M. (2021). Identifying the influence of the Halal logo on Muslim consumers' attitudes using fMRI technology. *Journal of Islamic Marketing*, *12*(6), 1159–1179. DOI: 10.1108/JIMA-01-2020-0026

Almourad, M., Bataineh, E., Hussein, M., & Wattar, Z. (2025). Strategic Placement of Branding Elements in Digital Marketing: Insights from Eye-Tracking Data. In *Proceedings of the 27th International Conference on Enterprise Information Systems* (pp. 417-423). DOI: 10.5220/0013281500003929

AlRoshoud, A. N., & El-Gohary, H. O. (2024). Exploring the Impact of Combining Neuromarketing and AI Adoption on the Perceived Effectiveness of Social Media Advertising Campaigns. *International Journal of Customer Relationship Marketing and Management, 15*(1), 1–28. Advance online publication. DOI: 10.4018/IJCRMM.361975

Alshaketheep, K., Mansour, A. M., Al-Ma'aitah, M. M. L., Dabaghia, M. N., & Dabaghie, Y. M. (2024). Leveraging AI Predictive Analytics for Marketing Strategy: The Mediating Role of Management Awareness. *Journal of System and Management Sciences, 14*(2), 71–89. DOI: 10.33168/JSMS.2024.0205

Alsharif, A. H., & Isa, S. M. (2025). Electroencephalography Studies on Marketing Stimuli: A Literature Review and Future Research Agenda. In *International Journal of Consumer Studies* (Vol. 49, Number 1). John Wiley and Sons Inc. DOI: 10.1111/ijcs.70015

Alsharif, A. H., Md Salleh, N. Z., Baharun, R., & Rami Hashem, E. A. (2021). Neuromarketing research in the last five years: a bibliometric analysis. In *Cogent Business and Management* (Vol. 8, Number 1). Cogent OA. DOI: 10.1080/23311975.2021.1978620

Alsharif, A. H., Salleh, N. Z. M., Baharun, R., Alharthi Rami Hashem, E., Mansor, A. A., Ali, J., & Abbas, A. F. (2021). Neuroimaging techniques in advertising research: Main applications, development, and brain regions and processes. In *Sustainability (Switzerland)* (Vol. 13, Number 11). MDPI AG. DOI: 10.3390/su13116488

Alsharif, A. H., Salleh, N. Z. M., Abdullah, M., Khraiwish, A., & Ashaari, A. (2023). Neuromarketing Tools Used in the Marketing Mix: A Systematic Literature and Future Research Agenda. *SAGE Open, 13*(1). Advance online publication. DOI: 10.1177/21582440231156563/ASSET/4995F1D5-0A6A-4E37-9011-383BB2B68B56/ASSETS/IMAGES/LARGE/10.1177_21582440231156563-FIG4.JPG

Alsharif, A. H., Salleh, N. Z. M., Al-Zahrani, S. A., & Khraiwish, A. (2022). Consumer behaviour to be considered in advertising: A systematic analysis and future agenda. *Behavioral Sciences (Basel, Switzerland), 12*(12), 472. DOI: 10.3390/bs12120472 PMID: 36546955

Alsharif, A. H., Wang, J., Isa, S. M., Salleh, N. Z. M., Dawas, H. A., & Alsharif, M. H. (2025). The synergy of neuromarketing and artificial intelligence: A comprehensive literature review in the last decade. *Future Business Journal, 11*(1), 170. Advance online publication. DOI: 10.1186/s43093-025-00591-x

Alter, A. (2017). *Irresistible: The rise of addictive technology and the business of keeping us hooked*. Penguin Press.

Ambika, A., Shin, H., & Jain, V. (2025). Immersive technologies and consumer behavior: A systematic review of two decades of research. *Australian Journal of Management, 50*(1), 55–79. DOI: 10.1177/03128962231181429

Andreoletti, D., Luceri, L., & Peternier, A. (2021). The virtual emotion loop: Towards emotion-driven product design via virtual reality. In 2021 16th Conference on Computer Science and Information Systems (FedCSIS) (pp. 1–10). DOI: 10.15439/2021FCSIS.12345678

Anil Kumar, J., & Ramesh Babu, S. (2025). Strategic Marketing and Customer Analytics. In *Strategy Analytics for Business Resilience Theories and Practices* (pp. 73–88). Springer Nature Switzerland. DOI: 10.1007/978-3-031-82369-5_5

Apicella, A., Arpaia, P., Mastrati, G., & Moccaldi, N. (2021). EEG-based detection of emotional valence towards a reproducible measurement of emotions. *Scientific Reports, 11*(1), 21615. DOI: 10.1038/s41598-021-00812-7 PMID: 34732756

Aprilianty, F., Takahashi, M., & Matsuura, Y. (2024). Bridging Brains and Bots: The Impact of AI on Neuromarketing. *Procedia Computer Science, 246*(C), 1830–1839. DOI: 10.1016/j.procs.2024.09.687

Aral, S. (2021). The hype machine: How social media disrupts our elections, our economy, and our health—and how we must adapt. *Journal of Marketing, 85*(1), 129–133. DOI: 10.1002/asi.24604

Ariely, D., & Berns, G. S. (2010). Neuromarketing: the hope and hype of neuroimaging in business. *Nature Reviews Neuroscience 2010 11:4, 11*(4), 284–292. DOI: 10.1038/nrn2795

Arnould, E. J., & Thompson, C. J. (2005). Consumer culture theory (CCT): Twenty years of research. *The Journal of Consumer Research, 31*(4), 868–882. DOI: 10.1086/426626

Arora, R. (2024). Bridging the Gap Between Offline and Online Presence in E-commerce: The Role of Artificial Intelligence. *INTERANTIONAL JOURNAL OF SCIENTIFIC RESEARCH IN ENGINEERING AND MANAGEMENT, 08*(12), 1–6. DOI: 10.55041/IJSREM33002

Arya, K., Bhardwaj, V., Kumari, V., & Singh, D. (2025). From Brain To Business: The Role of Neuroscience In Marketing, HR, and Finance Along With Ethical Issues. *Academy of Marketing Studies Journal, 29*(5).

Asudani, D. S., Nagwani, N. K., & Singh, P. (2023). Impact of word embedding models on text analytics in deep learning environment: A review. *Artificial Intelligence Review, 56*(9), 4873–4910. DOI: 10.1007/s10462-023-10419-1 PMID: 36844886

Aurangzeb, K., Ayub, N., & Alhussein, M. (2021). Aspect-based multi-labeling using SVM-based ensembler. *IEEE Access : Practical Innovations, Open Solutions*, *9*, 26026–26040. DOI: 10.1109/ACCESS.2021.3055768

Ayoubi, S. B. A., Ayoubi, M. M., & Aria, N. (2025). Augmented and Virtual Reality in Consumer Decision-Making: Impact on Engagement, Confidence, and Purchase Intentions. *Journal of Optimization and Supply Chain Management*, *2*(1), 33–45.

Babiker, A., Baashar, Y., Alkahtani, A. A., Faye, I., & Alkawsi, G. (2021). Towards detection of interest using physiological sensors. *Applied Sciences (Basel, Switzerland)*, *11*(3), 1318. DOI: 10.3390/app11031318

Babiloni, F., & Cherubino, P. (2023). Consumer neuroscience: A neural engineering approach. In *Handbook of neuroengineering* (pp. 2861–2889). Springer Nature Singapore. DOI: 10.1007/978-981-16-5540-1_74

Bag, S., Srivastava, G., Al Bashir, M. M., Kumari, S., Giannakis, M., & Chowdhury, A. H. (2022). Journey of customers in this digital era: Understanding the role of artificial intelligence technologies in user engagement and conversion. *Benchmarking*, *29*(7), 2074–2098. DOI: 10.1108/BIJ-07-2021-0415/FULL/XML

Baharum, A., Ismail, R., Halamy, S., Rahim, E. A., Noor, N. A. M., & Deris, F. D. (2024, August). Enhancing UX Design Through Eye-Tracking and Image Processing: Practical Insights and Applications. In *2024 International Conference on Platform Technology and Service (PlatCon)* (pp. 1-4). IEEE. DOI: 10.1109/PlatCon63925.2024.10830718

Bajaj, R., Ali Syed, A., & Singh, S. (2024). Analysing applications of neuromarketing in efficacy of programmatic advertising. *Journal of Consumer Behaviour*, *23*(2), 939–958. DOI: 10.1002/cb.2249

Bajpai, A., & Islam, T. (2022). Impact of augmented reality marketing on customer engagement, behavior, loyalty, and buying decisions. *Cardiometry*, (23), 545–553.

Baldo, D., Viswanathan, V. S., Timpone, R. J., & Venkatraman, V. (2022). The heart, brain, and body of marketing: Complementary roles of neurophysiologicalmeasuresin trackingemotions,memory, and ad effectiveness. *Psychology of Marketing: Wiley*, *39*, 1979–1991. https://doi.org/DOI:10.1002/mar.21697

Bansal, S., Nangia, P., & Koles, B. (2025). Neuromarketing and the Marketing Mix: An Integrative Review and Future Research Agenda Using the TMC Approach. *International Journal of Consumer Studies*, *49*(3), e70072. https://doi.org/https://doi.org/10.1111/ijcs.70072. DOI: 10.1111/ijcs.70072

Banytė, J., Pūkienė, I., & Dargytė, G. (2025). The role of consumers' visual attention stimuli in advertising: traditional and neuromarketing research perspectives. *Innovative marketing., 21*(1), 296-313.

Bao, W., Cao, Y., Yang, Y., Che, H., Huang, J., & Wen, S. (2025). Data-driven stock forecasting models based on neural networks: A review. *Information Fusion, 113*, 102616. DOI: 10.1016/j.inffus.2024.102616

Barbierato, E., & Alvino, L. (2025). Neurowine insights: Exploring the impact of neuroscience on wine cue assessment. *International Journal of Wine Business Research, 37*(3), 425–444. DOI: 10.1108/IJWBR-06-2024-0033

Barocas, S., & Selbst, A. D. (2016). Big data's disparate impact. *SSRN, 104*(3), 671–732. DOI: 10.2139/ssrn.2477899

Barrera, K. G., & Shah, D. (2023). Marketing in the Metaverse: Conceptual understanding, framework, and research agenda. *Journal of Business Research, 155*, 113420. DOI: 10.1016/j.jbusres.2022.113420

Bazzani, A., Ravaioli, S., Trieste, L., Faraguna, U., & Turchetti, G. (2020). Is EEG Suitable for Marketing Research? A Systematic Review. In *Frontiers in Neuroscience* (Vol. 14). Frontiers Media S.A. DOI: 10.3389/fnins.2020.594566

Behl, A., Jayawardena, N., Shankar, A., Gupta, M., & Lang, L. D. (2024). Gamification and neuromarketing: A unified approach for improving user experience. *Journal of Consumer Behaviour, 23*(1), 218–228. DOI: 10.1002/cb.2178

Bekenova, G., & Orazgaliyeva, E. (2025). Neuromarketing Insights: Using Eye-Tracking and Machine Learning to Understand Consumer Preferences for University Promotional Products. *BUKETOV BUSINESS REVIEW, 11830*(2), 4–16. DOI: 10.31489/2025ec2/4-16

Bekler, M., Yilmaz, M., & Ilgın, H. E. (2024). Assessing feature importance in eye-tracking data within virtual reality using explainable artificial intelligence techniques. *Applied Sciences (Basel, Switzerland), 14*(14), 6042. DOI: 10.3390/app14146042

Benrimoh, D., Israel, S., Perlman, K., Fratila, R., Krause, M., & Lowe, M. (2021). AI and mental health: A new frontier for patient care. *Frontiers in Psychiatry, 12*, 573. DOI: 10.3389/fpsyt.2021.573

Bercea Olteanu, M. D. (2015). Neuroethics and responsibility in conducting neuromarketing research. *Neuroethics, 8*(2), 191–202. DOI: 10.1007/s12152-014-9227-y

Berčík, J., Mravcová, A., Nadal, E. S., Lluch, D. B. L., & Farkaš, A. (2024). FaceReader as a neuromarketing tool to compare the olfactory preferences of customers in selected markets. *Spanish Journal of Marketing - ESIC*. Advance online publication.

Beyari, H., Hashem, T. N., & Alrusain, O. (2024). Neuromarketing: Understanding the effect of emotion and memory on consumer behavior by mediating the role of artificial intelligence and customers' digital experience. *Journal of Project Management, 9*(4), 323–336. DOI: 10.5267/j.jpm.2024.9.001

Bhardwaj, S., Kaushik, N., & Arora, M. (2024). Does Your Brain Have a Buy Button?: A Neuro Marketing Approach With Sensory Branding. In *Sensible Selling Through Sensory Neuromarketing* (pp. 210–229). IGI Global. DOI: 10.4018/979-8-3693-4236-7.ch011

Bhardwaj, S., Rana, G. A., Behl, A., & Gallego de Caceres, S. J. (2023). Exploring the boundaries of Neuromarketing through systematic investigation. *Journal of Business Research, 154*, 113371. DOI: 10.1016/j.jbusres.2022.113371

Bhatt, P., & Singh, A. K. (2024). Impact of AI on Consumers' Purchase Intention Towards Online Grocery Shopping in India. *Journal of Reliability and Statistical Studies, 17*(2), 453–490. DOI: 10.13052/JRSS0974-8024.17210

Białowąs, S., & Szyszka, A. (2019). Eye-tracking in Marketing Research. *Managing Economic Innovations – Methods and Instruments*, 91–104. DOI: 10.12657/9788379862771-6

Bigne, E., Boksem, M., Casado-Aranda, L. A., García-Madariaga, J., Gier-Reinartz, N. R., Guerreiro, J., Loureiro, S., Kakaria, S., Smidts, A., & Wedel, M. (2025). How to Conduct Valuable Marketing Research With Neurophysiological Tools. *Psychology and Marketing, 42*(10), 2616–2649. DOI: 10.1002/mar.70002

Bigne, E., Simonetti, A., Guixeres, J., & Alcaniz, M. (2024). Visual attention and product interaction: A neuroscientific study on purchase across two product categories in a virtual store. *International Journal of Retail & Distribution Management, 52*(4), 389–406. DOI: 10.1108/IJRDM-02-2023-0067

Boerman, S. C., Willemsen, L. M., & Van Der Aa, E. P. (2017). "This post is sponsored": Effects of sponsorship disclosure on persuasion knowledge and electronic word of mouth in the context of Facebook. *Journal of Interactive Marketing, 38*(1), 82–92. DOI: 10.1016/j.intmar.2016.12.002

Bogomolova, S., Oppewal, H., Cohen, J., & Yao, J. (2020). How the layout of a unit price label affects eye-movements and product choice: An eye-tracking investigation. *Journal of Business Research, 111*, 102–116. DOI: 10.1016/j.jbusres.2018.10.049

Borawska, A., & Mateja, A. (2024). Unveiling the User Experience: A Synthesis of Cognitive Neuroscience Methods in Digital Product Design. In *Advances in Information Systems Development: Information Systems Development, Organizational Aspects, and Societal Trends* (pp. 199–218). Springer Nature Switzerland. DOI: 10.1007/978-3-031-57189-3_10

Böttcher, S., Vieluf, S., Bruno, E., Joseph, B., Epitashvili, N., Biondi, A., Zabler, N., Glasstetter, M., Dümpelmann, M., Van Laerhoven, K., Nasseri, M., Brinkman, B. H., Richardson, M. P., Schulze-Bonhage, A., & Loddenkemper, T. (2022). Data quality evaluation in wearable monitoring. *Scientific Reports*, *12*(1), 1–13. DOI: 10.1038/s41598-022-25949-x PMID: 36496546

Bozdog, L.-S., Naghi, R. I., Preda, G., & Prada, S. I. (2025). The Influence of AI Chatbots on the Purchase Intention of Sustainable Products. *Transformations in Business & Economics*, *24*(1 (64)), 238–261. DOI: 10.15388/Tibe.2025.24.1.11

Buhalis, D., Lin, M. S., & Leung, D. (2023). Metaverse as a driver for customer experience and value co-creation: Implications for hospitality and tourism management and marketing. *International Journal of Contemporary Hospitality Management*, *35*(2), 701–716. DOI: 10.1108/IJCHM-05-2022-0631

Buolamwini, J., & Gebru, T. (2018). Gender shades: Intersectional accuracy disparities in commercial gender classification. *Proceedings of Machine Learning Research*, *81*, 1–15.

Cadwalladr, C., & Graham-Harrison, E. (2018, March 17). Revealed: 50 million Facebook profiles harvested for Cambridge Analytica in major data breach. *The Guardian*. https://www.theguardian.com/news/2018/mar/17/cambridge-analytica-facebook-influence-us-election

Çakar, T., & Filiz, G. (2023). Unraveling neural pathways of political engagement: Bridging neuromarketing and political science for understanding voter behavior and political leader perception. *Frontiers in Human Neuroscience*, *17*, 1293173. Advance online publication. DOI: 10.3389/fnhum.2023.1293173 PMID: 38188505

Calderón Fajardo, V., Anaya-Sánchez, R., Rejón-Guardia, F., & Molinillo-Jiménez, S. (2024). Neurotourism insights: Eye tracking and galvanic analysis of tourism destination brand logos and AI visuals.

Cambria, E., & White, B. (2014). Jumping NLP curves: A review of natural language processing research. *IEEE Computational Intelligence Magazine*, *9*(2), 48–57. DOI: 10.1109/MCI.2014.2307227

Canhoto, A. I., Keegan, B. J., & Ryzhikh, M. (2024). Snakes and Ladders: Unpacking the Personalisation-Privacy Paradox in the Context of AI-Enabled Personalisation in the Physical Retail Environment. *Information Systems Frontiers*, *26*(3), 1005–1024. DOI: 10.1007/S10796-023-10369-7/FIGURES/3

Cao, X., & Zhang, J. (2021). Preference learning and demand forecast. *Marketing Science*, *40*(1), 62–79. DOI: 10.1287/mksc.2020.1238

Cardone, B., Di Martino, F., & Senatore, S. (2022). A fuzzy partition-based method to classify social messages assessing their emotional relevance. *Information Sciences*, *608*, 1178–1196. DOI: 10.1016/j.ins.2022.02.028

Casado-Aranda, L. A., Dimoka, A., & Sánchez-Fernández, J. (2019). Consumer Processing of Online Trust Signals: A Neuroimaging Study. *Journal of Interactive Marketing*, *47*(1), 159–180. DOI: 10.1016/j.intmar.2019.02.006

Casado-Aranda, L. A., Sánchez-Fernández, J., & García, N. (2022). Evaluating the neural mechanisms of exposure and retrieval of hedonic and utilitarian banners: A fMRI study. *Computers in Human Behavior*, *134*, 107317. DOI: 10.1016/j.chb.2022.107317

Casaló, L. V., Flavián, C., & Ibáñez-Sánchez, S. (2020). Influencers on Instagram: Antecedents and consequences of opinion leadership. *Journal of Business Research*, *117*, 510–519. DOI: 10.1016/j.jbusres.2018.07.005

Casarotto, S., Ricciardi, E., Romani, S., Dalli, D., & Pietrini, P. (2012). Covert brand recognition engages emotion-specific brain networks. *Archives Italiennes de Biologie*, *150*(4), 259–273. PMID: 23479459

Cenizo, C. (2025). A Neuromarketing Approach to Consumer Behavior on Web Platforms. *International Journal of Consumer Studies*, *49*(2), e70034. DOI: 10.1111/ijcs.70034

Chae, J. (2018). Explaining females' envy toward social media influencers. *Media Psychology*, *21*(2), 246–262. DOI: 10.1080/15213269.2017.1328312

Chakraborty, P., Ahmed, S., Yousuf, M. A., Azad, A. K. M., Alyami, S. A., & Moni, M. A. (2021). A human-robot interaction system calculating visual focus of human's attention level. *IEEE Access : Practical Innovations, Open Solutions*, *9*, 93409–93421. DOI: 10.1109/ACCESS.2021.3091642

Chand, T., Nair, V. S., Srinivasu, P. N., & Kumar, V. J. (2025). Prospects and challenges in decoding consumer behavior using neurotechnology. In Artificial intelligence applications for brain–computer interfaces (pp. 161–182). DOI: 10.1016/B978-0-443-33414-6.00011-3

Chandra, S., Verma, S., Lim, W. M., Kumar, S., & Donthu, N. (2022). Personalization in personalized marketing: Trends and ways forward. *Psychology and Marketing*, *39*(8), 1529–1562. DOI: 10.1002/mar.21670

Chan, E. Y. (2024). Consumer behavior in the future. In *Consumer behavior in practice: Strategic insights for the modern marketer* (pp. 251–263). Springer Nature Switzerland. DOI: 10.1007/978-3-031-50947-6_13

Chang, C. Y., Santra, A. S., Chang, I. H., Wu, S. J., Roy, D. S., & Zhang, Q. (2024). Design and implementation of a real-time face recognition system based on artificial intelligence techniques. *Multimedia Systems*, *30*(2), 114. DOI: 10.1007/s00530-024-01306-y

Chaudhary, U. (2025). Non-invasive Brain Signal Acquisition Techniques: Exploring EEG, EOG, fNIRS, fMRI, MEG, and fUS. In *Expanding Senses using Neurotechnology: Volume 1–Foundation of Brain-Computer Interface Technology* (pp. 25–80). Springer Nature Switzerland. DOI: 10.1007/978-3-031-76081-5_2

Cheng, K. H. (2022). The structural relationships among spatial presence, situational interest and behavioral attitudes toward online virtual museum navigation: A PLS-SEM analysis. *Library Hi Tech*, *40*(5), 1210–1225. DOI: 10.1108/LHT-09-2021-0301

Cheng, S., & Dey, A. K. (2019). I see, you design: User interface intelligent design system with eye tracking and interactive genetic algorithm. *CCF Transactions on Pervasive Computing and Interaction*, *1*(3), 224–236. DOI: 10.1007/s42486-019-00019-w

Cheng, S., Fan, J., & Hu, Y. (2023). Visual saliency model based on crowdsourcing eye tracking data and its application in visual design. *Personal and Ubiquitous Computing*, *27*(3), 613–630. DOI: 10.1007/s00779-020-01463-7

Chen, L., Zhong, X., Li, H., Wu, J., Lu, B., Chen, D., Xie, S.-P., Wu, L., Chao, Q., Lin, C., Hu, Z., & Qi, Y. (2024). A machine learning model that outperforms conventional global subseasonal forecast models. *Nature Communications*, *15*(1), 6425. DOI: 10.1038/s41467-024-50714-1 PMID: 39080287

Chen, S. (2024). The application of eye-tracking technology in chemistry education research: A systematic review. *Research in Science & Technological Education*, •••, 1–20.

Chen, X., & Chen, Z. (2017). Exploring visual attention using random walks based eye tracking protocols. *Journal of Visual Communication and Image Representation*, *45*, 147–155. DOI: 10.1016/j.jvcir.2017.02.005

Chen, X., Wang, S., Yang, X., Yu, C., Ni, F., Yang, J., Tian, Y., Ye, J., Liu, H., & Luo, R. (2023). Utilizing artificial intelligence-based eye tracking technology for screening ADHD symptoms in children. *Frontiers in Psychiatry, 14*, 1260031. DOI: 10.3389/fpsyt.2023.1260031 PMID: 38034916

Cherubino, P., Martinez-Levy, A. C., Caratù, M., Cartocci, G., Di Flumeri, G., Modica, E., Rossi, D., Mancini, M., & Trettel, A. (2019). Consumer behaviour through the eyes of neurophysiological measures: State-of-the-Art and future trends. *Computational Intelligence and Neuroscience, 2019*(1), 1976847. DOI: 10.1155/2019/1976847 PMID: 31641346

Chhajer, P., Shah, M., & Kshirsagar, A. (2022). The applications of artificial neural networks, support vector machines, and long–short term memory for stock market prediction. *Decision Analytics Journal, 2*, 100015. DOI: 10.1016/j.dajour.2021.100015

Chhaniwal, N., Rani, B., Jain, N., & Hushain, J. (2024). Impact of Virtual Reality on Consumer Purchase Intentions: A Neuromarketing Perspective.

Chintagunta, P., Hanssens, D. M., & Hauser, J. R. (2016). Marketing science and big data. In *Marketing Science* (Vol. 35, Number 3, pp. 341–342). INFORMS Inst. for Operations Res.and the Management Sciences. DOI: 10.1287/mksc.2016.0996

Chiu, M. C., Huang, J. H., Gupta, S., & Akman, G. (2021). Developing a personalized recommendation system in a smart product service system based on an unsupervised learning model. *Computers in Industry, 128*, 103421. Advance online publication. DOI: 10.1016/j.compind.2021.103421

Christopoulos, G. I., Uy, M. A., & Yap, W. J. (2019). The body and the brain: Measuring skin conductance responses to understand the emotional experience. *Organizational Research Methods, 22*(1), 394–420. DOI: 10.1177/1094428116681073

Chygryn, O., Shevchenko, K., & Tuliakov, O. (2024). Neuromarketing as a mechanism of communication with the consumer: The case for small business. *Marketing i menedžment innovacij, 15*(2), 26-38.

Ciceri, A., Russo, V., Songa, G., Gabrielli, G., & Clement, J. (2020). A neuroscientific method for assessing effectiveness of digital vs. print ads: Using biometric techniques to measure cross-media ad experience and recall. *Journal of Advertising Research, 60*(1), 71–86. DOI: 10.2501/JAR-2019-015

Cioffi, G. M., Pinilla-Echeverri, N., Sheth, T., & Sibbald, M. G. (2023). Does artificial intelligence enhance physician interpretation of optical coherence tomography: Insights from eye tracking. *Frontiers in Cardiovascular Medicine, 10*, 1283338. DOI: 10.3389/fcvm.2023.1283338 PMID: 38144364

Clement, J., Kristensen, T., & Grønhaug, K. (2013). Understanding consumers' in-store visual perception: The influence of package design features on visual attention. *Journal of Retailing and Consumer Services*, *20*(2), 234–239. DOI: 10.1016/j.jretconser.2013.01.003

Clement, S. (2025). Leveraging artificial intelligence for sustainable healthcare marketing: Opportunities and ethical challenges. *Academy of Marketing Studies Journal*, *29*(5), 1–9.

Clithero, J. A., Karmarkar, U. R., & Hsu, M. (2021). Toward an integrative conceptualization of maladaptive consumer behavior. *Journal of the Association for Consumer Research*, *6*(3), 334–341. DOI: 10.1086/714364

Cong, L., Luan, S., Young, E., Mirosa, M., Bremer, P., & Torrico, D. D. (2023). The application of biometric approaches in agri-food marketing: A systematic literature review. *Foods*, *12*(16), 2982. DOI: 10.3390/foods12162982 PMID: 37627981

Cordeiro, R., Reis, A., Ferreira, B. M., & Bacalhau, L. M. (2024). Neuromarketing: Decoding the Role of Emotions and Senses and Consumer Behaviour. *Cognitive Behavioural Neuroscience in Organizational Settings*, 83-100.

Cordova-Buiza, F., Grillo-Torres, C. M., & Vega, C. R. (2025). Gastronomic culture and social networks: The impact of digital strategies on the promotion of traditional colombian cuisine. *Geo Journal of Tourism and Geosites*, *59*(2), 587–594. DOI: 10.30892/gtg.59207-1439

Costa-Feito, A., González-Fernández, A. M., Rodríguez-Santos, C., & Cervantes-Blanco, M. (2023). Electroencephalography in consumer behaviour and marketing: A science mapping approach. *Humanities & Social Sciences Communications*, *10*(1), 1–13. DOI: 10.1057/s41599-023-01991-6

Cowls, J., Tsamados, A., Taddeo, M., & Floridi, L. (2023). The AI gambit: Leveraging artificial intelligence to combat climate change—opportunities, challenges, and recommendations. *AI & Society*, *38*(1), 283–307. DOI: 10.1007/S00146-021-01294-X/METRICS

Crawford, K. (2021). *Atlas of AI: Power, politics, and the planetary costs of artificial intelligence*. Yale University Press.

Cueva, C. J., Saez, A., Marcos, E., Genovesio, A., Jazayeri, M., Romo, R., Salzman, C. D., Shadlen, M. N., & Fusi, S. (2020). Low-dimensional dynamics for working memory and time encoding. *Proceedings of the National Academy of Sciences of the United States of America*, *117*(37), 23021–23032. DOI: 10.1073/PNAS.1915984117/SUPPL_FILE/PNAS.1915984117.SAPP.PDF

D'Aniello, G., Gaeta, M., & La Rocca, I. (2022). KnowMIS-ABSA: An overview and a reference model for applications of sentiment analysis and aspect-based sentiment analysis. *Artificial Intelligence Review, 55*(6), 4813–4846. DOI: 10.1007/s10462-021-10134-9

Dahouda, M. K., & Joe, I. (2021). A Deep-Learned Embedding Technique for Categorical Features Encoding. *IEEE Access : Practical Innovations, Open Solutions, 9*, 114381–114391. DOI: 10.1109/ACCESS.2021.3104357

Dang, C. N., Moreno-García, M. N., & Prieta, F. D. (2021). An approach to integrating sentiment analysis into recommender systems. *Sensors (Basel), 21*(3), 1012. Advance online publication. DOI: 10.3390/s21165666 PMID: 34451118

Daugherty, T., & Hoffman, E. (2016). Neuromarketing: Understanding the application of neuroscientific methods within marketing research. In Ethics and neuromarketing: Implications for market research and business practice (pp. 5–30). Springer International Publishing.

Davenport, T., Guha, A., Grewal, D., & Bressgott, T. (2020). How artificial intelligence will change the future of marketing. *Journal of the Academy of Marketing Science, 48*(1), 24–42. DOI: 10.1007/s11747-019-00696-0

Davis, F. D. (1989). Perceived usefulness, perceived ease of use, and user acceptance of information technology. *Management Information Systems Quarterly, 13*(3), 319–340. DOI: 10.2307/249008

De Martino, B., Kumaran, D., Seymour, B., & Dolan, R. J. (2006). Frames, biases, and rational decision-making in the human brain. *Science, 313*(5787), 684–687. DOI: 10.1126/science.1128356 PMID: 16888142

De Veirman, M., Cauberghe, V., & Hudders, L. (2017). Marketing through Instagram influencers: The impact of number of followers and product divergence on brand attitude. *International Journal of Advertising, 36*(5), 798–828. DOI: 10.1080/02650487.2017.1348035

Deckker, D., & Sumanasekara, S. (2025). AI and neuromarketing – Understanding consumer decision making with artificial intelligence – Systematic review. *Indonesian Journal of Business Analytics, 5*(2), 1929–1946. DOI: 10.55927/ijba.v5i2.13990

Dessart, L. (2017). Social media engagement: A model of antecedents and relational outcomes. *Journal of Marketing Management, 33*(5–6), 375–399. DOI: 10.1080/0267257X.2017.1302975

Dewandaru, B., Goncalves, M., & Rahmadi, A. N. (2023). IMPACT OF DIGITAL MARKETING, DIGITAL FINANCE, AND DIGITAL LITERACY ON BUSINESS PERFORMANCE SMEs. *Journal of Innovation Research and Knowledge, 3*(3). https://bajangjournal.com/index.php/JIRK/article/view/8788

Dewey, C. (2023). Metacognitive control in single- vs. dual-process theory. *Thinking & Reasoning, 29*(2), 177–212. DOI: 10.1080/13546783.2022.2047106;JOURNAL:-JOURNAL:PTAR20;WGROUP:STRING:PUBLICATION

Dignum, V. (2018). Ethics in artificial intelligence: Introduction to the special issue. *Ethics and Information Technology, 20*(1), 1–3. DOI: 10.1007/S10676-018-9450-Z/METRICS

Djafarova, E., & Trofimenko, O. (2019). 'Instafamous' – credibility and self-presentation of micro-celebrities on social media. *Information Communication and Society, 22*(10), 1432–1446. DOI: 10.1080/1369118X.2018.1438491

Douglas, B. D., Ewell, P. J., & Brauer, M. (2023). Data quality in online human-subjects research: Comparisons between MTurk, Prolific, CloudResearch, Qualtrics, and SONA. *PLoS One, 18*(1), e0280404. Advance online publication. DOI: 10.1371/journal.pone.0279720 PMID: 36917576

Dragolea, L., & Cotirlea, D. (2011). Neuromarketing: between influence and manipulation. *Polish journal of management studies, 3*, 78-88.

Drews, M., & Dierkes, K. (2024). Strategies for enhancing automatic fixation detection in head-mounted eye tracking. *Behavior Research Methods, 56*(6), 6276–6298. DOI: 10.3758/s13428-024-02360-0 PMID: 38594440

Duan, S., Wang, Z., Wang, S., & Chen, M. (2024). Emotion-aware interaction design in intelligent user interface using multi-modal deep learning. In 2024 5th International Conference on Artificial Intelligence and Computer Engineering (ICAICE) (pp. 1–6). DOI: 10.1109/ISCEIC63613.2024.10810240

Dwivedi, Y. K., Hughes, L., Wang, Y., Alalwan, A. A., Ahn, S. J., Balakrishnan, J., Barta, S., Belk, R., Buhalis, D., Dutot, V., Felix, R., Filieri, R., Flavián, C., Gustafsson, A., Hinsch, C., Hollensen, S., Jain, V., Kim, J., Krishen, A. S., & Wirtz, J. (2023). Metaverse marketing: How the metaverse will shape the future of consumer research and practice. *Psychology and Marketing, 40*(4), 750–776. DOI: 10.1002/mar.21767

Dwork, C., & Roth, A. (2014). The algorithmic foundations of differential privacy. *Foundations and Trends in Theoretical Computer Science, 9*(3–4), 211–407. DOI: 10.1561/0400000042

Edelman. (2021). *Edelman trust barometer 2021.* Edelman. https://www.edelman.com/trust/2021-trust-barometer

Eisenbeiss, M., Cornelissen, G., Backhaus, K., & Hoyer, W. D. (2014). Nonlinear and asymmetric returns on customer satisfaction: Do they vary across situations and consumers? *Journal of the Academy of Marketing Science*, *42*(3), 242–263. DOI: 10.1007/s11747-013-0366-1

Erensoy, A., Mathrani, A., Schnack, A., Elms, J., & Baghaei, N. (2024). Consumer behavior in immersive virtual reality retail environments: A systematic literature review using the stimuli-organisms-responses (S-O-r) model. *Journal of Consumer Behaviour*, *23*(6), 2781–2811. DOI: 10.1002/cb.2374

Eslami, M., Rickman, A., Vaccaro, K., Aleyasen, A., Vuong, A., Karahalios, K., Hamilton, K., & Sandvig, C. (2015). "I always assumed that I wasn't really that close to [her]": Reasoning about invisible algorithms in news feeds. *Proceedings of the 33rd Annual ACM Conference on Human Factors in Computing Systems*, 153–162. https://doi.org/DOI: 10.1145/2702123.2702556

Evans, J. S. B., & Stanovich, K. E. (2013). Dual-process theories of higher cognition: Advancing the debate. *Perspectives on Psychological Science*, *8*(3), 223–241. DOI: 10.1177/1745691612460685 PMID: 26172965

Evans, N. J., Phua, J., Lim, J., & Jun, H. (2017). Disclosing Instagram influencer advertising: The effects of disclosure language on advertising recognition, attitudes, and behavioural intent. *Journal of Interactive Advertising*, *17*(2), 138–149. DOI: 10.1080/15252019.2017.1366885

Farhud, D. D., & Zokaei, S. (2021). Ethical issues of artificial intelligence in medicine and healthcare. *Iranian Journal of Public Health*, *50*(11), i–v. DOI: 10.18502/ijph.v50i11.7600 PMID: 35223619

Feijóo, C., & Kwon, Y. (2020a). AI impacts on economy and society: Latest developments, open issues and new policy measures. *Telecommunications Policy*, *44*(6), 101987. Advance online publication. DOI: 10.1016/j.telpol.2020.101987 PMID: 32377031

Ferrell, M. L., Beatty, A., & Dubljevic, V. (2025). The Ethics of Neuromarketing: A Rapid Review. In *Neuroethics* (Vol. 18, Number 1). Springer Science and Business Media B.V. DOI: 10.1007/s12152-025-09591-8

Fici, A., Bilucaglia, M., Casiraghi, C., Rossi, C., Chiarelli, S., Columbano, M., Micheletto, V., Zito, M., & Russo, V. (2024). From E-commerce to the metaverse: A neuroscientific analysis of digital consumer behavior. *Behavioral Sciences (Basel, Switzerland)*, *14*(7), 596. DOI: 10.3390/bs14070596 PMID: 39062419

Filieri, R., Lin, Z., Li, Y., Lu, X., & Yang, X. (2022). Customer emotions in service robot encounters: A hybrid machine-human intelligence approach. *Journal of Service Research*, *25*(2), 267–285. DOI: 10.1177/10946705221103937

Floridi, L., Cowls, J., Beltrametti, M., Chatila, R., Chazerand, P., Dignum, V., Luetge, C., Madelin, R., Pagallo, U., Rossi, F., Schafer, B., Valcke, P., & Vayena, E. (2018). AI4People—An ethical framework for a good AI society. *Minds and Machines*, *28*(4), 689–707. DOI: 10.1007/s11023-018-9482-5 PMID: 30930541

Fortunato, V. C. R., Giraldi, J. D. M. E., & De Oliveira, J. H. C. (2014). A Review of Studies on Neuromarketing: Practical Results, Techniques, Contributions and Limitations. *Journal of Management Research*, *6*(2), 201. DOI: 10.5296/jmr.v6i2.5446

Frederick, D. P. (2022). Recent trends in neuro marketing–An exploratory study. [IJCSBE]. *International Journal of Case Studies in Business, IT, and Education*, *6*(1), 38–60. DOI: 10.47992/IJCSBE.2581.6942.0148

Furnham, A., & Boo, H. C. (2011). A literature review of the anchoring effect. *Journal of Socio-Economics*, *40*(1), 35–42. DOI: 10.1016/j.socec.2010.10.008

Gamage, G., De Silva, D., Mills, N., Alahakoon, D., & Manic, M. (2024). Emotion AWARE: An artificial intelligence framework for adaptable, robust, explainable, and multi-granular emotion analysis. *Journal of Big Data*, *11*(1), 1–25. DOI: 10.1186/s40537-024-00953-2

Ganeshkumar, M., Karunakaran, S., Muzhumathi, R., & Suguna, R. (2024, October). Ai-driven marketing insights: Harnessing machine learning for enhanced consumer engagement and personalization. In *2024 First International Conference on Software, Systems and Information Technology (SSITCON)* (pp. 1-6). IEEE. DOI: 10.1109/SSITCON62437.2024.10796558

Gao, E., Zhong, H., Yuan, R., Guo, J., & Chen, Z. (2025, May). "How Do You Understand? Your Eyes Show It": Explainable Artificial Intelligence for Cross-Language Comprehension Prediction Through Eye Movement. In *International Conference on Human-Computer Interaction* (pp. 323-348). Cham: Springer Nature Switzerland.

Gensler, S., Völckner, F., Liu-Thompkins, Y., & Wiertz, C. (2013). Managing brands in the social media environment. *Journal of Interactive Marketing*, *27*(4), 242–256. DOI: 10.1016/j.intmar.2013.09.004

Gervasi, R., Barravecchia, F., Mastrogiacomo, L., & Franceschini, F. (2023). Applications of affective computing in human-robot interaction: State-of-the-art and challenges for manufacturing. *Proceedings of the Institution of Mechanical Engineers. Part B, Journal of Engineering Manufacture*, *237*(6–7), 815–832. DOI: 10.1177/09544054221121888

Giannakopoulos, N. T., Sakas, D. P., & Migkos, S. P. (2024). Neuromarketing and big data analysis of banking firms' website interfaces and performance. *Electronics (Basel)*, *13*(16), 3256. DOI: 10.3390/electronics13163256

Gohain, T. T., Rajagopal, G., Firas Armosh, F. A., & Dwivedi, D. P. K. (2024). A study on role of neuromarketing in digital era business development. *Migration Letters : An International Journal of Migration Studies*, *21*(S4), 1600–1605.

Goncalves, M., & Dangelo, D. (2026). Consumer privacy and neuromarketing: Ethical implications and legal frameworks in California. In *Next generation entrepreneurship: Convergence of innovation, technology, and society* (pp. 443–471). Springer Nature Switzerland. DOI: 10.1007/978-3-031-98513-3_17

Goncalves, M., Hu, Y., Aliagas, I., & Cerdá, L. M. (2024). Neuromarketing algorithms' consumer privacy and ethical considerations: Challenges and opportunities. *Cogent Business & Management*, *11*(1), 2333063. DOI: 10.1080/23311975.2024.2333063;PAGE:STRING:ARTICLE/CHAPTER

Gowri, D. P. (2024). Impact of AI in personalized digital marketing: Boosting customer engagement through tailored content. *Journal of Communication Management (London)*, *3*(03), 216–221.

Greenwald, A. G., Poehlman, T. A., Uhlmann, E. L., & Banaji, M. R. (2009). Understanding and using the Implicit Association Test: III. Meta-analysis of predictive validity. *Journal of Personality and Social Psychology*, *97*(1), 17–41. DOI: 10.1037/a0015575 PMID: 19586237

Grewal, D., Guha, A., Satornino, C. B., & Schweiger, E. B. (2021). Artificial intelligence: The light and the darkness. *Journal of Business Research*, *136*, 229–236. DOI: 10.1016/j.jbusres.2021.07.043

Grewal, D., Hulland, J., Kopalle, P. K., & Karahanna, E. (2020). The future of technology and marketing: A multidisciplinary perspective. *Journal of the Academy of Marketing Science*, *48*(1), 1–8. DOI: 10.1007/s11747-019-00711-4

Grewal, D., Roggeveen, A. L., & Nordfält, J. (2017). The future of retailing. *Journal of Retailing*, *93*(1), 1–6. DOI: 10.1016/j.jretai.2016.12.008

Guo, R., Kim, N., & Lee, J. (2024). Empirical insights into eye-tracking for design evaluation: Applications in visual communication and new media design. *Behavioral Sciences (Basel, Switzerland), 14*(12), 1231. DOI: 10.3390/bs14121231 PMID: 39767372

Gupta, R., Kapoor, A. P., & Verma, H. V. (2025b). Neuro-insights: a systematic review of neuromarketing perspectives across consumer buying stages. In *Frontiers in Neuroergonomics* (Vol. 6). Frontiers Media SA. DOI: 10.3389/fnrgo.2025.1542847

Gupta, R., Kapoor, A. P., & Verma, H. (2025a). Exploring consumer neuroscience in marketing research: Theoretical foundations, methodological aspects, and future research directions. *Journal of Marketing Theory and Practice*, 1–27. Advance online publication. DOI: 10.1080/10696679.2025.2493816

Gurgu, E., Gurgu, I.-A., & Tonis, R. B. M. (2020). Neuromarketing for a better understanding of consumer needs and emotions. *Independent Journal of Management & Production, 11*(1), 208–235. DOI: 10.14807/ijmp.v11i1.993

Haleem, A., Javaid, M., & Vaishya, R. (2025). *The new era of Artificial Intelligence in consumption: Theoretical framing, review and research agenda*. Management Review Quarterly., DOI: 10.1007/s11301-025-00531-7

Hamelin, N., Moujahid, O., & Thaichon, P. (2017). Emotion and advertising effectiveness: A novel facial expression analysis approach. *Journal of Retailing and Consumer Services, 36*, 103–111. DOI: 10.1016/j.jretconser.2017.01.001

Hamelin, N., Thaichon, P., Abraham, C., Driver, N., Lipscombe, J., & Pillai, J. (2020). Storytelling, the scale of persuasion and retention: A neuromarketing approach. *Journal of Retailing and Consumer Services, 55*, 102099. DOI: 10.1016/j.jretconser.2020.102099

Han, D. I. D., Weber, J., Bastiaansen, M., Mitas, O., & Lub, X. (2020). Blowing your mind: A conceptual framework of augmented reality and virtual reality enhanced cultural visitor experiences using EEG experience measures. *International Journal of Technology Marketing, 14*(1), 47–68. DOI: 10.1504/IJTMKT.2020.105118

Haque, A., Akther, N., Khan, I., Agarwal, K., & Uddin, N. (2024). Artificial Intelligence in Retail Marketing: Research Agenda Based on Bibliometric Reflection and Content Analysis (2000–2023). *Informatics 2024, Vol. 11, Page 74, 11*(4), 74. DOI: 10.3390/INFORMATICS11040074

Hari, H., Sharma, A., Verma, S., & Chaturvedi, R. (2024). Exploring ethical frontiers of artificial intelligence in marketing. *Journal of Responsible Technology, 19*, 100103. Advance online publication. DOI: 10.1016/j.jrt.2024.100103

Harris, J. M., Ciorciari, J., & Gountas, J. (2018). Consumer neuroscience for marketing researchers. *Journal of Consumer Behaviour, 17*(3), 239–252. DOI: 10.1002/cb.1710

Hartmann, J., Heitmann, M., Siebert, C., & Schamp, C. (2023). More than a feeling: Accuracy and application of sentiment analysis. *International Journal of Research in Marketing, 40*(1), 1–20. DOI: 10.1016/j.ijresmar.2022.05.005

Heikkonen, A. (2024). *Viral video marketing on TikTok: effects on brands beyond views, likes and shares* (Master's thesis, A. Heikkonen). https://urn.fi/URN:NBN:fi:oulu-202405304095

Helen, J., & Siva Sankar, R. (2025). The Role of AI in Transforming Global E-commerce and Consumer Behaviour. *Thiagarajar College of Preceptors Edu Spectra, 7*(S1), 48–55. DOI: 10.34293/eduspectra.v7is1-feb25.006

Hillaire, S., Breton, G., Ouarti, N., Cozot, R., & Lécuyer, A. (2010, September). Using a visual attention model to improve gaze tracking systems in interactive 3d applications. [). Oxford, UK: Blackwell Publishing Ltd.]. *Computer Graphics Forum, 29*(6), 1830–1841. DOI: 10.1111/j.1467-8659.2010.01651.x

Ho, D. B., Duong, C. D., Tran, M. L., Luong, T. S., & Tran, T. P. H. (2025). Big data analytics powered by artificial intelligence and entrepreneurial resilience: A moderated mediation model of technological turbulence and business innovation model. *Journal of Open Innovation, 11*(3), 100611. Advance online publication. DOI: 10.1016/j.joitmc.2025.100611

Horowitz, T., Doyen, M., Caminiti, S. P., Yakushev, I., Verger, A., & Guedj, E. (2025). Metabolic brain PET connectivity. *PET Clinics, 20*(1), 1–10. DOI: 10.1016/j.cpet.2024.09.014

Horton, D., & Wohl, R. R. (1956). Mass communication and parasocial interaction: Observations on intimacy at a distance. *Psychiatry, 19*(3), 215–229. DOI: 10.1080/00332747.1956.11023049

Hossain, M. S., & Rahman, M. F. (2023). Customer sentiment analysis and prediction of insurance products' reviews using machine learning approaches. *FIIB Business Review, 12*(2), 158–169. DOI: 10.1177/23197145221115793

Hsu, L., & Chen, Y. J. (2020). Neuromarketing, subliminal advertising, and hotel selection: An EEG study. *Australasian Marketing Journal, 28*(4), 200–208. DOI: 10.1016/j.ausmj.2020.04.009

Hsu, M. (2017). Neuromarketing: Inside the consumer's mind. *Frontiers in Psychology, 8*, 774. DOI: 10.3389/fpsyg.2017.00774

Hsu, M. (2017). Neuromarketing: Inside the mind of the consumer. *California Management Review, 59*(4), 5–22. DOI: 10.1177/0008125617720208

Huang, M. H., & Rust, R. T. (2021). Artificial Intelligence in service. *Journal of Service Research, 24*(1), 3–21.

Hubballi, R. B., Selvakumar, P., Seenivasan, R., Basava Aradhya, S. G., Dinesh, N., & Seelam, P. K. (2025). Overview of current AI technologies in education. In Kyei-Blankson, L., & Ntuli, E. (Eds.), *Transformative AI practices for personalized learning strategies* (pp. 1–26). IGI Global Scientific Publishing., DOI: 10.4018/979-8-3693-8744-3.ch001

Huddleston, P., McAlister, A. R., & Alade, F. (2025). Through a child's eyes: Eye tracking to study children's consumer behavior. *Journal of Consumer Marketing, 42*(2), 174–192. DOI: 10.1108/JCM-11-2023-6396

Hu, L., Tan, C., & Deng, H. (2023). Product recommendation using online reviews with emotional preferences. *Kybernetes, 52*(5), 1573–1596. DOI: 10.1108/K-09-2021-0852

Hutchinson, J. W., Reimann, M., Knutson, B., & Huber, J. (2024). Commentaries on "Reconsidering the path for neural and physiological methods in consumer psychology". *Journal of Consumer Psychology, 34*(1), 214–221. DOI: 10.1002/jcpy.1398

Hwang, Y. M., & Lee, K. C. (2018). Using an eye-tracking approach to explore gender differences in visual attention and shopping attitudes in an online shopping environment. *International Journal of Human-Computer Interaction, 34*(1), 15–24. DOI: 10.1080/10447318.2017.1314611

Iloka, C. B., & Anukwe, G. I. (2020). Review of eye-tracking: A neuromarketing technique. *Neuroscience Research Notes, 3*(4), 29–34. DOI: 10.31117/neuroscirn.v3i4.61

Isa, S. M., & Anuar, N. N. A. (2024). Neuromarketing cues: An eye-tracking study on mother's visual attention to organic vegetable advertisement. *Neuroscience Research Notes, 7*(4), 363–1.

Ismagilova, E., Slade, E. L., Rana, N. P., & Dwivedi, Y. K. (2020). The Effect of Electronic Word of Mouth Communications on Intention to Buy: A Meta-Analysis. *Information Systems Frontiers, 22*(5), 1203–1226. DOI: 10.1007/s10796-019-09924-y

Jain, P., Jain, P., & Jain, A. (2024). Marketing's crystal ball: Where we are and where we could soon be with generative artificial intelligence in marketing. *Journal of Cultural Marketing Strategy, 8*(2), 134–150. DOI: 10.69554/JDOC2249

Jamil, N., & Belkacem, A. N. (2024). Advancing real-time remote learning: A novel paradigm for cognitive enhancement using EEG and eye-tracking analytics. *IEEE Access : Practical Innovations, Open Solutions, 12*, 93116–93132. DOI: 10.1109/ACCESS.2024.3422926

Jayapal, J. (2025). Unveiling the impact of AI-driven personalization on customer loyalty in online shopping: The moderating effects of privacy concerns. *Journal of Promotion Management, 31*(5), 865–894. DOI: 10.1080/10496491.2025.2525099

Jessie Chen-Yu, H., & Kincade, D. H. (2001). Effects of product image at three stages of the consumer decision process for apparel products: Alternative evaluation, purchase and post-purchase. *Journal of Fashion Marketing and Management, 5*(1), 29–43. DOI: 10.1108/EUM0000000007277

Jin, J., Jia, D., & Chen, K. (2022). Mining online reviews with a Kansei-integrated Kano model for innovative product design. *International Journal of Production Research, 60*(11), 3437–3454. DOI: 10.1080/00207543.2021.1949641

Jin, K., Zhang, Y., & Chen, J. (2025). Optimizing Urban Visual Identity: Eye-Tracking Insights for Outdoor Advertising Management. *Buildings (Basel, Switzerland), 15*(12), 2128. DOI: 10.3390/buildings15122128

Jin, S. V., & Ryu, E. (2020). "I'll buy what she's #wearing": The roles of envy toward and parasocial interaction with influencers in Instagram celebrity-based brand endorsement and social commerce. *Journal of Retailing and Consumer Services, 55*, 102121. DOI: 10.1016/j.jretconser.2020.102121

Jobin, A., Ienca, M., & Vayena, E. (2019). The global landscape of AI ethics guidelines. *Nature Machine Intelligence 2019 1:9, 1*(9), 389–399. DOI: 10.1038/s42256-019-0088-2

Jordan, M. I., & Mitchell, T. M. (2015). Machine learning: Trends, perspectives, and prospects. In *Science* (Vol. 349, Number 6245, pp. 255–260). American Association for the Advancement of Science. DOI: 10.1126/science.aaa8415

Jordao, I. L. D. S., Souza, M. T. D., Oliveira, J. H. C. D., & Giraldi, J. D. M. E. (2017). Neuromarketing applied to consumer behaviour: An integrative literature review between 2010 and 2015. *International Journal of Business Forecasting and Marketing Intelligence, 3*(3), 270–288. DOI: 10.1504/IJBFMI.2017.085371

Juarez, D., Tur-Viñes, V., & Mengual, A. (2020). Neuromarketing Applied to Educational Toy Packaging. *Frontiers in Psychology, 11*, 2077. Advance online publication. DOI: 10.3389/fpsyg.2020.02077 PMID: 32982857

Judijanto, L., Riatmaja, D. S., & Ajie, B. (2025). NEUROMARKETING INSIGHTS INTO BRAND LOYALTY FORMATION IN GEN Z CONSUMERS. *INTERNATIONAL JOURNAL OF FINANCIAL ECONOMICS, 2*(3), 970–985.

Jung, N. Y. (2025). AI-Powered personalization drives loyalty in retail. In *Leveraging AI-Powered Marketing in the Experience-Driven Economy* (pp. 105–146). IGI Global Scientific Publishing. DOI: 10.4018/979-8-3693-9561-5.ch004

K, L., Kumar, P., Chowdhury, S., & Madhavedi, S. (2024). Role of Neuromarketing and Artificial Intelligence in Futuristic Marketing Approach: An Empirical Study. *Journal of Informatics Education and Research, 4*(2), 560–567. http://jier.org

Kachhara, G., & Jain, J. (2025). Unleashing Synergy: A review of the Impact of AI and Neuromarketing on Business Success. *International Journal of Environmental Sciences, 11*(3s), 727–739.

Kahneman, D. (2011). *Thinking, fast and slow*. Farrar, Straus and Giroux.

Kahneman, D., & Tversky, A. (1979). Prospect theory: An analysis of decision under risk. *Econometrica, 47*(2), 263–291. DOI: 10.2307/1914185

Kajla, T., Raj, S., Kansra, P., Gupta, S. L., & Singh, N. (2024). Neuromarketing and consumer behavior: A bibliometric analysis. *Journal of Consumer Behaviour, 23*(2), 959–975. DOI: 10.1002/cb.2256

Kaklauskas, A., Abraham, A., Ubarte, I., Kliukas, R., Luksaite, V., Binkyte-Veliene, A., Vetloviene, I., & Kaklauskiene, L. (2022). A review of AI cloud and edge sensors, methods, and applications for the recognition of emotional, affective and physiological states. *Sensors (Basel), 22*(20), 7824. DOI: 10.3390/s22207824 PMID: 36298176

Kannan, P. K., & Li, H. (2017). Digital marketing: A framework, review and research agenda. *International Journal of Research in Marketing, 34*(1), 22–45. DOI: 10.1016/j.ijresmar.2016.11.006

Kaplan, A. (2021). Artificial intelligence, marketing, and the future of consumer behavior. *European Journal of Marketing, 55*(7), 1973–1994. DOI: 10.1108/EJM-12-2019-0936

Kaplan, A., & Haenlein, M. (2019). Siri, Siri, in my hand: Who's the fairest in the land? On the interpretations, illustrations, and implications of artificial intelligence. *Business Horizons, 62*(1), 15–25. DOI: 10.1016/j.bushor.2018.08.004

Kapoor, A., & Sindwani, R. (2025). Artificial Intelligence as a Catalyst for Advancing Contactless Payments: Unveiling Key Adoption Drivers. In *AI Marketing and Ethical Considerations in Consumer Engagement* (pp. 321–338). IGI Global Scientific Publishing. DOI: 10.4018/979-8-3373-3476-9.ch016

Kapoor, A., Sindwani, R., & Goel, M. (2021a). Prioritising the key factors influencing the adoption of mobile wallets: An Indian perspective in covid-19 era. *Journal of Information Technology Management, 13*(4), 161–182.

Kapoor, A., Sindwani, R., & Goel, M. (2021b). Ranking mobile wallet service providers using fuzzy multi-criteria decision-making approach. [IJEBR]. *International Journal of E-Business Research, 17*(4), 1–21. DOI: 10.4018/IJEBR.2021100102

Kapoor, A., Sindwani, R., & Goel, M. (2023a). Evaluating mobile wallet acceptance factors using best worst method. *International Journal of Process Management and Benchmarking, 13*(4), 449–469. DOI: 10.1504/IJPMB.2023.129822

Kapoor, A., Sindwani, R., & Goel, M. (2023b). Exploring quick commerce service experience: A moderated mediated investigation using SEM and fsQCA. *Total Quality Management & Business Excellence, 34*(13-14), 1896–1919. DOI: 10.1080/14783363.2023.2213653

Kapoor, A., Sindwani, R., & Goel, M. (2024). Exploring the symmetric and asymmetric effects of mobile wallet service experience on brand loyalty in India: Evidence from SEM and fsQCA. *Journal of Financial Services Marketing, 29*(4), 1524–1541. DOI: 10.1057/s41264-024-00280-w

Kapoor, A., Sindwani, R., & Goel, M. (2025a). A novel framework for understanding the interplay between the mobile wallet service quality dimensions and loyalty intention. *The TQM Journal, 37*(6), 1716–1741. DOI: 10.1108/TQM-12-2023-0422

Kapoor, A., Sindwani, R., & Goel, M. (2025b). Assessing mobile wallet service quality using analytic hierarchy process and fuzzy evaluation method. *International Journal of Services and Operations Management, 50*(2), 246–266. DOI: 10.1504/IJSOM.2025.144481

Kapoor, A., Sindwani, R., & Goel, M. (2025c). Unlocking India's mobile wallet potential: Identifying and prioritising key sustainable growth catalysts using best worst method. *International Journal of Process Management and Benchmarking, 21*(2), 218–230. DOI: 10.1504/IJPMB.2025.148685

Kapoor, A., Sindwani, R., Goel, M., & Shankar, A. (2022). Mobile wallet adoption intention amid COVID-19 pandemic outbreak: A novel conceptual framework. *Computers & Industrial Engineering*, *172*, 108646. DOI: 10.1016/j.cie.2022.108646 PMID: 36118531

Karmarkar, U. R. (2011). Note on neuromarketing. *Harvard Business School Background Note 512-031*.

Karthik, R. V., & Ganapathy, S. (2021). A fuzzy recommendation system for predicting the customers' interests using sentiment analysis and ontology in e-commerce. *Applied Soft Computing*, *102*, 107101. Advance online publication. DOI: 10.1016/j.asoc.2021.107396

Kaur, J., Mogaji, E., Paliwal, M., Jha, S., Agarwal, S., & Mogaji, S. A. (2024). Consumer behavior in the metaverse. *Journal of Consumer Behaviour*, *23*(4), 1720–1738. DOI: 10.1002/cb.2298

Kaur, K., & Sharma, T. (2024). Impulse buying in the digital age: An exploration using systematic literature review approach. *Journal of Consumer Behaviour*, *23*(5), 2553–2584. DOI: 10.1002/cb.2360

Kavya, G. B. (2024). IMPACT OF ARTIFICIAL INTELLIGENCE ON E-COMMERCE:"A STUDY OF CONSUMER BEHAVIOR". *EPRA International Journal of Environmental Economics. Commerce and Educational Management*, *51–54*. Advance online publication. DOI: 10.36713/epra18548

Keller, K. L., & Lehmann, D. R. (2006). Brands and branding: Research findings and future priorities. *Marketing Science*, *25*(6), 740–759. DOI: 10.1287/mksc.1050.0153

Kemora, H., Pasaribu, P., Marlina, A., & Himawan, E. N. (2024). Optimizing Digital Marketing Efforts Through Neuromarketing: Systematic Review. *Moneter: Jurnal Keuangan dan Perbankan, 12*(1), 32-44.

Kesarwani, J., Rai, H., & Kesarwani, R. (2025). A Neuromarketing Framework for Data-Driven Intelligent Automation in Marketing. *Handbook of Intelligent Automation Systems Using Computer Vision and Artificial Intelligence*, 449-469.

Khairunnisa, D., Salqaura, S. A., & Lestari, I. (2025). Pengaruh Viral Marketing dan Neuromarketing terhadap Keputusan Pembelian Konsumen Fore Coffee. *RIGGS: Journal of Artificial Intelligence and Digital Business*, *4*(2), 7373–7378. DOI: 10.31004/riggs.v4i2.1874

Khamoushi, E. (2024). AI in Food Marketing from Personalized Recommendations to Predictive Analytics: Comparing Traditional Advertising Techniques with AI-Driven Strategies. *Cornell University*. https://doi.org/https://doi.org/10.48550/arXiv.2410.01815

Khan, A. A., Khan, K. M., Habib, M. S., Islam, M., Rehman, B. U., Shahid, H., & Ullah, K. (2025). HAND GESTURE TO VOICE CONVERSION USING ARTIFICIAL INTELLIGENCE. *Spectrum of Engineering Sciences*, *3*(6), 762–777.

Khedher, M. (2014). Personal branding phenomenon. *International Journal of Information, Business and Management*, *6*(2), 29–40. DOI: 10.2139/ssrn.2541447

Khondakar, M. F. K., Sarowar, M. H., Chowdhury, M. H., Majumder, S., Hossain, M. A., Dewan, M. A. A., & Hossain, Q. D. (2024). A systematic review on EEG-based neuromarketing: recent trends and analyzing techniques. In *Brain Informatics* (Vol. 11, Number 1). Springer Science and Business Media Deutschland GmbH. DOI: 10.1186/s40708-024-00229-8

Khurana, V., Gahalawat, M., Kumar, P., Roy, P. P., Dogra, D. P., Scheme, E., & Soleymani, M. (2021). A Survey on Neuromarketing Using EEG Signals. *IEEE Transactions on Cognitive and Developmental Systems*, *13*(4), 732–749. DOI: 10.1109/TCDS.2021.3065200

Ki, C.-W., & Kim, Y.-K. (2019). The mechanism by which social media influencers persuade consumers: The role of consumers' desire to mimic. *Psychology and Marketing*, *36*(10), 905–922. DOI: 10.1002/mar.21244

Kim, C., Jeon, H. G., & Lee, K. C. (2020). Discovering the Role of Emotional and Rational Appeals and Hidden Heterogeneity of Consumers in Advertising Copies for Sustainable Marketing. *Sustainability 2020, Vol. 12, Page 5189, 12*(12), 5189. DOI: 10.3390/SU12125189

Kim, A. J., & Ko, E. (2012). Do social media marketing activities enhance customer equity? An empirical study of luxury fashion brand. *Journal of Business Research*, *65*(10), 1480–1486. DOI: 10.1016/j.jbusres.2011.10.014

Kim, D., Hyun, H., & Park, J. (2020). The effect of interior colour on customers' aesthetic perception, emotion, and behaviour in the luxury service. *Journal of Retailing and Consumer Services*, *57*, 102252. DOI: 10.1016/j.jretconser.2020.102252

Kim, J. Y., & Kim, M. J. (2024). Identifying customer preferences through the eye-tracking in travel websites focusing on neuromarketing. *Journal of Asian Architecture and Building Engineering*, *23*(2), 515–527. DOI: 10.1080/13467581.2023.2244566

Kim, T. Y., Ko, H., Kim, S. H., & Kim, H. D. (2021). Modeling of recommendation system based on emotional information and collaborative filtering. *Sensors (Basel), 21*(3), 1013. Advance online publication. DOI: 10.3390/s21061997 PMID: 33808989

Kim, Y.-K., & Sullivan, P. (2019). Emotional branding speaks to consumers' heart: The case of fashion brands. *Fashion and Textiles, 6*(1), 1–16. DOI: 10.1186/s40691-018-0164-y

Knutson, B., Rick, S., Wimmer, G. E., Prelec, D., & Loewenstein, G. (2007). Neural predictors of purchases. *Neuron, 53*(1), 147–156. DOI: 10.1016/j.neuron.2006.11.010 PMID: 17196537

Koc, E., Boz, H., & Arslan, A. (2020). Eye tracking: Evaluation, potential and limitations of field applications. In Eye tracking in tourism (pp. 45–60).

Ko, E. S., Kim, J. N., Na, H. J., & Kim, S. T. (2024). Changes in pupil size according to the color of cosmetic packaging: Using eye-tracking techniques. *Applied Sciences (Basel, Switzerland), 15*(1), 73. DOI: 10.3390/app15010073

Kondak, A. (2023). The Application of Eye Tracking and Artificial Intelligence in Contemporary Marketing Communication Management. *Scientific Papers of Silesian University of Technology. Organization & Management/Zeszyty Naukowe Politechniki Slaskiej. Seria Organizacji i Zarzadzanie*, (186).

Koorathota, S., Papadopoulos, N., Ma, J. L., Kumar, S., Sun, X., Mittal, A., . . . Sajda, P. (2023). Fixating on attention: Integrating human eye tracking into vision transformers. *arXiv preprint arXiv:2308.13969.*

Kotler, P., & Keller, K. L. (2016). *Marketing management* (15th ed.). Pearson Education.

Kotte, K. R., Attaluri, V., & Selvakumar, P. (2025). Revolutionising retail banking with AI and virtual technologies: AI-driven financial training. In Nair, A. J., Manohar, S., Limbu, Y. B., & Huhmann, B. A. (Eds.), *Intersecting natural language processing and FinTech innovations in service marketing* (pp. 421–440). IGI Global Scientific Publishing., DOI: 10.4018/979-8-3693-9944-6.ch020

Kovacova, M., Machova, V., & Bennett, D. (2022). Immersive extended reality technologies, data visualization tools, and customer behavior analytics in the metaverse commerce. *Journal of Self-Governance and Management Economics, 10*(2), 7–21.

Kühn, S., Strelow, E., & Gallinat, J. (2016). Multiple "buy buttons" in the brain: Forecasting chocolate sales at point-of-sale based on fMRI. *NeuroImage, 136*, 122–128. DOI: 10.1016/j.neuroimage.2016.05.021 PMID: 27173762

Kumar, P., Chowdhury, S., Madhavedi, S., & Lakshminarayana, K. (2024). Role of neuromarketing and artificial intelligence in futuristic marketing approach: An empirical study. *Journal of Informatics Education and Research*, *4*(2), 560–567.

Kunnathully, K., Satyanarayana, P., Anute, N., Sharma, M., Sureshkrishna, G., & Manjunath, T. C. (2025). Propaganda, social media and AI. In Vieira, A., Joaquim, A., & Duarte, A. (Eds.), *Digital populism and the use of neo-propaganda and fake news* (pp. 19–38). IGI Global Scientific Publishing., DOI: 10.4018/979-8-3693-9999-6.ch002

Kusá, A., & Beličková, P. (2023). The role of artificial intelligence in neuromarketing research: Insights and applications. *Media & Marketing Identity*, 269–275. DOI: 10.34135/mmidentity-2023-27

Kusters, R., Misevic, D., Berry, H., Cully, A., Le Cunff, Y., Dandoy, L., Díaz-Rodríguez, N., Ficher, M., Grizou, J., Othmani, A., Palpanas, T., Komorowski, M., Loiseau, P., Moulin Frier, C., Nanini, S., Quercia, D., Sebag, M., Soulié Fogelman, F., Taleb, S., & Wehbi, F. (2020). Interdisciplinary Research in Artificial Intelligence: Challenges and Opportunities. *Frontiers in Big Data*, *3*, 577974. Advance online publication. DOI: 10.3389/fdata.2020.577974 PMID: 33693418

Labib, E. (2024). Artificial intelligence in marketing: Exploring current and future trends. *Cogent Business & Management*, *11*(1), 2348728. DOI: 10.1080/23311975.2024.2348728

Labrecque, L. I., Markos, E., & Milne, G. R. (2013). Online personal branding: Processes, challenges, and implications. *Journal of Interactive Marketing*, *27*(1), 37–50. DOI: 10.1016/j.intmar.2010.09.002

LaChapelle, C., & Tucker, C. (2023). *Generative AI in political advertising*. Brennan Center for Justice.

Lakshminarayana, K., Kumar, P., & Madhavedi, S. (2024). Role of Neuromarketing and Artificial Intelligence in Futuristic Marketing Approach: An Empirical Study. *Journal of Informatics Education and Research*, *4*(2), 560. DOI: 10.52783/JIER.V4I2.809

Lamberton, C., & Stephen, A. T. (2016). A thematic exploration of digital, social media, and mobile marketing: Research evolution from 2000 to 2015 and an agenda for future inquiry. *Journal of Marketing*, *80*(6), 146–172. DOI: 10.1509/jm.15.0415

Latif, F. (2025). AI-POWERED PERSONALIZATION IN BRANDING: IMPACT ON CONSUMER ENGAGEMENT AND LOYALTY. *Contemporary Journal of Social Science Review*, *3*(4), 47–57. DOI: 10.63878/cjssr.v3i4.1825

Lee, S. M., Olson, D. L., & Trimi, S. (2010). Strategic innovation in the convergence era. *International Journal of Management and Enterprise Development*, *9*(1), 1–12. DOI: 10.1504/IJMED.2010.035304

Lemon, K. N., & Verhoef, P. C. (2016). Understanding customer experience throughout the customer journey. *Journal of Marketing*, *80*(6), 69–96. DOI: 10.1509/jm.15.0420

Li, F., Chen, C. H., Liu, Y., Chang, D., Cui, J., & Sourina, O. (2024). Autoencoder-enabled eye-tracking data analytics for objective assessment of user preference in humanoid robot appearance design. *Expert Systems with Applications*, *249*, 123857. DOI: 10.1016/j.eswa.2024.123857

Lim, W. M. (2018). What will business-to-business marketers learn from neuro-marketing? Insights for business marketing practice. *Journal of Business-To-Business Marketing*, *25*(3), 251–259. DOI: 10.1080/1051712X.2018.1488915

Lim, W. M., Gunasekara, A., Pallant, J. L., Pallant, J. I., & Pechenko, E. (2024). Advances in neuromarketing and improved understanding of consumer behavior: A comprehensive review. *Cogent Business & Management*, *11*(1), 2376773. DOI: 10.1080/23311975.2024.2376773

Lim, W. M., & Weissmann, M. A. (2023). Toward a theory of behavioral control. *Journal of Strategic Marketing*, *31*(1), 185–211. DOI: 10.1080/0965254X.2021.1890190

Lim, W. M., Yap, S. F., & Makkar, M. (2021). Home sharing in marketing and tourism at a tipping point: What do we know, how do we know, and where should we be heading? *Journal of Business Research*, *122*, 534–566. DOI: 10.1016/j.jbusres.2020.08.051

Liu-Thompkins, Y., Okazaki, S., & Li, H. (2022). Artificial empathy in marketing interactions: Bridging the human-AI gap in affective and social customer experience. *Journal of the Academy of Marketing Science*, *50*(6), 1198–1218. DOI: 10.1007/s11747-022-00892-5

Li, X., Luh, D. B., & Chen, Z. (2024). A Systematic Review and Meta-Analysis of Eye-Tracking Studies for Consumers' Visual Attention in Online Shopping. *Information Technology and Control*, *53*(1), 187–205. DOI: 10.5755/j01.itc.53.1.34855

Li, Z., Li, R., Yuan, L., Cui, J., & Li, F. (2024). A benchmarking framework for eye-tracking-based vigilance prediction of vessel traffic controllers. *Engineering Applications of Artificial Intelligence*, *129*, 107660. DOI: 10.1016/j.engappai.2023.107660

Lou, C., & Yuan, S. (2019). Influencer marketing: How message value and credibility affect consumer trust of branded content on social media. *Journal of Interactive Advertising*, *19*(1), 58–73. DOI: 10.1080/15252019.2018.1533501

Loureiro, S. M. C., Guerreiro, J., & Ali, F. (2020). 20 years of research on virtual reality and augmented reality in tourism context: A text-mining approach. *Tourism Management*, *77*, 104028. DOI: 10.1016/j.tourman.2019.104028

Luo, C., Hasan, N. A. M., Zamri bin Ahmad, A. M., & Lei, G. (2025). Influence of short video content on consumers purchase intentions on social media platforms with trust as a mediator. *Scientific Reports*, *15*(1), 1–16. DOI: 10.1038/s41598-025-94994-z

Lyu, D., Manas-Viniegra, L., & Xu, Z. (2025). Visual Attention Differences Toward Football Stadium's Naming Rights: An Eye Tracking Study. *Asia Pacific Journal of Marketing and Logistics*, *37*(1), 189–209. DOI: 10.1108/APJML-03-2024-0281

Macdonald, E., Wilson, H. N., & Konus, U. (2012). Better customer insight-in real time (Vol. 90). Harvard Business School Publishing. Huseynov, S., Kassas, B., Segovia, M. S., & Palma, M. A. (2019). Incorporating biometric data in models of consumer choice. *Applied Economics*, *51*(14), 1514–1531.

Makransky, G., & Lilleholt, L. (2018). A structural equation modeling investigation of the emotional value of immersive virtual reality in education. *Educational Technology Research and Development*, *66*(5), 1141–1164. DOI: 10.1007/s11423-018-9581-2

Mankutė, V. (2025). *The impact of visual attention on brand attitudes in social media using eye-tracking approach* (Doctoral dissertation, Vilniaus universitetas.).

Mansor, A. A., & Isa, S. M. (2020). Fundamentals of neuromarketing: What is it all about? *Neuroscience Research Notes*, *3*(4), 22–28. DOI: 10.31117/neuroscirn.v3i4.58

Mariani, M. M., Perez-Vega, R., & Wirtz, J. (2022). AI in marketing, consumer research and psychology: A systematic literature review and research agenda. *Psychology and Marketing*, *39*(4), 755–776. DOI: 10.1002/mar.21619

Martin, K. D., & Murphy, P. E. (2017). The role of data privacy in marketing. *Journal of the Academy of Marketing Science*, *45*(2), 135–155. DOI: 10.1007/s11747-016-0495-4

Martin, K., Borah, A., & Palmatier, R. W. (2017). Data privacy: Effects on customer and firm performance. *Journal of Marketing*, *81*(1), 36–58. DOI: 10.1509/jm.15.0497

Martin, K., & Murphy, P. (2017). The role of data privacy in marketing. *Journal of Business Ethics*, *143*(3), 467–481.

Mathur, M., Khan, S., Khan, S. W., Das, S., & Goel, V. (2025). Consumer Engagement in the Era of Personalization: The Strategic Role of AI-Driven Marketing. *Advances in Consumer Research. Association for Consumer Research (U. S.)*, *2*(4).

McKinsey. (2020). *How personalization drives value in retail*. McKinsey & Company. https://www.mckinsey.com/business-functions/marketing-and-sales/our-insights/how-personalization-drives-value-in-retail

Mehrabi, N., Morstatter, F., Saxena, N., Lerman, K., & Galstyan, A. (2021). A survey on bias and fairness in machine learning. *ACM Computing Surveys*, *54*(6), 1–35. DOI: 10.1145/3457607

Menaka, S., & Selvam, V. (2025). Bibliometric Analysis of Artificial Intelligence on Consumer Purchase Intention in E-Retailing. *International Journal of Computational and Experimental Science and Engineering*, *11*(1), 1138–1146. DOI: 10.22399/IJCESEN.1007

Meyerding, S. G., & Mehlhose, C. M. (2020). Can neuromarketing add value to the traditional marketing research? An exemplary experiment with functional near-infrared spectroscopy (fNIRS). *Journal of Business Research*, *107*, 172–185. DOI: 10.1016/j.jbusres.2018.10.052

Millagala, K., & Gunasinghe, N. (2024). Neuromarketing as a digital marketing strategy to unravel the evolution of marketing communication. In *Applying business intelligence and innovation to entrepreneurship* (pp. 81–105). IGI Global Scientific Publishing. DOI: 10.4018/979-8-3693-1846-1.ch005

Miller, D. (2023). Embracing the technological metamorphosis: Envisioning higher education for generation alpha in a shifting educational landscape. [IJSECS]. *International Journal Software Engineering and Computer Science*, *3*(2), 88–96. DOI: 10.35870/ijsecs.v3i2.1492

Miller, T. (2019). Explanation in artificial intelligence: Insights from the social sciences. *Artificial Intelligence*, *267*, 1–38. DOI: 10.1016/j.artint.2018.07.007

Miranda, M. L. S. L. P. (2025). Emotion-based image recommendation system [Master's thesis, Universidade de Lisboa, Faculdade de Ciências]. http://hdl.handle.net/10400.5/100177

Mishra, A. B. (2025). *Neuromarketing in the Phygital Era by Influencing Gen Z and Sustainable Consumer Behaviour in a Digitally Driven Retail World.* In *Organizational Risks, Challenges, and Barriers in Developing Sustainability Start-Ups* (pp. 239-252). IGI Global. DOI: 10.4018/978-1-6684-9872-9.ch012

Mitchell, M., Wu, S., Zaldivar, A., Barnes, P., Vasserman, L., Hutchinson, B., & Gebru, T. (2021). Model cards for model reporting. *Communications of the ACM*, *64*(12), 56–65. DOI: 10.1145/3562927

Mittal, S., Pandey, A., Chandel, A., & Hung, T. H. (2025). Leveraging Neuromarketing Technologies to Enhance Agile Marketing Strategies: A Study on Consumer Behavior Insights and Real-Time Adaptation. In *Digital Transformation Initiatives for Agile Marketing* (pp. 275-302). IGI Global.

Mitu, F.-G., Bota, M., Emanuel SAVAN, E., & Emanuel Savan, E. (2024). Unlocking the Shopper's Mind: How Emerging Technologies Like Artificial Intelligence Is Shaping the Future of Retail. *Studia Universitatis Babe -Bolyai Negotia*, 69–83. DOI: 10.24193/SUBBNEGOTIA.2024.4.04

Mogaji, E., Olaleye, S., & Ukpabi, D. (2020). *Using AI to Personalise Emotionally Appealing Advertisement*. 137–150. DOI: 10.1007/978-3-030-24374-6_10

Mohammad, S. M. (2022). Ethics sheet for automatic emotion recognition and sentiment analysis. *Computational Linguistics*, *48*(2), 239–274. DOI: 10.1162/coli_a_00433

Mohammed, S. M., & Alhumaid, M. T. (2025). The impact of managerial innovation skills on neuromarketing implementation in the pharmaceutical sector. *International Journal of Pharmaceutical and Healthcare Marketing*. https://doi.org/https://doi.org/10.1108/IJPHM-10-2024-0119

Montag, C., Lachmann, B., Herrlich, M., & Zweig, K. A. (2019). Addictive features of social media and freemium games in the context of psychological and economic theories. *International Journal of Environmental Research and Public Health*, *16*(14), 2612. DOI: 10.3390/ijerph16142612

Moqaddem, O. (2025). Investigating the impact of AI on personalization and customer engagement in intelligent marketing strategies. *European Journal of Management and Marketing Studies*, *10*(1). Advance online publication. DOI: 10.46827/ejmms.v10i1.1922

Moreno-Arjonilla, J., López-Ruiz, A., Jiménez-Pérez, J. R., Callejas-Aguilera, J. E., & Jurado, J. M. (2024). Eye-tracking on virtual reality: A survey. *Virtual Reality (Waltham Cross)*, *28*(1), 38. DOI: 10.1007/s10055-023-00903-y

Morgan, R. M., & Hunt, S. D. (1994). The commitment-trust theory of relationship marketing. *Journal of Marketing*, *58*(3), 20–38. DOI: 10.1177/002224299405800302

Morhart, F. M., Malär, L., Guèvremont, A., Girardin, F., & Grohmann, B. (2015). Brand authenticity: An integrative framework and measurement scale. *Journal of Consumer Psychology*, *25*(2), 200–218. DOI: 10.1016/j.jcps.2014.11.006

Morin, C. (2011). Neuromarketing: The New Science of Consumer Behavior. In *Society* (Vol. 48, Number 2, pp. 131–135). Springer Science and Business Media, LLC. DOI: 10.1007/s12115-010-9408-1

Müller, V. C. (2020). *Stanford Encyclopedia of Philosophy.* https://plato.stanford.edu/entries/ethics-ai/#ManiBeha

Müller, V. C. (2021). Ethics of artificial intelligence. In *The Routledge Social Science Handbook of AI* (1st ed.). Taylor & Francis Group., https://www.taylorfrancis.com/chapters/edit/10.4324/9780429198533-9/ethics-artificial-intelligence-vincent-m%C3%BCller DOI: 10.4324/9780429198533-9

Munar, A. M., & Jacobsen, J. K. S. (2014). Motivations for sharing tourism experiences through social media. *Tourism Management, 43*, 46–54. DOI: 10.1016/j.tourman.2014.01.012

Muñoz-Leiva, F., Hernández-Méndez, J., & Gómez-Carmona, D. (2019). Measuring advertising effectiveness in Travel 2.0 websites through eye-tracking technology. *Physiology & Behavior, 200*, 83–95. DOI: 10.1016/j.physbeh.2018.03.002 PMID: 29522796

Murti, A., & Ghosh, R. (2023). The Impact of Emotional Appeals in Neuro-Marketing: Analyzing the Brain Responses of Consumers to Emotional Advertising Campaigns. In *International Journal of Enhanced Research in Management & Computer Applications* (Vol. 12).

Musole, E. (2025). The Role of Neurotechnology in Shaping Business Decisions: A Comprehensive Literature Review. *Open Journal of Business and Management, 13*(2), 985–999. DOI: 10.4236/ojbm.2025.132053

Najafi, F., Shetab Boushehri, S. N., Khatibi, A., & Azmsha, T. (2024). Comparison of Customers' Visual Attention in the Online Shopping Process of Sports Products with a Neuromarketing Approach. *Journal of Advanced Sport Technology, 8*(3), 1–14.

Neely, J. H. (1977). Semantic priming and retrieval from lexical memory: Roles of inhibitionless spreading activation and limited-capacity attention. *Journal of Experimental Psychology. General, 106*(3), 226–254. DOI: 10.1037/0096-3445.106.3.226

Neiroukh, S., Emeagwali, O. L., & Aljuhmani, H. Y. (2024). Artificial intelligence capability and organizational performance: Unraveling the mediating mechanisms of decision-making processes. *Management Decision.* Advance online publication. DOI: 10.1108/MD-10-2023-1946

Niedziela, M. M., & Ambroze, K. (2021). Neuroscience tools: Using the right tool for the right question. In *Emotion measurement* (pp. 559–592). Woodhead Publishing. DOI: 10.1016/B978-0-12-821124-3.00017-X

Nilashi, M., Yadegaridehkordi, E., Samad, S., Mardani, A., Ahani, A., Aljojo, N., Razali, N. S., & Tajuddin, T. (2020). Decision to adopt neuromarketing techniques for sustainable product marketing: A fuzzy decision-making approach. *Symmetry*, *12*(2), 305. DOI: 10.3390/sym12020305

Nisbett, R. E., & Wilson, T. D. (1977). The halo effect: Evidence for unconscious alteration of judgments. *Journal of Personality and Social Psychology*, *35*(4), 250–256. DOI: 10.1037/0022-3514.35.4.250

Northoff, G. (2012). Neuroethics: The ethical impact of neuroscience in marketing. *Business Ethics Quarterly*, *22*(1), 35–67. DOI: 10.5840/beq20122213

Noseworthy, T. J., Wang, J., & Islam, T. (2012). How context shapes category inferences and attribute preference for new ambiguous products. *Journal of Consumer Psychology*, *22*(4), 529–544. DOI: 10.1016/j.jcps.2012.04.004

Nozari, H., & Samadi, S. (2025). AIoE-Powered Neuromarketing for Decoding the Consumer Brain. In *Artificial Intelligence of Everything and Sustainable Development* (pp. 39–53). Springer Nature Singapore. DOI: 10.1007/978-981-96-7202-8_3

O'Reilly, T., Strauss, I., & Mazzucato, M. (2024). Algorithmic attention rents: A theory of digital platform market power. *Data & Policy*, *6*, e6. DOI: 10.1017/dap.2024.1

Oberst, U., Wegmann, E., Stodt, B., Brand, M., & Chamarro, A. (2017). Negative consequences from heavy social networking in adolescents: The mediating role of fear of missing out. *Journal of Adolescence*, *55*(1), 51–60. DOI: 10.1016/j.adolescence.2016.12.008

Ohme, R., Matukin, M., & Pacula-Lesniak, B. (2011). Biometric measures for interactive advertising research. *Journal of Interactive Advertising*, *11*(2), 60–72. DOI: 10.1080/15252019.2011.10722185

Omar, B., & Dequan, W. (2020). Watch, share or create: The influence of personality traits and user motivation on TikTok mobile video usage. *International Journal of Interactive Mobile Technologies*, *14*(4), 121–137. DOI: 10.3991/ijim.v14i04.12429

Österle, B., Herrando, C., Köpsel, A., & Kuhn, M. (2024). "Business-to-Business-to-Brain?" Reviewing Neuroscience Research in B2B-Marketing Using TCCM Analysis. *Journal of Business-To-Business Marketing*, *31*(4), 421–445. DOI: 10.1080/1051712X.2024.2380671

Ozkul, E., Boz, H., Bilgili, B., & Koc, E. (2019). What colour and light do in service atmospherics: A neuro-marketing perspective. In *Atmospheric turn in culture and tourism: Place, design and process impacts on customer behaviour, marketing and branding* (pp. 223–244). Emerald Publishing Limited. DOI: 10.1108/S1871-317320190000016022

Panwar, D., Bhargava, A., Bohara, S., & Chaudhary, S. S. (2024). Neuromarketing insights for effective advertising strategies: A review and future research agenda. *Neuropsychological Trends*, (36), 107–132. DOI: 10.7358/neur-2024-036-panw

Papić, T., Mihajlović, A., & Gajić, J. (2023). Advanced Technologies as a Framework for Sustainable Marketing Campaigns (AI Application in Neuromarketing). *Sinteza 2023 - International Scientific Conference on Information Technology, Computer Science, and Data Science*, 180–184. DOI: 10.15308/SINTEZA-2023-180-184

Pariser, E. (2011). *The filter bubble: What the Internet is hiding from you*. Penguin Press.

Parmaxi, A., Stylianou, K., & Zaphiris, P. (2017). Enabling social exploration through virtual guidance in Google Expeditions: An exploratory study. In *Interactive mobile communication, technologies and learning* (pp. 397–408). Springer International Publishing.

Patil, D. (2024). *Artificial Intelligence in Retail and E-Commerce: Enhancing Customer Experience Through Personalization, Predictive Analytics, And Real-Time Engagement*. DOI: 10.2139/SSRN.5057420

Peer, E., Rothschild, D., Gordon, A., Evernden, Z., & Jablonski, B. (2022). Data quality of platforms and panels for online behavioral research. *Behavior Research Methods*, *54*(4), 1643–1662. DOI: 10.3758/s13428-021-01694-3 PMID: 34590289

Peng, Y., Yao, S., Li, A., Xiong, F., Sun, G., Li, Z., Zhou, H., Chen, Y., Gong, X., Peng, F., Liu, , Zhang, C., & Zeng, J. (2024). Investigating quantitative approach for microalgal biomass using deep convolutional neural networks and image recognition. *Bioresource Technology*, *403*, 130889. DOI: 10.1016/j.biortech.2024.130889

Pentina, I., Zhang, L., Bata, H., & Chen, Y. (2018). Exploring source effects in online product reviews: A mental imagery processing perspective. *Journal of Retailing and Consumer Services*, *45*, 131–139. DOI: 10.1016/j.jretconser.2018.08.004

Pereira, R., Córdova, F. M., & Díaz, H. A. (2021). Some experiences in Neuromarketing: Moving from White papers to Scientific inquiries. *Procedia Computer Science*, *199*, 1409–1415. DOI: 10.1016/j.procs.2022.01.178

Perumallaplli, R. (2014). AI in E-Commerce Leveraging Predictive Analytics for Personalization. SSRN *Electronic Journal*. DOI: 10.2139/SSRN.5228531

Petty, R. E., & Cacioppo, J. T. (1986). The elaboration likelihood model of persuasion. *Advances in Experimental Social Psychology, 19*, 123–205. DOI: 10.1016/S0065-2601(08)60214-2

Pillarisetty, R., & Mishra, P. (2022). A Review of AI (Artificial Intelligence) Tools and Customer Experience in Online Fashion Retail. *International Journal of E-Business Research, 18*(2), 1–12. DOI: 10.4018/IJEBR.294111

Pine, B. J., & Gilmore, J. H. (1999). *The Experience Economy*. Harvard Business School Press.

Pinhal, R., Estima, A., & Duarte, P. (2025). See, like, and book: Eye-tracking the power of visual attention in destination marketing. *Journal of Marketing Communications*, •••, 1–21. DOI: 10.1080/13527266.2025.2511144

Piper, L., De Cosmo, L. M., Prete, M. I., Mileti, A., & Guido, G. (2024). Effectiveness of pictorial warnings on food fat content: Consumers' perception and neurological responses. *British Food Journal, 126*(6), 2328–2348. DOI: 10.1108/BFJ-02-2023-0123

Pires, P. B., Santos, J. D., & Pereira, I. V. (2024). *Digital marketing*. DOI: 10.1201/9781003384960

Plassmann, H., Ramsøy, T. Z., & Milosavljevic, M. (2012). Branding the brain: A critical review and outlook. *Journal of Consumer Psychology, 22*(1), 18–36. DOI: 10.1016/J.JCPS.2011.11.010

Plassmann, H., Venkatraman, V., Huettel, S., & Yoon, C. (2015). Consumer neuroscience: Applications, challenges, and possible solutions. *JMR, Journal of Marketing Research, 52*(4), 427–435. DOI: 10.1509/jmr.14.0048

Poushneh, A., & Vasquez-Parraga, A. Z. (2017). Discernible impact of augmented reality on retail customer's experience, satisfaction and willingness to buy. *Journal of Retailing and Consumer Services, 34*, 229–234. DOI: 10.1016/j.jretconser.2016.10.005

Pozharliev, R., Rossi, D., & De Angelis, M. (2022). A picture says more than a thousand words: Using consumer neuroscience to study Instagram users' responses to influencer advertising. *Psychology and Marketing, 39*(7), 1336–1349. DOI: 10.1002/mar.21659

Pragna, K. P., Shetty, S., Kodipalli, A., Devamane, S. B., & Martis, R. J. (2025, January). Comprehensive Analysis of Machine Learning Approaches for Phishing Website Detection. In *2025 International Conference on Cognitive Computing in Engineering, Communications, Sciences and Biomedical Health Informatics (IC3ECSBHI)* (pp. 776-781). IEEE.

Prahalad, C. K., & Ramaswamy, V. (2004). Co-creation experiences: The next practice in value creation. *Journal of Interactive Marketing*, *18*(3), 5–14. DOI: 10.1002/dir.20015

Presti, P. (2023). The processing of emotional body expressions within architectural experience: electroencephalography and eye-tracking studies in virtual reality.

Priporas, C. V., Stylos, N., & Fotiadis, A. K. (2017). Generation Z consumers' expectations of interactions in smart retailing: A future agenda. *Computers in Human Behavior*, *77*, 374–381. DOI: 10.1016/j.chb.2017.01.058

Przybylski, A. K., Murayama, K., DeHaan, C. R., & Gladwell, V. (2013). Motivational, emotional, and behavioural correlates of fear of missing out. *Computers in Human Behavior*, *29*(4), 1841–1848. DOI: 10.1016/j.chb.2013.02.014

Pupchenko, D. (2022). *Importance of Neuromarketing Technologies in the Success of an Advertising Strategy: The Case of KEX LLP.* Bachelor's Thesis, Kazakhstan.

Qishu, L. (2024). Implementation method of intelligent emotion-aware clothing system based on nanofibre technology. *Industria Textila (Bucuresti)*, *75*(1), 1–6. DOI: 10.35530/IT.075.01.202379

Quan, H., Li, S., Zeng, C., Wei, H., & Hu, J. (2023). Big data and AI-driven product design: A survey. *Applied Sciences (Basel, Switzerland)*, *13*(16), 9433. Advance online publication. DOI: 10.3390/app13169433

Quiles Pérez, M., Martínez Beltrán, E. T., López Bernal, S., Horna Prat, E., Montesano Del Campo, L., Fernández Maimó, L., & Huertas Celdrán, A. (2024). Data fusion in neuromarketing: Multimodal analysis of biosignals, lifecycle stages, current advances, datasets, trends, and challenges. *Information Fusion*, *105*, 102231. Advance online publication. DOI: 10.1016/j.inffus.2024.102231

Qutb, M. M., Nada, M., & Azmy, A. (2024). An Innovative Methodology in Neuromarketing for Supporting Technology-Enabled Companies. *International Design Journal*, *14*(1), 491–634. DOI: 10.21608/idj.2024.330635

Rabindranath, M., & Singh, A. K. (2024). Advertising research. In *Advertising management: Concepts, theories, research and trends* (pp. 225–247). Springer Nature Singapore. DOI: 10.1007/978-981-99-8657-6_7

Rachmad, Y. E. (2023). *Digital Influence Theory*. Alexandria Bibliotheca Kitab Nashr. https://doi.org/DOI: 10.17605/osf.io/aursv

Radojević, I., Slijepčević, M., & Popović Šević, N. (2025). The Role of Artificial Intelligence in the Modern Approach to Neuromarketing. In *Multidisciplinary Approaches to Contemporary Marketing: Digital Trends, Social Issues and Economics* (pp. 45–73). Springer Nature Switzerland. DOI: 10.1007/978-3-031-78026-4_2

Rahmaini, R., & Salqaura, S. A. (2024). Pengaruh Viral Marketing Dan Neuromarketing Terhadap Keputusan Pembelian Cromboloni Roti'o Di Cabang Manhattan Square Medan. [JIMBI]. *Jurnal Ilmiah Manajemen Dan Bisnis*, *5*(2), 302–310. DOI: 10.31289/jimbi.v5i2.5341

Rajan, B., & Nagpal, M. (2024). AI-powered marketing: What, where, and how? *International Journal of Information Management*, *77*, 102783. Advance online publication. DOI: 10.1016/j.ijinfomgt.2024.102783

Raji, M. A., Olodo, H. B., Oke, T. T., Addy, W. A., Ofodile, O. C., Oyewole, A. T., Raji, M. A., Olodo, H. B., Oke, T. T., Addy, W. A., Ofodile, O. C., & Oyewole, A. T. (2024). E-commerce and consumer behavior: A review of AI-powered personalization and market trends. Https://Gsconlinepress.Com/Journals/Gscarr/Sites/Default/Files/GSCARR-2024-0090.Pdf, *18*(3), 066–077. DOI: 10.30574/GSCARR.2024.18.3.0090

Rancati, G., Nguyen, T. T. T., Fowler, D., Mauri, M., & Schultz, C. D. (2024). Customer experience in coffee stores: A multidisciplinary neuromarketing approach. *Journal of Consumer Behaviour*, *23*(1), 243–259. DOI: 10.1002/cb.2184

Rane, N., Choudhary, S., & Rane, J. (2023). Metaverse for enhancing customer loyalty: effective strategies to improve customer relationship, service, engagement, satisfaction, and experience. *Service, Engagement, Satisfaction, and Experience (November 1, 2023)*.

Rane, N., Choudhary, S., & Rane, J. (2023). Hyper-personalization for enhancing customer loyalty and satisfaction in Customer Relationship Management (CRM) systems. *Available at SSRN* 4641044. DOI: 10.2139/ssrn.4641044

Rawnaque, F. S., Rahman, K. M., Anwar, S. F., Vaidyanathan, R., Chau, T., Sarker, F., & Al Mamun, K. A. (2020). Technological advancements and opportunities in Neuromarketing: a systematic review. In *Brain Informatics* (Vol. 7, Number 1). Springer Science and Business Media Deutschland GmbH. DOI: 10.1186/s40708-020-00109-x

Reinecke, K., Yeh, T., Miratrix, L., Mardiko, R., Zhao, Y., Liu, J., & Gajos, K. Z. (2013). Predicting users' first impressions of website aesthetics with a quantification of perceived visual complexity and colourfulness. In *Proceedings of the SIGCHI Conference on Human Factors in Computing Systems* (pp. 2049–2058). https://doi.org/DOI: 10.1145/2470654.2481281

Rifan, M. (2024). The Convergence of Artificial Intelligence and Digital Marketing. *Proceeding of The International Seminar on Business, Economics, Social Science and Technology (ISBEST), 4*(1). DOI: 10.33830/isbest.v4i1.3266

Riswanto, A. L., Ha, S., Lee, S., & Kwon, M. (2024). Online reviews meet visual attention: A study on consumer patterns in advertising, analyzing customer satisfaction, visual engagement, and purchase intention. *Journal of Theoretical and Applied Electronic Commerce Research, 19*(4), 3102–3122. DOI: 10.3390/jtaer19040150

Robaina-Calderín, L., & Martín-Santana, J. D. (2021). A review of research on neuromarketing using content analysis: Key approaches and new avenues. *Cognitive Neurodynamics, 15*(6), 923–938. DOI: 10.1007/s11571-021-09693-y PMID: 34790262

Rostami, M., Vardasbi, A., Aliannejadi, M., & Crestani, F. (2024). Emotional insights for food recommendations. In *European Conference on Information Retrieval* (Vol. 13185, pp. 3–17). DOI: 10.1007/978-3-031-28241-6_1

Rowlands, J. (2021). Interviewee transcript review as a tool to improve data quality and participant confidence in sensitive research. *International Journal of Qualitative Methods, 20*, 1–9. DOI: 10.1177/16094069211066170

Ruan, T., Liu, Q., & Chang, Y. (2025). Digital media recommendation system design based on user behavior analysis and emotional feature extraction. *PLoS One, 20*(1), e0281234. Advance online publication. DOI: 10.1371/journal.pone.0322768 PMID: 40388444

Russel, S., & Norvig, P. (2010). *Artificial Intelligence: A Modern Approach* (3rd ed.). Prentice Hall: Pearson., http://repo.darmajaya.ac.id/5272/1/Artificial%20Intelligence-A%20Modern%20Approach%20(3rd%20Edition)%20(%20PDFDrive%20).pdf

Russo, V., Bilucaglia, M., & Zito, M. (2022). From virtual reality to augmented reality: A neuromarketing perspective. *Frontiers in Psychology, 13*, 965499. DOI: 10.3389/fpsyg.2022.965499 PMID: 36160557

Rutkowska, A. (2022). Modern Neuroimaging Methods in Contemporary Neuroeconomics and Neuromanagement. *Olsztyn Economic Journal, 17*(2), 247–263. DOI: 10.31648/oej.8767

S, R. (2025, April 9). *Role of Artificial Intelligence in Shaping Consumer Experience and Loyalty in Fashion E-Commerce – IJSREM*. https://ijsrem.com/download/role-of-artificial-intelligence-in-shaping-consumer-experience-and-loyalty-in-fashion-e-commerce/

Sáez-García, J., Sáiz-Manzanares, M. C., & Marticorena-Sánchez, R. (2024). A proposed method of automating data processing for analyzing data produced from eye tracking and galvanic skin response. *Computers*, *13*(11), 289. DOI: 10.3390/computers13110289

Saffari, F., Kakaria, S., Bigné, E., Bruni, L. E., Zarei, S., & Ramsøy, T. Z. (2023). Motivation in the metaverse: A dual-process approach to consumer choices in a virtual reality supermarket. *Frontiers in Neuroscience*, *17*, 1062980. DOI: 10.3389/fnins.2023.1062980 PMID: 36875641

Sakthivel, M., Jaganathan, A., & Mohanraj, M. Mohit, & Manjunath, T. (2025). Brand loyalty through AI and personalisation AI-generated content for financial marketing. In A. J. Nair, S. Manohar, Y. B. Limbu, & B. A. Huhmann (Eds.), Intersecting natural language processing and FinTech innovations in service marketing (pp. 77–96). IGI Global Scientific Publishing. DOI: 10.4018/979-8-3693-9944-6.ch006

Samal, A., & Bhargav, J. S. K. M., Selvakumar, P., Sharma, M., & T. C. M. (2025). Measuring brand performance with AI tools. In Z. Hussain, M. Sharipudin, A. Albattat, & A. Khan (Eds.), Strategic brand management in the age of AI and disruption (pp. 279–302). IGI Global Scientific Publishing. DOI: 10.4018/979-8-3693-9461-8.ch011

Samuel, A., White, G. R., Thomas, R., & Jones, P. (2021). Programmatic advertising: An exegesis of consumer concerns. *Computers in Human Behavior*, *116*, 106657. DOI: 10.1016/j.chb.2020.106657

Sandoval, P. S., & García-Madariaga, J. (2024). Impact of emotional appeal on non-profit advertising: A neurophysiological analysis. *Journal of Consumer Behaviour*, *23*(1), 203–217. DOI: 10.1002/cb.2168

Saxena, N., & Aggarwal, R. (2020). Biometric data regulation: Current frameworks and future challenges. *Journal of Cyber Policy*, *5*(2), 240–257. DOI: 10.1080/23738871.2020.1779431

Schäfer, H., Sapi, G., & Stephens, P. (2022). Dark nudges and consumer manipulation: Regulation, AI, and the future of marketing. *Journal of Business Ethics*, *176*(1), 43–61. DOI: 10.1007/s10551-020-04632-6

Schmitt, B. (2012). The consumer psychology of brands. *Journal of Consumer Psychology*, *22*(1), 7–17. DOI: 10.1016/j.jcps.2011.09.005

Scholz, J., & Duffy, K. (2018). We ARe at home: How augmented reality reshapes mobile marketing and consumer-brand relationships. *Journal of Retailing and Consumer Services*, *44*, 11–23. DOI: 10.1016/J.JRETCONSER.2018.05.004

Selvarajan, G. P. (2021). Harnessing AI-Driven Data Mining for Predictive Insights: A framework for Enhancing Decision-Making in Dynamic Data Environments. *International Journal of Creative Research Thoughts*, *9*(2), 5476–5486.

Sembiring, N. S. B., Sinaga, M. D., & Sianturi, N. E. (2024, November). Implementation of Adaptive Neuro-Fuzzy Inference System (ANFIS) Algorithm for Customer Credit Prediction. In *2024 6th International Conference on Cybernetics and Intelligent System (ICORIS)* (pp. 1-6). IEEE.

Semwal, R., Tripathi, N., Rana, A., Dafouti, B. S., Bairwa, M. K., & Mathur, V. (2024, May). AI-powered personalization and emotional intelligence integration for enhanced service marketing in transformative tourism experiences. In *2024 International Conference on Communication, Computer Sciences and Engineering (IC3SE)* (pp. 1851-1856). IEEE. DOI: 10.1109/IC3SE62002.2024.10592909

*Sephora Creates an Online "In-store" Experience through Generative AI.* (n.d.). Retrieved July 9, 2025, from https://etailasia.wbresearch.com/blog/sephora-creates-an-online-in-store-experience-through-generative-ai?utm_source=chatgpt.com

Serbin, V., & Yashkina, O. (2024). Systematization of research on the use of artificial intelligence in the transformation of marketing strategies of e-commerce enterprises. *Marketing and Digital Technologies*, *8*(4), 92–109. DOI: 10.15276/MDT.8.4.2024.8

Sestino, A., Prete, M. I., Piper, L., & Guido, G. (2020). Internet of Things and Big Data as enablers for business digitalization strategies. *Technological Forecasting and Social Change*, *155*, 119908. DOI: 10.1016/j.techfore.2020.119908

Shah, M. A., & Kumar, P. (2024). Leveraging Machine Learning Techniques to Project Customer Behaviour Through Predictive Analysis and Ethical Marketing. In *Market Grooming* (pp. 121–138). Emerald Publishing Limited. DOI: 10.1108/978-1-83549-001-320241006

Shahzad, K., Khan, S., Raza, F., Kamal, M. H., & Ullah, S. (2025). Emotions, Triggers, and Traits: A Thematic Analysis of Neuromarketing in Digital Buying. *Pakistan Journal of Humanities and Social Sciences*, *13*(1), 570–586. DOI: 10.52131/pjhss.2025.v13i1.2800

Shalev-Shwartz, S., & Ben-David, S. (2014). *Understanding Machine Learning: From Theory to Algorithms*. Cambridge University Press. DOI: 10.1017/CBO9781107298019

Shareef, F., Ajith, R., Kaushal, P., & Sengupta, K. (2024). RetailGPT: A Fine-Tuned LLM Architecture for Customer Experience and Sales Optimization. *2024 2nd International Conference on Self Sustainable Artificial Intelligence Systems (ICSSAS)*, 1390–1394. DOI: 10.1109/ICSSAS64001.2024.10760685

Sharma, A. (2023). Analyzing the Role of Artificial Intelligence in Predicting Customer Behavior and Personalizing the Shopping Experience in Ecommerce. *INTERANTIONAL JOURNAL OF SCIENTIFIC RESEARCH IN ENGINEERING AND MANAGEMENT*, *07*(02). Advance online publication. DOI: 10.55041/IJSREM17839

Sharma, K., Giannakos, M., & Dillenbourg, P. (2020). Eye-tracking and artificial intelligence to enhance motivation and learning. *Smart Learning Environments*, *7*(1), 13. DOI: 10.1186/s40561-020-00122-x

Sharma, R., Mithas, S., & Kankanhalli, A. (2014). Transforming decision-making processes: A research agenda for understanding the impact of business analytics on organisations. *European Journal of Information Systems*, *23*(4), 433–441. DOI: 10.1057/ejis.2014.17

Sherly Steffi, L., Subha, B., Kuriakose, A., Singh, J., Arunkumar, B., & Rajalakshmi, V. (2024). The impact of AI-driven personalization on consumer behavior and brand engagement in online marketing. In Harnessing, A. I. (Ed.), *Machine Learning, and IoT for Intelligent Business* (Vol. 1, pp. 485–492). Springer Nature Switzerland.

Shi, R., Wang, M., Liu, C., & Gull, N. (2023). The influence of short video platform characteristics on users' willingness to share marketing information: Based on the SOR model. *Sustainability (Basel)*, *15*(3), 2448. DOI: 10.3390/su15032448

Shiri, F. M., Perumal, T., Mustapha, N., & Mohamed, R. (2024). A Comprehensive Overview and Comparative Analysis on Deep Learning Models. *Journal on Artificial Intelligence*, *6*(1), 301–360. DOI: 10.32604/jai.2024.054314

Shmueli, G., & Koppius, O. R. (2011). Predictive analytics in information systems research. In *MIS Quarterly: Management Information Systems* (Vol. 35, Number 3, pp. 553–572). University of Minnesota. DOI: 10.2307/23042796

Singh, P., Alhassan, I., & Khoshaim, L. (2023). What Do You Need to Know? A Systematic Review and Research Agenda on Neuromarketing Discipline. In *Journal of Theoretical and Applied Electronic Commerce Research* (Vol. 18, Number 4, pp. 2007–2032). Multidisciplinary Digital Publishing Institute (MDPI). DOI: 10.3390/jtaer18040101

Singh, P., Alhassan, I., & Khoshaim, L. (2023). What Do You Need to Know? A Systematic Review and Research Agenda on Neuromarketing Discipline. *Journal of Theoretical and Applied Electronic Commerce Research 2023, Vol. 18, Pages 2007-2032, 18*(4), 2007–2032. DOI: 10.3390/JTAER18040101

Singh, A., & Kakkar, A. (2025). Marketing in the age of hyper-personalisation: Lessons from analytics-driven brand success. *Applied Marketing Analytics, 11*(1), 72–86. DOI: 10.69554/XQVW6761

Singh, J., & Modi, N. (2024). A robust, real-time camera-based eye gaze tracking system to analyze users' visual attention using deep learning. *Interactive Learning Environments, 32*(2), 409–430. DOI: 10.1080/10494820.2022.2088561

Singh, K., & Kumar, A. (2026). Exploring the evolving landscape of neuromarketing ethics. *International Journal of Market Research, 68*(1), 108–131. DOI: 10.1177/14707853251383629

Sinha, S., Sinha, D., & Dalmia, T. (2024). Role of AI in Enhancing Customer Experience in Online Shopping. *2024 11th International Conference on Reliability, Infocom Technologies and Optimization (Trends and Future Directions) (ICRITO)*, 1–5. DOI: 10.1109/ICRITO61523.2024.10522285

Skaramagkas, V., Giannakakis, G., Ktistakis, E., Manousos, D., Karatzanis, I., Tachos, N. S., Tripoliti, E., Marias, K., Fotiadis, D. I., & Tsiknakis, M. (2021). Review of eye tracking metrics involved in emotional and cognitive processes. *IEEE Reviews in Biomedical Engineering, 16*, 260–277. DOI: 10.1109/RBME.2021.3066072 PMID: 33729950

Skriabin, O. M., Sanakoiev, D. B., Sanakoieva, N. D., Berezenko, V. V., & Liubchenko, Y. V. (2021). Neurotechnologies in the advertising industry: Legal and ethical aspects. *Innovative Marketing, 17*(2), 189. DOI: 10.21511/im.17(2).2021.17

Slager, E. (2023). Unravelling the adoption of neuromarketing techniques in marketing organisations: insight from (neuro) marketing professionals (Master's thesis, University of Twente).

Smidts, A., Hsu, M., Sanfey, A. G., Boksem, M. A. S., Ebstein, R. B., Huettel, S. A., Kable, J. W., Karmarkar, U. R., Kitayama, S., Knutson, B., Liberzon, I., Lohrenz, T., Stallen, M., & Yoon, C. (2014). Advancing consumer neuroscience. *Marketing Letters, 25*(3), 257–267. DOI: 10.1007/S11002-014-9306-1/METRICS

Smith, T. (2020). Engaging the micro-moment: Building brand equity in the mobile age. *Journal of Marketing Communications, 26*(5), 487–506.

Snyder, H. (2019). Literature review as a research methodology: An overview and guidelines. *Journal of Business Research, 104*, 333–339. DOI: 10.1016/j.jbusres.2019.07.039

Sokolova, K., & Perez, C. (2021). You follow fitness influencers on YouTube. But do you really trust them? *Journal of Retailing and Consumer Services, 58*, 102276. DOI: 10.1016/j.jretconser.2020.102276

Šola, H. M., Qureshi, F. H., & Khawaja, S. (2024). AI Eye-Tracking Technology: A new era in managing cognitive loads for online learners. *Education Sciences, 14*(9), 933. DOI: 10.3390/educsci14090933

Šola, H. M., Qureshi, F. H., & Khawaja, S. (2024). Predicting behaviour patterns in online and PDF magazines with AI eye-tracking. *Behavioral Sciences (Basel, Switzerland), 14*(8), 677. DOI: 10.3390/bs14080677 PMID: 39199073

Šola, H. M., Qureshi, F. H., & Khawaja, S. (2025). AI and Eye Tracking Reveal Design Elements' Impact on E-Magazine Reader Engagement. *Education Sciences, 15*(2), 203. DOI: 10.3390/educsci15020203

Šola, H. M., Qureshi, F. H., & Khawaja, S. (2025). Human-centred design meets AI-driven algorithms: Comparative analysis of political campaign branding in the Harris–Trump presidential campaigns. *Informatics (MDPI), 12*(1), 30. Advance online publication. DOI: 10.3390/informatics12010030

Soltanizadeh, S., Ahmadisharif, M., & Rousta, A. (2025). A Qualitative Model of Customer Purchase Decision-Making Based on Neuromarketing (FMCG Industry). *Digital Transformation and Administration Innovation*, 1-11.

Song, G., Gazi, M. A. I., Waaje, A., Roshid, M. M., Karim, R., Rahaman, M. A., Min, Z., & Senathirajah, A. R. B. S. (2025). The Neuromarketing: Bridging Neuroscience and Marketing for Enhanced Consumer Engagement. In *IEEE Access* (Vol. 13, pp. 40331–40353). Institute of Electrical and Electronics Engineers Inc. DOI: 10.1109/ACCESS.2025.3545742

Spanjaard, D., Young, L., & Freeman, L. (2014). Emotions in supermarket brand choice: A multi-method approach. *Qualitative Market Research, 17*(3), 209–224. DOI: 10.1108/QMR-10-2012-0049

Stanton, S. J., Sinnott-Armstrong, W., & Huettel, S. A. (2017). Neuromarketing: Ethical implications of its use and potential misuse. *Journal of Business Ethics, 144*(4), 799–811. DOI: 10.1007/s10551-016-3059-0

Stanton, S. J., Sinnott-Armstrong, W., & Huettel, S. A. (2017). Neuromarketing: Ethical Implications of its Use and Potential Misuse. *Journal of Business Ethics, 144*(4), 799–811. DOI: 10.1007/S10551-016-3059-0

Štefko, R., Ondrijová, I., Miško, D., & Tomková, A. (2025). Analysis of Flight Search on the Web Using Eye-Tracking. *Journal of Sensory Studies, 40*(4), e70066. DOI: 10.1111/joss.70066

Sundar, S. S., & Kim, J. (2019). Machine heuristic: When we trust computers more than humans with our personal information. In Taddeo, M., & Floridi, L. (Eds.), *The responsibilities of online service providers* (pp. 195–212). Springer., DOI: 10.1145/3290605.3300768

Sung, B., Wilson, N. J., Yun, J. H., & Lee, E. J. (2020). What can neuroscience offer marketing research? *Asia Pacific Journal of Marketing and Logistics, 32*(5), 1089–1111. DOI: 10.1108/APJML-04-2019-0227

Suomala, J., Palokangas, L., Leminen, S., Westerlund, M., Heinonen, J., & Numminen, J. (2012). Neuromarketing: Understanding Customers' Subconscious Responses to Marketing. *Technology Innovation Management Review, 2*(12), 12–21. http://www.theseus.fi/handle/10024/151224

Susser, D., Roessler, B., & Nissenbaum, H. (2019). Online manipulation: Hidden influences in a digital world. *Georgetown Law Technology Review, 4*(2), 1–45.

Swaminathan, V., Sorescu, A., Steenkamp, J. B. E., O'Guinn, T. C. G., & Schmitt, B. (2020). Branding in a hyperconnected world: Refocusing theories and rethinking boundaries. *Journal of Marketing, 84*(2), 24–46. DOI: 10.1177/0022242919899905

Tadimarri, A., Jangoan, S., Kumar Sharma, K., Gurusamy, A., & Radius, H. (2024). AI-Powered Marketing: Transforming Consumer Engagement and Brand Growth. *IJFMR - International. Journal of Multidisciplinary Research, 6*(2). Advance online publication. DOI: 10.36948/IJFMR.2024.V06I02.14595

Tajfel, H., & Turner, J. C. (1986). The social identity theory of intergroup behaviour. In Worchel, S., & Austin, W. G. (Eds.), *Psychology of intergroup relations* (pp. 7–24). Nelson-Hall.

Tang, Y., & Chen, C. (2024). Can stylized products generated by AI better attract user attention? Using eye-tracking technology for research. *Applied Sciences (Basel, Switzerland), 14*(17), 7729. DOI: 10.3390/app14177729

Tao, L., Nakamura, S., Wang, X., Kawahara, T., Tamura, G., & Yamasaki, T. (2024). A large-scale television advertising dataset for detailed impression analysis. *Multimedia Tools and Applications, 83*(7), 18779–18802. DOI: 10.1007/s11042-023-14704-7

Teepapal, T. (2025). AI-driven personalization: Unraveling consumer perceptions in social media engagement. *Computers in Human Behavior, 165*, 108549. DOI: 10.1016/j.chb.2024.108549

Thakur, N. (2025). Neuromarketing Techniques in Shaping Purchase Decisions: A Sales Perspective. *Journal of Marketing and Sales Management ISSN: 2457-0095 (Online), 9*(1).

Thanyawatpornkul, R. (2024). Implementing AI-driven Customer Relationship Management (CRM) systems: Enhancing customer experience in the retail industry of Thailand. *World Journal of Advanced Research and Reviews, 24*(1), 1691–1699. DOI: 10.30574/wjarr.2024.24.1.3154

*The hidden persuaders: How businesses are using neuroscience to make you buy | WIRED.* (n.d.). Retrieved July 9, 2025, from https://www.wired.com/story/neuromarketing-is-a-go/?utm_source=chatgpt.com

Theodorakopoulos, L., Theodoropoulou, A., & Klavdianos, C. (2025). Interactive Viral Marketing Through Big Data Analytics, Influencer Networks, AI Integration, and Ethical Dimensions. In *Journal of Theoretical and Applied Electronic Commerce Research* (Vol. 20, Number 2). Multidisciplinary Digital Publishing Institute (MDPI). DOI: 10.3390/jtaer20020115

Thompson, C. J., Arnould, E. J., & Giesler, M. (2013). Discursivity, difference, and disruption: Genealogical reflections on the consumer culture theory heteroglossia. *Marketing Theory, 13*(2), 149–174. DOI: 10.1177/1470593113477889

Tipper, S. P. (1985). The negative priming effect: Inhibitory priming by ignored objects. *The Quarterly Journal of Experimental Psychology. A, Human Experimental Psychology, 37*(4), 571–590. DOI: 10.1080/14640748508400920 PMID: 4081101

Tirandazi, P., Bamakan, S. M. H., & Toghroljerdi, A. (2023). A review of studies on internet of everything as an enabler of neuromarketing methods and techniques. *The Journal of Supercomputing, 79*(7), 7835–7876. DOI: 10.1007/s11227-022-04988-1

Tiutiu, M., & Dabija, D.-C. (2023). Improving Customer Experience Using Artificial Intelligence in Online Retail. *Proceedings of the International Conference on Business Excellence, 17*(1), 1139–1147. DOI: 10.2478/PICBE-2023-0102

Trauthig, I., & McKay, C. (2025, August 7). Then and now: How does AI electoral interference compare in 2025? *Centre for International Governance Innovation*. https://www.cigionline.org/articles/then-and-now-how-does-ai-electoral-interference-compare-in-2025/

Tukachinsky, R. (2011). Para-romantic love and para-friendships: Development and assessment of a multiple-parasocial relationships scale. *American Journal of Media Psychology, 4*(1/2), 73–94.

Tversky, A., & Kahneman, D. (1974). Judgment under uncertainty: Heuristics and biases. *Science, 185*(4157), 1124–1131. DOI: 10.1126/science.185.4157.1124 PMID: 17835457

Ullah, K., Mumtaz, I., Zia, M. A., & Razzaq, A. (2022). Text-based emotion detection by using classification and regression model. In Lecture notes on data engineering and communications technologies (Vol. 144, pp. 414–419). DOI: 10.1007/978-3-031-10388-9_30

Ulman, Y. I., Cakar, T., & Yildiz, G. (2015). Ethical issues in neuromarketing: "I consume, therefore I am!". *Science and Engineering Ethics, 21*(5), 1271–1284. DOI: 10.1007/s11948-014-9581-5 PMID: 25150848

Uppal, A., Banerjee, S., Agarwal, V., & Yadav, P. (2025). Emotion-Driven Intelligent Segmentation for Hyper-Personalized Customer Experiences: A Rule Mining Approach. *Metallurgical and Materials Engineering, 31*(4), 972–981. DOI: 10.63278/1541

Usman, F. O., Eyo-Udo, N. L., Etukudoh, E. A., Odonkor, B., Ibeh, C. V., & Adegbola, A. (2024). A critical review of AI-driven strategies for entrepreneurial success. *International Journal of Management & Entrepreneurship Research, 6*(1), 200–215. DOI: 10.51594/ijmer.v6i1.748

Vallabhaneni, A. S., Perla, A., Regalla, R. R., & Kumari, N. (2024). The power of personalization: AI-driven recommendations. In *Minds unveiled* (1st ed.). Productivity Press., https://www.taylorfrancis.com/chapters/edit/10.4324/9781032711089-9 DOI: 10.4324/9781032711089-9

Van Loo, E. J., Grebitus, C., Nayga, R. M.Jr, Verbeke, W., & Roosen, J. (2018). On the measurement of consumer preferences and food choice behavior: The relation between visual attention and choices. *Applied Economic Perspectives and Policy, 40*(4), 538–562. DOI: 10.1093/aepp/ppy022

Varan, D., Lang, A., Barwise, P., Weber, R., & Bellman, S. (2015). How reliable are neuromarketers' measures of advertising effectiveness: Data from ongoing research holds no common truth among vendors. *Journal of Advertising Research, 55*(2), 176–191. DOI: 10.2501/JAR-55-2-176-191

Varghese, P. (2022). Neuromarketing and artificial intelligence for effective future business. *IUJ Journal of Management, 1*(1), 240–254.

Vecchiato, G., Maglione, A. G., Cherubino, P., Wasikowska, B., Wawrzyniak, A., Latuszynska, A., Latuszynska, M., Nermend, K., Graziani, I., Leucci, M. R., Trettel, A., & Babiloni, F. (2014). Neurophysiological tools to investigate consumer's gender differences during the observation of TV commercials. *Computational and Mathematical Methods in Medicine, 2014*(1), 912981. DOI: 10.1155/2014/912981 PMID: 25147579

Velammal, R. S., Leo, A., Abraham, J. M., Fortuna, C. M., & Kumar, V. (2025). Electroencephalography (EEG)-Based Neuromarketing: Predicting Favourable and Unfavourable Consumer Reactions Using ML Techniques. *BRAIN. Broad Research in Artificial Intelligence and Neuroscience, 16*(3), 153–168. DOI: 10.70594/brain/16.3/12

Veltmeijer, E. A., Gerritsen, C., & Hindriks, K. (2023). Automatic emotion recognition for groups: A review. *IEEE Transactions on Affective Computing, 14*(1), 1–20. DOI: 10.1109/TAFFC.2021.3065726

Venkatesh, V., Morris, M. G., Davis, G. B., & Davis, F. D. (2003). User acceptance of information technology: Toward a unified view. *Management Information Systems Quarterly, 27*(3), 425–478. DOI: 10.2307/30036540

Venkatraman, V., Dimoka, A., Pavlou, P. A., Vo, K., Hampton, W., Bollinger, B., Hershfield, H. E., Ishihara, M., & Winer, R. S. (2015). Predicting advertising success beyond traditional measures: New insights from neurophysiological methods and market response modeling. *JMR, Journal of Marketing Research, 52*(4), 436–452. DOI: 10.1509/JMR.13.0593/SUPPL_FILE/PREDICTINGADVERTISING.PDF

Vergura, D. T., & Luceri, B. (2018). Product packaging and consumers' emotional response. Does spatial representation influence product evaluation and choice? *Journal of Consumer Marketing, 35*(2), 218–227. DOI: 10.1108/JCM-12-2016-2021

Verhoef, P. C., Broekhuizen, T., Bart, Y., Bhattacharya, A., Qi Dong, J., Fabian, N., & Haenlein, M. (2021). Digital transformation: A multidisciplinary reflection and research agenda. *Journal of Business Research, 122*, 889–901. DOI: 10.1016/j.jbusres.2019.09.022

Vij, M., Vij, A., Kumar, P., & Shameem, B. (2024, February). Impact of AI-Driven Customer Insights on Brand Engagement and Loyalty in Tourism Marketing. In 2024 2nd International Conference on Cyber Resilience (ICCR) (pp. 1-6). IEEE.

Vlačić, B., Corbo, L., Costa e Silva, S., & Dabić, M. (2021). The evolving role of artificial intelligence in marketing: A review and research agenda. In *Journal of Business Research* (Vol. 128, pp. 187–203). Elsevier Inc., DOI: 10.1016/j.jbusres.2021.01.055

Vozzi, A., Ronca, V., Cherubino, P., & Trettel, A. (2021). Measuring the emotional and cognitive consumers' responses during interaction. In Decision-making in management: Methods and behavioral tools (p. 137).

Walla, P., Brenner, G., & Koller, M. (2011). Objective measures of emotion related to brand attitude: A new way to quantify emotion-related aspects relevant to marketing. *PLoS One*, *6*(11), e26782. DOI: 10.1371/journal.pone.0026782 PMID: 22073192

Wang, Q., Yang, S., Liu, M., Cao, Z., & Ma, Q. (2014). An eye-tracking study of website complexity from cognitive load perspective. *Decision Support Systems*, *62*, 1–10. DOI: 10.1016/j.dss.2014.02.007

Wedel, M., & Kannan, P. K. (2016). Marketing analytics for data-rich environments. *Journal of Marketing*, *80*(6), 97–121. DOI: 10.1509/jm.15.0413

Wedel, M., Pieters, R., & van der Lans, R. (2019). Eye tracking methodology for research in consumer psychology. In *Handbook of Research Methods in Consumer Psychology* (pp. 276–292). Routledge.

Westen, D. (2008). *The political brain: The role of emotion in deciding the fate of the nation*. PublicAffairs.

Westlin, C., Theriault, J. E., Katsumi, Y., Nieto-Castanon, A., Kucyi, A., Ruf, S. F., Brown, S. M., Pavel, M., Erdogmus, D., Brooks, D. H., Quigley, K. S., Whitfield-Gabrieli, S., & Barrett, L. F. (2023). Improving the study of brain-behavior relationships by revisiting basic assumptions. *Trends in Cognitive Sciences*, *27*(3), 246–257. DOI: 10.1016/j.tics.2022.12.015 PMID: 36739181

Wilson, E., Sendhilnathan, N., Burlingham, C. S., Mansour, Y., Cavin, R., Tetali, S. D., & Proulx, M. J. (2025, May). Eye Gaze as a Signal for Conveying User Attention in Contextual AI Systems. In *Proceedings of the 2025 Symposium on Eye Tracking Research and Applications* (pp. 1-7). DOI: 10.1145/3715669.3727349

Winterhalter, L., Kofler, F., Ströbele, D. A., Othman, A., & von See, C. (2024). AI-assisted diagnostics in dentistry: An eye-tracking study on user behavior. *Journal of Clinical and Experimental Dentistry, 16*(5), e547–e555. DOI: 10.4317/jced.61491 PMID: 38988762

Wu, D. C., Zhong, S., Wu, J., & Song, H. (2025). Tourism and hospitality forecasting with big data: A systematic review of the literature. *Journal of Hospitality & Tourism Research (Washington, D.C.), 49*(3), 615–634. DOI: 10.1177/10963480231223151

Xiao, L., Li, X., & Mou, J. (2024). Exploring user engagement behaviour with short-form video advertising on short-form video platforms: A visual-audio perspective. *Internet Research*. Advance online publication. DOI: 10.1108/INTR-07-2023-0521

Xin, Q., He, Y., Pan, Y., Wang, Y., & Du, S. (2023). The implementation of an AI-driven advertising push system based on an NLP algorithm. *International Journal of Global Economics and Management, 6*(1), 1–15. https://pdfs.semanticscholar.org/72cd/00135b5bab08597f2248a7a4fa0c7cc6e24c.pdf

Xue, Y., Feng, T., & Wu, C. (2024). How technical and situational cues affect impulse buying behaviour in social commerce? Evidence from bored consumers. *Frontiers in Psychology, 15*, 1405189. DOI: 10.3389/fpsyg.2024.1405189

Yadav, T. (2024). AI in Neuromarketing: Understanding Consumer Emotions and Behavior through Machine Learning. *IJFMR - International. Journal of Multidisciplinary Research, 6*(5). Advance online publication. DOI: 10.36948/IJFMR.2024.V06I05.28154

Yadete, F. D., & Kant, S. (2023). Neuro-Marketing in Understanding Consumer Behavior: Systematic Literature Review. *Journal of Social Sciences and Management Studies, 2*(2), 1–12. DOI: 10.56556/JSSMS.V2I2.483

Yao, X., & Wang, Y. (2024). Using neural data to forecast aggregate consumer behavior in neuromarketing: Theory, metrics, progress, and outlook. *Journal of Consumer Behaviour, 23*(4), 2142–2159. DOI: 10.1002/cb.2324

Yin, R. K. (2017). *Case study research and applications: Design and methods*. No Title.

Younus, M., Nurmandi, A., Mutiarin, D., Manaf, H. A., Prianto, A. L., Irawan, B., & Malik, I. (2025). A Comprehensive Study of Neuro Marketing Techniques. In *Impact of Sensory Marketing on Buying Behaviour* (pp. 1–34). IGI Global.

Yrjölä, M., Hautamäki, P., & Ranta, R. (2024). Value propositions of artificial intelligence in retailing. *International Review of Retail, Distribution and Consumer Research.* Advance online publication. DOI: 10.1080/09593969.2024.2411209;WGROUP:STRING:PUBLICATION

Yu, J., Dickinger, A., So, K. K. F., & Egger, R. (2024). Artificial intelligence-generated virtual influencer: Examining the effects of emotional display on user engagement. *Journal of Retailing and Consumer Services, 76,* 103560. DOI: 10.1016/J.JRETCONSER.2023.103560

Zacharia, A. B., & Hamelin, N. (2021). An analysis of subliminal static images and words using eye tracking techniques. In *Developing digital marketing: Relationship perspectives* (pp. 155–180). Emerald Publishing Limited. DOI: 10.1108/978-1-80071-348-220211009

Zed, E. Z., Kartini, T. M., & Purnamasari, P. (2024). The Power Of Personalization: Exploring The Impact Of Ai-Driven Marketing Strategies On Consumer Loyalty In E-Commerce. *Jurnal Ekonomi, 13*(04), 1303–1314.

Zenozain, E. A. M. (2025). Deciphering Purchase Decisions in Neuromarketing: A Systematic Review of the Last Decade Using Neutrosophic Z Numbers. *Neutrosophic Sets and Systems, 84*(1), 264–280. https://digitalrepository.unm.edu/nss_journal/vol84/iss1/22

Zenozain, E. A. M., Salvador, E., & Salvador, S. (2025). Deciphering Purchase Decisions in Neuromarketing: A Systematic Review of the Last Decade Using Neutrosophic Z Numbers. In *Neutrosophic Sets and Systems* (Vol. 84). https://digitalrepository.unm.edu/nss_journal/vol84/iss1/22

Zhang, J., & Tao, D. (2021). Empowering Things with Intelligence: A Survey of the Progress, Challenges, and Opportunities in Artificial Intelligence of Things. In *IEEE Internet of Things Journal* (Vol. 8, Number 10, pp. 7789–7817). Institute of Electrical and Electronics Engineers Inc. DOI: 10.1109/JIOT.2020.3039359

Zhang, H., Yin, L., & Zhang, H. (2024). Using subjective emotion, facial expression, and gaze direction to evaluate user affective experience and predict preference when playing single-player games. *Ergonomics, 67*(12), 1863–1883. DOI: 10.1080/00140139.2024.2359123 PMID: 38832783

Zhang, R., Walshe, C., Liu, Z., Guan, L., Muller, K., Whritner, J., Zhang, L., Hayhoe, M., & Ballard, D. (2020, April). Atari-head: Atari human eye-tracking and demonstration dataset. *Proceedings of the AAAI Conference on Artificial Intelligence*, *34*(04), 6811–6820. DOI: 10.1609/aaai.v34i04.6161 PMID: 32901213

Zhang, W., & Liu, H. (2017). Toward a reliable collection of eye-tracking data for image quality research: Challenges, solutions, and applications. *IEEE Transactions on Image Processing*, *26*(5), 2424–2437. DOI: 10.1109/TIP.2017.2681424 PMID: 28362586

Zhang, Y., Thaichon, P., & Shao, W. (2023). Neuroscientific research methods and techniques in consumer research. *Australasian Marketing Journal*, *31*(3), 211–227. DOI: 10.1177/14413582221085321

Zheng, J., Huang, Y., Chen, Y., Guan, L., & Liu, Q. (2022). Subjective preference and visual attention to the attributes of ornamental plants in urban green space: An eye-tracking study. *Forests*, *13*(11), 1871. DOI: 10.3390/f13111871

Zhou, R., Zhang, Z., Fu, H., Zhang, L., & Li, L. (2023). PR-PL: A novel prototypical representation-based pairwise learning framework for emotion recognition using EEG signals. *IEEE Transactions on Affective Computing*. Advance online publication. DOI: 10.1109/TAFFC.2023.3280747

Zhuk, A., & Yatskyi, O. (2024). The use of artificial intelligence and machine learning in e-commerce marketing. *Technology Audit and Production Reserves*, *3*(4(77)), 33–38. DOI: 10.15587/2706-5448.2024.305280

Zhu, P., Liu, Z., Li, X., Jiang, X., & Zhu, M. X. (2023). The influences of livestreaming on online purchase intention: Examining platform characteristics and consumer psychology. *Industrial Management & Data Systems*, *123*(1), 1–20. DOI: 10.1108/IMDS-07-2022-0430

Zhu, S., Qi, J., Hu, J., & Hao, S. (2022). A new approach for product evaluation based on integration of EEG and eye-tracking. *Advanced Engineering Informatics*, *52*, 101601. DOI: 10.1016/j.aei.2022.101601

Ziv, G. (2016). Gaze behavior and visual attention: A review of eye tracking studies in aviation. *The International Journal of Aviation Psychology*, *26*(3-4), 75–104. DOI: 10.1080/10508414.2017.1313096

Zong, Z., & Guan, Y. (2024). AI-Driven Intelligent Data Analytics and Predictive Analysis in Industry 4.0: Transforming Knowledge, Innovation, and Efficiency. *Journal of the Knowledge Economy*, *16*(1), 864–903. Advance online publication. DOI: 10.1007/s13132-024-02001-z

Zuboff, S. (2019). The age of surveillance capitalism: The fight for a human future at the new frontier of power. *Journal of Information Technology*, *34*(2), 199–201. DOI: 10.1177/1350508419842708

Zuschke, N. (2020). An analysis of process-tracing research on consumer decision-making. *Journal of Business Research*, *111*, 305–320. DOI: 10.1016/j.jbusres.2019.01.028

# About the Contributors

**Fernando Ortiz-Rodriguez** is a Full Professor and Head of the Artificial Intelligence and Innovation Lab at Tamaulipas Autonomous University. He was the Executive Director at the International Institute of Studies (IIES). He created the First Business School in Tamaulipas, Mexico. He worked as the Information Technology Manager at Emerson Electric, where he developed more than 40 pieces of software, some of them used globally in Emerson, and he achieved technology convergence by implementing the first efforts on IoT and Industry 4.0. Fernando is a member of National Systems Researchers (SNI) Level 1 of the National Council of Science and Technology (CONACYT) and INDEX IT Advisor

**Miguel Sahagun** High Point University hired Miguel Angel Sahagun as assistant professor of marketing. Sahagun teaches Principles of Marketing in the university's new marketing major in the Phillips School of Business. Sahagun, who relocated to High Point from Brownsville, Texas, has a wide-ranging interest in studying the decision-making process individuals go through in various situations. His expertise includes the product adoption process of consumers prior to purchasing products, the process of customers becoming loyal consumers, students' perspective on ethics in college sports, and high school students' process of selecting higher education institutions to attend. "I see my new job at HPU as an opportunity to help students find what gives their professional lives meaning and purpose, and direct their energy and effort toward continually bettering themselves through the acquisition of new knowledge," Sahagun says. Prior to HPU, Sahagun worked as research assistant, teaching assistant, instructor and program director for various undergraduate and graduate courses and programs. He is an active member of professional organizations such as the American Marketing Association, and has presented and published his research. Prior to his career in education, he worked for various manufacturing companies in the automotive and furniture industries as an industrial engineer, ergonomics coordinator and plant manager. Sahagun earned a doctoral degree in

Business Administration with a concentration in Marketing from the University of Texas-Pan American. He earned a master's degree in business administration from the University of Texas at Brownsville and a bachelor's degree in industrial engineering from the Instituto Tecnológico y de Estudios Superiores de Occidente at Guadalajara, Mexico.

**Anuj Kumar** is a Professor and Global Country Head at Rushford Business School, Switzerland, where he also leads the Research and Doctor of Business Administration (DBA) program. He is a Post-Doctoral Fellow in Malaysia and holds a dual Ph.D. from Aligarh Muslim University (India) and the All-India Management Association, New Delhi. Dr. Kumar also earned an M.Sc. in International Business from the Michael Smurfit Graduate Business School, University College Dublin, Ireland. In addition, he holds three postgraduate degrees and a bachelor's degree in technology from Guru Gobind Singh Indraprastha University, Delhi, India. Dr. Kumar currently serves as an Honorary Research Fellow at INTI International University, Malaysia; Honorary Professor at the European Global Institute of Innovation & Technology, Malta; and Visiting Faculty at the VNU University of Economics and Business, Vietnam. He is also the Editorial Head at Confab 360 Degree, India's first IAF–ISO certified organization.

**Nishu Ayedee** is the Founder and CEO of Confab 360 Degree. Confab 360 Degree is an ISO 9001: 2015 certified company that has its operations in India, Dubai, London, Vietnam, Germany, and other countries. Confab 360 Degree is famous for its global conferences and training programs in different domains. Nishu has 14 years of professional experience across marketing, sales, and academia. She is committed to fostering quality and collaboration in professional development. She is also a research fellow at INTI International University. She has published papers in quality Scopus and Web of Science-indexed journals. She has been invited to India and other foreign countries as a keynote speaker, guest of honor, and chief guest in different programs.

***

**A.A.Jayashree Prabhakar**, is working as a Professor in Vels Institution of Science, Technology and Advanced Studies, Department of English,School of Languages, VISTAS, Chennai, since 2013.She has 25 years of teaching experience and 16 years of Research Experience. She has produced 13 Doctorates.She has published 10 Patents, 10 Chapters, 8 Books and 80 Research papers . She has received 4 Faculty Excellence Award from VISTAS and 7 Awards from different organizations.She has done 10 NPTEL courses .She is the Topper of NPTEL Online Course Technical English for Engineers.

**Shuvasree Banerjee** is a Asst. Professor with over nine years of teaching experience in Tourism and Hotel Management Institutes. She holds a Bachelor of Business Administration (BBA) in Tourism and Hospitality from Burdwan University, West Bengal, followed by a Post Graduate Diploma in Management (PGDM) in Travel & Tourism Management from the Indian Institute of Tourism and Travel Management (IITTM) Bhubaneswar, an autonomous body under the Ministry of Tourism, Government of India. Additionally, she has completed a Master of Business Administration (MBA) in Tourism and Hospitality from the National Institute of Tourism and Hospitality Management (NITHM), Hyderabad, under affiliation with Jawaharlal Nehru Technological University, Hyderabad. She is awarded a PhD degree in Tourism and Hospitality from Chandigarh University. As an active research scholar, she has presented papers at 14 international conferences from 2022 to 2025 and has 16 publications to their credit. Her scholarly contributions include one paper published in a Scopus Q1 journal and 8 book chapters, with 2 paper and 8 chapters indexed in Scopus.

**C. Karpagavalli**, B.A. (English), M.A., M.Phil., PGDELT, Ph.D., earned a Ph.D. in Indian Writing in English, with a comparative study of the novels of Amitav Ghosh and Aravind Adiga. I have 19 years of teaching experience in higher education and have published over seven research papers in reputed national and international journals, along with three papers in conference proceedings. My academic interests include Indian English literature, comparative literary studies, postcolonial narratives, and contemporary trends in fiction. I continue to engage actively in teaching, research, publication, and academic development.

**Manju.C**, MA, M.Phil, PGDELT, B.Ed, Ph.D, holds an esteemed position as Assistant Professor in the Department of English at Dharmamurthi Rao Bahadur Calavala Cunnan Chetty's Hindu College - Shift 2. With 18 years of experience, she has established herself as an accomplished, student-focused English professor and a good mentor. Her specializations include Indian and American Literature, and she has expertise in handling soft skills classes for PG students. She has published papers in national and international conferences and has organized and attended workshops, seminars, and FDPs to enhance her skills

**Jomon Jose M.** (Post-Doc.) is an Associate Professor and Research Supervisor at Sahrdaya Institute of Management Studies, Thrissur, Kerala, India. With expertise in sustainable business practices, digital economy, and consumer behavior, he has published extensively in Scopus and international journals. His research interests include Industry 6.0, circular economy, behavioral finance, and AI applications in management. Dr. Jose also guides doctoral research and has presented papers at leading global conferences.

**Sneha Kapoor** received her Bachelor's degree from University of Delhi. Currently she is pursuing Masters in Business Administration from J.C. Bose University of Science and Technology, YMCA, Faridabad, India. With a strong academic foundation and a keen interest in marketing, leadership and innovation, she aspires to make a meaningful impact in the business world. She actively engages in co-curricular activities, case study competitions and industry interactions to broaden her learning. Sneha envisions a career that blends creativity with strategy, driving growth and transformation.

**Sunayna Khurana** is an accomplished academician, with 22 years of experience, currently working as Professor & Dean, University School of Management Studies, Rayat Bahra University.She has guided several research scholars for a Ph.D. in the field of Marketing. More than 64 research papers in the National/International Journals/Conferences are credited to her name. Besides, she has organized numerous conferences, seminars, workshops, and short-term training programs etc. She also received a grant from AICTE for organizing an International conference and from ICSSR for a 10-day Research Methodology workshop. Her impressive research portfolio includes one (awarded), 3 published, and 2 filed patents, and 3 copyrights. 5 research scholars have completed PhD under her supervision, and 3 scholars are pursuing. She authored 4 textbooks, edited 2 books, and also reviewed 5 textbooks of International Publishers like McGraw Hill Higher Education and Cengage Learning India Pvt. Ltd.

**Jonika Lamba** is currently working as an Assistant Professor (Finance) in Amity College of Commerce & Finance, Amity University. Prior to this she has worked as Assistant Professor in SOMC, K R Mangalam University, Sohna Gurugram. Presently She is pursuing Master's of Business Law Programme from National Law School of India University, Bengaluru. She holds a Ph.D. in Stock Market Studies from The NorthCap University and brings with her a strong academic background and multifaceted professional experience in the field of finance and commerce. A dedicated researcher and innovator, Dr. Lamba has authored more than 23 research publications, several of which are indexed in reputed databases such as Scopus and Web of Science. Her contributions to research and academia are further evidenced by five patents registered with the Government of India, reflecting her commitment to innovation and advancement in the fields of finance, law, and technology.

**Jyothis Rachel Mathews** is an Assistant Professor at Ahalia School of Management, Palakkad, Kerala, India. Her academic focus lies in strategic management, sustainability, and organizational behavior. She has authored and co-authored several research papers in peer- reviewed journals and actively contributes to academic-industry collaborations.

**N. S. Vishnu Priya** has been working as Associate Professor in the Department of English in VIT, Vellore. She has more than 23 years of experience. She has produced 6 doctorates and is currently guiding 4 scholars for their doctorate. She is both a short story writer and a translator. She has published more than 50 papers in peer reviewed journals out of which 14 are scopus indexed.

**Nasib** is a faculty member of the Magister Management program at the Institute of Business Information Technology and Business. His research interests include Marketing Management, Consumer Behavior, and Marketing Strategy. He holds a Bachelor's degree in Education (S.Pd) from Universitas Setia Budi Mandiri, a Master of Management (MM) from Universitas Muhammadiyah Sumatera Utara, and a Doctorate (Dr) from Universitas Prima Indonesia. His research has been published in several renowned international journals such as the Journal of Logistics Informatics and Service Science, Quality Access to Success, International Journal of Advanced and Applied Sciences, and Journal of System and Management Sciences. He can be reached via email at nasibwibowo02@gmail.com.

**P. Selvakumar** is currently an Associate Professor in the Department of Science and Humanities at Nehru Institute of Technology, Coimbatore, Tamil Nadu, India. Prior to joining Nehru Institute of Technology, he held positions as an Assistant Professor in the Department of Science and Humanities various engineering colleges in Coimbatore, Tamil Nadu, India, spanning from 2011 to 2023. Dr.P. Selvakumar's academic and research interests lie primarily in the field of phytochemistry. He has made significant contributions to his field, with an impressive record that includes 30 journal publications, 12 patents, and 20 conference papers. Additionally, he has organized 5 seminars and conferences, further demonstrating his commitment to academic and scientific exchange. Throughout his career, Dr. P.Selvakumar has been recognized for his dedication and excellence in teaching, having been honored with several awards, including the Best Teacher Awards. He holds a prominent position in the academic community, contributing actively to research.

**Majdi Anwar Quttainah** earned his Ph.D. degree in Management from Rensselaer Polytechnic Institute, Lally School of Management & Technology (USA); MBA degree with merits from the Business School & Entrepreneurship at Newcastle University (UK), and bachelor's degree in International Business from the American International University in London (UK). Dr. Quttainah is an associate professor of management in the College of Business Administration at Kuwait University. His research and teaching interests are corporate governance and strategies, entrepreneurship & small businesses, and organizational development. In addition, as a recognition of his research, he was awarded the Best Young Researcher academic year 2016/2017 Kuwait University. He is an active scholar, presently working as senior editor of FIIB Business Review (Scopus Q1, WoS, Published by the Sage Publishing). His research won several recognition and awards including the Best Paper Award at the 76th Annual Meeting of the Academy of Management Anaheim, CA, the Best Paper Award at the AGBA's 12th Annual World Congress, Kuantan City (State of Pahang), Malaysia, and the Best Paper Award of the Gorontalo International Conference of Project Management (ICPM) - Gorontalo/Indonesia. Also, at the home country level the best paper award for the Kuwait Economic Researcher Award by the Central Bank of Kuwait; May 2019 and 2022.

**Shivansu Sachan** is Pursuing Ph.D. in Management, a Master's holder from Integral University, Lucknow, Bachelor's from IHM, Lucknow. Academic and professional accomplishments of 6 years with renowned organizations and institutes. His Teaching Career has been very satisfying and have continuously upgraded the skills and knowledge by attending many courses and training programs, seminars, conferences organized by different organizations and also delivered many lectures as a Hospitality sector. He is working as an Assistant Professor at Chhatrapati Shahu ji Maharaj University Kanpur .

**Bhaskar Sailesh** is an academic and researcher in the field of hospitality and tourism studies, with a strong focus on postcolonial culinary narratives, sustainable tourism, hospitality marketing and cultural heritage. He currently teaches at PES University, Bengaluru, and has contributed extensively to scholarly publications and curriculum design in hospitality education. His work bridges historical inquiry and contemporary practice in Indian food culture.

**Siti Alhamra Salqaura** SE., M.Si. is a distinguished academic, researcher, and educator. Born in Jakarta on August 24, 1988. Dr. Salqaura completed her undergraduate studies at the Universitas Pendidikan Indonesia (UPI) from 2006 to 2010. She then pursued a Master's degree in Management Sciences at Universitas Sumatera Utara (USU) between 2014 and 2016. Dr. Salqaura continued her academic journey in 2020 by earning a Doctorate in Management from USU in 2023. In addition to her degrees, she has participated in various advanced programs at prestigious institutions, including Harvard University, the University System of Maryland, and Curtin University. Currently, Dr. Salqaura serves as a faculty member at the Universitas Medan Area, where she is dedicated to nurturing the next generation of leaders in management and economics. Her academic interests span marketing management, digital marketing, entrepreneurship, social entrepreneurship, economic policy, and sustainable business practices, with a focus on enhancing business efficiency in emerging markets. Through her extensive research and publications in reputable journals, she has made significant contributions to both academic knowledge and practical solutions for policymakers and business leaders. Dr. Salqaura's work aims to bridge the gap between theory and practice, ensuring that her research translates into actionable insights for improving business and economic systems in Indonesia. With her commitment to advancing the body of knowledge, she hopes that this book will inspire and contribute to the acceleration of societal welfare.

**Rajiv Sindwani** is working as Associate Professor in the Department of Management Studies at J C Bose University of Science and Technology, YMCA, Faridabad, India. He received his PhD degree in area of Service Quality Management. He is having 20 years of experience in various sectors including consumer durables, banking, teaching and research. He has published many papers in international journals of repute indexed in SSCI, Scopus and ESCI. He has presented papers in various international conferences. He has also chaired many conference sessions.

**Mohammad Badruddoza Talukder** is an Associate Professor in the College of Tourism and Hospitality Management at IUBAT–International University of Business Agriculture and Technology, Dhaka. He holds a PhD in Hotel Management and has over fifteen years of combined academic, administrative, and industry experience in tourism, hospitality, and hotel management education. Dr. Talukder has served in leadership roles as Head of Department at multiple institutions and has extensive industry exposure in food and beverage management. His research interests include tourism and hospitality service quality, food service management, sustainable tourism, digital marketing, and emerging technologies such as artificial intelligence in hospitality, with numerous publications in Scopus-indexed journals, book chapters, and edited volumes.

**V.N. Sudheer** Unfolded his teaching profession in 2004 as a Lecturer of English and served up to 2006 in a Science and Arts Degree College, Chittoor, A.P. Later, he switched over to an Engineering Institution and Management Studies an Autonomous organization in 2006 and served organization till 2021as an Assistant Professor of English and took up the charge as an Academic Director for CBSE senior secondary school 2021 to 2022. Further, to continue his research and to spread the acquired knowledge and to upgrade in his carrier, he joined as an Associate Professor of

English for CMR University, Bangalore and serving in the existing position since August, 2022.Besides guiding research scholars in the field of ELT and English Literature, he is also handling the subjects of Professional Communication, Oral and Written Communication, and English Verbal ability for students' placements.

# Index

# D

## E



## G



## H



## I



## L



## M

## N



## O



## P



## R

www.ingramcontent.com/pod-product-compliance
Lightning Source LLC
LaVergne TN
LVHW062330300926
849161LV00007B/1638